HUMAN
Communication

Principles and Contexts

Eleventh Edition

STEWART L. TUBBS

Eastern Michigan University

SYLVIA MOSS

**McGraw-Hill
Higher Education**

Boston   Burr Ridge, IL   Dubuque, IA   New York   San Francisco   St. Louis
Bangkok   Bogotá   Caracas   Kuala Lumpur   Lisbon   London   Madrid   Mexico City
Milan   Montreal   New Delhi   Santiago   Seoul   Singapore   Sydney   Taipei   Toronto

The McGraw·Hill Companies

Mc Graw Hill Higher Education

Published by McGraw-Hill, an imprint of The McGraw-Hill Companies, Inc., 1221 Avenue of the Americas, New York, NY 10020. Copyright © 2008, 2006, 2003, 2000, 1994, 1991, 1987, 1983, 1980, 1977, 1974. by The McGraw-Hill Companies, Inc. All rights reserved. No part of this publication may be reproduced or distributed in any form or by any means, or stored in a database or retrieval system, without the prior written consent of The McGraw-Hill Companies, Inc., including, but not limited to, in any network or other electronic storage or transmission, or broadcast for distance learning.

Some ancillaries, including electronic and print components, may not be available to customers outside the United States.

This book is printed on acid-free paper.

2 3 4 5 6 7 8 9 0 DOC/DOC 0 9

ISBN: 978-0-07-128363-2

MHID: 0-07-128363-3

DEDICATION

To Gail, Brian, Michelle, Connor, Kelly, John, and Baby Campbell
Harry, Sara, Michael, and Sarah

BRIEF CONTENTS

CONTENTS

Chapter 11

Interviewing   353

Chapter 12

Small-Group Communication   385

PREFACE

This eleventh edition of *Human Communication* continues a long and engaging collaboration in which we have traced many new developments in our field and have each explored areas of special interest. It is designed to give students a broad-based and up-to-date survey of the entire discipline. As always, we are committed to presenting students with a comprehensive theoretical base and an understanding of how modern communication has evolved and continues to grow, resulting in changes that affect numerous aspects of their everyday lives.

Once again we have focused on the traditional concerns of this discipline while expanding upon specific areas of interest for today's curriculum. Along with our traditional approach of fusing current and classical communication theories, concepts, and skills, we have also expanded our treatment of media and technology and its effects on communication, conflict as it relates to business communication, and the complexities of intercultural communication and ethics.

As a result of this focus, we have tried to create a text that has immediacy and relevance for students and instructors, one that reflects our long-term goals of understandability while introducing rich concepts and theories without oversimplification and using language that is clear, vivid, and precise.

NEW TO THIS EDITION

Among our changes are revised or expanded coverage of the following topics:

- **Conflict:** New sections on ethnic conflict management and an expansion of our treatment of conflict as it relates to business communication.

- **Relationships:** New sections on the effects of deception in close relationships, the changing nature of marriage and families, and new research on dating.
- **Mass Communication and the New Technologies:** New discussion of agenda setting; the potential of the Internet; extensive discussion of media influences on society, including politics; how the use of new technologies is changing our world; and a new section on video games.
- **The Verbal Message:** Coverage of recent controversies in the media regarding celebrities and offensive language; slang; and expanded coverage on language and sexism.
- **Ethics:** Expanded material on ethical decision making; privacy and disclosure; the complexities of leaks; and the implications of lying.
- **Intercultural Communication:** Expanded treatment of intercultural understanding, including a new section on furthering greater tolerance and harmony, as well as new research on stereotyping, ethics, and values.

Other changes include:

- Seven new tables and figures to enhance the visual program of the text, including a media map of News Corporation, several items from the Reading the Mind in the Eyes test, and a table on singles and their relationships. There are also four new *Issues in Communication* boxes.
- More than 250 new citations and research references.

These revisions incorporate our responses to changes in current theories, issues, and research in communication.

PLAN OF THE BOOK

Chapter 1 introduces the process of human communication. It includes new research from *Harvard Business Review* about how to deal with the "conversational dead zone" resulting from spouses both working long hours; changes in the curricula at such universities as Dartmouth, Harvard, Michigan, MIT, and Stanford to include more emphasis on communication skills, including interpersonal, group, public, and organizational as well as conflict management and listening; Microsoft's new software, "immortal computing," for leaving messages and insights from one generation to future generations of family members; communication channels and the different ways of using the Web versus face-to-face, phone, text messaging, blogging, and e-mail; and use of communication technologies such as video-conferencing, group discussion spaces, and online communities.

Chapter 2 on person perception explores how we learn to view ourselves, how we form impressions of other people both face-to-face and online, as well as the accuracy of those perceptions. There are new findings on self-concept, self-esteem, and self-fulfilling prophecies as well as a new section on the attribution of humanness. There is also new discussion of how initial impressions can influence election outcomes and our perception of political candidates. A new *Issues in Communication* box discusses empathy and a new theory regarding empathic qualities. We also discuss new research findings on accurate person perception, including the concept of interpersonal sensitivity.

Chapter 3 on the elements of verbal communication has new interpretations of the Sapir-Whorf hypothesis, the use of language in branding such famous brands as "American Idol"; new-age technology terms creating a new form of slang; and coverage of the controversies over the use of offensive language by celebrities such as Michael Richards, Mel Gibson, Don Imus, and Isaiah Washington, even though some of it is commonly used in rap and hip-hop music.

In **Chapter 4** on nonverbal communication we move from the interpretation of nonverbal communication to spatial, temporal, and then vocal cues. There are new research findings and discussion concerning body orientation, the face as a source of information, cultural display rules, and doctor-patient communication. A new *Issues in Communication* box examines cues of power and dominance as well as the sometimes related cues of poise and self-confidence. There is also new material on major hand gestures. New discussion of deception cues includes recent research findings and an outline of nonverbal behaviors that are reliably associated with deception.

Chapter 5 on listening discusses types of listening and tips for improving listening skills. The chapter also discusses different communication styles and their effects on listening difficulties; listening and success in getting a job in sales and as a manager; as well as listening and effectiveness in academic advising.

Chapter 6 on conflict and negotiation has new and expanded sections on emotional intelligence and its relation to conflict management; intergroup conflicts, including large ethnic systems; ethnic conflict management; diagrammatic reasoning as a set of negotiation skills; as well as negotiation styles and support systems.

In **Chapter 7** we approach ethics as a continuum extending from interpersonal to mass communication. This chapter includes a new view of moral decision making that is the result of recent findings of neuroscience and linguistics. Also new to this chapter is a discussion of the three most common principles people use in ethical decision making. Lying and misrepresentation are considered not only in relation to public and mass communication but also to the behavior of college students and faculty. There are new discussions of scientific misrepresentation and fraud and of the consequences of academic fraud—both for students and teachers. There is also new material on issues of privacy and disclosure. This chapter introduces the concept of moral courage, viewed within the context of recent cases of whistleblowing. We also look at the complexities of leaks and confidential sources and how they can destroy professional reputations. The cases of outed CIA agent Valerie Plame and nuclear scientist Wen Ho Lee are discussed.

Chapter 8 on relationship processes has a new section that includes discussion and new research concerning close relationships as they are affected by lying and deception (as well as self-deception). In addition to a new section on minimal daters, another on online dating includes research on singles, their levels of commitment, and their interest in romantic relationships. Our discussion of family communication re-examines the concept of family and includes recent research findings about the changing nature of marriage and cohabitation.

The first of our chapters on communication contexts, **Chapter 9** on interpersonal communication is designed to dovetail with the relationship processes discussed in Chapter 8. We have added a new section on self-disclosure and self-presentation in Internet dating. There is also a new *Issues in Communication* box on how expectations of intimacy and dependency in a relationship with a spouse can affect other close relationships. Also included are new discussions and research findings on attachment style; unreciprocated love; and cohabitation, marriage, and later marital stability.

Chapter 10 on intercultural communication has a new section on promoting intercultural understanding. It includes and extends earlier discussions of ethnocentrism, stereotyping, and polarization and goes on to consider recent research on intergroup relations and dialogue as well as community actions and the proposals of scholars from several disciplines for furthering communication and tolerance. This chapter also has new research findings on values and ethics. There is also new material on ways in which selected events are perceived and interpreted by members of different cultures and how such distinctions shed light on a recent international incident.

Chapter 11 on interviewing discusses types of interviews, how to prepare for a job inter-

view, and tips on how to handle tough interview questions. The chapter also includes material on the SHARE method of interviewing in difficult conversations and new sections on cognitive interviewing and motivational interviewing.

Small group communication is the subject of **Chapter 12.** New to this chapter is coverage on the growing use of collaborative software, on the use of groups to influence communities, and research on the power of group decisions on such television shows as *Who Wants to Be a Millionaire?* and *The Apprentice.*

Chapter 13 on public communication covers presentations, speech anxiety, and the importance of credibility. New to this chapter are examples from the 2008 presidential race involving Joe Biden, Barack Obama, and Mitt Romney; speaking tips from experts; and the implications of the high demand for top public speakers such as Bill Clinton, at $250,000 a speech, and Dana Carvey at $75,000. Also new to this edition is information on the use of improvisational training to help speakers and effective use of humor in speeches.

Chapter 14 on organizational communication has new research on the usefulness of informal communication in organizations, studies of communication effectiveness and financial success in companies, and the use of speed-dating techniques for business networking. The chapter also includes new information on the impact of miscommunication, with examples of global companies like Airbus and Ferrari experiencing multibillion-dollar problems. Cases of organizational culture problems at Wal-Mart and at Disney that resulted in scandals and firings of top executives are also discussed.

Our final chapter, **Chapter 15** on mass communication and the new technologies, once more has numerous changes. There is a new section on agenda setting and an expanded discussion of framing. New material on media consolidation now includes a media map. This chapter also includes an extensive discussion of presidential and congressional elections and whether voting choices are influenced by the various media. There is also a new *Issues in Communication* box on political satire, news, and spin. There are new research findings on how Americans use the Internet as well as new sections on video games and on cell phones. The discussion of social networks such as MySpace.com is new to this edition, and there are new research findings on the complex issue of whether the Internet affects social relationships. The potential of the Internet for international engagement is also considered.

RESOURCES

Human Communication continues to incorporate a variety of teaching and study aids throughout the text that we hope will benefit both students and instructors. Each chapter has a list of *Key Terms,* a *Summary,* a set of *Review Questions, Exercises,* and an annotated list of *Suggested Readings* of both popular and scholarly works.

The chapter pedagogies are supported by the text's free Online Learning Center (OLC) Web site, *www.mhhe.com/tubbsmoss11,* which provides further study aids with updated *PowerPoint* presentations, *Learning Objectives, Glossary,* and Web links. The updated *Instructor's Manual* and revised *Test Bank* are also available on the Web site.

ACKNOWLEDGMENTS

For their valuable reviews and critique of the tenth edition, we wish to thank the following reviewers: Michael Dues, University of Arizona; Jeff Farrar, University of Connecticut; Steven Pratt, University of Central Oklahoma; Kyle Tusing, University of Arizona; and Robin Vagenas, University of Delaware.

We wish to express our thanks to our editors at McGraw-Hill: Suzanne Earth, our sponsoring editor, for her commitment and support; Erika Lake, our developmental editor, for her invaluable assistance and enthusiasm; and Paul Wells, our production editor, for guiding our book through the various stages of production. Special thanks as well to Jennie Katsaros of McGraw-Hill for her expertise; Phillip Butcher for his editorial guidance and contribution to the online aspects of this revision; Anne Draus of Scratchgravel Publishing Services for her excellent production management of this project; and our copy editor, Carol Lombardi.

Stewart Tubbs would also like to thank Lena Aganesova, Maher Jafar, Matt Rall, and Hollie Rowe for their invaluable research support. Sylvia Moss is grateful to the research librarians of the Larchmont Library for their efforts to secure many sources and to the Columbia University libraries for the use of their outstanding collections.

Stewart L. Tubbs

Stewart L. Tubbs is the Darrell H. Cooper Professor of Leadership in the College of Business at Eastern Michigan University and former Dean of the College of Business. He received his doctorate in Communication and Organizational Behavior from the University of Kansas. His master's degree in Communication and his bachelor's degree in Science are from Bowling Green State University. He has completed postdoctoral work in management at the University of Michigan, Harvard Business School, and Stanford Graduate School of Business. He is also a visiting professor at Koc University in Istanbul, Turkey.

Dr. Tubbs has also taught at General Motors Institute, and at Boise State University, where he was Chairman of the Management Department and, later, Associate Dean of the College of Business.

He has been named an Outstanding Teacher five times, has consulted extensively for *Fortune 500* companies, and is former Chairman of the Organizational Communication division of the Academy of Management. In 1994, he received the Outstanding Leadership Award in London from the Academy of Business Administration and was also inducted into the Distinguished Alumni Hall of Fame by Lakewood High School in Lakewood, Ohio.

Dr. Tubbs is the author of *A Systems Approach to Small Group Interaction* and *Keys to Leadership: 101 Steps to Success,* and coauthor of *Interpersonal Communication* with Sylvia Moss. He is listed in *American Men and Women of Science, Contemporary Authors, Directory of American Scholars,* the *International Who's Who in Education,* and *Outstanding Young Men of America.*

Sylvia Moss

Sylvia Moss is a professional writer with a strong interest in the social sciences. She received her undergraduate education at Barnard College and the University of Wisconsin and holds graduate degrees from Columbia University and New York University. She is the author, with Stewart Tubbs, of *Interpersonal Communication* and has contributed to several college textbooks in the social sciences.

She is also the author of *Cities in Motion,* a collection of poetry selected by Derek Walcott for The National Poetry Series and published by the University of Illinois Press. She has received a Whiting Writer's Award and twice been a Yaddo Fellow. Selections from her work also appear in the bilingual poetry anthology *Six Poets* (St. Petersburg) as well as in the *Grolier Poetry Prize Annual* and such literary journals as *New Letters, Helicon Nine,* and *Foreign Literature* (Moscow).

Ms. Moss has taught at the College of New Rochelle and is a former Random House and Knopf editor. Her translations of contemporary Russian poetry have appeared in *International Poetry Review,* and she is currently working on a book-length collection of English translations of Russian poems. Asia is her area of special interest and training. She is the editor of *China 5000 Years: Innovation and Transformation in the Arts,* published by the Guggenheim Museum.

PART ONE

Principles

The Process of Human Communication

Chapter Objectives

After reading this chapter, you should be able to:

1. Define the term "communication."
2. Explain the term "input" as it is used in the communication model.
3. List four types of messages and give an example of each.
4. Distinguish between technical and semantic interference and give an example of each.
5. Describe the impact of feedback on behavior.
6. Identify seven different contexts of communication and explain how each is distinctive.
7. Define effective communication in terms of five possible outcomes of human communication.

Human communication is the most important skill that you can learn! A study of 975 business managers published in the *Harvard Business Review* showed that many people are so overloaded today that they have reached a "conversational dead zone," which wreaks havoc on communication at home (Schellenberger, 2007). However, some couples have avoided this by talking on the phone during the day; others schedule time after the children are in bed to "debrief." This example illustrates both the importance of communication and some promising methods for overcoming communication challenges.

In another case, premier schools such as Harvard, Michigan, MIT, Dartmouth, and Stanford have beefed up their emphasis on communication skills—including interpersonal communication, listening, interviewing, leading meetings, managing conflict, public speaking, and organizational communication—to better equip their graduates for the real world of work (Dvorak, 2007). Warren Bennis, professor at the University of Southern California and former president of the University of Cincinnati, states that, "It isn't just nice—these interpersonal skills. It's about stuff that's necessary to lead a complex organization"(Dvorak, 2007, p. B3).

At home and at work, effective communication skills can make you or break you. This book is dedicated to helping you improve your communication skills in all the various contexts of your life.

Following is perhaps the most telling example that we can offer about how to be a successful communicator. A woman was given the opportunity to meet two of the most famous men in England, William Gladstone and Benjamin Disraeli. Afterward she was asked her impressions. She said that after meeting Gladstone she was convinced that she had been talking to the most important person in England. However, after meeting Disraeli, she said that she was convinced that she was the most important person in England.

Unsuccessful communication can also have a large impact on the opinions, attitudes, and feelings of the audience. In 2004, after Democratic presidential candidate Howard Dean's public "I Had a Scream" speech, his popularity took a nosedive ("Editorial," 2004, p. A14). The goal of his fiery rhetoric was to rally and energize his supporters. However, after his performance, the media deemed Dean "the angry candidate," and he was perceived by the recipients as unpresidential, costing Dean both his supporters and his campaign (Williams, 2004, p. A1).

The communicated message is therefore not just about the speaker's intention, but about how the message is received. Throughout this book, we will be offering many examples and concepts as well as practical guidelines designed to help you improve your communication.

For many years it has been thought that the speech function was unique to modern Homo sapiens. However, recent evidence indicates that the first creatures to use spoken communication were Neanderthals—more ancient Homo sapiens dating back 60,000 years. Garrett (1989) reports: "Now an international research team has found what it believes is the Neanderthal version of a bone that is a key to modern human speech . . . Baruch Arensburg of Tel Aviv University and his team unearthed the hyoid bone while digging in Israel's Kebara cave . . . The hyoid is a U-shaped bone that supports the tongue and its muscles" (p. 560).

Begley and Gleizes (1989) report this additional evidence:

Early Orators: Although Neanderthal's brain was bigger than ours, ever since his discovery "he was considered dull-witted and inarticulate," says neuroanatomist Terrence Deacon of Harvard University. Now that prejudice is yielding. Fossil brain casts show a well-developed language area, says Dean Falk of the State University of New York at Albany. His speech was only slightly inferior: using skull fossils to infer the position of the voice box in early humans, . . . [researchers concluded that] Neanderthals had a more restricted vocal range than we do. They had nasal voices, but could probably pronounce every consonant and vowel sound except "oo" and "ee," adds Deacon. "They were articulate, intelligent humans we would be able to understand and interact with," he says. (p. 71)

Communication begins very early in life. Roberta Michnick Golinkoff, PhD, author of *How Babies Talk: The Magic and Mystery of Language in the First Three Years of Life,* says that "language begins in the womb" and that after only seven months in the womb, babies have the hearing capability to "eavesdrop" on their mother's conversations (Howard, 2004, p. 69)!

In 2003, 50 million people in the United States and Canada all lost power. The blackout was initially caused by sagging electric lines in a grove of trees, but the cascading impact of the blackout was largely blamed on a breakdown in communications between Ohio energy supplier FirstEnergy and neighboring systems. Computer systems and networks are vulnerable, but communication between individuals working with these systems was critical and could have prevented the blackout from becoming so widespread ("Lessons from a Blackout," 2004, p. A18). As a result, cell phone networks became overloaded by people trying to communicate with one another across the nation. Without power, there were no e-mails, no instant messages, no televisions, and no fax machines. People sat on their porches, met their neighbors for the first time, had picnics, and had a moment's rest from electronic communications, estimated to total 192 messages per person per day (Clark, 1999).

In addition to all of these personal messages, mass delivered consumer messages have become overpowering. Companies now advertise during movie previews and video games. Computer pop-up advertisements have increased, as have spam messages. It is becoming more and more difficult to filter out the noise to concentrate on the messages that we want to receive. Nicknamed *information pollution,* information overload can actually steal away our time while increasing stress and decreasing the time we spend with our families and friends. In 2003, author Tim Sanders teamed with HeartMath, a research organization whose mission is to increase performance and health while decreasing stress (*www.heartmath.com*), revealed that a significant relationship exists between perceived information overload, hours on the Internet, and depression. Other symptoms of information overload that emerged included exhaustion, trouble sleeping, and memory problems (Dempsey, 2003, p. E3).

Keep in mind that all of the messages that make up information pollution do not even include all the interpersonal communication events we experience. It is no wonder that we need to learn more about human communication!

For over 60,000 years men and women have been communicating. Yet we still feel the need, perhaps more than ever, to find ways to improve these skills.

THE IMPORTANCE OF HUMAN COMMUNICATION

According to numerous research studies, for your entire life you have spent about 75 percent of each day engaged in communication. Therefore, you may be wondering why you need to study communication at all. There is a good reason: Quantity is no guarantee of quality. Given the number of divorces, unhappy workers, and ruptured parent-to-offspring relationships, quantity and frequency of communication are clearly no measure of how effectively people communicate with each other.

In another example of the importance of communication, Microsoft researchers are investigating ways that we can save messages for delivery to our descendants in later decades, centuries or even longer. Labeled "immortal computing," this project would allow us to offer insights to our grandchildren and future generations, thus capturing the lessons we have spent our lifetimes learning. It will even be able to capture visual images, much like electronic photo albums (Bishop, 2007).

Among other things, communication has been linked to *physical well-being*. Stewart (1986) indicates that socially isolated people are more likely to die prematurely; divorced men die at double the normal rate from cancer, heart disease, and strokes, five times the normal rate from hypertension, five times the normal rate from suicide, seven times the normal rate from cirrhosis of the liver, and ten times the normal rate from tuberculosis. Also, poor communication skills have been found to contribute to coronary heart disease, and the likelihood of death increases when a marriage partner dies.

Communication is also closely associated with one's *definition of self*. Rosenberg (1979) relates the story of the "wild boy of Aveyron," who was raised by wolves. He developed no identity as a human being until he began to interact with humans. Individuals gain a sense of self-identity by being paid attention to and getting feedback from others. Also, a sense of identity and worth develops from comparing ourselves with others.

General education needs revolve around communication. The highly regarded Carnegie Foundation for the Advancement of Teaching has recommended that teaching communication be one of the highest possible priorities for undergraduate education. Communication was the only subject field identified in their recommendations (Kenny, 1998)!

On-the-job communication is constantly cited as one of the most important skills in "getting ahead." Whetten and Cameron (2005) identified 402 individuals rated as highly effective managers in their own organizations in such fields as

Most Frequently Cited Skills of Effective Managers
1. Oral communication (including listening)
2. Managing time and stress
3. Managing individual decisions
4. Recognizing, defining, and solving problems
5. Motivating and influencing others
6. Delegating
7. Setting goals and articulating a vision
8. Self-awareness
9. Team building
10. Managing conflict (p. 8)
As you will see, many of these topics are covered in this book.

business, health care, education, and government. They interviewed the individuals to determine what attributes were associated with their effectiveness. The table above shows the top ten list of most frequently cited skills of effective managers.

These research findings have been confirmed by a 10-year study conducted by researchers at Carnegie Mellon University, which identified the most important skills that distinguished average job performers from outstanding job performers (Kelley, 1998). They found that interpersonal communication, relationship building, leadership, teamwork, networking, and persuasion were some of the most important skills for career success.

In this book, we shall explore each of these aspects of human communication—all the way from the first impressions we form of one another to how human relationships are maintained and sometimes terminated.

WHAT IS HUMAN COMMUNICATION?

What do you think of when the word "communication" is used? Students answering this question may mention anything from the use of electric circuits to prayer. Communication is a subject so frequently discussed that the term itself has become too meaningful—that is, it has too many different meanings for people. Agreeing on a working definition is the first step toward improving our understanding of this complex phenomenon.

Communication has been broadly defined as "the sharing of experience," and to some extent all living organisms can be said to share experience. What makes human communication unique is our superior ability to create and to use symbols; this ability enables humans to share experiences indirectly and vicariously. A symbol can be defined as something used for or regarded as representing something else. Briefly, then, human communication is the process of creating a meaning between two or more people. We will expand this partial definition in discussing communication outcomes later in this chapter under "What Is Effective Communication?"

What are some of the complications that have arisen as a result of the increased communication through such media as telephones, cell phones, fax messages, and e-mail? How do you resolve some of the difficulties? Audrey Glassman (1998) raised some of the following issues:

Telephones

1. How do you feel when you are on a call and someone takes another call on "call waiting"?

2. How do you feel when someone puts you on a speaker phone and your side of the conversation is more or less public?

3. What do you do if you are on a conference call and you cannot clearly hear one or more parties on the other end because of a bad connection?

Cellular Phones

4. Have you ever had any unusual experiences in which a person is talking on a cell phone while driving?

5. Can you think of any situations in which it is appropriate to receive cell phone calls when you are in a movie theater?

6. What are some examples of locations that you feel may be inappropriate for cell phone usage?

Fax Messages

7. When is it appropriate to send your résumé by fax if you are applying for a job?

8. Should you send confidential messages by fax? Are there any exceptions?

E-mail Messages

9. How many pages long should your messages usually be?

10. Have you ever had your message forwarded to someone you didn't expect? What should you do to anticipate this?

11. Have you ever sent a message when you were angry? Have you learned anything from this?

12. Have you ever exchanged messages with someone who has copied in another party to exercise authority or make a point? How did this make you feel?

13. What emotions do e-mails in all uppercase letters send to the recipient? What about a message scribed in all lowercase letters?

A MODEL OF HUMAN COMMUNICATION

Since human communication is an intangible, ever-changing process, many people find it helpful to use a tangible model to describe that process. Actually, a motion picture would be a better form for modeling communication. As you read this book,

Figure 1.1   *The Tubbs Communication Model*

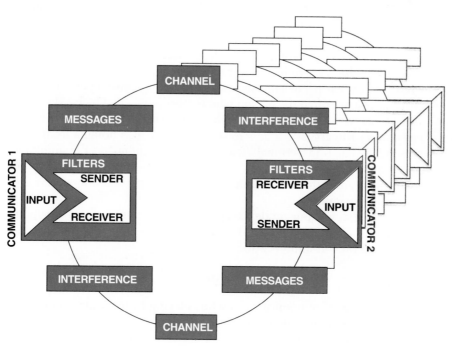

think of the model that follows as one frame of a motion picture—a momentary pause in an ongoing process. The model is not an end in itself; it is only a means to help explain the ways in which the various component parts interact.

Figure 1.1 is a model of the most basic human communication event; it involves only two people. Initially, we shall call them Communicator 1 (the sender/receiver) and Communicator 2 (the receiver/sender). In actuality, both are sources of communication, and each originates and receives messages simultaneously. In addition, both parties are simultaneously being influenced by one another in the transaction. Communicator 1 may originate the first message, and Communicator 2 may be the first person to perceive the transmitted stimuli, but most of our daily communication activities are spontaneous and relatively unstructured, so that these are overlapping roles.

Thus, as represented in the present model, a great many transactions can be initiated from either the right or the left side. For example, when you got up this morning, did you speak to someone first, or were you spoken to first? You probably don't even remember because who spoke first was a matter of chance. In an important sense, it is arbitrary to call yourself either a sender or a receiver: You are both. Even while you are speaking, you are simultaneously observing the other person's behavior and reacting to it. This is also true of the other person as he or she interacts with you.

The transactional view also emphasizes that you change as a result of the communication event. Have you ever been drawn into an argument so intense that the more you told the other person how angry you were, the angrier you became? The reverse is also possible. If a man tells a woman how much he cares for her and goes out of his way to do something thoughtful for her, what is the result? Typically, he increases his feeling of closeness to her, even though she may not respond well to his gesture. The research on self-persuasion shows that when you give a persuasive presentation to others, you are often the person who is most persuaded by it. Alcoholics Anonymous has worked with this principle for many years. The people who get up at meetings and try to persuade others to stay sober are also doing a lot to keep themselves persuaded. The transactional viewpoint, then, emphasizes the simultaneous and mutually influential nature of the communication event. The participants become interdependent, and their communication can be analyzed only in terms of the unique context of the event.

As you read more about our model, keep in mind the transactional viewpoint with its emphasis on the extent to which the two or more people involved create a relationship as part of their communicating.

Communicator 1: Sender/Receiver

Let's take a closer look at Communicator 1, who is trying to transmit a message—a process that requires sending a message from Communicator 1's nervous system to that of Communicator 2, with the intention of creating a meaning similar to that in the sender's mind. Keep in mind that both people are simultaneously sending and receiving all the time. What characteristics of this person would be important in the communication process? Obviously, mental capacities are of central importance. Inside the human brain are millions of nerve cells that function together to store and utilize knowledge, attitudes, and emotions. We want to know what makes Communicator 1 distinct from any other. Like those of any other human being, Communicator 1's senses are continually bombarded by a wealth of stimuli from both inside and outside the body. All that he or she knows and experiences—whether of the physical or the social world—comes initially through the senses. Borrowing from computer terminology, we call these raw data **input**—*all the stimuli, both past and present, that give us our information about the world.*

All of this affects the message Communicator 1 will send.

From the accounts of explorers, castaways, and prisoners of war, we can learn what it is like to experience a long period of isolation, but even in these extreme situations there has been some sensory stimulation. The effect of radically decreased input—in solitary confinement, for example—is more difficult to imagine. You can get some notion of how dependent you are on a steady flow of stimuli by supposing that your senses were shut off one by one. Imagine what it would be like without them for a day or just an hour or even 15 minutes.

Messages

Looking again at the model in Figure 1.1, we can think of the messages that Communicator 1 transmits as being conveyed. These **messages** may be verbal or nonverbal, and they may be intentional or unintentional. Thus four types of messages are possible: (1) intentional verbal, (2) unintentional verbal, (3) intentional nonverbal, and (4) unintentional nonverbal. As we examine these categories individually, keep in mind that most messages contain two or more types of stimuli and that they often overlap.

Verbal Messages

A **verbal message** is *any type of spoken communication that uses one or more words.* Most of the communicative stimuli we are conscious of fall within the category of *intentional verbal messages;* these are *the conscious attempts we make to communicate with others through speech.* Undoubtedly, the most unique aspect of human communication is the use of verbal symbols. It is somewhat of a miracle that we can look at ink marks on a piece of paper or listen to sounds carried on air waves and be able to create images in each other's brains. In fact, the process works so well that we often are surprised when problems occur.

For example, a friend once commented to her mother (who came to this country from Europe) that she had just received a new VISA card. Her mother responded by saying, "Oh really, I didn't know you were planning a trip." To the mother, the term "visa" referred to a permit used to travel to foreign countries. In fact, this "visa" was a charge card. This example illustrates the common principle that words themselves do not contain any meaning. Haney (1992) calls this the "Container Fallacy." In other words, it is a fallacy to believe that meanings are carried or contained by words. If it is possible to have misunderstandings using words that refer to such tangible objects as charge cards, imagine how difficult it is to be able to communicate to another person what we mean by such abstract terms as "truth," "justice," and "fair." Many labor contracts state that if a dispute arises, it must be resolved "within a reasonable period of time." Imagine how much confusion could potentially occur trying to agree on the meaning of "reasonable."

Unintentional verbal messages are *the things we say without meaning to.* Freud argued that all the apparently unintentional stimuli we transmit—both verbal and nonverbal—are unconsciously motivated. We cannot discuss the merits of this argument here, but we can cite an amusing example of a slip of the tongue described by one of Freud's colleagues: "While writing a prescription for a woman who was especially weighed down by the financial burden of the treatment, I was interested to hear her say suddenly: 'Please do not give me *big bills,* because I cannot swallow them.' Of course, she meant to say *pills*" (Freud, 1938, p. 82).

Everyone makes slips occasionally. In 2004 in New Orleans, a member of Mayor C. Ray Nagin's office slipped when describing the success of the year's Carnival celebration. The mayor's spokesperson wrote, "Early economic indicators reveal that this year's Carnival celebration was slightly better than average when it comes to the number of *revealers* and the economic impact" (italics added). Clearly, the spokesperson meant to say "revelers" ("Staffer of New Orleans Mayor . . . ," p. 1)!

Sometimes it's only when we get feedback from others (laughter, for instance) that we become aware we have transmitted such messages. Even in mass communication, which generally involves a great deal of planning and control, such unintentional messages make their appearance. Obviously, those people who represent the mass media are expected to be skilled communicators.

Nonverbal Messages   **Nonverbal messages** cannot be described as easily as verbal messages, probably because the category is so broad. They include all the nonverbal aspects of our behavior: facial expression, posture, tone of voice, hand movements, manner of dress, and so on. In short, *they are all the messages we transmit without words or over and above the words we use.* Each school year, controversy arises in high schools regarding the dress code, especially for women. The so-called Shakira look, with low hip-hugging pants and bare midriff, is usually not allowed. More recently, teenagers have resurrected the 80s fashions, which included colorful jelly bracelets. However, in 2004, wearing a certain colored bracelet represented certain specific sexual activity in which that person had participated. Some high school students stopped wearing them because of the impression they might be giving.

Let us first consider *intentional nonverbal messages, the nonverbal messages we want to transmit.* Sometimes we rely exclusively on nonverbal messages to reinforce verbal messages. For example, you can greet someone by smiling and nodding your head, or you can say "Hello" and also smile or wave. At times we deliberately use nonverbal messages to cancel out a polite verbal response and indicate our true feelings: The verbal message may be positive, but the tone and facial expression indicate that we mean something negative.

Much of what we are as a person "communicates" itself every time we behave. Much of this behavior is unintentional. Some writers on the subject go so far as to assert that what we communicate in this way is what we are. *Unintentional nonverbal messages* are *all those nonverbal aspects of our behavior transmitted without our control.* For example, one of the authors once told a student speaker to relax. "I am relaxed," the student replied in a tight voice, trembling, and speaking over the rattling of a paper he was holding. A problem frequently raised in management classes is that store managers unintentionally communicate anger or impatience to their customers.

Ralph Waldo Emerson phrased it well when he remarked to a speaker, "What you are speaks so loudly that I cannot hear what you say." As your communication skills improve, you may find that the number of unintentional messages you transmit will decrease significantly.

Channels

If you are talking on a cell phone, the channel that transmits the communicative stimuli are the air waves via phone towers. The *channels* of face-to-face communication are the sensory organs. Although all five senses may receive the stimuli, you rely almost exclusively on three: hearing, sight, and touch. For example, you listen to someone state an argument, or you exchange knowing glances with a friend, or you put your hand on someone's shoulder. In addition to the sensory organs, the channels of organizational communication include company e-mail messages, newsletters, bulletin boards, printed memoranda, media advertising, and annual reports. In mass communication, the primary channels would be newspapers, films, radio, television, and the Internet.

In the less formal contexts of communication, we rarely think about communication channels. Usually, a person becomes aware of them only when one or more are cut off or when some sort of interference is present. For example, imagine how you have felt when your e-mail stops working or when your cable television goes down. In another example, we all become very aware of communication channels when there is static on our cell phone, making it impossible to hear another person. The presence of communication channels becomes readily apparent in the absence of these resources. These instances reveal channels to the communicators and are often a single channel experience using either hearing, sight, or touch.

Videoconferencing presents some interesting problems with face-to-face communication. Not only are sight and hearing critical, but delays, static or choppy video, or sound problems may affect the communicators' abilities to react to facial cues. In other words, face-to-face communication is a multichannel experience, including hearing, sight, and touch in many cases. Simultaneously, we receive and make use of information from a number of different channels. In general, the more channels being used, the greater the number of communicative stimuli transmitted.

Each communication channel serves its specific purpose, but each possesses merits and limitations. Not all messages belong equally on all channels. In professional as well as in other types of communication "knowing which medium is best suited to your particular communication needs is the key to ensuring that your message is received and understood" (Larkin, 2005). For example, the Web is best suited for quick information retrieval, as the Web's strength lies in the ease of information search, not ease of comprehension (Larkin, 2005).

> The Web's use of hyperlinks is the reason for its lower comprehension. Links focus the mind on navigating, squeezing out the mental energy left for comprehending. Click one and you may be taken to the definition of a highlighted word; click another and you may be taken to a picture; click yet another and a video commentary begins, or an e-mail page opens inviting your comments to the site host. Thinking about where to go next is the dominant mental activity, not understanding the content. (Larkin, 2005)

Be wary of relying on the Internet too much while preparing for your exams: The additional mental task of navigating links on the Web steals mental resources away from comprehension (Spyridakis, 1998)! Demonstrating this point further, researchers Hailey and Hailey (1998) found that engineering students using Web pages with links missed 33 percent more test questions than students using the same Web pages without links.

When the material is complex, its communication requires a different medium: paper. Paper is, thus, best suited for learning new, long, complicated ideas (Larkin, 2005).

> Paper's strength is comprehension. People use the Web; they read paper. When reading from paper, employees can devote all their mental resources to

understanding. On paper, the author controls the navigation: The reader turns the page, reads, then turns another page. (Larkin, 2005)

When the purpose of communication is overcoming someone's resistance to change, face-to-face communication is the best channel (Larkin, 2005).

People change their behavior when someone in their group whom they know and trust adopts the new behavior and recommends it to the others. Formal communication from a faraway source (town hall meetings, company newspapers, Web sites, broadcast e-mails) does not change employee behavior. The words that change employees' behavior appear in informal conversations. (Larkin, 2005)

Consider an example of just how effective this communication channel can be: Consumer behavior research shows that a word-of-mouth recommendation is 13 times more powerful than print or television advertising when it comes to buying a product for the first time (Sultan et al., 1990).

A recent study of effectiveness of different media in organizational communication found that employees considered the information about their job most satisfactory when it was received from rich communication channels such as face-to-face meetings with their bosses, phone conversations, and departmental meetings. In contrast, employees were more satisfied with information about the company when it was delivered via lean communication media, such as the quarterly meetings, the employee newsletter, or written memos and notices (Byrne and LeMay, 2006).

A recent study conducted by Switzerland's largest telecommunication company, Swisscom, provides interesting insights into the latest behavioral trends of consumers faced with rapidly increasing numbers of available communication channels. The study's main conclusion is that as the communications options available to us expand, we tend to narrow the uses and audiences for each (Giussani, 2006). "SMS is to tell you I miss you, e-mail is to organize our dinner, voice is to say I'm late, and IM is to continue our conversation," writes Stefana Broadbent, the author of the study. Broadbent's findings are summarized as follows:

- The fixed phone is the collective channel: "a shared organizational tool for the whole household," with most calls done in "public," because they are relevant to other members of the household. Only 25 percent are done "privately," from one's bedroom or study.
- Mobile voice is "the micro coordination channel": It is "the preferred channel for last-minute adjustment of plans or updates on where people are and what they are doing." Surprisingly, "80 percent of all exchanges are with only four people."
- SMS, or short messaging, is "for intimacy, emotions, and efficiency. Only the most intimate sphere of friends and family are contacted by SMS, and the content of the messages is often related to 'grooming' and emotional exchanges."

- E-mail is "the administrative channel," used to support online activities such as travel reservations and shopping, for coordination with extended social groups (clubs, friends, acquaintances), or for exchanging pictures, music, and other content with close social networks.
- IM and VoIP are "the continuous channels": "users open an instant messaging channel for the day and then just keep it open in the background while they do other activities; they multitask—and step in and out of a conversation."
- Blogging is the broader networking channel: "Personal pages are often primarily a center of communication with friends and people online in general." (Giussani, 2006)

In addition, says Broadbent, with the emergence of new communication channels, the existing media are being constantly redefined. "IM is currently redefining usage of short messaging; blogging is redefining the usage of e-mail; VoIP is changing the nature of a phone call. New patterns of communication emerge slowly, stabilize for a period, and then change again when new channels come along" (Giussani, 2006).

Blogging is a good example of such redefining. Having originated as personal online diaries where people kept accounts of their personal lives, blogs are increasingly attracting attention of businesses that view them as a useful communication channel for receiving customer feedback or early warning systems for product or service problems (Carr, 2006). Dell, Microsoft, and Apple are currently running such corporate blogs. In addition, Dell is reaching out to bloggers to reinforce company's corporate strategy of selling directly to buyers; Microsoft, to promote its new products (Xbox); and Wal-Mart, to improve its battered image (Barbaro, 2006). Along with the definition, the rules for blogging behavior are also changing:

> Anything that goes up on the Internet is immediately available to a worldwide audience of billions—and it becomes a permanent part of the public record. Independent bloggers may not have to think before they post, but corporate bloggers do. (Carr, 2006)

Interference

After initiating a message, the sender almost always assumes that it has been received. The sender is puzzled or annoyed if he or she is misinterpreted or gets no response, as shown in recent Cingular/AT&T commercials on TV. The sender may even have taken special pains to make the message very clear. "Isn't that enough?" the sender asks. In effect, he or she wants to know what went wrong between the transmission and reception of the message.

The communication scholar would answer, **interference,** or **noise**—that is, *anything that distorts the information transmitted to the receiver or distracts him or her from receiving it.* In communication theory, "interference" and "noise" are synonymous terms. "Interference" is probably a more appropriate word, but because "noise" was the term first used in studies of telecommunication, you should be familiar with it too. One recent example is fashionable clothing. High school dress codes now prohibit clothing that is considered a distraction. This includes plunging necklines, low-riding jeans paired with midriff-baring T-shirts and tops with spaghetti straps (Stone-Palmquist, 2001, p. A1). This interference is also present in the workplace. Many companies have dress codes to prevent distraction due to inappropriate attire. Presenters and interview candidates should also pay close attention to their attire to make sure that they are not distracting from their intended message.

Remember that there are many kinds of noise, not just sound. A smoke-filled, overheated classroom; a student who has made abundant use of a very strong perfume; and a lecturer dressed in weird clothing can all become sources of interference.

We can distinguish between two kinds of interference: technical interference and semantic interference. **Technical interference** refers to *the factors that cause the receiver to perceive distortion in the intended information or stimuli.* And the sender may create the distortion: A person who has a speech impediment or who mumbles a great deal may have difficulty making words clear to someone else. At a party, one person may not be able to hear the response of another because the stereo is blaring or because other people standing nearby are speaking so loudly. In this case, the interference is simply the transmission of the sounds of other people in conversation.

Semantic interference occurs when *the receiver does not attribute the same meaning to the signal that the sender does.* For example, a city official and a social worker got into a heated argument over the causes of crime. The city official argued that the causes were primarily "economic," and the social worker maintained, quite predictably, that they were largely "social." Only after considerable discussion did the two begin to realize that although they had been using different terms, essentially they were referring to the same phenomenon. Bear in mind, however, that no two people will attribute exactly the same meaning to any word and that it is also possible to attribute different meanings to nonverbal messages.

As we have seen, interference can exist in the context of the communication, in the channel, in the communicator who sends the message, or in the one who receives it. Some interference will always be present in human communication.

Communicator 2: Receiver/Sender

Traditionally, emphasis has been given to the communicator as message sender, but equally important to any viable model of human communication is an analysis of the communicator as receiver. For most communication, visual perception will be an essential aspect of message reception. Another critical aspect of message reception is *listening.*

Listening

Consider this ancient Chinese saying, "From listening comes wisdom, from speaking repentance." Listening and hearing are far from synonymous. When Communicator

2 (the receiver/sender) listens, four different yet interrelated processes will occur: attention, hearing, understanding, and remembering.

Thus far we have discussed the transmission and reception of a single message. At this point, however, our model departs from several current models that create the illusion that all human communication has a definite starting point with a sender and a termination point with a receiver. When Communicator 2 in Figure 1.1 has received a message, we have come only halfway through the continuous and ongoing process that is communication. For each receiver of a message is also a sender of messages—hence, the term "receiver/sender." Moreover, that person's uniqueness as a human being ensures that his or her attempts to communicate will be very different from those of the other person in the model. For example, Communicator 2's cultural input may be quite unlike that of Communicator 1. His or her filters, both physiological and psychological, will be different. The stimuli he or she transmits will be different. Even the selection of channels and sources of difficulty, or interference, may differ.

The present model includes these differences as inherent parts of the communication process. Although the left half of the model lists the same elements as the right half—input, filters, messages, channels, interference—and these elements are defined in the same way, they are always different in content from those in the right half.

Feedback

The transmission and reception of a single message are only part of our model. Face-to-face communication in particular is characterized by its interdependent participants and the explicit and immediate feedback between them. Even in organizational and mass communication, where the sender/receiver may represent a social organization, the receiver/sender is still able to supply feedback. It may take any number of forms, from a union slowdown in response to the visit of a time-study analyst to an angry letter to the editor of a major newspaper.

A common definition of **feedback** is *the return to you of behavior you have generated.* When we examine feedback solely in interpersonal terms, we can be more specific and say that feedback reinforces some behaviors and extinguishes others. For example, one story has it that a psychology instructor who had been teaching the principles of instrumental learning was actually conditioned by his own class. The students decided to give him reinforcement by taking lots of notes, looking attentive, and asking questions whenever he moved to his right. Whenever he moved to his left, they tried to extinguish this behavior by not taking notes, being inattentive, and not asking questions. He was just about teaching from the right front corner of the room when he realized what was happening.

Knapp and Hall (1997) also observed,

> many times we talk about our relationships with people as if we had no relation or connection to them—as if our behavior had nothing to do with what the other did. In actuality, however, we have a lot more to do with our partner's responses than we may wish to acknowledge. (p. 11)

In our personal and professional lives, this interdependence must be recognized in order to ensure effective communication in the workplace. Emotional intelligence, a term coined by author Daniel Goleman, includes self-awareness, which allows individuals to understand their own behavior and communications and the effect that these behaviors and communications have on others. Other aspects of emotional intelligence include ability to empathize and ability to control emotions (Valentis, 2004, p. 1). These are especially critical in communication. Individuals with high emotional intelligence recognize their interdependence and are more effective partners or leaders. As a result, companies are hiring executive coaches to teach emotional intelligence to their leaders.

Thus, feedback is an essential characteristic of relationships as well as an important source of information about yourself. (If you would like to know more about yourself, check out the Keirsey Temperament Sorter at *www.keirsey.com/ keirsey.html.*)

Time

Once Communicator 2 responds to Communicator 1, their interaction can be represented by a circle. But as their exchange progresses in time, the relationship between them is more accurately described by several circles. In fact, all but the briefest exchanges entail several communication cycles. Thus, time itself becomes the final element in our model.

Figure 1.1 conveys the presence of time by representing communication in a form somewhat like a spiral, or uncoiled spring. Some writers prefer to symbolize time as a helix; the only difference between these forms is that the spiral is usually regarded as two-dimensional whereas the helix is thought of as three-dimensional. We shall treat them as identical.

The spiral also illustrates that participants in the communication process can never return to the point at which they started. The relationship must undergo change as a result of each interaction.

Throughout this text, we shall point out the effects of time on communication. Implicit in this emphasis is our belief that time is one of the most relevant variables in the study of human communication. If it does nothing else, the spiral or transactional model should remind us that communication is not static and that it thus requires methods of analysis different from those applied to a fixed entity.

The model identifies some of the major elements that exist in all human communication. We have discussed such communication only in its simplest form. As we add more communicators, change the kind or amount of interference, or vary the messages transmitted, our subject increases in complexity. We shall see this especially when we turn to the study of **communication contexts.** As you read on, you may want to look at other models, some of which are mentioned in the books listed at the end of this chapter. You may even want to try your hand at developing a model of your own. In either case remember that each communication event you will study has something unique about it, and no model can be used as a blueprint of the communication process.

COMMUNICATION CONTEXTS

Human communication occurs in several kinds of situations. Seven different contexts seem to be widely agreed upon in the communication literature: (1) interpersonal, (2) intercultural, (3) interviewing, (4) small group, (5) public communication, (6) organizational communication, and (7) mass communication. Keep in mind that while each of these contexts has some unique characteristics, all of them share *the process of creating a meaning between two or more people.* And all of these contexts sometimes involve intercultural communication, another variable we will examine.

Interpersonal Communication

Interpersonal communication is the basic unit of communication. Although it may occur among three or more individuals in some special circumstances, our communication model depicts this context as occurring between two people. Some scholars believe that the most important defining element in interpersonal communication is the level of closeness or intimacy between the parties. That is felt to be more important than the number of individuals participating. However, we believe that interpersonal communication also includes most of the informal, everyday exchanges that we engage in from the time we get up until the time we go to bed. While a lot of very informal and superficial communication may occur between two people (i.e., a dyad), this is also the context that includes the most intimate relationships we ever experience.

In Mitch Albom's best-selling book *Tuesdays with Morrie,* he tells the true story of his last conversations with his former teacher, Morrie Schwartz, who was dying of ALS (Lou Gehrig's disease). He writes,

> "I don't know why you came back to me. But I want to say this . . ."
> He paused and his voice choked.
> "If I could have had another son, I would have liked it to be you."
> I dropped my eyes, kneading the dying flesh of his feet between my fingers. For a moment I felt afraid, as if accepting his words would somehow betray my own father. But when I looked up, I saw Morrie smiling through tears and I knew there was no betrayal in a moment like this. All I was afraid of was saying goodbye. (Albom, 1997, p. 168)

This passage illustrates the deep love that can develop through interpersonal communication.

Intercultural Communication

Another category we shall be exploring is *intercultural communication*—that is, *communication between members of different cultures (whether defined in terms of racial, ethnic, or socioeconomic differences, or a combination of these differences).* **Culture** is *a way of life developed and shared by a group of people and passed down* *from generation to generation.* Gudykunst and Kim (1992) offer the following example of intercultural communication:

> Consider a visit to North America by strangers from a culture with a communication rule requiring that direct eye contact always be avoided . . . If the strangers do not look them in the eye when talking, the North Americans will assume that the strangers either have something to hide or are not telling the truth. (p. 35)

Similarly, Chin, Gu, and Tubbs (2001) write, ". . . being outgoing, as it is normally understood in the U.S., may be perceived as being rude in other cultures, thereby provoking rather than preventing social isolation" (p. 21).

The significance of intercultural communication will only increase as companies strive toward global operations. Along with globalization of the market comes globalization of knowledge, which today is perceived as a vital tool in maintaining a company's core competencies. Companies that have implemented knowledge management programs have been increasingly confronted by the fact that cultural barriers today are major obstacles to the success of any such program (Kaweevisultrakul, 2007).

This dimension of experience cuts across all communication contexts: It may occur in two-person communication, interviews, small groups, or any of the other categories we examine in Part Two. Thus intercultural communication will be discussed not only in Chapter 10 but also in many other chapters of this text—for example, in relation to person perception, human attraction, and verbal and nonverbal communication. In a society such as our own, with its rich mix of cultures, intercultural communication will be especially relevant.

Interviewing

An *interview* is often defined as *a communication transaction that emphasizes questions and answers* (Camp, Vielhaber, and Simonetti, 2001). Whether it is talking to a physician to help diagnose an illness, to a prospective employer for a job, to a professor for help in a course, to a market researcher to identify strengths in a product, or to a prosecuting attorney from the witness stand, interviewing is often targeted toward accomplishing a specific purpose. Since interviewing is such a stylized form of communication, specific techniques can be used to best accomplish the interviewer's purpose. These techniques, along with specific types of interview questions, and so on, can be observed on such television programs as *60 Minutes, 20/20,* and *Meet the Press.*

Small-Group Communication

Small-group communication is defined as *"the process by which three or more members of a group exchange verbal and nonverbal messages in an attempt to influence one another"* (Tubbs, 2007, p. 5). Since this context involves three or more people, the degree of intimacy, participation, and satisfaction tends to be lower than in two-person communication. Small-group communication occurs in churches, in social situations, in organizations, and in therapeutic settings, to name a few examples. Group dynamics is a well-researched field of study and tends to focus on small groups that engage in problem solving and decision making. Small-group communication, therefore, tends to focus on the ways to improve the work that can be accomplished in groups. Work teams are but one example of small groups dedicated to improving organizational performance (see Maxwell, 2001).

Public Communication

Often referred to as "public speaking," this is a distinct context in a number of ways. First, it occurs in public rather than private places—that is, in auditoriums, classrooms, ballrooms, and so on. Second, public communication is relatively formal as opposed to informal, unstructured communications. Usually, the event is planned in advance. Some people are designated to perform certain functions (such as introducing the speaker). In a commencement exercise, for example, there may be several speakers, as well as a prayer and a ceremony in which degrees are awarded. And third, there are relatively clear-cut behavioral norms (Lucas, 2001). For example, questions are usually addressed to the speaker after the speech is completed. Thus, *public communication* usually requires that the speaker do significantly more preparation, and he or she should expect a more formalized setting than in two-person or small-group communication.

Organizational Communication

Organizational communication is defined as *"the flow of messages within a network of interdependent relationships"* (Goldhaber, 1990, p. 11). This definition fits not only businesses but also hospitals, churches, government agencies, military organizations, and academic institutions. Here we are concerned not only with the effectiveness of the individual communication but with the role of communication in contributing to or detracting from the effective functioning of the total organization.

A study of U.S. hospitals conducted by the *Wall Street Journal* found that communication problems occurring when a patient is handed over to a new nurse or doctor during a shift change are the "single largest source of medical error" ("*Wall Street Journal* Examines . . . ," 2006). According to the *Journal*, hospitals generally have hand-off arrangements that "vary from unit to unit or even nurse to nurse," resulting in errors that range from giving a patient the wrong medication to reviving a patient who has a "do not resuscitate" order.

To address the problem, the Joint Commission on Accreditation of Healthcare Organizations has begun requiring hospitals to develop formal procedures addressing hand-off communications. For example, when St. Joseph Medical Center in Chicago implemented a communication model called SBAR (Situation, Background, Assessment, and Recommendation)—which originally was used to quickly brief nuclear submariners during a change in command—the rate of adverse events dropped to 39.6 from 89.9 per 1,000 patient days in the first year ("*Wall Street Journal* Examines . . . ," 2006).

The return from increased communication effectiveness merits the effort spent on its improvement. The Watson Wyatt 2005/2006 *Communication World* ROI Study of 335 North American companies demonstrated a strong correlation between communication effectiveness, organizational turnover, and financial performance. For example, the study found that companies with highly effective communication practices have a 19 percent higher market premium, 57 percent shareholder returns over five years, and a level of employee engagement that is 4.5 times higher than that of the competition (Finney, 2006).

The nature of organizations is radically changing, and the complexity of organizational communication increases as companies enter the global market. The same study also found that most companies competing internationally (60 percent of surveyed companies had global operations)—even those with a high degree of communication effectiveness—often fall short when it comes to global communication mainly because what companies regard as communicating is often merely translating (Finney, 2006).

The use of an intranet greatly increases the role communication can play in an organization. Because of the number of assignments at distant locations, Banco do Brasil, a large financial services company in South America, has used an intranet to successfully improve the quality of intradepartment communication, as well as communication with clients (Correia and Menezes De Faria, 2004, p. 32).

Greater emphasis than ever is being placed on "continuous improvement." In Japan, this is known as *kaizen* (*kai* means "change," and *zen* means "good" or "for the better") (Liker, 2004). An example of this is the story about several customers who are waiting in line for service (it could be anywhere). One person at the front of the line gets mediocre service, and everybody else gets mad. They say, "Who do you think you are, getting mediocre service—you are supposed to get lousy service like the rest of us!" This is just one indication of why organizations need to be striving toward *kaizen*.

While modern communication channels increase the efficiency of communication among company's employees, they also bring a greater risk of release of sensitive information, intentional or unintentional (Vandermeer, 2006). E-mail, being the preferred communications venue for employees today, presents the greatest risk. According to a recently completed audit of e-mail traffic of several *Fortune* 500 companies, approximately 2 to 5 percent of all corporate e-mail messages contain data or information that is legally protected or considered proprietary to the business from which it originates (Vandermeer, 2006).

Mass Communication

This last context involves *communication that is mediated*. That is, the source of a message communicates through some print or electronic medium. And mediated encounters differ from personal encounters (Avery and McCain, 1982). In addition, the message is intended for masses of individuals rather than for only a small number of individuals. Of the seven contexts of human communication discussed in this book, *mass communication* is the most formal—and the most expensive. Television advertisements during the Super Bowl each year will cost millions of dollars per minute! Saddam Hussein was captured on Saturday, December 13, 2003. After official confirmation, the news spread throughout the entire world by the following Sunday morning. In addition, the opportunities for feedback in mass communication are more limited, especially when compared with interpersonal or small-group communication. The audience is relatively large, heterogeneous, and anonymous to the source. Finally, communication experience is characterized as public, rapid, and fleeting.

Bernard Goldberg states in his book *Bias* (2002) that in his many years as a television correspondent for CBS News, he noticed a systematic liberal bias in the coverage, not only in his network, but at ABC and NBC. He carefully documents numerous specific examples of this bias starting with the coverage of "conservative millionaire" Steve Forbes as a presidential candidate in 2000. If you are interested in this topic, you also would enjoy the opposing point of view expressed in the book by James Carvill and Paul Begala entitled *Buck Up, Suck Up . . . and Come Back When You Foul Up* (2002). Both of these are really great treatments of some of the issues regarding mass communication.

COMMUNICATION TECHNOLOGIES

We are all becoming increasingly familiar with what was once considered complex communication technology. For example, laptop computers have become a daily tool for many. Students walking across campus are often talking on their cell phones. Fax machines are so popular that fast-food restaurants like McDonald's use them to take orders.

The most powerful technological wonder that has revolutionized human communication is the Internet. Although this has had positive effects, there have been some downsides too. One major study at Carnegie Mellon University (Harmon, 1998*) found that people who spend even a few hours a week online experience higher levels of depression and loneliness than people who use the computer less. The researchers concluded that Internet use itself appeared to cause a decline in psychological well-being. The study was funded by high-tech companies such as Hewlett-Packard, AT&T Research, Intel, Apple Computer, and the National Science Foundation, and the findings were exactly the opposite of what researchers were expecting to find. The researchers also concluded that the study "raises some troubling questions about the nature of 'virtual' communication and the disembodied relationships that are often formed in the vacuum of cyberspace" (p. A4).

Another study looked into so-called Internet addiction (Lorek, 1998). How would you answer the following questions, using: 1, not at all; 2, rarely; 3, occasionally; 4, often; and 5, always.

---

*See Chapter 15 for more on the social effects of Internet use.

Do you stay online longer than you intended?

Do you prefer the excitement of the Internet to the intimacy of your partner?

Do you check your e-mail before something else that you need to do?

Do you lose sleep at night due to late-night log-ons?

Do you choose to spend more time online than going out with others?

If you scored 5–9, you have average online use. If you scored 10–17, this would indicate some tendency toward Internet problems. If you scored 18–25, this would indicate a stronger tendency toward Internet problems. This is according to Kimberly Young at the University of Pittsburgh, who is cofounder of the Center for Online Addiction.

Even farmers have gone high tech. Kageyama (1992) reports that some farmers in Japan have outfitted their cattle with beepers. He reports that "he dials the cows' number on a portable phone to get their attention, and 'they look up immediately from eating the grass.' Usually they head for the feeding station, but sometimes they ignore the beeps and continue grazing" (p. A3).

Few areas have been affected by computer-based communication technologies more profoundly than the areas of learning and education. Today's learning groups often interact solely by means of technology; the participants may be colleagues, friends, or even strangers (Imamoglu, 2007). The benefits of today's distant learning, or e-learning, include

- Video-Conference Classrooms that eliminate the boundaries of place-dependent, face-to-face classrooms so that two or more distinct social networks can be joined together.
- Group Discussion Spaces that provide a site for a working group, such as a project team, consulting team, or student learning team.
- Online Communities—Internet-based forums that anybody can join to discuss themes of common interest. (Imamoglu, 2007)

With all this high-tech communication potential, human communication is at once more possible and perhaps less human. Regardless of your sentiments regarding these innovations, there is no question that they are having a profound and permanent impact on human communication.

Communication Ethics

This edition includes a chapter on ethics in communication. It seems that hardly a day goes by without some controversy being reported, whether it's deciding whether to clone human beings, or corporations abusing the environment, or Stanford University being accused of misusing overhead expense accounts from research grants.

Ethical questions also arise about how information is communicated to mass audiences, especially through television. For example, during the 2004 Super Bowl,

Janet Jackson revealed her breast during the half-time show. The Super Bowl audience is traditionally a family audience. The FCC has attempted to regulate the material allowed on network television, but there are often discrepancies between programs allowed on network television and cable stations.

Advertisements on television and magazines also present what may be considered unethical behavior. Ads tout harmful products such as cigarettes and promote unrealistic body images to young audiences. The chapter on communication ethics should provide you with some helpful insights and guidelines on how to avoid difficulties in all of these areas.

WHAT IS EFFECTIVE COMMUNICATION?

Have you ever wondered what they teach in an "information literacy" class? Or what exactly a vendor who "offers printing solutions" does? These and other examples are the reason that communication expert Gerard Braud says that he finds himself asking the question "What does that mean?" more and more often. "In an age of information overload, audiences don't have time to decipher techno-speak, doublespeak, acronyms, and *make it up so I sound smarter than you*–speak" (Braud, 2007, italics in original). "While preparing someone for an interview or writing notes for the spokesperson and organization, I have to ask 'What does that mean?' no less than three times before I can get to what the person is really trying to say" (Braud, 2007).

> A charity needed help with its messaging. In a role-playing media training interview, one executive said, "Our clients have barriers to employment." My first "What does that mean?" came because I wanted an explanation of the word clients. I was told it meant the people who come to the charity for help. My second "What does that mean?" came as I asked about "barriers to employment." The executive's response was that some individuals are unable to obtain employment because of barriers related to their social, economic and/or physical conditions. In my third attempt at clarification, I asked if it was because they were poor, divorced, uneducated, living without a car, raising children as single parents, or living with a physical or mental disability. The answer was yes, all of the above. The organization's new clarified key message is: "Our goal is to help people find jobs, whether it's people with physical limitations, single mothers, people with no transportation, or a variety of other issues that keep them from getting and keeping a good-paying job." (Braud, 2007)

The following few simple rules, Braud says, are essential for effective communication:

Rule No. 1: Make it clear.

Rule No. 2: Say what you mean.

Rule No. 3: Avoid acronyms and abbreviations.

Rule No. 4: Get to the lowest common denominator.

Earlier in this chapter we said that we would be concerned not only with human speech communication but with the concept of effective communication. But what are the criteria that make for effective communication? Students sometimes say that communication is effective when a person gets his or her point across. This is but one measure of effectiveness. More generally, communication is effective *when the stimulus as it was initiated and intended by the sender, or source, corresponds closely to the stimulus as it is perceived and responded to by the receiver.*

If we let *S* stand for the person who is the sender or source of the message and *R* for the receiver of the message, then communication is whole and complete when the response *S* intends and the response *R* provides are identical:

$$\frac{R}{S} = \frac{receiver's\ meaning}{sender's\ meaning} = 1$$

We rarely reach 1—that is, perfect sharing of meaning. As a matter of fact, we never reach 1. We approximate it. And the greater the correspondence between our intention and the response we receive, the more effective we have been in communicating. At times, of course, we hit the zero mark: There is absolutely no correspondence between the response we want to produce and the one we receive. The drowning man who signals wildly for help to one of his friends on a sailboat only to have her wave back is not accomplishing his communication objective to say the least.

The example of the drowning man is extreme. By now you may be wondering just how important effective communication is on a day-to-day basis. A long-term study of Massachusetts Institute of Technology (MIT) graduates who were interviewed several times over a 15-year period has revealed that even for those very talented, technically competent graduates of a prestigious school, effectiveness in communication was one of the most important skills in achieving a successful and fulfilling life, if not the *most* important. On the basis of his research, the author of this study stresses the increasing importance of interpersonal competence as a skill critical "not only for dealing with self and family development, but for career advancement as well" (Schein, 1978, p. 77).

But how do we measure our own effectiveness? We can't judge our effectiveness if our intentions are not clear; we must know what we are trying to do. What makes that first definition of effectiveness inadequate ("when a person gets his or her point across") is that in communicating, we may try to bring about one or more of several possible outcomes. We shall consider five of them here: understanding, pleasure, attitude influence, improved relationships, and action.

Understanding

Understanding refers primarily to *accurate reception of the content of the intended stimulus.* In this sense, a communicator is said to be effective if the receiver has an accurate understanding of the message the communicator has tried to convey.

(Of course, the communicator sometimes conveys messages unintentionally that are also quite clearly understood.)

The primary failures in interpersonal communication are failures to achieve content accuracy. For example, the service manager of an oil company had a call one winter morning from a woman who complained that her oil burner was not working. "How high is your thermostat set?" he asked. "Just a moment," the woman replied. After several minutes she returned to the phone. "At 5 feet 3½ inches," she said, "same as it's always been." This confusion is typical of a failure to achieve understanding. Most misunderstandings of this kind are relatively easy to remedy through clarifying feedback and restatement.

As we add more people to a communication context, it becomes more difficult to determine how accurately messages are being received. This is one of the reasons that group discussions sometimes turn into free-for-alls. Comments begin to have little relation to one another, and even a group with an agenda to follow may not advance toward the resolution of any of its problems. Situations such as these call for more clarifying, summarizing, and directing of group comments.

With respect to public communication, much has been written about how to improve understanding when speaking to inform—with "understanding" often being referred to as "information gain." What the public speaker must remember is that the feedback he or she receives is often quite limited; the speaker should therefore make a concerted effort to be as objective and precise as possible in explaining his or her subject. The use of supporting materials—examples, analogies, and the like—helps clarify an explanation of almost any subject.

Within an organizational setting, accurate understanding is one of the most basic desired outcomes. It is not possible, for example, for an organization to function efficiently unless employees understand what they are expected to do at their jobs. This may involve understanding not only verbal directives from immediate superiors but also information disseminated through interoffice memos, employee handbooks, and other restatements of company policies.

In mass communication, the dissemination of information is also a primary objective on many occasions. (Newscasts, documentaries, and videotape programs immediately come to mind.) Presumably, those who work in the mass media have developed their communications skill to a high degree so that they are able to organize, present, and interpret information in a way that promotes understanding. For example, in a single hour a television special can present a program on depression: its symptoms, causes, and possible treatment. Because feedback is so limited in this setting, however, it is difficult to assess the level of information gain within the audience.

Pleasure

Not all communication has as its goal the transmission of a specific message. In fact, the goal of the transactional analysis school of thought is simply to communicate with others in a way that ensures a sense of mutual well-being. This is sometimes referred to as a *phatic communication,* or maintaining human contact. Many of our brief exchanges with others—"Hi"; "How are you today?"; "How's it going?" have this purpose. Casual dates and cocktail parties are more structured occasions on which we come together to enjoy the company and conversation of others. The degree to which we find communication pleasurable is closely related to our feelings about those with whom we are interacting. Recent research on cell phone usage shows that the average U.S. teenager uses his or her cell phone 500 minutes a month, but 800 or 900 minutes per month is not unusual (LeDuc, 2001). Also, according to a study by Context, the cell phone has become such a primary mode of communication for teenagers that they may even unintentionally avoid contact with friends who don't have cell phones (Batista, 2003).

The purpose of public communication can also be pleasure; the after-dinner speech and the speech intended to entertain fall into this category. Much of the informal communication within an organization takes place during lunch hours, coffee breaks, company picnics, and management club dances. And certainly in movies, situation comedies, and televised sports events, we see entertainment provided on a grand scale.

Attitude Influence

Understanding and agreement are by no means synonymous outcomes. When you understand someone's message, you may find that you disagree with him or her even more strongly than you did before.

Products created in response to the latest diet trend in 2004, the "low-carb diet," are advertised everywhere. Now you can buy almost anything in a new low-carb version, even beverages. Coca-Cola has launched a new product, Coke Zero, a low-carb version of Coke, to market to those who have jumped on the low-carb bandwagon (Oglesby, 2004). As more products are developed and the diet hype continues, consumers are influenced to purchase and consume certain types of foods. On one hand, a consumer may feel the pressures of choosing low-carb foods because of all the advertising and focus on the diet. On the other hand, the feelings of those who do not agree with the diet may grow even deeper when the hype is all around them.

Influencing attitudes is a basic part of daily living. In many situations, we are interested in influencing a person's attitude as well as in having him or her understand what we are saying. The process of changing and reformulating attitudes, or *attitude influence,* goes on throughout our lives. In two-person situations, attitude influence is often referred to as "social influence." In the counseling interview, it might be called "gentle persuasion." Attitude influence is no less important in the small-group or the organizational setting. For example, consensus among group members is an objective of many problem-solving discussions. And industries often try, especially through the mass media, to influence public attitudes toward big business by presenting themselves in a flattering light. (For example, Exxon commercials about ecology suggest that the fuel industry is greatly concerned about the pollution problems caused by industrial waste.) When applied to public and mass communication contexts, the process of attitude influence is usually referred to as "persuasion." Studies of mass communication are particularly concerned with the persuasive impact of the message on various opinion leaders within the larger mass audience.

In determining how successful your attempts to communicate have been, remember that you may fail to change a person's attitude but still get that person to understand your point of view. In other words, a failure to change someone's point of view should not necessarily be written off as a failure to increase understanding.

Improved Relationships

It is commonly believed that if a person can select the right words, prepare his or her message ahead of time, and state it precisely, perfect communication will be ensured. But total effectiveness requires a positive and trusting psychological climate. When a human relationship is clouded by mistrust, numerous opportunities arise for distorting or discrediting even the most skillfully constructed messages. Voters may well be suspicious of their mayor's promise that if reelected, he will fulfill all the campaign promises he failed to keep during his first term in office. A young man will probably discount a young woman's assurances that she is very interested in him after she breaks a date for the third or fourth time. A professor may begin to doubt the excuses of a student who is holding court at the student union an hour after the student was too sick to take the midterm.

We mentioned that the primary failures in communication occur when the content of the message is not accurately understood. By contrast, secondary failures are disturbances in human relationships that result from misunderstandings. They stem from the frustration, anger, or confusion (sometimes all three) caused by the initial failure to understand. Because such failures tend to polarize the communicators involved, they are difficult to resolve. By acknowledging that the initial misunderstandings are a common occurrence in daily communication, we may be able to tolerate them better and avoid or at least minimize their damaging effect on interpersonal relationships.

Still another kind of understanding can have a profound effect on human relationships: understanding another person's motivations. At times each of us communicates not to convey information or to change someone's attitude but simply to be "understood" in this second sense. Throughout this text, we shall discuss various facets of human relationships: motivation; social choice; confirmation, self-disclosure, trust; group cohesiveness; and source credibility in public and mass communication. We hope to show that all these concepts are bound together by a common theme: The better the relationship between people, the more likely it is that other outcomes of effective communication in the fullest sense will occur.

Action

Some would argue that all communication is useless unless it brings about a desired action. Yet all the outcomes discussed thus far—understanding, pleasure, attitude influence, improved relationships—are important at different times and in different places. There are instances, however, when action is an essential determinant of the success of a communicative act. In the sales interview, an automobile salesman who wants you to think more favorably of his car than his competitor's also wants you to act by buying a car; his primary objective is not attitude change. A math tutor is far from satisfied if the student she is coaching says he understands how to do a set of problems but fails to demonstrate that understanding on his next exam. And we might question the effectiveness of a finance committee that reaches consensus on how to balance a budget yet fails to act on its decision.

Eliciting action on the part of another person is probably the communication outcome most difficult to produce. In the first place, it seems easier to get someone to understand your message than it is to get the person to agree with it. Furthermore, it seems easier to get that person to agree—that he or she should exercise regularly, for example—than to get the person to act on it. (We realize that some behaviors are induced through coercion, social pressure, or role prescriptions and do not necessarily require prior attitude change. Voluntary actions, however, usually follow rather than precede attitude changes.) If you are trying to promote action on the part of the receiver, you increase your chances of getting the desired response if you can (1) facilitate understanding of your request, (2) secure agreement that the request is legitimate, and (3) maintain a comfortable relationship with the receiver. The desired action does not follow automatically, but it is more likely to follow if these intermediate objectives have first been accomplished.

The difficulties of eliciting action on the part of the receiver are further compounded in organizational and mass communication settings. The plant manager's abrasive memo on absenteeism, for example, may trigger more absenteeism, or the sick calls may taper off and some form of sabotage appear in the products turned out on the assembly line. Certainly, the mass media are often concerned with promoting audience action—whether it be promoting a particular brand of detergent, getting mothers to immunize their children against rubella, or changing audience voting patterns. Yet researchers have questioned the effectiveness of mass communication in changing behavior. It has been found, for example, that political campaigns conducted through the mass media have little direct influence on changes in voting behavior. One interesting new development intended to improve action as a result of communication is that the Federal Communications Commission has directed cell phone companies to start issuing phones that determine their locations through transmission towers or by global positioning satellites. In some cases, the accuracy must be within 150 feet. This is so that emergency crews can respond more quickly to urgent phone calls. However, it also raises the question of privacy, since all calls can be traced to the sending location. You may want to discuss the pros and cons of this in your class (Kanaley, 2001).

In short, the five possible outcomes of effective human communication are understanding, pleasure, attitude influence, improved relationships, and action. At different points in this book, we will give special attention to each of them. For example, the concepts of attitude similarity, status, social influence and consensus, and persuasion all have some bearing on attitude influence. Similarly, the concepts of trust, cohesiveness, and source credibility are all relevant to improved human relationships.

The five outcomes we have discussed are neither exhaustive nor mutually exclusive. Thus, a look at the relationship aspects of communication in Chapter 8 will illustrate that defensive behaviors distort understanding, that the so-called disconfirming responses are not pleasurable. In the chapters that follow, we will show some of the many ways in which communication outcomes are interdependent and to demonstrate that this is true for many different communication contexts, or settings.

Summary

In this book, we view human communication as the process of creating a meaning between two or more people. Today, many communication scholars emphasize the transactional nature of the communication process so that one person's communication can be defined only in relation to some other or others.

In this chapter, we presented a model to help us conceptualize the relationships between the elements of human communication. Like all human beings, both communicators in our model originate and perceive messages. Both depend on the steady flow of physical, social, and cultural input, and both select from the total input through their perceptual filters and sets.

We then discussed the components of a message in terms of the types of stimuli transmitted: verbal and nonverbal, intentional and unintentional. We learned that, though all five senses are potential channels for receiving stimuli, face-to-face communication relies primarily on hearing, sight, and touch and is usually a multichannel experience. The channels of organizational communication would extend to newsletters, memos, e-mails, and the like, whereas those of mass communication would include newspapers, films, radio, the Internet, and television. Anything that distorts the information transmitted through the various channels or that distracts the receiver from getting it would be considered interference.

We saw that all the elements in Communicator 1's half of our communication cycle—input, filters, verbal and nonverbal messages, channels, and interference—are different for Communicator 2 because of his or her uniqueness as a human being. Emphasis was given to the receiver as listener. We examined the importance of feedback, and we examined the effect of time, represented in the model by a spiral, as a crucial variable in all studies of communication.

Much of the time people spend communicating involves interpersonal communication. But in studying human communication, we are also concerned with contexts in which a great many parties are involved, feedback is limited, and messages are transmitted through such media as newspaper, radio, and television. We are interested therefore in the principles of human communication as they apply not only to the two-person setting and the interview but to small-group, public, organizational, and mass communication. We are also interested in communication behaviors that are ethical.

After a brief discussion of each of the communication contexts, we turned to an examination of what constitutes effective communication. It was established that communication is effective to the degree that the message as it is intended by the sender corresponds with the message as it is perceived and responded to by the receiver. We learned that effectiveness is closely linked with intention and that in communicating, we usually want to bring about one or more of several possible outcomes. Five of the major outcomes—understanding, pleasure, attitude influence, improved relationships, and action—were considered here, with emphasis on their application to the various communication contexts. Another area of interest is intercultural communication, which cuts across all the contexts we shall be discussing.

Key Terms

Communication	Feedback	Messages	Technical
Communication	Input	Nonverbal message	interference
context	Interference	Semantic interference	Verbal message

Review Questions

1. Provide your own personal definition of "communication." How is it similar to, or different from, the definitions given in this text?

2. What is input, and how does it influence a person's communication?

3. Name the four types of messages. Give a specific example of each from your own experience.

4. Explain the difference between technical and semantic interference and give an example of each.

5. Discuss the influence of various kinds of feedback.

6. List seven different communication contexts. Explain the distinctive characteristics of each.

7. What is effective communication? Think of arguments for and against the types of communication effectiveness that have been described in this chapter. Are there some that the text has not included? Are there some it has discussed that you think should not be included? What do you think is the most important outcome of face-to-face communication?

Exercises

1. Start a personal log on the computer in which you record your daily reaction to perhaps 10 members of your class. Only some will impress you (favorably or unfavorably) at first. Note details of their behavior. Describe your own responses as candidly as possible.

2. a. Draw and label a model of human communication. If possible, include components that can be appropriately labeled as Communicator 1 (sender/receiver), Communicator 2 (receiver/sender), input, filters, messages, channels, interference, and time.

   b. Examine the model carefully and formulate five statements that describe how two or more components of the model may influence communication effectiveness as defined in this chapter.

3. Write a short paper in which you analyze the strengths and weaknesses of the communication model in this chapter. Compare and contrast it with some other models, which may be found in the books in the suggested readings.

4. Divide the class members into groups of five or six; then have each group member discuss a personal problem in communication. Have each group select its "best" example of a communication problem as well as a spokesperson to present the example to the entire class. Then analyze each example in terms of the communication model given in this chapter.

5. Observe several communication events and keep a record of their outcomes. Which outcomes occurred most frequently? Under what conditions did these outcomes seem to occur? How can you explain these results?

6. Write a one-page case study of a communication failure that you have experienced or observed. Then write an analysis of its causes, and suggest a way to resolve it.

7. Think of two people you know, one an excellent communicator, the other quite ineffective. Write a highly specific description of each; then write a comparison of the two in which you contrast and evaluate their communication styles. On the basis of this analysis, set yourself three specific objectives for improving your own communication behaviors.

8. Check out the Internet for sources of information regarding communication.

Suggested Readings

Acuff, Frank L. *How to Negotiate Anything with Anyone Anywhere around the World,* 2nd ed. New York: American Management Association, 1997.

This excellent book helps explain how to apply communication principles in 41 countries. It is a very valuable resource.

Gladwell, Malcolm. *BLINK.* Boston: Little Brown and Company, 2004.

This best-selling book offers numerous principles and examples of communication in society.

Goldberg, Bernard. *Bias: A CBS Insider Exposes How the Media Distort the News.* Washington, D.C.: Regnery Publishing, 2002.

This best-selling book details a carefully researched account of the liberal bias in television news.

Hartman, Laura P., and Joe Desjardins, *Business Ethics: Decision-Making for Personal Integrity & Social Responsibility.* New York: McGraw-Hill, 2008.

This is an excellent book with many examples of thorny ethical decisions for readers to make.

Samovar, Larry A. *Public Speaking in a Multicultural Society.* Los Angeles: Roxbury Publishing Company, 2007.

This little paperback book demonstrates the ways that public speaking can be adapted to today's much more global society.

Tapscott, Don. *Growing Up Digital: The Rise of the Net Generation.* New York: McGraw-Hill, 1998.

An excellent source of information about how the Internet is and will be used as a growing communication alternative at work, at play, and as a learning tool.

Welch, Jack, with Suzy Welch. *Winning.* New York: Harper Business, 2005.

The former CEO of General Electric discusses how to be successful in business. Many of his subjects relate to topics in this book.

 ## For Supplementary Information

Log onto the Online Learning Center at *www.mhhe.com/tubbsmoss11.*

Person Perception

Chapter Objectives

After reading this chapter, you should be able to:

1. Explain the difference between a perceptual filter and a psychological set and discuss the selective nature of all perception.
2. Describe how person perception differs from object perception and explain the implications of such differences for communication.
3. Discuss the development of self-concept as well as its relationship to gender.
4. Explain some of the variables that influence self-esteem and state current research findings about self-esteem, shyness and Internet use, and the Pygmalion effect.
5. Describe the concepts of private personality theory, central traits, primacy, and empathy.
6. Discuss several variables, including perceived traits, physical attractiveness, expressiveness, and charisma, that influence our impressions of others.
7. Distinguish between personal generalizations and stereotypes, and discuss the effects of stereotyping.
8. Discuss how work, student, gender-linked, and marital roles influence person perception.
9. Describe several variables including interpersonal sensitivity involved in forming accurate perceptions of others, and identify three ways to improve person perception and communication effectiveness.

Maybe, as soon as a face is there, you know whether to trust it.
                                        —**Willis and Todorov (2006, p. 597)**

When it comes to first impressions, how much time does it take after seeing a person's face before you make up your mind? One new study asked people to make judgments of unfamiliar faces (Willis and Todorov, 2006) and found that you can form such a judgment within a tenth of a second. "In fact, for all judgments—attractiveness, likeability, trustworthiness, competence, and aggressiveness—increased exposure time [to viewing a face] did not significantly increase the correlations" (p. 592). Most scholars agree that impressions based on facial appearance tend to be fast and intuitive.

On the other hand, with increased time, research finds, your confidence about your judgments also increases and impressions about the traits of others become more differentiated. People become more individualized. For example, the effects of facial attractiveness seem to decrease over time.

In this chapter we examine many of the variables that affect our initial perceptions of others. For example, we will consider what we judge to be physically attractive in others as well as other traits we regard as central in forming such judgments. Our impressions of others form the basis for countless decisions throughout our lives—not only about romantic relationships, but about choosing a roommate, a friend, a business partner, an advisor, or a doctor. In the following pages, we will consider the initial process by which all such impressions of other human beings are formed but, equally important, we will also examine how we look at ourselves.

PERCEIVING PEOPLE AND OBJECTS: A COMPARISON

Our total awareness of the world comes to us through our senses. Thus, all our perceptions—whether they be of drawings, household objects, or other people—have a common basis. Yet, as we've seen countless times, two people often disagree sharply in their judgments about a third. Have you ever been "fixed up" with someone described to you as just your type, only to be thoroughly disappointed from the very beginning of the evening? You might have even asked yourself whether the person who arranged the date perceived you or the other party with any accuracy. The reasons for such varying perceptions should become apparent as we consider similarities between interpersonal perception and perception in general.

Two Kinds of Filters

Your capacity to register sensory stimuli is limited. You cannot take in everything. Nor do you always want to. You choose certain aspects of your environment over others. What you are aware of at any time is determined in part by what you as a receiver select out of the total input. "You hear what you want to hear," mutters the irritated father to his teenage son, "This is the third time this afternoon I've asked you when you're going to get around to washing the car." Later that day, the same man may sit at the dinner table reading the Sunday paper, oblivious to a family quarrel that is taking place across the room. *The ability to process certain of the stimuli available to us while filtering out others* is called **selective attention.**

The American philosopher and psychologist William James explained the process of selection at work here in terms of interest: "Millions of items of the outward order are present to my senses which never properly enter into my experience. Why? Because they have no *interest* for me. *My experience is what I agree to attend to.* Only those items which I *notice* shape my mind—without selective interest, experience is an utter chaos" (James, 1950, p. 402).

Each of us, then, perceives only part of the available stimuli while filtering out other stimuli. There are two kinds of filters through which all input or sensation will pass: physiological and psychological.

Perceptual Filters and Psychological Sets

Among the inherent structures of our sense organs are our **perceptual filters,** *physiological limitations that are built into human beings* and cannot be reversed. Such limitations on our capacity to perceive exist whether we are experiencing an object or a person. And they vary considerably from one individual to another so that we differ in the degree to which our various senses are accurate.

To the human communicator one extremely troublesome perceptual filter is the limit on one's ability to hear. Sometimes we think we hear a person say one thing when actually he or she said another. We then act on the basis of what we think that person said. Or we may act without hearing what a person said at all. Many communication difficulties are rooted in this kind of misunderstanding.

A psychological set is a second type of filter that influences our perceptions. Our **psychological sets**—that is, *our expectancies or predispositions to respond*— have a profound effect on our perception of objects. Similarly, psychological set affects our perception of other people. Suppose you were asked to interpret the scene in Figure 2.1. How would you answer? Is the young woman sitting with her laptop annoyed with the man beside her? Is she waiting for someone else? Or is she attracted to him? And why is he looking toward her? Has he just said something sarcastic—or flattering? Is he flirting? Do the two know each other well? An almost infinite number of interpretations can be evoked by an ambiguous photograph such as this one. Each of us has a story for this scene; with a little prodding, each of us could elaborate on it.

If you've been involved in a recent romantic relationship, you might be more inclined to perceive these people in a more positive way because you've come to expect and anticipate caring behavior. On the other hand, the two might be having a difficult time or they might be strangers with little connection to each other. Whatever your interpretation, it reveals much about your own expectations and past experiences. As you read on, you will see that past experience is a strong influence

Figure 2.1

on what you select from all the available stimuli; and often you are judging another person, at least initially, by the group or context in which he or she is first seen. This will certainly be apparent when we discuss stereotyping.

Culture and Perception

One of the most powerful determinants of psychological set is culture. Consider the two parallel straight lines in Figure 2.2. Which would you say is longer? Chances are that if you live in a Western culture, you will perceive the bottom line as being the longer of the two. If you measure them, though, you will see that they are actually the same length. This is a well-known phenomenon called the *Müller-Lyer illusion*. It is an illusion in visual perception that Western peoples are particularly likely to experience and one to which certain non-Western peoples are much less susceptible.

One explanation for the Müller-Lyer illusion is that people who live in a visual environment in which straight lines and right angles prevail—a "carpentered world" constructed with tools such as the saw, the plane, and the plumb bob—learn to make certain visual inferences. For example, they tend to interpret acute and obtuse angles as right angles that are extended in space. This is what happens when Westerners look at Figure 2.2. From the two-dimensional drawing they make inferences about perspective, thus seeing the two lines as unequal in length. People who live in a culture that has very few structures made up of straight lines and corners—people from Ghana, for example—are not likely to experience the Müller-Lyer

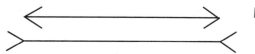

Figure 2.2

illusion because they do not tend to make such inferences about perspective (Segall et al., 1969). This is just one way in which culture influences our perception.

We have sets not only about objects and words but about other human beings—what they should look like, how they should act, and what they will say. In the United States, a businessperson expects people to be on time for appointments, and in turn those people do not expect to be kept waiting for long periods of time. When such expectancies are shared by all involved, they are often useful in facilitating communication. Other sets interfere with our ability to perceive accurately and respond appropriately. For example, some people—especially in telephone conversations—are so accustomed to being asked how they are that after saying "Hi" or "Hello," they answer "Fine" to whatever the other party has just said.

A great deal of interpersonal conflict stems from people's unawareness of the limits on their perceptual capacities. If they do realize the fallibility of their senses, they may be too defensive to acknowledge their mistakes. There is now convincing evidence that in some situations, if such a person is pressed, opposition to our point is likely to be reinforced instead of reversed, even though the person appears to be agreeing with us.

As two people communicate, each formulates ideas that become the content of the communication event. How accurately a message is received depends on the other person's perceptual filters and sets. Remember that psychological and physiological characteristics will influence which stimuli are selected and how they are perceived.

Selective Perception, Organization, and Interpretation

Today we don't believe, as early philosophers did, that the human mind is a blank tablet on which impressions are imprinted. We know that perception is not a passive state in which stimuli are received and automatically registered. Quite the opposite. Perception is an active process: Each of you *selectively* perceives, organizes, and interprets what you experience.

In general, you perceive stimuli that are intense, repetitive, or in the process of changing. Nonetheless, each person actively chooses what to attend to depending on personal interests, motivations, desires, and expectations. Entranced by a young woman's appearance, a man sitting next to her at a party may notice what great legs she has and pay little attention to what she's saying. Someone else in the group may be more interested in her remarks about working in the personnel department of a large company because he is looking for a job.

In addition to the selective perception of stimuli, you tend to organize stimuli selectively—that is, you order the stimuli with which you are presented into a "whole," a complete, sensible picture. Psychological tests with ambiguous scenes such as the one in Figure 2.1 are based on this notion.

People organize stimuli according to different schema and expectations: They attribute cause and effect uniquely. A quarrel between husband and wife in which he claims to withdraw because she nags while she claims to nag because he withdraws is such an example: The differences in organizing the sequence are at the heart of their different perceptions. Asked to explain, the husband maintains his withdrawal is his sole defense against his wife's nagging. She, in turn, sees his explanation as a deliberate distortion of "what 'really' happens"—that the reason for her critical attitude is the husband's passivity (Watzlawick et al., 1967, pp. 56–57).

After stimuli are selectively perceived and selectively organized, they are selectively interpreted—that is, the stimuli are assigned meanings unique to the perceiver. Personal interpretations are based on the perceiver's past experiences, assumptions about human behavior, knowledge of the other's circumstances, present moods/wants/desires, and expectations.

Perceiver/Object/Context

Like perceiving objects, perceiving other people may be thought of in terms of three elements: the perceiver, the object of perception (in this instance, another human being), and the context within which the object is viewed. As the perceiver, you are of course influenced by your own attributes. For example, people seem to have predispositions to make generally negative or positive evaluations of others; certainly we have all met someone who feels that "people are no damn good" or, at the other end of the spectrum, someone who would say that there's good to be found in all of us. It is through the eyes of the perceiver that all the attributes of that second person (the object, if you will) are filtered. Remember, though, that because person perception is a transactional process, those attributes do not always remain constant. If early in our first conversation you act as if I'm a terrible bore, you might find that my behavior changes from mildly friendly to just plain obnoxious. As for the third element, the context or setting within which the process of interpersonal perception occurs is both physical and psychological, as we shall see.

To some degree, however slight, we assume that the other person shares some of our characteristics, that we resemble each other in some ways. We are—or so we think—familiar with some of the other person's experience. Such assumptions may help us perceive more accurately. For example, if I know that you have just returned from a funeral, on the basis of my own experiences I will probably interpret your silence as depression rather than indifference. On the other hand, we often misinterpret what we perceive precisely because we assume other people are like us. If I assume that your taste in music is like mine, when I offer to play some country music, I may interpret your remark "Oh, great!" as genuinely enthusiastic though it is clear to most people from your facial expression that your reply was sarcastic.

Another way in which perceiving people differs from perceiving objects is that our perceptions and misperceptions influence and keep on influencing our interactions with others—because they keep responding to these perceptions. Sometimes people correct our misperceptions. But occasionally one misinterpretation leads to another, and we get further and further afield.

Person perception then is a special form of perception. As we go on to examine how impressions of others are formed, we will also give some attention to how members of other cultures tend to be perceived.

FORMING IMPRESSIONS

Our concern with the process of forming impressions involves the discussion of many variables, but it begins with you, the perceiver, and how you view yourself.

Looking at Yourself

If asked to describe yourself, what information would you give—a physical description, your age, gender, membership in an ethnic group? Perhaps you would define yourself by certain traits or by what you do. You might say you are a student, that you are outgoing and interested in politics, or that you are athletic and somewhat shy. For some, self-description is an uncomfortable process. For example, one college application asks prospective students to describe themselves by using ten adjectives. One reason college applications can be so difficult to fill out is that they often require statements about self-concept.

Self-Concept

Your **self-concept,** *your relatively stable impressions of yourself,* includes not only your perception of your physical characteristics but your judgments about what you "have been, are, and aspire to be" (Pearson et al., 1995). Self-concept develops partly out of the feedback you receive from the people around you. In fact, some early theorists believe that there is a **"looking glass self"** that develops out of our relations and interactions with others. In other words, you evaluate yourself primarily on the basis of how you *think* others perceive and evaluate you. You combine all these reflected perceptions, ways in which you think others see you, and they make up what Mead (1934) calls "the generalized other."

Such a view gives great weight to your experiences as a child. If, for example, Maria's parents, relatives, and school friends all come to think of her as "the good student," she may learn to regard herself in the same way and strive even harder to do well in classes. Academic performance may become an essential aspect of the way she thinks of herself. Conversely, if Jermaine is viewed by his parents, relatives, and neighbors as "the black sheep," he may come to see himself in this light.

A later theory related to the formation of self-concept is the **self-expansion model** proposed by Aron and Aron (1986). In this view, *expanding the self* to achieve various goals and desires is a basic human motivation, and a major way in which we do this is by *"including others in the self through close relationships so that the other's resources, perspectives, and identities are treated to some extent as one's own"* (Aron et al., 2006, p. 608). Like the earlier theory of the looking glass self, the self-expansion model emphasizes how the self develops in relation to—that is, out of interactions with—other people. We know that self-concept can change when close relationships develop and are later terminated (Lewandowski et al., 2006). (See Chapter 8 for a discussion of the life cycle of human relationships.)

Self-concept not only grows out of your social interactions but changes with your age as well as your situation—for example, you might see yourself very differently when at home than you do when you are away at college (Hinde et al., 2001, p. 190). Self-concept can vary so much with context that some suggest viewing the self "not as a unitary structure, but as multiple." It's been proposed also that different people who know us know different aspects of the self. "And the self must be seen as an active agent, providing expectancies and directing attention to whatever is of significance to the individual" (pp. 190–191).

Self-concept also has a comparative dimension. For example, Kagan writes: "Although a particular child is a female, Canadian, Catholic, with brown eyes, she is also prettier than her sister, smarter than her best friend, and more fearful of animals than her brother" (1989, p. 244). So a good part of how you think about yourself may have to do with how you judge yourself in relation to others.

Self-Concept and Gender

The way you see yourself in terms of what your culture regards as masculine or feminine traits is an important part of your self-concept, an aspect of gender as distinct from sex. *Sex* refers to *your biological and physiological characteristics, what makes you male or female.* **Gender,** a broader, more complex concept, *is in part shaped by culture and includes your "biological sex (male or female), psychological characteristics (femininity, masculinity, androgyny), attitudes about the sexes, and sexual orientation"* (Ivy and Backlund, 2004, pp. 32–34, 75).

Your attitudes toward gender affect both how you look at yourself and how you look at others. For example, one recent study found that people who have sexist attitudes also used gender as a basic category in perceiving others and that this contributed to gender stereotyping (Harper and Schoeman, 2003).

Much has been written about women valuing social relationships more than men do. In a study in which young adults were asked to write 20 sentences about themselves, young men used twice as many statements that were based on their membership in groups as women did. These included such sentences as "I am a Northwestern student" and "I am a member of Pi Kappa Alpha." Young women, on the other hand, were almost twice as likely as men to describe themselves in terms of their close relationships—for example, "I am Amanda's best friend" and "I am Pam's sister." This does not mean that one gender showed more interdependence than the other. Social bonds were of importance to both men and women, but they were expressed differently. When stressed, women tended to turn more to their close relationships, men to their social groups. Many studies confirm these findings

(Gardner and Gabriel, 2004). "Belonging is an essential component of the human experience" (p. 186).

When men and women from 12 countries were asked to describe themselves in terms of masculinity or femininity, "men in all countries described themselves as more masculine than women." But when asked to describe their ideal self, both men and women "wished to be 'more masculine' than they thought they were." This recent cross-cultural study also found greater similarity between the self-concepts of men and women in more developed countries and where women had worked outside their homes and had attended college (Best and Thomas, 2004, p. 303).

In general, many scholars now believe that we can best view the ways in which men and women are similar and different as a continuum, not a dichotomy (Beall, Eagly, and Sternberg, 2004, p. 4).

Self-Esteem

One of the chief measures of self-concept is **self-esteem,** *your feelings of self-worth.* Your self-esteem might be linked with your physical appearance, intelligence, work, any number of qualities, traits, and affiliations, but self-esteem may be entirely subjective. The research on self-esteem is becoming increasingly complex (Kernis, 2006). In "Your Money or Your Self-Esteem," a fascinating new series of studies (Zhang and Baumeister, 2006) looks at whether a person's self-esteem can interfere with sound judgment when it comes to financial decision making. Findings indicate that sometimes people pay a considerable financial price and emotional price when their self-esteem is threatened because they end up committing further resources to investments that they made based on bad decisions. In other words, when egotism is threatened, people are more likely to become trapped in losing situations. And "by persisting in the losing endeavor, they lost both money and whatever self-esteem they may have sought" (p. 890).

These studies give support to the view that threats to the ego may result in behaviors that are self-defeating, as the authors point out in reviewing previous research:

> Laboratory findings and field studies simply confirm what has been noted as a recurrent tragedy in everyday life: People get locked into unpromising career choices . . . , supervisors become overcommitted to those employees about whom they had expressed favorable opinion in hiring decisions, . . . coaches grant more playing time to higher drafted players in the NBA and keep them longer than the players' performance would warrant . . . , senior executives in banks escalate their institution's commitment to problem loans . . . , and entrepreneurs and venture capitalists become entrapped in unprofitable projects. (Zhang and Baumeister, 2006, p. 881)

Some theorists believe that at times we try to protect our self-esteem in areas where social comparisons are made—for example, if you don't do as well as your brother or sister who excels in academic work, you may find friends whose grades are not as high. There is, they suggest, a *frog pond effect.* According to this theory, being a "big frog in a small pond," or a success in a relatively unsuccessful group, is preferred over situations in which the performance of an individual's group may outshine the individual's own successes. (Gardner and Gabriel, 2004, p. 183)

Other research indicates that "self-esteem is not in and of itself a strong predictor of success" (Johnson, 1998). There may be no direct relationship between your actual traits, achievement, or competence and your feelings of self-worth (Sternberg and Kolligian, 1990). For example, a study of 1,000 women who achieved considerable success in their careers finds that many described themselves as "shy," "sensitive," and "self-critical" (Rimm, 1999, p. 8). Other research on exceptionally bright students shows that academic excellence does not necessarily make for high self-esteem.

Many studies of children report differences in self-esteem between boys and girls. In general, boys tend to overestimate their sense of competence while girls usually play down their own abilities.

And one summary of research on self-esteem includes these differences:

- Men have a higher expected success rate on nonsocial skills than do women; even when men do not perform better, people perceive that they do.
- Single women have higher self-esteem than do married women.
- Older children score higher on self-esteem than do younger children.
- Similarity in self-esteem appears to be a factor in selecting someone to date or have a relationship [with]. (Pearson et al., 1995)

Because it is linked with individualism, self-esteem is often highly regarded in the United States, but it's not only some high achievers who have high self-esteem—so do gang members and violent criminals. Indeed, "aggressive, violent, and hostile people consistently express favorable views of themselves" and when those views are threatened, the potential for violence is unleashed if the person in question is unstable or has an inflated sense of self (Baumeister et al., 1999). A survey of self-esteem research (Baumeister, 1998) summarizes the findings:

First, high self-esteem is linked to various positive outcomes and low self-esteem to bad outcomes, but often the self-esteem is the result rather than the cause. Second, high self-esteem does seem to make people feel better. . . . Third, high self-esteem has a small number of practical material benefits, such as greater persistence in the face of failure. Fourth, most social and personal problems are not caused by a lack of self-esteem, so raising self-esteem is unlikely to solve them. Fifth, high self-esteem, especially when not grounded in actual accomplishments, may breed interpersonal violence and other possible undesirable consequences. (p. 699)

Other research (Schütz, 2001) found that high self-esteem, though it has many benefits, can sometimes be disruptive socially, fostering a negative attitude toward other human beings. Certain interpersonal strategies for presenting yourself can also put down other people. For example:

Presenting yourself positively while criticizing others.

Overemphasizing your own abilities and devaluing those of other people.

Overestimating your own attractiveness and minimizing your responsibilities for social conflicts. (Adapted from p. 172)

It seems, then, that high self-esteem is not always a predictor of positive attitudes toward others.

Feedback

Feedback often has a direct effect on level of self-esteem. When people are asked to predict their own performance on a test—whether it be of social, intellectual, or physical competence—and are later given feedback on how well they scored, they revise their predictions for the next experimental task in the direction of that feedback. This is true regardless of whether the feedback is accurate.

Numerous studies of speech communication feedback suggest that this commonsense hunch is correct: When you get positive feedback, you gain in self-confidence. Negative feedback can make you flustered and cause disruptions in your delivery, whether this is indicated by the loudness of your voice, rate of speech fluency, nervousness, stage fright, eye contact, or body movement.

Current research on how we *perceive* our own abilities supports the view that our relationships with others make up the foundation out of which we develop a sense of self and competence. Some researchers believe that earlier theories about self-concept are still useful as a base for further studies on how the self develops in social contexts (Hinde et al., 2001).

There seem to be some gender differences with respect to feedback. Because women tend to give more importance to how others evaluate them, research has found, "women were more likely to consider . . . feedback accurate and to take it seriously (unrelated to any differences in self-confidence)—in other words, feedback had more information value for women than for men" (Deaux and LaFrance, 1998, p. 810). For example, the effect of negative stereotyping by employers would seem to influence a woman's evaluation of herself more than it would a man's self-evaluation.

Shyness

"Do you consider yourself to be a shy person?" This is one of the questions with which Zimbardo began his pioneering studies of shyness over 25 years ago. According to Zimbardo, "the average person you meet is either shy, used to be shy, or is easily shy in certain situations." In fact, "only about 10 percent of Americans say they've never felt shy" (Kutner, 1992; Zimbardo, 1990).

We take for granted our sense of self. If you have been raised in a Western culture, you probably tend to see yourself as independent of others—you make choices, decide for yourself, and feel relatively autonomous. Yet theorists are finding that there may be great cultural variation in self-concept—that is, in how the self is conceived. Western culture tends to promote *an independent self* that values self-direction, personal self-esteem and achievement, and freedom in relationships. Other cultures, including those from East Asia, seem to promote *an interdependent self* that places highest value on connection, collective self-esteem, group achievements, and being part of the in-group (Ting-Toomey, 1999, p. 29).

Thus Japanese students are more responsive to situations and self-criticism than students from the United States are (Kanagawa et al., 2001). For example, to someone Japanese describing yourself as kind or attractive might not be appropriate because that judgment should be made by the person you are with (p. 101). While American culture encourages developing "an independent view of the self—to be unique, to express the self, and to realize [your] own

thoughts, feelings, and capacities," Kanagawa finds the Japanese emphasize their similarity to others and how they fit into different social situations (p. 99).

Like Japanese culture, Chinese culture seems to foster an interdependent self. The emphasis in Confucianism is on relatedness to others—often in a hierarchical relationship. In Chinese, for example, there is no word for brother. Instead, there is one word for older brother and a different word for younger brother.

"For the Chinese," writes Stella Ting-Toomey, "the 'self' is both a center of relationships and a dynamic process of development within a network of relationships. In Chinese culture, to be aware of one's relations with others is an integral part of *zuo ren*, or 'conducting oneself properly' in getting along with others . . . Chinese can never separate themselves from obligations to others and Chinese sense of self-worth is closely tied with kinship and social networks" (Ting-Toomey, 1999, p. 78).

What has shaped your own self-concept? Do you think of yourself as more independent or more connected with others?

Today much is known about shyness. For example, researchers have found that some people have a "temperamental bias," or genetic predisposition, toward shyness; interestingly enough, this includes some physical traits such as light-colored eyes. Shyness has many physical symptoms, and these vary from one person to another—trembling, rapid heartbeat, dry mouth, sweating, blushing. Shy people date less frequently, have fewer friends, "tend to have low-esteem and are preoccupied with the thought that they are socially inadequate" (Cheek and Cheek, 1990, p. 15).

Because they have lower self-esteem, they also tend to apply for jobs beneath their level of skills and to settle for the first job offer that comes along. In general, they earn less and advance less in their work because, as researchers explain, "shy people self-select themselves out of high-paying careers" (Cheek and Cheek, 1990, p. 176).

Now new studies suggest that in some situations shy people can overcome their reticence. In making the transition to the social setting of the university, first-year students enter a new social setting that is unfamiliar to them. They are also in a setting in which they are evaluated on an ongoing basis: Professors are evaluating their intellectual capacities; and other students, most of whom are strangers, are evaluating their "intellectual, social, and sexual attractiveness." Certainly, this is a time in life that one would expect to intensify feelings of shyness. Yet in a study of students at Berlin University, Asendorpf (2000) found that leaving home to start at the university was apparently not threatening to shy students. And although it took more time for shy students to expand their social network of peers, they too forged new relationships. For shy students a major difference seemed to be that a considerable number were often lonely, and while other first-year students described themselves as in love "at any point in time," this was true of only a third of shy students. Then too, even when love and support were present in their relationships, shy students tended to feel more loneliness than students who were not shy.

More encouraging results come from several studies on the effects of technology use—specifically, use of the computer to access the Internet. There is considerable evidence that shy people reduce their levels of shyness online and that sometimes as a result of online successes they then reduce levels of shyness offline (Roberts et al., 2000).

A growing body of research and case material shows that shyness is sometimes outgrown and that it is treatable. You can find out more about approaches to treatment of shyness and a new study on social interaction and technology at *www. shyness.com.*

Self-Fulfilling Prophecies

For artists, writers, and scientists, early rejection has usually been "the rule rather than the exception"—the careers of architect Frank Lloyd Wright, dancer Martha Graham, sculptor Louise Nevelson, and novelist James Joyce offer just a few examples. After studying people who have a sense of their own competence, two psychologists observe:

> The power of efficacy [competence] beliefs to affect the life paths of men and women . . . is clearly revealed in studies of career and choice development. . . . Those who have a strong sense of personal efficacy consider a wide range of career options, show greater interest in them, prepare themselves better for different careers, and have greater staying power in their chosen pursuits. (Bussey and Bandura, 2004, p. 100)

Our expectations also have an influence on our impressions of other people. People who expect to be accepted by others and who perceive others as friendly are often outgoing and congenial; and their behavior accounts in good measure for their popularity and the positive way in which others respond. On the other hand, people who expect to be rejected often are (Adelmann, 1988). Perceiving others as hostile or unfriendly, they often act defensive or superior; this behavior may very well set in motion the rejection they fear. And a person who thinks his relationship with someone is casual rather than exclusive may therefore spend little time with the other person so that indeed the relationship never deepens (Honeycutt and Cantrill, 2001, p. 166).

Because of their psychological set, these people help to confirm their own expectations so that a favorable self-concept may lead to success, an unfavorable self-concept to failure. This phenomenon is called a **self-fulfilling prophecy.**

A Greek myth tells the story of Pygmalion, a young sculptor who created an exquisite ivory statue of a beautiful woman and fell in love with it. Pygmalion prayed to Aphrodite, the goddess of love, that the statue might come to life, and the ivory figure became flesh and moved on her pedestal. Pygmalion named her Galatea, and the two were married in the presence of Aphrodite.

In a much-discussed experiment, Rosenthal and others studied what came to be known as the *Pygmalion effect, a self-fulfilling prophecy in which "one person's expectation for another person's behavior can quite unwittingly become a more accurate prediction for its having been made"* (Rosenthal and Jacobson, 1992, p. vii, emphasis added). Essentially, Rosenthal's study found that when, at the beginning of the school year, elementary school teachers were given information that led them to believe certain pupils ranked higher than others in intellectual competence (supposedly measured by IQ tests), those "special" children showed dramatic intellectual growth and ranked far above the "ordinary" children. A striking example of self-fulfilling prophecy, the Pygmalion effect has been observed in educational, medical, and many other contexts.

Recent research finds that the inaccurate beliefs of mothers about the alcohol use of their children had distinct effects on their children's later use of alcohol. Over time unfavorable beliefs of mothers were shown to have a cumulative negative effect, increasing alcohol use by children who were "consistently exposed to unfavorable versus favorable beliefs year after year" and contributing to a self-fulfilling prophecy (Madon et al., 2006, p. 911). Another recent study finds that in close relationships romantic partners who view things in an optimistic light (expecting positive outcomes) tended to be more satisfied in their relationships (Srivastava et al., 2006)—another instance of the long-lasting effects of self-fulfilling prophecy.

The Attribution of Humanness

Do you think of yourself as being more "human" than others? In recent studies of *humanness*, researchers report, *"people attributed human nature traits to the self more than to the average other or to an in-group:* They judged themselves to embody human nature—openness, warmth, and emotionality—better than other people" (Haslam and Bain, 2007, p. 58, italics added).

It seems we think of ourselves as "more essentially human" regardless of our level of self-esteem, and we also think of members of our in-groups, groups to which we belong, as having more humanness than members of out-groups, groups to we do not belong. We also attribute human uniqueness to our in-groups more than we do to out-groups (p. 58; Haslam et al., 2005). The implications of this will become clearer in Chapter 10 on intercultural communication.

As for how our view of humanness can change, Haslam and Bain (2007) conclude:

> The extent to which we see ourselves as better and more human than others is reduced when we make others the focus of our attention and when we represent them concretely by individuating them. (p. 66)

Often, then, to intensify our perceptions of others and to learn more about them can lead to heightened, more accurate social perception.

Behavior Attribution

There seems to be another major difference between the way you perceive yourself and the way you perceive others. A series of studies on **behavior attribution** suggests that *you see your own behavior as a sequence of responses to the demands of a given situation, but you view the same behavior in others as generated by their disposition,* that is, their stable traits or needs. Lee, for example, sees himself as cutting down on his expenses and living more economically because he's saving up for a car; but he tends to think of Adam, his roommate, as cheap. Or "She is arrogant," but "I was provoked." In addition, a consistent finding in attribution research is that we tend to attribute the causes of our success to ourselves and the causes of our failures to external factors (Nurmi, 1991).

Two reasons for these perceptual differences in behavior attribution have been proposed. First, the information available to the actor (the one who performs the action) and the observer may be different. The observer does not—cannot—know firsthand the actor's history, experiences, motives, or present emotional state; these can only be inferred. Thus, if we see a person overreact to a mildly critical remark, as observers we may not know what events preceding this episode made it the straw that broke the camel's back. A second possibility is that, even when the same information is available to both actor and observer, they process it differently because different aspects of it are salient to each of them.

These information differences may exist in actor and observer because their points of view are literally quite different. You do not see yourself acting; under ordinary circumstances you cannot be an observer of your own behavior. And while as an actor you watch the situation in which you find yourself, the other person spends most of his or her time observing you, not the situation (Storms, 1973). One study (Hancock and Dunham, 2001) found that the impressions people formed during *computer-mediated communications* (**CMC**) are less detailed than they are in face-to-face settings, but personality attributions are more intense and extreme. Earlier studies had shown no differences.

Suppose we reverse the viewpoints of actor and observer. Storms found that after seeing ourselves on tape, we are much more likely to explain our behavior as a reflection of personal disposition than as a response to the environment. But videotape is not the answer. What we need is a more balanced view of ourselves and of others, a view that enables us to interpret behavior in terms of both disposition and environment. By combining information about ourselves that is available only to us with an awareness of how other human beings perceive us, we may begin to see ourselves in sharper perspective.

Looking at Others

In many situations, we find ourselves making several judgments about others—and all at once. For example, Chandra was at a New Year's party. Mixed in with the old crowd were four people she didn't know. But by the end of the evening she had, at least to her own satisfaction, sized up all the newcomers. The young woman in the red dress was lively and pleasant; she liked her right away. But her husband was a terrible snob—and so self-involved. The tall blonde was too nervous, but the older man seated next to her was easygoing with a great sense of humor. And she noticed how confident he was—they spent quite a bit of time talking.

Like Chandra, most of us form impressions of others quite easily; yet we find it difficult to explain the process. In fact, many feel that they make their judgments intuitively. Recall the Willis and Todorov study (2006) discussed on page 36.

In one study of how people form impressions of others in cyberspace, Jacobson (1999) looked at online expectations and offline experiences in text-based virtual communities called MOOs. One woman explained how she perceived the difference:

> On MOO everything can seem larger than life—it can be quite a surprise to
> realize the people are ordinary. People here can seem more witty and amusing
> and clever and sexy than the people one knows irl [in real life]. People project
> a persona here sometimes, and when you meet them they are shyer or whatever.
> A friend of mine said he was disappointed when he first started meeting people
> from the MOO. He had the impression they were demi-gods. (p. 12)

"Impression" is a word we use about our personal judgments. We speak of being "under the impression," or of someone making a "lasting impression," a "false impression," or a "good impression." We know that our initial impressions also influence election outcomes. For example, a study of the 2000, 2002, and 2004 congressional elections (Todorov et al., 2005) finds that inferences about the competence of various candidates that were based exclusively on their facial appearance successfully predicted the election outcomes. These inferences were made with only a one-second exposure to candidates' faces. And it turns out that competence was the trait that subjects considered most important for all candidates.

Our legal system certainly reflects the degree to which we rely on snap judgments. Before a trial begins, prospective jurors are screened by the defense and the prosecution. In addition to raising specific objections to certain candidates for the jury, both the defense and the prosecuting attorneys are allowed to reject a certain number of would-be jurors without stating their reasons. Attorneys often make their decisions rapidly, though they are complex ones and are probably based on several considerations. They will probably take into account their perception of the potential juror and the client and the impression they feel that the client will make upon that juror. And, of course, the attorney for one side might be more than willing to accept a juror whom opposing counsel finds objectionable.

Attorneys usually seem to be rather skilled perceivers, accustomed to formulating judgments about others very quickly. But think of the members of the jury. They will be meeting and evaluating many people for the first time and presumably doing this entirely on their own. In a short time each juror will probably have formed an impression of most if not all of those involved in the case—including the witnesses, the defense attorney, the prosecuting attorney, and even the judge.

Research on person perception in legal settings confirms that a juror's perception of an attorney's credibility and of the defendant's guilt will be influenced not only by the attorney's opening statements but by various nonverbal cues in delivering those statements. We know that a juror's early impressions of a defendant can be influenced by the defendant's race. Now some studies (Sargent and Bradfield, 2004) suggest that in subtle ways a defendant's race can affect how jurors process the information within the defendant's testimony. Much more research is needed on this subject.

Because a juror's final judgment about the person on trial can have dramatic consequences, it is important to consider how he or she forms initial impressions and whether those impressions will have any effect on later perceptions. Our own evaluations of people also have important if less dramatic consequences, so we might all benefit from looking more closely at how an impression of another person is formed.

The First Impression

One of the major uses of evaluating personality is to explain and predict behavior on the basis of very limited information. How do we put this information together and come up with a first impression? Actually, each of us seems to hold a **private theory of personality** (sometimes known as "implicit personality theory"). Essentially, the term refers to *how we select and organize information about other people on the basis of what behaviors we think go together.*

Suppose you are given the following list of words describing a man you have never met and are then asked to write a personality sketch of him:

energetic	ironical
assured	inquisitive
talkative	persuasive
cold	

In a classic experiment, Solomon Asch (1946) used this list to learn more about how impressions of others are formed. He read the list to a group of students and asked them to write a full impression of the person described by these adjectives. There were two important findings.

Unity   Asch's first finding was unity. All the students were able to organize the scanty information they received and create a consistent, unified impression, though there was a great deal of variation in their personality sketches, and they all went beyond the terms of the original description. Here is a sample:

> Possibly he does not have any deep feeling. He would tend to be an opportunist. Likely to succeed in things he intends to do. He has perhaps married a wife who would help him in his purpose. He tends to be skeptical. (Asch, 1946, p. 261)

Central Traits   Second, Asch found that certain traits are more *central,* more influential than others in forming impressions of personality. When one of the adjectives on the list was replaced by its opposite, the personality descriptions were radically different. Whether a person is warm or cold was more important than whether he is blunt or polite.

For a long time, theorists believed that impressions of others were interpreted on the basis of the *halo effect,* the tendency to extend a favorable or unfavorable impression of one trait to other traits. Thus, you might think of Kate as honest and polite, just because you consider her intelligent. Or if you feel Justin is cheap, you might attribute several other undesirable traits to him. This explanation sounds reasonable, but we now know that the halo effect is too simple a concept to account completely for the way we interpret our perceptions.

Indirectly, experiments tell us that certain traits carry weight and are clearly more decisive in our judgments than others. Somehow we manage to make all the information we have about a person—all those distinct verbal and nonverbal cues—fit together (Asch and Zukier, 1984; Bruner, 1986). If they don't seem consistent, we build in an explanation.

People seem more reliable, more knowable, when we can predict some aspects of their behavior. Perhaps that explains our need to perceive another human being as a "personality"—to see that personality quickly; to see it vividly, with certain dominant or central traits; and, most important, to see it as a unity.

The Primacy Effect

Time is one of the most significant variables in our communication model. Thus, it seems natural to ask what effect the first impression you form will have on your later perceptions of another person. Ideally, as you learn more about someone, you continually revise or refine your impressions in the light of new information. But is this in fact so? Does a first impression enhance or interfere with later knowledge, or does it have no effect at all?

Earlier research on attraction found that first impressions tend to have long-term consequences. People in long-term romantic relationships often make judgments soon after getting acquainted and feel that their impressions are confirmed during the first few weeks. A newer study strongly supports these findings that first impressions can be "strong and lasting" and that we may know something about

2.2 ISSUES IN COMMUNICATION

Simon Baron-Cohen, professor of psychology and psychiatry at Cambridge University and head of its Autism Research Centre, proposes a controversial theory about an essential difference between the male and the female brain. On the basis of research, he theorizes that the male brain is "predominantly hardwired for understanding and building systems," whereas the female brain is "predominantly hardwired for empathy" (2003, p. 1).

He is not saying that males, because of their capacity for systemizing, are more intelligent. Nor that women are all more empathic than men. There are many exceptions. Not only that: These qualities—empathizing and systemizing—are present in both sexes and differ among individuals. There are women in whom systemizing rather than empathic abilities will be dominant, men in whom empathic abilities will be dominant. In effect, what he is describing are two predominant qualities of the human brain.

Whether or not his theory proves valid, his characterization of empathy is of great interest to those who study person perception. Empathy, he maintains, has two components: "understanding the other's feelings and the ability to take their perspective" is a cognitive ability; being able to make "appropriate emotional response[s] to another person's emotional state" is an ability involving feelings (p. 26).

Empathy is fundamental to communication—an ongoing process that ensures genuine exchange between people and involves an awareness of how the other is thinking and feeling, sensitivity to subtle changes in the other person's mood, as well as an ability to respond spontaneously and adapt conversation when needed. Hence, says Baron-Cohen, it is "a defining feature of human relationships" (p. 23).

Imagine yourself being asked whether you strongly agree, slightly agree, slightly disagree, or strongly disagree with statements such as the following:

"I am quick to spot when someone in a group is feeling awkward or uncomfortable."

"If I see a stranger in a group, I think that it is up to them to make an effort to join in."

"Friends usually talk to me about their problems as they say that I am very understanding."

"If anyone asked me if I liked their haircut, I would reply truthfully, even if I didn't like it." (pp. 201–207)

Because the measurement of empathy is central to his work on autism—a condition characterized by a deficiency in this dimension—Baron-Cohen has developed a test that measures a person's empathic abilities. The questions above and many others, 60 in all, are from that test. How would you rate your own empathic abilities? To determine your Empathy Quotient or EQ, see the complete test in Baron-Cohen (2003, pp. 201–207).

how a relationship will develop as early as within the first few weeks or even days of meeting the other person (Sunnafrank and Ramirez, 2004, p. 377).

Among early studies of impression formation, those of Luchins have been very influential. In one of Luchins's experiments, subjects read two paragraphs describing a young man named Jim. One paragraph described actions of Jim that were predominantly introverted; the other described actions that were predominantly extroverted. All subjects read the same paragraphs; only their order varied. Luchins found that a **primacy effect** did exist—that *the first information we receive about a person is the most decisive in forming our impression* (Luchins, 1957). So first meetings—especially the very first minutes of those meetings—are important.

Primacy has a clear-cut effect on communication. If you look once more at the model in Figure 1.1 (page 9), you can see that each communicator should be receiving input and feedback. The primacy effect blocks both. It is, in our terms, a source of technical interference, and this time the interference is within the communicator. If Sandra, after spending five minutes with her roommate's brother Bill, is sure that he is overbearing and phony, she is not going to be very interested in getting any feedback about her impression of him. Most of you have been in Bill's place at least once. It's as though you suddenly had become invisible. No matter what you said or did, the other person no longer seemed to respond; you couldn't change that first impression of you.

Rightly or wrongly, most people feel quite confident about their judgments. For example, in Luchins's experiment almost all the subjects were very willing to answer questions about Jim's behavior that were totally unrelated to the information they had read about him. Given information about some of his behavior, they inferred several other things about him and confidently predicted how he would behave in other social situations. Only a few asked how they were expected to know such things (Brown, 1986). But as we will see in Chapter 3, all inferences involve some measure of risk, and this is true of inferences about personality.

We all know how often first impressions can be mistaken ones, and we also know how often decisions depend on first impressions. Imagine that you are being interviewed for your first job after graduation. You look very nervous and were 10 minutes late for the interview. Then you make an obvious grammatical mistake in speaking. What is likely to be the outcome?

It's disturbing to think that first impressions can have such dramatic effects on judgment. But Luchins found that if people were warned not to make snap judgments, the primacy effect was reversed or eliminated completely. Several other studies confirm that the primacy effect is not inevitable (Fletcher et al., 2004).

Physical Attractiveness

In some ideal world we will all be beautiful. Until that time, however, it seems likely that those of us who are physically attractive will have a slight edge—at least initially—on those of us who are not (Maner et al., 2003). Among scholars there is general agreement: Physically attractive people are considered by others to be more sociable, more popular, more sexual, more successful, and more persuasive. Frequently they are thought to be happier and to have more appealing personalities (Berscheid and Reis, 1998). Two scholars sum up research findings on the social benefits of physical attractiveness over the lifespan:

Figure 2.3

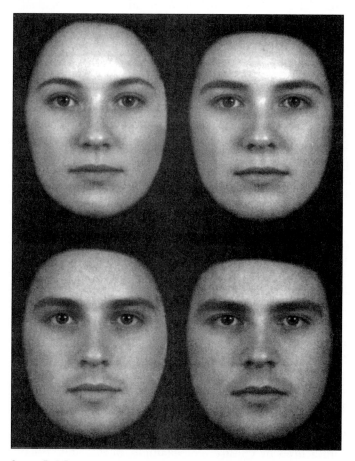

Source: D. I. Perrett, K. J. Lee, I. Penton-Voak et al., "Effects of Sexual Dimorphism on Facial Attractiveness," *Nature* 394 (August 27, 1998).

"In infancy, more attractive babies are preferred by their own parents."

"More attractive people are more likely to marry and, among those who do marry, those who are more attractive marry sooner. . . ."

"More attractive adults also have more occupational success."

"Physically attractive defendants are less likely to be convicted and, if convicted, they receive more lenient sentences than those convicted of equally serious crimes." (Adapted from Zebrowitz and Rhodes, 2002, pp. 61–62)

Several researchers are using composite images to study the human face in relation to standards of beauty, personality judgments, and perceiver accuracy (Penton-Voak et al., 2006; Bodenhausen and Macrae, 2006). For example, take a careful look at the faces in Figure 2.3, part of a cross-cultural study of standards of beauty (Perrett et al., 1998). After examining the two female faces in the top half of this figure and the two male faces below them, which would you select as ideally feminine and masculine?

These faces are computer composites—images blended to emphasize certain features, including face shape, associated with each sex. The woman's face at the upper left (masculinized at the right) has been feminized so that the bottom half of her face is narrower and her cheeks are higher and rounded. The man's face at the lower left has also been feminized, in contrast to the masculinized male image at the lower right, with its square shape, enlarged jaw, and heavy brow. This intriguing study finds that people of both sexes think that feminine features in both women and men are more attractive. And this is true of both Caucasian and Japanese subjects. Subjects also attributed such traits as being warmer and more emotional, honest, and cooperative to the feminized male face.

One of several qualities we associate beauty with is symmetry and we are attracted by it. For example, in Western faces we know that average faces and symmetrical faces are regarded as attractive. An attractive face will also seem more familiar to us and therefore we tend to like it more (Monin, 2003). One study looked at averageness and symmetry in Chinese and Japanese faces, using composite images that enhanced these qualities. The researchers found the same preferences and suggest that these standards of beauty may turn out to be biologically based (Rhodes et al., 2001).

Classic research on facial attractiveness shows that even infants as young as two to three months old prefer attractive faces. People of many cultures seem to agree on which faces are perceived as attractive, which also suggests that this response may be universal (Zebrowitz and Rhodes, 2002, p. 263). But two important research questions remain: How much do individual cultures value attractiveness? And how does a person's behavior modify our perception of his or her attractiveness? (Dion, 2002).

Although some standards of beauty may be universal, several other aspects of attractiveness seem to be influenced by culture. For example, in the United States being attractive is often associated with thinness, so that one of the unpardonable sins—at least for women—is becoming "fat." Witness the alarming number of women suffering from such eating disorders as anorexia and bulimia: As many as 22 percent of college women may be affected (Gustafson et al., 2001). The National Eating Disorders Association reports that every day thousands of people log on to Internet clubs and websites that discuss and advise about weight loss and that ultimately promote eating disorders ("Anorexia's Web," 2001).

We take many of our images of beauty from the mass media, yet consider the following statistics:

- The average American woman is 5′ 4″ tall and weighs 140 pounds.
- 80 percent of American women are dissatisfied with their appearance.
- The average American model is 5′ 11″ tall and weighs 117 pounds.
- Most fashion models are thinner than 98 percent of American women. (*www.edap.org*)

Many studies of body images that appear in women's magazines confirm what most of us already know: Ads do not represent a diversity of body types. Instead they promote the stereotype of a "thin ideal," which has become a social and cultural norm associated not only with beauty but success (Gustafson et al., 2001).

Aside from liking physically attractive people because they are good to look at, we sometimes like them because we feel that by being seen with them, we will enhance our own image. The college man who consistently dates beautiful women is very likely to improve his own image among both his male friends and his prospective female acquaintances. The woman who dates handsome men is also increasing her own self-esteem. One article described arrangements in which a man or woman seeks "arm candy," a good-looking escort for an evening out—someone who will make others envious.

Attractiveness may also be linked with perceptions of power and status. A recent study of how physical and vocal attractiveness affects our perception of political candidates had subjects rate hypothetical candidates for competency, trustworthiness, qualification (competence), and leadership ability (Surawski and Ossoff, 2006). Researchers found a stronger halo effect for political candidates who were physically attractive than for candidates whose voices were attractive. When candidates were physically attractive but had an unattractive voice, they received lower ratings. We will discuss both physical and vocal attractiveness in more detail in Chapter 4 on nonverbal communication.

In academic life, physical attractiveness can affect student evaluations of teaching. When college students were asked to evaluate their college professors, those professors perceived as attractive were given more favorable evaluations (Riniolo et al., 2006). This was not an isolated finding. Evaluations for both female and male professors were higher for those perceived as attractive, but other studies report that physical attractiveness in male professors has a greater influence.

Despite the association of beauty with talent, however, career success for women is not furthered by their good looks. Studies point to a bias against good-looking women in managerial and executive positions (Zebrowitz, 1997). Attractive women who run for public office, unlike their male counterparts, also seem to be at a disadvantage. The so-called beauty backlash applies only to women.

The influence of physical beauty seems to be most powerful early in a relationship; as we acquire more and more information about a person, the effects of physical appearance diminish considerably.

Expressiveness and Charisma

Faces are attractive, appealing, or "charismatic" in that they have the power to draw people into a relationship, whether it be as mates, lovers, caregivers, fans, or followers.

—Keating (2002, p. 155)

Today there is a growing body of research about expressiveness and charisma. According to recent findings, **expressiveness,** *a dimension of nonverbal communication* that influences our first impressions, has been linked with animation, dynamism, expansiveness, and intensity of both nonverbal and verbal behaviors (DePaulo and Friedman, 1998; Guerrero and Floyd, 2006). On the basis of their work, Boone and Buck (2003) confirm that the influence of emotional expressiveness—their research was on nonverbal expressiveness—on a first impression is immediate and that often we believe emotionally expressive people are more trustworthy. In addition, this often functions as a signal for cooperative behavior. Expressive people are also thought to be higher in self-esteem as well as more extroverted and less inhibited (pp. 171–177).

When it comes to faces, "female faces with the expressive features of arched eyebrows, dilated pupils, wide mouths, and full lips, and male faces with large smiles, are seen as more attractive than their less expressive counterparts" (Cunningham et al., 2002, p. 210). Expressiveness also seems to reflect physical well-being. People who are considered more expressive usually attract more attention, and we usually think of them as more attractive. They tend to create first impressions that are extremely favorable, and such impressions tend to be sustained over time.

> [E]xpressiveness makes one seem more attractive, as does one's ability to regulate nonverbal behaviors in ways that are appealing . . . Studies of personal charisma, which examine both fixed attractiveness and expressiveness, suggest that expressiveness is at least as important as physical attractiveness—perhaps even more so—in account[ing] for immediately favorable first impressions. Many charismatic actors would be judged plain and unappealing from photographs alone; conversely, one's perceptions of a striking beauty can be obliterated by the first few minutes of a conversation. (DePaulo and Friedman, 1998, pp. 13–14)

Charisma has been defined as *"personal magnetism that enables an individual to attract and influence people" (Random House Webster's,* 2000) and as *a divinely conferred power or talent (Shorter OED,* 2002). The origin of the word itself is Greek and means "divine gift." Sometimes charisma is associated with what is "attractive and influential"—notice the word "influential." It implies the power to move people. Actors are sometimes referred to as having charisma. Many religious and political leaders have also been considered charismatic. One fascinating study analyzed the facial features of three charismatic presidents: Kennedy, Reagan, and Clinton (Keating, 2002).

We can say that while charisma and expressiveness may sometimes be linked, charisma is a more rare and elusive quality. Who would you describe as charismatic?

Personal Generalizations and Stereotypes

For good or ill, your private theory of personality is in large part based on generalizations, many of which derive from personal experience. If Jane favors boys of fraternity XYZ, for example, then she may be attracted to Phil simply because he is a member. Similarly, if she thinks economics students are geeks, then she may refuse a first date with one regardless of whether he fits her personal definition of economics students. If your luggage is stolen while you are traveling in Italy, you may come to feel that Italians are dishonest. If you have seen several Swedish films starring beautiful actresses, perhaps you have come to believe that all Swedish women are beautiful.

In saner moments, we realize that although generalizations are necessary to the organization of any perceptions, generalizations based on very limited personal experience are often inaccurate and misleading. Jane may find that the next member of fraternity XYZ she dates is a geek. You may get to know members of a wonderful Italian family who practically take you into their home. The first Swedish girl you actually meet may be unattractive.

But how we perceive other human beings also depends on generalizations derived from our shared experiences as members of a given culture or society. In discussing the Müller-Lyer illusion, we observed that culture is a determinant of visual perception. From the standpoint of human communication it is even more significant that culture can be a determinant of person perception.

Culture   The influence of a culture on the person perception of its members is most directly seen in its stereotypes. A **stereotype** is *a generalization about a class of people, objects, or events that is widely held by a given culture.* We cannot say categorically that all stereotypes are false. According to one hypothesis, there is a kernel of truth in all of them. Thus, we can at least acknowledge that some are accurate enough to provide a very limited basis for making judgments about groups of people we hardly know. But when applied to a specific individual, most stereotypes are inappropriate and highly inaccurate—and many are false. Relying on stereotypes rather than on direct perceptions can result in embarrassing social situations and inappropriate responses.

There can be no doubt that race membership affects our perceptions of others. For example, an early study finds that we are better at recognizing pictures of members of our own race than of members of another (Malpass and Kravitz, 1969). And we often make false assumptions—and actually perceive inaccurately—when we judge on the basis of race. For example, consider the experience of many African Americans. In his book *Member of the Club,* Lawrence Otis Graham (1995), a prominent attorney, writes about a certain New York restaurant that he does not patronize

> . . . because its maitre d' is never at the second floor entry landing upon a guest's arrival, which has left me on three occasions to fend off incoming patrons who handed me their hats, jackets, and umbrellas for the coat check. And I almost always avoid restaurants with valet parking because of the times I've been handed keys by incoming white patrons who assume that I am there to park cars rather than waiting to have my own car delivered to the front door as I leave. (p. 91)

Even positive stereotypes can have damaging effects on intercultural communication. In the United States, Asian Americans have generally been singled out as America's most "successful" minority, sometimes fostering resentment by others and subtle forms of discrimination (Han and Hsu, 2004). The mass media seem to have given special emphasis to the "success story" of Asian Americans. "Intelligent," "hard-working," "quiet," "soft-spoken," "well-mannered"—these were some of the all-too-predictable terms (Taylor and Stern, 1997). One Asian American reporter sees the problem this way:

> I think Asians are seen in one of three stereotypical ways: 1) victims or perpetrators of crime, 2) immigrant owners of Laundromats, restaurants or corner stores where the owners feud with the local black residents, or, 3) the brainiac students, nerd doctors, engineers or hi-sci experts with pocket protectors. HELLO!!!??? (Cited in Mansfield-Richardson, 2000, p. 298)

Physical Attributes   Stereotypes also extend to physical attributes. Think of the longstanding American stereotype concerning the advantages of being blonde. A wide variety of rinses and dyes are available to all who wish to cover even the earliest signs of gray hair or simply to choose the hair color of the moment.

In discussing attractiveness, we saw that physical attributes have considerable influence on our first impressions. Each culture emphasizes certain facial cues. It might be the amount of makeup a woman wears or how she wears her hair or even whether she wears glasses. For example, in some cultures, people are regarded as more intelligent, reliable, and industrious when they wear glasses (Kleinke, 1986, p. 79). No doubt you have seen people who are aware of the power of this stereotype and exploit it to create an impression. It's the same impulse that makes the budding "professorial type" sport a pipe or the femme fatale take to smoking little cigars.

Do you know anyone your age with a baby face? People with baby faces have larger eyes in proportion to the rest of their face; their eyebrows are high and fine, their noses tend to be smaller, and their lips are also more childlike. The baby-face stereotype, as it's called, also describes a person with fuller cheeks, a rounder face. The look of babies is disarming. We are drawn to them, and now current research shows that we are also drawn to baby-faced adults (Rhodes and Zebrowitz, 2002; Zebrowitz, 1997). What's more, the baby-face stereotype is universal across cultures.

Baby-faced people are perceived as warm, trusting, and trustworthy. People talk to and confide in them more readily—and research finds that "a baby face is likely to be helpful in the early stages of making friends and in the evocation of intimacy in established relationships" (Zebrowitz, 1997, p. 98). The downside of having a baby face is that you tend to be perceived as having less expertise and as being naive and submissive—and this can influence not only your social life but your professional life as well.

Stereotyping certainly exists in computer-mediated communication. For example, one study of text-based virtual communities found that often the participants formed images of other players on the basis of screen names. For example:

timberwolf is a broad shouldered man who wears cotton flannel shirts with the sleeves rolled up and likes to spend a lot of time outdoors. He wears gold wire-frame glasses and his somewhat unruly brown hair is starting to go gray. He's from the Pacific Northwest so that explains the flannel shirt, pseudo-lumberjack outdoorsman part. The graying hair goes with his being a professor, as do the glasses, although the fact that they are gold wire-rim has more to do with his name and the fact that he doesn't capitalize it, a sort of understated elegance. (Jacobson, 1999, p. 8)

Some Effects of Stereotyping   In these examples of stereotyping, a person is considered to have attributes generally ascribed to the group of which he or she is a member. That person is not perceived as a unique human being but as a member of a certain category of human beings, whether it be actresses, Asian Americans, or college professors. In a sense, the person is judged in terms of context. Although some generalizations about categories are valuable to us in daily experience, generalizations about human beings—especially generalizations about how they think and how they are likely to behave—tend to distort our perceptions and to interfere with our ability to make accurate judgments. Unfortunately, personal generalizations or stereotypes cannot be eliminated simply by alerting the perceiver to their dangers.

One analysis of research about stereotypes finds at least four statements that seem warranted. First, stereotyping results from "cognitive biases stemming from illusory correlations between group membership and psychological attributes." Second, our stereotypes influence the way we process information—we remember less favorable information about out-groups and more favorable information about in-groups. Third, "stereotypes create expectancies (hypotheses) about others, and individuals try to confirm these expectancies." And last—and perhaps most significant from the standpoint of intercultural communication—our stereotypes operate as a constraint upon the communication behaviors of others, giving rise to behavior that then confirms our stereotypic expectations (Gudykunst and Ting-Toomey, 1988, pp. 136–137). (See Chapter 10 for a further discussion of stereotyping.)

Social Roles

Among the several social roles that influence how we perceive others and are ourselves perceived by others are work roles, student roles, sex-linked roles, and marital roles.

Work Roles

A classic example of how our work roles may alter perception is Zimbardo's so-called prison experiment (1971) in which students randomly assigned to be "guards" and others designated "prisoners" quickly came to see and respond to each other in stereotypical guard-prisoner fashion: The guards became cruel and unjust, the prisoners rebellious. Although planned to last for two weeks, the experiment was stopped after only six days. Students no longer thought like students, but like guards and prisoners. They truly lived their parts.

Later research on Hispanics and whites (Jones, 1991) supports the view that perceived differences in social status (as defined by work roles) influence ethnic stereotypes and that "occupational status . . . is often used to make rather confident judgments of personal attributes." According to this study, "occupational title appears to be a more central trait than ethnicity in determining American students' perceptions of people" (p. 475).

Student Roles

As for student roles, research on perceptions in the classroom finds that teachers perceive the model student as a communicator—"well-behaved, patient, controlled, and polite. He or she waits before speaking, listens intently and politely, sits quietly while others talk, and contributes clear and germane comments" (Trenholm and Rose, 1981, p. 24). Teachers describe the model student as one who willingly does all assignments, "never criticizes the teacher or gives way to frustration, and accepts and even welcomes criticism" (p. 24). According to these findings, compliance rather than inquiring behavior would be rewarded. What a contrast with the way most students feel about unquestioning compliance.

Another aspect of student–teacher roles is the perception of power in the classroom. Although teachers and students generally agree on power bases, some important differences exist. Both groups see most power as stemming from the teacher's ability to give rewards (e.g., high grades, approval), ability to make the student identify with the teacher, and perceived expertise. Again students, as you might expect, have a less positive view of the teacher's use of power (McCroskey and Richmond, 1983).

Gender-Linked Roles

That gender-linked roles also influence perceptions is confirmed by many research summaries. The consensus is that women are perceived as more supportive than men, laughing more often, intruding less on others, and being more deferential. Men, on the other hand, are considered more dominant and more achievement- and task-oriented. These descriptions reflect the more stereotypical views that women place a higher value on establishing and maintaining relationships while men tend to perceive the world more as a place to "win" or "achieve" (Rosenthal and DePaulo, 1979; LaFrance and Mayo, 1979; Pearson et al., 1995).

Some argue that a person whose self-concept is highly sex-typed may strive to behave consistently with various internalized standards for that role and to suppress behavior seen as inappropriate. They cite Bem's suggestion "that an androgynous self-concept might allow individuals to engage freely in both masculine and feminine behaviors and allow greater human potentiation" (Veenendall and Braito, 1987, p. 32).

Marital Roles

Perceptions of marital roles have undergone considerable change in the last decades, particularly with the great number of married women who have joined the workforce (Cherlin, 1998). A study attempting to predict marital and career success among dual-working couples (Hiller and Philliber, 1982) identifies four major marital types: These are based on how the husband and wife perceive themselves.

In a *traditional marriage relationship,* the husband sees himself as masculine and the wife sees herself as feminine. For example, although both work outside the home, the husband is perceived as bringing home the proverbial bacon whereas the wife has sole responsibility for all the housework. Housework is her province, and he won't help with any of it.

In a *reluctant wife marriage relationship,* the wife views herself as feminine and her husband sees himself as androgynous (having both masculine and feminine characteristics). If the wife in this relationship does not perceive herself as furnishing most of the emotional support, she may perceive her husband as "too feminine." And if her husband helps with the housework, sharing these tasks because she is so busy as a result of her successful career, she may feel guilty—both because she neglects "her duties" at home and because her professional skills seem "unfeminine."

On the other hand, in a *reluctant husband marriage relationship,* the husband sees himself as masculine and his wife sees herself as androgynous: He may feel threatened by her broad range of activities if he defines her role more narrowly. Suppose, for example, that she wants to split all the housework whereas he believes that if she hasn't the time for all the domestic concerns, she should spend less time at the office.

In the *androgynous marriage relationship,* the fourth type, both spouses see themselves as androgynous: Both engage in so-called masculine and feminine behaviors, making adaptation easier. He may even do most of the cooking; she may do most of the cleaning and laundry. Problems may still arise based on social expectations of appropriate or "proper" husband/wife roles.

It might be interesting to try classifying the marriages of those you know—relatives, friends, neighbors—and see whether you can discover any pattern related to age, work, and psychological makeup of the spouses involved. Or ask yourself which type of marriage you have or expect to have. (For a further discussion of marital roles, see Chapter 9.)

We've looked at several factors influencing our impressions of others. In addition to their physical attractiveness, expressiveness, and social roles, our own self-perceptions, our notions of personality, and the stereotypes we hold and our own generalizations also come into play. So we turn in the final section of this chapter to questions concerning the accuracy of these impressions.

SOME VARIABLES INVOLVED IN ACCURATE PERCEPTION

Granted the selective quality of human perception, we must ask what are the other variables that will affect the accuracy of our perceptions. Early studies suggest that at least three generalizations can be made:

1. Some people are easier to judge than others—perhaps because they are more open about themselves.
2. Certain traits are easier to judge than others—e.g., it is much easier to identify people who are not shy than it is to pick out people who consider themselves shy (Zimbardo, 1990).
3. People are better at judging those who resemble themselves.

The desire to improve one's accuracy in judging others seems to be virtually universal. Following are several of the important variables that researchers have examined:

Context   Some communication scholars believe that the ability to judge other people may be quite specific to context. For example, students were asked to view a person bargaining, first in a very cooperative situation and later in a very competitive one. Group influence was so strong that when their perception of the bargainer did not correspond to the perceptions of other group members, subjects denied what they had seen with their own eyes. In fact, they came to believe the opposite of what they had seen. Majority or group opinion is just one instance in which context—the third element of perception—exerts its subtle influence.

Interpersonal Sensitivity   Research on accurate person perception increasingly refers to the concept of **interpersonal sensitivity,** sometimes defined as *"success in decoding nonverbal communication"* or *"the accurate recall of another person's nonverbal behavior"* (Noller, 2006, p. 404; Hall et al., 2006, p. 141; italics added).

A good deal of recent research confirms that women are more accurate than men in their recall and decoding of nonverbal cues. For example, at least nine studies show that women have an advantage over men in recalling the physical appearance of others (Mast and Hall, 2006). And in judging the meaning of nonverbal cues, women have higher accuracy than men when it comes to personality traits, intelligence, facial expressions, and vocal expressions of emotion; on the other hand, women are no more accurate than men when it comes to judging cues for deception or dominance (J. Hall, 2006). We will look at findings on gender differences again and some possible explanations in Chapter 4.

Perceiver Self-Confidence   For a long time, psychologists have tried to establish whether some people are indeed better judges than others. Certainly, we all know people who feel their perceptions to be extremely accurate. But is there a relationship between self-confidence and accuracy? Does self-confidence about our ability to judge others make a difference in how we see them?

In terms of our communication model, we might say that a person who forms impressions of others solely on the basis of personal expectations avoids the task of person perception. Researchers have found no correlation between confidence in our perceptions of others and the accuracy of those perceptions.

Other Perceiver Traits   Despite the fact that accurate person perception varies from one situation to another, theorists generally agree that certain characteristics are associated with sound perceptions of others.

First, *intelligence* is a prime factor. Second, *the ability to draw inferences about people from their behavior* seems related to accurate perception. Third, people who score low on tests of authoritarianism tend to be better judges of others. They are *less rigid* in their *expectations,* judging more from what they know about the person and assuming less that he or she is like themselves. And fourth, those with *a high degree of objectivity* about themselves tend to have insight into the behavior of others. Openness and awareness of our own shortcomings seem to play a part in this process.

In "The Good Judge Revisited," a study of the accuracy of personality judgments, Christiansen and others examined a range of individual differences in judgment that they argue can be explained by "a combination of cognitive and personality factors" (2005, p. 144). They studied accuracy in employment interviews and found the best predictor of accuracy was "dispositional intelligence (knowledge of how personality is related to behavior)" (p. 123):

More accurate judges are higher in cognitive ability and openness to experience, which appears to affect accuracy by way of general knowledge of how personality relates to behavior. Overall, judgments of people known fairly well will be most accurate when this knowledge is possessed by individuals who are more conscientious and more agreeable. (p. 144)

The importance of openness has been confirmed in a number of other communication contexts.

A survey of *empathic accuracy and inference,* how good we are at reading the thoughts and feelings of other people, finds that intelligence, cognitive complexity, positive adjustment, and interpersonal trust as well as social sensitivity—in combination—all play a part (Davis and Kraus, 1997, p. 163). And though women are generally regarded as being more intuitive and more empathic, Graham and Ickes say that although the stereotype of "women's intuition" might have a "proverbial kernel of truth," gender differences in empathic skills and dispositions appear to be small rather than large and specific rather than general in their scope" (1997, pp. 139–140). For more on empathy, see page 53.

How can this information be applied to improving our effectiveness as communicators? We certainly cannot improve our intelligence directly—and the ability to draw valid inferences about people from their behavior probably depends in part on intelligence. Nor can we simply tell ourselves to be less rigid or authoritarian. Research demonstrates that attitudes are rarely changed so easily. One thing we can do is become conscious of, and less defensive about, our own limitations. And the more sensitive we become to cues outside ourselves, the more we listen instead of projecting our own feelings onto others, the more accurate we are likely to be in our evaluations of others.

IMPROVING PERCEPTION AND COMMUNICATION

Failures in communication frequently occur because people have inaccurate perceptions of each other. If a man is told that a woman he knows only casually is snobbish and standoffish, he is not very likely to ask her out. If you feel that a particular instructor is stubborn and somewhat hostile, you probably won't consider questioning her about your low grade on the last exam. But how do you know you are right? In many ways, your perceptions of others can determine not only the kind of communication that takes place but whether you attempt to communicate at all.

It would seem then an easy matter to facilitate communication by simply improving the accuracy of our perceptions. Yet the three elements of perception—perceiver, object, and context—are so interwoven that one cannot be analyzed apart from the others. One of the most important things the perceiver can do is take into account the need to make perceptual adjustments as any of these three components varies.

Among the primary elements in accurate person perception is an awareness that your own perceptions may be inaccurate. Improved perception and communication can occur only if you are willing to acknowledge that your perceptions are subjective.

Another requirement is empathy. **Empathy** involves *experiencing the other's perception—that is, seeing and feeling things as the other does.* We've already seen in the research on behavior attribution how people tend to view their own behavior as response to a given situation and to interpret the same behavior in another person as an expression of stable traits or needs. For example, you lose your temper and explain you've had a hectic and frustrating day, but when one of your co-workers loses his temper, you say he has "a short fuse."

Ideally, we work toward developing the kind of sensitivity or responsiveness to others that actually extends perception. Many scholars believe empathy is the key to effective listening and therefore to communication. In Chapter 5, the role of empathy in listening and in resolving conflicts should become clear: Perceiving something the way the other person perceives it—taking the other's perspective—provides insights and paves the way for effective relationships.

It would be utopian to say that more accurate person perception always makes for more effective communication. Nevertheless, communication in both long-term and short-term relationships is often enhanced when the participants perceive each other accurately. The same principles apply to marital and dating relationships and to many less intense interpersonal encounters including job interviews.

We have tried to suggest that interpersonal sensitivity is important to both long- and short-term encounters. In the chapters that follow, we shall also see that although early impressions depend to a great extent on the perceiver's preconceptions and stereotypes and on the other person's physical appearance, as contact with a person continues, the content of his or her messages (both verbal and nonverbal) plays a greater role in modifying our perceptions of that person.

Summary

In this chapter, we looked at person perception as an active process in which communicators selectively perceive, organize, and interpret what they experience. We also showed how person perception affects intercultural communication. We began by considering the physiological and psychological filters that affect all our perceptions. After suggesting some parallels between object and person perception, we looked first at how we form our perceptions about ourselves. Thus, we examined some of the many variables that influence self-concept including gender and self-esteem and looked at recent research findings about shyness and trait attribution. We then focused on how our impressions of other human beings are formed. We spoke of how we tend to view our own behaviors as opposed to those of others.

We discussed trait centrality and associations of traits, primacy, empathy, and the effects of physical attractiveness, expressiveness, and charisma. Personal generalizations and stereotypes and the influence of work, student, gender-linked, and marital roles were also discussed.

We saw that our impressions, while formed with relative ease, are not necessarily accurate. Some characteristics of perceivers were mentioned, including interpersonal sensitivity, but judging ability itself was seen as sometimes specific to context. In concluding, we discussed inaccurate perception as a source of communication failures and how improved perception enhances communication. Empathy was seen to be one of the crucial elements in this process.

Key Terms

Behavior attribution	Gender	Primacy effect	Self-concept
Charisma	Interpersonal	Private theory of	Self-esteem
CMC	sensitivity	personality	Self-expansion model
Empathy	Looking glass self	Psychological sets	Self-fulfilling prophecy
Expressiveness	Perceptual filters	Selective attention	Stereotype

Review Questions

1. Distinguish between a perceptual filter and a psychological set.

2. Discuss two ways in which person perception is different from object perception. What are the implications of these differences for communication?

3. Discuss the formation of self-concept, including recent findings about self-concept and gender and recent theory about self-expansion.

4. Explain recent findings about the attribution of humanness.

5. Discuss two important influences on self-esteem as well as recent research findings.

6. Describe some of the new research findings about shyness, including shyness and Internet use.

7. What is the Pygmalion effect? Discuss some of the research on it.

8. Identify the single most significant implication of behavior attribution research for the study of person perception.

9. Explain the concept of central traits and its significance for person perception.

10. What is the primacy effect? How might it influence communication?

11. Give a brief summary of the major research findings on physical attractiveness and its influence on first impressions.

12. Explain how expressiveness and charisma affect person perception.

13. How do personal generalizations and stereotypes differ?

14. List four statements about stereotypes that are supported by recent research.

15. Describe the influence of work, gender-linked, student, and marital roles on how we perceive and are ourselves perceived by others.

16. What three generalizations can you make from the research studies cited here about how various traits of the perceived affect the accuracy of person perception?

17. What is interpersonal sensitivity?

18. Discuss four perceiver characteristics associated with accurate perception of others.

19. What are two ways in which person perception and communication effectiveness can be improved?

20. Explain the concept of empathy and its significance for accurate person perception.

Exercises

1. Write a description of yourself in which you use 10 adjectives. Then ask a person in your class to describe you in the same way and compare the results. You might try this again with a close friend.

2. Go to *www.shyness.com* and answer the 35 questions on the Henderson/Zimbardo Shyness Questionnaire. Then to get your ShyQ or rating (Not Shy to Very Shy), go to the results section. Share these results with two friends. Do you think the rating is accurate? Do your friends? You can also participate in research on computer-mediated communication by filling out the Social Interaction and Technology Use Questionnaire at the same website.

3. Write down some of the perceptions you have of your classmates. Then refer to your earlier comments in the personal log on the computer that you began in Chapter 1, exercise 1. Have you changed or confirmed some of your original impressions?

4. Reread your descriptions (in exercise 4) of people who really impressed you at first. Write a list of words describing each person. Then try to identify the specific verbal and nonverbal behaviors that led you to draw up each list. Now that you know each of these people better,

what additional experiences have shaped your perception of each of them?

5. Write a paragraph describing someone you think is an effective communicator. List all attributes that seem to contribute to this effectiveness. Now think of a poor communicator. What characteristics seem to cause the ineffectiveness?

6. What characteristics do you possess that affect how you perceive these two people?

7. Have the class split up into groups of five. Your instructor will give you copies of the "Preliminary Scale of Interpersonal Perceptions." Fill out these forms, giving your perceptions of each of the other members in your group. Do not put your own name on the forms. When everyone has filled out all the forms, exchange them so that each person has a rating from every other group member. Then look at the ratings you received from the rest of the group. You might want to discuss these with others in the group to gain additional feedback.

8. Interview a person who does a lot of interviewing. Discuss communication and person perception with that person. Have the interviewer elaborate on how he or she perceives interviewees and selects cues in assessing them.

Suggested Readings

Baron-Cohen, Simon. *The Essential Difference: The Truth About the Male and Female Brain.* New York: Basic Books, 2004.

This fascinating and controversial book developed out of the author's work on autism. Can we really describe brains as predominantly male or female? What would be the advantages or disadvantages of each?

Cole, Jonathan. *About Face.* Cambridge, MA: Bradford Books, 1999.

A study of the human face, its expressiveness, and what happens to people who lose their capacity to make facial expressions. The author presents research on the importance of the face in the development of communication and emotion.

Crozier, W. Ray (ed.). *Shyness: Development, Consolidation and Change.* New York: Routledge, 2000.

An important collection of work on the study of shyness. For the advanced student.

Gladwell, Malcolm. *Blink: The Power of Thinking Without Thinking.* New York: Back Bay Books, 2007.

An informative and entertaining book about the way people make snap judgments. Several of the leading researchers on the subject are discussed.

Goleman, Daniel. *Social Intelligence: The New Science of Human Relationships.* New York: Bantam Books, 2006.

On the basis of new findings in neuroscience and biology the author discusses the development of "social intelligence" in human beings, including a built-in bias for empathy and altruistic behavior.

Ickes, William, ed. *Empathic Accuracy.* New York and London: Guilford, 1997.

An excellent collection of essays on many aspects of empathic accuracy. See, especially, Chapter 5 on the limits of women's intuition and Chapter 6 on the relationship between personality and empathic accuracy.

Paul, Annie Murphy. *The Cult of Personality.* New York: Free Press, 2004.

The author examines the uses and misuses of personality tests not only by psychologists but by the corporate world in its hiring practices. Specialized reading on the methods and biases of personality testing, this book is controversial, intriguing, and well written.

Zebrowitz, Leslie A. *Reading Faces: Window to the Soul?* Boulder, CO: Westview Press, 1997.

A fascinating discussion of research and theory about self-fulfilling prophecies as well as responses to baby-faced people and physical attractiveness in general.

 ## For Supplementary Information

Log onto the Online Learning Center at *www.mhhe.com/tubbsmoss11.*

3

The Verbal Message

Chapter Objectives

After reading this chapter, you should be able to:

1. Explain what is intended by the statement "The word is not the thing" and distinguish between denotation and connotation.
2. Differentiate between private and shared meanings and explain the concepts of overlapping codes and codeswitching.
3. Discuss two theories about how message encoding skills develop.
4. Summarize the Sapir-Whorf hypothesis and describe two ways in which language and thought are related.
5. Specify five problem areas in our use of language and give an example of each.
6. Explain how one's cultural frame of reference influences communication and give examples from two different cultures.
7. Discuss the effects of sexist language on communication, how male and female language usage differs, and several language forms perceived by others as powerful.
8. Explain the concept of metacommunication and give an example.

In the spring of 2007, radio talk show host Don Imus created a firestorm of controversy, which led to his firing. He referred to the tough-looking and tattooed members of the Rutgers University women's basketball team (who had nearly won the national championship) as ". . . some nappy-headed ho's."

Not much earlier, the famous comedian Michael Richards, known as Kramer from the sitcom *Seinfeld*, had a racial rant at the Laugh Factory in Los Angeles. In response to an African-American audience member's heckling, Richards started using the "n word" repeatedly and made many other racial comments. A few months earlier, actor and director Mel Gibson had a similar incident: When he was pulled over by the police, he began yelling anti-Semitic comments, saying that, "The Jews are responsible for all the wars in history" (Hamilton, 2006). In each instance, these outbursts have permanently tainted society's perception of these celebrities. In communication terms, the saying "You can't unring a bell" applies to all three events. In other words, no amount of apology can ever reverse the damage.

In the spring of 2004, the Federal Communications Commission (FCC) ruled that Bono was indecent and profane for describing one of the 2003 Golden Globe movie award winners as "f——brilliant." At about the same time, Howard Stern was slapped with three indecency fines for his radio broadcasts, two against Infinity Broadcasting and one against Clear Channel Communications. To avoid a repeat incident at the Golden Globes broadcast in 2005, NBC instituted a 10-second delay, and ABC did the same with its telecast of the Academy Awards show (Salant, 2004).

In the fall of 2001, eight U.S. senators and movie stars along with Rabbi Chaim Feld, head of Aish Hatorah, an international Orthodox Jewish educational organization, launched a media campaign to stop the harmful use of words in our society. Their organization is called Words Can Heal (see *www.wordscanheal.org*). Some of the spokespeople have included stars Tom Cruise and Goldie Hawn, and politicians Rudolph Giuliani, John McCain, and Bob Dole. This is one of the most public pronouncements demonstrating people's awareness of the positive and negative power of words (Reuters "Gossip," 2001, p. 5A).

The word "conversation" is the same in English and French, but as Raymonde Carroll explains, "It is far from signifying the same thing in the two cultures." Words per se cannot be said to "contain" meaning. As we will see, even for people who share a common language, words often generate very different associations (Carroll, 1988, p. 23).

As we examine verbal messages in this chapter, we will take up four major concerns. The first is the relationship between words and meaning. Thus, we will be talking about the symbolic nature of language, the descriptive and associative aspects of words (denotation and connotation), as well as private and shared meanings.

A second section takes up the complex process of formulating verbal messages and how we all learn to do this. As we examine the third issue, how language and thought are related, you will learn about a highly influential theory on the subject, the Sapir-Whorf hypothesis, and then look at several ways in which language use—abstraction, for example—affects your thinking.

In the fourth section, you will also learn about the influence of language usage on feelings and behavior. You will be looking at sexist language, gender differences in the use of language, and the linguistic forms considered most powerful or effective.

Let's turn first to a consideration of the nature of language.

WORDS AND MEANING

We saw in Chapter 1 that the communication process involves sending messages from one person's nervous system to another's with the intention of creating a meaning similar to the one in the sender's mind. The verbal message does this through words, the basic elements of language, and words, of course, are verbal symbols.

Symbols and Referents

In Chapter 1, we defined a symbol as *something used for or regarded as representing something else.* Thus, the image of a lion can serve as a symbol of courage, a red-and-white striped pole as a symbol of a barber shop. Durkel (2002) defined symbols as "representations of an event, action, object, person, or place that can be used to communicate about the event, action, object, person, or place." Symbols can take many forms, including words. In English, the word "sun" is the verbal symbol used to designate the star that is the central body of our solar system; the French use another symbol, "soleil"; and the Germans a third, "Sonne." All three symbols represent the same star.

Consider the term "disk." "Disk" is the name given to a flexible, round magnetic recording medium or storage device. The term is arbitrary. It was assigned to the recording device so that we could communicate about it without pointing each time we referred to it. "Disk" might have been called "soft record" or "blank" or even "urg." So initially, no real association exists between a word we agree to call something and its referent, *the object for which it stands.* Clearly, the word is not the thing. A word is merely a verbal symbol of the object it represents. Such words as "teletext," "modem," "Internet," and "e-mail" are but a few of those that have entered our language as a result of the new communication technologies.

For the most part when a company changes its name it is usually to increase sales—except for when AT&T and Cingular merged in 2005. AT&T and their owners, SBC, spent over $4 million to increase brand awareness of Cingular and made it the most popular carrier among the younger generation by using *American Idol* as one of its liaisons. In spite of this successful and expensive campaign, the company elected to replace "Cingular" with "AT&T" after the merger (Hood, 2006).

Another recent example is the Amway company, which sometimes uses high-pressure tactics to sell products through friendship networks. Amway launched its e-commerce business with a new name, Quixtar, in October of 2000. The corporate leaders wanted to differentiate its new line of business from the traditional Amway view. It also changed the Amway name to Alticor for the same reason. Amway had just developed a negative brand image (Bott, 2000, p. F1; see also *www.quixtar.com*).

Once we agree on a system of verbal symbols, we can use language to communicate. Of course, if all the words we used referred only to objects, our communication problems would be eased considerably. We could establish what referents we were speaking about with somewhat less difficulty. But words also refer to events, properties of things, actions, relationships, concepts, and so on.

The relationship between meaning and referent becomes especially clear when we encounter words in a foreign language. If we see МИР, the Russian word for "peace" and "world," for the first time, we have no way of determining what concepts that word represents simply by looking at the word itself. Even with new words in our own language, we have to learn what concepts they represent. Notice how we carefully avoided saying, "what the words mean." Meanings are not inherent in words. Words in and of themselves are meaningful only after we have associated them with some referents. It is human beings who assign meanings to words.

Denotation and Connotation

In discussing meaning, some students of language make the traditional distinction between "denotation" and "connotation." We have said that words are meaningful only after we have associated them with some referents. When we speak of **denotation,** we refer to *the primary associations a word has for most members of a given linguistic community.* When we speak of **connotation,** we refer to *other, secondary associations a word has for one or more members of that community.* Sometimes the connotations a word has are the same for nearly everyone; sometimes they relate solely to one individual's experience or, more often, to the experience of a particular subgroup.

The connotations of words have many uses and focus on the personal meanings that words have in our minds. For example, poets use the connotations of words in order to utilize words in a variety of symbolic ways, allowing the reader to create a new referent for a word that they may never have identified before (Chandler, 2002, p. I9). However, the connotations of words are often the occasion of misunderstanding in other contexts.

Culture has a large impact on the connotation of words. For example, the word "red" in Russian, "krasnyj," is a positive term and is a root of the word for "beautiful," which is "prekransyj." In English, the word "red" has connotations such as "blood" (Ministry of Education, 1996) or "stop" as on a stop sign.

Did you know that after ten years of falling sales, the prune industry decided to officially change the name of that fruit to "dried plums"? The California Prune Board spent over $10 million in 2001 to market its new brand image. The term "dried plums" tested much more positively by 90 percent of those surveyed. Similarly, Kiwi fruit used to be known as Chinese gooseberries, but the name was changed for better marketing and sales (Condor, 2001, p. 5H).

In the new age of technology and the high use of the Internet, the Urban Dictionary helps us decode the new slang that is being spoken across the United States. This useful resource can be found on the Internet and in its printed form. The Urban

Dictionary (2007) is a guide for pop culture (*www.urbandictionary.com*); some of its newer and most popular entries are the following:

Babysit: To pay little or no attention to your alcoholic beverage, letting it sit idle, while you pretend to nurse it.

Betty: Hot chick.

Biff: To fall hard.

Brokeback: Used to describe anything of questionable masculinity; originated from the 2005 motion picture *Brokeback Mountain*.

Five: Akin to the words "cool" and "awesome."

Gore Effect: The phenomenon that leads to unseasonably cold temperatures, driving rain, hail, or snow whenever Al Gore visits an area to discuss global warming—hence, the Gore Effect.

Hater: A person that simply cannot be happy for another person's success, so rather than be happy, they make a point of exposing a flaw in that person.

Heisman: A rejection given to a member of the opposite sex, a job, or anything no longer wanted; named after the Heisman trophy, which depicts a football player giving a stiff-arm block to a tackle.

January joiner: Someone who joins the gym in January as part of a New Year's resolution and by February is back to being a couch potato. Example: "I can't get a treadmill until February because the January joiners are all using them."

Kfed: Kevin Federline, Britney Spears's now–ex-husband.

Punked: A way to describe someone ripping you off, tricking you, or teasing you. It is also known for the TV show *Punk'd*.

Surge protector: Those who oppose an increase in troops in Iraq, like most Democrats and a few Republicans.

Did you also know that SPAM means a spiced lunch meat product made of pork shoulders and ham that is sold by Hormel Foods Corporation? To many young people spam means junk (unwanted) e-mail. Hormel Foods went to court to ensure that when you use the word in uppercase letters—SPAM—it refers to their product and when you use spam in lowercase letters it refers to junk e-mail. According to one source, "The slang meaning of 'spam' is said to have been inspired by a skit by British comedy troupe Monty Python in which a group of Vikings mutter 'spam, spam, spam,' with an ever increasing volume, drowning out normal conversation" (Reuters "SPAM," 2001, p. B13; see also *www.spam.com*).

In 2003, the restaurant menus in the three House of Representatives office buildings changed the name of french fries to freedom fries and french toast to freedom toast. The name change stemmed from anger over France's refusal to support the U.S. position on Iraq. Walter Jones, R–North Carolina, proposed the new terminology to include "freedom" as a reminder of the thousands of deployed troops who have a deep love for the freedom of this nation and their desire to fight for the freedom of those who are oppressed overseas ("House Restaurants Change Name . . . ," 2003).

When scientists recently retracted Pluto's status as a planet, a new form of the word "pluto" emerged: as a verb. The meaning of "to pluto" is "to demote or devalue someone or something" (*www.cnn.com*). One might say, for example, that "She was plutoed like the trash." A similar noun-to-verb transformation occurred with "google," which was originally a proper noun. "Plutoed" was the American Dialect Society's 2006 Word of the Year.

Negative-Positive Connotation

Because words can elicit such powerful emotional reactions, they are often said to have negative or positive connotations for people. Today, many people prefer to be called "senior citizens" rather than "elderly." And though parents may take equal pleasure in hearing their children referred to as "brilliant" or "gifted," those with "retarded" children are sensitive to the many negative connotations of the word.

In another example, a few years ago Reebok named a women's running shoe "Incubus" without knowing that the term "incubus" means a mythical demon who rapes sleeping women. Reebok later said that it was "horrified" about the mistake and immediately discontinued the use of the offensive name ("Shoemaker's Foot in Mouth," 1997).

In research on word connotations, subjects were exposed to various words on a tachistoscope, and their galvanic skin responses were measured. Although nonsignificant differences occurred between responses to "good" words (e.g., "beauty," "love," "kiss," and "friend") and "aversive" words (e.g., "cancer," "hate," "liar," and "death"), some words caused significant reactions in both men and women. These were called "personal" words and included the subject's first name, last name, father's first name, mother's first name, major in school, year in school, and school name. Subjects were more physiologically aroused by the personal words than by either the good or the aversive words (Crane et al., 1970). (For a discussion entitled "What Makes Bad Language Bad?" see Davis, 1989.)

The Semantic Differential

Some of the most influential research on the measurement of meaning has been conducted by Osgood and his associates (1957), who developed an instrument called the *Semantic Differential*. With the Semantic Differential, a researcher *can test a person's reactions to any concept or term*—sex, hard rock, mother, political correctness, apartheid, ego, cigarettes, Madonna, capital punishment—and then compare them with those of other people.

The test itself is a seven-interval scale with limits defined by sets of bipolar adjectives. "The words used to anchor the scales," explains Griffin (1991), "are

Figure 3.1   *Example of a Semantic Differential Scale*

Commitment

Sharp	___ : ___ : ___ : ___ : ___ : ___ : ___	Dull
Courageous	___ : ___ : ___ : ___ : ___ : ___ : ___	Cowardly
Dirty	___ : ___ : ___ : ___ : ___ : ___ : ___	Clean
Hot	___ : ___ : ___ : ___ : ___ : ___ : ___	Cold
Good	___ : ___ : ___ : ___ : ___ : ___ : ___	Bad
Fair	___ : ___ : ___ : ___ : ___ : ___ : ___	Unfair
Powerful	___ : ___ : ___ : ___ : ___ : ___ : ___	Weak
Deceitful	___ : ___ : ___ : ___ : ___ : ___ : ___	Honest
Fast	___ : ___ : ___ : ___ : ___ : ___ : ___	Slow
Cruel	___ : ___ : ___ : ___ : ___ : ___ : ___	Kind
Active	___ : ___ : ___ : ___ : ___ : ___ : ___	Passive

concerned with feelings (connotation) rather than a description (denotation)" (p. 32). Figure 3.1, for example, is a Semantic Differential for the word "commitment." The subject rates the concept by checking the interval between each pair of adjectives that best describes it. The researcher then draws a line connecting each point made by the subject, thus creating a profile of the subject's concept of commitment.

Statistical analysis of the work of Osgood and his associates suggests that our judgments have three major dimensions: evaluation, potency, and activity. Thus, we say that commitment is good or bad and cruel or kind (evaluation), that it is powerful or weak and hot or cold (potency), and fast or slow and active or passive (activity).

Culture and Connotation

The subjects of Osgood's early research were Americans, but he was intrigued by the possibility of cross-cultural studies and went on to explore the dimensions of affective meaning in 26 different language communities (Osgood, 1974a; 1974b). According to Osgood, the major dimensions of affective meaning in all these cultures were the same: evaluation, potency, and activity.

ISSUES IN COMMUNICATION

A Word about Semantics

When do words make a difference? When you give someone your "word," what does that imply? Have you ever seen communication difficulties arise over the use and assumed meaning ascribed to certain words?

When Chevrolet introduced the Nova into Spanish-speaking countries, it had disappointing sales. *No va* means "it does not go" in Spanish. How could this have been avoided?

When AT&T lays off 40,000 employees, it is called "downsizing" or "restructuring." What do you think it would be called if 40,000 people

were permanently put out of work by an act of nature?

Some authors (Tubbs, 2007) have referred to different types of words as "purr" words versus "snarl" words. Imagine a work situation in which someone has just submitted a report and you want to give the person some feedback that you think it has some good aspects, but it could be improved. Try creating two scenarios in which you give the feedback using "snarl" words and another using "purr" words.

From his cross-cultural research, Osgood has compiled the *Atlas of Affective Meanings*. The 620 concepts in this atlas run the gamut from "accepting things as they are," "accident," "marriage," and "masculinity," to "master," "yesterday," "youth," and "zero." Although Osgood found certain definite cultural variations, many concepts were evaluated similarly by members of a great many different cultures. One such concept was "the days of the week." Monday was generally evaluated as the worst day in the week; things tended to improve after that, gathering momentum on Friday and reaching a peak on Sunday, the best day. For Iranians, on the other hand, the worst day was Saturday (comparable to our Monday), and Friday (the Muslim holy day) was the best (Osgood, 1974b, p. 83).

The great appeal of the Semantic Differential is its flexibility. The procedure is so general that it can be precisely tailored to the needs and interests of the experimenter, who can test the emotional valence of any concept at all.

Griffin (1991) offers this assessment of Osgood's work:

Of course, many anthropologists doubt the validity of Osgood's conclusion that evaluation, potency, and activity are universal dimensions of affect. Anyone who claims they've punched a hole in the language barrier is bound to draw fire. But a decade of rigorous cross-cultural testing with the semantic differential suggests that Osgood has made a quantum leap in understanding the meaning of meaning. (p. 36)

Private and Shared Meanings

In psychology and semantics, much research is based on the distinction between denotation and connotation. The Semantic Differential, for example, is said to measure "connotative meaning." But when we examine it closely, the distinction between denotation and connotation seems to break down. All people who speak English are members of the same linguistic community; yet within that community certain groups exist for whom even the primary associations, or denotations, of a given word are different.

Take the case of the Americans and the British. In England you take a "lift," not an "elevator"; if you ask for the "second floor," you get the "third." You take the "underground," not the "subway." You "queue up"; you don't "stand in line." You go to a "chemist's," not a "pharmacy." The list seems virtually endless.

Private Meaning

We can all use language idiosyncratically, assigning meanings to words without agreement and, in effect, creating our own private language. We can decide, for example, to call trees "reds" or "cows" or "haves." Schizophrenic speech is often private in this way, but schizophrenics are unaware that they sometimes use language in a way that is not shared by others: They use the words they have recreated and expect to be understood. When one young patient was admitted to a hospital, she continually referred to her father, a lawyer by profession, as "the chauffeur." Everyone with whom she spoke found this reference bizarre. Only in treatment was it learned that when she called her father a "chauffeur," she meant that he was completely under her mother's domination. In his book *Philosophical Investigations,* philospher Ludwig Wittgenstein defined private language as follows: "The words of this language are to refer to what can be known only to the speaker; to his immediate, private, sensations. So another cannot understand the language" (Candlish, 2004).

Shared Meaning

Presumably, if we assign private meanings to words, we are aware that we can use them to communicate with someone only if we let that person know what the referents of these words are. **Shared meaning** requires *some correspondence between the message as perceived by the sender and the receiver.* Two friends, a husband and wife, an entire family, or a group of physicists may decide to use language in a way that makes little sense to others. Among themselves, however, they can communicate with no difficulty.

Shared meaning is essential in building culture within organizations. Organizations have their own terminology, industry vocabulary, acronyms, and definitions within the environment. It is easy to spot an outsider to an organization while a group is within the throes of conversation using shared language. This sharing creates a sense of belonging to the organizational culture. Can you think back on your own experience on the first day of a job and how it felt to suddenly be immersed in a new culture with shared meanings that you did not yet understand? How did you feel once you understood these meanings?

The ever-growing popularity of text messaging has led to the formation a new "language" for the individuals who use cell phones for more than the average phone call. Most of those who fit into this group are teenagers and young adults across the globe; they have created an abbreviated version of their existing languages to type faster. Below are some examples of English language text-messaging shorthand, according to *www.netlingo.com* (2007):

CUL8R—see you later

BRB—be right back

2BZ4UQT—to busy for you cutie

@TEOTD—at the end of the day

LOL—laughing out loud

P911—parent alert

TNX—thanks

The same phenomenon occurs among members of many other kinds of groups. Actors understand each other when they talk about scenes being "blocked." Physical therapists refer in their work to "trigger points" and "jelling pain." An extensive vocabulary describes the various moves possible on a skateboard, such as "ollies," "bonelesses," "720s," "thread the needles," and "slob airs." For the subgroup that uses this language, the meaning of "bonelesses" and "thread the needles" is always clear.

One writer described the insider language of those who approve screenplays for major motion pictures such as producers, directors, and lead actors. He wrote that when people use the following terms they really mean something else: "Wonderful means change it. Fantastic means change it. Terrific means change it. Thank you means you're fired" (Applebome, 1998, p. E1).

Group members have no difficulty understanding one another when they use language in this way because they share a code. Communication difficulties emerge only when they expect meaning to be shared by those outside the group. This is a recurring expectation, especially in a country such as the United States, where so many different ethnic groups coexist.

Overlapping Codes and Codeswitching

In intercultural communication, the sender and the receiver often have overlapping codes, *"codes which provide an area of commonality but which also contain areas of unshared codification"* (Samovar and Porter, 1972, p. 291, emphasis added). Even if the code they use at home is very different, members of minority groups are usually compelled to learn and make some use of the language of the majority because in education, business, and politics this language dominates.

Restricted codes of communication seem to be common among intimate dyads. A study of young lovers (Bell et al., 1987) found the number of personal idioms they used—that is, "words, phrases, or nonverbal signs they had created that had meaning unique to their relationship" (p. 47)—to be highly correlated with love, commitment, and closeness. This proved to be true for both premarital and marital relationships. The couples studied had private idioms, which they used only when they were alone, and public idioms, which they could use when others were present: The private idioms were usually sexual references or euphemisms and sexual invitations (e.g., "Let's go home and watch TV"), whereas the public idioms were often nicknames, confrontations, teasing insults, and requests.

Shifts in codes occur in many different communication contexts. An analysis of such American television interviewers as Larry King, Oprah Winfrey, and Katie Couric (Scotton, 1988) argues that a pattern of frequent codeswitching within a single conversation can be used by a speaker for the purpose of negotiating power. *Codeswitching* is referred to here as *shifting to different styles* (casual, quasi-literary, and so on) *and introducing shifts in vocabulary or syntax.* Codeswitching is used in many contexts. For example, salespeople must be able to codeswitch in both developing customer relationships and in negotiations. They must mirror the communication style of the customer in many cases to develop the relationship and be able to shift into a mode of negotiation when necessary. Additionally, there are many contexts in which codeswitching establishes or reinforces intimacy. Novelist Amy Tan (1991), author of *The Joy Luck Club,* writes of speaking to an audience about her life and work when suddenly her talk sounded "wrong." Her language was formal and literary, but her mother, who was born in China, was in the audience and had never heard her speaking this formally. Tan goes on to describe how later, when taking a walk with her mother, she once more became aware of the English she was using:

> We were talking about the price of new and used furniture and I heard myself saying this: "Not waste money that way." My husband was with us as well, and he didn't notice any switch in my English. And then I realized why. It's because over the twenty years we've been together I've often used the same kind of English with him, and sometimes he even uses it with me. It has become our language of intimacy, a different sort of English that relates to family talk, the language I grew up with. (p. 197)

The several "Englishes" used by Tan will also be familiar to other children of bilingual families.

LANGUAGE AND THOUGHT

In discussing message encoding, we've seen that language and thought are often said to be interrelated. But the nature of their relationship is far from clear. Is language a precondition of human thought? Is thinking simply inner speech? There are no easy answers. Students of communication have been particularly concerned with the question: Does language shape our ideas, or is it merely an instrument of thought?

The Sapir-Whorf Hypothesis

One version of the view that our thought is shaped by the language we speak is the **Sapir-Whorf hypothesis** that *the world is perceived differently by members of different communities and that this perception is transmitted and sustained by language.* Benjamin Lee Whorf (1956), whose work was shaped by that of the great linguist Edwin Sapir, regards language as the primary vehicle of culture. In short, the language we speak influences our experience of the world, while the evolution of language also reflects changes in the predominant modes of expression.

Whorf supports this theory with findings from studies of Native American languages. In English, he points out, we tend to classify words as nouns or verbs; in Hopi the words tend to be classified by duration. For example, in Hopi "lightning," "flame," " wave," and "spark" are verbs, not nouns; they are classified as events of brief duration. In Nootka, which is spoken by the inhabitants of Vancouver Island, categories such as things and events do not exist; thus it is said that "A house occurs" or "It houses."

The Sapir-Whorf hypothesis is based on two types of determinism, which define how our language determines how we view the environment. "Strong" determinism is the belief that language has the power to determine our thoughts; "weak" determinism is the belief that our way of viewing the world and our thoughts are influenced by language but not controlled by it. The latter type of determinism is the most important line of thought among current cognitive psychologists. Alison Motluk (2002), a writer for the British magazine *New Scientist,* wrote an article titled "You Are What You Speak." She noted differences in language construction and how individuals see the world. She cites the following example: When describing 11 pens lying on a table, a person from Russia would have to consider the gender of the pens in the answer, a Japanese person has to look at the shape of the pens, and an English speaker just has to count the pens. She questioned if these linguistic differences actually change how we think about the world ("Sapir-Whorf Hypothesis Redux," 2002/2003, pp. 456–457). In spite of opposing lines of thought, the current consensus is that language does have some influence on our thoughts, but does not determine them.

As stated before, Whorf's hypothesis that language can determine the nature and content of thought is useful in explaining this peculiar evidence. A linguist from Columbia University did a study on the Piraha tribe and discovered that they use a three-word number system ("one-two-many"). This addresses the classic Whorfian question about whether language can determine thought. Results of numerical tasks with varying cognitive demands show that numerical cognition is clearly affected by the lack of a counting system in the language (Gordon, 2004).

In an even more significant example, Stoltz (1997) cites brain research that shows that the language we use can shape our perception of success and even our ability to be successful. Those individuals who tell themselves that their shortcomings are long lasting tend to have more failures than those who see setbacks as temporary. Similarly, those who see setbacks as a result of their lack of abilities tend to have more failures than those who see their failures as a result of not having given their best effort. This research has major implications for helping people improve their career and life successes.

Relabeling skills are what Losoncy (1997) calls the ability to use language in more constructive ways. For example, one can relabel setbacks as "annoyances," catastrophes as "hindrances," failures as "growth experiences," or rejections as "inconveniences."

The specific mechanism for increasing success is self-talk, which refers to the messages we communicate to ourselves. When an event occurs, such as our boss criticizing us on a task, we can use positive or negative self-talk. This results in either a positive or a negative feeling or behavior. To quote one source: "The difference between a really good day and a really awful day is not in what happened but in what you tell yourself about that day" (Whiteman et al., 1996, p. 196).

Language does two important things. First, it serves as an aid to memory. It makes memory more efficient by allowing us to code events as verbal categories. Researchers have shown, for example, that we find it easier to recognize colors of low codability again if we named them for ourselves the first time we saw them (Brown and Lenneberg, 1954). It is now believed that an adult's memory is primarily verbal. And second, language also enables us to abstract indefinitely from our experience, which is especially important in communicating about abstract relationships (something animals are unable to do).

Language Problems

Ideally, language is a valuable instrument of thought; yet we know that language can sometimes interfere with our ability to think critically. Although Whorf was best known for his writings on linguistics, he was trained as an engineer. When he became an accident investigator, he began to realize that a certain percentage of accidents occurred as a result of what might be called "careless thinking." For example, people would be very careful around barrels labeled "gasoline" but would smoke unconcernedly around barrels labeled "empty gasoline barrel," though the fumes in the empty barrels were more likely to ignite than the actual gasoline (Whorf, 1956, p. 135). Imprecise use of language can interfere with our thought processes in many ways. We shall examine several that have a direct influence on our communication.

Abstract Language

When people use *abstract* language, they frequently cause communication difficulties that have to do with the *vagueness of words*. As concepts become more vague, or abstract, it gets harder and harder to decode the intended meaning. S. I. Hayakawa has written several books on semantics, and in one he included the so-called abstraction ladder we see in Figure 3.2.

In general, the more abstract the term, the greater our chances of misunderstanding. Consider this exchange between father and teenage son:

Father: Have a good time, and don't stay out late.

   Son: Thanks, I will. Don't worry. I'll be home early.

Figure 3.2   *Abstraction Ladder*

Start Reading from the bottom *UP*

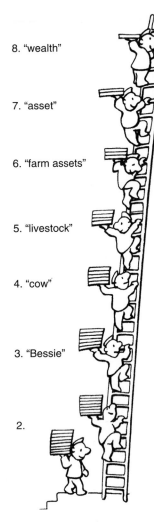

8. "wealth"

7. "asset"

6. "farm assets"

5. "livestock"

4. "cow"

3. "Bessie"

2.

8. The word "wealth" is at an extremely high level of abstraction, omitting *almost* all reference to the characteristics of Bessie.

7. When Bessie is referred to as an "asset," still more of her characteristics are left out.

6. When Bessie is included among "farm assets," reference is made only to what she has in common with what all other salable items on the farm.

5. When Bessie is referred to as "livestock," only those characteristics she has in common with pigs, chickens, goats, etc., are referred to.

4. The word "cow" stands for the characteristics we have abstracted as common to cow_1, cow_2, cow_3 . . . cow_n. Characteristics peculiar to specific cows are left out.

3. The word "Bessie" (cow_1) is the *name* we give to the object of perception of level 2. The name is not the object; it merely *stands for* the object and omits reference to many of the characteristics of the object.

2. The cow we perceive is not the word, but the object of experience, that which our nervous system abstracts (selects) from the totality that constitutes the process-cow. Many of the characteristics of the process-cow are left out.

1. The cow known to science ultimately consists of atoms, electrons, etc., according to present-day scientific inference. Characteristics (represented by circles) are infinite at this level and ever-changing. This is the *process level.*

Source: From *Language in Thought and Action*, 4th ed. by S. I. Hayakawa. Copyright © 1978. Reprinted with permission of Heinle, a division of Thomson Learning. *www.thomsonrights.com.* Fax 800-730-2215.

The next day they may get into a disagreement because they were not thinking the same things when they used the words "early" and "late." Perhaps the son purposely did not clarify what the father meant by "late" because he didn't want to be held to a strict time limit. And the father may have been vague intentionally so that his son would have a chance to exercise judgment and learn to become more adult. On the other hand, if the son came home at 4:00 a.m., both father and son would probably agree that he had indeed stayed out "late."

The following may help you understand the abstract meaning of "love":

> Take *love* as an example. You have heard and used that word since you were three or four years old. Does it mean to you now what it meant to you when you were five? when you were ten? when you were fourteen(!)? I am sure you will share my certainty that the word changes meaning when we marry, when we divorce, when we have children, when we look back at lost parents or spouses or children. The word stays the same, but the meaning keeps changing. (Friedlander, 2007)

Often, in an attempt to avoid ambiguity, we use very precise wording to clarify meaning. Legal contracts are such an example. But no amount of care is sufficient to avoid all ambiguity of interpretation. We need only look at the differences in how Supreme Court justices have interpreted the Constitution, or at the different ways in which the Bible has been interpreted, to see the inherent ambiguity in our use of language. Keep in mind the abstraction ladder, however, for some terms are considerably more abstract, and therefore more subject to misinterpretation, than others.

Inferences

An *inference* is *a conclusion or judgment derived from evidence or assumptions.* Every day you make dozens of inferences. When you sit down, you infer that the chair will support your weight. When you go through a green light, you infer that the traffic moving at right angles to you will stop at the red light. When you drive down a one-way street, you infer that all the traffic will be going in one direction. You may have good reason to expect these inferences to be correct, but there is also some uncalculated probability that events will not always go as you expect. Drivers who have been involved in traffic accidents frequently say that the accident occurred because they inferred that the other party would act in a certain way when in fact he or she did not. Every year we read of people who were accidentally shot with guns they inferred were not loaded.

As students of communication, we are concerned with the inferences implicit in verbal messages. If you say, "It is sunny outside today," your statement can be easily verified. It is a factual statement based on an observed and verifiable event. If you say, "It is sunny outside; therefore, it is sunny 50 miles from here," you draw a conclusion based on more than what you have observed. You have made a statement based in part on an inference.

Consider a more complex situation. Sheila Waring has broken off a substantial part of one of her front teeth. Her dentist takes an x-ray, covers the tooth with a temporary, and gives her an appointment for the following week; she may, he mentions, need root canal work. The next week Sheila returns, and as she walks into the office, the dentist says, "I'm sorry, Sheila. You do need root canal work. This calls for a heroic effort." Hearing this, Sheila is terrified and during the next hour sits in the chair awaiting the awful pain that never comes. "There. Finished—" says the dentist, "I've taken out the nerve." "But I didn't feel it at all. I thought you said I would have to be heroic about it." "No. I said 'a heroic effort,' " answers the dentist. "I didn't say *your* effort."

We make inferences in every imaginable context, and it is neither possible nor desirable to avoid them entirely. Nevertheless, to use language more precisely and to be more discerning when we hear others speak, we should learn to distinguish between factual and inferential statements. "You spend a great deal of time with my roommate" is a statement of fact. It involves a low level of uncertainty, it is made as a result of direct observation, and it can be verified. Add to it "I'm sure he won't mind if you borrow his coat," and you have an inferential statement that may well jeopardize a friendship. In becoming more conscious of inference making, we can at least learn to calculate the risks involved.

To compound the problem, our language is structured so that no distinction is made between facts and inferences. It is the verb "to be" that creates the difficulty: no grammatical distinction is made between a fact verified through sense data (e.g., "She is wearing a red coat") and a statement that cannot be verified through sense data and is merely an inference (e.g., "She is thinking about her upcoming date this weekend").

Dichotomies

Dichotomies, or *polar words,* are frequently responsible for another type of language problem. Some semanticists classify English as a "two-valued" rather than a "multi-valued language." By this they mean that English has an excess of polar words and a relative scarcity of words to describe the wide middle ground between these opposites. Obviously, every person, entity, or event can be described in terms of a whole array of adjectives ranging from very favorable to very unfavorable. (Recall the Semantic Differential, discussed earlier in this chapter, which uses a seven-interval scale.) Yet we tend to say that a student is a "success" or a "failure," that a child is "good" or "bad," that a woman is "attractive" or "unattractive." Try, for example, to think of some words to describe the spots marked on the continua in the scale of dichotomies in Figure 3.3. As you search for words, you begin to see that there are a lot of distinctions for which we lack single words. The continua also illustrate how our language suggests that certain categories of experience are mutually exclusive, when in truth they are not.

Consider the first set of terms, "success" and "failure." Every human being undoubtedly meets with some success and some failure during the course of a lifetime.

Figure 3.3

SCALE OF DICHOTOMIES

Success	___	___	X	___	___	___	___	Failure
Brilliant	___	___	___	X	___	___	___	Stupid
Handsome	___	___	X	___	___	___	___	Ugly
Winner	___	___	___	X	___	___	___	Loser
Honest	___	___	___	X	___	___	___	Dishonest
Black	___	X	___	___	___	___	___	White

Source: Reprinted from the *Journal of Applied Behavioral Science,* 6, "The Fifth Achievement," by Blake and Mouton, p. 418, copyright © 1970. Reprinted by permission of Sage Publications via Copyright Clearance Center.

An insurance broker unemployed for many months and unable to find work may also be a supportive and much-loved father and husband. Yet our language suggests that he be classified as either a success or a failure. Similar difficulties crop up if we are asked to apply such adjectives as "brilliant" and "stupid" or "winner" and "loser" to other people. Is the math major with a straight A average brilliant or stupid if she can't learn to drive a car or ride a bike? If the author of a recent best-seller is divorced for the third time, is he a winner or a loser?

When polar terms are used in a misleading way, they suggest false dichotomies, reducing experience in a way that it need not be reduced. Differences are emphasized and similarities are overlooked, and in the process a great deal of information is lost. This is certainly true in our country at election time.

One way to avoid making false dichotomies, as Haney (1992, p. 374) has pointed out, is to make use of the questions "How much?" and "To what extent?":

How much of a success am I?

How much of a change is this from his former stand on gun control?

To what extent is he honest?

To what extent is her plan practical?

With the aid of such questions, perhaps we can keep in mind that we have many options, that we need not cast our messages in black-and-white terms, and that we need not accept these either-or distinctions when they are made by others.

Euphemisms

Through *euphemisms* we *substitute mild, vague, or less emotionally charged terms for more blunt ones*—"campaign of disinformation" for "smear campaign," "security review procedure" for "censorship," "discomfort" for "pain," "memory garden" for "cemetery," "powder room" for "bathroom," "attack" for "rape." "Portly," "stout," and "heavyset" are ways to avoid saying "fat." Of course, they lack the specificity of "fat" as well as the affect attached to the word. If we hear that a woman was "attacked," we don't know if she was assaulted or raped. Often the problem created by using euphemisms is that the intent may be conveyed but not the degree to which the intent is felt. So-called empty words are euphemisms because they are pleasant sounding yet indirect enough to avoid being blunt: "nice," "wonderful," and "pleasant" appear to be all-purpose euphemisms. They make for dull conversations. And on many occasions, euphemistic language is used to misrepresent what is being said. For example, one high school counselor revealed several phrases he used in writing student recommendations for college applications: describing a student with serious emotional problems as "having peaks and valleys"; saying a student "likes to take risks" when referring to a drug problem; characterizing an arrogant student as "pushing against the limits" (Carmody, 1989, p. B6).

Equivocal Language

Misunderstandings often occur because people assume that a word, a phrase, or even a sentence is unequivocal—that is, it has only one meaning. Hayakawa refers to this as "the 'one word, one meaning' fallacy" (1978). But much of the language we use is *equivocal*; it has *two or more possible interpretations*.

We've seen the problems created by disagreements over the referents of such words as "peace," "truth," and "freedom." Misunderstandings are also quite common when the words and phrases in question sound far more concrete. If your date says, "Let's get a drink after the show," the drink may refer to an alcoholic beverage, continuing the evening in a club, or a desire to stay together for simple conversation.

There seem to be two sources of confusion about words or phrases. First, people may assume that because they are using the same word, they agree, when in fact each interprets the word differently. In a comical incident, a woman asks a pharmacist for a refill of her prescription for "the pill." "Please hurry," she adds, "I've got someone waiting in the car." Much humor is based on such double meanings. In daily communication, this type of confusion may not be so funny. For example, one of the authors and spouse—and we're not saying which one—were drawn into a needless argument:

Husband: You know, the travel literature on Switzerland that I borrowed is still in the house. Since we're not going, I'd better return it to that fellow in my office. Could you get it together for me so I can take it in tomorrow?

Wife: I don't know where it is.

Husband: What kind of answer is that? If it's too much trouble, forget it.

Wife: What do you mean, "What kind of answer is that?" How can I do anything with it if I can't find it?

Husband: There's nothing to do. All I asked you to do was find it. You don't have to give me a smart answer.

Wife: But you said "get it together." I thought you meant put it in some sort of order.

Husband: I meant "find it." Don't you know what "get it together" means?

Wife: Well, I didn't know it meant that.

Husband: If you didn't know, why didn't you ask me?

Wife: Because I thought I knew. I speak English, too, you know.

For a time this misunderstanding created a lot of ill feeling. Both husband and wife were insulted—the husband because he felt his wife had refused to do something relatively simple for him, and the wife because she felt her husband had insulted her intelligence.

A second type of misunderstanding occurs when two people assume that they disagree because they are using different words when actually they may agree on the concept or entity represented by those words. That is, they use different terms that have the same referent. For example, a school psychologist and a guidance counselor were discussing a student who was failing several of her classes though she was of above-average intelligence. A disagreement developed when the counselor insisted that the girl definitely needed "help." "She certainly does not," countered the psychologist. "She needs psychological intervention." "That's what I'm saying," said the counselor. "She should be getting psychological counseling." "Well, then we agree," answered the psychologist. "When you said 'help,' I thought you were talking about tutoring." The psychologist and counselor were able to resolve their apparent differences because they did stop and redefine their terms.

Although our attention has been given to words or phrases, most messages take the form of sentences. "It's a rainy day," remarks Jack to Jill. What could be clearer than the meaning of that sentence? Yet Laing (1972) suggests five ways in which Jack might intend his statement. Perhaps he wishes to register the fact that it is a rainy day. If yesterday Jack and Jill agreed to go for a walk instead of going to a movie, he might be saying that because of the rain he will probably get to see the movie. He might be implying that because of the weather Jill should stay at home. If yesterday the two argued about what the weather would be like, he might mean that Jill is right again or that he is the one who always predicts the weather correctly. If the window is open, he might be saying that he would like Jill to close it. No doubt each of us could come up with several other interpretations. The point is that any message derives a great part of its meaning from the context in which it is transmitted. Our knowledge of the speaker and the speaker's use of language, our own associations with the words he or she chooses, our previous relationship, and the messages we have already exchanged should all play a part in how we interpret what is said.

Culture as Our Frame of Reference

Although all our behaviors have possible meaning for a receiver, language is by far our most explicit form of communication. In using it, we usually desire to facilitate thought, not to obscure it. Language is potentially the most precise vehicle we have for human communication. Even if we grant the infinite richness of language and the precision it is capable of expressing, however, a look at intercultural communication makes clear that often people are divided, not because of a failure to understand grammar or vocabulary, but because of a failure to understand rhetoric or point of view.

Kenneth Kaunda, the former president of Zambia, insists that Westerners and Africans have very different ways of seeing things, solving problems, and thinking in general. He characterizes the Westerner as having a "problem-solving mind." Once a Westerner perceives a problem, he or she feels compelled to solve it. Unable to live with contradictory ideas, the Westerner excludes all solutions that have no logical basis. Supernatural and nonrational phenomena are regarded as superstition. The African, on the other hand, allows himself or herself to experience all phenomena, nonrational as well as rational. The African has a "situation-experiencing mind." Kaunda believes that "the African can hold contradictory ideas in fruitful tension within his mind without any sense of incongruity, and he will act on the basis of the one which seems most appropriate to the particular situation" (Legum, 1976, pp. 63–64).

In ancient India, according to Kirkwood (1989) and other students of Indian rhetoric, truthfulness was considered the prime standard for speech. Emphasis was placed not only on the value of truthful speech to listeners but on the profound effects for the speaker as well. The practice of speaking truthfully was regarded as spiritually liberating, and the performance itself—the act of speaking the truth—brought with it self-knowledge as well as freedom, thus transforming the speaker. Such ideas date back to the tenth century B.C. and are an enduring aspect of India's culture.

On the other hand, a study of Chinese and Japanese attitudes toward speech communication in public settings offers several reasons for the lack of argumentation and debate in the Far East. According to Becker (1991), social history contributed to an aversion to public debate. For example, in the Chinese and Japanese traditions, "taking opposite sides of an argument necessarily meant becoming a personal rival and antagonist of the one who held the other side. The more important concomitant of this idea was that if one did not wish to become a lifelong opponent of someone else, he would not venture an opinion contrary to the other person's opinions in public. Even the legal system was set up in such a way that it avoided direct confrontations" (p. 236).

In addition, various linguistic features of Chinese and Japanese (e.g., Chinese lacks plurals and tenses) as well as great differences between Western and Eastern philosophy and religion all presented powerful barriers to the widespread use of debate and argumentation for considering new proposals or strategies for implementing social and political change (Becker, 1991, p. 242). Becker emphasizes that the Westerner's ideal speech situation requiring "equality of participants, freedom from social coercion, suspension of privilege, and free expression of feeling . . . [would be] both impractical and even theoretically inconceivable to traditionally educated Chinese and Japanese" (p. 242).

In looking at different cultural frames of reference, we seem to have come full circle, recalling elements of the Sapir-Whorf hypothesis. To some degree, linguistic traditions help shape our thought processes, but for members of different cultures, these traditions can be a barrier.

We've considered several language-related problems that interfere with your ability to think and communicate clearly. Of course, there are numerous others. But just being aware of the *possibility* that language can be a source of misunderstanding should enable you to be more perceptive about verbal messages.

WORDS IN ACTION

In this final section of our chapter, we will examine some ways in which words influence human actions, both directly and indirectly. In ancient times, people of many diverse cultures believed that words had magical powers. For example, in ancient Egypt a man received two names: his true name, which he concealed, and his good name, by which he was known publicly. Even today many primitive societies regard words as magical. Members of some cultures go to great lengths to conceal their personal names. They avoid saying the names of their gods. The names of their dead are never uttered. Presumably, we moderns are far more sophisticated. Yet we have our own verbal taboos. And the euphemisms we've just talked about are part of our everyday vocabulary. Thus, we often hear not that someone "died" but that he or she "passed away." And a sudden drop in the stock market is often termed a "correction."

Recently, the use of the term "mother" has come into some controversy. According to one source, "In Massachusetts and many other states, only the woman who gives birth is presumed to be the mother and can have her name on the original birth certificate. The law does not address women becoming mothers by having embryos implanted in a surrogate . . . More than a month after they were born, a baby boy and his twin sister still have no birth certificates. The paperwork is being held up in a dispute over the legal definition of the term mother" (Lavoie, 2001, p. A7).

Some empirical studies of word power examine the ways in which a speaker's use of profane words affects our judgment of his or her credibility. (See Chapter 13 for a discussion of credibility.) Three classes of profanity were used: religious, excretory, and sexual. Although religious profanity was less offensive when circumstances appeared to justify it, sexual profanity—whether provoked or unprovoked—always seemed to bring the speakers significantly lower credibility ratings. These results are surprisingly consistent: They are the same for males and females, older and younger women, and first-year and graduate students (Rossiter and Bostrom, 1968; Bostrom et al., 1973; Mabry, 1975).

Writers on public communication traditionally refer to the effective use of language as "eloquence." In public speaking, eloquence describes a more dramatic, stirring use of language—often for the purpose of inspiring or persuading others. One thinks of the famous speech of Dr. Martin Luther King, Jr., "I Have a Dream," through which thousands were inspired to work for equal rights:

> I have a dream that one day, even the state of Mississippi, a state sweltering with the heat of injustice, sweltering with the heat of oppression, will be transformed into an oasis of freedom and justice . . .
> With this faith we will be able to hew out of the mountain of despair a stone of hope. With this faith we will be able to transform the jangling discords of our nation into a beautiful symphony of brotherhood.

With these words, Dr. King was able to move people's feelings more powerfully than he could have with more commonplace language. Lamenting the "eloquence gap" in contemporary politics, poet Michael Blumenthal expressed his sense that "a nation that no longer expects and demands eloquence and statesmanship from its politicians no longer expects and demands grandeur from itself—or precision of belief from those who lead it" (1989, p. 18).

Sometimes our decisions are based in part on how a thing is labeled. For example, certain words clearly have greater prestige than others. A "classic car" is better than an old one. "Vintage clothing" is more appealing than old second-hand clothing. The same desk commands different prices when it is called "used," "secondhand," or "antique." "Doctor" is another powerful word. In many situations, for example, it is undeniable that "Dr." Bradley will get more attention than "Ms." Bradley or "Mr." Bradley.

Sexist Language

Since the late 1960s many students of language, a good many feminists among them, have argued that our language is sexist, that it reflects a bias affecting how women are perceived and treated by others and sometimes how they regard themselves. For example, words associated with the descriptions of males often have positive connotations—"confident," "forceful," "strong," and the like—whereas females are more often described as "fickle," "frivolous," "timid," and so forth (Heilbrun, 1976).

In studies at three different universities, Pearson and her associates (1991) found that when students were asked to list all the terms for men and women, the list of words for women was longer and generally much less favorable than the one for men. (See Table 3.1.) It's the group in power, these writers point out, that "typically does the naming or labeling. In our culture men tend to name people, places, and things."

Table 3.1	Terms for Women and Men				
Women			**Men**		
Chick	Wife	Honey	Gent	Boy	
Girl	Old maid	Madam	Man	Stud	
Old lady	Bitch	Whore	Guy	Hunk	
Piece	Lady	Dog	Male	Bastard	
Female	Broad	Cow	Husband		
Prostitute	Woman	Old biddy			

Source: From *Gender and Communication,* by Judy Cornelia Pearson. Copyright © 1985. Reprinted by permission of the author.

Of the differences in the labeling of men and women, Pearson et al. (1991) note, "names for women are sometimes created by adding another word or a feminine marker to a name for men" (thus, "waitress," "actress," and so on). In addition, terms for women tend to be more frequently sexual, often with connotations that the women are the objects of sexual conquest.

Some words in the English language indicate a lower status for females. An example that illustrates this is how the English language makes a distinction between "Mrs." and "Miss," which shows that a woman is either married or single, respectively. Conversely, males only have "Mr.," which gives no indication of marital status (Lei, 2006).

The following are some examples from Lei (2006) of occupational nouns and job titles ending in "-man" that make the presence of women unclear in such professions and positions as well as some alternative terms:

policeman—police officer

businessman—business executive

chairman—chair, chairperson

clergyman—member of the clergy

weatherman—meteorologist

The metaphors used for men and women also differ. Metaphors involving food are often used when referring to women—"tomato," "cookie," "sugar," "piece of cake," and so on. Sometimes animal names are used in referring to women, but these tend to be the names of baby animals ("chick" or "kitty," for example)—names that connote weakness or vulnerability. If men are linked with animals, it's with the names of far more powerful animals ("wolf" is an example). Pearson et al. (1991) point out that the terms for men and women are often polar opposites with the male term being positive, the female term negative; "bachelor" and "old maid" are a case in point.

Women tend to be referred to by euphemisms far more frequently than men are. And although men are not often called "gentlemen" or "boys," "ladies" and "girls" are terms still frequently heard by women as forms of address. Women use them too—hence such comments as "I'm going out for lunch with the girls."

A more subtle but extremely influential form of sexist language is the high frequency of familiar—or overly familiar—terms applied to women, terms that reflect lower social status. Although men are more frequently addressed formally ("Sir," "Mister," and so on), it is quite common for women to be called by their first names, or even to hear themselves called "honey," "hon," "baby," "sweetie," "dear," or the like—and sometimes by people they've never met before (Pearson et al., 1991, p. 100).

The implication that men are the more important members of the human race can be changed in many ways. For example, "manhood" may be replaced by the term "adulthood," "firemen" by "firefighters," and so on. The use of such words as "chairperson," "businessperson," and "he/she"—for all their attendant awkwardness—attempts to address this problem.

The insistence of many groups on such changes is legitimate because, as we have tried to indicate, words shape perceptions and self-concepts. Linguistic changes evolve slowly, but they are taking place.

Male and Female Language Use

Are there true differences between the ways males and females use language? Most research supports the stereotypic view that in contrast to males, females are more submissive, affected by social pressure, and responsive to the needs of others. It has been found that, although women seem to respond more to the remarks of other people, work harder at maintaining conversations, and give more "positive minimal responses," men generally initiate as well as receive more interaction. Men also interrupt others more and ignore the remarks of others more frequently than women do. Such differences are often explained in terms of the greater social power men enjoy in most communication contexts (Haslett, 1987, p. 216).

Language differences that give rise to these perceptions have been described in this way: Females use more words, intensifiers, questions (including tag questions, such as "That's great, isn't it?"), and affect words (i.e., words implying emotion) than males use (Berryman and Wilcox, 1980). Male speech, on the other hand, shows more instances of incorrect grammar, obscenities, and slang (Liska et al., 1981). Apparently both males and females expect males to use more verbally aggressive strategies and females to use strategies that are more social and less verbally aggressive (Burgoon et al., 1983).

The *Dilbert* joke (Figure 3.4) helps illustrate the difference in male and female language usage. In the joke, the male's only focus is the work aspect of Yvonne, whereas the woman is focused more on the personal aspects.

In *You Just Don't Understand,* a popular book that became a national bestseller, sociolinguist Deborah Tannen (1990) proposes that communication difficulties between men and women often originate in gender differences in conversational style.

Figure 3.4

Source: © Scott Adams, Inc./Dist. by UFS, Inc.

She makes the distinction between "report talk" and "rapport talk." Tannen argues that most men use conversation primarily as a language of **report,** that is, "as *a means to preserve independence and negotiate and maintain status in a hierarchical social order*" (1990, p. 77). This conversational style emphasizes demonstrating knowledge and skill and in general having the right information. "From childhood," writes Tannen, "men learn to use talking as a way to get and keep attention" (p. 77). Thus in the world of many men, "conversations are negotiations in which people try to achieve the upper hand if they can, and protect themselves from others' attempts to push them down and push them around" (p. 24).

To most women conversation is, for the most part, "a language of *rapport,*" with which they have learned since childhood to *establish connections and negotiate relationships, often for greater closeness.* What women emphasize in their talk are their similarities with other people and their comparable experiences ("I'm just like that," "The same thing happened to me . . ."). Women also have interests in achievement or status goals, says Tannen (1990), but they tend to go after them "in the guise of connection." Similarly,

> Men are also concerned with achieving involvement and avoiding isolation, but they are not focused on these goals, and they tend to pursue them in the guise of opposition. (p. 25)

According to Tannen, it's these differences in style that account for so many misunderstandings. She gives a striking example:

> Though both women and men complain of being interrupted by each other, the behaviors they are complaining about are different.
> In many of the comments I heard from people I interviewed, men felt interrupted by women who overlapped with words of agreement and support

and anticipation of how their sentences and thoughts would end. If a woman supported a man's story by elaborating on a point different from the one he had intended, he felt his right to tell his own story had been violated. (p. 210)

Feminist critic Deborah Cameron identifies two current approaches to the language styles of men and women. She contrasts *theories of difference,* such as Tannen's, with *theories of dominance.* In theories of dominance, "Women's style is seen as the outcome of power struggles and negotiations . . . played out under the surface of conversation" (Cameron, 1990, p. 25). This, for example, is how a theory of dominance would interpret research findings about questions:

Women ask more questions than men . . . not because insecurity is part of [their] psychology and therefore of [their] speech style . . . but because men in a dominant position often refuse to take responsibility for the smooth conduct of interpersonal relations . . . Asking them a question is thus an effective strategy for forcing them to acknowledge and contribute to the talk. It can be argued that features like question-asking are not deferential at all . . . (p. 25)

Theories such as these are a source of spirited debate and will be most valuable if they generate further research in language studies.

Powerful and Powerless Language

As we speak, many of us use tag questions—for example, "Let's go to the movies, okay?"—in making simple statements. We also use hedges—"kinda" and "I think"—or disclaimers such as "I probably shouldn't say this" and "I'm not really sure." In examining seven message types of differing **power,** Bradac and Mulac (1984) found that the language forms just described as well as hesitations such as "uh" and "well" are perceived by other people as forms of powerless and ineffective speech; on the other hand, speech free of such usage is considered both powerful and effective.

A more recent study explored the relationship between language style and gender stereotypes (Quina et al., 1987). Researchers found that individuals using a so-called feminine style of speech characterized by politeness, exaggeration, hedging, and illogical sequence—one that was generally nonassertive—were perceived as having greater warmth but less competence than those having a "masculine" style. The authors remind us that "a polite, warm linguistic style is not consistent with the popular image of American corporate success or achievement" (p. 118). Nonetheless, qualities associated with a feminine style included sensitivity, friendliness, and sincerity.

In general, communicators who use a powerful style are considered more competent and attractive. Legal situations are different, however; plaintiffs and defendants using a more powerful style are also considered more blameworthy, perhaps because they seem "in control" of themselves. Less powerful speakers are more often seen as victims (Bradac et al., 1981).

Metacommunication

In addition to trying to use a more powerful language, there's another very important way to increase the effectiveness of verbal messages. With practice, you can use language to change your relationship to others through **metacommunication**—that is, *communication about communication*. This is a concept closely linked to the relationship level of human encounters. For example, if you say to your mother, "Tell him to mind his own damned business," and she replies, "I wish you wouldn't swear so much. You do it more and more, and I don't like it," she is responding not to the content of your remark but to your method of getting your point across. The topic of her communication is communication itself.

Any comment directed at the way in which a person communicates is an example of metacommunication. For years the procedure in public-speaking classes has been for students to give practice speeches and then have the instructor and class members give their reactions to the speaker and the speech. Such comments as "I thought you had excellent examples," "You could have brought out your central idea more explicitly," and "Try to be a little more enthusiastic" are all instances of metacommunicating.

Writing about families, Galvin and Brommel (1991) observe:

> Metacommunication occurs when people communicate about their communication, when they give verbal and nonverbal instructions about how their messages should be understood. Such remarks as "I was only kidding," "This is important," or "Talking about this makes me uncomfortable" are signals to another on how to interpret certain comments, as are facial expressions, gestures, or vocal tones. (p. 18)

Both humans and other animals give nonverbal instructions about how their messages should be understood. For example, dogs change their posture when signifying that they want to play to make sure that the recipient understands the intention of their message. Monkeys use actual facial expressions when communicating to express intentions as well (Wain, 2004).

Metacommunication is not always explicit, even when it is verbal. Sometimes conversations that begin at the content level become forms of metacommunication. We can best illustrate with an anecdote. Ahmet and Sunita dressed for a night on the town, have just stepped out of a cab. As they stand at the corner waiting for the light to change, they rapidly become involved in a heated argument:

Sunita: Next time try to pick me up earlier so we can be on time.

Ahmet: It's only a party. Next time tell me beforehand if you think it's so important to be there at eight sharp. And don't sound so annoyed.

Sunita: But you're always late.

Ahmet: I'm not always late. Don't generalize like that.

Sunita: Well, you're late a lot of the time. Why do you always put me down when I say something about you?

Ahmet: I don't "always" put you down. There you go again, generalizing.

Although they may well remember it simply as a quarrel about lateness, Ahmet and Sunita are arguing about how they communicate with each other. He tells her not to sound so annoyed, he informs her that she makes too many generalizations, she counters that he puts her down, and so on. In effect, they are arguing about their relationship.

As we will see in Chapter 6, when there are serious conflicts about relationships rather than content, metacommunication is often especially difficult (Sillars and Weisberg, 1987). Two people may lack the skill to use metacommunication; and the source of the conflict may be "diffuse and selectively perceived. Attempts to communicate are therefore frustrated by a failure to agree on the definition of the conflict and by an ability to metacommunicate" (p. 151).

In a more supportive situation, the use of metacommunication might help people become aware of ways in which their communication practices are ineffective. For example, one teenage girl finally confided to her mother that she was embarrassed when the mother tried to sound "hip" in front of the daughter's teenage friends. It is sometimes awkward to provide such feedback. When given in a kind rather than a hostile way, however, it can be a valuable impetus to self-improvement.

Summary

Our analysis of verbal communication began with a consideration of the concept of meaning. In discussing the symbolic nature of language, we saw that symbols and referents are associated with each other only by convention and that it is human beings who assign meanings to words. We reviewed the traditional distinction between denotation and connotation and suggested that it might be more useful to distinguish between private and shared meanings. In this connection, we discussed overlapping linguistic codes and codeswitching.

Our next concern was the relationship between thought and language, and after examining the Sapir-Whorf hypothesis, we considered several language problems created through abstracting, inferences, dichotomies, euphemisms, and equivocal meanings. We went on to observe that when people of different cultures communicate, they may be separated not so much by grammar or vocabulary as by frame of reference.

To study words in action, we examined sexist language, differences between males and females in their use of language (these seem to be context-bound), and the language forms perceived by others as powerful or powerless. In closing, we saw that metacommunication (communication *about* communication) is potentially a means of improving one's relationships.

Key Terms

Connotation
Cultural frame of
 reference

Denotation
Metacommunication
Power

Sapir-Whorf hypothesis   Shared meanings
Sexist language

Review Questions

1. What is intended by the statement "The word is not the thing"?

2. What is the difference between denotation and connotation?

3. What is the Semantic Differential? Give an example of a differential.

4. Explain the difference between private and shared meanings.

5. What are the concepts of overlapping codes and codeswitching?

6. What is the Sapir-Whorf hypothesis?

7. Discuss two ways in which language affects thought.

8. Describe the concept of abstracting and give examples.

9. Describe at least four problem areas in our use of language. Give an example of each.

10. What is the influence of viewpoint or frame of reference (as distinguished from grammar and vocabulary) on communication between cultures? Give two examples.

11. Discuss the use of sexist language and give two examples.

12. What are some of the differences between how males and females use language?

13. Specify the difference between the ways males and females use language on the job.

14. Identify powerful and powerless language and explain its relationship to communication style.

15. What is metacommunication? Give an example.

Exercises

1. a. Construct a Semantic Differential consisting of ten bipolar adjectives. Assess the potential marketability of a fictitious product name by asking several classmates to react to two or more names using the Semantic Differential. The sample scale below shows two names for a perfume.

Bouquet		Summer Nights	
Good X _ _ _ _ _ _ Bad		Good _ _ _ _ _ X _ Bad	
Sharp _ X _ _ _ _ _ Dull		Sharp _ _ _ _ _ _ X Dull	
Active _ _ _ X _ _ _ Passive		Active _ _ _ X _ _ _ Passive	
Pretty _ _ X _ _ _ _ Ugly		Pretty _ _ _ X _ _ _ Ugly	

b. How do the responses on the Semantic Differential reflect the difference between denotation and connotation; between private and shared meaning?

2. Construct a two-column list with proper names in one column and stereotypical occupations associated with those names in the second. Mix up the order of names and occupations in each column. Present the lists to several people and ask them to match the names and occupations. A sample list appears follows:

Miss Flora   Ballet dancer
Spencer Turnbull   Teacher
Harry Hogan   Car thief
Speedy   Banker
Dominique Dubois   Hairdresser
Ken Sharp   Wrestling coach

a. To what extent do people agree in their responses? How do the results relate to the statement "The word is not the thing"?
b. How do the results relate to the three factors that affect stereotype perceptions (see Chapter 2)?
c. What implications do these results suggest about the relationship between language, stereotyping, and communication effectiveness?

3. Interview two people who are ostensibly very different—a local politician and an artist, for example. Ask each of them to make a list of adjectives describing (a) himself or herself and (b) a member of the other group. Compare the lists to see how differently each group member perceives himself or herself from the way he or she is perceived by the other person. Notice how the perceptual differences are manifested in the words chosen for the descriptions.

4. Prepare an oral persuasive message in two forms. Use the most tactful language possible in one and the most inflammatory terms you can think of in the other. Give the messages to two groups and try to assess their reactions on an attitude scale. Which message is more effective? If the audiences are similar and your messages alike except for word choice (and assuming the nonverbal cues are similar), any difference in your results should be due to the difference in the language you use.

5. In a chance conversation, deliberately assume that individual words have only one meaning and try to interpret them in a way that the other person does not intend. What are the results?

6. Prepare a short presentation in two forms. In the first, use words that are high on the ladder of abstraction (i.e., vague); in the second, use much more concrete, highly specific words. Discuss class reactions to these different presentations.

Suggested Readings

Bate, Barbara, and Anita Taylor, eds. *Women Communicating*. Norwood, NJ: Ablex, 1988.

An important collection of studies on women's talk.

Bennett, William J. *The Death of Outrage*. New York: Free Press, 1998.

Analyzes the rhetoric of President William J. Clinton and analyzes his use and misuse of language.

Donnellon, Anne. *Team Talk: The Power of Language in Team Dynamics*. Cambridge: Harvard Business School Press, 1996.

This excellent book analyzes teams from the standpoint of their members' language. It offers an
excellent framework for analyzing and improving teams.

Ivy, Diana, and Phil Backlund. *Gender Speak*, 3rd ed. New York: McGraw-Hill, 2004.

This book is one of the best in the field of gender communication. It is a "must read" for those interested in this topic.

www.slanguage.com

A website that monitors current and changing slang words and expressions. It focuses on the slang terms used by Generation X. Beautifully illustrates the ever-changing nature of language.

Tannen, Deborah. *The Argument Culture: Moving from Debate to Dialogue.* New York: Random House, 1998.

This outstanding author relates the use of language to improving communication in conflict situations.

The book includes information on communication between genders, communication across cultures, and the role of technology.

 # For Supplementary Information

Log onto the Online Learning Center at *www.mhhe.com/tubbsmoss11.*

4

The Nonverbal Message

Chapter Objectives

After reading this chapter, you should be able to:

1. Describe four categories of communication, distinguishing between verbal and nonverbal as well as vocal and nonvocal, and give an example of each.
2. Discuss the kinds of information conveyed by nonverbal and verbal messages and three ways in which they are related.
3. Identify several of the nonverbal cues associated with power and dominance.
4. Discuss the concepts of personal space and interpersonal distance.
5. Explain how we communicate through our use of time and how timing can interfere with intercultural communication.
6. Identify the major visual cues given by facial expression and head and body movements and discuss the kinds of messages they convey.
7. Describe how one's choice of physical objects, including clothing, communicates messages to others.
8. Explain the concept of paralinguistics and identify four kinds of vocal cues, giving an example of each. Discuss some gender differences in vocal cues.
9. Discuss deception cues and recent research findings on accuracy in reliably judging deception and the mutual influence of deceivers and detectors.

Figure 4.1

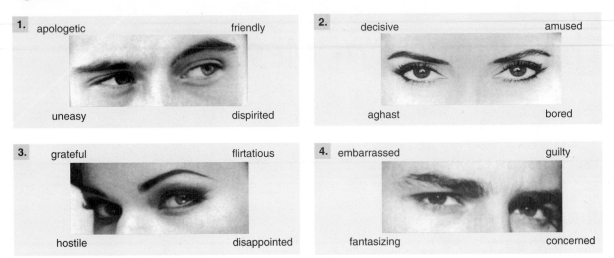

Source: From "The 'Reading the Mind in the Eyes' Test," *The Essential Difference: The Truth About the Male and Female Brain* by Simon Baron-Cohen. Reprinted by permission of Basic Books, a member of Perseus Books Group and Penguin Group (UK).

The photographs above in Figure 4.1 are from "The Reading the Mind in the Eyes Test." Before you read any further, for each photograph select one of the four surrounding words that best describes what the person in the photograph is thinking or feeling (see page 120 for the answers). Later in this chapter you'll learn something about your accuracy in judging facial expressions on the basis of eyes.

In this chapter we look at the broad spectrum of nonverbal communication behaviors. We begin by considering the relative weight people give to verbal and nonverbal messages. Thus, we will look at how nonverbal messages are interpreted, what types of information we receive through them, and how they interact with verbal messages.

INTERPRETING NONVERBAL MESSAGES

The literal definition of nonverbal communication, communication without words, is something of an oversimplification, because written words are considered "verbal" although they lack the element of sound. Stewart and D'Angelo (1980) propose that if we distinguish verbal from nonverbal and vocal from nonvocal, we have four types of communication. *Verbal/vocal communication* refers to *communication through the spoken word.* For example, Mira and her father discuss the new car Mira wants to buy and her plans for getting together the money. In *verbal/nonvocal communication, words are involved but no speaking takes place:* If she writes a letter to her father about the car, her communication is verbal but nonvocal. Or suppose that Mira asks her father for a loan for the car, and he simply groans. Such *groans, or vocalizations, constitute a form of* nonverbal/vocal communication. A fourth kind of communication, **nonverbal/nonvocal communication**, *involves only gestures and appearance*—imagine Mira's father looking angry or pleased. Seen in these terms, **nonverbal communication** *conveys nonlinguistic messages.*

Such messages take any number of forms. You raise your hand to vote yes at a committee meeting, hail a cab, exchange signals with someone on your basketball team. You sit on the edge of your seat in a dull class and keep twisting a lock of your hair. You touch the arm of a friend to reassure him. You buy a red sports car because you think it's more your kind of car than a brown sedan. In this chapter, we will be looking at nonverbal messages of all kinds, and one of the first issues we will explore is the division often made between meanings conveyed by nonverbal and verbal communication.

The Verbal/Nonverbal Split in Meaning

Nonverbal communication—indeed the entire communication process—must be viewed as a whole that is greater than the sum of its parts. Outside the laboratory we do not depend on isolated **cues**, or *hints*. In face-to-face communication, all cues, both verbal and nonverbal, are available to us. Even in communicating on-line, we have access to some though limited nonverbal cues. As much as 65 percent of all social meaning in face-to-face communication is conveyed through nonverbal cues.

There are many times when we give greater credence to nonverbal cues. These include when we judge interpersonal style; when we respond to questions requiring interpretation; when we evaluate a person's genuine emotions, ideas, and attitudes from "inconsistent expressions"; and when we judge credibility and leadership qualities (Burgoon et al., 1996, p. 137). According to one study, nonverbal responsiveness in students significantly increases both teacher liking and compliance in granting student requests (Mottet et al., 2004).

As we've seen in Chapter 2, nonverbal cues also have greater influence when it comes to forming first impressions. And we give greater weight to nonverbal over verbal cues when they are contradictory. When it comes to deceptive behavior, nonverbal as well as verbal, it seems to be easier to tell the difference between liars and truth-tellers when we judge by all those behaviors—including, it turns out, how much they move. According to recent studies, both children and adults make fewer movements when they are lying (Vrij et al., 2004; Vrij, 2006).

Communication scholars agree that in most messages we get information from several nonverbal channels at once:

> Consistent multichanneled messages communicate sincerity, honesty, and believability because each channel provides additional weight to the overall message. Also, it is hard to lie in ten channels, whereas verbal lies are relatively easy to achieve . . . However, this same multichanneled system has the capacity to send simultaneously contradictory messages such as approach and avoidance, ecstasy and guilt, joy and sorrow, or love and hate. (Andersen, 1999, p. 22)

Nonverbal Information

We learn most about the meaning of nonverbal messages by studying them in relationship to verbal messages. Essentially, a nonverbal message functions in one of three ways: It replaces, reinforces, or contradicts a verbal message.

A nonverbal message that substitutes for a verbal one is often easy to interpret. Our culture provides us with gestures and expressions that are the equivalents of certain brief verbal messages: "Yes," "No," "Hello," "Good-bye," "I don't know," and so on. Likes and dislikes can also be expressed without words—for example, by smiling, clapping, smirking, or frowning.

When a nonverbal message reinforces a verbal message, meaning is conveyed quickly and easily, and with increased comprehension. Sometimes a single cue such as a hand movement or a long pause gives special emphasis to one part of a message so that we are able to discern what the speaker feels is most important.

Nonverbal cues predominate by sheer number. In general, if as receivers we are caught between two discrepant messages, we are more inclined to believe the nonverbal message. Nonverbal cues, we assume, give information about our intentions and emotional responses. Thus, in business many people still prefer face-to-face communication—whether it be meeting for lunch or in the formal setting of an office—to a fax, e-mail, letter, or telephone call when solving problems or negotiating critical decisions. In negotiation, much is learned from watching the other person's facial expression and gestures so that you can adapt your own responses. (The use of teleconferencing, which provides a wealth of nonverbal cues, is also on the increase.)

Another reason the nonverbal message seems to have greater impact is the popular belief that body movements, facial expressions, vocal qualities, and so on cannot be simulated by the average person. Even children are quick to sense gestures or expressions that are not spontaneous.

Nonverbal channels convey primarily relational messages, messages about the feeling/emotional level of our communication, rather than the thoughts (best communicated by verbal communication); also, nonverbal messages are ambiguous for the most part, except perhaps for certain gestures. Ambiguous facial expressions and gestures have sometimes been the cause of subway violence and street fights.

We all have some sensitivity to nonverbal cues, or we would not be able to communicate with the ease we do. Still, we know there are differences among people in how skilled they are in interpreting what they perceive. Through tests such as the popular Profile of Nonverbal Sensitivity Test—the PONS—researchers have confirmed that some people do have greater sensitivities to nonverbal cues. "Success in decoding nonverbal communication" is important not only in forming our initial impressions of others but in maintaining our close relationships (Noller, 2006; Guerrero and Floyd, 2006).

As we discussed in Chapter 2, there are gender differences not only in interpersonal sensitivity but in the ability to recall the physical appearance of others (Hall et al., 2006; Mast and Hall, 2006). Women seem to have the advantage in both cases. To explain this some scholars have proposed that, for women, social status and appearance are more closely linked and that women themselves are often judged on the basis of appearance so that possibly they are more aware of appearance and more competitive about it (J. Hall, 2006).

Most of our problems in interpreting meaning arise when we receive a nonverbal message that contradicts a verbal message. Suppose, for example, that a supervisor always cautions her employees not to postpone discussing problem areas in their work. "Don't wait till it's too late to remedy the situation. I want you to come and tell me when you run into problems," she repeats. Yet as one of the assistant managers enters her office, she looks up annoyed and gives him an icy stare. Then, as the employee starts to back out of her office, the supervisor says, "Well, don't stand there looking so frightened. Tell me what's on your mind."

Birdwhistell (1970) uses the term **kinesic slips** for mixed messages—*contradictory verbal and nonverbal messages.* Imagine this conversation between a couple who have just had a bitter quarrel. She asks, "Honey, are you still angry?" "No," he replies, "it's all right." "But you sound as though you're still angry," she insists. "I'm telling you I'm not angry!" he answers. His words give one message, his voice and frowning face another. He may not even be aware of the second. Which message is she likely to believe?

Verbal/Nonverbal Interaction

For purposes of analysis we speak of verbal and nonverbal messages as distinct, yet in daily life we are rarely able to separate their effects. For example, what we say is qualified, modified, by how we say it—tone of voice, facial expression, eye contact, and so on—as well as by the almost instantaneous verbal and nonverbal responses of others. And this interaction is ongoing.

Consider the counterpoint of the verbal and nonverbal responses in this scene from Jhumpa Lahiri's story "A Temporary Matter." A young husband and his wife, who had recently had a stillborn child, are at home. They have just finished a candlelit dinner, which he prepared. Shoba, the wife, blows out the candle and turns on the light switch, then sits down once more:

> She set her plate aside and clasped her hands on the table. "I want you to see my face when I tell you this," she said gently.
>
> His heart began to pound. The day she told him she was pregnant, she had used the very same words, saying them in the same gentle way, turning off the basketball game he'd been watching on television. He hadn't been prepared then. Now he was.
>
> Only he didn't want her to be pregnant again. He didn't want to have to pretend to be happy.
>
> "I've been looking for an apartment and I've found one," she said, narrowing her eyes on something, it seemed, behind his left shoulder. It was nobody's fault, she continued. They'd been through enough. She needed some time alone. She had saved up money for a security deposit . . . She had signed the lease that night before coming home.

Guerrero and Floyd (2006) distinguish between power, "having the ability and potential to influence others as well as to resist the persuasive attempt of others," and interpersonal dominance, "communication strategies that people use successfully to gain or express power" (p. 160).

Their extensive survey of research finds that nonverbal cues of power and dominance are numerous and often interrelated. For example, people who are powerful have greater control of personal space and also establish dominance visually. In meetings, they tend to position themselves centrally, whether seated at a table or standing in a room. They look at people more directly when they are speaking than when they are listening. When speaking, they can express power by choosing to stand when others are seated, thus reinforcing their height. Often, they speak more than others in conversation, also interrupting and changing topics of conversation more frequently.

These and other dominant behaviors often associated with strong social skills include direct gaze; expressiveness, both in touch and voice; frequent eye contact when conversing; open arms and open body positioning; a strong and relatively loud voice; smiling and generally pleasant facial expressions (pp. 133–161).

One of the most interesting aspects of this research summary concerns nonverbal cues that convey poise and self-confidence:

> *[People] judged as dominant typically appear poised, relaxed, and composed. . . . Poise and relaxation are communicated nonverbally through a set of behaviors that include asymmetrical leg and arm positions, sideways leaning, arm openness, open body position, expressive gestures, less swiveling, and less random leg and foot movement. . . . Greater facial pleasantness, smiling, eye contact, and proximity can also send messages of poise, relaxation, and composure. . . .* (2006, p. 152)

Do you think of yourself as powerful? dominant? How would you rate your own nonverbal behavior in terms of poise and self-confidence?

She wouldn't look at him, but he stared at her. It was obvious that she'd rehearsed the lines. All the time she'd been looking for an apartment. . . . (1999, p. 21)

The statement is often made that we cannot *not* communicate, that everything we do—or refrain from doing—communicates something. The playwright George Bernard Shaw once wrote, "Silence is the most perfect expression of scorn." But that is just one state of feeling that can be conveyed by silence. Being motionless and silent can convey confusion, awe, resistance, doubt, withholding, agreement, boredom, rejection—a seemingly infinite variety of responses.

In the remainder of this chapter, we shall see how through their nonverbal messages people give us many cues—spatial, temporal, visual, and vocal—about their emotions, their intentions, their personalities, and even their social status.

SPATIAL AND TEMPORAL CUES

Only when we interact with people of other cultures do we begin to realize that some of our most cherished ideas about what is appropriate conduct are norms, or rules, whether stated or unstated, about behavior; that is, they are relative, not absolute, values. Indirectly, our culture teaches us to communicate in many ways—through our voices, our gestures, and even our style of dressing. Yet each of us interprets and expresses these conventions somewhat differently.

Culture has an even more subtle and pervasive influence on nonverbal communication, however. Each culture continually provides its members with input about how the world is structured. (See the Müller-Lyer illusion in Chapter 2.) Slowly we develop preconceptions about the world. It is the cues derived from these preconceptions that we take most for granted and that imperceptibly set the limits for our style of communication. Our cues about space and time are among those most significantly influenced by culture and sometimes the source of difficulties in intercultural communication.

Space

Personal Space

Personal space centers on the body and can be thought of as *a person's portable territory, which each individual carries along wherever he or she may go.* Robert Sommer, a psychologist at the University of California–Davis, refers to it as *"an area with invisible boundaries surrounding a person's body into which intruders may not come"* (1969, p. 26; italics added).

In research in libraries and parks, Sommer took on the role of intruder, systematically violating the personal space of others and observing the resulting tensions and anxieties. Much research on personal space focuses on the relationship between spatial arrangements (architectural elements, interior design, seating, and so on) and human feelings and interaction. For instance, in the study halls of college libraries, students tend to protect privacy by sitting as far away from each other as possible. One way of communicating this need is by occupying a corner position. Or students sprawl out, resting their legs on a nearby chair. If they get up from the table, they may "reserve" the place by spreading out books and papers or leaving clothing draped over the chair (Sommer, 1969, pp. 46–47). How far you go in defending your personal space will depend, of course, on both your personality and your communication style. If you sit too close to me in the library, I may get up and move. But reverse our roles and you may glare at me and even spread out your notebooks and papers so that they take up a good part of the table.

Other research finds that personality variables such as need for affiliation influence the size of one's personal space (Rosenfeld, 1965). In his study of prison inmates who had committed violent crimes, Kinzel (1969) observed that these men had a personal space, or "body buffer zone," twice as large as that of nonviolent prisoners. Recently, it's even been suggested that "air rage" is related to a perceived invasion of personal space.

Another familiar aspect of personal space is the greater feeling of confidence when we are within our own surroundings:

> To allow yourself to be summoned voluntarily to someone else's home turf is a show of weakness. Inexperienced diplomats and politicians learn this only after having made too many concessions to adversaries or having lost the respect of allies. The recognized territorial advantage is the reason for insisting on a neutral locale for summit meetings and other serious talks. (Burgoon et al., 1996, p. 307)

Interpersonal Distance

Students of nonverbal communication are indebted to the anthropologist Edward Hall for his cross-cultural studies of space as well as time. Hall has given the name **proxemics** to *the study of how human beings communicate through their use of space.* If you were to enter a restaurant with only one customer in it, chances are that you would not sit down right next to him or her. Hall explains that though this behavior seems natural to a North American, an Arab might have a very different notion of appropriate distance between strangers. By contrast, if you visited a new doctor and she sat down in the chair next to you rather than behind her desk, her closeness might communicate warmth and a lack of formality far beyond the norm.

Social scientists make use of the Scale of Social Distance, an instrument that uses the term "distance" figuratively, to indicate degree of liking or preference. Hall (1959) goes a step further and speaks of four measurable distances between people: intimate, personal, social, and public. Each distance is differentiated by a close and a far phase within which different behaviors occur (Figure 4.2). There is nothing arbitrary about these distances, as he explains:

> It is in the nature of animals, including man, to exhibit behavior which we call territoriality. In so doing, they use the senses to distinguish between one space or distance and another. The specific distance chosen depends on the transaction, the relationship of the interacting individuals, how they feel, and what they are doing. (p. 128)

Here we look briefly at the four distances and Hall's findings about what they mean to most North Americans.

Intimate Distance   At *intimate distance, 18 inches or less,* the presence of another person "is unmistakable and may at times be overwhelming because of the greatly stepped-up sensory inputs" (Hall, 1959, p. 116). In its close phase (6 inches or less) intimate distance lends itself primarily to nonverbal communication. This distance is usually reserved for very close friends and family. Subjects discussed are usually top secret. The far phase (6 to 18 inches) is often used for discussing confidential matters, with the voice usually kept to a whisper. Such close proximity is

Figure 4.2 *Interpersonal Distance Zones*

		Close phase	Far phase
Intimate Distance 0–18 in.			
	Voice:	Soft whisper	Audible whisper
	Message:	Top secret	Very confidential
Personal Distance 1.5–4 ft.			
	Voice:	Soft	Slightly lowered
	Message:	Personal subject matter	Personal subject matter
Social Distance 4–12 ft.			
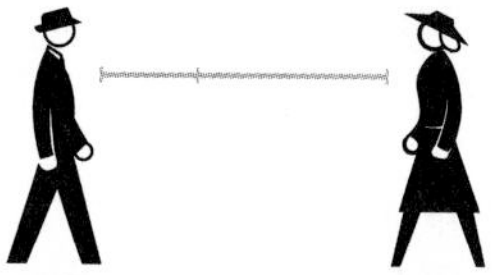	Voice:	Full	Full with slight overloudness
	Message:	Nonpersonal information	Public information for others to hear
Public Distance 12–25 ft. or more			
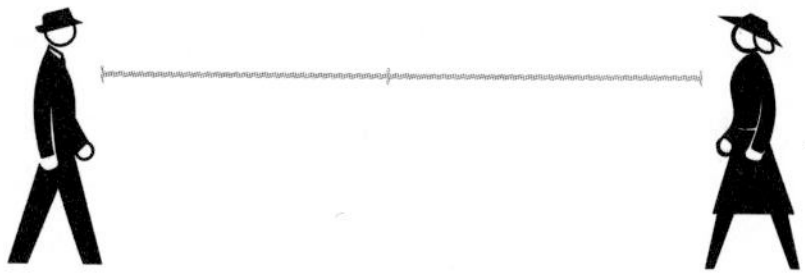	Voice:	Loud, talking to a group	Loudest
	Message:	Public information for others to hear	Hailing, departures

Source: From *The Silent Language* by Edward T. Hall, Copyright © 1959, 1981 by Edward T. Hall. Used by permission of Doubleday, a division of Random House, Inc.

considered improper for public places, though dormitories seem to be exceptions to the rule. In general, Americans try hard to avoid close contact with people they do not know on buses and other public vehicles.

Personal Distance *Personal distance,* from *1½ to 4 feet,* can be thought of as "a small protective sphere or bubble that an organism maintains between itself and others" (Hall, 1959, p. 119). Topics discussed would still be personal. The close phase (1½ to 2½ feet) is still a distance reserved for very close relationships; the far phase (2½ to 4 feet) is a comfortable distance for conversing with friends.

Social Distance   *Social distance,* ranging from *4 to 12 feet,* is a psychological distance, "one at which the animal apparently begins to feel anxious when he exceeds its limits. We can think of it as a hidden band that contains the group." The close phase (4 to 7 feet) is suitable for conversations at social gatherings and business discussions. The far phase (7 to 12 feet) is appropriate for meetings in a business office. People who are in the room but outside the 7-foot boundary can be ignored without being offended. Those who violate the 7-foot boundary tend to be surprised if we do not acknowledge their presence, unless we are very busy. Humans have extended social distance by means of the telephone, radio, television, fax, computer (e-mail), and teleconferencing.

Public Distance   *Public distance, 12 feet or more of space,* is the largest of the zones and it exists only in human relationships. In fact, the public relationships and manners of Americans and Europeans are considerably different from those of other cultures. At the close phase (12 to 25 feet), a more formal style of language and a louder voice are required. At the far phase (25 feet or more), further accommodations to distance are usually made: Experienced public speakers exaggerate body movements, gestures, enunciation, and volume while reducing their rate of speech. Figure 4.2 is a brief summary of how message content and vocal shift vary with distance between communicators.

High- and Low-Contact Cultures   Within a culture as diverse as the United States, various co-cultures may develop their own proxemic norms. (A **co-culture** is *a group having sufficient distinctive traits to distinguish it from other members of the same dominant culture.*) In research on intercultural communication, the distinction is often made between high-contact and low-contact cultures. Members of **high-contact cultures** *touch each other more often, sit or stand closer to each other, make more eye contact, and speak louder.* Members of **low-contact cultures** *touch each other less often, maintain more interpersonal distance, and are more indirect in facing each other and in their eye contact. They also tend to use a lower, softer tone of voice.* French, Italian, Latin American, Russian, Arab, and African cultures are some high-contact cultures; German, Danish, and East Asian cultures include those seen as low-contact (Figure 4.3). Moderate-contact cultures include the United States, New Zealand, Australia, and Canada (Ting-Toomey, 1999, p. 129).

Though there is a tendency to generalize about distance norms within Europe, it seems that people from northern European cultures—Sweden and Scotland, for example—require greater interpersonal distance than people from Mediterranean countries such as Italy and Greece.

Researchers are not saying that we calculate these differences while communicating. On the contrary, our sense of what distance is natural for a given interaction is so deeply ingrained in us by our culture that we automatically make spatial adjustments and interpret spatial cues. Latin Americans, Arabs, and the French, for example, stand so close to each other that if they exercise their own distance norms while conversing with a North American, they may arouse hostile or sexual feelings.

Figure 4.3   Selected High- and Low-Contact Cultures

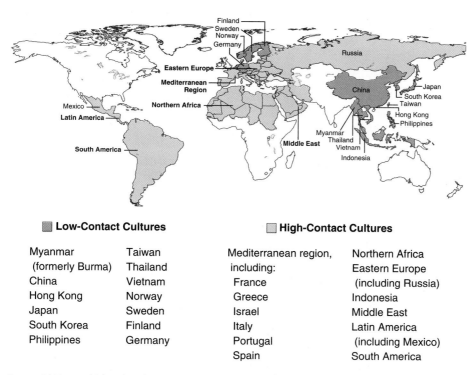

■ Low-Contact Cultures

Myanmar (formerly Burma)	Taiwan
China	Thailand
Hong Kong	Vietnam
Japan	Norway
South Korea	Sweden
Philippines	Finland
	Germany

■ High-Contact Cultures

Mediterranean region, including:	Northern Africa
France	Eastern Europe (including Russia)
Greece	Indonesia
Israel	Middle East
Italy	Latin America (including Mexico)
Portugal	South America
Spain	

Source: "A Range of Selected High- and Low-Contast Cultures" from *Nonverbal Communication: Forms and Functions,* 2nd Edition, by Peter A. Andersen. Copyright © 2007. Published by Waveland Press. Reprinted by permission of Peter A. Anderson.

If you want, test this concept the next time you converse with someone. See how close you can get before the other party starts backing away.

Orientation   Your **orientation**—that is, *the angle of your body as you interact with another person,* may also reflect the nature of the relationship between the two of you. For example, some studies of British and North American seating patterns have shown that a 90-degree-angle orientation facilitates conversation, face-to-face orientations tend toward competitive behaviors, and side-by-side orientations are more often viewed as showing cooperation (Hargie et al., 1987, p. 27). In Figure 4.4 we see several preferences in orientation for sitting at a table. Notice how situation often determines choice of orientation.

According to psychiatrist Albert Scheflen, you use certain frames, or positions, to define your space when you interact with others. For example, in the *side-by-side frame* you are sometimes closer to the other person (shoulder to shoulder), but you have no eye contact. In the *vis-à-vis frame,* you face the other person, modulate the distance between you, and maintain eye contact. It is striking, one consultant on

Figure 4.4   *Seating Preferences at a Rectangular Table*

Type of interaction	Position of participants	Suggested situations
Conversation		• Counseling interview • Employer interviewing an employee • Some progressive job interviews
Cooperation		• Friends meeting in a pub • Teacher helping a pupil in his work • Staff cooperating on the same project
Competition		• Some job interviews • Principal interviewing pupil • Playing games such as chess, poker, etc.
Coaction		• Strangers in a public eating place • Unfamiliar students working at same library table • Strangers sharing a seat on the train

Source: Adapted from *Social Skills in Interpersonal Communication* by Hargie et al., 1987. Reprinted by permission of Taylor & Francis.

nonverbal communication points out, that the side-by-side frame is preferred by men, the vis-à-vis frame by women (Nelson, 2004, pp. 164–165).

Research on doctor-patient communication confirms the importance of how doctors orient themselves toward their patients:

> One of the most well-documented interrelationships is between gaze and body orientation. . . . Although different segments of the body (e.g., the head, torso, and legs) can be oriented in different directions . . . , there remains a socially understood body-segment hierarchy in terms of [a person's] levels of attention and engagement. Specifically, though gaze orientation communicates . . . [a person's focus] of attention, relative to upper-body segments (e.g., the head), lower body segments (e.g., the legs) more strongly communicate . . . dominant orientation. (Robinson, 2006, p. 452)

This applies, of course, to many forms of interpersonal communication.

Time

A study of 36 cities across the United States finds many differences in the pace or tempo of life: Researchers used four measures—the walking speed of pedestrians, work speed, concern with clock time (e.g., whether people wore watches), and talking speed. The fastest city was—no, not New York—but Boston, with New York ranking third. "The fastest overall times were in the northeast, followed by the midwest, the south and then the west" (Levine, 1997, pp. 146–151).

When we study *how human beings communicate through their use of time,* we are concerned with **chronemics.** At what time in the evening is it too late to call someone? How many days or weeks in advance can a first date be arranged? How quickly do you expect a friend to reply to an e-mail from you? In each case, timing leads to certain expectations that influence the face-to-face communication that subsequently occurs. Being very late for a job interview can have a disastrous effect, not just a dramatic one. Much of the ensuing verbal communication may be spent explaining away the nonverbal message that has already been conveyed.

Conceptions of what is "early" or "late" vary from culture to culture. Americans tend to be "busy" people. They tend to like schedules and agendas. They value doing things "on time." So it is sometimes jarring to see themselves as others do. For example, *In the Time of the Butterflies,* a novel by Julia Alvarez, is set in the Dominican Republic. A woman from the United States phones to set up an appointment to meet Dedé:

"So if I'm coming from Santiago I drive on past Salcedo?" the woman asks.
"*Exactamente.* And then where you see a great big anacahuita tree, you turn left."
"A . . . great . . . big . . . tree . . . ," the woman repeats. She is writing all this down!
"I turn left. What's the name of the street?"
"It's just the road by the anacahuita tree. We don't name them," Dedé says, driven to doodling to contain her impatience . . .
The voice laughs, embarrassed. "Of course. You must think I'm so outside of things." *Tan afuera de la cosa.*
Dedé bites her lip. "Not at all," she lies. "I'll see you this afternoon then."
"About what time?" the voice wants to know.
Oh yes. The gringos need a time. But there isn't a clock time for this kind of just-right moment. "Any time after three or three-thirty, four-ish."
"Dominican time, eh?" The woman laughs.
"*Exactamente!*" Finally, the woman is getting the hang of how things are done here. (1994, p. 4)

Hall (1984; 1999) distinguishes between monochronic and polychronic conceptions of time (Table 4.1). **Monochronic** time is time thought of as *linear and segmented.* In cultures with monochronic time, people perceive time as "almost tangible," speaking of it, says Hall, as if it were money (time gets "saved," "spent," "wasted," "lost"). People like to do one thing at a time, and their preference is for precise scheduling. Making appointments and deadlines is highly valued. In cultures with a **polychronic** conception of time, on the other hand, *many things are going on at once.* Nor is there great surprise when delays or interruptions occur. Indeed, they seem to be expected, and people take them in stride.

The new technologies seem to be influencing how people handle their use of time, even in monochronic cultures. Have you ever talked to someone on the phone only to hear him using his computer as he spoke with you? A recent cartoon showed a woman sitting alone and speaking on her cell phone. "Are you multitasking me?" she asks the person she is talking to. Some cognitive scientists caution that there are limits to how many activities we should be involved in at a given time and that doing several things at once sometimes interferes with the ability to concentrate and results in mistakes. According to one expert, "Disruptions and interruptions are a bad deal from the standpoint of our ability to process information" (Lohr, 2007, p. 1).

It has been said that for the American businessperson discussion is simply "a means to an end: the deal." Moreover, it's a sign of good faith to agree on major issues, assuming that details will be worked out later on. But like the Latin American, the Greek businessperson engages in what may seem to others as prolonged discussion and an excessive preoccupation with details. For the Greek, these concerns usually signify goodwill (Hall and Whyte, 1966, p. 568; see also Storace, 1997).

Do you think of yourself as monochronic or polychronic? Some of the differences between monochronic people and polychronic people are listed in Table 4.1.

Table 4.1   *Some Differences between Monochronic and Polychronic People*

Monochronic People	Polychronic People
Do one thing at a time	Do many things at once
Concentrate on the job	Are highly distractible and subject to interruptions
Take time commitments (deadlines, schedules) seriously	Consider time commitments an objective to be achieved if possible
Are low-context and need information	Are high-context and already have information
Are committed to the job	Are committed to people and human relationships
Adhere religiously to plans	Change plans often and easily
Are concerned about not disturbing others; follow rules of privacy and consideration	Are more concerned with those who are closely related (family, friends, close business associates) than with privacy
Show great respect for private property	Borrow and lend things often and easily
Emphasize promptness	Base promptness on the relationship
Are accustomed to short-term relationships	Have strong tendencies to build lifelong relationships

Source: From *Understanding Cultural Differences* by Edward T. Hall and Mildred R. Hall, Intercultural Press. Copyright © 1990 Edward T. Hall Associates. Published by Intercultural Press, Inc.

Hall believes that these approaches to time are learned. And if his distinction is a valid one, the culture your family is from probably influenced your own use of time.

VISUAL CUES

The second category of nonverbal cues we will discuss is extremely broad, ranging from facial expressions and body movements to the clothing we wear and the objects we display. Let's begin with an anecdote.

At the end of the nineteenth century, a German horse named Hans was reported to know how to add. If you asked him to add 2 and 6, for example, he pawed the ground eight times. The curious thing was that Hans could do sums only in the presence of human beings. His mysterious talent was later explained rather simply: When he unwittingly reached the answer, he saw his audience relax, and he stopped pawing.

The people who came to see Hans perform would have been shocked to learn that they were, by their body movements, transmitting the correct answers visually. Yet they were probably leaning forward eagerly to take in every aspect of the spectacle before them, for we all know how much we gain by seeing a performer, a lecturer, or any person we are speaking to. In fact, members of discussion groups interact more frequently when seated facing each other rather than side by side. In other words, the greater our visibility, the greater our potential for communicating. And, as we saw in Chapter 1, the greater the number of channels the sender uses, the more information is received.

Visual cues add to the information transmitted through other channels and at times stand alone. Specific motions of the head, for example, give the equivalents of certain brief verbal messages such as yes and no, and these movements may vary from culture to culture. Even head orientation, the direction in which we turn our heads, communicates something. Mehrabian (1967) found that a person who gives more head orientation while speaking conveys more positive feeling.

The British actress Helen Mirren won an Academy Award in 2007 for her performance as Queen Elizabeth in *The Queen*. Asked during an interview how she had prepared for this commanding role, she spoke, among other things, of posture; she said she projected authority in part by the way she stood, the way she carried herself. In playing Elizabeth, she said she learned to carry herself as the police do, with her arms at her sides, never folded, since folding one's arms conveys being submissive. Mirren has played a London police inspector, the present queen of England, and Elizabeth the First—all roles that demanded the projection of great power.

A pioneering figure in research on nonverbal communication, Ray Birdwhistell (1952) introduced the term **kinesics** to refer to *the study of body movements in communication.* "Body movements" is used in a broad sense and refers also to movements of the head and face. Birdwhistell has estimated that over 700,000 possible physical signs can be transmitted via body movement. The first group of visual cues we will look at has to do with facial expression.

Facial Expression

The human face is so mobile that it can effortlessly register boredom, surprise, affection, and disapproval one after another in a few seconds. *We constantly read expressions from people's faces.* In fact, *facial cues* are the single most important source of nonverbal communication. Comments such as "If looks could kill" and "It was all over her face" bear witness to the significance we give to facial expression.

We make use of information about the face in many ways:

1. To identify a person's social category memberships
2. To discern others' personality traits
3. To detect the direction of their attention
4. To gauge the sincerity of their verbal behavior
5. To understand [their] thoughts and minds

(Bodenhausen and Macrae, 2006, p. 511)

During the last 25 years there has been an upswing in research on the human face, and it's being led by researchers in neuroscience. Nonetheless, a review of past and current research emphasizes that contributions from many disciplines are needed to add to this growing fund of knowledge (Zebrowitz, 2006). What's particularly interesting is that there seems to be what some refer to as "a kernel of truth" about the judgments we make about character or personality based on facial traits (Penton-Voak et al., 2006).

We like a face or we don't; we think it's animated or relatively inert. These are general impressions. But what do we see that makes us judge someone to be sad or happy or frightened or angry? Isolating which facial cues specify particular emotions is more difficult than simply judging a face.

The study of facial cues as expressions of specific emotions has a long history. One of the most eminent scientists to examine this subject was Charles Darwin, who tried to find out whether the facial behaviors associated with particular emotions are universal. One method he used was to ask subjects to identify specific emotions from still photographs of people's faces. Darwin concluded that most of a human being's expressive actions, like those of other animals, are instinctive, not learned behaviors. For example, "We may see children, only two or three years old, and even those born blind, blushing from shame" (Darwin, 1959, p. 398).

Darwin's argument was supported by several studies done more than half a century later. Ekman and Friesen (1971) asked members of a preliterate New Guinea culture to judge emotions from the facial expressions of Westerners. The subjects had had virtually no exposure to Western culture. Yet they made the same identifications that Westerners made, with one exception: They were not able to differentiate between fear and surprise. The researchers concluded that, at least in some respects, expressive facial behavior is constant across cultures. They acknowledged that cultural differences exist but argued that the differences are reflected "in the circumstances which elicit an emotion, in the action consequences of an emotion and in the display rules which govern the management of facial behavior in particular social settings" (p. 129).

According to anthropologist Melvin Konner (1987), smiling seems to be a human social display that is universal. For example, Eibl-Eibesfeldt's films from many remote parts of the world show smiling as a "consistent feature of greeting, often in combination with raising of the eyebrows" (p. 42). How our smiles are interpreted, however, will depend on many variables including physical attractiveness (Forgas, 1987). We know, for example, that in Japan a smiling face is often interpreted as more "feminine" than is a serious face (Kawamura and Kageyama, 2006, p. 210).

Research on more than 30 different cultures suggests that there is a high level of agreement in judging emotions from photographs of people's facial expressions. Most interesting, though, is the finding that there are cultural differences in the degree to which such expressions are recognized and also in how their intensity is rated. Happiness, fear, and surprise seem to be more universally recognized but judging contempt and disgust vary more from one culture to another (Biehl et al., 1997).

Matsumoto (2006) and many other scholars maintain that there is convincing evidence for the universality of facial expressions of emotion. The six universal expressions he identifies are disgust, fear, happiness, sadness, surprise, and anger. They can also be found in animals.

Nonetheless, there seem to be cultural differences in the expression of emotion. Through *cultural display rules,* rules that we learn in early childhood, we manage and adapt how we express emotion. Matsumoto and colleagues, who created the DRAI (the Display Rule Assessment Inventory), have also found that *control* over the expression of various emotions varies from one culture to another. For example, among Russians, Americans, and Japanese, "Americans and Russians both expressed anger and contempt more than Japanese, Americans expressed fear and distrust more than Russians, and Americans expressed happiness more than did Russians and Japanese" (2006, pp. 226–227).

And it may be that we have an advantage in judging emotion of a given cultural group when we ourselves are members of that group. We also differ culturally in judging how intense expressions are. We need more research to determine the validity of that statement.

There is also a growing body of research about emotional contagion (Andersen and Guerrero, 1998) and how perceiving an emotional expression—a smile, for example—might cause us to mimic that expression and thereby experience that state of feeling. The implication is that we "catch" another person's emotions, through feedback from either the face or the body (Doherty, 1997). Generally, our accuracy in identifying emotions seems to increase with the number of cues we receive.

We mimic others—that is, we tend to repeat their gestures, their mannerisms, and the way they move—but most of the time we are not doing this consciously. One of your authors observed a woman who always visited the local library and sat in a chair scowling. She decided to smile at this woman and discovered that each time she did, the woman's face relaxed and she smiled broadly. Several researchers believe that this *chameleon effect,* as nonconscious mimicry is sometimes called, actually promotes our relationships with other people and results in increased liking and affiliation. They argue that this two-way relationship is evidence that "mimicry has played an important role in evolution" (Lakin et al., 2003, p. 145).

In a recent experiment on cross-cultural understanding of facial expressions, Elfenbein observed that accuracy in judging emotion on this basis is "a core component of emotional intelligence" (2006, p. 21). Her study of improving accuracy through feedback is particularly interesting because she found greater improvement of accuracy skills when subjects were judging cultural groups more distant from their own familial backgrounds. She suggests that perhaps this occurs because the feedback had "greater novel information" (p. 21). Her work would seem to contradict Matsumoto's findings about familiarity, but her conclusions are only concerned with the influence of feedback. Further research is needed, although Elfenbein's study offers more evidence that accuracy in our judgments about emotions can be improved.

Oculesics

"In the right context, even a glance held a fraction longer than normal may be perceived as an act of intimacy. The glance penetrates the private psychological space of the other, and also reveals one's own" (Bates, 2001, p. 113). Prolonged eye contact, of course, can also be seen as aggressive. The many rules implicit in our culture about looking at others are a tacit admission that eye contact is perhaps the single most important facial cue we use in communicating. *The study of the role of eye behaviors such as eye contact, eye movements, and pupil dilation in communicating* is called **oculesics.**

Answers to Figure 4.1: (1) uneasy, (2) decisive, (3) flirtatious, and (4) concerned.

Although the face has been called "the major nonverbal liar" (Ekman and Friesen, 1984), cues given in eye contact seem to reveal a good deal about emotion, personality, and intention. Hence, the belief that "The eyes are the windows of the soul." Apparently, we have greater control of the muscles in the lower part of our face than we do of the muscles around our eyes. (There are exceptions, of course. Machiavellian individuals and con artists are able to sustain good eye contact even when telling lies.) It has even been suggested that "the lower face may follow culturally transmitted display rules while the eyes may reveal the spontaneous or naked response" (Libby and Yaklevich, 1973, p. 203).

At present most of the research on eye behaviors has to do with eye contact. One study estimates that in group communication we spend 30 to 60 percent of our time in eye contact with others (10 to 30 percent of the looks last only about a second). Four unstated rules about eye contact are:

1. A looker may invite interaction by staring at another person who is on the other side of a room. The target's studied return of the gaze is generally interpreted as acceptance of the invitation, whereas averting the eyes is a rejection of the looker's request.

2. There is more mutual eye contact between friends than others, and a looker's frank gaze is widely interpreted as positive regard.

3. Persons who seek eye contact while speaking are regarded not only as exceptionally well-disposed by their target, but also as more believable and earnest.

4. If the usual short, intermittent gazes during conversation are replaced by gazes of longer duration, the target interprets this as meaning that the task is less important than the personal relation between the two persons. (Argyle, 1985)

The second rule is corroborated by other researchers: Frequent eye contact does seem to be a sign of affection or interest. For example, flirting will often begin "with a quick upward glance, followed by averting the gaze and then another bout of eye contact, and a friendly smile" (Bates, 2001, p. 113). "Eye contact," writes Andersen, "does more than signal availability: it is an invitation to communicate" (1999, p. 191). A recent review of research on nonverbal communication and interaction between physicians and their patients reports one study in which "physicians' eye contact while patients spoke was positively associated with physicians' psychodiagnostic abilities" (Robinson, 2006, p. 441). And in the absence of such gaze orientation on the part of the doctor, patients were less likely to disclose information about themselves.

Even in public communication, frequency of eye contact affects the message sender. When an audience gives negative feedback (including poor eye contact), a speaker tends to lose fluency and to do poorly in presenting his or her message. In turn, audiences prefer a speaker who gives good eye contact. Researchers report that the best nonverbal predictor of perceived social support and coping is eye contact.

Why is eye contact so rewarding to others? Perhaps it is because the eyes are considered such a valuable source of information. Hess's studies (1965; 1975) confirm that the size of your pupils is a sensitive index of your interest in what you're looking at. And apparently in dating, your unconscious awareness that the other person's pupils are dilated can increase your attraction to that person. Eye contact with friends can also help us to cope with stressful events (Winstead et al., 1992).

There are several popular beliefs about what can be learned from watching someone's eyes. For example, two people who exchange knowing glances at a party seem able to communicate without words. Being able to look another person in the eye traditionally implies that you are being truthful and that your intentions are not to be questioned. Conversely, the person who averts his or her eyes is thought to be hiding something. In the Mediterranean, belief in the power of eyes is seen, for example, in the eye painted on Greek boats and the glass eyeball worn as a charm (sometimes on a key chain or bracelet) that is thought to protect the wearer against the curse of "the evil eye."

Knapp and Hall (2002) summarize current research by identifying several functions of eye contact:

1. Regulating the flow of communication—opening the channels of communicating and assisting in the turn-taking process

2. Monitoring feedback

3. Expressing emotions

4. Communicating the nature of the interpersonal relationship, for example, variations due to status, liking, and disliking. (p. 369)

(See Chapter 10 on the intercultural aspects of eye contact and cultures in which avoiding eye contact is a sign of respect.)

Body Movements

If during a party you were asked to record and classify all the body movements of two people in conversation during a five-minute period, you would probably find this an impossible task. Nothing short of a film captures the rapid, often subtle changes of the body.

Take flirting, for example. What are the nonverbal behaviors that signal flirting? The classic work of Scheflen (1965) grew out of his filming and analysis of patterns of "quasi-courtship" that he noticed between males and females during psychotherapy as well as at conferences and business meetings. After studying films, he was able to classify typical behaviors. Some were simply movements to establish greater rapport and closeness between participants; others were signs of nonverbal flirting. For example, how we position our arms and legs transmits cues about who we include and exclude, as in Figure 4.5: (a) "We're not open to others" and (b) "I'm with you—not him" (Knapp and Hall, 2002, p. 429).

Signs of *courtship readiness* included *preening* by playing with the hair, pulling at stockings, adjusting the tie, and so on.

Positioning was another source of cues about interpersonal attraction. For example, two people might face each other and lean forward eagerly. Sometimes they sat with the upper half of their torsos turned in an open position so that a third person might enter the conversation but with their legs forming a circle and thus excluding the intruder.

Actions of appeal included flirtatious glances and head cocking. Women signaled sexual invitation by crossing the legs, exposing the thigh, exhibiting the palm of the hand, and protruding the breast.

To find out how people choose a mate, Steven Gangestad, an evolutionary psychologist, has studied the universality of flirting behaviors: In all cultures there

Figure 4.5   *Positional Cues*

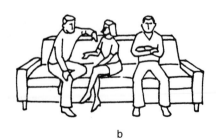

a   b

Source: From *Nonverbal Communication in Human Interaction*, 5th ed., by Mark L Knapp and Judith A. Hall, © 2002. Reprinted with permission of Wadsworth, a division of Thomson Learning. *www.thomsonrights.com.* Fax 800-730-2215.

seems to be a set of gestures we use to express sexual interest. Some researchers including David Givens, an anthropologist, and Timothy Perper, a social psychologist, have studied flirting in cocktail lounges and bars: It seems that "if all went well, a couple would invariably progress from touching themselves to touching each other" (Rodgers, 1999, p. 39). One study (Simpson et al., 1993) found that, though the sets of nonverbal behaviors were different for men and women, there was a clear-cut pattern. Men who were flirting smiled and laughed more often, showed more flirtatious glances, and looked downward less frequently than men who were not flirting. In flirting women, body movements seemed to be more pronounced; women tended to cant their heads during conversation and to lean forward; of course, by leaning forward you maximize other cues from your face and head. Although earlier researchers have connected head canting with communicating submissiveness, this seems not to be the case here. Women who canted their heads were actually rated not only as more engaging but slightly more dominant (p. 456). Future research may explain these discrepancies.

According to the findings of Ekman (1965), cues from the head and face suggest what emotion is being experienced whereas the body gives off cues about how intense that emotion is. The hands, however, can give us the same information we receive from the head and face.

Hand Gestures

Anthropologists distinguish humankind from other animals by their use of language and their superior manual dexterity. Flexible hands enable human beings to use tools and to draw on a wide range of gestures in communicating. As a mode of nonverbal communication, *hand gestures rank second in importance only to facial cues.*

The palm of the hand conveys some of the "least-noticed, but most powerful, body signals," according to Pease and Pease (2006, p. 36). They identify three *major palm-command gestures:*

Palm-Up: The upward facing palm is nonthreatening, a sometimes submissive gesture. "If you want someone to talk, you can use the Palm-Up as a 'handover' gesture to let them know you expect them to talk and that you're ready to listen." A throwback, perhaps, to earlier times when the open palm was an indication that the person was not carrying any weapons.

Palm-Down: In contrast, the palm that is facing downward conveys authority immediately, so that when you use this gesture "the other person will sense that you've given them an order . . . and may begin to feel antagonistic toward you, depending on your relationship with him in a work environment" (pp. 36–37).

Palm-Closed-Finger-Pointed: A closed palm and pointed finger is, according to this research, "one of the most annoying gestures anyone can use while speaking, particularly when it beats time to the speaker's words." It is considered an insult in some cultures (p. 38). Apparently, this gesture elicits the least positive response from listeners and the least recall of what the speaker has said.

Sometimes pointing is solely nonverbal, and pointing at others is often considered an offensive gesture. This author recalls an incident in a crowded restaurant in which someone at her table proceeded to collect all the empty plates, put them on top of his own, and then point at a busy waiter and point down at the pile of plates, gesturing for the waiter to take them away immediately. The atmosphere became decidedly frosty. The pointing gesture not only offended the waiter but the other guests at the table.

It is not only broad, expansive gestures that communicate mood. Less animated people often communicate inadvertently by means of their hands. The rather reserved husband of a lawyer we know repeatedly drums his fingers on a table or chair whenever his wife speaks about her practice. This behavior is the only sign of his impatience with her deep involvement in her profession.

Even those who were born blind gesture with their hands when they speak. Although our hand gestures can convey nonverbal messages on their own, when we gesture with our hands we actually enhance our ability to think (Goldin-Meddow, 2003). When children are prevented from gesturing—for example, using their hands when explaining a mathematical method that had been taught to them—they remember less of what they'd been taught (Watts, 2006, p. 1384). And when people are lying, there is an increase in the number of their metaphoric hand gestures (those that are pictorial and represent abstract ideas—for example, drawing a shape with one's hands, such as a fist to indicate strength). The number of pointing gestures also decreases (Caso et al., 2006).

Hand gestures sometimes substitute for verbal communication. Deaf-mutes use a system of hand signals so comprehensive that it literally replaces spoken language. The signals themselves are arbitrary. Many of our hand movements are culturally determined. Hand gestures may be used differently even within a single location. In New York there are at least 100 ways of greeting someone by shaking hands. Between 2003 and 2004 Michael Britton and his crew filmed many kinds of New York handshakes for a one-hour documentary called "Gimme Five: History of a Hundred Handshakes" (Moynihan, 2004, B1). Imagine—an entire hour of handshakes.

The same gestures can convey different things to members of different cultures, and, over time, gestures change even within the same culture. To an American, for example, making a circle with one's thumb and forefinger and extending the other fingers means "okay," but to a Brazilian it is an obscene sign of contempt.

Desmond Morris and his colleagues in England (1979) have identified what they call twenty key gestures used in Europe. They are shown in Figure 4.6. Some of these, such as the nose thumb (no. 3), the forearm jerk (no. 7), the ring (no. 9), and the palm-back V-sign (no. 20), are quite familiar to us. Others, however, such as the cheek screw (no. 5), the horizontal horn-sign (no. 11), the chin flick (no. 14), and the fig (no. 12) are almost completely unknown in the United States. They found that different meanings were assigned in different countries. The fig, for example, is interpreted in many different ways including as sexual comment, sexual insult, or protection. Similarly, the nose tap (no. 19) has several interpretations—among them, complicity, be alert, you are being nosey, I'm alert, he is clever, and awareness that a threat is present.

Figure 4.6 Key Gestures

Source: From *Gestures* by Desmond Morris, P. Collett, P. Marsh, and M. O'Shaughnessy, 1979. Reprinted by permission of Desmond Morris.

Haptics

Touch is one of our most important means of communicating nonverbally. **Haptics,** *the study of how we use touch to communicate,* has been receiving increasing attention among communication scholars.

We know that touch is essential for psychological and physical development in children and emotional well-being in adults. In our culture, being able to touch other human beings seems to be linked with high self-esteem and sociability. And our experience of intimacy, connectedness with others and satisfaction in relationships is intensified by being touched (Prager, 2000). In the play *Dinner with Friends* by Donald Margulies, one of the characters describes when he finally decided to divorce his wife: He notices that during an entire week she has never touched him once.

In addition to conveying nurturance and caring, touch is also used to signify a professional relationship (being touched by a barber, for example); a social relationship (handshakes); friendship (for example, touching the upper arm); intimacy (hugs, for instance); and sexual arousal (for example, certain types of kisses). In each instance, touch is a bonding gesture (Heslin and Alper, 1983).

Touching is thought by scholars to vary with gender and culture. A recent study attempted to test the widely held theory that "touching behavior is an expression of dominance" by examining whether in traditional male-dominated cultures men will touch more than women will (Dibiase and Gunnoe, 2004, p. 49). The study also looked at whether men will touch more with their hands. Those who participated were young men and women from Italy, the United States, and the Czech Republic. Results showed that women did more nonhand than hand touching. The most significant differences between men and women were in the Czech Republic, which, like Italy, is a high-contact culture. In the Czech Republic, where the society is more stratified by gender, there were more gender differences in hand touching. And Italians, who belong to a high-contact culture, "touched significantly more than Czechs, who touched more than Americans" (p. 59).

We also use touch to persuade or influence other people; in fact, touching increases self-disclosure and compliant behavior. The influence of touching on compliance has been demonstrated in several fascinating studies. For example, subjects touched lightly on the arm were more likely to sign a petition than those who were not touched (Willis and Hamm, 1980). Besides the need for touch to establish and develop our relationships with others, some touch appears to have unambiguous symbolic content or meaning. Further, the codes of interpersonal touch encompass a great range of meanings, so we use touch to convey many different things, some far more ambiguous than others.

Research (Jones, 1999; Jones and Yarbrough, 1985) identifies seven types of touches:

Positive affect touches include touches of support, appreciation, inclusion, affection, physical attraction, and sexual interest.

Playful touches show playful affection or playful aggression.

Control touches gain compliance or attention or emphasize a response.

Ritualistic touches are more formal touches that signal greeting or departure.

*Hybrid touche*s are those of greeting or departure that express affection.

Task-related touches might accompany a task (e.g., helping someone put on a coat) or be used along with a comment ("I like your coat," said while touching the coat).

Accidental touches are perceived as unintentional (e.g., brushing past someone on the street). (Adapted from Jones, 1999, pp. 196–200)

Touch is involving; it is an approach form of behavior. On the other hand, **touch avoidance,** is *"a negative attitude toward touch that also affects [your] proxemic behavior and other types of nonverbal communication"* (Andersen, 1999, p. 173). Touch avoidance is not about how much you touch others but your feelings and attitude about touching and being touched; it can be thought of as reflecting your general level of intimacy. Touch avoidance is also a good predictor of how much interpersonal distance we maintain, particularly when the other person is female (Anderson and Sull, 1985).

In discussing proxemics, we examined the distinction between high- and low-contact cultures. Edward Hall (1959) identifies the United States and Northern European cultures as low-contact cultures, but one study of patterns of touch (McDaniel and Andersen, 1998) finds a broad range of touching behaviors in members of most cultures. The exception is to be seen in Asian countries, especially in Northeast Asia. Like many others, the authors cite Confucianism as a possible influence on the "East Asian reluctance toward interpersonal touch" (p. 70). Other variables affect patterns of touching—among them the degree of familiarity between people, their status, and, of course, the communication context itself.

Physical Appearance and the Use of Objects

It is said that when Albert Einstein was asked by his wife to change his clothes to meet the German ambassador, Einstein replied: "They want to see me. Here I am. If they want to see my clothes, open my closet and show them my suits."

There are not many people who show such complete disregard for appearance. **Objectics,** *the study of how we select and make use of physical objects in our nonverbal communication,* is concerned with every kind of physical object—from the clothing you wear to the furniture you choose to the car you drive. For example, whether you intend to or not, you often project a personal style through how you dress. Clothes may not make the person, but dress, general physical appearance, and grooming are often the basis of first and relatively long-lasting impressions.

Martha Stewart, a high-visibility defendant, seemed unaware that the French handbag she wore at her trial, an exclusive model that cost upward of $6,000, would create an uproar. It was widely commented on by reporters, and there was also some question as to whether the cost of the bag had been discussed among the jurors. Because her trial concerned whether she lied about selling a stock illegally to protect an investment, wearing the handbag in the courtroom was probably an unfortunate choice, conveying a degree of affluence that did not serve her case.

Even whether you wear glasses can affect the way you are perceived by others. It's well known that among architects the *style* of glasses they wear is always noted. Although glasses are often associated with intelligence and deliberately used to convey it (see Stephen Colbert's parody of newscasters on "The Colbert Report"), glasses are sometimes interpreted as conveying sincerity. Consider this description of a character in Eileen Chang's story "Red Rose, White Rose":

> Zhenbao wasn't tall, but he was vigorous and quick. He . . . wore black-rimmed glasses, with something peculiarly untouched in his facial expression. His posture was excellent and he didn't joke around—unless, that is, it was appropriate to joke. He seemed frank and open, a man you could take in at a glance—and if you couldn't quite pinpoint the sincerity in his eyes those eyeglasses were proof enough. (2007, p. 256)

A women's magazine makes clear what the associations of different hair styles often are. Among eight classic hairstyles, they list:

> *Long and Straight:* "In the '60s, long straight hair becomes a symbol of feminine power and rebellion—and it never really goes out of style"

> *The Flip:* "The official hairstyle of the '60s suburban housewife, a neat flip always favors optimism and control over sexuality"

> *The Bob:* "With its neat, high-maintenance, geometric shape, the bob has long been the cut for high-style, high-class, no-nonsense types." (Einstein and Van Gelder, 2004)

For those in the public eye, even a change in hairstyle can reinforce an impression. For example, after Angelina Jolie made unflattering statements about one of her children in a widely publicized video interview, her appearance at the 2007 Golden Globes drew this criticism: "And while she looked ultra-glamorous at the premiere of her latest film, 'The Good Shepherd,' the perfectly upswept hair and self-contained demeanor of her recent appearances have also made her seem plastic" (James, 2007, E7).

Men are not exempt from scrutiny. Although mustaches are sometimes associated with masculinity and power, they don't always make a good impression on mothers and girlfriends. A popular article on style begins "Are mustaches cool? Uncool? Or so painfully uncool that they are actually kind of hip? . . . No other style of male grooming sends so many potent—and often mixed—signals" (Burns, 2006, G3). The popularity of beards, on the other hand, seems to be cyclical (Kleinke, 1986, p. 78).

Uniforms tell us a great deal about rank and status. In several studies, people received greater help or compliance with their requests (e.g., signing a petition) when they were formally or neatly dressed than they did when their dress was casual or careless (Kleinke, 1986, pp. 77–78).

How formally you dress can be another sensitive indicator. Most people tend to comply with office dress codes, which until recently were extremely casual. There seems to be a return to more formal dress not only for job interviews but in the workplace, at least for meetings with bosses and clients. "Credibility," says one young lawyer, "is a suit" (Parnes, 2001, p. G1). (For more on dress as well as other nonverbal cues during job interviews see Chapter 11.)

The clothing you wear often communicates your compliance or noncompliance with traditional values. And being overdressed for a social function can suggest a lack of sophistication. Interestingly, it's people with higher status who usually have the option of dressing up or down (Andersen, 1999).

Even your choice of color can may be interpreted as communicating something about you. For example, the novelist Sandra Cisneros created an uproar in a historic district of San Antonio when she painted her house purple. At times, your choice of accessories or equipment suggests a desire to communicate status or power—for example, through a Rolex watch, a state-of-the-art laptop, or a BlackBerry. In fact, high-end cell phones have been compared to cars: "Phones, like cars, are fashion items: people generally replace them long before they actually wear out. Both are social technologies that bring people together and act as symbols of independence for teenagers" ("Phones Are the New Cars," 2006, p. 16).

Objects can also come to have symbolic value. Following the terrorist attacks on New York and Washington, many people displayed American flags on their cars, and we heard of one Sikh who started wearing a turban that was red, white, and blue. Similarly, a small pink triangle on an envelope conveys support for gay rights, and wearing a red ribbon may draw attention to AIDS awareness. A nose ring may signal something about the wearer's unconventionality. In general, cosmetics, jewelry, and tattoos or decals—seen even on high-fashion models—often evoke strong responses from others.

And, of course, choices vary from one culture to another. The manager of Porsche in China, a country of many new millionaires, explained that the Chinese are not interested in sports cars and that the luxury car of choice there is a 911 convertible rather than a coupe, "the opposite of Germany and the States," because "in a convertible, people can see you" (Smith, 2004, p. 14). And while Rolls-Royces in most other parts of the world are owner-driven, in Asia they are chauffeur-driven because owners want to be seen being driven.

Whether or not your intention is to communicate, the way you choose and display physical objects is taken by others as a source of information about you. It should go without saying that such information is not always accurate.

We have discussed a great many visual cues individually, but remember that as a communicator you are also taking in and interpreting cues about space and time as well as vocal cues, which we will look at in some detail.

VOCAL CUES

When they are online, many people also add nonverbal cues to their text-based messages (Walther, 2006; Hancock and Dunham, 2001; Jacobson, 1999). When they want to create an impression or express feelings, or convey variations in tone or volume, they use capital and lowercase letters differently, typing errors, exclamation points, and other punctuation marks and emoticons (sometimes called smileys) along with their verbal messages.

Early in this chapter, we described communication that was verbal/vocal—that is, both verbal and vocal. One difference between the verbal and the vocal message is the difference between what is said and how it is said.

Take the sentence "I hate you." Imagine these words being said to show anger or in a much different way to sound seductive. The simple sentence "I'm glad to meet you" can sound cold and insincere despite its verbal message. Or suppose you go to a friend's apartment and she opens the door and says, "Oh, it's you." The vocal cues, perhaps in combination with several visual cues, tell you whether she is really pleased to see you, indifferent, or even disappointed. Of course, if she simply groans when she opens the door, this is an example of nonverbal/vocal communication.

The study of vocal phenomena, **paralinguistics** or *paralanguage, refers to something beyond or in addition to language itself.* Paralanguage has two components: *voice qualities,* such as *pitch, range, resonance, lip control, and articulation control;* and *vocalizations,* or *noises without linguistic structure, such as crying, laughing, and grunting* (Trager, 1958). So using paralinguistic cues online such as those mentioned above is another attempt to go beyond communicating simply by verbal means.

Several distinct emotions can be accurately identified solely on the basis of vocal cues, but the more similar the emotions—admiration and affection, for example—the greater our difficulty in identifying them.

Much research on vocal characteristics and emotions parallels the studies of facial expressions. Mehrabian (1968) found that people are easily able to judge the degree of liking communicated vocally. One team of researchers identified four categories of emotion: positive feeling, dislike, sadness, and apprehension or fear. The results confirm that "voice sounds alone, independent of semantic components of vocal messages, carry important clues to the emotional state of a speaker" (Soskin and Kauffman, 1961, p. 78; Knapp and Hall, 2002, p. 410). People can detect aggressiveness from a tape recording of a speaker's message, though not from a written transcript, and can judge intensity of emotion from vocal characteristics. We cannot assume, though, that vocal cues are similar across cultures.

A common problem in interpreting vocal cues is misunderstanding sarcasm. This is especially true for children and people with poor listening and/or intellectual skills.

Vocal cues are sometimes the basis for our inferences about personality traits. If people increase the loudness, pitch, timbre, and rate of their speech, we think of them as more active and dynamic. If they use more intonation, higher speech rates, more volume, and greater fluency in their speech, we find them more persuasive (Knapp and Hall, 2002, p. 410). In computer-mediated communication, even limited paralinguistic cues can influence how people form impressions of others; this is true, for example, in online communities (Jacobson, 1999).

It's interesting that judgments about status can be made quite rapidly (for example, after listening to a sample of a person's speech for only 10 or 15 seconds). Apparently, we can make such inferences with a high degree of accuracy.

Despite wide agreement about certain relationships between voice qualities and personality traits, no conclusive evidence supports such inferences. They seem to derive from vocal stereotypes. Even if our beliefs have no basis in fact, however, they have striking effects on our response to others; we act on what we believe to be true. Thus, when the talkies appeared, several stars of the silent films were ruined because the public expected their voices to sound consistent with their screen personalities. The great lover with the high-pitched voice was too great a disappointment.

Volume

One precondition of effective verbal communication is adequate *volume.* If your voice is so low that you can barely be heard, people rapidly become too tired or too embarrassed to ask you to repeat your last remark. In this case, it is you, the message sender, who becomes a source of interference for the receiver. In organizational communication, vocal intensity can reinforce or enhance a person's power base and convey a sense of confidence. For example, an employee who speaks loudly is more likely to enhance the perception of his or her expertise. And higher volume also seems to be one of the cues associated with perceived dominance (Tusing and Dillard, 2000).

Most people link volume to certain personality traits: Thus it is commonly thought that an aggressive person speaks in a louder voice than one who is reserved and shy. Volume, however, is not necessarily a function of personality. Our models in childhood also influence our volume level.

Feedback from the receiver is the best check on volume. If you are not getting through or if you're coming on too strong, adjust your voice accordingly.

Rate and Fluency

Your **rate of speech** is the *number of words you utter within a specified time.* The unit most often used is one minute, and the average speaking rate is about 125 to 150 words per minute.

Speech rates are highly stable for individuals. For this reason, a faster rate (as well as shorter comments and more frequent pauses) seems to be linked to fear or anger and a slower rate to grief or depression (Barnlund, 1968, p. 529). Some people are able to control their rate of speaking despite their emotions, but the strain of maintaining this control is often expressed in other vocal or facial cues. There is no optimum speaking rate. Like many other vocal qualities, rate of speech is more effective when adapted to the verbal content of the message and to the specific receiver.

The **fluency,** or *continuity,* of our speech is closely related to rate, and pauses, of course, affect fluency. The person who pauses continually, whose speech is full of vocalizations such as "um," "er," and "ah," may destroy his or her effectiveness as a communicator. Pauses that are frequent, long, and vocalized, and that come in the middle of an idea, are usually unsettling and undermine the sender's purpose. When used for emphasis and variation, pauses often enhance the verbal message—particularly if they are infrequent, short, and silent, and are used at the end of an idea.

Pitch

Pitch is *the frequency level (high or low) of the voice.* Your pitch range is determined by the size and shape of the vocal bands within your larynx, or voice box. Optimum pitch, the level most comfortable for you, is usually one-third above the lowest pitch you are capable of producing. Most untrained speakers use a pitch somewhat higher than their optimum pitch, but it has been found that lower pitches are most pleasant to listen to.

Although women's voices tend to be more high-pitched than men's, the difference may not simply be a question of biology:

> When women's and men's voices are compared to the respective size of their vocal tracts, women talk as if they are physically smaller than they actually are. Their voices are pitched to the upper range, the decibel level is reduced, and vowel resonances are thinned. These paralinguistic elements are not the effect of biology but of socialization and learning—the imperative [for women] to be soft-spoken. (Nelson, 2004, p. 209)

Pitch is an important element in people's judgments about a speaker. A voice with unvaried pitch is monotonous and usually disliked; in fact, a monotone seems to be as unpopular as a poker face. People sometimes derive information about emotions from changes in pitch. Pitch can even influence our judgments about a doctor's professional competence and social attractiveness.

Apparently, pitch level does influence your attitude toward the communicator and the content of the message. Exaggerated pitch changes are even more unpopular than the monotone. A naturally expressive voice has a variety of pitch levels that are spontaneous and unforced changes.

Quality

Think of a violin, a viola, and a cello. Each is a stringed instrument but has a different size and shape. The same note played on each of these instruments will therefore have a different *resonance—a distinctive quality of sound.* Similarly, each of you has a distinctive voice quality because the resonance of your voice—which to a great

ISSUES IN COMMUNICATION

Gender and Vocal Cues

Audrey Nelson, a communication consultant for business and government organizations, also writes on communication differences between men and women. Here are some of her suggestions about vocal cues:

- Credibility is associated with determined, short speech. Though some women enjoy conveying the whole story, they might be more effective in their interactions with men if they cut to the chase.

- Meaningless chatter undermines credibility. Women are advised to keep this under control in business situations.

- Soft-spoken women are at a disadvantage when negotiating or trying to persuade. In these situations, it's important to speak up and command the floor with other nonverbal cues.

- Tag questions [a direct statement with a question at the end—e.g., "I need the critique by Friday, okay?"] can cause listeners to doubt a speaker's resolve. They are to be avoided unless the speaker invites cooperation and discussion. A lower pitch at the end of a sentence indicates that a decision is final.

- Silence can make men seem remote, even if they don't want to be. They should notice if their habitual silence undermines their relationships with female co-workers and friends.

- Although vocal cues such as deeper pitch, less inflection, and greater volume convey authority and persuasion, men may need to monitor them when interacting with women. (Nelson with Golant, 2004, p. 224)

Do you think her suggestions are helpful? Do you think any are sexist?

extent determines its quality—is a function of the size and shape of your body as well as of your vocal cords.

There seems to be wide agreement in responses to vocal qualities. Judges could reliably distinguish voices described as shrill or harsh from those considered pleasant, or "resonant." In our culture, several voice qualities considered particularly unpleasant are hypernasality (talking through the nose), denasality (which sounds as though the speaker has a constant head cold), hoarseness, and harshness (or stridency). Voices considered attractive and influential are "more resonant and calm, less monotonous, lower-pitched (especially for males), less regionally accented, less nasal, less shrill, and more relaxed" (Andersen, 1999, p. 71). Differences in gender also influence how vocal quality is interpreted. For example:

A female speaker with a breathy voice is perceived as pretty, petite, feminine, high-strung, and shallow; a male speaker with a breathy voice is perceived as young and artistic . . . Women with "throaty" voices are perceived as more masculine, lazier, less intelligent, less emotional, less attractive, more careless,

less artistic, more naive, more neurotic, less interesting, more apathetic, and quieter. On the other hand, throatiness in men resulted in their being perceived as older, more mature, more sophisticated, and better adjusted. (Pearson et al., 1994)

Having an attractive voice is a distinct advantage, and apparently we operate from a "what sounds beautiful is good" hypothesis. People with voices that are clear, warm, expressive, and robust are more likely to be seen as powerful, dominant, assertive, and socially skilled. This is especially the case when you use voice mail and answering machines, which rely so heavily on vocal cues. One study of messages left on business answering machines found that when people left taped excuses for not taking their phone calls, a person whose voice was attractive was seen—no matter what the excuse was—as "more competent, likeable, and dominant" (Semic, 1999, p. 153). So know how you sound and sharpen those vocal skills.

Through practice and training, almost all of us can improve our vocal quality. One of the best media available for studying communication style is the videotape recorder, though even videotape loses some nuances of vocal inflection, eye contact, postural cues, and the like. The audiotape recorder is another valuable aid.

Summing up research findings on vocal cues, Knapp and Hall (2002) point out:

> You should be quick to challenge the cliché that vocal cues only concern how something is said; frequently they are what is said. What is said might be an attitude ("I like you" or "I'm superior to you"); it might be an emotion; it might be the coordination and management of the conversation; or it might be the presentation of some aspect of your personality, background, or physical features. (p. 410)

For discussion purposes, we have isolated three categories of nonverbal cues. But as we pointed out early on, people interpret messages on the basis of multiple nonverbal and verbal cues. This is certainly the case with deception.

DECEPTION

One of the defining characteristics of successful salespeople, politicians, and poker players is their ability to appear truthful when their truthfulness is challenged. Even daily life seems to require this ability, because diary studies suggest that everyone admits to lying a few times daily.

—Frank and Ekman (2004, p. 486)

It seems that in judging whether people are deceiving us or telling the truth, we're not that accurate. According to one source, "the accuracy rate for detecting deception is only about 55 percent to 60 percent, with people less likely to be accurate when a person is lying compared to telling the truth. This percentage does not improve with close relationships." On the other hand, researchers find that we tend to be far more accurate in judging when people are telling the truth (Guerrero and Floyd, 2006, pp. 197, 181).

So just because we know a person well—a friend or romantic partner or sibling—doesn't mean that we will be able to detect when he or she is not telling the truth. Our confidence that we know the other person very well may lead us astray.

As you might guess, when the stakes are high, people who are lying tend to give more nonverbal cues that might indicate deception. For example, there might be less foot and leg movement, less arm and hand movement, an increased rate of speech, and more pauses (Vrij, 2006).

According to Aldert Vrij, many of us are looking at the wrong nonverbal cues. First, we often mistakenly believe that people who are lying will increase their movements, and also that they tend to avoid looking at the other person. But in fact it seems that "liars tend to *decrease* rather than increase their movements . . . " (2006, p. 352). Some of our ideas about deceptive behavior are acquired from the media. And there may be a "confirmation bias" so that we select data that reinforces our own beliefs. Then, too, since we rarely get feedback on whether we were right about someone we think was deceiving us, we have no way to determine how accurate our judgments have been (p. 352).

Guerrero and Floyd's recent review of reliable nonverbal indicators of deception (2006) discusses facial, vocal, and kinesic behaviors. Counter to what many of us believe, direct gaze, maintaining eye contact, and smiling do not seem to be completely reliable cues concerning truthtelling. Some researchers—notably Ekman and his colleagues, whose work is known worldwide—have distinguished between "felt" and "false" smiles. Unlike felt or genuine smiles (sometimes referred to as "Duchenne smiles"), which involve not only muscles around the mouth but the eyes, smiles that are false seem to involve only the muscles around the mouth.

As for nonverbal cues involving the eyes, it is not, as many of us believe, maintaining briefer or less frequent eye contact that is a reliable predictor of truthfulness. Two other cues from the eyes that involve less control—blinking and the dilation of the pupils—seem to be more reliable. Apparently, when we are under stress—and this includes when we are behaving deceptively—we blink more often than we do when we are relaxed, including when we tell the truth. And when we are deceptive, as when we are generally aroused or emotional, our pupils dilate. Blinking is difficult to control, and dilation of the pupils is completely automatic behavior.

Vocal cues that seem to be important indicators of deception include more frequent errors in speaking, longer pauses and more pauses filled with sounds such as "ah" and "um", markedly higher pitch, and greater "vocal stress."

The third category outlined by Guerrero and Floyd, kinesic behaviors, involves "movement-oriented nonverbal behaviors, including gestures, head movements, postural shifts, and foot and leg movements" (2006, p. 179). Although you might expect people to move more when they are lying rather than when they are telling the truth, research suggests that deception cues involve fewer movements of the hands, fingers, legs, and feet. For a summary of all these cues, see Table 4.2.

Table 4.2 *Nonverbal Behaviors Reliably Associated with Deception*		
Facial Behaviors	*Vocalic Behaviors*	*Kinesic Behaviors*
Smiling: Deceivers use more fake smiles than truthtellers; no difference in overall amount of smiling Eye behaviors: Deceivers blink more and have more pupil dilation; no difference with respect to eye contact	Pitch: Deceivers have higher pitch than truthtellers Vocal stress: Vocal stress and nervousness are elevated during deception Speech errors: Deceivers commit more speech errors than do truthtellers	Deceivers engage in fewer hand/finger movements, fewer foot/leg movements, and fewer illustrator gestures than do truthtellers

Source: From *Nonverbal Communication in Close Relationships* by Laura Guerrero and Kory Floyd (Lawrence Erlbaum, 2006), p. 181.

The kinds of **leakage,** or *signals of deception,* that take place depend on whether the lie is spontaneous or rehearsed and whether we are concealing something emotional or factual. Deception cues are most likely to be given when the deceiver wants to hide a feeling experienced at that moment or feels strongly about the information being hidden. They also tend to occur when a person feels anxious, or guilty, or needs to think carefully while speaking.

One study found that deceivers delivering a prepared lie respond more quickly than truth tellers mainly because less thinking is necessary (Greene et al., 1985). When they are unprepared, however, deceivers generally take longer than both prepared deceivers and truth tellers. Those telling the truth generally maintain more eye contact than deceivers. Deceivers also show less body movement, probably in an attempt to avoid leakage cues. At the same time, they laugh and smile more often, presumably trying to keep their faces from displaying other expressions that may turn out to be leakage cues. It's especially interesting that these people continue to behave "deceptively" even when telling the truth. They probably fear that they will lose control if the situation in which they need to lie should recur (Greene et al., 1985). We must note here the great potential for intercultural misunderstandings when cultural conventions of little gesturing and infrequent eye contact may be interpreted as deception.

Another study of naive and able liars (Anolli and Ciceri, 1997) argues that lying is for the most part a vocal act, one that is very demanding. The study emphasizes that lying, a "strategic act," is intellectually demanding because the liar, who knows the truth, is trying to be more persuasive—and also to conceal the emotional arousal that is sometimes created by the act of lying (especially if the liar is unprepared). At times the control a liar must exert is transformed into overcontrol so that the voice becomes flat and deeper in tone.

Voice stress analysis, which detects very minute changes in a person's voice that are then displayed on a computer screen, is not a new technology—it has been available for almost 15 years, but its use is growing. Those who market it claim that voice changes can be interpreted as registering subtle emotional changes including stress (Heingartner, 2004).

Much deception research has focused on the nature of deception cues and on how information is leaked, but research by Buller and others looks at mutual influence in deception and the actual communication exchange between deceivers and detectors. One study (Buller et al., 1991) examines how effective probing is as a strategy for detection and whether knowing the source—that is, the deceiver—affects our ability to distinguish what is truthful. Buller found that as receivers we communicate whether we accept or suspect a message, and we also communicate our suspicion nonverbally through our increased vigilance. When receivers were suspicious, they "spoke slower, were less fluent, and lacked clarity in their messages. When probing . . . [they showed] longer response latencies [delays] as the conversation progressed" (p. 18). In fact, they may have tried to conceal their suspicion by asking fewer probing questions—in effect, they themselves become less truthful. Deceivers, in turn, can judge our reactions to see how successful they have been and sometimes even modify their behavior to appear more truthful.

Most deception studies have used college students as subjects. Over the last 25 years of research, Ekman and Sullivan observe, "people have not been very accurate in judging when someone is lying" (1991, p. 913). One study of professional lie catchers looked at members of the U.S. Secret Service, federal polygraphers, judges, police, psychiatrists, a diverse group of working adults, and college students. Most groups did no better than college students. Secret Service people were the only ones who had greater than chance accuracy in detecting liars.

The study of deception has much to teach us not only about individual nonverbal cues but about the interaction of verbal and nonverbal behavior. Even though analysis often requires that we speak of verbal and nonverbal messages as if they could be separated, in practice this is nearly impossible. Face-to-face communication is a total experience. No matter what a person is trying to say, you can see his or her face, body movement, clothing, and so on, and you are responding, whether you are aware of it or not, to all these cues.

Summary

Nonverbal communication is going on all the time. In discussing the interpretation of nonverbal messages, we saw that a significant percentage of all social meaning is conveyed through nonverbal stimuli. We also saw that nonverbal channels convey primarily relational messages—messages about the emotional level of our communication—and that a nonverbal message can replace, reinforce, or contradict a verbal message. Yet verbal and nonverbal responses qualify each other in so many ways that they are not totally separable.

Three broad categories of nonverbal cues were examined. First we discussed space and time, cues that have a subtle but pervasive influence on communication style and are, to a great degree, determined by one's culture. We saw that assumptions about nonverbal cues may create misunderstandings in intercultural communication. Visual cues from facial expressions, eye contact, body movements (particularly hand gestures), touching, physical appearance, and the use of objects were analyzed. We found that these cues give us information about human emotions and intentions; they are also the basis for some of our judgments about personality and social status. Vocal cues are another source of information, and we discussed volume, rate and fluency, pitch, and quality, as well as gender differences.

In closing, we looked at an area of nonverbal behavior that cuts across all the individual nonverbal cues, the study of deception. We examined some conditions under which signals of deception are most likely to occur as well as new research findings about accuracy in decoding deception cues and the mutual influence of deceivers and detectors.

Key Terms

Chronemics
Co-culture
Haptics
High-contact culture
Interpersonal distance

Kinesic slips
Kinesics
Leakage
Low-contact culture
Monochronic

Nonverbal
 communication
Objectics
Oculesics
Orientation

Paralinguistics
Personal space
Polychronic
Proxemics
Touch avoidance

Review Questions

1. Specify four categories of communication associated with verbal and vocal communication.

2. What is the relative weight we assign to verbal and nonverbal messages? What type of information does each convey?

3. What are three ways in which nonverbal messages relate to verbal messages?

4. What is a mixed message or kinesic slip? How does it relate to both verbal and nonverbal communication?

5. Specify five or more nonverbal cues associated with power and dominance.

6. What is personal space? Give an example.

7. Specify four kinds of interpersonal distance. Give an example of each kind.

8. What are some differences between high-contact and low-contact cultures?

9. What is chronemics? Give an example of how timing might interfere with intercultural communication.

10. Explain the difference between monochronic and polychronic time, giving an example of each.

11. What is kinesics?

12. What are four unstated rules in our culture about eye contact?

13. Describe three categories of nonverbal courtship behavior. Give an example of each type.

14. What is the relationship between head and body movements in communicating emotion?

15. What are the three major palm-command gestures and what do they convey?

16. What is haptics?

17. Describe how touch might influence bonding, dominance, compliance, and self-disclosure.

18. What is touch avoidance? Give an example from your own experience.

19. Describe how one's choice of physical objects can communicate messages to others.

20. What is paralinguistics? Give some examples of paralinguistic cues.

21. What four categories of emotion are consistently identified by paralinguistic cues? Give some examples of gender differences in vocal cues.

22. Discuss several of the nonverbal behaviors reliably associated with deception.

23. Identify the conditions under which signals of deception are most likely to occur.

24. Describe the possibilities for mutual influence between detectors and deceivers and discuss recent research findings about accuracy in decoding deception cues.

Exercises

1. Form several two-person teams consisting of one male and one female. Have each team select a place where several people are likely to pass by. Have both members take turns asking strangers the time of day or some other standard question. While speaking, slowly violate the stranger's proxemic norms until you are very close to him or her. The other member of the team should observe and record the stranger's reactions. When all the teams have collected data, discuss these questions in light of the data collected:

   a. In what ways did the strangers demonstrate nonverbal/vocal and nonverbal/nonvocal communication?

   b. How did the strangers respond to the questioner as he or she began to violate proxemic norms?

   c. Did male and female strangers respond differently to proxemic norm violation depending on whether a male or female did the violating?

2. Repeat the exercise just described, but this time have one questioner dress very neatly and the other look sloppy and unkempt. Discuss the differences in the strangers' reaction to the questioner.

3. Go to *www.members.aol.com/nonverbal2* and access *The Nonverbal Dictionary*. Read all the entries on facial expressions including the "blank face" and "zygomatic smile." Find three unposed examples of both in current online sources, magazines, or newspapers and identify each by context.

4. Make a list of the various paralinguistic and vocal cues discussed in this chapter. Tape-record a series of short messages presented by a male and a female that illustrate the various types of paralinguistic and vocal cues. Construct a Semantic Differential similar to the one suggested in exercise 1a in Chapter 3. Then ask a number of people to listen to the taped messages and rate the speakers using the Semantic Differential. How did the various paralinguistic and vocal cues affect the listeners' perceptions of the speaker? Relate the results to the concepts discussed in Chapter 2 on person perception.

5. The next time you get angry with someone, try to observe your own nonverbal behavior. Most people look and sound like their parents or other members of their family. Facial expressions, posture, gestures, and vocal cues are often similar among family members. Do you notice similarities and differences? Can you account for these similarities and differences?

6. Select three shopping sites on the Web and find three magazine ads that advertise (a) clothing, (b) furniture, or (c) cars. Analyze and compare what the advertisers suggest would be the nonverbal messages—for example, status, intelligence, power, physical attractiveness—the consumer would be able to convey by purchasing and using these items.

Suggested Readings

Andersen, Peter A. *Nonverbal Communication: Forms and Functions.* Mountain View, CA: Mayfield, 1999.

   This is an excellent survey of nonverbal communication, organized in an original and very useful way. Chapter 4 on cultural cues, Chapter 5 on gender differences, and Chapter 6 on nonverbal communication in intimate relationships are of special interest.

Bates, Brian, with John Cleese. *The Human Face.* London: BBC, 2001.

A popular book, written in connection with the BBC presentation of a documentary on the face. It's informative and easy to read; it has a host of wonderful illustrations and photographs. Try getting hold of the BBC video of the same title.

Ekman, Paul. *Emotions Revealed: Recognizing Faces and Feelings to Improve Communication and Emotional Life.* New York: Times Books, 2003.

An expert in the study of human expressions looks at how we experience and interpret emotions and explains how to develop better communication skills by learning more about basic emotions. The Appendix has a test for reading faces.

Hall, Edward T. *The Dance of Life: The Other Dimension of Time.* Gloucester, MA: Peter Smith, 1996.

The author views time as culture and explores how, both consciously and unconsciously, time is formulated, patterned, and used in diverse cultures.

Hall, Stephen S. *Size Matters: How Height Affects the Health, Happiness, and Success of Boys—and the Men They Become.* Boston: Houghton Mifflin, 2006.

This book examines the psychological and social effects of height on males from childhood on. Not all will agree about the advantages of height, but the studies, anecdotes, and arguments are interesting.

Knapp, Mark L., and Judy A. Hall. *Nonverbal Communication in Human Interaction,* 6th ed. Belmont, CA: Wadsworth, 2005.

An excellent resource for the student of nonverbal communication. The approach is research-based and comprehensive. Chapter 4 covers the effects of the environment—including architectural design, color, and structure—on communication.

Martin, Judith N., and Thomas K. Nakayama. *Intercultural Communication in Contexts,* 4th ed. New York: McGraw-Hill, 2007.

The authors of this intercultural text present their subject from three different perspectives. Chapter 7 is devoted to nonverbal codes and cultural space.

Nelson, Audrey, with Susan K. Golant. *You Don't Say: Navigating Nonverbal Communication between the Sexes.* New York: Penguin Group, 2004.

A popular book about misunderstandings between men and women because of gender differences in nonverbal communication. It has many engaging examples and a great deal of practical advice.

Pease, Alan, and Barbara Pease. *The Definitive Book of Body Language.* New York: Bantam Books, 2006.

The revision of a popular book on interpreting body language. The authors include many simple and instructive illustrations and some amusing photographs.

 # For Supplementary Information

Log onto the Online Learning Center at *www.mhhe.com/tubbsmoss11*.

Listening

5

Chapter Objectives

After reading this chapter, you should be able to:

1. Identify the most- to least-used modes of communication.
2. Identify the variables that influence arousal level.
3. Give examples of four different types of listening.
4. Identify four different methods of supporting a speaker's points.
5. Evaluate the various propaganda devices.
6. Differentiate between situations requiring critical listening from empathic listening.
7. Explain how "anticipatory set" can be used to improve listening.
8. Explain four ways in which "spare time" can be used to improve listening.

Most leaders die with their mouths open. Leaders must know how to listen—and the art of listening is more subtle than most people think it is. But first, and just as important, leaders must want to listen.

—**Ronald Heifetz (2005)**

Why do we have difficulty communicating with some people and not others? It is because we are from different planets, figuratively speaking (Walston, 2006). When it comes to communication, some styles are inherent to the individual. To help explain the difference, Walston (2006) makes the analogy to planets and explains that some people are Saturn and some people are Neptune. To understand these people better, you first need to identify which planet they come from. Saturns are logical, process-oriented, and more interested in facts than big ideas. Neptunes are intuitive, nonlinear, and more likely to leap to conclusions. When styles clash, communication is derailed: People may use negative listening practices, such as finishing the other person's sentences, providing an answer without knowing the question, and speaking too much about oneself. In contrast, positive listening practices—being open to other ideas and perspectives, asking questions about the other person's concerns—will open the communication channels.

Walston suggests specific ways to talk to people from the other planets: To talk to a Saturn, be specific, provide documents, use concrete language and step-by-step information. To communicate with a Neptune, emphasize the end result, focus on the big picture, and talk in general terms. When you employ the techniques of positive listening, you will be able to communicate effectively with people from other planets and avoid misunderstandings while building trust and respect.

Mark Twain once said, "The first person in a conversation to draw a breath should be declared the listener!" The world turns away from the person who preaches at us, but turns toward the listener. In probably 95 percent of conversations, when Person A is speaking, Person B, instead of really listening to understand, is busy evaluating or thinking, "What should I say next?" Listening with true empathy is one of the keys to successfully winning others over.

WHY LISTEN?

Deborah Tannen's best-selling book *You Just Don't Understand* (1990) is a riveting explanation of many of the misunderstandings between men and women. In one example she writes,

> Eve had a lump removed from her breast. Shortly after the operation, talking to her sister, she said that she found it upsetting to have been cut into, and that looking at the stitches was distressing because they left a seam that had changed the contour of her breast. Her sister said, "I know. When I had my operation I felt the same way." Eve made the same observation to her friend Karen, who said, "I know. It's like your body has been violated." But when she told her husband Mark how she felt, he said, "You can have plastic surgery to cover up the scar and restore the shape of your breast."

Eve had been comforted by her sister and her friend, but she was not comforted by Mark's comment. Quite the contrary, it upset her more. Not only didn't she hear what she wanted, that he understood her feelings, but far worse, she felt he was asking her to undergo more surgery just when she was telling him how much this operation had upset her. (p. 50)

Tannen writes that Eve had wanted understanding, but Mark had given her advice. He was trying to act as a problem solver, when instead, she wanted him to confirm her feelings and give her support.

Communication between the sexes is just one very important reason why learning to listen more effectively is a valuable skill to learn in life. In fact, we spend more time listening than we spend at any other method of communicating. As early as 1926, it was found that we spend 70 percent of our waking hours communicating—that is, reading, writing, speaking, and listening. When the time spent on these activities was broken down, the results showed that we spend 42 percent of our communicating time listening, 32 percent talking, 15 percent reading, and 11 percent writing (Rankin, 1926).

In a more recent study, Barker and associates (1981) found that college students averaged 53 percent of their waking hours listening (see Figure 5.1). Given students' heavy reading and writing assignments, it seems plausible that the listening percentage for nonstudents is even higher. Research reported by Hargie and associates (1987) confirms the earlier findings. If we spend more time listening than talking, then why is listening a problem?

One study showed that of the four communicative behaviors—speaking, writing, listening, and reading—listening was second only to reading as the least arousing of the four activities. Speaking was the most arousing, then writing, then listening, then reading (Crane et al., 1970). In another study, those who talked most frequently in a small-group discussion were most satisfied with the group discussion, and those who participated least were least satisfied (Bostrom, 1970). It is obvious that, in general, talking is more enjoyable than listening to someone else talk. This is due to a number of factors including gaining social recognition, maintaining a topic of interest to you, and attracting attention to yourself.

Listening is like physical fitness or wearing seat belts: Everybody knows it is desirable but finds it difficult to do on a regular basis. One psychotherapist we know observes that after a session with a patient he is drenched with perspiration and often feels exhausted, and he feels this is primarily the result of intensive listening. It would be hard to listen that intensively through much of every day, but most would agree that when it comes to listening, each of us has room for improvement.

According to Murphy (1992),

American Airlines has achieved over $180 million in cost savings by tuning into ideas and

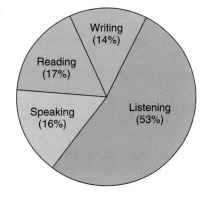

Figure 5.1

Waking Hours

Source: From "An Investigation of Proportional Time Spent in Various Communication Activities by College Students," by Larry Barker, *Journal of Applied Communication Research* 8, 1981, pp. 101–109. Used by permission of the National Communication Association.

suggestions of their employees . . . In January of 1992, over 160 employees who made significant contributions to the IdeAAs in Action program were invited to take the maiden voyage on a new Boeing 757 that was purchased with $50 million of savings generated by employee ideas and suggestions. (pp. 1, 204)

If I listen, I have the advantage; if I speak, others will have it.
—**Arabic saying (Acuff, 1993, p. 96)**

IMPORTANCE OF LISTENING

Listening is an art and takes on many forms in which human beings translate sounds into meaning. We have the ability to listen to sounds and patterns and translate their meaning through language. In 1816, Rene Laennec invented the stethoscope to *listen* to his patient's hearts in order to determine their ailment and to avoid the embarrassment of having to put his ear to the chests of his female patients. For almost two centuries, doctors have been relying on their ability to listen to and translate patterns that they hear with stethoscopes into medical terminology. There is a current belief that doctors are now neglecting the art of listening and prematurely relying on echocardiograms and other complex instruments to determine irregularities of the heart when the human ability to listen can reveal many complicated diagnoses (Blanchard, 2004, p. C.1).

Listening behaviors can also determine social and professional success. Your listening skills could make the difference between getting a job and being passed over for another candidate. Rowh (2006) gives the example of a job applicant who was asked a question in an interview and answered with a response that had nothing to do with the question. This caused the interviewer to suspect that the individual was not up to her standards; hence, she hired another candidate. The candidate likely thought he had wonderful listening skills and would never have imagined that he would lose an opportunity based on listening. Rowh points out that this is why listening skills are often overlooked: We think we already know how to do it and that we do it well. The reality is often the opposite.

Think of the impression you get of a person who makes what he thinks is an original comment but is merely repeating what was uttered only moments before by another in the group. The importance of listening is shown imaginatively in the movie *What Women Want* (2000). Mel Gibson's character is a chauvinist advertising executive in a Chicago agency, who doesn't have a clue as to what women think and what they want. In an unusual accident, he slips in a bathtub and accidentally shocks himself. After the incident, he finds that he has acquired the ability to read women's minds, which makes him not only a more creative advertiser, but much more popular with women.

McCormack (1984, p. 9) tells the story of how Pepsi-Cola had tried to get Burger King to use their product and had assumed that Burger King would never dream of dropping Coca-Cola. After approaching Burger King with a new product strategy concept that linked Pepsi and Burger King, the Pepsi people were told, "We've been trying to tell you that for months. I'm glad someone finally listened."

How are your listening skills? Julie Fuimano, personal career coach, author, and motivational speaker for *NurturingYourSuccess.com* (2004), compiled a set of self-assessment questions to measure your listening skills. The following list is an adaptation of Fuimano's list. A "yes" answer to any of these questions means that you can improve your listening skills. How many questions did you answer yes to? What will you do to improve these areas?

- Do you interrupt or jump in before another person finishes his or her thought?

- Do you formulate a reply in your head while the person is still speaking only later to find out that you missed an essential part of the message?

- Do you finish other people's sentences for them and find that you are often incorrect?

- Are you fully present or are you thinking about other things going on in your life while you are listening to someone?

- Are you focused on having an answer rather than listening for the needs of the other person?

- At work, do you try to read e-mail and type on the computer while listening to another person who is either in person or on the phone?

A listening study was conducted to test the hypotheses of several previous studies related to listening skills and how it pertains to academic advising (Nadler and Simerly, 2006). The study looked at a student's level of trust generated by the perception that the advisor was listening as well as how that ultimately leads to satisfaction and commitment with the advisor. The study was conducted through surveys with 438 students at a large southeastern U.S. university. The survey results demonstrated strong correlations between listening and perceived benevolence, listening and competence, listening and dependability/reliability, listening and likeability, and listening and honesty. Overall, the study provided further credibility to the belief that listening is an effective communication tool.

Management has a tendency to shut themselves off from their employees, and in doing so, they can miss out on crucial information or suffer from misinformation being broadcast throughout the organization. One simple answer to this issue is getting out of your office and connecting with the people in the organization (Dulye, 2006). In order to effectively communicate and start listening, you have to get up from behind that desk and computer and leave your cell phone, BlackBerry, and any other distractions behind. In most organizations, the manager is the main conduit of information; however, too often the choice of communication is formal, such as presentations and documents. These kinds of communication do not convey to employees that the manager is listening to them, but informal communication can. Informal communication conducted by walking around and engaging in conversations and really listening to what people are saying can achieve several goals at once. For example, it leads to mutual trust between management and employees, it garners meaningful feedback, and it contributes to a consistent message from management about what is happening in the organization. If you ever find yourself in a management position and you haven't tried walking around, get up, get out of your office, and start listening to what people have to say!

In Chapter 1 we presented a communication model, and we also discussed the importance of active participation by the parties involved in the communication event. For the communicative cycle to be complete, the party receiving a message must respond accordingly. Without effective listening, the appropriateness of a receiver's response is severely diminished. Both from a practical and from a theoretical standpoint, then, effective listening becomes a vital element in human communication.

WHAT IS MEANT BY LISTENING?

One reason for misconceptions about "listening" stems from the ambiguity of the term. Listening is actually a complex process involving four elements: (1) hearing, (2) attention, (3) understanding, and (4) remembering. Thus, a suitable definition of listening would be "the selective process of attending to, hearing, understanding, and remembering aural symbols."

Hearing

On October 8, 2001, radio commentator Rush Limbaugh revealed that he had lost virtually all of his hearing within the previous few months. The prognosis was not good; however, doctors successfully placed a cochlear implant and restored about 70 percent of his hearing electronically. Without this procedure, Limbaugh would have had to give up his $30 million a year job in radio through which he reaches some 20 million listeners a day through nearly 600 stations (*www.msnbc.msn.com/id/3920488*).

The first element in the listening process is hearing, which is the automatic physiological process of receiving aural stimuli. At this stage, a defect in a person's physical hearing apparatus may cause difficulty in the listening process. Human speech frequencies range from 125 to 8,000 cycles per second; most words fall between 1,000 and 7,500 cycles per second, which is the critical range of auditory ability (Brooks, 1981, p. 82).

Typically, sound waves are received by the ear and stimulate neurological impulses to the brain. However, any physical defect that interrupts this normal chain of events can result in a hearing difficulty. Research indicates that very loud sound (measured in decibels) can and does produce both temporary and permanent hearing losses. For example, excessively loud rock music has been found to produce hearing losses in listeners.

The human ear can cope with 55 to 85 decibels. However, rock concerts can pose a problem because the noise level can reach as high as 100 decibels (the level of a plane taking off). Government regulations are now in effect to ensure that workers are protected from hearing losses that might otherwise result from loud industrial noises. For the most part, if we assume that our hearing apparatus is functioning properly, problems in listening do not typically stem from physical problems in hearing.

Second, we place these sounds in a meaningful order or sequence so that they may be recognized as words. Third, we recognize words in a pattern that constitutes a language, which then helps to convey the message from the communicator to us.

Another factor in hearing is the speaker's rate. The average speaker's rate is between 100 and 150 words per minute. However, the research on compressed speech shows that most of us are able to comprehend rates up to 400 to 500 words per minute (Goss, 1982, p. 91).

Although the ability to process information four times faster than the average person speaks would seem to be an advantage, it turns out that it is instead a part of the problem in that three-fourths of our listening is "spare time." This means that we are able to comprehend what we hear much more quickly than a speaker is able to articulate his or her thoughts; thus, we may get bored and begin to daydream. This fact tends to account for the findings that show speaking to be more interesting than listening. Later in this chapter we will look at ways of using our "spare time" to improve our listening ability.

Attention

Malone (1998) has identified **concentration** as one of the most important aspects of listening. Concentration is really just *paying close attention.*

Business leaders who keep their mouths shut and their ears open have a better chance of being heard, especially when they learn to use silence as a listening tool (Moore, 2005). Kenny Moore, a former monastic priest turned businessman, uses his experience of 15 years in a monastery to demonstrate how silence in the corporate setting is a valuable tool that can be used to communicate with fellow employees. Now an executive at KeySpan Corporation, Moore and a colleague set up group meetings with managers to get their input regarding departmental goals. Instead of doing a lot of talking at these meetings, Moore and the other executive leaders spent a lot of time just listening to the other managers talk to each other. They found that executives don't have as much credibility among the employees and are often not listened to because they are seen as paid envoys of the corporation. However, employees do lend credibility to their co-workers, who they perceive as more sincere. In the end, Moore believes that executives ultimately gain more insightful information from those working for them by saying less and listening more. He suggests that as an executive, you may want to consider silence to be the most important thing you contribute to these conversations—and you may be surprised by the results.

Attending to stimuli in our environment is like focusing our conscious awareness on certain specific stimuli. In Chapter 2, we pointed out that our sensory receptors are constantly bombarded with so many stimuli that we cannot possibly respond to all of them at once. Specific cells in our nervous system (inhibitory neurons) serve to filter out some of these incoming sensations, keeping them from our conscious awareness. One writer stated that, were it not for these inhibitory neurons, we would experience sensations similar to an epileptic seizure every time we opened our eyes (Kern, 1971, p. 48). In spite of these neurological limitations, we still are not able to focus on a single event for more than just a few seconds at a time because of the other stimuli usually competing for our attention.

In today's fast-paced world of meetings and growing responsibilities, people more often find themselves driven to distraction by multitasking (Schmid, 2007). The reality is that the accepted and expected conduct is for people to be doing many things at once. For example, it is no longer considered rude for a person at a meeting to be typing e-mails on a BlackBerry under the table while listening to someone speak. The reason for this is that multitasking is considered a point of pride and that the more you can do at a time, the more productive you are perceived to be. However, this all comes at the cost of not being able to focus upon and really listen to others. It is nearly impossible to listen to someone when you are doing something else at the same time. Schmid's (2007) message is to convince us that we need to "uni-task" and not multitask. When we are listening to someone, it should be our only task—not typing an e-mail or doing some other chore that will distract our senses from what they should really be doing.

The phenomenon whereby we attend to certain stimuli while filtering out others is referred to as **selective attention.** In order to better understand this phenomenon, take out a piece of paper and a pen or pencil. Then, in a moment, stop reading and listen to the sounds around you. Now make a list of these sounds. How many sounds did you write down? Were you aware of them while you were reading? Can you now focus on them or ignore them at will? Probably not, but perhaps you can better understand what we mean when we say that numerous stimuli compete for our attention most of the time. In fact, students who want to improve their study habits are often told to find a place that has the fewest distractions that could promote daydreaming (e.g., pictures of your girlfriend or boyfriend, windows, chairs facing doorways where people walk by, posters). All of these stimuli are usually more pleasant to attend to than the study materials at hand.

A part of this selective attention process that has been experimentally studied is called the "cocktail party problem" (Bostrom, 1988)—namely, how do you listen to one voice when more than one person is speaking at the same time? The next time you are in such a situation, try to focus on one voice at a time. Numerous studies have shown that a person will normally do this, rather than flitting attention from one person's voice to another (Broadbent, 1958). This is probably because we have a greater interest in a continuous message than in several interrupted messages. Another finding is that we are able to sort out a single voice much easier when it comes in only one ear while a competing message is coming in the other ear than if both messages are heard by the same ear. Research using headphones and tape-recorded messages indicates that selective attention from "*dichotic* presentation (when one message is presented to one ear, another to the other) was markedly superior to *monaural* presentation (where both messages were presented to the same ear)" (Moray, 1969, p. 17). The author concludes that "it is clear that a listener is able to exercise considerable voluntary control over what he will hear" (p. 88).

An issue related to attention is the concept of threshold, which is defined as the minimum level of stimulus intensity that enables us to pay attention. Think of surround sound at the movies and how certain sounds are strategically placed and pitched to get your attention over other noises occurring in the movie. These sounds are just at your auditory threshold. The important thing to remember is that our attention thresholds vary depending on several things, including our own motivational state. Later in this chapter we will show how this fact relates to improving our listening behaviors.

One final element that affects attention is a person's **arousal level.** Arousal level is directly related to the thresholds we have for listening. Obviously, we do not listen well when we are asleep. Nor do we listen well when we are drowsy. General alertness, then, affects our ability to attend to aural stimuli and subsequently to listen more effectively. Not only is general arousal important, but specific arousal also has a bearing on our listening behavior. A mother may sleep through a loud noise only to awake at the cry of a small baby. A man in a noisy restaurant may "perk his ears up" when he hears his name paged, and a child alone in a house after watching a spooky movie on TV may hear many more creaks and sounds than she normally would. Our specific state of arousal, then, to some extent determines our threshold for paying attention to auditory stimuli.

We are bombarded every day by a multitude of external messages through the television, telephone, radio, and Internet, to name only a few of the channels. The word "advertise" comes from a Latin root word meaning "to pay attention." These messages compete for our attention by taking advantage of our selective attention, thresholds, and arousal levels. These messages leave little time for us to listen to other people. This concept of paying close attention will also be related to some advice on improving your listening later in this chapter.

Understanding

The third and most complicated element in listening is understanding, also referred to as auditing. Understanding usually refers to the process whereby we assign a meaning to the words we hear that closely corresponds to the meaning intended by the person sending the message. This process was discussed in Chapter 1.

Since the process of understanding by definition requires us to associate a message with our past experiences, we also tend to accept or reject (i.e., evaluate) the message as we are trying to understand it. The famous psychologist Dr. Carl Rogers has written that "the major barrier to mutual interpersonal communication is our very natural tendency to judge, to evaluate, to approve or disapprove, the statement of the other person, or the group" (1961, p. 330). Losoncy (1998) refers to this as using sensitive-listening skills. He writes that this occurs "when you listen to accept another person's point of view without the obstruction of your own need to judge, moralize, advise, or appear to 'know it all' " (p. 27). This is sometimes called "aerobic" listening, since it is hard work!

If we can focus more of our listening effort on trying to understand the meaning that the speaker is intending to convey, temporarily withholding our tendency to judge or evaluate that message, we should considerably improve our ability to listen more effectively.

There has often been a disconnect between managers and employees when it comes to how the employee perceives the listening skills of the manager. One study showed that a quarter of those surveyed believed that their managers did not consider their views and act without consulting them (Beagrie, 2005). This leads employees to believe that their managers are not really listening when they speak to them. To combat this, managers must endeavor to listen meaningfully, which is an overall description of a number of different techniques you can utilize to listen more effectively to others. Suggestions for meaningful listening include finding a place to talk where there are no distractions and focusing on the person talking to you. You should not engage in other activities (such as checking e-mail) while you are conversing. Furthermore, you should maintain eye contact with the other individual, refrain from interrupting or finishing his or her sentences, and pay close attention to body language. Utilizing these techniques, especially in the manager/employee relationship, will result in positive perceptions among employees that they are being listened to and acknowledged in the workplace.

Interpreting a message is literally giving it meaning. It is based on (at the least) understanding the grammar of the language, recognizing and understanding the source's intent (sarcastic, joking, serious), understanding the implications of the situation (including the physical environment, the relationship shared with the other person, and the climate of the encounter), and sharing assumptions about the world and how it operates (what is and is not realistic).

Remembering

Most tests of listening to some extent test how much we remember of what we heard and understood. **Remembering** is *the storing of information for later retrieval.* If a person gives you directions to a particular place and you understand them but forget the directions before you can write them down, then your listening was not as useful as it might have been.

There are two types of memory—short-term memory (STM) and long-term memory (LTM). Short-term memory is what allows us to remember a telephone number long enough to dial it but not well enough to recall it even five minutes later. Short-term memory is said to be able to handle about five items of information at one time. You can recognize this limitation by trying to remember several names when you are introduced to a large group at a social gathering.

Verbal material stored in STM appears to be encoded by the sound of the material rather than the sight. For example, if we see the letter Q but later mistakenly recall that letter, we are more likely to remember it as a U (which sounds similar to Q) than as an O (which looks more like a Q). Thus, the information coding and retrieval mechanism of the brain appears to be in part based on the sound of a word, probably as a result of the way we learn the names for things.

Long-term memory stores those items of information that we usually think of as being "committed" to memory (e.g., our hometown, our parents' first names). Basically the difference between STM and LTM is the amount of repetition and rehearsing that occurs with an individual item of information and the ease with which the item fits into already stored information. Active listening is a technique for rehearsing material in the STM. It helps you remember the material longer. Thus, active listening is much like programmed learning, which assumes that learning is most effective when learners periodically test themselves on how much they are remembering, then review what they have learned.

Research summarized by Barker (1971) indicates that immediately after we hear something we remember only half of it. Eight hours later we remember only 35 percent, and two months later we remember 25 percent. Obviously, this assumes we were paying attention in the first place, and that the message was brief and relatively uncomplicated. The "bottom line" with respect to listening is the residual message, the kernel the listener remembers.

In this section, we have looked at the four interrelated elements that constitute listening. They were (1) hearing; (2) attention; (3) understanding, or auditing; and (4) remembering. In the next section, we will discuss different types of listening.

TYPES OF LISTENING

If you were to list some of the typical reasons you listen to others, what would they be? Probably any list would include at least four types of listening. These four are not mutually exclusive or exhaustive but merely representative.

Pleasurable Listening

The first type of listening would be **pleasurable listening.** Children often wonder how adults can just talk to each other for hours at social gatherings. As we grow out of childhood, we become more oriented toward *talking as a means of socializing* and less oriented toward acting (e.g., playing games) as a means of socializing. Obviously, some types of listening experiences must be pleasurable or enjoyable. Pleasurable listening might also include movies, plays, television, music, and many other forms of entertainment. Although we may benefit intellectually or professionally from this type of listening, these gains are by-products and are not the main reason for engaging in pleasurable listening (Nadig, 2004).

Discriminative Listening

A second type of listening is **discriminative listening.** This is a more serious type of listening and *is primarily used for understanding and remembering* (as discussed in the previous section). Discriminative listening would include most of the serious listening situations in which we find ourselves—attending in the classroom, listening on the job, listening to instructions, and many others. As a general rule of thumb, the more important the situation (e.g., listening to directions on how to react in an emergency situation), the more important it is to be able to employ this type of listening.

Critical Listening

The third type of listening is **critical listening,** which *is usually needed when we suspect that we may be listening to a biased source of information and when we need to make a choice about something.* Imagine that you are trying to select a new stereo from several competing models. You would have to rely on your critical listening skills when deciphering the opinions of potentially biased salespersons, your friends, and anyone else trying to help you out in your decision. You must also rely on your own determination of which stereo actually sounds better to you during trials. Anthony Armstrong (2004) offers a newsletter on critical listening in stereo selection. He defines critical listening as "the practice and skill of evaluating the quality of audio equipment by careful listening" and deems it key to evaluating different stereos.

Whether you are evaluating stereos, separating opinion from fact, or ruling out potential bias in messages that you receive, critical listening is essential. Part of developing critical listening skills is learning to identify the techniques of persuasion being used.

The means of developing a point in a discussion are often called methods of support or materials of support. There are at least four specific methods of support, including (1) analogy, (2) example, (3) statistics, and (4) testimony or quotation.

Analogy

An **analogy** may be the most concise and graphic way to get a complex idea or a point across. In a discussion of the increasing arrests of young people on drug charges, one student commented: "Relaxing the law would indeed reduce the number of arrests, but it would be like loosening your tie to relieve sweating. It is only a temporary measure that does nothing to eliminate the problem causing the arrests." As it stands, this analogy effectively conveyed the student's position. Suppose, however, that she had gone on to argue that laws, like ties and other articles of clothing, are unnatural constraints that should be discarded. She would then have been on very shaky ground.

An analogy *draws parallels between two things or situations,* but as we have observed, it is only a partial comparison. If the objects of comparison are dissimilar enough to invalidate the attempt to juxtapose them, the analogy is a poor one. In listening critically, we must first determine the appropriateness of the speaker's analogy to the subject at hand and then the limits of its use. For example, in one debate a speaker compared a government policy to putting a new muffler on a defective car. "It only makes the car sound better," he commented. "It doesn't solve the problem." His opponent, responding to what he felt was a poor analogy, commented, "Without the new muffler, the car's occupants would be asphyxiated in a matter of minutes. So the new policy is needed immediately."

The test for the critical listener is to determine how accurate or reasonable the comparison is. Analogies are metaphorical ways of explaining ideas, and at some point the analogy breaks down. In other words, the situations usually involve some differences that are important enough to invalidate the comparison being made.

However, analogies may be a very useful and legitimate method to bring about understanding of an idea.

Listeners often recall the examples or analogies used by the speaker and miss the point the speaker intends to illustrate. In analyzing all materials of support, it is critical first to identify the speaker's point and then to evaluate the method of support used to prove it. Remember that materials of support do not in themselves constitute an argument.

Example

The second *method of supporting an idea* is using an **example.** We have used examples throughout this book to illustrate many of the concepts we are trying to convey. Examples may be very brief specific instances, or they may be quite extended. Examples usually make meaning much clearer for the listener. However, examples, like analogies, can be misused. The critical listener will try to determine if the example being used is actually representative of the point that the communicator is trying to make. In a propaganda device called the **hasty generalization,** one or two examples are cited to prove a point. When using this propaganda device, *the speaker jumps to a conclusion on the basis of very limited evidence.* It is the receiver who must decide, first, whether an example is appropriate to a speaker's point and, second, whether it is being used in lieu of an argument. Consider this example from a student discussion: "My grandparents have lots of money, so I don't think old people need Medicare benefits." Most of us tend to generalize from our own personal experiences (or lifelong sets of examples). However, those experiences are often misleading. Examples can be used or abused; the critical listener must make subjective judgments to detect the difference.

Statistics

Statistics *are numerical methods of describing events or ideas.* Statistics can be rather difficult for listeners to understand, but when used in conjunction with other methods of support, they can help to clarify points considerably. In a discussion of teenage marriages, a person may use an example of a couple who had an unsuccessful marriage, then go on to cite that the divorce rate for couples who marry in their teens is double that of older married couples, and that even the divorce rate of older couples is fairly high. Here statistics are used to show that the conclusion drawn from the example is in fact valid and not a hasty generalization.

Statistics can also be abused, however. Advertisements are often misleading when they state, "Skyhighs now relieve pain twice as fast." The assumption is that they act twice as fast as some competitor's product. But perhaps they only relieve pain twice as fast as they did two years ago and indeed take effect no faster than any of the competing products. We don't know. We would have to ask, "Twice as fast as what?" What are the terms of the comparison? This use of statistics, like the propaganda devices of card stacking or half-truths, is misleading in that it presents a biased or distorted view of the truth.

Another propaganda device that makes use of statistics is the **bandwagon appeal.** One student survey of college cheating showed that certain percentages of students cheat on exams. Using statistics from this survey, a speaker could claim that cheating is acceptable since other people do it too. Statistics, then, can be used properly or improperly depending on the user and the situation. This is illustrated by the old adage "Statistics don't lie, but liars may use statistics."

The critical listener must attempt to determine if the speaker clearly reveals and defines what unit of measure is being used in the statistics and what is being compared (e.g., is a product being compared to itself or to its competitor?).

Testimony or Quotations

The fourth method of supporting an idea is through the use of **testimony or quotations.** Ideas often are more acceptable to listeners if they think the ideas are accepted by others, especially if those others are either prestigious or expert. For example, in arguing the effects of marijuana, a speaker might use quotations from medical authorities to show that her point or position is supported by expert opinion. Lawyers in the courtroom frequently use this technique to establish the probable validity of their cases. Consider, for example, this courtroom comment:

> Ladies and gentlemen of the jury, the coroner's report showed that the time of death was between midnight and six a.m. on the night of May 16th. We have established that my client was nowhere near the scene of the crime on the night of the 16th. Therefore, my client could not have committed the murder.

In this case, the coroner's expert testimony helps prove the innocence of the client.

In many informal conversations, we cite trusted or respected others who support a given point as a means of making our point more believable. However, testimony and quotations, like other methods of support, can be misused. Often people who are expert in one field have strong opinions in fields where they have little or no expertise. The critical listener may catch this and realize that the testimonials used are not valid. Rev. Jerry Falwell's opinions on religion, for example, would probably be acceptable as expert authority; his opinions on apartheid, however, would not have the same validity.

The propaganda device of **plain folks** represents another misuse of testimony. Middle-aged professors who dress like their students in an attempt to identify with their listeners often look ridiculous. Politicians who try to overidentify with their constituents (by milking cows or wearing ten-gallon hats) may be using the plain folks approach.

Probably the most crucial point to remember about critical listening is that you must first listen and be able to identify the point the speaker is trying to make, then listen for and evaluate the method of support the speaker uses to prove that point. So often in conversations listeners will remember the example a speaker uses and miss the point that the example was supposed to illustrate.

Empathic Listening

The final type of listening is **empathic listening.** As the term suggests, *the listener tries to demonstrate empathy for the speaker.* "When was the last time you paid attention to someone? I mean really gave your complete and undivided attention to another person?" In 2003, Lawrence Cohen, practicing licensed psychologist and writer, asked his *Boston Globe* readers this question. Cohen believes that very few of us are "really good" at listening and that we exercise bad habits such as filling in the gaps with our own beliefs and neglecting the "deeper feelings" of the person that we are listening too (p. H5). In essence, we fail to *empathize* with others as we listen to them. All of us like to feel that a person is being sympathetic during times of difficulty. In fact, in some cities "Dial a Friend" or "warm lines" have been established for just such a purpose. Stephen Covey, in his best-selling book *The 7 Habits of Highly Effective People* (1990), offers the following advice:

> "Seek first to understand" involves a very deep shift in paradigm. We typically seek first to be understood. Most people do not listen with the intent to understand; they listen with the intent to reply . . . When I say empathic listening, I mean listening with intent to understand. I mean seeking first to understand, to really understand. (pp. 239–240)

Empathic listening can also be described as listening "between the lines." When we listen between the lines we heighten our awareness and interpersonal sensitivity to the entire message a person may be trying to communicate.

The very culture of an organization in its approach toward listening can reveal a great deal about communication problems that they may be facing. The leaders of an organization have a great deal of say in how the culture of an organization is created and thus they have to be aware of the need for fostering deep inquiry and listening (Walters, 2005). Deep inquiry means that you endeavor to ask the right questions at the right time in order to get the whole picture of a situation. Too often, we nod our heads as if we agree with what is being said to us, but in reality we are only skimming the surface of the message. Deep inquiry involves multiple probing questions designed to complete the information picture. In conjunction with deep inquiry, deep listening is utilized, which dictates that you listen below the surface into what is truly being said. Taken together, deep inquiry and deep listening remind us that there is more to communication than what is obviously apparent. One must go deeper and delve into the multiple layers of communication to truly foster a proper culture of listening in an organization. The example starts at the top with key leaders, but from there, becomes the responsibility of everyone to maintain.

A good definition of this approach to listening is illustrated by the following point of view. "Empathy is perception and communication by resonance, by identification, by experiencing in ourselves some reflection of the emotional tone that is being experienced by the other person . . . Empathy continues throughout life as the basic mode of significant communication between adults" (Pearce and Newton, 1963, p. 52).

"Empathy" comes from the word *einfühlung* used by German psychologists; it literally means "feeling into." One friend who was having a problem with his girlfriend talked for over an hour without our saying much more than that we knew how he felt and we sincerely hoped he could work things out. By the end of the hour he had seen a way to resolve the difficulty and left saying, "Thanks so much for helping me figure this thing out!" We really had been concerned, and we really had listened, but we hadn't offered any suggestions on how to solve the problem. Yet our friend needed someone to talk to, and this opportunity to share his problem with concerned listeners helped him gain a new attitude toward the situation. Empathic listening serves as a reward or encouragement to the speaker. It communicates your caring and acceptance and reaffirms the person's sense of worth. This style of listening seems to be most important in terms of strengthening or improving a positive interpersonal relationship.

Empathic listening is often an important part of any client-counselor relationship, such as that between the patient and the psychotherapist. Theodore Reik (1948), a psychoanalyst, coined the phrase "listening with the third ear" to symbolize this type of listening. Actually, it refers to being as sensitive to visual cues as to vocal cues, but it represents another way of thinking about this style of listening. He describes listening with the third ear in this manner:

> The analyst hears not only what is in the words; he hears also what the words do not say . . . In psychoanalysis . . . what is spoken is not the most important thing. It appears to us more important to recognize what speech conceals and what silence reveals. (p. 125)

The way people sit, the way they dress, their eye movements and other visual cues are integral to the spoken word. In the process of carefully listening to someone, you must pay attention to these implicit messages, which may reveal subtle nuances that the spoken word could not. Useful suggestions for improving the listening power of your third ear involve taking a bird's eye view of the situation, being with the action, not in it; refraining from focusing on your own agenda; and observing everyone in the group instead of focusing on individuals (Guttman, 2005).

Take another example of an incident that occurred in 2003 when the Chicago Cubs were five outs away from advancing to the World Series for the first time since 1945. A foul ball was hit and a fan in the stands reached for it, which then prevented Cubs player Moises Alou from making the catch. Cub fans gave full blame to the interfering fan, Steve Bartman, for the loss of the series and a chance at the World Series. Bartman was given a police escort from the stands and was literally afraid to show his face in public due to threats he received. However, later Bartman gave a statement: "To Moises Alou, the Chicago Cubs organization, Ron Santo, Ernie Banks, and Cub fans everywhere, I am so truly sorry from the bottom of this Cub fan's broken heart" (Fox News Channel, 2003). After this statement, many fellow Cubs fans were more empathic and realized they would probably have done the same thing in the same situation.

One difficulty with trying to practice empathic listening is that it often requires the opposite frame of mind from that required for critical listening. Empathic listening implies a willingness not to judge, evaluate, or criticize but rather to be an accepting, permissive, and understanding listener. Thus, what might be the proper way to improve listening in one context may be the very opposite of what is required to be a good listener in another context. The difficult task for the listener is to determine which skills are most important in which situations.

Two psychologists from Harvard University (Athos and Gabarro, 1978) offer some excellent guidelines on how to use empathic listening (or what they refer to as the "reflective response"):

> At the most general level, we can describe reflective responses by several simple characteristics:
>
> - A greater emphasis on listening than on talking.
> - Responding to that which is personal rather than abstract.
> - Following another in his exploration rather than leading him into areas we think he should be exploring.
> - Clarifying what the other person has said about his own thoughts and feelings rather than asking questions or telling him what we believe he should be thinking, seeing, or feeling.
> - Responding to the feelings implicit in what the other has said rather than the assumptions or "content" that he has talked about.
> - Trying to get into the other person's inner frame of reference rather than listening and responding from our own frame of reference.
> - Responding with empathic understanding and acceptance rather than with disconcern, distanced objectivity, or overidentification (i.e., internalizing his problem so that it also becomes our own). (p. 417)

Although these brief generalizations may appear to suggest that reflection requires passive and generally inactive behavior on the part of the person who is trying to help or understand, quite the opposite is true. The reflective technique requires very careful and focused listening. It also requires a high degree of selectivity in choosing what to respond to in what the person has said. (Athos and Gabarro, 1978; see also Pearce, 1991.)

HOW TO IMPROVE LISTENING

Most of the experts agree that the first step to becoming a better listener is to develop an awareness of the problem. We have tried to accomplish that objective thus far in the chapter. The second step to improvement is to develop the desire or motivation to behave differently. The third step is to change, or activate new behaviors.

Listen Effectively

It is not uncommon in the business environment to find ourselves in situations where negotiation skills are necessary. In such circumstances, listening skills can be very useful. There are five basic rules you can utilize if you would like to improve your negotiating listening skills, all of which begin with R so they are easy to remember (Munoz, 2006). The first is to *Relinquish* old habits. This means consciously trying to avoid our learned bad habits, like multitasking when listening, and practice good habits, like remembering to wait for the other side to finish before speaking. The next R is *Reviewing* and setting aside your preconceived assumptions. When you are negotiating with another person or party, do not automatically assume you know what side they will take; doing so will prevent you from listening effectively. Following with the next R, we come to *Respect*. It does not matter who is across the table from you in a negotiation, you still must show them an appropriate amount of respect. Showing respect naturally leads to better listening skills in the other party. Next, you must *Reflect* during the negotiations to put the message from the other person in a context in which you can think clearly about its meaning. Reflecting involves repeating in your own words what the other person has said to you in order to ensure that you are interpreting the message correctly. Taking this extra step can avoid misunderstandings between the parties. The final R is *Request clarification*. Similar to reflecting, requesting clarification can lead to a better understanding of the situation at hand. It is necessary in a negotiation to ask the question "why" frequently and listen carefully to the responses. Crucial information that might not otherwise have been revealed is sometimes brought to the table simply by asking questions. Taken together, the Five R's can be an easily remembered set of tips that will come in handy during your next experience in negotiations.

Ineffective listening may take any of the forms described below:

Hearing problems is the general term that covers *any of the myriad problems that can decrease or eliminate the range of sounds that can be heard*. This is especially important when you consider that hearing is the first step in the listening process. Without adequate hearing, there can be no listening whatsoever.

Overload is the problem associated with *hearing too much, having to attend to too many stimuli*. The result can be stress, withdrawal, or not being able to focus attention.

Rapid thought goes along with the section on using your "spare time." The problem is that the time is "wasted" as the listener allows his or her mind to wander.

Noise is the general term used to describe anything that interferes with the communication process. With respect to listening, we can identify noise connected with the physical environment, the channel, and the psychological environment (the matters demanding attention that are on the listener's mind).

Inappropriate approaches to listening is the general category for a host of inappropriate listening behaviors. The most inappropriate is "ambush listening." This is listening for the little piece of information that can be used as the basis for an attack on the speaker. "Insensitive listening" is accepting the speaker's words at face value and not taking into account all the things that affect meaning. "Dan Ayckroyd listening" is listening only for the facts. "Touchy-feely listening" is listening only for the emotions. "Pseudolistening" is pretending to listen (which many of us were taught—to be polite and act as if we are paying attention even if we aren't).

Pay Attention

Before we can react appropriately to what a person says, we must pay attention to it. Unfortunately, most people tend to think they are better at this than they really are. William Keefe (1976) writes:

> Not all in this situation see themselves for what they are. Many believe themselves to be good listeners. But they cannot back up their laudatory self-analysis. The Opinion Research Corporation of Princeton, New Jersey, carried out a survey in four large companies. The findings showed that 77 percent of the supervisors interviewed felt themselves to be good listeners. Other data (from their subordinates) gave them the lie. (p. 14)

Earlier in this chapter we stated that the threshold for listening could be improved (lowered to detect more stimuli) by changes in a person's motivation. Thus, a determined effort to pay attention has been found to improve a person's listening considerably.

In addition, those who are otherwise good speakers may not be good listeners. Brilhart (1965) showed that there is no necessary correlation between skill as a speaker and skill as a listener. In fact, several of her findings suggested that good speakers were relatively poor listeners (i.e., there were negative correlations). Thus, if you feel yourself to be a relatively effective speaker, you are even more likely to need listening improvement.

Perhaps you are wondering if it is ever possible to improve a person's listening ability. Numerous studies indicate that dramatic improvements are possible even with minimal training (Keller, 1960).

Listen for Main Points or Ideas

A second way to improve your listening is to maintain your motivation to pay attention by listening for the specific main ideas in a message. Earlier in this chapter, we discussed the role that attention plays in listening. Numerous experimental studies indicate that simply paying attention is one of the most important ways of improving your listening.

Keller (1960) describes the techniques this way:

> *Anticipatory set* is defined as the ability to say to oneself as he listens, "I imagine that what the speaker is trying to say is . . . ." This anticipation and comparing of

expectation with outcome may cause the listener to pay attention in order to see if he is right. (p. 30)

Use Your Spare Time

One of the reasons that paying attention seems to be such a problem for listeners is that the human brain can process information much faster than a person can talk. Research has been conducted in the area of time-compressed speech in which a tape-recorded message is electronically speeded up without changing the pitch level (unless pitch is controlled, the recording begins to sound like a chipmunk as the speed is increased). Depending on the message's complexity, organization, and such, we can understand information relatively well, even up to a rate of 400 to 500 words per minute. The average speaking rate, however, is only 125 to 150 words per minute (Goss, 1982). As a consequence, our minds are seldom fully occupied while listening, and we have a tendency to daydream.

Several listening experts have suggested that this "spare time" (while our mind is working faster than the speaker's rate of speech) may be used to do some extra thinking about what the speaker is trying to say. This may be a bit tricky and seems more suitable for an audience member or group member than for a participant in a two-person conversation.

Ralph Nichols (1957), the nation's respected authority on listening, suggests that you first anticipate the speaker's next point. From the context of his or her past remarks, you may be able to predict the next point in advance (sometimes you may be surprised). Second, mentally rehearse or review the points that the speaker has already covered. As we stated earlier, this rehearsal is the key factor in transferring information from short-term memory (STM) to long-term memory (LTM). Third, use the tests of critical thinking discussed earlier in this chapter. Listen for the validity and quality of the analogies, examples, statistics, and testimonials the speaker uses. Fourth, listen "between the lines" for what the speaker doesn't say but may be communicating nonverbally through tone of voice or even with visual cues. As we pointed out in Chapter 4, these cues may carry as much or more meaning than the verbal messages. The spare time that is available to the listener can be used for daydreaming and faulty listening, or it can be used more profitably to improve understanding and retention of a speaker's message.

Aerobic Listening

According to *The Wall Street Journal,* the resignation some time ago of Coca-Cola's CEO, Doug Ivestor, was because the board members felt that he simply wasn't listening to them. Why is it that we so often hear of poor listening as a problem? It is primarily due to a lack of motivation. It is like maintaining the proper weight. We all know that we should, it just takes more motivation and discipline than most of us can muster. However, it may also be due to lack of the appropriate skills. So, if you would like to work on improving your listening, here are four skills that may be helpful. Think of the acronym *CARE.*

*C*oncentrate. We need to maximize the amount and accuracy of information we receive. Our brains can process up to 600 words per minute, but the average person speaks at about 125 to 150 words per minute. The natural result is that most of us let our attention wander. As a result, we often lose out on key information. One of the biggest drawbacks to being in a leadership position is that you can't keep up with all the relevant information in your organization. There is at once too much information and not enough of the right information. The key is to really pay attention. At Coke, Ivestor was told repeatedly that he was making some major errors, but he refused to pay attention to the feedback. *Fortune* magazine reports that one board member, Don Keough, sent him a six-page letter reiterating constructive suggestions, given orally, on how Ivestor could improve his situation. The response was a one-line reply thanking him for his input. It is clear that the advice wasn't followed.

*A*cknowledge. The second skill is to actively acknowledge that you understand what the person is saying. Find a quiet place with minimal distractions. Also, sit down while listening. Give the person your undivided attention, if only for a few minutes. Look the person in the eye. Ask questions, paraphrase and restate what he or she is saying. Test to see if you really have understood the message. One of your authors once had a job interview in which the interviewer sat with his back to us and looked out the window with his feet on the windowsill while he was asking questions. We didn't get the feeling that he cared much about the interview, or us.

The National Retailers Association recently asked workers to list in order of importance their reasons for working. The number one reason given was "appreciation for what I do." The third reason was money. All of us have a deep need to feel validated. In the 1999 movie *Anna and the King,* the king asks Anna if she agrees with what the newspapers are saying critically about him. She says that she does not. He responds, "Thank you ma'am for humble validation." Even kings, queens, and CEOs (and board members) need to feel that they are acknowledged and validated.

*R*espect. The National Retailers Association survey also found that "respect" was also one of the top three reasons people gave for working. Using information given to us by other people shows them that we respect their input. Ignoring it sends the opposite message. Often, busy and knowledgeable people tend to assume that they already know what the other person is going to say. However, Oliver Wendell Holmes reminds us that "It is the province of knowledge to speak. And it is the province of wisdom to listen."

*E*mpathize. A recent study by Agilent Consulting identified empathy as one of the key leadership skills of the new century. People who really actively listen and empathize say that it is like an "aerobic workout." It is hard work, yet it energizes you. Think of it as *"aerobic listening."* Genuinely caring about the person is not enough; you need to demonstrate your active involvement with your body positioning, your follow-up questions, and your accurate paraphrasing of their comments, as well as the feelings they convey. Watch the person's body language and listen to his or her tone of voice. All of these are ways that we can demonstrate empathy.

Ideally, we should convey that what a person is saying is the most important thing in our life at that moment.

We may not all be in sales, but the skills that an effective sales professional utilizes can be applied to a variety of different situations. In business, we often find ourselves trying to "sell" our idea or proposal to a co-worker, manager, or business partner. In such situations, the power of active listening can work wonders in your efforts to bring the other side to your point of view (Brooks, 2006). First, it is important to remember that the more intently you listen to someone, the more he or she will listen to you when your turn comes to speak. That fact alone underlies the practices of active listening. To practice active listening, there are several key things you can do, such as avoid negative feelings about the person you are listening to, and do not let your opinion of the person interfere with the objectives you are trying to accomplish. In addition, do not act preoccupied, as this will lessen the respect the other party has for you and what he or she will do for you if asked. Never assume you know what the other person is going to say and intently listen as the words are being spoken. One of the most important things you can do to build respect with the other party is to never interrupt, but be interruptible. This will go a long way in showing that you care about the other person, which can help close a sale or bring the other side to the decision you wish him or her to make.

Remember, Aristotle once said that "We have two ears and but one tongue so that we may listen more than we speak."

Summary

In this chapter, we have attempted to answer the question "Why listen?" by showing how professional and social success may be affected by listening. We discussed the different phases of listening, including hearing, attention, understanding, and remembering. We discussed the different types of listening—pleasurable, discriminative, critical, and empathic—and pointed out that these may call for quite different behaviors. Finally, we suggested that most of us could benefit by improving our listening behaviors, and we presented ways in which this might be accomplished. They include paying closer attention, listening for main points, and using the spare time between thought rate and speech rate.

Key Terms

Analogy	Empathic listening	Overload	Statistics
Arousal level	Example	Plain folks	Testimony or
Bandwagon appeal	Hasty generalization	Pleasurable listening	quotations
Concentration	Hearing problems	Rapid thought	
Critical listening	Ineffective listening	Remembering	
Discriminative listening	Noise	Selective attention	

Review Questions

1. Which of the four modes of communicating do we use most, and which do we use least?

2. What are some of the variables that influence a person's arousal level? How does this knowledge relate to listening?

3. Give examples of pleasurable, discriminative, critical, and empathic listening.

4. Develop an essay on any topic and use one of each of the following methods of support to amplify your point: (a) analogy, (b) example, (c) statistics, and (d) quotation or testimony.

5. Describe some of the ways the methods of support may become devices of propaganda.

6. Describe and differentiate between the situations in which critical listening and empathic listening may be more appropriate. Use illustrations from your experiences to support your point of view.

7. How may "anticipatory set" be used to improve listening?

8. Discuss the four techniques of using the spare time between your thought speed and a communicator's speaking speed. After trying these techniques, evaluate their usefulness.

Exercises

1. Form the class into a circle of about 20 people (more than one circle if necessary). Have the first person give his or her name and mention something he or she likes. Then have the second person tell about himself or herself and the first person. Then have the third tell about himself or herself and the first two. For example, the third person says: I'm Sally and I like strawberries, and he's Jack and he likes guitar, and she's Pam and she likes backpacking. Keep this up until you have gone around the entire circle.

2. Make a tape recording of yourself either in an informal conversation or in a formal speech situation. Play the tape and write an analysis of the factors that make your speech hard to listen to. Then make a list of suggestions on how you might improve your speaking.

3. Write a description (i.e., a case study) of an experience in which a breakdown in listening played an important part. Then write an analysis of how the problem might be avoided or the situation improved in the future.

4. As you listen to a speech given in your class, try to outline it, including (a) the thesis idea, (b) the main points, and (c) the types of supporting

materials used (identify and evaluate them). Then compare your outline to that of the speaker.

5. Practice listening to very difficult or unfamiliar information, applying the suggestions in this chapter (i.e., paying attention, listening for the main points, using the "spare time," developing empathic listening).

6. Write a paragraph of factual information. Have one person read it to the class after three students have left the room. Call one student in and read the paragraph again, then have this student try to repeat it from memory to another who left, who in turn will repeat it to the third. Tape-record this if possible. Analyze the way the original message gets changed.

7. Analyze a television commercial, a political speech, or an informal conversation for the use and misuse of materials supporting the person's ideas (i.e., analogy, example, statistics, and testimony). Write an evaluation of their effectiveness.

8. Have a two-person conversation (dyadic encounter) with someone you choose from your class. Try to find out more about each other than the superficialities of hometown, major subjects, and such. Then (if you agree to beforehand) have

each person write a short description of the other person in each dyad and reproduce a copy of each description for each member of the class. This will motivate you to listen carefully to each other and will help class members to get to know more about each other.

9. In a group discussion, either in class or elsewhere, try to test your listening by restating or paraphrasing a point that has been stated but that you are not sure you understand. You may also try to summarize the main points that have been brought out in the discussion, both to help orient you and the other group members to what the group has already accomplished and to see how well you have been listening to the progress of the discussion.

10. In a discriminative listening situation, try (really try) as often as possible to apply the suggestions offered in this chapter. After a reasonable length of time (e.g., a month), evaluate whether this has improved your listening ability.

Suggested Readings

Burley-Allen, Madelyn. *Listening: The Forgotten Skill.* New York: Wiley, 1995.

This little paperback book is a practical and easily readable book on listening. It contains tips on how to put effective listening to work for you, professionally, socially, and personally.

Helgesen, Marc, Steven Brown, and Dorolyn Smith. *Active Listening,* 3rd ed. Cambridge, England: Cambridge University Press, 1997.

Offers numerous listening exercises to build listening skills.

Hughes, Richard, Robert Ginnett, and Gordon Curphy. *Leadership,* 5th ed. New York: McGraw-Hill, 2006.

This excellent book shows how listening is a crucial leadership skill.

Murphy, Kevin J. *Effective Listening.* Salem, NH: ELI Press, 1992.

A good practical handbook on how to improve your listening. The book is filled with self-tests. It also emphasizes applications to professional settings.

Stewart, John, and Carol Logan. *Together: Communicating Interpersonally,* 5th ed. New York: McGraw-Hill, 1998.

This excellent book has a wonderful chapter on listening that is well worth the time spent reading it.

Tannen, Deborah. *Talking from 9 to 5.* New York: Avon Books, 1995.

This best-selling book is a must for all to read in order to improve communication between the sexes, especially on the job.

Wolvin, Andrew, and C. G. Coakley. *Listening,* 5th ed. Dubuque, IA: Brown, 1996.

One of the most complete books available on this subject.

 # For Supplementary Information

Log onto the Online Learning Center at *www.mhhe.com/tubbsmoss11.*

6

Conflict and Negotiation

Chapter Objectives

After reading this chapter, you should be able to:

1. Define conflict and discuss the important elements in the definition.
2. Define and discuss the four levels of conflict.
3. Discuss and explain the Kilmann-Thomas conflict resolution model.
4. Define negotiation.
5. Identify and use the six-step process in negotiations.
6. Identify and discuss five assumptions of successful negotiation.
7. Define principled negotiation and discuss four basic rules of thumb.
8. Identify and discuss five techniques of principled negotiation.

CONFLICT

If two people are honestly talking, they cannot be hitting each other.

—**Dzwonkowski (1998)**

Many times communicating with others is enjoyable and fun. However, conflict sometimes arises and then communicating is not fun at all. It can be agonizing. It can keep you awake at night. It can tie your stomach in knots. It can lead to violence and death. The world events resulting from the attack on the World Trade Center and the Pentagon on September 11, 2001, and the war in Iraq have once again reminded us of the intense need for improving our conflict management and negotiation skills. The presidential campaign of 2004 became one of the most divisive in our country's history. Roughly one-half of the nation supported Senator John Kerry, while the other half supported President George W. Bush. Friends and even families found themselves in conflict over their choice for president.

This chapter is about communicating in conflict situations and negotiating your way through to possible resolution.

On a somewhat lighter note, a friend of ours recalls that her three-year-old son, seeing his parents in a heated argument, stepped in between them, held his arms straight out, and said, "Now just a minute, you two." Many of us go out of our way to avoid conflict and might characterize ideal relationships as free of argument. However, by the time we become adults, we've usually been at least a witness to a great many conflicts both minor and intense. Few young people reach adulthood without experiencing some conflict with their parents, siblings, or peers.

Theorists tend to regard conflict as a natural part of human relationships, one that is not necessarily destructive, although, as we'll see in Chapter 10, in some cultures it is traditional for conflict to go unexpressed.

Conflict is defined as *"an expressed struggle between at least two interdependent parties who perceive incompatible goals, scarce resources, and interference from others in achieving their goals"* (Wilmot and Hocker, 1998, p. 34). Let's briefly examine each of the important elements in the definition.

Expressed Struggle   An interpersonal communication approach to this topic focuses on the communication exchanges that compose the conflict. In other words, there must be communication messages exchanged in order for the conflict to be expressed.

Interdependence   If we don't have some need for the other person to cooperate, then there is no conflict. It is only when we are interdependent that the conflict exists. For example, you agree to play tennis with another person. If either of you doesn't show up, neither can play. The two of you are interdependent.

Perceived Incompatible Goals   Two or more people may have a conflict that is based solely on perception (see Chapter 2). They may actually agree, but

Fisher, Ury, and Patton (1991) have suggested an approach referred to as "principled negotiation." They contend that negotiation and conflict resolution can be more successful if you follow their guidelines. What do you think are the advantages and disadvantages of each of these guidelines?

Separate people from the problem. This means that you should try not to get angry with the other party. Try to remain neutral toward the person, even if he or she is arguing a point of view that you feel is very distasteful.

Focus on interests, not positions. Look for common interests and avoid sticking to a certain fixed position, like how much you want to get if you are selling a car.

Invent various options for mutual gain. Look for a variety of possible solutions, not just *x* versus *y* as your only possible solutions.

Use objective criteria to determine outcomes. See if you can find information that both parties agree is accurate as guidelines for finding a solution.

think they don't. Or they may in fact have goals that are in conflict. You may like to stay home and your spouse may want to eat out. Or, two parties may be in love with the same person. In the story of Camelot, King Arthur and Sir Lancelot both love Queen Guinevere. What really complicates things is that Arthur also considers Lancelot his closest friend. Try to imagine how psychologically painful that would be. In the present context, we would say that they have incompatible goals.

Perceived Scarce Resources   Again, the problem may solely be in the perception. Or, there may simply not be enough to go around. If there truly are insufficient resources, it can often create conflict. As one clergyman has said, "Lack of money is the root of all evil." Stephen Covey, in his famous book *The 7 Habits of Highly Effective People* (1990), writes eloquently about the perception part of this type of conflict. He feels that there are two types of attitudes, (1) a scarcity mentality and (2) an abundance mentality. Those with the scarcity mentality feel that if you gain, they must lose. They feel jealous or threatened if you get positive recognition or success. He writes, "The abundance mentality, on the other hand, flows out of a deep inner sense of personal worth and security. It is the paradigm that there is plenty out there and enough to spare for everybody" (p. 220). The scarcity mentality's analogy is that if one person gets a bigger piece of a pie, then others get less. The abundance mentality says that all can get more if you work together to create a bigger pie.

Perceived Interference   If we would like something and another person keeps us from getting it, then interference has occurred. Let's say that you would like to get a promotion and your boss won't do it. How would you feel toward her or him?

Levels of Conflict

Intrapersonal Conflict   One way of classifying types of conflict is by level (Lewicki et al., 2007). The first level of conflict takes place within the individual. This is called intrapersonal conflict. Sources of internal conflict can include ideas, attitudes, emotions, values, or personality drives that are in conflict with each other. Certainly, you have found yourself torn between, for example, wanting to go out with friends versus staying in and studying! This is an example of intrapersonal conflict. Since intrapersonal conflict is felt inwardly but not yet expressed, it would not be included in Wilmot and Hocker's definition of conflict. However, some would argue that the more an individual is internally conflicted, the more likely he or she is to become involved in conflicts with others (Losoncy, 1998). So there is a possible connection between intrapersonal conflict and interpersonal conflict.

In the example above, if a person has a hard time deciding between the need for affiliation (going out with friends) and the need for achievement (staying in to study), this could lead the person to "snap" at the other person who is inviting him or her to go out. Another similar example is the difficulty of saying no to things people ask us to do. Part of us wants to be liked, but part of us doesn't want to do certain tasks that others ask of us.

Interpersonal Conflict   A second major level of conflict occurs between individuals. This is called interpersonal conflict. This can occur between friends, roommates, fraternity or sorority members, family members, co-workers, lovers, or total strangers (as in cases of "road rage"). Witness the popularity of television and radio programs that frequently show people involved in conflict. The *Jerry Springer Show* was the source of much controversy a few years back because it showed outlandish displays of conflict. Often television and radio shows will have people who represent both sides of a controversy, first in order to show both sides of an issue, but more importantly, because conflict is interesting and improves their viewer and listener ratings. Examples are numerous—*Survivor, Lost,* other so-called "reality TV shows," Maury Povich, Dr. Laura Schlessinger, Rush Limbaugh, Al Sharpton, Howard Stern, and many others.

In interpersonal conflicts the parties usually communicate directly with one another. Most of the principles of conflict and conflict resolution relate to interpersonal conflict, since this is the basic unit of interpersonal communication and interpersonal relations.

Interpersonal conflict is the most common type of conflict occurring in the workplace. Its causes may be numerous, but they chiefly stem from unfulfilled or ignored human needs. Common human needs found in the workplace include: acceptance, acknowledgement, affirmation, appreciation, autonomy, belonging, clarity, collaboration, completion, compassion, consideration, cooperation, fun, freedom, help, honesty, humor, inspiration, order, participation, planning, power, reassurance, respect, structure, support, to contribute, to share, tolerance, trust, understanding, variety (Janetta, 2006).

Intragroup Conflict   A third major level of conflict is within a small group. It can take place within a family, between team members, on a committee, or in any small group of individuals. Individual differences can affect how small groups interact during conflict situations. We mentioned before that there are cultural differences in expression and results of conflict. Nibler and Harris (2003) investigated the relationships between intragroup conflict and group effectiveness of groups across cultures. The study looked at groups of U.S. friends and strangers and groups of Chinese friends and strangers in decision-making contexts. In U.S. groups of strangers, there was little conflict, which resulted in poor performance, while in groups of friends, higher comfort levels with conflict and openness led to more success on tasks. Conversely, Chinese groups of friends and groups of strangers performed worse when there was more conflict and open exchange of ideas (p. 613). Researchers (Goleman, 2001) have identified four categories of emotional competencies needed for effective emotional self-managements as well for effectively relating to others in a group: self-awareness, self-management, social awareness, and relationship management (cited in Hede, 2007).

The first, self-awareness, is seen as the ability to monitor one's own emotions, to accurately self-assess and to be self-confident (Goleman, 2001, cited in Hede, 2007).

> "If an individual has low inner-awareness . . . it will actively seek an emotional trigger to . . . unleash itself onto the group in relationship conflict." (Hede, 2007)

The second set of competencies in the Goleman (2001) model is self-management. It involves such skills as emotional self-control, adaptability, conscientiousness, trustworthiness, achievement, drive, and initiative. The key skill here is the ability to control one's own emotional reactivity. This involves being able to

- Identify one's own habitual emotional triggers.
- Detect the physical warning signs of an "emotional hijacking" (e.g., increased heart rate, rush of blood, surge of adrenaline). (Goleman, 1995)
- Avoid identification with the reactive thoughts that accompany an acute emotional response.
- Implement effective protocols for defusing one's own emotional reactivity, thereby avoiding any behavioral outburst. (Hede, 2007)

The third set of emotional competencies proposed by Goleman (2001) is social awareness consisting of empathy, service orientation, and organizational awareness. In relation to shadow group management, empathy plays a crucial role. As Goleman has pointed out:

> An emotionally intelligent team . . . has the collective equivalent of empathy, the basis of all relationship skills. (Goleman, 2004, p. 182)

If group members have a high level of empathy, they understand each other's sensitivities and can read each other's emotional state. This enables them to anticipate a negative emotional reaction in another group member and to avoid behaviors that could trigger an outburst (Hede, 2007).

The fourth and final set of emotional competencies in the Goleman (2001) model is relationship management. This includes the following skills: developing others, influence, communication, conflict management, visionary leadership, catalyzing change, building bonds, teamwork, and collaboration (Hede, 2007).

Having analyzed a number of conflict situations according to the Goleman's model, Hede formulated several viable conflict management hypotheses:

- Individuals who have high inner-awareness are less likely to experience negative emotionality in groups.
- Individuals are most likely to experience relationship conflict with the group member they perceive as the most opposite to themselves.
- Escalation of task into relationship conflict is more likely to occur in groups that use the same terminology for "debates" and "fights." (Hede, 2007)

We deal more with intragroup conflict in Chapter 12.

Intergroup Conflict   This final level of conflict occurs between groups. This could involve feuding families, labor and management, rival street gangs, some groups and the U.S. government, and even warring nations. Communication at this level of conflict is often through representatives. When conflict gets to this level, it is often very complicated since it involves more people and may even involve centuries of history. Of course, conflicts may also occur at more than one of these levels simultaneously.

Some scholars would add another conflict type to this classification: conflicts between large ethnic systems or civilizations. Such approach derives from the works of the great fourteenth-century Arab historian Ibn Khaldoun and was further developed in the twentieth century by Arnold Toynbee (1889–1975) in his principal work *A Study of History*. In recent years, this view was espoused most notably by two scholars: Lev Nikolayevich Gumilev (1912–1992) in Russia and Samuel Huntington (b. 1927) in the United States.

For both Gumilev and Huntington, the key notion governing intercultural (intercivilizational) relationships is a subconscious sense of sympathy or antipathy shared by the members of an ethnic group, which serves to determine the distinction between "one's own" and "strangers" (Goudakov, 2006). This stands in contrast with the more common approach among many historians and political scientists who speak of political will as the force behind intercivilizational cultural exchanges.

While these issues may have seemed largely theoretical 10 to 15 years ago, today they are becoming more practical in light of the recent extension of European Union toward the east as well as NATO expansion. When in 2004 EU extended membership invitations to Romania and Bulgaria, this stirred intense debates across Europe. An even more intensely debated issue is the prospect of Turkey joining the European Union.

Stages of Conflict

Every conflict is believed to occur in stages, and each stage is characterized by different communication patterns. Brahm (2003) summarized the six phases of conflict: latent conflict, emergence, escalation, de-escalation, resolution, and reconciliation.

Latent Conflict and Emergence

The initial phase is represented by a lack of overt conflict where only latent, or potential, conflict exists. Latent conflict is the existence of opposing goals. If some event triggers the latent conflict, then the conflict may emerge and become overt. These triggers can take many forms. First, an unfortunate comment or verbal interchange is the most common trigger. Second, if one party does not hear the other party accurately, a comment may be taken as negative when it was not intended to be. (Chapter 5 discussed the importance of effective listening; listening is critical in the prevention of emergent conflict.)

Third, differences in semantics can be blamed for conflict emergence. Words must not be used that have negative connotations to the other party. For example, the concept of "reasonable spending" may mean entirely different things to a husband and a wife. Fourth, body language can speak volumes. If someone says something with a sneer on his or her face, for example, the perception of the verbal message will be combined with the negative facial expression. Negative comments, ineffective listening, semantic differences, and inconsistent body language can all act as triggers resulting in the emergence of a latent conflict (Akin, 2003).

Escalation and Resolution

The emergent conflict may then, and often does, escalate to a higher level of intensity. A conflict generally escalates until both parties have reached a "stalemate" where neither party feels that they can "win" the argument. A stalemate generally causes the parties to decide to de-escalate or negotiate to reach conflict resolution. Negotiation will be discussed later on in this chapter.

A resolved conflict may still leave behind damaged relationships and hurt feelings. Reconciliation must occur as the final phase of conflict to ensure that the residual negativity released by the conflict has abated and both parties can move forward productively (Brahm, 2003).

Of course, conflict does not always follow these general phases in a prescribed order and can return to escalation after resolution, or can skip escalation altogether. There is no set prescription for conflict, but only a model that can assist in understanding and improving our chances for conflict management. Conflict resolution is the goal of all episodes of conflict as you will see in the next section.

Conflict Resolution

One of the best models for conceptualizing conflict resolution has been offered by Kilmann and Thomas (1975). Their two-dimensional model is illustrated in

Figure 6.1   The Kilmann-Thomas Conflict Model

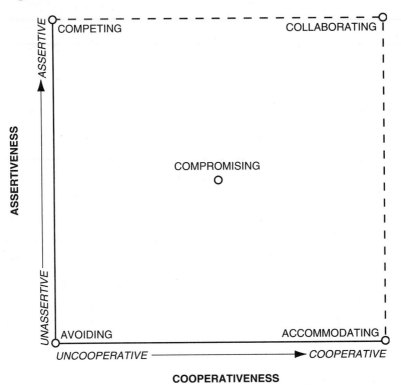

Source: This two-dimensional model of conflict handling behavior is adapted from "The Kilmann-Thomas Conflict Model" by Kenneth Thomas. Reprinted by permission of Grid International, Inc.

Figure 6.1. The model suggests that individuals may have a preferred style for resolving conflicts. However, as we develop a broader range of style flexibility, our skill in dealing with a broad range of conflict situations is enhanced. We shouldn't limit ourselves to using only one style. The model offers five basic styles of conflict resolution: (1) avoidance, (2) competition, (3) compromise, (4) accommodation, and (5) collaboration. Let us look a bit at each of these styles.

Avoidance

Winston Churchill once remarked that he and his wife had decided at the beginning of their marriage that, if they were going to remain married, they should never have breakfast together.

The first choice in trying to resolve conflict is whether to deal with it at all. The easiest way is just to avoid it. Some of us may have grown up in a home in which the prevailing advice when it came to conflict was "The less said the better." Avoidance behaviors include a wide spectrum of evasive strategies intended to head off a confrontation. In simple **denial,** unelaborated statements are made denying that there is a conflict ("Who's fighting? I'm not angry at all!"). **Underresponsiveness** is a *"failure to acknowledge or deny the presence of a conflict following a statement or inquiry about the conflict by a partner"* (Sillars, 1986) ("I still don't think you've fixed the car. What if it stalls again on the highway?" "You'll manage"). In addition to **shifting** and **avoiding topics,** other tactics you probably recognize include semantic focus, abstractness, joking, ambivalence, and pessimism.

Semantic focus is an especially interesting dodge. The *person trying to avoid conflict focuses on what is being said, then makes statements about what the words mean or how to characterize the ongoing conflict and this discussion of words.* So terminology or "semantics" replaces the original conflict issue. Often, as we suggested in Chapter 2 and in the discussion of confirmation, the issue is about relationships, not about content. Pessimistic remarks tend to downplay or undermine a discussion of causes of conflict ("Let's not rehash everything. We've been through this over and over").

Postponement, although it is sometimes a strategy for avoidance, can work well, but only if both parties will work out a discussion time that is not too far in the future (Wilmot and Hocker, 1998). Planning to have a discussion two weeks after the incident that sparked the disagreement is unlikely to be very beneficial.

The advantage of the **avoidance** approach is that you avoid saying things that sometimes may escalate the conflict. All of us have probably said things in the heat of the moment that we later wished we could take back. The disadvantage of this style is that the conflicts never get resolved and the tension tends to mount as the conflict festers. Another disadvantage is that as the conflicts go unresolved the anger may increase within one or more parties so that, when there is a discussion, the angry feelings explode.

Unfortunately, avoidance seems to work only in the short run. Eventually, the conflicts need to be addressed in order to be resolved.

Competition

In the **competition** style of conflict, *one party tries to use aggression or power to beat the other party.* The conflict is seen as a "battleground." People sometimes get caught up in the excitement of the fight. Competition may also be exhibited in an assertive way rather than an aggressive way. The difference is whether you are injuring the other party while trying to accomplish your goals. Competition may take the form of threats, criticisms, confrontational remarks, or extreme language choices.

Sillars's schema includes several competitive tactics. These include faulting (direct personal criticism, such as "You look like a mess"), hostile questioning ("How can you stand to live like that?"), hostile joking ("If your friends jumped off a cliff, would you jump too?"), presumptive attribution, avoiding responsibility, and prescription.

Presumptive attribution refers to *making statements that attribute to the other person feelings, thoughts, or motives that he or she does not acknowledge.* Examples: "You're just saying that because you know it makes me angry." "You'd like to see me make a fool out of myself." "So you think I can't stand up to my boss."

One of the most competitive and forceful of the strategies is **prescription,** which can take many forms. The confrontational person makes requests or demands, threatens, or argues for a given behavior change in the other person that presumably would resolve the conflict. Examples: "Get the job done by tomorrow or I'm not paying." "Clean up your room or you're grounded for the weekend." "If you leave this apartment, don't come back." Threats are among the most frequent responses people use during conflict, and there are times when they can generate change, but only if the person being threatened believes, and cares, that the threat will be carried out. For example, the "tough love" program for working with juvenile delinquents is based on this premise.

The advantages of competition are that it can stimulate creativity and energize people to a very high degree. Witness the enthusiasm at many sporting events. The disadvantages of competition are that it usually runs the risk of harming the relationship between the parties involved. Winning takes a higher priority than building the relationship. Competition may also drive the other party "underground" if he or she is not in a position to respond openly. The best example of this is the sabotage that employees resort to when they feel abused by their bosses. Perhaps the greatest disadvantage is violence. All you have to do is look at the news each day to witness the many cases in which conflict escalates into violence.

Compromise

Many times, in order to resolve a conflict, both parties have to give in a bit so as to reach a compromise solution. Note the definition of "negotiation" later in this chapter as finding mutually acceptable tradeoffs. The key here is that the tradeoffs must be mutually agreeable. Sometimes compromises are just poor solutions in which nobody really gets what he or she wants. The classic example comes from the Bible: Wise King Solomon is asked to settle a dispute between two women who both claim to be a baby's mother. He says that in order to satisfy them both he will cut the baby in half and give each woman one-half. The baby's birth mother offers to give the baby to the other woman to save the child's life. King Solomon gives the baby to the birth mother instead, because only the birth mother would rather give up the child than see it harmed. In many modern-day legal cases, lawyers refer to a judge's decision as "cutting the baby in half." This simply means that if one party is suing the other for $1 million damages, the judge will settle on $500,000. This is a typical example of a compromise solution.

One advantage of compromise is that it does often lead to resolution of the conflict. It can also be used as an alternative when other styles such as competition have failed. A disadvantage is that it can be used as the easy way out. It may also be that $500,000 is still much too much for the party to pay in damages. Compromise may also be used instead of more creative solutions that might be better and even more satisfying to both parties. Compromise does not involve a strong drive for the relationship and for the substantive goals, but rather a half-hearted attempt to meet both.

Compromise happens every day—even in apparently silly situations. Recently, in Canton Township, Michigan, a controversy occurred over a Big Boy restaurant's icon, a fiberglass 6-foot-tall statue. A Canton ordinance prohibits businesses from having more than one monument-size sign on their property. The issue was taken to court, where the judge recommended the statue be considered a piece of art instead of a sign. After the prosecution realized this wasn't worth all the trouble, they compromised and changed the ordinance to make the Big Boy statue legal ("Canton Township . . . ," 2004).

We once heard about a faculty committee that could not decide whether to adopt textbook A or textbook B. They compromised on textbook C, a book that no committee members really felt excited about. This is an example of the downside to compromise as a conflict-resolving style.

Accommodation

In this style, the *person suppresses his or her substantive needs and emphasizes harmony with the other party* ("Go ahead and do it your way. I don't want to fight about this"). This approach is also called **appeasement** or smoothing over the conflict. Again, this appears to be a short-term strategy. All of us have human needs, as we shall discuss in the section on negotiation. If we chronically suppress these needs in order to please another person, sooner or later the unmet needs will rise to the surface.

However, this style has the advantage in the short run of demonstrating to the other person our willingness to put the relationship above our own selfish needs. We are reminded of this in the story "The Gift of the Magi," by O. Henry, in which a man sells his watch to buy jeweled combs for his wife's hair, while she sells her hair to buy a chain for his gold watch. Each person is thinking first of the other. It would seem that this style would work best in the family or among very close friends. The disadvantage is that the sacrifice may be one-sided and the relationship will eventually suffer anyway.

Collaboration

Collaboration requires the highest level of commitment to the relationship of any of the conflict-resolving styles. It involves a high degree of concern for achieving the goals of both parties, as well as a high degree of concern for the relationship between the parties. This is often very difficult to accomplish. The discussions continue until both parties are satisfied. In the best cases, the relationship can be strengthened in the process.

Sillars (1986) provides a summary of the following collaborative tactics. Description is just that, not blaming or making evaluations of the other. It involves simply describing (not "You never want to go out," but rather "I'm feeling depressed because we don't go out as much as I would like").

Qualification *involves limiting the subject at issue* ("Let's not get into why we don't have enough money. Can we figure out how we can manage what we have right now to make it less stressful for both of us?"). By disclosing your own thoughts and feelings and soliciting disclosures from the other person, you are trying to establish a supportive climate in which conflict may be resolved ("When you talk about dating other people, I get anxious. Are you trying to say that you want to stop seeing me?"). Negative inquiries also help to elicit disclosures and greater openness from the other person ("Honey, if there's some way in which I've hurt your feelings, I'd really like to know about it").

Two important ways in which we can be confirming and still move toward resolution are by showing empathy or support ("It's rough right now. We seem to be at each other's throats all the time, and I suppose you're feeling as down about it as I am") and by emphasizing commonalities ("Well, we may not agree on how to cut the budget, but can't we come up with something to save our department from being eliminated?"). Other behaviors that may facilitate conflict resolution are accepting responsibility ("We've both been at fault. I know I was getting more and more hostile, and I just had to get it off my chest") and initiating problem solving ("What would be best for the kids? Let's try to work this out").

The advantage is that collaboration can lead to some of the most effective conflict resolutions achievable. The disadvantage is that many times only one party is willing to utilize this style. Unless both parties are willing to use this style, it is not very likely to work. It also takes a lot of time, energy, and skill. But the results are often worth it.

However, all in all, this style appears to have the most promise for effective conflict resolution. Keep in mind that none of us uses any one style in the textbook sense. In real life we often see a mixture of different styles. The Kilmann-Thomas model, an excellent way of conceptualizing the process, offers an idealized way of attempting to improve our conflict-resolving skills.

Who desires peace, should prepare for war.

—Vegetius (*De Re Militari*)

Some conflicts may not follow the Kilmann-Thomas model. Consider the following situations (Bester and Warneryd, 2006):

1. Two countries negotiate about the division of fishing waters located between them. If negotiations break down, they go to war.
2. A buyer and a seller of a good try to renegotiate the terms of a trading contract. If they fail to reach an agreement, they go to court.
3. Two political parties try to form a coalition. If their negotiations are unsuccessful, they enter the elections on uncoordinated policy platforms.

These examples represent bargaining in the absence of well-defined property rights (Bester and Warneryd, 2006). In his *Problem of Social Cost* (1960), Coase offered a theoretical framework for conflict resolution in such situations. He argued that, although lack of well-defined property rights is an obstacle to reaching efficient agreements in settings where agents have the potential for outright conflict, mutually beneficial agreements are possible even under such circumstances. "As long as the parties' relative strengths in an outright conflict are common knowledge among them, they would, if risk-neutral, accept an agreement that gave each of them at least their expected value under conflict" (Bester and Warneryd, 2006). Several conclusions of Bester and Waneryd's work are

- Outright conflict is less likely when the costs of conflict are high (i.e., when conflict more directly destroys the resources under dispute).
- Conflict is less likely the more powerful each party appears to the other.
- The likelihood of conflict depends on the entire distribution of strength, not just its expectation.

Ambiguity and Disorder

Despite the repeated emphasis on constructive conflict resolution through communication skills, some theorists acknowledge that not all conflicts are amenable to resolution. Sillars and Weisberg (1987) have discussed some of the variables that a "skills approach" often fails to take into account. "Conflict," they point out, "simply cannot be fully appreciated from a highly rational view of human behavior. Sometimes people lose control over conflict—not because they are naïve, but because the process itself has disorderly and irrational elements" (p. 148).

Ambiguity, disorder, and confusion are part and parcel of many conflicts. What starts out as a simple argument over "nothing" can heat up and can quickly become chaotic. They write:

> Private arguments do not necessarily conform to public standards of reasonableness, consistency, or relevance in argumentation because a dyad defines its own sense of "correct" or "appropriate argument . . . In fact, a striking feature of intense interpersonal conflict is the disintegration of conventional patterns of conversation." (Sillars and Weisberg, 1987, p. 149)

In the midst of a vehement argument, conversation may become increasingly emotional and volatile. It may not even be relevant. One person, or both, may suddenly bring up all sorts of past resentments. This intensifies and confuses the initial conflict. After a time, two people may even lose sense of what they started arguing about.

Perhaps you have been involved in this kind of argument yourself. One factor that contributes to the disorder and ambiguity is confusion about the source of the conflict. We don't always know why we are angry, and we don't always know why the other people respond, or "overreact," the way they do. Tempers escalate, and we're off.

Relationship conflicts can be bitter and chaotic: "A vague sense of dissatisfaction over core relationships may have a rippling effect, creating conflict over many peripheral issues." For example, a couple's argument about when to leave a party may also reflect a struggle over which person has the decision-making power.

Often conflict is also disorganized because it is embedded in daily activities. Many interpersonal conflicts carry a strong element of surprise. They seem to surface out of nowhere and to have no boundaries. For example, conflict can come up just as two people are leaving their house for work, then break off, unresolved, only to recur several days later—perhaps at another inopportune moment. Many interpersonal conflicts resist scheduling and are experienced as outside our control.

Conflicts in which all concerned have a clear perception and understanding of their goals and focus on a single delimited issue are more suited to a skills approach, but serious conflicts about relationships are extremely difficult to disentangle. However, we believe the guidelines below will help improve your chances of successfully resolving conflict:

- Pick your conflicts. Don't argue over everything.
- Develop a reputation as someone who admits when you are wrong.
- Provide an alternative for ideas you oppose. Don't knock down the ideas of others without having something else to suggest.
- Let the other person speak first. This will encourage the other person to listen better. You will also gain insight into what it takes to satisfy him or her.
- Base your statements on facts. Avoid exaggeration.
- Don't lose your temper.
- Avoid sarcasm, disbelief, and caustic humor.
- Develop a win-win mentality. Aim to meet both your needs and the other person's. Avoid simply trying to defend your position. Never try to win by destroying the other person. (Adapted from Deep and Sussman, 1998, p. 59)

Ethnic Conflict Management

Most conflict resolution methods described above are relevant in individual and small group conflict situations. The twentieth century was probably the most conflict-saturated period in human history. While World War II remains the most tragic among them, a less-known fact is that over 40 million lives have already been lost since its end—many to ethnic clashes, such as conflicts in former Yugoslavia; conflict between Armenia and Azerbaijan over Nagorny Karabakh; the Tibetan revolt; conflicts between Ethiopia, Somalia, and Eritrea; conflicts in Congo, Rwanda, and Sudan. Areas where the potential for ethnic conflicts remains high today include Cyprus, Kosovo, Georgia/Abkhazia in the Caucasus region, and the Kurd situation in the Middle East.

In ethnic conflict situations, territorial autonomy for minority groups has traditionally been regarded as the most desired solution. However, because such solution is often not feasible, an alternative approach—known as functional, overlapping, and competing jurisdictions—has recently received increased attention by both scholars (Kyriacou, 2006) and governments. This concept is not new. As early as the fifteenth century, the Ottoman Empire recognized some non-Muslim ethnic groups as separate entities and granted them rights to administer their own affairs in matters of education, religion, and family law. Having analyzed a number of past and present ethnic conflicts, Andreas Kyriacou concludes that functional autonomy is, in many situations, a preferred method for distribution of power among ethnic groups.

> The functional devolution of powers which is intrinsic to Functional, Overlapping and Competing Jurisdictions may be preferable to territorial devolution when

minority groups are either not spatially concentrated or, when this is the case, they are in a numerical minority in their region. Even when minority groups are in a majority in their region functional rather than territorial devolution may dampen secessionist fears among members of the majority. Moreover, a case can be made for a degree of functional devolution to complement territorial devolution when territorial devolution aimed at protecting one particular minority leaves other ethnic groups in a minority situation. (Kyriacou, 2006)

NEGOTIATION

When Jeffrey Katzenberg was CEO of Disney Studios, he described his style of negotiating in the following way:

> I operated like a mercenary soldier . . . If someone poked me in the chest, I would hit them with a baseball bat. And if they hit me with a bat, I would blast them with a bazooka. And I would escalate this until I reached nuclear-bomb time. This was the way I was taught . . . It's a hostile and predatory way to live life. The truth is, if you asked me to look back and say, because I behaved that way, that's why I was successful, I would now say: No. If I had been more conciliatory, I would have been more successful. (In Cloke and Goldsmith, 2005, p. 45)

Negotiation is another set of methods for resolving conflicts between and among people. It is defined as "the process of resolving differences through mutually acceptable tradeoffs" (Walker and Harris, 1995, p. 2).

Fairness

Inherent in all social exchanges are both elements of cooperation and competition. The outcome of such of such exchanges is often affected by whether the exchange partners perceive each other's behavior as fair. Sociological research defines fairness primarily as justice judgment, but it has also been suggested that such perception is directly linked to the nature of exchange in which the parties are involved—reciprocal or negotiated (Molm et al., 2006). "The more competitive and conflictual the actors perceive their relationship, the more likely they are to perceive the inequalities as unjust and their partners as unfair" (Molm et al., 2006). It follows, therefore, that parties in negotiated exchanges are more likely to perceive their partner's behavior as unfair than in reciprocal exchanges. In other words, reciprocal exchanges are perceived as more fair than negotiated exchanges because they are perceived as less conflictual and competitive (Molm et al., 2006). It is useful to keep this in mind when planning a negotiation process.

Six-Step Model

Many times negotiations seem to be a mystery. However, there are ways of organizing the negotiation process that help to simplify and demystify it.

Walker and Harris (1995) have identified the following six predictable steps in the negotiation process: (1) analyzing the negotiation situation, (2) planning for the upcoming negotiation, (3) organizing, (4) gaining and maintaining control, (5) closing the negotiations, and (6) continuous improvement. Let's look at each of these steps a bit more closely.

Step 1: Analyzing the Negotiation Situation

In this step, you can begin to establish what your objectives are or what you hope to accomplish from the negotiation. For example, if you want to sell your used car, what price do you need to feel that you have been successful?

You need to determine what your "bottom line" is, but you also need to determine an acceptable range of alternatives just to give yourself some bargaining room. You should also think about what the other person's needs are. What attributes or benefits can you sell about your car that will help meet this person's needs? What is there about the environment that will affect the negotiation? For example, if you have a convertible and it is summer, the physical environment will be more favorable to the sale than if it is the dead of winter. A good economic environment will help your sale, as compared to when the economy is weak. How many others are competing for your buyer? Is it a buyer's market or a seller's market? All of these are questions that you will want to consider in your analysis.

Sometimes you may have a best alternative to a negotiated agreement (BATNA). This is your best way of satisfying your interests without the other's agreement (Ury, 1993, p. 20). In this case, you don't need the other person's cooperation, and the two of you are not interdependent. For example, it is better to keep your used car than to sell it for too little money.

Step 2: Planning for the Upcoming Negotiations

Henry Kissinger negotiated many diplomatic agreements and has been quoted as saying that 50 percent of negotiation time is spent in planning prior to the actual negotiation. The inexperienced negotiator tends to underestimate the need for careful preparation.

As one researcher notes, negotiations are often "complex, ill-structured, and evolving tasks, which require sophisticated decision support" (Lim and Yang, 2007). Moreover, human negotiations are often susceptible to various "stumbling blocks," such as cognitive biases as well as emotional complications (Lim and Yang, 2007). These stumbling blocks, combined with the increasing complexity of negotiated issues, have led to development of the notion of Negotiation Support Systems (NSS). The purpose of NSS is "to assist negotiating parties in reaching mutually satisfactory decisions by supporting information analysis and communication protocols" (Lim and Yang, 2007). NSS may be especially helpful during the planning stage of negotiations as in many cases planning is the key element. For example, one challenge faced by business negotiations (e.g., buyer-seller, labor-management, international business merger) is to jointly identify and set ranges on critical issues to be negotiated prior to the actual negotiation (Lim and Yang, 2007).

Most negotiations revolve around three basic components: (1) money, (2) people, and (3) timing. As you plan the negotiation, you should consider what goals you have for each of these three key components.

Another important consideration is what communication strategies and tactics you will plan to use. What kind of psychological climate would you like to establish in the negotiation? Are you trying to gain a win-win outcome or a win-lose outcome? A lose-lose outcome is also possible.

In a formal negotiation you can begin to work out the structure of the negotiation with such items as: Where will it take place? What will be the agenda (what points will be discussed)? Who will be involved? When will the sessions occur? Who will take minutes or notes of the agreements reached? How many sessions will there be? All these are items that may need to be negotiated. During the Vietnam War era, it took 18 months for the two sides to agree on the shape of the negotiating table and who the participants would be in the negotiations! A key thing to remember is that everything is potentially negotiable.

Step 3: Organizing

The first thing to do in this phase is to determine who will be the most effective people for your negotiation team. In a business setting, the sales and purchasing people may be supported by legal, financial, or other technical experts. In common life situations, you may be negotiating alone or you may bring a significant other. Often two heads are better than one.

The second thing is to develop your game plan, which means determining your objectives for the negotiation. If you are buying a home, some of your objectives should include (1) an affordable purchase price, (2) occupancy date when you need it, (3) a good mortgage rate, (4) negotiating what is included in the purchase price, and perhaps, (5) an inspection paid for by the seller.

Third, you should determine ahead of time your opening offer, then what your next offer might be, and finally what is the highest you can afford to offer.

Fourth, you should conduct a mock negotiation to practice how you will react to issues brought up by the other party.

Finally, expect surprises. Negotiation is by its very nature highly unpredictable!

Step 4: Gaining and Maintaining Control

Sometimes negotiations can get out of control. Emotions tend to escalate, voices are raised, positions become polarized, and agreement becomes less and less likely to occur. One way to gain some control is to create the draft agenda. Then you can ask for the reaction to it, and you may make adjustments. If you leave the agenda to the other party, he or she will often gain control of not only the agenda but other items as well. A typical agenda will include the following items:

Date	List of topics
Attendees	Order of the topics
Time	Length of time for each topic
Location	Beginning and ending times
Ground rules for the sessions	

A good exercise would be for you to practice by creating an agenda for an upcoming negotiation to develop your familiarity with this process.

Step 5: Closing the Negotiations

The information on brainstorming covered in Chapter 12 will also be valuable in negotiations. Many times agreements can be achieved if people are creative enough to invent options that are not immediately obvious. We may be limited primarily by our own lack of creativity. Once, one of the authors was negotiating with a moving van company over the price of a cross-country move. In order to save money in the cost of the move, the following items, among many others, were brainstormed:

- Packing some household items instead of having the movers do it.
- Packing boxes of bed linens.
- Shipping boxes of books instead of having them hauled in the moving van.
- Having a garage sale to cut down on the amount to be moved.
- Getting used boxes instead of buying new ones from the mover.
- Changing the type of insurance to reduce costs.

However, the two parties still remained about $500 apart. So the moving company representative came up with the idea of a customer endorsement and awarded us a $500 discount if we would write a letter as a satisfied customer, which the company could then use in their advertising. This became an ingenious way to accomplish a very satisfying agreement for both parties.

Step 6: Continuous Improvement

This is perhaps the least often practiced step. Once the negotiation is over, there is real value in going back over the process and analyzing ways to improve. You can go back over each of the previous steps and look for things that could be done differently. For example, Were your objectives met? How well did your outcomes match your "bottom line"? Was your planning sufficient? Did your organization plan work? How would you do it next time? Were you able to gain and maintain control? If not, what did you learn that you could do more effectively next time? How well were you able to close the negotiation? It has been said that the mark of a really good negotiation is that both parties would come to the same agreement again if they had it to do over. Keep in mind that people can negotiate for many years and still learn more about it. Negotiation is a highly complex set of communication skills, as we shall see in the next section.

Negotiation Strategy and Tactics

A survey by the J. D. Powers company (1992) found that 68 percent of car buyers dreaded negotiating with the auto salesperson for a new car, whereas 32 percent said that they enjoyed it. In our culture we are not used to negotiating. We pretty much pay whatever price is shown on a product. However, as we saw in the moving van example above, there is often some room to negotiate.

Negotiation Styles and Outcomes

Personal traits of negotiators often affect negotiation outcomes. It is therefore of practical value to understand various negotiating behaviors.

Cheung and colleagues (2006) identified five negotiating styles: integrating, obliging, avoiding, dominating, and compromising. They are characterized as follows:

Integrating

- I collaborate with the other to come up with a decision acceptable to us.
- I try to bring all concerns out in the open so that the issues can be resolved in the best possible way.
- I exchange accurate information with the other so that we can solve the problem together.
- I try to work with the other to find solutions to a problem that will satisfy our expectations.
- I try to investigate an issue with the other to find a solution that will be acceptable to everyone involved.
- I try to work with the other for a proper understanding of a problem.

Obliging

- I try to satisfy the expectations of the other.
- I usually try to accommodate the wishes of the other.
- I generally try to satisfy the needs of the other.
- I give in to the wishes of the other.
- I often go along with the suggestions of the other.
- I usually allow concession to the other.
- I attempt to avoid being "put on the spot" and try to keep my conflict with the other to myself.

Dominating

- I use my authority to make a decision in my favor.
- I use my influence to get my ideas accepted.

- I sometimes use my power to win a competitive situation.
- I am generally firm in pursuing my side of the issue.
- I use my expertise to make a decision in my favor.

Compromising

- I try to find a middle course to resolve an impasse.
- I negotiate with the other so that compromise can be reached.
- I try to integrate my ideas with the other to come up with a decision jointly.
- I use "give and take" so that a compromise can be reached.
- I try to avoid unpleasant exchanges with the other.

Avoiding

- I try to stay away from disagreement with the other.
- I avoid an encounter with the other.
- I try to keep my disagreements with the other to myself to avoid hard feelings.

These distinctions are more than merely theoretical. In their study of negotiating styles and dispute resolution outcomes in highly conflict-saturated Hong Kong construction industry, Cheung and colleagues (2006) found that the use of obliging, dominating, and avoiding styles was less influential in achieving functional negotiation outcomes. Integrating style was found to be useful in achieving the functional negotiation outcomes while the use of compromising style was practical in resolving disputes.

Assumptions

Before actually entering into a negotiation, we should first check our assumptions. The following are a few assumptions often recommended by experienced negotiators.

Both Parties Have Some Needs to Be Met   If you are selling a car, then the buyer obviously has some need for transportation. He or she also has financial needs, time constraints, psychological needs, and so on. The more we are able to recognize the other party's needs, the more likely we are to be successful in negotiating.

Both Parties Should Avoid a Win-Lose Philosophy   Sometimes it may seem that the negotiation is a one-shot experience. This may lead us to conclude that we don't have to worry about the ethics involved. However, many times we cross paths with the same people again, so our long-term reputations are very important. People have long memories. If we mistreat them, they are likely to want to return the favor at some future date. This is especially true in ongoing relationships—in families, with friends, and at work, experienced negotiators work hard to have the other party feel good about the negotiation's outcome.

Many Issues Are (Potentially) Negotiable When we see a formal contract such as a printed form, the power of authority leads us to feel that we do not have the discretion to change any of the terms in that contract. This may be a false assumption (Cohen, 1996). One of the authors was once trying to hire a very prestigious man. His attorney presented us with a formal employment agreement on behalf of this man. The terms of employment were very extreme. It seemed he was asking for a lot more than we would ever be able to provide in the way of salary, benefits, travel budget, clerical support, and so on. When we actually sat down to negotiate in person with the man, he said the document was only intended to get the discussion started. He ended up agreeing to work for a grand total of $1 per year (since he was wealthy enough to work without need for pay). He did, however, have psychological needs that were met by his affiliation with our organization.

Think about a top-performing basketball player such as Rasheed Wallace. The Detroit Pistons were eager to sign Wallace after he helped the Pistons win the national title in 2004. At one point, the Pistons were just waiting for a "yea" or a "nay" from Wallace. "And the 'nay' is just to bump it up (meaning salary) a little more" (Lage, 2004). After negotiation, Rasheed signed a deal worth $57 million over 5 years.

It is said that even the definition of who is dead and who is alive has been changed. A few years ago the definition of death was renegotiated between the American Bar Association and the American Medical Association. In order to harvest organs from a donor, there has to be an agreed-upon definition of when the donor is legally dead. Prior to the redefinition, a person was dead when his or her heart stopped beating. With the new definition, a person is dead when he or she is "brain dead," even if the heart continues to beat. This seemingly extreme example shows that even the distinction between dead and alive is negotiable.

One of the most flexible or negotiable issues is a deadline. For example, someone may ask you to complete a task by a certain deadline. You might want to try negotiating that deadline as you begin to gain more experience as a negotiator. You may have already negotiated with a professor for an extension on a deadline for an assignment. To be sure, you will encounter some situations in which there may be no room to negotiate. That is why we hedge when we say that many issues are (potentially) negotiable.

To Be Successful, You Must Consider the Other Person's Needs As with all forms of communication, you must analyze your audience in order to tailor your communication strategies and tactics to the particular situation. You would certainly behave differently in trying to ask one of your parents for something as opposed to asking a friend. Always keep in mind that in order to negotiate successfully, you must keep the other person's needs in mind.

Meanings and Standards Are Not Always the Same In Chapter 3, we saw that there is a great deal of potential for misunderstanding based on the use of language. In negotiating, it is very important to keep in mind that there is great potential to assume that we are using meanings the same way, when in fact we are not. For example, in many labor contracts it is written that things will be done within a "reasonable period of time." You can imagine how this is open to many different interpretations. On the other hand, so-called weasel words (called this because they enable you to weasel your way out of a firm commitment) are sometimes used on purpose, to allow both parties flexibility.

Different people interpret language in different ways. For example, in real estate contracts, it is typical to include language that states the draperies, wall coverings, carpeting, and other items that are affixed by screws, nails, glue, and so on will be included in the property. However, once one of the authors bought a house and discovered upon taking occupancy that the mailbox had been taken off its post, all the light bulbs had been taken out of their sockets, and a number of other items had been removed as well.

The above example may appear trivial, but it points to a fundamental cognitive problem of conflict management: "Whatever happens in negotiations will be interpreted and framed by stakeholders based on their different belief-value systems and world views" (Hoffman, 2005). An example of this discrepancy occurred in 2000, during the Camp David summit between Israeli Prime Minister Barak and Palestinian Chairman Arafat. The issue of sovereignty over Jerusalem's holy places was discussed—namely, the problem of what for Israel is the "Temple Mount" and for Palestinians "Haram al-Sharif." Among formulations offered as framework for an agreement for the division of Israeli and Palestinian sovereignty was the following: "Israeli sovereignty over the Western Wall and the space sacred to Judaism of which it is a part" or "the Western Wall and the holy of holies of which it is the part" (cited in Hoffmann, 2005). One of Barak's advisors clarified that while historically "holy of holies" referred to the "four square meters that the High Priest would enter on Yom Kippur," Barak used it to refer to the territory that included Haram al-Sharif (Hofmann, 2005). Such interpretation, however, directly contradicted the Palestinian idea of sovereignty of the Haram. Since Arafat could not know how "the sacred places of Judaism" or the "holy of holies" would be interpreted by his counterparts, agreement on the issue was not reached.

Principled Negotiation

Roger Fisher and his colleagues at Harvard University have devised a method for bringing a higher level of professionalism to negotiation. Fisher, Ury, and Patton (1991) write persuasively that negotiators typically see negotiations as either soft or hard. They reject this view and suggest that a third approach is the better way. This is **principled negotiation,** or deciding an issue based on its merits rather than by taking positions and trying to get the other party to come to our position. As we shall see, principled negotiation has four primary rules of thumb: (1) separate people from the problem; (2) focus on interests, not positions; (3) invent various options for mutual gain; and (4) use objective criteria.

Separate People from the Problem   As we mentioned above, people have psychological needs as well as substantive needs in a negotiation. Most negotiation

Herb Cohen is one of the country's foremost negotiation experts. Here are a few tips from his book *Negotiate This!* (2003):

- Detach yourself emotionally.
- Set high goals.
- Remember, "no" does not mean never.
- Generally, begin in an amiable fashion.
- Keep the ultimate decision maker out of the nitty-gritty dealmaking.
- Display respect.

- Start with mutual interests.
- Try to acquire information about the other party's beliefs, motives, values, and needs.
- View yourself as a problem solver.
- Attempt to see the problem through their eyes.
- When we care too much the adrenaline starts flowing, causing us to become doped up and dumbed down.
- Strive for an attitude of caring, but not t-h-a-t much.

takes place in the context of an ongoing relationship. In some cases, the relationship is far more important than any one specific negotiation. In negotiations, often tempers flare and the disagreement over issues tends to erode or even destroy the relationship. The lesson here is that we can be more effective if we treat each other with respect than if we get sarcastic, insult each other, or call each other names. Fisher, Ury, and Patton (1991) put it this way: "[Be] hard on the problem, [but] soft on the people" (p. 54). If the other party behaves emotionally, it is usually best not to escalate the conflict by reacting in kind. The following is an excerpt from an actual conversation that occurred in the presence of one of the authors.

Nahal: Would you enter the accounts payable a different way next time? I think this new method would streamline the process.

Heather: Why is it that you can't do things our way? You're not even from this country!

Nahal: Well, I wouldn't talk! You can't even keep a husband! How many times have you been divorced?

What do you think is the likelihood of these two people ever reaching agreement on the accounting system (or much of anything) after that exchange?

Focus on Interests, Not Positions

One of the authors was in a negotiation recently in which there were three people on one side and five people on the other. In the opening remarks, the speaker on the one side stated that the discussion was to center on three alternatives (positions). Much arguing followed and a lot of time was wasted until someone suggested that we start over and look at what we all could agree was in our mutual best interests. Then a lot of ideas were suggested, and resolution came about rather quickly.

The second approach in this example focused on mutual interests rather than on the three specific positions. Most negotiators focus on positions because they may not be aware of the alternative approach. If you try to decide where to meet, you may say, "My place or yours?" This is a very common way to decide things. However, it is not always the best way when parties have a hard time agreeing. Perhaps a better alternative would be to ask, "Where would you feel comfortable meeting?" One natural outcome of positional bargaining is that once you have stated your position, it makes you look and feel foolish if you have to "back down." This causes you to "lose face" or feel embarrassed. Thus, it is better to take the focusing-on-interests approach rather than the focusing-on-positions approach in the first place.

Fisher, Ury, and Patton (1991) offer the following example. At one point, the Egyptian-Israeli peace negotiations reached an impasse because the Egyptians wanted the Sinai Peninsula returned to them, whereas Israel insisted on keeping the territory. Both sides were focusing on positions.

When they looked at interests instead of positions, they found that Israel's interests were in security. The Israelis did not want Egyptian tanks near their border, ready to strike. Egypt's interests were focused on national sovereignty. The Sinai had been part of Egypt since the time of the Pharaohs. The two parties eventually agreed to a plan that returned the Sinai to Egypt, but made it a demilitarized zone (with no tanks or guns), so that both parties could satisfy their interests (Fisher, Ury, and Patton, 1991, pp. 41–42).

Focusing on interests usually involves each side's asking questions instead of making statements. The more information that is shared, the easier it is to determine what the other party is seeking. Keep in mind that the motivation behind many actions is rooted in such basic interests as:

- Security
- Economic well-being
- A sense of belonging
- Recognition
- Control over one's life

If you keep these in mind, you improve your chances of negotiating effectively. Also keep in mind that the more complex the negotiation, the harder it is to use positional bargaining. There may be simply too many issues. One of the authors was once on a management team that negotiated with labor union representatives on a contract worth over $300 million. There were a total of 1,013 articles in the union contract and each one had to be negotiated. As you can imagine, it would be pretty hard to formulate positions on that many issues.

Invent Various Options for Mutual Gain   As we shall see in Chapter 12, problem solving and decision making can be complex processes. One of the most common mistakes is to jump immediately to the solution phase without carefully looking at the definition of the problem, the symptoms of the problem, the root causes of those symptoms, and the criteria for an effective solution. Only after we take those steps can we begin to effectively brainstorm multiple potential solutions to be compared to our criteria. The same is true in negotiation situations.

Use Objective Criteria   Imagine that you are trying to negotiate with your boss for a pay increase. How would you go about proving your case? One way is to compare what you are doing with others who are doing the same thing with the same number of years' experience. What if you are trying to sell a house? How do you decide what to ask for it? The typical method in real estate is to get three other examples of "comparable" property in comparable locations and look at their value. When you plan to buy or sell a used car, you can use the *Kelley Blue Book*, which lists the values of all makes and models of cars of each model year. In the labor contract negotiations mentioned above, both management and the union used national studies that showed what the pay rate was for comparable employees. Both sides also showed agreements from other comparable institutions that had recently completed their contract negotiations. The union showed other organizations that had given large percentage increases, while management showed settlements that had given smaller percentage increases. These are all examples of using objective criteria on which to base your discussion.

Using objective criteria tends to make a negotiation efficient, especially if both parties can agree on the criteria at the beginning of the negotiation. The alternative is to argue different perceptions, which often gets us nowhere. One party thinks workers are underpaid; the other thinks the opposite. In a divorce settlement, a way of using this method would be for the two parties to decide on rights for visiting the children, before deciding which parent gets custody. No methods are foolproof, but principled negotiation methods tend to offer an alternative to the traditional cut-throat methods often encountered.

The following are a few principled negotiation techniques that are very helpful:

"Correct me if I'm wrong." One party may say, "You have mentioned that this program would have to operate at a loss. Correct me if I'm wrong, but hasn't this program made a profit for the organization?" This conveys the message that you think the facts are different from the ones that have been stated, but leaves open the possibility that you may not have all the facts.

"We appreciate what you have done." This shows that you are recognizing the other party's efforts. It acknowledges the need in all of us to have our efforts, patience, consideration, creativity, and so on appreciated.

"Let me check to see if my facts are correct." It helps to say something like, "According to my notes, we have agreed on the following four items. Would you agree with these as I have stated them?" Negotiations can often become complicated. This technique gives both parties the opportunity to review and to make sure that misunderstandings have not occurred.

"Let me see if I understand what you are saying." One party may say, "As I understand it, you are saying that if I loan you my tennis racket this Saturday, you will let me borrow five CDs for our party." Again, this restatement gives both parties the opportunity to double-check to see whether they have misunderstood one another.

"Here is where I have trouble following your reasoning." Another way to say this is "Help me understand your reasoning on this point." This is a nonthreatening way to ask the other person to explain his or her thinking a different way. You can also ask, "Can you explain that a different way? I am not following your line of reasoning." The goal is to clarify the understanding without antagonizing the other party.

We have found these five principled negotiation techniques to be invaluable over many years of negotiations. We recommend that you try them to see if they work as well for you. Remember that principled negotiation is only effective if you use effective communication techniques. Sam Horn, author and speaker, takes a close look at effective communication techniques in conflict and negotiation. She defines the martial arts of communication as "Tongue Fu®" (Horn, 2004). The goal of Sam Horn's organization is "to create a diplomatic group dynamic in which everyone has an incentive to get along." If people get along, then they can effectively negotiate to reach commonality in their goals. Effective communication is critical in this pursuit (Horn, 2004).

Horn (2004) illustrates some of the Tongue Fu practices that can lead to more effective conflict resolution and conflict diffusion. For example, Horn recommends asking questions to get to the root of the problem instead of responding to the verbal attacks of an opposing party. She suggests using hand gestures to pause a heated discussion, such as using the "time out" symbol instead of verbally jumping into the conflict.

Horn stresses the use of empathy and listening and warns against the use of the word "but." Imagine that you are in a negotiation and the opposing party says something like, "I agree with your plans on addressing the issue *but* I still think that you could have worked more effectively with the team." You automatically only hear the part of the sentence that occurs after the "but."

You can read these steps in detail along with information about her earlier book, *Tongue Fu!® How to Deflect, Disarm, and Defuse Any Verbal Conflict* on her Web site at *www.SamHorn.com*.

In addition, we suggest that you try to use the following guidelines for negotiation:

- Establish a cooperative tone at the outset.
- Strive for a win-win outcome.
- Ask lots of questions and really listen to the answers. Knowledge of the other person's needs, expectations, preferences, pressures, and strategies will help you reach an understanding.

- Find a line of reasoning that meets your needs while also meeting the other party's needs at the least cost to you.
- Know your "bottom line." Don't give away more than your maximum or accept less than your minimum.
- Stay calm. If you feel you are losing your temper, call for a break.
- Don't appear too anxious for a solution. Avoid snap judgments.
- If you reach an impasse, either suggest a recess or restate the consequences of not reaching an agreement. You may also suggest a trade of items from each party. (Adapted from Deep and Sussman, 1998, p. 61)

If you practice effective communication when you find yourself in a conflict situation, you can facilitate the negotiation and resolution processes to the benefit of both parties. Effective communication is essential in making progress toward mutually beneficial solutions.

Summary

In this chapter, we have focused on communication situations that involve conflict and negotiation. There is potential for conflict in virtually every arena of human communication. It is a normal and predictable part of the communication process. Therefore, the better equipped we are to manage conflict, the more likely we are to improve this aspect of our communication skills.

We discussed the definition of conflict and several different levels of conflict. We also discussed the Kilmann-Thomas model of conflict resolution, as well as several tactics and techniques for resolving conflicts. In the negotiation section, we defined negotiation and examined a six-step model of the negotiation process. We then described negotiation strategy, including some important assumptions and several negotiating styles that offen affect outcomes. Five techniques for conducting "principled negotiation" were also discussed.

Key Terms

Appeasement	Denial	Postponement	Semantic focus
Avoidance	Intergroup conflict	Prescription	Shifting
Avoiding topics	Interpersonal conflict	Presumptive attribution	Underresponsiveness
Competition	Intragroup conflict	Principled negotiation	
Conflict	Intrapersonal conflict	Qualification	

Review Questions

1. Define and discuss the definition of "conflict" given in this chapter.

2. Discuss the important elements in this definition.

3. Define and discuss the four levels of conflict discussed in this chapter.

4. Discuss and explain the Kilmann-Thomas model of conflict resolution. Discuss each of the major parts of the model.

5. Define negotiation.

6. Identify and discuss the six-step process in negotiations.

7. Identify and discuss five assumptions of successful negotiation.

8. Define principled negotiation and discuss four primary rules of thumb.

9. Identify and discuss five techniques of principled negotiation.

10. Write an essay discussing the most important ideas that you feel you have learned from this chapter. How can you put these to use?

Exercise

1. Use the Kilmann-Thomas conflict model to identify your preferred style. In small groups, discuss the advantages and disadvantages of each style.

Suggested Readings

Acuff, Frank. *How to Negotiate with Anyone Anywhere around the World.* New York: AMACOM, 1997.

This excellent book covers negotiations with people from different cultures.

Borisoff, Deborah, and David A. Victor. *Conflict Management,* 2nd ed. Englewood Cliffs, NJ: Prentice-Hall, 1998.

A communication skills approach to conflict management.

Camp, Jim. *Start With No.* New York: Crown Business, 2002.

This book advocates a very hard line style of negotiation. It is useful to learn one of a wide range of styles.

Cloke, Kenneth, and Joan Goldsmith. *Resolving Conflicts at Work,* 2nd ed. San Francisco: Jossey-Bass, 2005.

This book offers eight strategies for resolving conflicts on the job.

Cohen, Herb. *Negotiate This!* New York: Warner Books, 2003.

Once again Herb Cohen has written a very readable book filled with practical advice for any negotiator.

Coltri, Laurie. *Conflict Diagnosis and Alternative Dispute Resolution.* Upper Saddle River, NJ: Pearson/Prentice-Hall, 2004.

This book is for the very advanced student. It is excellent in that its approach is unique and well grounded in legal issues.

Fisher, Roger, and Danny Ertel. *Getting Ready to Negotiate.* New York: Penguin, 1995.

A little workbook that helps you prepare for upcoming negotiations.

Fisher, Roger, William Ury, and Bruce Patton. *Getting to Yes: Negotiating Agreement without Giving In,* 2nd ed. New York: Penguin, 1991.

A groundbreaking book on "principled negotiation."

Karrass, Chester. *Give and Take,* 2nd ed. New York: William Morrow, 1995.

A worthwhile list of many negotiation strategies and tactics. This is the most exhaustive list available.

Lewicki, Roy, Bruce Barry, and David Saunders. *Negotiation: Readings, Exercises and Cases,* 5th ed. New York: McGraw-Hill, 2007.

This excellent book is a comprehensive look at negotiation principles and practices.

Reardon, Kathleen. *Becoming a Skilled Negotiator.* New York: John Wiley & Sons, 2005.

This book takes a more quantitative approach and is somewhat more advanced.

Walker, Michael A., and George L. Harris. *Negotiation: Six Steps to Success.* Upper Saddle River, NJ: Bantam Books, 1995.

A comprehensive explanation of the six-step model for structuring the negotiation process discussed in this chapter.

Whetten, David, and Kim Cameron. *Developing Management Skills,* 6th ed. Upper Saddle River, NJ: Prentice-Hall, 2005.

This book has a chapter on managing conflict that is worth reading.

Wilmot, William, and Joyce L. Hocker. *Interpersonal Conflict,* 5th ed. New York: McGraw-Hill, 1998.

A theoretical book with an excellent coverage of the topics.

 # For Supplementary Information

Log onto the Online Learning Center at *www.mhhe.com/tubbsmoss11.*

7

Ethics and Communication

Chapter Objectives

After reading this chapter, you should be able to:

1. Define ethics and identify three of the most common principles people use in making ethical decisions.
2. Discuss Aristotle's concept of the golden mean and give two examples of it.
3. Compare and contrast the ethical views of Kant and the utilitarians.
4. Discuss the concept of the veil of ignorance and its relationship to a theory of justice.
5. Identify the excuses people give in defending lies and discuss three ethical issues concerned with lying. Give examples from at least three communication contexts.
6. Discuss three forms of intentional misrepresentation.
7. Define plagiarism and explain the difference between plagiarism and paraphrasing.
8. Discuss three issues concerning the disclosure of information. Give four examples of contexts in which they might occur.
9. Discuss the ethical issues that grow out of the use of the new technologies.
10. Explain the difference between whistleblowing and leaking information. Discuss the ethical issues raised by each and the concept of moral courage.

There is something terribly unsettling about Tom Ripley, the main character in Patricia Highsmith's novel *The Talented Mr. Ripley* and the film of the same name. Tom (played in the film by Matt Damon) is a young American down on his luck who meets Mr. Greenleaf, a wealthy businessman. They strike a bargain: Greenleaf will pay Tom $1,000 to go to Europe and persuade his playboy son Dickie to return home from Europe, where he is living the life on the Italian Riviera. Tom sets off for Italy where he befriends Dickie (Jude Law) and his girlfriend Marge (Gwyneth Paltrow), and slowly their lives become entwined as Tom moves in to share their house. Tom later deceives, impersonates, and ultimately murders Dickie, taking on his identity. Theft, lying, manipulation, harrowing chase scenes follow as Tom is about to be cornered and unmasked. The viewer watches as Tom's actions become increasingly brazen, always waiting for him to be caught. But this is not an ordinary mystery. In the last scene we suddenly understand that Tom Ripley will walk away scot-free.

Why is this ending so troubling? In the film, as in the novel, we inhabit a world where none of the moral distinctions between right and wrong, none of the ethical principles or distinctions we have learned, matter. Today we live in a world dominated by questions about ethics in the public sphere—political ethics, business ethics, and media ethics. We live private lives but, like it or not, we are touched by public events. In this chapter we look at ethics as a continuum that extends from the public sphere to the private decisions that color all our actions and personal relationships.

The study of communication has always reflected an interest in ethics. Confucius wrote on ethics in the sixth century B.C., and in the fourth century B.C. Aristotle discussed the importance of appeals to *ethos,* personal qualities such as honesty and credibility, in communication. This chapter considers some of the thorny issues related to ethics in communication, or "communicating with integrity."

Ethics has been defined as *the study of the general nature of morals and of the specific moral choices to be made by a person.* Notice the word "choices." Ethics involves communication choices so that, by examining and becoming more aware of our own values, we become more responsible for the consequences of our actions.

Yet our moral choices and subsequent actions often lead to conflict when people feel we are trying to impose our own ethical values on them. How to reconcile the claims of personal freedom with those of moral responsibility has been debated over the centuries. The communications scholar Nick Couldry writes:

> By *ethics,* I mean neither a specific moral code . . . nor an agreed list of specific, narrowly circumscribed "virtues" . . . but rather an open-ended process of reflecting on how we need to act so that we can live well, both individually and collectively. (2006, p. 102)

Giving thought beforehand to the basis of our ethical choices enables us to think through rather than rationalize our decisions:

> If ethical principles are to be a guide to future behavior rather than a rationalization of acts already performed, it's important for us to stake out our

moral turf before we are thrust into a specific situation . . . The motivation to act ethically can be self-imposed, socially mandated, or divinely inspired. But regardless of the impetus, we need to have a way to determine the difference between right and wrong, good and bad, virtue and vice. (Griffin, 2006)

Many theories have been proposed about the basis for our ethical choices. *Moral Minds,* a recent book by Harvard professor Marc Hauser, brings together the findings of several disciplines including neuroscience, linguistics, and evolutionary biology. He argues that human beings have evolved a moral instinct, "a capacity that naturally grows within each child, designed to generate rapid judgments about what is morally right or wrong based on an unconscious grammar of action" (2006, p. xviii).

In other words, the moral instinct itself is universal, and human beings build moral systems that are specific to the culture they grow up in. Once our own moral limits are fixed, Hauser explains,

we may be as perplexed by another community's moral system as we are by their language. Appreciating the fact that we share a universal moral grammar, and that at birth we could have acquired any of the world's moral systems, should provide us with a sense of comfort, a sense that perhaps we can understand each other. (p. 426)

In this chapter we begin by looking at some of the major ethical principles proposed by Western thinkers and then examine several issues that arise in many different communication contexts including the many challenging problems that have emerged with the use of the new technologies.

PRINCIPLES

The Golden Mean

Aristotle is thought of by many scholars as the founder of the communication discipline. A Greek biologist—and a tutor to Alexander the Great—he believed that ethics had to do with inner character rather than just overt behaviors.

Perhaps no concept in philosophy has been more widely cited than Aristotle's **golden mean.** According to Aristotle, *morality is to be found in moderation.* Aristotle views moral virtues as choices or modes of choice. He considers each virtue as the mean, *the middle path between two extremes—excess and deficiency.* We can see this most clearly with the virtue of temperance, the mean between eating and drinking too little or too much. Similarly, courage would be the mean between the extremes of fear (deficiency) and overconfidence (excess). Truthfulness would be the mean between false modesty and boastfulness; justice would be the mean between distributing too few goods (or punishments) and too many (Aristotle, 1947, pp. 333–337).

Some have interpreted Aristotle as saying that good is that which is desirable for its own sake—in other words, it is an end in itself. Since Aristotle was a biologist, he might have been interested in modern studies showing that people who report having committed fewer acts they consider immoral also report significantly lower levels of stress; other studies find that those who volunteer to help others actually live longer (Schuller, 1991, p. 97).

Though Aristotle is emphasizing what is within the range of human possibility, it is important not to misinterpret the principle of the golden mean. To advocate moderation is not to say that all behaviors are acceptable: "There is no mean for adultery, murder, theft . . . Not every action nor every passion admits of a mean" (1947, p. 341). Similarly, Aristotle condemns lying; saying that "truth is noble and full of praise."

The aim of ethics for Aristotle is the happiness of the individual; the aim of politics involves the welfare of the entire community. Although Aristotle believed personal ethics to be subordinate to politics, this did not create a conflict of loyalties:

> This principle does not entail that the individual must sacrifice his interests to those of the community, except under unusual conditions such as war, because he assumed that the needs of both normally coincide. (Abelson, 1967, p. 85)

Our own interests, Aristotle would say, are usually in harmony with those of our society.

The Categorical Imperative

Suppose that every time you made a decision about ethics and acted on it, your decision became a universal law. This is the guiding principle proposed by the eighteenth-century German philosopher Immanuel Kant:

> Act only according to that maxim by which you can at the same time will that it should become a universal law. (1959, p. 39)

Kant's principle is known as the **categorical imperative**—that is, *a command or obligation to act (an "imperative") that is absolute ("categorical")—one with no exceptions or conditions.*

A categorical imperative makes certain behaviors unacceptable under any circumstances. For example, to Kant telling the truth is a sacred duty. There are no circumstances under which it would be acceptable for us to lie because, says Kant, we always harm someone by telling a lie: If we don't harm a particular person, still we do harm to humankind by undermining the nature of law. Take an extreme case—one that Kant himself considered: Would you tell a lie to prevent a murder? Kant argues that telling a lie even to prevent a murder would not be justified.

For Kant morality is measured by our intentions to obey universal laws of morality rather than by the consequences or outcomes of our actions—even if they will spare another's feelings or protect that person's welfare.

Many consider Kant's most significant contribution to ethical theory to be his requirement of "universal obedience to a rule of action":

> It expresses more precisely and unambiguously the "golden rule" to be found in all the great religions, and it has been incorporated, in one form or another, in most modern systems of ethical theory. (Abelson, 1967, p. 95)

We find an emphasis on universals similar to that of Kant in many religious systems and writings, including the Ten Commandments of the Old Testament and Saint Augustine's prohibition that all lies are sins:

> To use speech, then, for the purpose of deception, and not for its appointed end, is a sin. Nor are we to suppose that there is any lie that is not a sin, because it is sometimes possible, by telling a lie, to do service to another. (Augustine, 1961)

Utilitarianism

In sharp contrast to Kant, British philosophers Jeremy Bentham and John Stuart Mill place primary value not on our moral intentions but on *the outcomes or consequences of our actions.*

Bentham proposed a "hedonistic calculus," in which the amount of pleasure an action creates is weighed against the amount of pain it causes. Mill refers to the foundation of utilitarianism as the Greatest Happiness Principle:

> Actions are right in proportion as they tend to promote happiness, wrong [insofar] as they tend to produce the reverse of happiness. (Mill, 1968, p. 249)

Happiness is the greatest good, and for Mill "happiness" refers to "pleasure and the absence of pain," unhappiness to pain and the lack of pleasure. Mill extends the notion of happiness to include not simply pleasure but quality, so that pleasure is defined more broadly and includes intellectual pleasure and other values.

Mill's later formulation of **utilitarianism** in the nineteenth century is the best known:

> Seek the greatest happiness for the greatest number.

Utilitarianism grew out of concern for political and social reforms—hence its emphasis on what will benefit the greatest number of people—and was responsible for English legislative reforms during the nineteenth century (Abelson, 1967, p. 96). According to this view, the claims and welfare of individuals or smaller groups have to be subordinated to the claims of the greatest number of people.

Justice and the Veil of Ignorance

The contemporary American philosopher John Rawls argues for a principle of justice rather than utility. In *A Theory of Justice* (1971), a book on political and social philosophy, he suggests a fair procedure by which we can agree on common ethical principles: To free ourselves of bias and self-interest because of our social position, education, and so on—what are sometimes called "accidents of birth"—Rawls proposes that we should all be placed behind a **veil of ignorance:**

> First of all, no one knows his place in society, his class position or social status; nor does he know his fortune in the distribution of natural assets and abilities, his intelligence and strength, and the like. Nor, again, does anyone know his conception of the good, the particulars of his rational plan of life, or even the special features of the psychology such as his aversion to risk or liability to optimism or pessimism. More than this, I assume that the parties do not know the particular circumstances of their own society. (p. 137)

Because we do not know our situations in society or our natural assets, argues Rawls, "no one is in a position to tailor principles to his advantage" (p. 139). We don't know which principles would be in our own interest. This also eliminates the possibility of groups banding together to form a coalition, for they do not know how to favor themselves. Once all these factors are corrected for, we make an ethical decision in which there will be unanimity of choice—fairness: No single person, group, or generation will be favored. (Rawls believes the "notion of the veil of ignorance is . . . implicit in Kant's ethics" [p. 140].)

Imagine the world as redesigned by Rawls:

> The participants may be male or female, 10-years-old or 90, a Russian or a Pole, rookie or veteran, black or white, advertising executive or sales representative for a weekly. As we negotiate social agreements in the situation of imagined equality behind the veil of ignorance, . . . we inevitably seek to protect the weaker party and to minimize risks. In case I emerge from the veil as a beginning reporter rather than a big-time publisher, I will opt for fair treatment for the former. The most vulnerable party receives priority in these cases and the result, Rawls would contend, is a just resolution. (Christians et al., 1998, p. 8)

Rawls proposes then that a principle of justice or fairness must include protection of those whose position in the society is weakest—whether due to age, illness, status, or income—and that what is moral is what is fair for all.

Rushworth Kidder, who founded the Institute for Global Ethics, identifies three of the most common principles people use in ethical decision making (2005):

> *Ends-based principles* are exemplified by those we saw in discussing utilitarianism. The focus here is to reach "good outcomes and results rather than on the motives or rules that guided us in our choices" (p. 93).

> *Rule-based principles,* such as the categorical imperative, stress the unchanging, universal codes of behavior. The focus is on duty and obligation.

> *Care-based principles* ask, "What would we want others to do to us?" Kidder links care-based principles with compassion. The Golden Rule is a prime

example: "This principle of reciprocity or reversibility calls on us to imagine that we are in another's shoes, about to be impacted by the very actions we're contemplating" (p. 93). Hauser writes that we find the Golden Rule "in one form or another in all cultures, through either explicit religious doctrine or implicit social norms" (Hauser, 2006, p. 410).

After observing thousands of people in seminars at the Institute for Global Ethics, Kidder has concluded that "most people have more than one principle to which they appeal as the basis for moral choice" (2005, p. 92).

Ethical principles from many other cultures and other times could, of course, be represented here. Our hope is that those we have looked at will serve as a springboard for discussion and reflection as you consider some of the issues involved in making ethical choices about communication.

ISSUES

Lying and Misrepresentation

Truth exists as a human need in two ways: First, in the sense that human beings do not wish to lose their relation to tangible reality . . . Second, human beings feel that communication between them is worthy of respect only if the criterion of truth is given its proper place. Otherwise, communication between human beings is felt to be disrespect. Thus, we can speak of truth as a threefold need of human beings: in relation to reality, to oneself, and to other people. (Mieth, 1997, p. 90)

Perhaps one of the most obvious breaches of ethics is lying. Distorting the truth is so common that over the last decade people have become increasingly disenchanted with politics. At times loss of credibility has also led to the public's disenchantment with the mass media. In his memoir *A Million Little Pieces,* James Frey described spending three months in jail and recounted his addiction and recovery. Highly acclaimed, the book sold over 3 million copies, was praised in literary circles and singled out as an Oprah Book Club selection. Then it was discovered that much in the book had been invented by the author. Oprah Winfrey made a public apology for at first having defended Frey. He appeared on her television show, during which she questioned him, "getting him to admit that he'd inflated his story partly out of a need to look macho and partly because he (correctly) suspected it would sell better" (Freedman, 2006, p. 53):

Writers do not write only for themselves. The events that Frey inflated or invented—jail time, the suicide of a friend, the severity of his stay in a rehab clinic—went right to the core of his story of debasement and redemption. If he never bottomed out the way he described it and if his recovery was not one long, sadistic humiliation, then he is conning readers, passing off snake oil as an antibiotic.

Fiction isn't the spackle you use to fill in the cracks of your research. Fiction and nonfiction make fundamentally different compacts with a reader and are held to fundamentally different standards. . . . In return for the allegiance to factuality, nonfiction can present what may seem implausible and tell a reader, *But that's what really happened.* (p. 53)

Notice the use of the word "compacts"—a compact is an agreement between two parties. Anyone who writes a memoir has made an implicit agreement with the reader that what he or she writes will be true.

Similarly, we expect a newspaper account to be true. Consider the case of Jayson Blair, a well-regarded journalist who had worked at *The New York Times* for five years, advancing from an intern to a national reporter. Then, in 2002, his work at the newspaper came into question. One incident involved a reporter who noticed that one of her stories appeared as part of a story by Blair, but without her byline.

On May 11, 2003, a four-page article about Blair appeared in the *Times:*

The reporter, Jayson Blair, 27, misled readers and *Times* colleagues with dispatches that purported to be from Maryland, Texas and other states, when often he was far away, in New York. He fabricated comments. He concocted scenes. He lifted material from other newspapers and wire ser vices. He selected details from photographs to create the impression he had been somewhere or seen someone, when he had not.

And he used these techniques to write falsely about emotionally charged moments in recent history, from the deadly sniper attacks in suburban Washington to the anguish of families grieving for loved ones killed in Iraq. (Barry et al., 2003, A1)

In one instance Blair reported in a front-page article that he had talked to six wounded marines in a Bethesda naval hospital, but he had never been there and some of the marines were not even in the hospital on the dates he mentioned (Hassan, 2003).

The *Times* itself called Blair's actions "a profound betrayal of trust and a low point in the 152-year history of the newspaper" (Barry et al., 2003, p. A1). Among journalists there was much concern about how Blair's deception could have gone undetected for so long and revived discussion about the issue of plagiarism.

Of course, plagiarism occurs in many different communication contexts (see Wiener [2007], for example). Here **plagiarism** is broadly defined as *using or present-ing as your own the ideas, images, or words of another source—for example, from books or online information—without acknowledgment or permission.* It need not in-volve the use of a written text; it might be an idea for a screenplay, a passage of music, song lyrics, or an image created by an artist. Legal scholar Richard Posner writes that "concealment is at the heart of plagiarism. . . . It is not a mere failure to acknowledge copying" (p. 2007, p. 17). **Paraphrasing,** on the other hand, is *using your own words to express or restate someone else's words or ideas,* and appropriately acknowledging all your sources is a legitimate way to do academic work (Fox, 2004).

When it comes to plagiarism and misrepresentation, academic life is not exempt. For example, how would you feel about one of your professors giving higher grades to student athletes even though they were undeserved? What about someone who received a research grant and did not use any of the money received on the project for which it was intended? Many dramatic instances of fraud and misrepresentation with wide repercussions for the public and for academic life involve misconduct in scientific research. Consider the case of Dr. Hwang Woo-suk of South Korea, who falsely claimed that he had cloned a human embryo in his laboratory and produced stem cell lines from it. In 2004 he was proclaimed a national hero. By 2006 he was disgraced and had admitted to charges of altering his data as well as to the misuse of state funds.

Another recent case is that of Eric Poehlman, a faculty member of the University of Vermont, who falsified data on clinical research: The studies of aging, menopause, and obesity that he supervised in his lab were used in support of other medical experiments. "He presented fraudulent data in lectures and in published papers, and he used this data to obtain millions of dollars in federal grants from the National Institutes of Health" (Interlandi, 2006, p. 98). He was brought to trial in 2005 because a young research assistant at his lab, who had looked up to him as a mentor, began questioning and cross-checking Poehlman's data.

> More frequent, according to a study published in *Nature* in June 2005, are smaller lapses in ethical judgment, like failing to present data that contradicts your previous research or inappropriately assigning author credit. (Interlandi, 2006, p. 101)

Though at times they seem remote, ethical questions occur in many other academic contexts—for example, in graduate study. After the oral defense of her thesis, a doctoral candidate in psychology we know was told by an eminent psychologist on her dissertation committee that he wanted her to add his name to her forthcoming research. In actuality, he was a guest reader and had nothing to do with her work. She refused. Some graduate students have also seen their research papers used, without credit, in the publications of their supervising professors.

Cheating and academic fraud have many unforeseen consequences. This is certainly true of teachers who pad grades or even alter student answers on tests. In *Freakonomics*, economist Steven Levitt and his coauthor discuss the case of a grade-school teacher who cheats by changing the answers of her grade-school students on a high-stakes test so that their grades will be higher and they will be promoted. Incentives for the teacher might include praise and professional advancement. She might even rationalize that she was helping her students to succeed, but as the authors point out, "these students (and their parents) would be in for a terrible shock once they reached the seventh grade" (2006, p. 30). The very students who most need to be identified as weaker so that they get appropriate help and placement are thus promoted to the next grade, where the possibility of failing only increases.

On a personal level, what is your feeling about cheating and plagiarism in school? If a good many classmates do it, does this make it all right? Results of research conducted nationwide by the Center for Academic Integrity and released in 2005 show that cheating and plagiarism are on the upswing:

> On most [college] campuses, 70% of students admit to some cheating. Close to one-quarter of the participating students admitted to serious test cheating in the past year and half admitted to one or more instances of serious cheating on written assignments.

The figures for high-school students are also high:

> Studies of 18,000 students at 61 schools, conducted in the last four years [show] over 70% of respondents at public and parochial schools admitted to one or more instances of serious test cheating and of plagiarism using the Internet. 60% admitted to some form of plagiarism. Slightly less than half of the respondents from private schools admitted similar behaviors. About half of all students admitted they had engaged in some level of plagiarism using the Internet. (*www.academicintegrity.org*)

At schools that had honor codes, there was a significantly lower incidence of both cheating on tests (33 to 50 percent) and on assignments (25 to 33 percent).

In her study of lying, philosopher Sissela Bok defines a **lie** as "*any intentionally deceptive message that is stated*" (1999, p. 13; italics added). Thus, she emphasizes a person's intention to deceive or mislead through verbal communication. Paul Ekman, whose research on deception in nonverbal communication we looked at in Chapter 4, also links lying with the liar's intention either to conceal by "leaving out true information" or to falsify, "presenting false information as if it were true" (1985, p. 41).

There is less agreement on how to regard ambiguous or equivocal communication. We've already spoken of euphemisms and unintentionally equivocal language in Chapter 3. Bavelas and her colleagues (1990) define "equivocation" as "avoidance," "communication that is not straightforward: it appears ambiguous, contradictory, tangential, obscure, or even evasive" (p. 28). They argue that the person who equivocates "is not the cause of equivocation. Rather [equivocation] is the result of the individual's communicative situation" (p. 54). In our discussion, the assumption will be that we can and do make choices about ethical and unethical behaviors.

Movies such as *The Lives of Others, The Croupier, Closer, Glengarry Glen Ross*, and *House of Games*, deal with issues of trust, lying, and deception. In *Glengarry Glen Ross*, several real estate salesmen try to hustle and swindle customers into buying large land deals. At one point in the film, a customer is having second thoughts and wants his large check back. The salesman played by Al Pacino says that it has not been cashed by the home office yet, and the customer has nothing to worry about, whereupon another salesman comes into the office and says that he has in fact sent the check in. Later Pacino's character virtually explodes over the incident, telling the other salesman that he is never supposed to open his mouth in front of a customer until he knows what the customer has already been told. In other words, any lie is all right as long as it gets the sale.

Although these films portray an absolute low in personal and business ethics, situations in which we encounter lying are not always so sharply drawn. People have even cited moral reasons for lying. Thus, a perennial question in ethics is whether there are circumstances in which telling a lie is acceptable.

Jensen (1997) makes two important distinctions about truth telling. The first concerns terminology:

> A message that is truthful, full of truth—implies that a communicative act is either fully truthful or fully untruthful. The terminology sets up a two-valued image of polarized options. But there are degrees of truthfulness, twilight zones of truth, gray areas that some call near lies. (p. 87)

Second, he suggests that we think of truth in terms of both accuracy and completeness. Your answer to a question may be accurate yet incomplete; it may not cover everything. But a lack of completeness in your response does not necessarily signify your intention to deceive. Of course your incomplete response may be intended to protect someone. Suppose you're going out to a party and your roommate was not invited. If you just say you're going out for a while but don't say where you are going, are you telling the truth? Are you lying?

Bok finds that, in giving excuses to defend their lying, people appeal to four principles:

- Lying to produce some benefits
- Lying to avoid harm
- Lying for the sake of fairness
- Lying for the sake of truth (usually a truth not known to others) (1999, pp. 73–89)

To some degree, this analysis overlaps with the results of a study of deception in which people gave five reasons for lying: to protect or acquire material resources (for example, money, an apartment, or a job); to decrease or increase their affiliation with others; to protect themselves either by avoiding self-disclosure or enhancing or protecting their self-image; to avoid conflict; to protect other people (Lippard, 1988).

Let's consider a lie that is told to avoid harm by protecting someone else's feelings. In discussing the many behaviors and strategies people use to maintain close relationships, Knapp and Vangelisti (2000) include lying:

> For most couples, the real issue is whether a lie will have a damaging effect on the relationship and whether the motivation for lying is well intended or not. (p. 264)

They then propose three questions in thinking about a lie:

(1) Will this lie help both of us? If the lie is solely for the benefit of one partner, it is more likely to be viewed negatively and incur more relationship damage . . .

(2) Is the lie consistent with the rules of fairness in the relationship?

(3) Does your partner (the lied to) believe you have his or her best interests at heart—both generally and in this specific situation? (p. 264)

Imagine yourself as the person lied to in this relationship and consider your own views. Would you want to know if someone you loved was unfaithful to you, or would you prefer to be spared the pain (Knapp, 2006)? A related issue here is whether a lie such as this, which seems to protect, actually does. Granted, it avoids conflict, one of the reasons people frequently give for lying; but what does it protect—the relationship itself, the person lied to, the liar? Is it in your best interest to remain in the same relationship to the other person, or might you be better off finding out "the worst," trying to hammer out the difficulties, and having the option of ending the relationship?

Consider a more structured two-person relationship. Suppose you are a doctor who discovers that your elderly patient is suffering from a terminal illness and has only a few months to live. Your patient is terrified of even the slightest illness. Do you tell him the truth about his condition?

We know that Kant's categorical imperative would prohibit lying under any circumstances. Aristotle's golden mean might suggest some middle ground between assuring the patient he is fine and telling him everything about his condition, including the amount of time he has to live. On the other hand, a utilitarian might argue that the patient would be happiest not knowing—happiness here being defined as pleasure, or the absence of pain. We also know that it's on such grounds that the family of a patient often asks a doctor not to tell the truth: A utilitarian might think of this decision as producing the greatest happiness for the greatest number. A principle of justice is more difficult to apply, unless we agree on what constitutes "protection." If everyone must be treated equally, the doctor's decision will be the same for all patients.

In a recent article on medical ethics, several doctors affirmed their obligation to tell the truth, unless patients had made clear that if they were dying they did not want to be told. Patients, it was suggested, should state early on the level of information they are comfortable with. This position is a subject of ongoing debate even among doctors.

Issues about lying arise in virtually every communication context. For example, would you lie about having been fired from your last job? Or during a job interview suppose you say you have far more computer experience than you do because you think that will ensure getting hired. If you then go home and learn what you need before you get the job, would you say this is a "white lie," one that is not meant to harm anyone? Many people seem to have a repertoire of lies they identify as harmless—for example, statements that flatter others or statements made to protect people's feelings. "What a perfect gift!" "Mr. Thomas is out for the day." "I have to work late tonight." "I'd love to stay, but I have so much work to do this evening." Do you think white lies are harmless?

Suppose you have just graduated from college and will be going to graduate school in September. You need to earn money over the summer and find a job listing that seems to fit your qualifications perfectly. At the interview you find there is only one hitch. The interviewer makes clear that this is a permanent job and wants a commitment from you of at least a year. There are very few summer jobs. What do you do?

Although you might argue that saying you will stay for the year is a harmless lie, from the employer's point of view it is not. You may do your work well over the summer, but the employer has lost an investment of time and training. It's also a lie that works against you; you certainly can't list this job on your résumé. As Bok points out, many lies described as harmless are not and telling white lies may later necessitate more frequent lies—sometimes lies that are more serious. "And even those lies which would generally be accepted as harmless are not needed whenever their goals can be achieved through completely honest means" (1999, p. 72).

In public and mass communication, lying is sometimes defended for the sake of producing benefits, even for the sake of truth. The ethical dimension of public communication raises many questions, especially about communication from government sources, where so much depends upon public trust. There have been times when governmental decisions about deception were later justified as being in the interest of national security. For example, as more information about the Iran-contra scandal unfolded, it became clear that many denials had been issued by government officials at the same time that incriminating documents were being shredded. In public communication, as in other communication contexts, we can see how initial lying, whatever its motivation, often leads to an intricate web of lies.

Let's consider arguments in mass communication about lying for the sake of some greater truth. For example, suppose a reporter is writing about the welfare system, and, to gain access to inside information, she misrepresents herself: Under an assumed name, she applies for welfare by posing as a homeless person. Suppose also that her intention is to write an article that will not only sell newspapers but may institute possible reforms. Is her lying justified—and if so, on what grounds?

We might return again to the ethical principles looked at earlier. It seems difficult here to follow the golden mean. Given the extremes of identifying oneself as a reporter or posing as a welfare applicant, perhaps a middle path could be taken if the reporter requested interviews with administrators (noting too if they declined to give information) and also interviewed many applicants to the system.

Kant's universal rule suggests that our reporter's deception is just plain wrong; regardless of her motive, the means cannot justify the end. In contrast, utilitarians might argue that the negative consequence of lying (the harm it might cause to the few deceived) would be far outweighed by the number of others who would benefit so that the ends justify the means. (The assumption here, of course, is that we can be sure of the consequences of our actions.) A theory of justice requiring fairness for all might argue against unfairness to those being lied to.

Issues about the media's obligation to its audience are well framed in the following questions:

Does the press have a legitimate advocacy function, or does it best serve
democratic life as an intermediary, a conduit of information and varying
opinions? In a similar vein, should the press mirror events or provide a map

that leads its audience to a destination? The kind of responsibility for justice that a particular medium is seen to possess often depends on how we answer these intermediate questions about the press's proper role and function. (Christians et al., 1998)

Misrepresentations in the mass media have enormous ramifications because of the size of the audience and the frequently high credibility of the sources. As members of a mass communication audience, we must also be able to distinguish between fact and public relations information, between an editorial reflecting the opinion of a newscaster and an advertisement, between information gathered by reporters and information disseminated to them by public relations firms who are working for a large corporation or other special interests. Carole Gorney (1993), a professor of journalism at Lehigh University, observes:

> Public relations consultants should be held accountable for participating in litigation journalism. The practice counters the groups' codes of ethical standards requiring consultants to avoid corrupting the channels of communication and the processes of government. (p. A15)

To avoid such problems, sources should be clearly acknowledged and conflicts of interest made explicit. Misrepresentation in public communication also violates public trust and results in a loss of credibility (see Chapters 13 and 15 on credibility). Journalists who face ethical problems can access several Web sites that will respond to their questions—for example, *www.poynter.org/oncall* and *www. ethicsadvicelineforjournalists.org*. The first is run by the Poynter Institute of Media Studies, the other by Loyola University Chicago and Chicago's chapter of the Society of Professional Journalists.

The new technologies have compounded ethical problems, creating an enormous potential for deception. For example, throughout school you've probably seen students cheat on exams, exchange work on assignments, or hand in papers they didn't write themselves. Students can copy someone's work through fax or e-mail, download material from the Internet, and hand it in without crediting the source; they can even download an entire paper. Web sites with digital libraries of term papers on every subject—sometimes at no charge to the user—and other term-paper sources are widely available.

Ironically, the same technology that makes forms of cheating so widespread is also being used to check this form of plagiarism. Through *www.turnitin.com*, *www.mydropbox.com*, and other sites teachers can—and increasingly are—able to discover plagiarism by comparing student work "against millions of websites, a database of previous submissions and papers offered by the so called term-paper mills" (Hafner, 2001, G6). Students who make use of such papers not only misrepresent themselves by handing in such work; they also undermine the original work of fellow students and affect grading for the entire class.

How do the new technologies affect personal relationships? We know that today many relationships are established over computer networks through chat rooms and forums, and that people meet for the first time and develop relationships online, some of which later become face-to-face relationships. We develop our identities as members of online communities and form impressions of others who are online. (For how people represent themselves in online dating, see Chapter 9.)

Consider the case of a young neuropsychologist who uses a wheelchair after being in a car accident that had disfigured her and killed her boyfriend. Although she had also lost her ability to speak, Joan began making online friends through CompuServe, where her upbeat attitude and emotional strength made her a source of support for many other disabled people. Over a period of two years, Joan formed many friendships and even became involved in some online romances. Then came an extraordinary discovery:

> Joan was revealed as being not disabled at all. More to the point, Joan, in fact, was not a woman. She was really a man we'll call Alex—a prominent New York psychiatrist in his early fifties engaged in a bizarre, all-consuming experiment to see what it felt like to be female, and to experience the intimacy of female friendship. (Cited in Lea and Spears, 1995, p. 199)

Misrepresenting one's identity—even gender—is not that uncommon in online communication, though the outcome and repercussions are usually not so dramatic. Yet this kind of manipulative interpersonal deception is part of what some communication scholars describe as "the darker side of relationships" (p. 224).

Other sources of misrepresentation online are **hate sites**, which target groups as various as Jews, homosexuals, Muslims, women, African Americans, and "foreigners." HateWatch, a nonprofit organization that monitors *online bigotry*, is Web-based. Here is their definition:

> *Online bigotry, which can take the form of a website, usenet post or other forms of electronic communication, is defined as,* "an organization or individual that advocates violence against or unreasonable hostility toward those persons or organizations identified by their race, religion, national origin, sexual orientation, gender or disability. Also including organizations or individuals that disseminate historically inaccurate information with regard to those persons or organizations for the purpose of vilification." (*www.HateWatch.org*; italics in original)

Hate sites not only foster false information about groups of people, they also sometimes describe and publish means of enacting violence (e.g., instructions on making bombs). And further, they protect the anonymity of those who post messages of hate (Wood and Smith, 2001). According to one estimate, there were 803 hate groups in the United States in 2005. In Chapter 10 we will discuss further issues about hate groups and the problems they create. For a map of active hate groups in the United States see *www.splcenter.org/intel/map/hate.jsp*. You can also learn more about hate groups by visiting *www.tolerance.org*.

For complex issues involving freedom of speech and allegations of bias on the college campus, see Box 7.1 on academic freedom.

Secrets, Disclosures, and Privacy

Issues about disclosures and secrecy naturally dovetail with those about lying. Many philosophers and theologians have debated the ethics of lying. But what about the ethics of disclosing information known to us—particularly the secrets of other people? What are your obligations? Do you have to protect others? Do you always have to make known what you know? And how should you protect yourself when your welfare seems to depend upon exposing others?

Take a case in which disclosing what you know about someone's behavior will probably result in disciplinary action. Vijaya and her three roommates are first-year college students. They live in a two-bedroom suite that has its own bathroom. Vijaya and Lisa share a bedroom, and so do their suite-mates, Karen and Deborah. In this dormitory students are allowed to sign in guests who can then sleep overnight. The problem begins when Lisa starts signing in guests who stay several days at a time, take drugs in the room, and camp out in the bathroom. The other three roommates become very ill at ease. They never know who might turn up in the suite or exactly what will happen. More significant—they don't know what is the right thing to do about it.

If you were one of these three students, what would you do? Consider some of your alternatives. You start by ignoring the parade of visitors, but suppose it only gets worse, and you find you can't study in the room or even feel comfortable when you go to sleep. Do you decide on a moderate course of action and make a firm request that Lisa tell her friends to leave? If that fails, what are some of your options—calling your parents, talking to the dean, going to the residential assistant (RA) in your dorm? For these students, the next step seemed to be going to the RA, the resident for their floor in the large dormitory. Even then, they felt a conflict—Lisa's behavior was endangering their welfare, yet appealing to a higher authority felt like turning someone in, "ratting" on her.

Here's an instance in which a conflict can arise not about whether to lie but whether to tell the truth. In a sense, this is an issue about loyalties—about getting a fellow student in trouble even though you feel that what she is doing is wrong. (This is what makes the honor system so difficult to enforce.) By disclosing information about someone else, you know that you will affect her welfare. Her parents might find out. She might be expelled. Perhaps Vijaya also fears that she may be harmed when Lisa's friends learn what has happened.

Issues concerning disclosure of information occur in many different communication contexts. For example, imagine yourself as a reporter for the school newspaper. As part of your job, you interview a university official, and she gives you some controversial information on the promise that you will not reveal her as the source: Grades of several athletes have been altered to raise their academic averages. Later a heated debate is stirred up by your article, and the dean of students demands to know the source of your information. Of course, the dean also controls the budget for your paper, and though he does not threaten to take money away, there is always that possibility. What would you do? What are your loyalties to the newspaper, the source, and the dean?

At Columbia University a dispute between students and faculty over the Middle East and Asian Language and Cultural Studies (MEALAC) department has touched off a fierce debate about bias and academic freedom—that is, "*liberty to teach, pursue, and discuss knowledge without restriction or interference, as by school or public officials*" (*American Heritage Dictionary*, 2004). In '*Columbia Unbecoming*,' a low-budget 40-minute film, several Columbia students allege that three pro-Palestinian professors in the MEALAC department have intimidated them in the classroom because of their pro-Israel sentiments. The film also critiques the political writings of the three and their alleged intimidating behavior toward students outside of class (Kleinfield, 2005). One criticism of the film has been that it fails to distinguish between what goes on in the classroom and outside it.

Since the film was shown in spring of 2004, the controversy has only escalated—dividing faculty members as well as students. The three MEALAC professors "accused of being intimidating and anti-Semitic" have received hate mail and death threats, and the president of Columbia has appointed a panel to investigate (Kleinfield, 2005).

But this is by no means an isolated controversy. In a time of much political division and intercultural conflict, the concept of academic freedom is being tested and debated at many colleges and universities. How far does that freedom extend and what of First Amendment rights to protect free speech and freedom of expression? At Columbia, Professor Patricia Williams suggests that if there is to be "any hope of reconciliation," the focus should be questions such as these:

- What are the limits of academic freedom for professors?
- Must all courses be "fair and balanced"— that is, neutral and impartial?
- To what extent should students have the ability to influence course content? (adapted from Williams, 2005, p. 9)

What is your opinion and what has been your experience in the classroom?

Even more difficult situations present themselves within families. Put yourself in the place of Derek, a college junior so concerned with his older sister's drinking problem that he struggles with whether to tell his parents, who have already asked him if something is wrong. Would they be able to help? Would his sister ever trust him again? And what would be the effect on their close relationship?

And we face far more dramatic tests of our loyalties. Consider the many reported planned attacks on schools after the Columbine High School massacre in Littleton, Colorado. In almost 75 percent of school shootings since 1974, the person or people who planned the attack had told someone else about it in advance, and usually the person told was a fellow student ("See Evil," March 19, 2001). In a California college and at high schools in Kansas, Colorado, and New York, authorities were tipped off by students who learned about peers who were stockpiling weapons and planning massacres. Here the consequences of a failure to disclose far outweighed any sense of concern about loyalty to a peer group. In such volatile situations, the decision was loyalty to the greater student body.

In mass communication troubling questions concerning disclosure and the right to privacy have been raised by a growing number of memoirs and biographies. "The fact is," writes one columnist, "we are not sure where we want to draw the line when it comes to knowing about other people's lives" (Franklin, 1998, p. 12). We have an appetite for information about people's private lives, especially public figures. The reclusive fiction writer J. D. Salinger, author of *Catcher in the Rye*, is the subject of a recent memoir by Joyce Maynard, who had a brief affair with him when she was 18 and he was in his forties.

What is the contract between a biographer and the subject of the biography? If a biographer has been given free access to the documents that re-create the life of a famous living person, what allegiance, if any, is owed to the subject? Ronald Suresh Roberts is the biographer of the South African writer Nadine Gordimer. Published in South Africa in 2005, as of this writing his biography *No Cold Kitchen* has not been published in the United States or England although the book was contracted by the American publisher Farrar, Straus and Giroux and the British publisher Blooms-bury. Nadine Gordimer, the book's subject, is one of South Africa's most acclaimed authors, the winner of the Nobel Prize and many other honors.

She first met Roberts, who is also South African, in 1997 and over several years granted him extensive interviews as well as free access to her private correspondence, diaries, and many other personal documents. According to one newspaper account, after reading the manuscript of the Roberts book, she expressed objections to certain passages and asked that he make revisions. "Among other things, Gordimer objected to the way he characterized an affair she had in the early '50s, Roberts said. She also found distasteful Roberts's account of the slow decline and death . . . of her second husband . . ." (Donadio, 2006). Roberts maintains that there were also conflicts over Gordimer's political views on the Middle East, about which he was critical, and over her position on apartheid, which since early in her writing career—Gordimer is now in her eighties—she had staunchly opposed.

Roberts refused to revise his manuscript after Gordimer had read it and made objections. He maintained that such criticisms infringed on his independence as a writer. Although the book was published to much critical acclaim in his own country, neither a British nor an American edition has yet to appear.

The ethical issues raised here are numerous and have a complexity that defies easy answers. Gordimer had disclosed much, entrusting very personal information to Roberts. The issues were further complicated when Roberts wrote that a few details in a personal essay by Gordimer for *The New Yorker* had been been invented. Yet this is a far cry from the fabrications in James Frey's memoir discussed earlier. What rights, if any, does Gordimer have in suppressing information about her life? We may also ask whether this biographer would have been able to complete his book without the open access to Gordimer and the documentation she freely gave.

In a book on the American poet Anne Sexton, who committed suicide at the age of 45, the biographer Diane Wood Middlebrook made use of a type of source material that had never before been used in the biography of a major American figure: over 300 audiotapes of Sexton's therapeutic sessions with her psychiatrist.

Although the tapes were used with the consent of Sexton's daughter, Sexton herself left no instructions about whether this was allowable (Stanley, 1991).

The book created an intense controversy, and several ethical questions emerged. The first is what many psychiatrists saw as a dramatic violation of medical ethics by Sexton's psychiatrist, Dr. Martin Orne. Sessions between doctor and patient are strictly confidential. Several prominent psychiatrists spoke of Orne's betrayal of both his patient and profession.

The right to privacy, so often discussed as an ethical issue, becomes particularly complex in connection with all the mass media—not merely with books. Journalists are repeatedly faced with the need to balance concerns about what is often called "the public's right to know" against concerns about an individual's right to privacy. Is it, for example, the public's right to know that a person is a homosexual? Is it the public's right to know the name of a rape victim in a much-publicized trial?

For example, privacy became an issue in a court case against Kobe Bryant, a basketball star who was accused of raping a young woman in 2003. After her name and other private information about her was published in several newspapers, she refused to appear in court and the case never came to trial. But after she had filed a civil suit in her own name seeking financial compensation, she was named by another newspaper even though an advocacy organization had asked that her privacy be protected (Simpson, 2004).

Questions about the public's right to know are especially common in political reporting, and there has been an increasing demand for full disclosure of all kinds of personal information about public figures—from their love lives to their medical history. In "'The President Is Fine' and Other Historical Lies," presidential historian Richard Norton Smith (2001) explains that traditionally "journalists have covered up White House illnesses as much as they have covered them." The public never knew, for example, that John F. Kennedy had Addison's disease or how seriously President Reagan had been shot in an assassination attempt by John Hinckley.

Things have certainly changed. For example, today it is expected that presidential candidates will release all necessary information about their health. In spring of 2007, presidential hopeful John Edwards and his wife announced his intention to continue his campaign after disclosing a recent recurrence of his wife's breast cancer, which her doctor said was now treatable but not curable. Public opinion ran the gamut from high praise to criticism of his decision. During the 2000 presidential campaign, questions were raised about Dick Cheney's viability as a political candidate because he had already had several heart attacks. After he became vice president, there was heightened concern when it was learned he had suffered another heart attack and had to undergo further medical procedures. Some felt the administration had failed to disclose the actual state of Cheney's health, and press coverage was extensive. The seriousness of a political figure's failure to disclose a medical condition and of the reaction of the press was dramatized in episodes of NBC's *West Wing.* President Josiah Bartlett, played by Martin Sheen, was forced to disclose that he has had multiple sclerosis for several years. Most of his staff had not been told, and his press secretary was forced to deal with the fallout.

Regarding invasion of privacy issues, Christians and others (1998) point out that

> . . . the law that conscientiously seeks to protect individual privacy excludes
> public officials. [Chief Justice] Brandeis . . . while condemning intrusion in
> personal matters, . . . insisted on the exposure of all secrets bearing on public
> concern. In general, the courts have upheld that political personalities cease to be
> purely private persons. (p. 109)

Since the press has tremendous latitude in deciding what is newsworthy and has
sometimes catered to tastes for gossip and sensationalism, these writers advocate
"additional determinants . . . to distinguish gossip and voyeurism from information
necessary to the democratic decision-making process" (p. 169).

Ethical questions concerning privacy are reversed somewhat in connection with
the new technologies. Because we often give out personal information on the Internet—
for example, when trying to get information or buying something online—there is
increasing concern over the scams that lead to identity theft. And did you know that
many Web sites place cookies on your computer? **Cookies** are *small files that a Web
site can use to track a visitor's preferences*—data you reveal when you are making a
purchase or just surfing the Net; the sites you access can gather information you type
in about yourself and store it. This is usually done without online notification. If you
are concerned about privacy, you should be aware that cookies are quite difficult to
remove from your computer (Schwartz, 2001).

More questions about the protection of our privacy are raised by electronic
surveillance. For example, should the government have the right to monitor
your e-mail? What about your activities while you are online? According to The
Pew Internet & American Life Project, a year after 9/11 people were "evenly divided" on the issue (Rainie, Fox, and Madden, 2002). What about surveillance
of employees on the job, an increasingly common practice? Employees sometimes
abuse their access to computers at work. They may be researching their interests
on company time, job hunting, playing games, writing personal e-mails, or even
watching pornography. Given such abuses of company time, however, do you
think that there should be monitoring of employees' online habits—and if so,
should they be told?

Whistleblowing

As members of groups, we enact certain roles and adopt specific behavioral
norms. Many of these are implicit, unstated, but nonetheless they are expectations about our behavior as a group member. Each professional organization
also has its principles and standards of behavior that all members promise to
uphold. In **whistleblowing,** *a member of a group makes a charge about the
violation of ethical standards or norms within that group itself*. A journalist
publishes a story about how another journalist has misled a criminal into giving
self-incriminating information. A doctor on the staff of a large hospital accuses
the chief surgeon of malpractice.

Issues of privacy and whistleblowing overlap in the case of Russell Tice. He is a former intelligence agent at the National Security Agency (NSA), a high-level government secret agency. Tice admitted to being one of the sources for a *New York Times* article in December 2005 concerning how the NSA had been eavesdropping electronically—without a warrant—on thousands of U.S. citizens. In 2006 he testified before Congress that he felt domestic spying was a violation of the Fourth Amendment and that the use of electronic surveillance in the future might have ramifications for millions of citizens ("NSA Whistleblower . . . ," 2006). Tice was fired in 2005 and is now a member of the National Security Whistleblower Coalition.

Bok identifies three elements that make whistleblowing particularly charged: dissent, breach of loyalty, and accusation (1989, pp. 214–215). First, it is a form of *dissent* because "it makes public a disagreement with an authority or majority view" but also has "the narrower aim of casting light on negligence or abuse, of alerting the public to a risk and of assigning responsibility for that risk." Second, the message itself is viewed "as a *breach of loyalty* because it comes from within. The whistleblower, although he is neither coach nor referee, blows the whistle on his own team." The third element, *accusation,* "singles out specific groups or persons as responsible"—and furthermore, the accusation is about "a present or an imminent threat" (pp. 214–215).

As in many other forms of ethical decision making, in whistleblowing the stakes can be extremely high, requiring great courage. Kidder considers the concept of **moral courage,** what he defines as "the courage to be moral," and describes it in terms of "adhering to the five core moral values of honesty, respect, fairness, responsibility, and compassion" (2005, p. 10).

For him, morally courageous action involves three interrelated elements: "a commitment to moral *principles,* an awareness of the *danger* involved in supporting those principles, and a willing *endurance* of that danger" (p. 7). Think of the three as intersecting, as we see in Figure 7.1.

"The point," he writes, "at which the circle of our deepest values, or principles, intersects with the twin circles of danger and endurance is the point at which we find moral courage most clearly in evidence" (p. 10).

Whistleblowing is an act that often requires great moral courage. Jensen (1997) emphasizes that it is an intentional public act and that its objective is "to enlist support from a large outside audience" with the aim of informing and arousing that audience (pp. 74–75). In addition, whistleblowers "usually act alone, they tend to be subordinate to those whom they are accusing, and to be well-informed." This last point is extremely important: "They possess something others do not possess—valuable inside information—which makes them potentially powerful communicators" (p. 76).

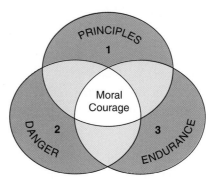

Figure 7.1

The Three Elements of Moral Courage

Source: From *Moral Courage* by Rushworth M. Kidder, Figs. 2 (p. 51) and 7 (p. 73). Copyright © 2004 by Rushworth M. Kidder. Reprinted by permission of HarperCollins Publishers.

In recent years, whistleblowing has become extremely common in many types of organizations—even in government. On May 21, 2002, Coleen Rowley, a Special Agent and Minneapolis Chief Division Counsel of the FBI, wrote a letter to FBI Director Robert Mueller. In it she described how, in the weeks before the attacks of September 11, the FBI's Washington supervisors had dismissed repeated requests by Minneapolis agents for greater authority to broaden their investigation of Zacharias Moussaoui, who had been identified as a terrorist threat after a call about his flight training. (He was later indicted as a conspirator in the 9/11 attacks.) Here is the opening of her letter:

Dear Director Mueller:

I feel at this point that I have to put my concerns in writing concerning the important topic of the FBI's response to evidence of terrorist activity in the United States prior to September 11th. The issues are fundamental ones of INTEGRITY and go the heart of the FBI's law enforcement mission and mandate. . . .

To get to the point, I have deep concerns that a delicate and subtle shading/ skewing of facts by you and others at the highest levels of FBI management has occurred and is occurring. The term "cover up" would be too strong a characterization which is why I am attempting to carefully . . . choose my words here. . . .

I feel that certain facts, including the following, have, up to now, been omitted, downplayed, glossed over and/or mis-characterizd in an effort to avoid or minimize personal and/or institutional embarrassment on the part of the FBI and/or perhaps even for improper political reasons. . . .

Rowley's letter, which was 13 pages long, goes on to describe her concerns in detail and closes this way:

. . . I hope my continued employment with the FBI is not somehow placed in jeopardy. I have never written to an FBI Director in my life before on any topic. Although I hope it is not necessary, I would therefore wish to take advantage of the federal "Whistleblower Protection" provisions by so characterizing my remarks.

Sincerely,
Coleen Rowley
Special Agent and Minneapolis Chief Division Counsel
(Coleen Rowley, cited in *time.com/time/covers*)

Rowley's letter is striking not only in its content but in her acknowledgment that whistleblowing involves great risk for the person who initiates it. By the end of the year she had testified before Congress and her letter had been leaked and widely published in major newspapers. In a 2002 issue of *Time* magazine, she was one of three women who appeared on the cover; the other two—Sherron Watkins and Cynthia Cooper—were business executives. Named "People of the Year," all three were whistleblowers (Lacayo and Ripley, 2002).

Sherron Watkins, an Enron vice president, sent an anonymous memo to Kenneth Lay, CEO of Enron, then the premier energy company in the country. Her memo was long and detailed and discussed the company's alarming business practices. She later met with Lay, but her concerns were ignored. When Enron was investigated, Watkins's testimony was crucial.

The second executive singled out by *Time* was Cynthia Cooper, a vice president of internal auditing at WorldCom. She uncovered bookkeeping practices that inflated company earnings by $3.9 billion. After she presented her discoveries to WorldCom's controller as well as to its CFO, they told her to postpone her audit. But Cooper continued and contacted the audit committee of the chairman of the board. "Two weeks later WorldCom announced it would restate earnings by $3.9 billion—the largest restatement ever" (Colvin, 2002, p. 56).

Writing about corporate whistleblowing, Geoffrey Colvin of *Fortune* suggests that it may be no accident that at Enron and WorldCom the whistleblowers were women:

> When a business needs shaking up, the best candidate is often an "insider outsider"—someone who has long experience with the company (an insider) but who works away from headquarters or in a noncore division (an outsider); more generally, it's someone who knows where the bodies are buried yet isn't tied deeply to the established powers. (Colvin, 2002, p. 56)

Whistleblowing requires great courage regardless of gender, and the consequences of whistleblowing have often been severe. People have been ostracized by colleagues, lost their jobs, been threatened, and been put at risk in many ways. For example, Jeffrey Wigand, a biochemist with the tobacco company Brown & Williamson, came forward to object to company practices including knowingly manipulating the nicotine levels of tobacco products to intensify the impact. He lost his job, was sued by the company for appearing on a television program about his accusations (he had signed a confidentiality agreement), and is now a high school teacher. Wigand's story is dramatized in the film *The Insider*. Another excellent film about whistleblowing is *Silkwood*.

More recently, Peter Rost, a former vice president of Pfizer, the largest drug company in the world, became one of a number of outspoken critics of the pharmaceutical industry and their efforts to withhold information that would affect their profits. He has not only spoken out for off-label marketing but also filed a whistleblower lawsuit against Pfizer alleging that Pharmacia, acquired by Pfizer in 2003, had tried to market Genotropin, a growth hormone, for inappropriate uses. The government did not join the suit, and Pfizer subsequently fired Rost. He went on to gain attention from the media when he advocated reimporting lower-cost prescription drugs from other countries. Rost has appeared on *60 Minutes* and continues to write and lecture on the pharmaceutical industry (Rost, 2006). Numerous other whistleblowers have taken on the drug companies. Other lawsuits include those in which sometimes-fatal side effects of drugs were concealed or drugs were kept off the market because they affected profits from drugs still under patent.

Whistleblowing occurs not only in business organizations and government, but in many other kinds of groups. Law enforcement officers have reported cases of police brutality, doctors who work for HMOs have blown the whistle on health insurance companies, and as we've seen, there have been controversial cases involving misconduct in scientific research. Here issues of whistleblowing can be further complicated by the status, reputation, and credibility of the people involved (Glazer, 1997). A recent article on professional ethics in a British medical journal was titled "Whistleblowing or Professional Assassination?"

Although motives remain a question in whistleblowing cases—a whistleblower may be awarded a significant sum from monies reclaimed by the government—the consequences of whistleblowing are well documented. A recent column asks "Whistleblowing Workers: Becoming an Endangered Species?" and cites research by Spherion Workplace (*www.spherion.com*):

> Although 34% of the respondents said they have seen unethical activities at the workplace, only 47% said they are likely to blow the whistle for such activities. ("Whistleblowing Workers . . . ," 2006, p. 9)

For many the costs of whistleblowing are simply too high—from being ostracized by friends and co-workers to losing one's job and even being sued. In sum, "whistleblowers are viewed by many in their group as traitors and by many of the public as heroes" (Jensen, 1997, p. 77).

Leaks

Another way of making information public is through a **leak**—*previously unknown information is made known to others, but its source,* unlike that of whistleblowing, *remains anonymous,* at least to the general public. For example, information might be leaked to the press by someone who may be a familiar source but whose identity is concealed. Of course, leaking information protects the source and often evades the responsibility of confirming the truth about the information that is given.

Leaks often have serious ramifications for people's personal lives. For example, a violation of confidentiality about your medical records can affect your employment. In formal contexts, the repercussions of leaks may be immediate and widespread. A leak to the news media about the ineffective leadership of a large corporation's president may not only damage reputations but also have disastrous effects on the company's stock, thus affecting thousands of shareholders as well as employees. Similarly, a leak about the imminent merger of a company can be a manipulation that artificially drives up stock values. Now the anonymity or possible concealment of sources on the Internet makes it another potentially dangerous channel for the communication of leaked information. And if you use search engines fairly often, you will probably run into shadow pages. The source of a **shadow page** is anonymous; it is *a Web page "established to attack the reputation of a person, corporation, or another site"* (Wood and Smith, 2001, p. 67).

Leaks often destroy professional reputations, as in the case of Dr. Wen Ho Lee. Part of the headline for a *Washington Post* story in 2006 reads "News Organizations Pay to Keep Sources Secret."

> Wen Ho Lee, the U.S. nuclear scientist once identified in news reports as the target of a spying operation [a charge that was later withdrawn], will receive more than $1.6 million from the federal government and five media organizations, including *The Washington Post,* to settle allegations that government leaks violated his privacy. (Farhi, 2006)

Notice the statement in the story's opening paragraph: *The Washington Post* discloses that it was one of the five media organizations involved.

When leaks to the media concern government information, sources are often accused of being motivated by partisanship, which is almost impossible to verify. In recent years, we have been inundated by leaks about politics and government. The timing of leaks is often manipulated to head off the response to unfavorable news or scandal, as when the government leaks the news to the press so that it is published at the end of the work week. Friday is notorious as the day to leak bad news because the assumption is that people will be preoccupied with personal affairs over the weekend.

Leaks have plagued the presidencies of political figures as different as Richard Nixon, Ronald Reagan, Bill Clinton, and, most recently, George W. Bush. One of the longest controversies during the Bush administration has been over who leaked information to the press about the identity of Valerie Plame as a CIA undercover agent.

In early July of 2003, Joseph Wilson, a former ambassador, wrote an Op-Ed piece in *The New York Times* titled "What I Didn't Find in Africa." In it he alleged that President George W. Bush's claim that Iraq had tried to buy uranium from Niger—for the purpose of building weapons of mass destruction—was untrue. The basis of Wilson's criticism was that earlier the CIA had sent him on a mission to Niger to investigate whether Iraq had tried to purchase uranium; Wilson had found no evidence of such a purpose and concluded that it was highly unlikely. His report (then classified) was available well before President Bush in his 2003 State of the Union address referred to Iraqi attempts to purchase the uranium. "Mr. Wilson concluded that the administration later manipulated intelligence about whether Iraq had sought to buy uranium from Niger" (Liptak, 2004, p. 18).

On July 14, 2003, eight days after the Wilson article was published, Robert Novak, a syndicated columnist with the *Chicago Sun-Times,* published a story in which he said that, according to two senior administration officials, Valerie Plame, Wilson's wife, was an undercover CIA agent and that she had worked in Niger. (Novak's column is published in over 300 papers, so its circulation is wide.)

Wilson then accused the administration of leaking information about his wife to the press and blowing her cover. It's a felony to disclose the identity of a covert intelligence agent; it can put the agent's life in danger, and, of course, also has a direct effect on the agent's career.

A special prosecutor was appointed by the Justice Department to investigate who had leaked the information. Apparently, it had been leaked to at least six reporters. In 2004 the six reporters were subpoenaed to testify: Robert Novak, Tim Russert of NBC, Matthew Cooper of *Time,* Walter Pincus and Glenn Kessler of the *Washington Post,* and Judith Miller of *The New York Times.* It is customary for reporters to resist attempts to reveal the identity of confidential sources and while we know that four reporters testified (Liptak, 2004), Judith Miller refused. Although she had written no story about Plame or Wilson, she went to jail for 85 days until her source of information, Richard Armitage, U.S. deputy secretary of state, freed her of their confidentiality agreement. Columnist Richard Novak finally acknowledged that Armitage was his source and that Karl Rove, chief of staff to President Bush, had confirmed Plame's identity as an undercover agent to Novak (Carr, 2007).

As a result of the investigation, in 2007 Vice President Cheney's former chief of staff, I. Lewis Libby, was found guilty not of leaking Plame's identity to the press, but of perjury and obstruction of justice concerning the leak—lying to FBI agents and during the grand jury investigation.

The freedom of the press and the right to protect its confidential sources is an issue of utmost concern for journalists but also an issue of great complexity. In 2004, FAIR (Fairness & Accuracy in Reporting), a national media watch group, argued that several reporters had violated Valerie Plame's privacy and that they should not protect the identity of officials who outed her:

> Protecting the identities of confidential sources is a journalistic right that should be recognized by the courts, but only when it protects genuine whistle-blowers, not when it shields government wrongdoing. . . .
>
> The ability to protect confidential sources who reveal government wrongdoing is an important journalistic protection that deserves judicial respect. ("Media Advisory . . . ," 2004)

Although most of us may not be in a position to "leak" information in the strict sense of the term, gossip and rumor are common communication behaviors that raise ethical questions. (The subject of rumors will be discussed in more detail in Chapter 14.)

In 1992, a special Senate counsel investigated the leak of Anita Hill's previously confidential allegations of sexual harassment by Clarence Thomas. At the time of the disclosure, Thomas had been nominated for Supreme Court Justice, and the leaked information resulted in lengthy testimony by Hill, Thomas, and others during Judge Thomas's confirmation hearings. The journalist who broke the story, Timothy Phelps of *Newsday,* was called to appear before the Senate counsel. Asked to disclose his source of information, Phelps refused. In his opening statement he said:

> I respectfully decline to answer the special independent counsel's questions here today because they are posed for the explicit reason of seeking the identity of my sources.
>
> I do so not only in an assertion of my right under the First Amendment, but also of those of my readers and of the American people. They have a need and

a right to know that serious allegations had been made against a nominee to the Supreme Court. (Cited in Barringer, 1992, p. 20)

Phelps's argument that the First Amendment guarantees freedom of the press and protects the right of confidentiality for its sources has a long history among journalists. Arguments about the ethics of leaking information by the mass media are especially difficult to resolve; often they involve balancing claims for actions done for the public good against the very damaging loss of credibility and reputation for those people who are singled out. Freedom of the press is among the most important media issues today.

In comparing whistleblowing and information leaks, Bok (1989) weighs the consequences of each:

In fairness to those criticized, openly accepted responsibility for blowing the whistle should . . . be preferred to the secret denunciation or the leaked rumor— the more so, the more derogatory and accusatory the information. What is openly stated can be more easily checked, its source's motives challenged, and the underlying information examined. Those under attack may otherwise be hard put to it to defend themselves against nameless adversaries. Often they do not even know they are threatened until it is too late to respond. (p. 215)

As you think about the ethical issues we have been discussing, keep in mind that intercultural communication often increases their complexity. For example, we sometimes have no knowledge about another culture's ethical values. Rhetorical frames of reference may be very different: What is regarded as a lie in one culture may be understood by members of another as an exaggeration for the sake of politeness. And as we will see in Chapter 10, norms about disclosures and privacy also vary considerably. What is a harmless disclosure in one culture may constitute a betrayal in another.

With the emergence of new communication technologies and the growing number of clashes between people of different cultures, the need for an ethical base that is morally inclusive becomes an issue that affects us all. In writing about media ethics, two scholars propose a basic principle that underpins all systematic ethics: the sacredness of human life.

Its universal scope enables us to avoid the divisiveness of appeals to individual interests, cultural practices, and national prerogatives. . . .

A commitment to universals does not eliminate all differences in what we think and believe. . . . The only question is whether our values affirm the human good or not. (Christians and Nordenstreng, 2004, pp. 21, 24)

From this universal—the sacredness of human life—they derive three related ethical principles: respect for human dignity, truthtelling, and nonviolence. These "master norms" are based on an earlier study of ethical norms in 13 countries across five continents (Christians and Traber, 1997). We will look at these principles in more detail when we discuss intercultural communication in Chapter 10.

Summary

In this chapter, we explored ethical decision making in communication. To establish a baseline for discussion, we considered some representative ethical principles that have been proposed by Western thinkers. We examined Aristotle's concept of the golden mean, a middle path between two extremes. In Kant's categorical imperative, we saw human actions judged as ethical by their intent rather than their outcomes. In the utilitarian view, on the other hand, greatest value was placed on the outcomes or consequences of our actions, with moral choice being governed by the greatest good for the greatest number of people. And in Rawls's theory of justice the guiding principle was fairness for everyone in society, including the most vulnerable. We also looked at three of the most common principles people use in ethical decision making.

We then turned to several fundamental issues in ethics. We discussed lying and misrepresentation as well as the reasons often given to defend lying— for example, lying to avoid harm or to protect another person. Next, we examined questions about the ethics of secrecy, disclosures, and rights of privacy, in public, academic, and personal life. We examined as well the ethical questions raised by the increasing use of computer-mediated communication. Finally, we looked at the complex issues of whistleblowing, in which a group member makes an accusation about the violation of ethical standards within the group itself, and of leaking information, in which the source of information remains anonymous. We also considered the concept of moral courage.

As we have tried to show, difficult ethical questions surface not just in organizational, public, mass, and computer-mediated communication but also in the most informal and intimate contexts. Ethics are not lofty principles for other people; we are all involved in making moral choices—often on a daily basis.

Key Terms

Categorical imperative	Hate site	Paraphrasing	Veil of ignorance
Cookies	Leak	Plagiarism	Whistleblowing
Ethics	Lie	Shadow page	
Golden mean	Moral courage	Utilitarianism	

Review Questions

1. Give your definition of "ethics."

2. What is Aristotle's concept of the golden mean, and what is its implication for ethical choices? Give two examples.

3. Explain Kant's principle of the categorical imperative.

4. Discuss the basic ethical principle of the utilitarians.

5. Compare and contrast the views of Kant and the utilitarians on making decisions about ethics.

6. What is the concept of the veil of ignorance, and how does it relate to Rawls's theory of justice?

7. Identify three of the most common principles people use in making ethical decisions.

8. What are the four principles people often appeal to in defending lies?

9. Identify three ethical issues concerned with lying or misrepresentation and include examples from at least three communication contexts in your discussion.

10. Give your own definition of plagiarism and explain the difference between plagiarizing and paraphrasing.

11. What are some of the ethical issues that have developed out of increasing use of the Internet and other new technologies?

12. Summarize three ethical issues related to the disclosure of information. Describe four contexts in which they might arise.

13. Discuss the concept of moral courage.

14. Identify three elements that are present in whistleblowing and give two examples of it.

15. What is the difference between whistleblowing and leaking information?

16. What ethical issues are raised by whistleblowing and leaks?

Exercises

1. Describe three different situations, involving (a) your friend, (b) your parents, and (c) your employer, in which you had to make a difficult decision about ethics. In each case, discuss the basis and motives for your decision; then evaluate whether your decisions were consistent from an ethical standpoint. If not, why not?

2. At a small party, your friend reads aloud a very personal letter, identifies who wrote it, and then asks the entire group what they think of it. No one at the party knows the letter writer. Discuss the ethics of this behavior and of possible responses from people at the party.

3. Go to *www.tolerance.org* and read about hate groups. Select two from the Web links and analyze the language used, including the use of adjectives, equivocal language, and dichotomies discussed in Chapter 3. Then discuss whether you think that such sites should be censored.

4. Reread the discussion in this chapter concerning the Nadine Gordimer biography by Ronald Suresh Roberts. Have two members of the class role-play the situation described, each presenting the ethical issues involved from one point of view. Then have the class discuss the validity of each position.

5. Identify a controversial news story with international implications that involves an ethical issue discussed in this chapter. Compare and contrast coverage of the incident by two major U.S. newspapers, a tabloid, two television stations, a weekly newsmagazine, and two Web sites for news: for example, *www.cnn.com* and *www.guardian.co.uk*. Compare how the different media present the issues. In each case, how is the information presented? What kind of language is used to describe the people involved? Is the treatment objective or partisan? Which media seem most impartial?

Suggested Readings

Bennett, Lance W. *News: The Politics of Illusion*, 7th ed. New York: Pearson/Longman, 2006.

A recent update of this classic on the relationship between the news media and politics. The author looks at information biases in the news, freedom of the press, and the subtle relationship between government and the media. News sources, leaks, censorship, and a host of other ethical issues are examined.

Bok, Sissela. *Mayhem: Violence as Public Entertainment.* Reading, MA: Addison-Wesley, 1998.

In her examination of media violence and its long-term effects, the author, a contemporary philosopher, discusses issues of free speech and censorship. This is a timely book that suggests innovative ways of resolving a pressing moral dilemma.

———. *Lying: Moral Choice in Public and Private Life*, 2nd ed. New York: Vintage, 1999.

The author analyzes lying in terms of ethical theory and illuminates her discussion with examples from many different contexts. This book has become a classic.

Christians, Clifford G., Mark Fackler, Kim B. Rotzoll, and Kathy Brittain McKee. *Media Ethics: Cases and Moral Reasoning,* 7th ed. Reading, MA: Allyn & Bacon, 2004.

An excellent and comprehensive treatment of media ethics, with detailed case studies on each of the issues discussed.

Ibsen, Henrik. *An Enemy of the People.* In Henrik Ibsen, *Selected Plays,* New York: Modern Library, Random House, n.d.

A complex and provocative play about the effects of whistleblowing, written by a great Norwegian playwright of the nineteenth century.

The Insider.

This film examines the costs of whistleblowing and how an issue with ramifications for large corporations affects the ethics of the mass media.

Kidder, Rushworth M. *Moral Courage.* New York: HarperCollins, 2005.

This book examines what it means to stand up for your values—its costs, risks, potential hardships, and rewards. It combines practical analysis with many excellent examples of how ethical dilemmas are approached and resolved.

Levitt, Stephen D., and Stephen J. Dubner. *Freakonomics: A Rogue Economist Explores the Hidden Side of Everything.* Revised and expanded ed. New York: HarperCollins, 2006.

An engaging and unconventional book in which a maverick economist explores how people pursue what they want—including by cheating. Not one dull chapter here.

The Lives of Others

An award-winning German film about the effects of the Stasi, the German secret police, during the 1980s and how the network of spying intimidated and sometimes recruited civilians.

Posner, Richard A. *The Little Book of Plagiarism.* New York: Pantheon, 2007.

A very brief, thought-provoking book by a legal scholar on current issues about plagiarism.

Smith, Rebecca, and John R. Emshwiller. *24 Days: How Two* Wall Street Journal *Reporters Uncovered the Lies That Destroyed Faith in Corporate America.* New York: HarperCollins, 2003.

This is a firsthand account by two investigative reporters of their discovery that Enron used secret partnerships to hide their enormous losses and that many of Enron's top executives walked off with vast personal fortunes.

Wiener, Jon. *Historians in Trouble: Plagiarism, Fraud, and Politics in the Ivory Tower.* New York: New Press, 2007.

A specialized but intriguing study of selected cases in which historians were accused of plagiarism. The author, an investigative journalist and a professor of history, examines how academic politics and media coverage contributed to which historians were condemned and which escaped censure.

 # For Supplementary Information

Log onto the Online Learning Center at *www.mhhe.com/tubbsmoss11.*

Relationships in Process

Chapter Objectives

After reading this chapter, you should be able to:

1. Discuss the influence of proximity on attraction.
2. Describe the relationship between similarity and attraction and identify three variables that qualify predictions about similarity and attraction.
3. Discuss recent research on minimal daters, online dating, and singles and their relationships.
4. Differentiate between the setting and the climate of a relationship and discuss two critical measures of climate.
5. Discuss the concepts of time, trust, and information sharing as defining characteristics of relationships.
6. Describe the dimensions of affection and control and discuss how they influence relationship stability.
7. Outline both the building and the declining stages of a close interpersonal relationship as described by Knapp. Compare this theory with Duck's view of the four phases of relationship dissolution.
8. Discuss various strategies that have been proposed for maintaining relationships.
9. Discuss the defining characteristics of family, the risks of divorce, the role of family in gender development, the distinctive nature of family communication, and the stages of development in families with children.

In *Blink,* his book about how we make decisions that seem instantaneous, Malcolm Gladwell takes a look at speed-dating:

> Speed-dating has become enormously popular around the world over the last few years, and it's not hard to understand why. It's the distillation of dating to a single snap judgment. Everyone who sat down at one of those tables was trying to answer a very simple question: Do I want to see this person again? And to answer that we don't need an entire evening. Velma, for instance, . . . said that she picked none of the men and that she made up her mind about each of them right away. "They lost me at hello," she said, rolling her eyes. (2005, p. 65)

What Velma describes are first impressions (see Chapter 2). And yet, Gladwell writes, we're not at all insightful about explaining our choices. Psychologist Sheena Iyengar and economist Raymond Fisman, both at Columbia University, are jointly researching speed-dating decisions and tell Gladwell that

> what they find when they compare what speed-daters say they want with what they are actually attracted to in the moment is that those things don't match. For example, if Mary said at the start of the evening that she wanted someone intelligent and sincere, that in no way means she'll be attracted only to intelligent and sincere men. It's just as likely that John, whom she likes more than anyone else, could turn out to be attractive and funny but not particularly sincere or smart at all. (pp. 65–66)

In this chapter we look in depth at the complex processes that underlie and create human relationships and those that maintain or undermine the stability of those relationships, sometimes resulting in their decline or deterioration. This chapter is about friends, it's about lovers, and it's also about families.

In recent years, the study of close interpersonal relationships—both theory and research—has become an area of tremendous interest and activity for communication scholars (Guerrero and Floyd, 2006; Canary and Dainton, 2003; Hendrick and Hendrick, 2000). We begin by looking at the major variables of human attraction and several of the characteristics that define all our relationships.

BASES OF HUMAN ATTRACTION

Shauna can have lunch with you in the school cafeteria, but Stephanie can't. You'd love to go to the movies with Michael, but not with Dennis. You express your preferences when choosing friends, school leaders, roommates, dates—and eventually a marriage partner.

Even when forced to communicate with people you yourself have not chosen—classmates, the people you work with, and so on—you prefer some people to others. As we examine the major bases of *human attraction,* or *liking,* we shall be looking at many kinds of relationships. The principles discussed here have a bearing on marriage, friendship, family, small-group, and work relationships, for all of these can be seen within a single framework. You should be thinking, then, of the entire web of human relationships as you read about attraction.

Proximity

The most obvious determinant of attraction is **proximity**, or *geographic closeness*. Other things being equal, the more closely two people are located geographically, the more likely they are to be attracted to one another. The effects of proximity are seen in a number of ways. If you are not within a reasonable distance of another person, your chances of meeting and becoming friends are quite slim. How many of your friends live more than 3,000 miles away from you? Probably very few. In support of the notion that proximity fosters attraction, researchers have found that you are far more likely to marry a person who is geographically close to your home or school than someone living or studying far away.

Once you get to know people, proximity also affects whether your relationships will continue. A great number of friendships and courtships are damaged by the effects of physical separation. Perhaps the old saying "Out of sight, out of mind" has some validity simply because of the effort it takes to sustain relationships across many miles. Relationships that do continue despite this obstacle are maintained by the intensity of the rewards derived from them.

Much smaller distances also influence attraction, as seen in a classic study of residents in housing projects: Neighbors chose to socialize most with neighbors from the apartment next door and least with those at the opposite end of the floor (Festinger et al., 1950).

Why should a few feet make any difference in how friendships are formed, and why, in general, should proximity tend to foster attraction? One theory is that *if we know we are going to be in very close proximity to someone*—living next door or working side by side over a long period of time—*we tend to minimize or even overlook that person's less desirable traits*. It has also been proposed that proximity tends to intensify liking *because opportunities for communication clearly increase as a function of proximity*. For example, in a large company, people who work on the same floor are more likely to share coffee breaks and gossip, go out to lunch together, or even meet after work. And the more two people see of each other, the more likely they are to spend leisure time together, exchange confidences, and offer support in difficult times.

Other experiments (Zajonc, 1968) suggest that familiarity in and of itself may increase liking. According to Berscheid and Reis (1998), the early research demonstrates that it is "interaction, not distance per se, that is important" and they cite recent advances in telecommuting (see Chapter 15) to bear out this conclusion.

But when people in proximity are of equal status and start off without negative attitudes toward one another, we cannot predict which people will become friends. Given physical proximity, we still favor some people and reject others. In short, proximity is often a precondition of liking, but there are other bases for attraction.

A recent review of research summarizes several other variables associated with liking in general, and, more specifically, with romantic love:

Reciprocal liking: discovering that the other likes the self
Desirability of the other: kindness, intelligence, humor, good looks, social
    status, etc.
Similarity, especially of attitudes, personality, and demographic characteristics
Exposure and social appropriateness, support and encouragement from one's
    social network . . . (Aron et al., 2006, adapted from p. 602; emphasis added)

When it comes to falling in love, reciprocal liking and desirability seem to have the most influence.

Similarity

Despite the romantic notion that opposites attract, there is little evidence that this is so. And a look at online dating sites such as *match.com* and *personals.aol.com* and the personals columns of many newspapers and magazines will show you how important *similarity* is perceived to be: Most people want to meet others who share many of their interests, whether it be in sports, music, or travel, and they often seek someone of the same religion, race, and social background.

In a study of mate selection, Buss (1985) found substantial evidence for assortive mating—that is, mating based on similarities. For example, husbands and wives are usually similar in age, education, ethnic background, race, religion, and socioeconomic status (p. 47). These six variables show the strongest correlations. As for psychological characteristics, the greatest similarities are in attitudes, opinions, and worldviews. Other strongly correlated characteristics include verbal abilities and degree of quarrelsomeness, ingenuousness, and extroversion (p. 49). Romantic couples also tend to have comparable levels of physical attractiveness.

Buss and his colleagues (2001) found that men's and women's preferences in selecting a mate have changed over the last half century: For both men and women physical attractiveness and earning potential have increased in importance. Earlier, women placed more value on strong earning ability, and men placed more value on physical attractiveness (Sprecher et al., 1994). The importance men place on domestic skills also declined sharply. And for both sexes mutual attraction and love have become more important. They even agree in how they *rank* the importance of mate qualities.

These researchers suggest that this evolution in values is in part a response to cultural changes. Internet dating and the threat of AIDS have changed patterns of mating. Women's many gains in the workplace have increased their economic power and financial security. And we are immersed in a visual culture that, through television, film, as well as Internet images, places extraordinary value on physical appearance.

The force of similarity as a basis for attraction is seen not just in selection of mates, but in all types of human relationships and thus in many forms of communication. Observation, research, and theory all bear out the statement that we like people who appear to be similar to us. Over a hundred years ago Disraeli remarked, "An agreeable person is a person who agrees with me." In other words, "We tend to like people who have the same beliefs and attitudes we have, and when we like people we want them to have the same attitudes we have" (Heider, 1983). In addition, personality, style of dressing, socioeconomic level, religion, age, status, and so forth will affect our feelings toward others. We tend to attract and be attracted to people who are like us, and conversely, we tend to dislike and be disliked by those who differ from us.

If this is the case, then given adequate knowledge of people's attitudes, interests, values, and backgrounds, it should be possible to predict which members of a group will become friends. A classic study in how college friendships are formed (Newcomb, 1961) confirms this prediction. On a long-term basis, those who remained friends after college had shown many similarities when they first met.

Later researchers have focused on the dynamics of attitude similarity and attraction. Byrne's research, for example, conducted over some 30 years, came to be known as the "attraction paradigm" (1997). Studies have found a high correlation between attraction and perceived similarity of attitudes. For example, pairs of subjects who expected to be attracted to one another tended to be more similar in their attitude toward an issue—capital punishment, for example—than discussion partners who expected to be incompatible. In other words, as we communicate with someone we think is similar to us, we are more likely to become more similar to that person in our attitudes toward a given issue.

Here and elsewhere when we describe the link between similarity and attraction, we are speaking of *perceived* similarity. As we emphasized in Chapters 1 and 2, human perception is a selective process and not always an accurate one; often we are influenced by how we expect people to look or think or behave. For example, we expect our friends to agree with us on a wide range of topics, and we probably exaggerate the extent of this agreement. No doubt we also tend to overemphasize our differences with those we dislike.

According to the 2000 Census, the number of interracial and interethnic marriages is rising—3 million marriages, or 5 percent of married couples in the United States. In fact, since 1980 the figure has doubled, with the trend being strongest among young people ("Melting at Last?" 2000) so over time we may see the greatest similarities between mates become factors involving values rather than race or ethnic background.

Situations

We qualified our statement about the effect of proximity on attraction with the phrase "other things being equal," and we must temper statements about similarity and attraction in the same way. For things rarely are equal. As we saw in Chapter 2, variations in the behaviors and personal characteristics of others—physical attractiveness, for example—influence liking.

Several situations also qualify what can reasonably be predicted about your attraction to others.

Perceived Reciprocity of Liking

First, your attraction to others can depend on **perceived reciprocity of liking**—*whether you feel that the people you like also like you.* Your liking for a person is intensified by your feeling that he or she likes you too. When you like someone and your feeling is not reciprocated, you tend to lose interest in that person. Many studies report that reciprocity is "one of the most important predictors of attraction"; a recent one by Lehr and Geher on short- versus long-term dating contexts finds that reciprocity rather than attitude similarity is particularly important in predicting long-term relationships (2006, p. 434).

Finding out that another person likes you is rewarding because it increases your own self-esteem. Suppose, for example, that you are asked to serve on a prestigious committee by one of its members. Once you are on the committee, new elections are held, and the person who endorsed you is nominated for chairman. It is very likely, especially if the committee members are people you don't know, that you will want to vote for the person who picked you—not so much because you owe a favor as because you feel you like that person.

The explanation for such reciprocity is twofold: First, people who like you increase your sense of self-worth; and, second, their "liking" behavior is a compliment, and you return the compliment with reciprocal liking.

Changes in Self-Esteem

A second situation that may influence your choice of people is *a change in your level of self-esteem.* Consider this example. Carlos and Elsa have dated for almost six months when suddenly she drops him. Because he feels that he is not good enough for her, Carlos finds his self-esteem at an all-time low. Then along comes Kim. Carlos has never considered her as attractive or intelligent as Elsa, but she seems to be interested in him. Carlos strikes up a romance on the rebound.

The rebound phenomenon illustrates what can happen to attraction as a result of a change in the level of one's self-esteem. Studies suggest that when self-esteem has recently been lowered, our need for affiliation increases, and we become more accepting of affection from others. It's then that people we might have considered unappealing may seem more desirable as companions.

Anxiety

Anxiety affects your need to interact or affiliate with others. In a classic experiment, Schachter (1959) found that high-anxiety conditions (painful electric shock) produce a much more intense desire for affiliation than low-anxiety conditions. And though "misery loves company," it isn't just any company: Anxious subjects prefer to be with others who are anxious too (pp. 17–19).

Anxiety-producing situations can increase your need to be with others and also change your criteria for choosing companions. Imagine yourself stuck in a fogged-in airport for most of a day or waiting for hours in a hospital to visit a loved one in the intensive-care ward. Apparently, the need to be comforted when sharing unpleasant experiences supersedes other needs for associating with people. Boot camps have long operated on this principle. People who share relatively unpleasant experiences often become more cohesive as a group.

Isolation

Isolation from the rewards of others also influences your choice of receivers. Although brief isolation can sometimes be peaceful and pleasant, prolonged isolation is almost always unpleasant. Hence, in prisons, one of the severest forms of punishment is solitary confinement.

In general, social isolation tends to be less pleasant than interaction with others. Some researchers have found that as we are deprived of the rewards possible from human interaction, we become more receptive to those rewards. Thus, as we are deprived of social reinforcement, our strong need to interact with other human beings tends to override our standards for acceptable friends.

Some theorists believe that in addition to the many variables we have been discussing, some differences between people can also be a basis for attraction—particularly if the people involved have needs that are complementary—but little evidence supports this theory of complementary needs.

Minimal Daters

Minimal daters are *"a unique population of individuals who have few dates in a specific period of time . . . feel inhibited around members of the opposite sex . . . , and are dissatisfied with their current dating frequency"* (Leck, 2006, p. 550). In a recent study of first- and second-year college students, Leck found several variables linked with minimal dating, including shyness, introversion, lower social self-esteem, and loneliness. His findings related to loneliness were particularly interesting:

> For men, childhood popularity with same-sex peers predicts popularity with members of the opposite sex, but this is not necessarily true for women. . . . Women who date minimally have just as many friends as high-frequency dating women, whereas men who seldom date are often isolated and have few or no friends. . . . Women also report their same-sex friendships to be stronger and more rewarding than do men. . . . (p. 561)

Leck also observed that though first impressions of possible dating partners are initially influenced by physical attractiveness, dating frequency is more strongly linked with attractiveness in women than it is with men.

Online Dating

A survey by the Pew Internet & American Life Project (Madden and Lenhart, 2006) increases our knowledge not only about online dating but unmarried Americans in general. For example,

Table 8.1 *Singles and Their Relationships*	All single Americans	Single men	Single women
In committed relationships	26%	30%	23%
Not in committed relationship and not looking for partner	55	42	65
Not in committed relationship but looking for partner	16	23	9
Don't know/Refused	3	5	3

Source: *Pew Internet & American Life Project Online Dating Survey, September–December 2005* (retrieved July 16, 2007 from www.pewinternet.org/pdfs/PIP_Online_Dating.pdf). *Margin of error is ±3% for all singles, ±5% for single men, and ±4% for single women.*

> Most Internet users who are married or in committed relationships met each other offline. Only 16% of single Americans, or 7% of all adults, say they are hunting for a partner. (p. 6)

The survey makes clear that not all single Americans are actively seeking a romantic partner, and this is the case even among young adults.

When surveyed, relationship-seeking singles described how many dates they had been on in the past three months:

> 36% said they had been on no dates in the previous three months. 13% had been on one date. 22% had been on 2–4 dates. 25% had been on 5 or more dates. (Madden and Lenhart, 2006, p. 7)

Table 8.1 summarizes additional findings from this survey. For more about online dating, see Chapters 2, 9, and 15.

DEFINING CHARACTERISTICS OF RELATIONSHIPS

The authors of a study of platonic friendships among young adults (Kaplan and Keys, 1997) challenge the truth of Billy Crystal's line in the movie *When Harry Met Sally*— "No man can be friends with a woman [because] he always wants to have sex with her." According to the results of this study, "while sexual attraction is present in many cross-sex friendships and presents a challenge for a sizable minority of . . . friends, there is much more to these relationships than just sexuality." Supportiveness, trust and understanding, sharing of information, and several other factors clearly play a part. In the pages that follow, we shall be discussing five of the basic perspectives from which many kinds of relationships, however different they seem, may be described.

Context

The **context** of every relationship has two aspects: the setting and the social-psychological environment in which communication takes place and relationships develop.

Setting, or *physical environment,* has an important connection with the principle of similarity: We form relationships with people with whom we share a certain setting, probably because that shared setting is indicative of similarities. Work relationships, relationships with neighbors, relationships with those who participate in the same sport or are members of the same religion, each takes place within a given physical environment, and we are unlikely to have a relationship outside that setting. For example, your supervisor at the office is unlikely to visit you at home.

Although setting may be significant for some relations, **communication climate,** or *social-psychological context,* is important for all of them. Among the most critical measures of climate are confirmation and supportiveness.

Confirmation and Disconfirmation

In studying human communication, we distinguish between message *content* and the *relationship* between communicators. It seems obvious that every message has content, whether the information is correct or incorrect, valid or invalid, or even indeterminable. But every message also defines how it is to be interpreted and, consequently, something about the relationship between the people involved.

Suppose a man is driving and his six children, who are in the back of the station wagon, are arguing among each other. He might say, "Please stop it or I'm going to pull over"—a parental request that is serious but not intimidating. Or "Stop it right now"—a command that conveys parental power. Or, as Al Roker's father used to say in that situation, "DON'T MAKE ME STOP THIS CAR!"—a command that by its very tone is an immediate unspecified threat (2000).

Even the most casual, seemingly neutral message—for example, the statement "It's up to you"—exists on the relationship level: "Every courtesy term between persons, every inflection of voice denoting respect or contempt, condescension or dependency, is a statement about the relationship between the two persons" (Ruesch and Bateson, 1968, p. 213).* Thus, as we communicate, we expect more than a simple exchange of verbal and nonverbal information. Each person conveys messages that tell how he or she perceives the other and their relationship, and each expects to receive similar responses.

Perhaps the most satisfying interpersonal response we can hope to receive is total **confirmation,** or as Sieburg and Larson define it, *"any behavior that causes another person to value himself more"* (1971, p. 1; italics added). We can also think of this as any behavior that strengthens or reinforces the other person's self-esteem. The theologian Buber writes: "In human society, at all its levels, persons confirm one another in a practical way, to some extent or other, in their personal qualities and capacities, and a society may be termed human in the measure to which its members confirm one another" (1957, p. 101).

We can illustrate this through a series of brief exchanges between husband and wife. Suppose Kathy comes home after work and says to her husband, "Brian—guess what? I was promoted to divisional manager today. Isn't that great?" "That's

---

*For an extensive discussion of content and relationship levels of communication, see Watzlawick et al., 1967, pp. 51–54.

wonderful, Kathy," replies Brian. "You've been working so hard. You really deserve this." Here Brian responds to Kathy and agrees with the content of her statement, thus confirming her very existence as a person. Yet what if he says, "Well, it sounds like a pressure job to me. I hope this isn't going to interfere with our life at home." Brian responds, but rejects the central content of Kathy's statement (that the promotion is a positive thing) and by implication Kathy herself. His statement acknowledges that she received a promotion, but is disconfirming as to its value (for both of them). A third response is possible. Suppose Brian ignores Kathy's statement altogether and asks, "What's for dinner tonight?" This remark probably would have the same impact as complete silence. Both are totally disconfirming behaviors, behaviors that cause people to value themselves less; they reject both the speaker and what the speaker has to say (Sieburg and Larson, 1971).

Psychotherapeutic literature tells us that **disconfirmation** is *one of the most damaging interpersonal responses*: "While rejection amounts to the message 'you are wrong,' disconfirmation *says in effect 'you do not exist'*" (Watzlawick et al., 1967, p. 86). Consider the following experience. Martine, whose parents are Haitian, was born in Brooklyn and grew up in South Miami. She and her boyfriend are sitting at a dinner table in a New York restaurant with his parents, who are from Texas. She and her boyfriend announce that they plan on moving to Texas:

> My boyfriend's mother, under the influence of too much Chianti, would not be stopped. She and her husband began a conversation that went like this. As if I wasn't there:
>
> *Mother:* So I just want to tell you that we really like Martine. We think she's just wonderful.
>
> *Father:* Sue!
>
> *Mother:* She's smart.
>
> *Father:* Sue, shut up!
>
> *Mother:* I am just trying to say that we like her but . . .
>
> *Father:* Sue. Please.
>
> *Mother:* Texas is not New York.
>
> *Father:* I'm sorry, Martine. She's had too much to drink.
>
> *Mother:* No. Martine. Like I said, we think you're great. What do your parents think about all this?
>
> I ran to the bathroom to cry. (Bury, 2001, p. 103)

The practical question becomes: What kinds of responses are most confirming or disconfirming? We find part of the answer in the Sieburg and Larson (1971) study. Members of the International Communication Association were asked to describe the behaviors of the persons with whom they most enjoyed and least enjoyed

Figure 8.1   *Confirmation and Disconfirmation: Some Ways of Responding*

Confirming Responses	Disconfirming Responses
Direct acknowledgment "Yes. I see where you're coming from."	**Tangential response** ["Do you know what I mean?"] –"Yes, I'm thinking of going to the movies."
Expressing positive feeling "That's a very good idea."	**Impersonal response** "Well, that's one way of thinking about it."
Clarifying response "Could you explain? I'm not sure I understand."	**Impervious (disregarding) response** "Have you seen my computer case?"
Agreement "You're absolutely right."	**Irrelevant response** ["I'm afraid I might lose my job."] –"I wonder if he's going to ask me out?"
Supportive response "I'm sure you'll make a good decision."	**Incongruous response (mixed message)** "Of course, it's your decision. It's up to you." (frown and exasperated tone of voice)

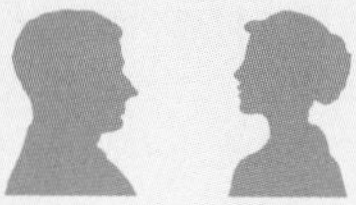

communicating. As we look at the results of this survey, two distinct response styles emerge. They are summarized in Figure 8.1, which gives selective examples of confirming and disconfirming responses.

These behaviors are by no means exhaustive, but they highlight the differences between a confirming response style, which generally acknowledges, supports, and accepts other human beings, and a disconfirming response style, which denies and undermines their personal sense of worth.

Confirmation/disconfirmation is a major dimension of human relationships with potential for influencing a range of communication outcomes. For example, perceived confirming behavior contributes to greater rapport between college roommates (Hawken et al., 1991, p. 306).

Yet to expect all your responses to others to be totally confirming would be unrealistic. There are times when you want to or must reject the communication of others, at least at the content level. Even in taking issue with others, however, keep in mind the importance of maintaining a confirming response style. Supportiveness is another important measure of climate.

Supportiveness and Defensiveness

A study (Schimel et al., 2001) finds that being accepted for who you are reduces your defensiveness. But it's not being liked for your accomplishments and achievements that makes you less defensive; it's the sense that you are liked for your intrinsic or true self. We can be supportive in all our interpersonal relationships if we know more about several of the responses that reduce or arouse **defensiveness**—that is, *behaviors used to protect ourselves from what we perceive to be a threat.*

In his classic work on interpersonal trust, Gibb (1961) contrasted two atmospheres that could be established through communication. He called them **supportive** and **defensive climates,** and he described them in terms of six sets of behaviors listed in Table 8.2.

Evaluative, or judgmental, behavior arouses defensiveness, but so does complete neutrality. We can reconcile this apparent contradiction if we recall that complete neutrality is disconfirming: It communicates a lack of concern, an indifference to the other person. Gibb points out that attempts to reassure a troubled person by saying that he is overanxious or should not feel bad may be interpreted as a lack of acceptance. It can be highly supportive, however, to show empathy with the person's emotions without trying to change him—for example, "I understand how concerned you are" rather than "Relax, there's nothing to worry about." Pearce and Newton (1963), who consider it "the basic mode of significant communication between adults," refer to **empathy** as *"perception and communication by resonance, by identification, by experiencing in ourselves some reflection of the emotional tone that is being experienced by the other person"* (p. 52, italics added). (See the discussion of empathic listening in Chapter 5.)

Table 8.2 *Supportive and Defensive Communication Climates*		
Defensive Climate	**Problem Created**	**Supportive Climate**
Evaluation	Feeling judged increases our defensiveness.	Description
Control	We resist someone trying to control us.	Problem orientation
Strategy	If we perceive a strategy or underlying motive, we become defensive.	Spontaneity
Neutrality	If the speaker appears to lack concern for us, we become defensive.	Empathy
Superiority	A person who acts superior arouses our defensive feelings.	Equality
Certainty	Those who are "know-it-alls" arouse our defensiveness.	Provisionalism

Source: From "Defensive Communications" by Jack R. Gibb, *Journal of Communication,* 11: 3, 1961, pp. 141–148. Reprinted by permission of the International Communication Association.

Statements that reflect an effort to control rather than solve a problem also arouse defensive responses. For example, compare the effect of "If you come home late again, you're grounded" to "Is there anything you can do differently so that you get home on time?" And compare statements that convey certainty—e.g., "You're making a big mistake by renting that apartment"—with those that reflect a provisional attitude—e.g., "Perhaps you should look a little more before you settle for an apartment that expensive." The first implies that the other person is foolish, the second simply suggests an alternative without telling her what to do.

From his survey Gibb concluded that when trust increases, efficiency and accuracy in communication also increase. To this, we might add that while a supportive climate is important even in short-term relationships, in more permanent relationships (e.g., in marriage or on the job) it has even greater possibilities for influencing all five communication outcomes. As we suggested in Chapter 1, the better the relationship between people, the more likely it is that the other outcomes of effective communication will also occur.

In addition to climate, time is another dimension that helps to characterize relationships.

Time

Time is required for all the qualities of a relationship to develop and evolve (Chelune et al., 1984). In general, our knowledge of another person is usually acquired slowly; interdependence, trust, and commitment also develop over time.

Time also affects the *intensity* of human relationships. For example, if you take a cross-country car trip with a friend, your relationship can become much closer than it would if you just met for an hour or two once a week. In terms of our model, it is as though one were pulling the ends of the spring in Figure 1.1 (Chapter 1, page 9) farther and farther apart. In other words, a human relationship is not constant; its intensity is affected by the amount of time that passes between encounters.

Communication style tends to change with the passage of time. When two people first meet, they usually try to be as explicit as possible. Even if the two share several interests, one does not assume knowledge of what the other is thinking or trying to say. This kind of insight develops only after long acquaintance. Sometimes two people get to know each other so well that each anticipates what the other is trying to say—they even finish each other's sentences, so to speak.

One very telling aspect of our relationships is the concept of investment: Notice how often the word "spent" is used in talking about time. In a measure designed to assess levels of investment, Lund (1985) included questions about how much time was spent with the other person rather than in doing things or seeing other people, and about the total length of time of the involvement. Her interest as a researcher was in predicting the continuity of personal relationships. No one can predict, of course, that time "invested" offers total security or constancy in a relationship—hence, the bitter complaint "I gave him the best years of my life" has no cogent answer.

Although time spent is a way of characterizing relationships, it is meaningful only when integrated with such dimensions as the *quality* of the time and the *desire to spend it*. Desire to spend time and the amount of time two people spend do not always mesh. For example, you may find yourself in a relationship where you and the other person want to be together almost constantly, yet circumstances make it impossible. On the other hand, a man and woman who have been married for many years may spend most of their free time with each other yet have little desire to do so. Or the wife may feel she always wants to spend her weekends with her husband, and the husband may have less desire to be with her; perhaps he'd rather go sailing some weekends even though she doesn't like sailing. Spending more time together is not always the solution. Many counselors and therapists advise that the quality of the time two people spend together—and the degree to which they express their mutual regard—can be more significant than the amount of time spent.

Currently, there is great interest in the long-term effects of living together. A study by Stafford and colleagues (2004) looked at married couples, couples who lived together and then married, and couples who simply lived together, tracking them over time in terms of their personal well-being and satisfaction with the relationship. Though the researchers report no significant differences, they did find that couples who lived together for many years but did not marry had more conflict and were more at risk of separating.

Information Sharing

Not all relationships foster the sharing of information—for example, some are quite guarded with little exchange on either side, others far more open with an ongoing series of exchanges, or with times of greater openness alternating with periods of concealment. Information sharing in a relationship can be described in terms of two dimensions: breadth and depth.

Breadth refers to *the variety of topics communicated*. For example, from conversations you may know that your lab partner is from Kansas, the oldest of four children, and an avid soccer player; yet you may still feel you know little about him. In many relationships the range of subjects you talk about is broad, yet discussion remains superficial.

What is lacking is **depth,** *the intimacy of what is communicated*. For example, you can tell someone about the work you do and thus add to the range of information she has about you, but your dissatisfaction with your job or your search for a new one is far more personal and revealing. Such information intensifies the depth of your relationship. Altman and Taylor (1983), who propose this distinction between breadth and depth, are concerned with interpersonal relationships in which both dimensions increase, yet their schema can characterize any relationships—those with our parents, friends, neighbors, or even our employers.

Whether or not we increase the breadth and depth of our communications—that is, whether we continue to talk superficially or begin the process of self-disclosure—depends on certain aspects of the relationship. Petronio and her colleagues (1984) found that in disclosing information, women assign more importance than men do to whether the other person is "discreet, trustworthy, sincere, liked, respected, a good listener, warm, and open." Women also feel more strongly than men that the person disclosing information "be accepted, be willing to disclose, be honest, frank, and not feel anxious, or be provoked into giving information" (p. 271). Note that the difference between males and females is one of degree, not kind: All the issues mentioned above are important to both sexes, but apparently more so to women.

What about online friendships that develop over time? Are they different from friendships that are face to face? One study of Internet users (Chan and Cheng, 2004) compared online and offline qualities of friendship: Face-to-face relationships were rated higher in several qualities including breadth (range of topics in conversation), depth (amount of self-disclosure and intimacy), understanding, and interdependence. The differences increased during the first year, but after that they tended to even out. "In other words, relationships developed online can also become personal, if given time, and relational partners can feel as intimate as they do in [face-to-face] interaction." Cross-sex friendship qualities were even higher within online friendships. This may be because online relationships are free of certain constraints such as social status, physical appearance, and nonverbal cues (p. 317).

Trust

Shaw (1997) proposes a working definition of trust as the "belief that those on whom we depend will meet our expectations of them." According to this view, trust begins when we assess the character or capabilities of the other person. "We trust those who meet our positive expectations" (p. 22)—in other words, you assess the other person's capacity to meet your needs.

Often associated with such concepts as fairness, integrity, and truthfulness, *trust* has also been defined as *the belief or feeling that no harm will come to you from the other person in the relationship.* In intimate relationships people are often devastated by a betrayal of trust. Some people are so shattered by betrayals of this kind that their loss of trust carries over into later relationships.

Trust is a necessary element of all relationships, not just intimate ones. When you make a new friend, speak frankly to an academic advisor, seek help from a doctor, or hire someone to move your furniture, a certain level of trust must exist. And trust is crucial in mass communication, as we'll see in Chapter 15.

Many scholars have emphasized the link between trust and *predictability.* We must be able to make reliable predictions about how others will behave toward us so that we can regulate our own behavior. Our ability to make predictions gives us "a sense of certainty about future actions and outcomes that permits [us to] make decisions and commitments" (Millar and Rogers, 1987, p. 122).

Trust has sometimes been studied by looking at how cooperative or competitive people are when they play games. And we know that when people are allowed to communicate face-to-face, their levels of cooperation increase. It seems then that, other things being equal, communication in and of itself sometimes raises the level of trust.

Writing about trustworthiness, Boone and Buck emphasize that knowledge of the other person's intention: "Predicting someone's trustworthiness is maximally useful in a prospective sense; while it is important to know when someone has cheated you, the real advantage is knowing when someone might cheat you" (2003, p. 172).

Lying and Deception

It might not surprise you to learn that people are often willing to lie to someone they consider a very attractive date. In one *Seinfeld* episode, the character George Costanza tries to impress a young woman by pretending to be a successful architect when actually he's not an architect and he's unemployed.

But what are the effects of lying between people who have already established a close relationship, presumably one based on trust? Whatever the lie, some would say, it was meant to protect the other person, to spare feelings. Communication scholar Mark Knapp's overview of lying and deception in close relationships (2006) finds that counter to what we might expect, partners may lie to each other more often than they do to other people. Sometimes the motive for such lying may simply be to maintain the existing bond. Much lying is done to maintain harmony or to protect the other's feelings and self-esteem. For example, despite voicing harsh criticism to her husband, a spouse may lie about having had the negative feelings: "Of course I love you. I was just kidding." But that may well have been her feeling at that moment. So total honesty is sometimes more ideal than real.

Knapp (2006) explores the consequences of what he calls "undiscovered lies." Reassuring someone of your love, even though you don't feel it at the time, is at times considered an altruistic lie. Many people openly acknowledge that they sometimes lie about their feelings. But lying to someone you're close to can make you feel angry, guilty, embarrassed.

"Sometimes lies are not uncovered, but suspicion has been aroused to such an extent that trust in one's partner is negatively affected" (Knapp, 2006, p. 527). Suspicions of *sexual infidelity* take questions of trust to an extreme. Fidelity in marriage is closely linked with issues of trust as well as intimacy. In marriage, sexual fidelity is a fundamental norm. According to a survey of marriage therapists, extramarital sex is among the most common problems for which couples enter therapy.

A study (Previti and Amato, 2004) examined whether extramarital sex is a cause or consequence of poor marital quality. Researchers found that among couples who had not been unfaithful "a high level of proneness to divorce (thinking that the marriage is in trouble, thinking about divorce, and talking about divorce with one's spouse or others) predicts that at least one spouse" is more likely to be unfaithful (p. 227). If infidelity does take place, it increases the likelihood of unhappiness in marriage as well as the probability of divorce. Infidelity can be seen, then, as both cause and consequence of the breakdown of the relationship.

Knapp reminds us that "self-deception clearly plays an important role in close relationships" (p. 521)—and there may be no more serious self-deception than one that involves infidelity. Sometimes we deny what seems clear to other people:

> *Little by little things were happening that didn't make sense, but I can remember making excuses for them myself . . . I didn't want to believe there was anything to find out. . . . I didn't confide in anyone, too, because I was afraid of what they would tell me. I wanted to believe everything was going to be fine and I wasn't deceived . . . But as much as I wanted to be a detective and find him out, I didn't*

want to either. Because the truth—I was afraid more of the truth than living in the lie kind of. (cited in Knapp, 2006, p. 522; italics in original)

Yet infidelity need not destroy a close relationship. For example, Dr. Keith Ablow (2006) has found that if a couple can learn why one of the spouses has been unfaithful, they may have an opportunity for change and the rebuilding of trust. Mitch, one of Ablow's patients, sought counseling after discovering that while on vacation with her girlfriends, his wife had met and been intimate with an old college sweetheart. Mitch was devastated and had initiated a divorce despite the fact that he still loved his wife and the couple had three children.

"There's a critical moment at hand," Dr. Ablow told Mitch, "And it could be the beginning of the best part of your marriage" (p. F5). He urged questioning and frank discussion between husband and wife about what had led to her actions and what changes—on both sides—needed to be made in the marriage.

In other kinds of relationships, people sometimes perceive *deception* either as a "normal" or necessary communication alternative. Research by Lippard (1988) with adolescents and young adults identified five primary motives for deception: resources, affiliation, self-protection, avoiding conflict, and protecting others.

One of the most interesting findings is a correlation between power, frequency of interaction, and deception. For example, those most often deceived were the subjects' parents—in other words, those who had the most control over their lives. This finding reinforces earlier research that deception "is frequently a power-balancing strategy" (p. 99). Note that almost 22 percent of all the deceptive actions involved loyalty to friends. And here women were reported to be more likely than men to lie in order to protect another person's feelings, a finding that supports stereotypical perceptions concerning women's behavior.

The subjects in this study were all young, of an age at which the shaping and preservation of one's self-identity seems to be a central task. Thus, further research must be done before it can be established that at other life stages—middle age, for example—the frequency of deception behaviors changes. Lippard (1988) shrewdly points out that "the easy resort to deception as a manipulative strategy does not truly change the power balance; rather, it reinforces the role relationship which creates the imbalance" (p. 102).

The final way in which we will characterize relationships is with respect to affection and control.

Affection and Control

More recent research supports original work by Leary (1957) proposing that relationships can be described in terms of two primary dimensions: affection and control. *Affection, the love/hate aspect of the relationship,* ranges from tender, cooperative, loving behaviors to those that are sarcastic, hostile, and aggressive. *Control,* a second and independent dimension, also *has two poles: dominance and submission.* At one extreme are behaviors we would characterize as competitive, exploitative, and domineering; at the other, we find those that are docile, dependent, and self-effacing. Of course there are many intermediate behaviors: You can be trusting without being overly dependent on someone else's judgment; you can act assertively without being overbearing.

Along the affection dimension, a given behavior, whether loving or hostile, tends to prompt behavior from the other person that is similar. So if Beth can't stand Carol and repeatedly acts hostile, it's more than likely Carol will come to respond in the same way to Beth. Conversely, friendly, cooperative behavior from Beth will tend to promote the same response from Carol.

The dominance/submission aspect of human relationships works differently. The control dimension, instead of eliciting similar behavior, tends to promote behavior that is *complementary*. For example, Jack's anxious, docile behavior may provoke his business partner, Don, into acting dogmatic and manipulative. Denise, a real go-getter with wonderful managerial skills, may marry someone who admires and respects these abilities and is relieved to let her take charge of most domestic and financial concerns. Whereas in the area of affection, stability occurs when two people are similar, in terms of control, the most stable relationship occurs when the two are *opposites*.

Without some agreement over the control aspects of a relationship, these have to be constantly renegotiated. Thus, two highly dominant people can find themselves locked in an ongoing power struggle, even over the most minor issues (who decides what hotel to stay at, who actually signs a legal form, who accepts an invitation). On the other hand, if two people both feel uncomfortable making decisions, each will try over and over again to get the other to assume responsibility.

As we said, affection and control are two independent dimensions, and relationships vary along both. No one should make the mistake of simply equating love with submission or dominance with hostility. A submissive wife may be very hostile toward her husband, although that hostility seems suppressed. By the same token, an extremely dominant husband may also be attentive and affectionate. Each of our actions reflects some measure of both dominance and submission and both love and hate, for affection and control are essential aspects of all our relationships.

Many other characteristics have been proposed for studying relationships. The five we have discussed—context, time, information sharing, trust, and affection and control—seem to us among the most essential. Clearly, no single characteristic suffices to describe the complexity of human relationships.

THEORIES OF RELATIONSHIP DEVELOPMENT

Potentially, every new person you meet may become that one lifelong friend in a relationship you treasure or the romantic partner with whom you want to spend your whole life. Although the odds are against it with most acquaintances, there is always that possibility.

Many scholars from communication and other disciplines have examined what they see as the linear development of personal relationships—viewing them as a sequence of stages or phases, each described by a particular set of behaviors. We will consider this approach by looking at the work of Mark Knapp.

A Theory on the Life Cycle of Relationships

Mark Knapp has written an extensive analysis of the stages of building, experiencing, and ending relationships and of the kind of communication that characterizes each stage. He sees these stages as building to a peak and sometimes declining—in his terms, "coming together" and "coming apart" (Knapp, 1984; Knapp and Vangelisti, 2000). The outline that follows pertains to relationships geared toward intimacy and permanence. This theory assumes that the projected stages may be sequential, that one often follows the other, but that sometimes relationships move more rapidly, skipping stages to move either forward (toward greater intimacy) or backward (toward dissolving).

Knapp proposes a staircase model, seen in Figure 8.2. Imagine yourself on the left side of the staircase (coming together). You are at the bottom (initiating) and as you develop a closer relationship with someone, you move up the steps (stages). The central staircase depicts states of possible equilibrium, or stabilizing, at each of the relationship stages.

Communication plays a different role at each stage in a relationship. During the early stages, it is aimed at learning about the other person so that decisions concerning the relationship can be made—whether to form a relationship, what subjects are open for discussion, how close or intimate the relationship should be. After this phase, communication is used to maintain, develop, and enhance the relationship as well as to negotiate differences that will increase the satisfaction derived from it. During the final stages, communication helps the partners terminate their relationship by providing a means of saving face, resolving feelings, and parting (ideally, on a positive basis).

Coming Together

Knapp proposes 10 stages in all: the first 5—"coming together"—describe the slow growth of interpersonal relationships.

Figure 8.2 A Staircase Model of Human Relationships

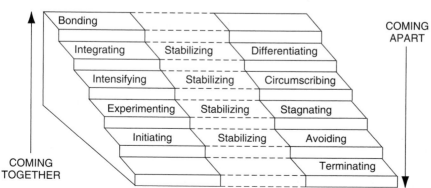

Source: From *Interpersonal Communication and Human Relationships*, 4th ed., by Mark L. Knapp and Anita L. Vangelisti. Published by Allyn and Bacon, Boston, MA. Copyright © 2000 by Pearson Education. Reprinted by permission of the publisher.

Initiating refers to the very first attempts you make at conversation with a new person. In Chapter 1, we referred to this as phatic communication: "Hi," "How's it going?" "Think it will rain today?" During this scanning process, communication is generally more cautious and conventional: You are trying to establish contact and express interest. Much of what we said about perception and first impressions in Chapter 2 relates to this stage of communication. Of course, these days the initiating phase may be taking place on the Internet.

Experimenting is the phase in which you try sample conversational topics in an attempt to gain some knowledge of the other person. Usually two people will ask a lot of questions and exchange a lot of small talk: "What's your major?" "What kind of music do you like?" "Where are you from?" Experimenting is a safe way of learning about similarities and differences. In this stage you're continually looking for ways of building on some area of common interest. Any commitments at this stage are generally very limited and the relationship is usually casual and relaxed: "Like it or not, most of our relationships probably don't progress very far beyond this stage" (Knapp and Vangelisti, 2000).

Intensifying marks the beginning of intimacy, sharing personal information, and the beginning of greater informality. This stage is marked by many changes in communication behaviors, both verbal and nonverbal, that take place when ac- quaintances become close friends. Physical closeness, hand holding, and greater eye contact are just a few of the various indicators that a relationship is intensifying. A greater degree of openness about yourself ("My parents are divorced"; "I'm not a very good student") is another. (We will have a great deal to say about self-disclosure in Chapter 9.) During the day you may be e-mailing each other at work, even if you are going to meet in the evening.

Integrating takes place when two people begin to consider themselves a cou- ple. Often this attitude is mirrored in the way others begin to treat them. At this time, they actively cultivate all the interests, attitudes, and qualities that seem to make them unique as a couple. They may also do this in a symbolic way, identify- ing a song as "our song," or even exchanging rings. As the two begin to value more and more of the same things, they intensify some aspects of their personalities and minimize others.

Bonding is a more formal or ritualistic stage. It may take the form of engage- ment or marriage, but even "going steady" is a form of bonding. Through bonding, the couple gain social or institutional support for their relationship and agree to accept a set of rules, or norms, governing their relationship. But bonding itself may change this relationship because it is now "more difficult to break out of . . . The contract becomes, either explicitly or implicitly, a frequent topic of conversation" (Knapp and Vangelisti, 2000).

Coming Apart

Relationships may stabilize at any of the building stages preceding bonding, the most intimate stage, but even relationships that reach the closest phase may begin to deteriorate. For Knapp, the termination of a relationship is not simply the reverse of what has been referred to as "coming together." People just don't "drift apart" or "separate"; only when both want to terminate the relationship is the process one of reversal, marked by decreasing contact, intimacy, and so on.

The other five stages seen on the right side of the staircase model describe the increasing deterioration that can occur in relationships that have been at the bonding stage—or in some cases, never achieved it.

Differentiating occurs when two people decide that perhaps their relationship may be too confining. This can be early on in a relationship. For example, a couple can pull back once a relationship intensifies and quickly begin to focus on their differences rather than their similarities. Or a couple who were at the bonding stage may decide they want to "do their own thing," "have a little breathing room"; in other words, they begin to emphasize their individuality. The most obvious change in communication is the increase in the number of fights.

Circumscribing refers to a stage in which couples begin to reduce the frequency and intimacy of their communication. Certain hot topics like money and sex tend to be avoided, since they are too likely to produce more quarreling. Greater formality returns, as if the two people didn't know each other very well. "Is it okay with you if I go for a walk now?" "I don't care. Do whatever you want to."

Stagnating reflects the increasing deterioration of a relationship that the participants are trying to hold together. It might be for religious or financial reasons, or for the sake of children involved, or because of other factors no longer having to do with attraction to the other person. Verbal and nonverbal messages become more and more like those conveyed between strangers. The relationship itself is no longer discussed.

Avoiding is a coping tactic to minimize the pain of experiencing a totally deteriorated relationship. Physical separation often takes place. Of course, this is easier if two people live apart, but we all know couples who live in the same house yet lead completely separate lives. Avoiding often takes place between neighbors or coworkers after a major argument. The participants still must remain physically close, but they manage to keep contact to a minimum.

Terminating is the final stage in any relationship. Knapp, who applies his theory to the briefest of encounters as well as to long-standing relationships, proposes that termination may occur after only a brief conversation or after a lifetime of intimacy. Generally, the longer and more meaningful the relationship, the more painful and drawn out its termination. Messages of distance and dissociation are often exchanged at this time, and usually these summarize and clarify what is happening between the two people—for example, "I don't ever want to see you again!" or "I'll always respect you, but I don't love you any more" (Knapp and Vangelisti, 2000). Movement down the staircase can also skip several steps, going for example from a bonding stage to a sudden rather than gradual termination—as when one person suddenly breaks off the relationship because he's found out that his partner was unfaithful.

Knapp's stage theory applies to same-sex as well as male–female relationships. And certainly some of the phases described are familiar to us all, but the lingering question is how well these categories account for the real discontinuities and jumps we find between stages and the degree to which we can generalize this theory of stages to a great number of relationships.

A Theory of Relationship Dissolution

The study of **relationship disengagement** or dissolution (what in Knapp's model constitutes "coming apart") has been given a great deal of attention (Duck, 1982; Baxter, 1982, 1984). Several variables will determine how a relationship ends. According to Baxter's research, how a relationship breaks up depends on who wants to end it (both people? only one?), whether problems came on suddenly, whether the partners confront each other directly, whether their discussions are long or short, whether the two parties want to "save" the relationship, and whether their goal is to change the relationship or to end it.

One theory that deals specifically with relationship dissolution has been proposed by Duck (1982, 1992, 1999) on the basis of his own work and the findings of Baxter and others. Duck believes there are four distinct phases, as seen in Figure 8.3.

The intrapsychic phase: The first phase in the breakdown of a relationship is usually internal. Although nothing is made overt, a great deal of dissatisfaction and reflecting on the relationship is going on. Partners are not yet speaking to each other about their growing unhappiness, but each may be focusing on the other's inadequacies, imagining how a breakup would affect their lives, or even thinking about starting a relationship with someone else. Sometimes it is only one person who has reached the point of thinking, "I can't stand this any more." "Just before exit from this phase," explains Duck, "people move up the scale of confidants so that they start to complain to their close friends" (1992, p. 95). (And for some people who are not in formal relationships, this may be where the breakup occurs.)

The dyadic phase: This phase is "the interpersonal mess"—the time when people actually confront each other. They may try talking out their differences, working out their difficulties, or ending the relationship and cutting their losses. Interestingly, Duck believes that people only talk about their relationships when things are not going well and that otherwise "the relationship" is usually a topic people avoid. This period is very stressful even for those who decide to stay in the relationship and attempt to repair it. They may resent the partner yet be unwilling to let go. It's a painful chaotic time—often full of hostility, guilt, and conflict. If the couple agree to break up, they enter the next phase.

The social phase: In this phase people start seeking advice from others—usually friends or family—in their social network about their decision. "It is no good just leaving a relationship: we need other people to agree with our decision or to prop us up and support what we have done" (Duck, 1992, p. 95). People want to feel confirmed in their action and to be thought of as acting in a responsible and justified way. While social networks may pressure a couple to stay together, once the breakup is imminent, they also spread the word that the couple is splitting up and help them recover after they do.

The grave dressing phase: To get over our distress we turn to others to justify ourselves. It seems we want to leave a relationship with some sort of narrative and,

Figure 8.3 *The Main Phases in Dissolving Personal Relationships*

BREAKDOWN: Dissatisfaction with relationship

Threshold: I can't stand this any more

INTRAPSYCHIC PHASE
Personal focus on partner's behavior
Assess adequacy of partner's role performance
Depict and evaluate negative aspects of being in the relationship
Consider costs of withdrawal
Assess positive aspects of alternative relationships
Face 'express/repress dilemma'

Threshold: I'd be justified in withdrawing

DYADIC PHASE
Face 'confrontation/avoidance dilemma'
Confront partner
Negotiate in 'our relationship talks'
Attempt repair and reconciliation?
Assess joint costs of withdrawal or reduced intimacy

Threshold: I mean it

SOCIAL PHASE
Negotiate post-dissolution state with partner
Initiate gossip/discussion in social network
Create publicly negotiable face-saving/blame-placing stories and accounts
Consider and face up to implied social network effects, if any
Call in intervention teams?

Threshold: It's now inevitable

GRAVE DRESSING PHASE
'Getting over' activity
Retrospection; reformulative post-mortem attribution
Public distribution of own version of break-up story

Source: From *Personal Relationships 5: Repairing Personal Relationships* by Steve Duck, 1984. Reprinted by permission of Elsevier.

in effect, prepare a story that makes us seem acceptable for future relationships. Now the social network becomes even more important:

> They can side with our version of events and our version of the partner's and the relationship's faults. ("I always thought he/she was no good," "I could

never understand how you two could get along—you never seemed right for each other.") . . . [O]nce the relationship is dead we have to bury it "good and proper"—with a tombstone saying how it was born, what it was like, and why it died. We have to create an account of the relationship's history. (pp. 95, 97)

Incidentally, several studies find that people tend to report that *they* were responsible for ending a previous relationship. "Apparently, individuals want to be the dumper rather than the dumpee" (Honeycutt and Cantrill, 2001, p. 152).

By emphasizing both the internal aspects of breakups—growing feelings of intense dissatisfaction and our misgivings about the relationship—and the role that people in social networks play when a couple is splitting up, Duck's theory broadens our understanding of how close relationships dissolve. His work also stresses that in ending a relationship both parties want to feel justified.

But are there truly set phases in interpersonal relationships? How do the theories you've been reading about correspond to your own experience? The concept of phases or stages enables us to categorize research findings about relational behaviors and to think of relationships in terms of movement and development. James Honeycutt (1993) and others argue that while the concept of phases in intimate relationships has been useful, it implies a final state—"bonding," for example, or "terminating"—although many actual relationships show continual fluctuations. Many relationships regress, become less intimate at times, but still endure. And even after divorce, formerly married couples may maintain some sort of relationship—and its quality may change many times. There are other difficulties with thinking in terms of stages. For example, how do we explain brief romances, one-night stands, and lifelong platonic friendships (p. 84)?

Honeycutt proposes a *memory structure approach* (Honeycutt and Cantrill, 2001). In this view, we all have expectations for relationship development. These are influenced not only by relationships we have actually had, but by what we have seen in the media, by observing our friends and family, and by what they tell us about their relationships. (If your best friend proposed to his wife three days after meeting her, "love at first sight" may be what you expect for yourself.) Our imagined interactions and fantasizing are also important.

In other words, we expect certain phases—each of which we associate with certain prototypes of behaviors—and these expectations affect how we interpret our relationships. Phases, Honeycutt believes, are constructed from our expectancies for relationships and exist in our memories, but the concept of stages may be helpful in looking at our perceptions and ideas about what should be happening over the span of a relationship (Honeycutt and Cantrill, 2001, p. 96).

MAINTAINING RELATIONSHIPS

A perfect day in the city always starts like this: My friend Leo picks me up and we go to a breakfast place called Rick and Ann's where they make red flannel hash out of beets and bacon, and then we cross the Bay Bridge to the gardens of the Palace of Fine Arts to sit in the wet grass and read poems out loud and talk about love.

—**Houston (1999, p. 143)**

The city is San Francisco and at the gardens of the Palace of Fine Arts newly married couples often come to have wedding photos taken. In this passage from Pam Houston's short story "The Best Girlfriend You Never Had," Lucille, the narrator, and her friend Leo do a great deal of talking, and when they talk about love it's often about love's failures. But they are not lovers; they're friends. Leo is an architect, and Pam is a photographer. Both grew up on the East Coast in what seem to be the same kind of families. Together they review their lives. "Is there anyone you could fall in love with besides Guinevere?" Lucille asks Leo. They talk about one of her ex-boyfriends, Gordon, who, it turns out, "had a jealous streak as vicious as a heat-seeking missile, and he could make a problem out of a paper bag" (p. 149). They console, humor, confide in, and support each other. By the end of that Saturday in November, they have switched from margaritas to lattes and they take a sailboat out in Sausalito "the way a real couple might on a Saturday afternoon." We don't have the sense that their story has a romantic ending, but that it will continue for a long, long time.

Today there is high interest in the study of **relationship maintenance**, or, in simpler language, *how people—whether they are friends, romantic partners, or family members—can maintain close and satisfying relationships*. The question is how, once we establish it, we can sustain a relationship.

Two people may establish what they think will be a lifelong friendship or marriage yet soon discover the pleasure that they felt when the initial bond was made is slipping away. It can be puzzling, even painful, to learn that some kind of effort is needed to keep a relationship going. If a close friend is easily insulted, keeping up the friendship may seem just too difficult to you. If your parents never fought, fighting with your spouse may seem to you a sign that your marriage is in danger. Often we have the idea that if we have to "work at" a relationship, it wasn't meant to be. But as we saw in Chapter 6, conflict is not always destructive. When two people can resolve their conflicts about relationship roles, it tends to enhance their relationship.

Theorists and researchers have identified many important routine behaviors as well as more conscious strategies that people use in maintaining close relationships (Canary and Dainton, 2003; Dindia, 2000; Duck, 1999; Knapp and Vangelisti, 2000): for example, disclosures or openness, verbal and nonverbal expressions of commitment and intimacy, constructive conflict, and—most surprisingly—lying.

According to some communication scholars (Duck, 1994; Duck and Pittmann, 1994), the very core of relational maintenance is in ordinary life—much of it everyday talk. It allows people to share their experiences. Through talk, however trivial, two people create shared meanings and project the future of their relationship. And it is these meanings that sustain their relationship.

> What is it that people are achieving by holding silly and insignificant conversations about trivial topics, telling one another jokes, discussing the clothing or demeanor of passersby, complaining about other people, speculating about other people's relationships, suggesting where to go for lunch, teasing one another, arguing and debating, or cajoling others? First, as *individuals,* they are giving off meaning . . . Second, as *partners,* they are colluding with the other partner in the embodiment of the relationship. (Duck, 1994, pp. 53–54)

Interestingly, talk between lovers is not rated as high in quality as talk between best friends. But research has shown that even everyday talk confirms two people in their agreement on how they experience the world (p. 56).

Certainly, in a close long-term relationship we come to expect an atmosphere of openness and trust in which two people will share a significant amount of personal information—thoughts, feelings, even responses to the relationship itself. We mentioned in discussing information sharing that women tend to be more self-disclosing than men. For example, when husbands believe their marriage is "going well," they see no need to speak about their relationship (Acitele, 1987). These and other findings lend some support to Tannen's observation that women tend to favor "relationship talk" and that for most women talk plays an essential role in maintaining intimacy (1990, p. 86).

Though people tend to talk less about their commitment to each other after the intensifying stage of their relationship, threatened relationships often require assurances, both verbal and nonverbal, that reestablish commitment:

> In troubled relationships, the "I love you" phrase may not be enough to convince one's partner he or she is loved. It has become an empty phrase because there have not been enough follow-up behaviors that specifically testify to the declaration of love . . . *Intensity* has a lot to do with the perceived strength of the commitment talk. This may involve rapt attention and focus achieved through long mutual gazes and close proximity; voice volume ("He just kept yelling 'I love Linda' as we walked down the street. It was embarrassing, but it meant a lot to me"); or absolute statements ("I'll *always* love you," or "I'll *never* leave you"). (Knapp and Vangelisti, 2000, p. 298)

As we saw in Chapter 3, when two people are intimate, they often develop a private language. Intimacy can be conveyed through personal idioms—from pet names to private ways of talking about sex. In a study of intimate play, a less serious aspect of personal relationships, Baxter (1992) includes private verbal codes, physical play, role-playing, teasing, and gossiping games. "Private verbal code play (i.e., playful idiomatic expression) appears to be a particularly strong indicator of intimacy" (p. 359). In many studies, play is not only used as a measure of intimacy but is thought to promote it. Considered a "low risk" or safe communication strategy, it enables people to moderate conflict and tensions.

Knapp notes how important it is that we initiate behaviors that maintain a relationship instead of simply receiving them. For example, a young woman we know once referred to her husband as "a guest in the marriage." Researchers have identified at least five maintenance strategies that have proved most successful in long-term romantic relationships:

Positivity: Being cooperative, cheerful, optimistic, not criticizing, being patient and forgiving, trying to build the other person's self-esteem (through compliments and other means).

Openness: Encouraging the other person's disclosure of thoughts and feelings, stating your feelings about the relationship, discussing the quality of the relationship as well as past relationship decisions, and what you need and want from it.

What are the qualities you most value in your best friend? Maeda and Richie (2003) looked at the concept of *shinyuu*—(best/close) friends—among Japanese college students as compared with college students from this country. While other studies have found that students from both Japan and the United States value several of the same qualities in friendship—particularly, closeness and dependability—these researchers tried to account for some of the subtle differences.

Among the valued categories for the Japanese students are some that might not be familiar. For example.

- "Does not pry . . . : does not interfere in others' affairs too much, does not ask too much about my private life, we keep a certain distance from each other."
- "A rival in a good sense: a good rival, we stimulate each other." (pp. 597–598)

In our culture we might find these somewhat puzzling, but the researchers explain that there are several valued qualities in Japanese culture that do not appear in studies of the West. Among them are "interdependence, group conformity, self-defense, and rivalry" (p. 582).

As we'll see in Chapter 10, in contrast to the individualist society of the United States, Japan is a collectivist society, one that emphasizes interdependence—for example, family and social obligations rather than uniqueness. Thus, the researchers suggest, there may be "a strong need to balance . . . social/group identity and personal/individual identity" so that maintaining your personal identity in a close friendship is more important in Japanese society (2003, p. 582). This may explain such values as rivalry and self-defense.

And it may be that the role of close friend is itself perceived differently in the two cultures:

One factor hindering the development of intercultural friendships may be differences in ideas and expectations of friendship. For instance, close friendship may involve acting like a family member in some cultures, whereas it might mean not interfering with a friend's family matters in other cultures. (p. 580)

For students planning to study abroad or simply developing friendships with people of other cultures, this is sound advice.

Assurances: Stressing commitment to the other person, implying the relationship has a future, showing love and faithfulness.

Networks: Spending time with common friends; showing willingness to be with the other person's friends or family, including them in activities.

Tasks: Sharing duties and tasks jointly including household chores and other responsibilities. ("Doing my fair share of the work we have to do.") (Canary and Stafford, 1992, adapted from pp. 262–263; 1994; Canary and Dainton, 2003)

Of these behaviors, sharing tasks is the most underrated and openness the most overrated (Dindia, 2000, p. 291). Other strategies mentioned are conflict management and giving advice.

In maintaining close friendships three kinds of behaviors seem especially important (Fehr, 2000):

Self-disclosure: Openness between friends, sometimes used consciously to sustain and enhance the friendship. A good part of friendship includes self-disclosure. Often friendships break down when one person starts withholding information from the other. This is especially true of friendships between women. (Married women sometimes say that they disclose more to their friends than they do to husbands. In fact, a good part of friendship between women involves talking about personal problems together. Men tend to see friendships as based primarily on doing things together [Tannen, 2001, p. 32].)

Supportiveness: Friends seem to have an unwritten understanding that they will be there for each other—for example, listening and offering advice when a friend has a problem with a girlfriend, parents, or grades. And friends expect support through loyalty. Most young adults rely on peers for social support.

Spending Time Together: Though it seems obvious, friends keep their relationship going by doing things together—seeing movies, taking trips, shopping, celebrating holidays and birthdays. When they can't be together, they keep in touch through telephone calls, e-mail, letters, and cards (adapted from Fehr, 2000, pp. 77–78).

In the story "The Best Girlfriend You Never Had," Leo and Lucille maintain their friendship through all these behaviors. They openly disclose and discuss their intimate feeling about his girlfriends, her boyfriends, their parents. They provide social support by listening to each other's problems and empathizing. And they routinely arrange to spend a great deal of free time together. (See Box 8.1 for a discussion of close friendships in other cultures.)

As you think about relationship maintenance, keep in mind that the concepts we speak of here are examined in many parts of this book. For example, we will look at other aspects of openness and commitment in Chapter 9. And remember that at times researchers define the same variable by somewhat different terminology and that there is no magic list of behaviors: You have to maintain and negotiate each relationship on its own terms.

FAMILY COMMUNICATION

Clearly, the relationships that matter most to us are those in our family: The family represents a very special constellation of relationships.

Currently, there is much debate about what constitutes a family. In their book on family theory (2006), Leslie Baxter and Dawn Braithwaite identify the five properties often used to define the concept of family:

Long-term commitment

Relations created through biology, law, or affection

Enmeshment in a kinship organization

Ongoing interdependence

Institutionalization (that is, legal or institutional recognition of the bond)

Baxter and Braithwaite give special emphasis to two qualities: commitment and interdependence. They define a family as "a social group of two or more persons, characterized by ongoing interdependence with long-term commitments that stem from blood, law, or affection" (Baxter and Braithwaite, 2006, p. 3).

Another broad and useful definition of **family** is "*networks of people who share their lives over long periods of time; who are bound by ties of marriage, blood, or commitment, legal or otherwise; who consider themselves as family; and who share future expectations of connected relationship*" (Galvin et al., 2003). So in addition to stepfamilies (also called remarried families) and single-parent families, such a definition includes heterosexual and same-sex couples who live together and who may or may not have children.

According to one source on traditional marriage, "Half of all divorces occur within the first seven years of marriage." Several of the risk factors for divorce or separation during the first 10 years of marriage appear in Table 8.3 (Shellenbarger, 2004).

Although research suggests that divorce rates may be declining, the divorce rate among couples over age 50 has increased. And it seems that in later life it is women rather than men who initiate the majority of divorces (Enright, 2004). This may be due, in part, to the increased ability of women to support themselves.

Today people's family histories are growing more complex as each year "half of all the marriages that take place in the United States are remarriages for one or both partners" (Coleman et al., 2001). And by 2010, it's thought that remarried families will be the most common type in this country. The 2000 Census also reports a considerable rise in the number of gay and lesbian families, and an increasing number of them are raising children.

Table 8.3 The First Ten Years of Marriage: Some Risk Factors	
Divorce rates can vary significantly. Here are the percentage-point increases in the probability of divorce or separation during the first 10 years of marriage, depending on a variety of factors:	
Annual income under $25,000 vs. over $50,000	+30%
Having a baby before marriage vs. seven months or more afterward	+24%
Marrying under 18 years of age vs. 25 or over	+24%
Own parents divorced vs. intact family of origin	+14%
No religious affiliation	+14%
High school dropout vs. some college	+13%
Central city vs. suburb dweller	+9%

Source: National Center for Health Statistics. Adapted from Sue Shellenbarger, "No Comfort in Numbers: Divorce Rate Varies Widely from Group to Group," *The Wall Street Journal,* April 22, 2004, D1 (with change in title of table). Copyright © 2004 Dow Jones and Co. Reprinted by permission of Dow Jones and Co. via Copyright Clearance Center.

Stephanie Coontz, the author of a number of books on marriage and family life including *Marriage, a History: How Love Conquered Marriage* (2006a), sums up some interesting findings:

> For the first time in 150 years, [U.S.] households headed by single adults and unmarried couples now outnumber married-couple families. [This figure may be misleading, however. For example, there's been a slight decline in the divorce rate. And one reason for the greater number of unmarried households is that people now marry later—27 is now the median age for men, just about 26 for women. You're less likely to divorce if you marry later in life.]
>
> Thirty million unmarried men and women live alone, in their own household rather than with roommates or parents.
>
> The number of heterosexual couples who live together outside of marriage has soared from 500,000 in 1970 to more than five million today.
>
> Forty percent of cohabiting couples, compared to 45 percent of married couple households, have children in the home.
>
> Elders are the fastest growing segment of the cohabiting population. (Coontz, 2006b)

To read a variety of articles on marriage, go to *www.stephaniecoontz.com/articles*. Be sure to take the pop quiz on marriage. You may be quite surprised.

Gender Development and the Family

Gender, we saw in Chapter 2, is an essential aspect of self-concept, and it is within the family that early consciousness of gender begins for the developing child. Even an infant as young as seven months knows the difference between a male and female face and voice. Parents begin to communicate a sense of gender orientation when a child is quite young (Bussey and Bandura, 2004, p. 101). Through the family a child first learns about culture, its expectations and rules for behavior, and, in part, what is considered feminine and masculine.

Parents communicate expectations and gender roles early on not only verbally but nonverbally when they choose their children's names, clothing, room furnishings and color scheme, and toys:

> Boys are provided with a greater variety of toys than girls. These play materials orient boys' activities to gender roles usually performed outside the house. By contrast, girls are given toys directed toward domestic roles such as homemaking and child care. Thus, the gender-linked play materials arranged for children channel their spontaneous play into traditionally feminine or masculine roles. (Bussey and Bandura, 2004, p. 102)

In both Western and non-Western cultures, there is more rough play with boys—by both parents, "closer physical proximity" to girls, and a tendency to think that girls will require more help: "Girls are encouraged to participate in activities that keep them close to their homes and families, while boys are given more opportunities for play and other activities away from home and independent of adult supervision . . ." (Ivy and Backlund, 2004, p. 84). A young girl who is adept at completing puzzles and block building might be told that someday she may work for an architect whereas a boy with comparable skills might be told that someday he may be an architect. Some studies of moral development even propose that because most women are brought up to emphasize caring and responsibility for others rather than autonomy and independence, they tend to develop different moral value systems than men (Gilligan, 1993; Gilligan et al., 1989).

The Family as a System

Current theorists view the family as a system, emphasizing family relationships rather than individual members. Looking at the family in this way, as a whole rather than the sum of its individual members, shifts attention to patterns of relationships and cycles of behavior rather than causes and effects: "Every member influences the others but is in turn influenced by them" (Bochner and Eisenberg, 1987, p. 542).

In her innovative work with families, therapist Virginia Satir distinguishes between closed and open family systems:

> The main difference between them is the nature of their reactions to change, both from the inside and from the outside. In a closed system the parts are rigidly connected or disconnected altogether. In either case, information does not flow between parts or from outside in or inside out. When parts are disconnected, they often appear as if they are operating: Information leaks in and out but without any direction. There are no boundaries.
>
> An open system is one in which the parts interconnect, are responsive and sensitive to one another, and allow information to flow between the internal and external environments. (1988, pp. 131–132)

For Satir, disturbed families are closed systems; nurturing families are open systems. In a closed system, communication is "indirect, unclear, unspecific, incongruent, growth-impeding": Rules are covert and out-of-date, with people changing their needs to conform to the rules. In an open system, communication is "direct, specific, congruent, growth-producing": Rules are open and up-to-date, changing "when need arises" (pp. 134–135).

Communication Rules

Today theorists emphasize the uniqueness of all families, happy or unhappy; they regard each as distinct, with its own history, values, and behavioral norms. Just as families have their own sets of values and expectations for their members, they have their own expectations about communication. There seem to be acceptable times to speak about certain topics, issues that are never raised, certain family members who should be approached or not approached, and so on. In other words, each family has a virtual handbook of understood communication rules.

In your family, for example, dinner conversations may be reserved for current things, news, movies. Serious problems and possible changes may be discussed late at night—and only with one parent. Your brother's low grades may be something the family never speaks about openly. There may be a family member from whom much information is kept (e.g., a grandmother). If you need money, you may always go to your mother, never your father. Or you may have a rule that you never interrupt your father when he is speaking, even if he is telling you something you already know. Communication rules are unique to each family, and over time these rules sometimes have to be revised.

Cohesion and Adaptation

Of the many variables theorists use to describe families, two of the most important are cohesion and adaptation to change. Both these dimensions influence and are influenced by communication (Galvin et al., 2003; Bochner and Eisenberg, 1987).

Cohesion refers to how closely connected or bonded family members are. At the high end of the spectrum are families "so closely bonded and overinvolved that individuals experience little autonomy or fulfillment of personal needs and goals" (Galvin et al., 2003). Such families have few boundaries. Family members are all implicated in each other's lives, and there is little privacy: Everyone knows everyone else's business. They share everything, and the level of emotional or physical intimacy tends to be very high.

In families with very low levels of cohesion, on the other hand, family members are so physically and emotionally separated, so uninvolved, that there often seems little connection between them. Few activities are shared, family functions have a low priority, and each person may seem to be on a separate schedule. Writing about how modern technology has eroded contemporary life, one psychologist describes this pattern when he speaks about "the microwave relationship" in family life, with the home becoming "less a nesting place than a pit stop" (Gergen, 2000, p. 66).

Cohesion is sometimes more wished for than actual. In John Cheever's short story "Goodbye, My Brother," four adult children and their families meet at their childhood summer home for a vacation. The narrator, one of the older brothers, begins:

> We are a family that has always been very close in spirit. Our father was drowned in a sailing accident when we were young and our mother has always stressed the fact that our familial relationships have a kind of permanence that we will never meet again. (Cheever, 1978, p. 3)

Yet the narrator is preoccupied by Lawrence, his youngest brother, and resents his repeated criticisms and withdrawals ("goodbyes") from the rest of the family. The story ends with a confrontation on the beach in which the narrator strikes his brother on the head, giving him a bloody wound. Lawrence and his wife leave early the next morning.

Another important dimension by which families are described is *adaptation to change:* Although earlier theorists looked on the family as a system that remains in balance and essentially constant, it has become clear that "family systems not only remain the same, they also change, sometimes suddenly" (Bochner and Eisenberg, 1987, p. 543). The family may be affected by developmental changes in younger children and by later changes, as children grow older, leave home, marry and introduce new spouses into the family. In the course of time, families also face crises such as divorce, economic reversals, significant illness, or deaths. There seem to be no families exempt from such stresses.

At the high end of the adaptability spectrum are families adapting themselves to any and every change in a way that becomes chaotic. Families who are extremely low in adaptability are described as rigid; they cannot accommodate themselves to change and live by inflexible rules. (Satir [1988] writes that in a closed system rules are inhuman [p. 134].) Most families fall somewhere in between these extremes and at times vary in their adaptability to change.

Although all families undergo stress, researchers propose that it's how the family deals with stress that determines its health. In healthy families, according to one analysis of research findings, family members don't take oppositional attitudes; they don't blame each other. Nor are they preoccupied with themselves; they don't "overanalyze." They tend to emphasize wit and to enjoy themselves. And the family boundaries tend to be conventional. In general, therapists "view adaptability as more critical to the functioning of the family than cohesion" (Bochner and Eisenberg, 1987, p. 556).

Stages in Family Development

The nuclear family has undergone drastic changes. Men and women now marry approximately four years later than they did a half-century ago, and an increasing number of women have children without marrying. Women have joined the workforce in increasing numbers: In 2000, almost 75 percent of married women who had school-age children were either employed or seeking work.

For all its shortcomings, the family is still one of the most important sources of gratification in our lives. From a study of the research on family communication Pearson (1993) has identified three stages in the development of families with children.

Families with Preschool Children

In this stage, birth to age six, children are in their peak years for language learning. We saw in Chapter 3 that the major part of language acquisition comes from the family—particularly from interaction between the child and the primary caretaker, usually the mother. Children begin by using single words. Between 18 and 24 months, two-word phrases appear. By age two children have developed a vocabulary of about 300 words. By age three they have about 1,000 words, and from age four to five, they add about 50 words a month!

Families with School-Age Children

Children experience increasingly greater independence with each year of maturation. Family communication, while still the dominant force, begins to share influence to an increasing degree with communication from outside. Two dimensions of parent-child communication become important: acceptance-rejection and control-autonomy.

All of us need to feel accepted; however, the degree of acceptance we need will vary with the amount we received from our parents. It is thought that the more accepting our parents, the less we feel a need for acceptance as we grow older. In other words, we have developed a feeling of self-worth. Furthermore, if we are raised in a family in which parents exhibit strict control, we tend to feel a higher need for control in later life.

Families with Adolescent Children

This stage tends to be characterized by increased conflict due to the increasing independence of the children. Issues of autonomy and control are very keen during these years. Adolescent children increasingly move away from family communication and toward communication with peers. Due to the intense physiological and psychological changes adolescents experience, certain topics become the focal point of communication. Acceptable topics might range from classes, grades, jobs, sports, future plans, to family news. Taboo topics include sex, parties, alcohol, drugs, and boyfriends and girlfriends.

For stepfamilies several issues compound the difficulties. One of these is conflicts over loyalty. For example, a 16-year-old girl observed:

> I guess when Eric [my stepfather] tries to discipline or tries to provide input my dad gets mad. You know, he tries to say that [Eric] doesn't have any authority in the family—he shouldn't have any say in what happens between us kids. So that causes friction for me because I'm put in the middle because you can't take sides. They both talk about each other and tell you stuff—like when they're in fights and mad at each other my mom will tell me stuff about my dad and my dad will tell me stuff about my mom. (Coleman et al., 2001, p. 65)

Two specialists in family therapy (McGoldrick and Carter, 1999) have identified the most common issues in stepfamilies with adolescents:

1. Conflict between the need for the remarried family to coalesce and the normal concentration of adolescents on separation. Adolescents often resent the major shifts in their customary family patterns and resist learning new roles and relating to new family members when they are concerned with growing away from the family.
2. . . . difficulty for a stepparent in attempting to discipline an adolescent.
3. Adolescent attempts to resolve their divided loyalties by taking sides . . . or actively play[ing] one side against the other.
4. Sexual attraction between stepsiblings or stepparent and stepchild, along with the adolescent's difficulty in accepting the biological parent's sexuality. (p. 425)

For all families with children the adolescent years are probably the most trying times with regard to communication. If parents and children can successfully weather the storms, smoother sailing tends to follow.

Children grow up and leave the house, yet in later life we may also take care of our aging parents so that these relationships alter, sometimes dramatically. And whether we have children or not, most of us will interact with siblings (and sometimes the siblings of our partners) for the rest of our lives. In the next chapter we consider some research findings about sibling relationships as part of an in-depth look at intimacy, self-disclosure, and other variables that play a part in the dynamics of all close relationships.

Summary

This chapter was concerned with relationship processes, and its first focus of attention was the bases of human attraction. Other things being equal, we found, the closer two people are geographically, the more likely they are to be attracted to each other. Although proximity is usually a precondition of attraction, people tend to attract and be attracted to those they perceive as similar to themselves. Conversely, they tend to dislike and be disliked by those perceived as different. Several variables qualify generalizations about the similarity thesis—including perceived reciprocity of liking, changes in self-esteem, anxiety, and isolation. We also looked at research on minimal daters, online dating, and simgles and their relationships.

We then turned to five defining characteristics of all relationships. We stressed the importance of social-psychological environment and spoke of what makes for confirming and supportive climates. Time, information sharing, and trust were also examined as were two primary dimensions of all relationships: affection and control. Lying and deception as they affect close relationships were also discussed.

The next part of our chapter examined a theory about stages in the life cycle of a relationship and another about how people end their relationships. We also considered recent findings about the behaviors and strategies people use to maintain satisfying relationships. And in our final section, on family communication, we looked at gender development, divorce, the family as a system of communication rules, the variables of cohesion and adaptability to change, as well as stages of development in families that have children.

Key Terms

Breadth	Depth	Perceived reciprocity of liking	Relationship maintenance
Communication climate	Disconfirmation	Proximity	Setting
Confirmation	Empathy	Relationship disengagement	Supportive climate
Context	Family		
Defensive climate	Minimal daters		
Defensiveness			

Review Questions

1. What are two ways in which proximity influences interpersonal relationships?

2. How is similarity related to attraction?

3. Describe four variables that qualify generalizations about attitude similarity.

4. Summarize some of the recent findings about minimal daters, online dating, and singles and their relationships.

5. Explain the difference between communication climate and setting.

6. What are the major differences between confirming and disconfirming response styles? Give some examples.

7. How do supportive and defensive climates of communication differ?

8. In what ways can we define relationships in terms of time?

9. What is the essential difference between depth and breadth of information sharing in any relationship?

10. What is the relationship between trust, accuracy, and effectiveness in human relationships?

11. Discuss lying and deception, their frequency and effects, in close relationships.

12. Explain how the dominance/submission (control) dimension of a relationship functions. Give an example.

13. How does the love/hostility (affection) dimension of human relationships function?

14. Identify the building and declining stages of human relationships as defined by Knapp.

15. Describe Duck's four phases of relationship dissolution.

16. Explain the memory structure approach to human relationships.

17. Discuss at least three strategies that have proved most effective for maintaining romantic relationships.

18. Discuss the three most effective strategies for maintaining friendships.

19. Explain at least three defining characteristics of families and what makes family communication distinctive. Discuss gender development and the family.

20. Give three risk factors for divorce in the first ten years of marriage.

21. Discuss two major variables in family communication.

22. List and briefly explain three stages in the development of families with children.

Exercises

1. Have some friends rate a number of topics on a scale such as the one shown here. Then create two paragraphs, one agreeing with the general attitude of the class on each issue—legalizing gay marriage, for example—and one disagreeing. Put a byline on each of the two paragraphs, using fictitious names. Then have your friends indicate the extent of their attraction to the authors. See whether they prefer the person whom they perceive as holding an attitude similar to their own. This would validate the theory that perceived attitude similarity yields attraction.

Strongly agree	Agree	Neither agree nor disagree	Disagree	Strongly disagree
5	4	3	2	1

2. Create a composite description of the kinds of people you are attracted to. What does this composite tell you about yourself?

3. Find 10 people in your classes or among your friends who have met someone through the Internet, whether it was a dating service such as *match.com* or *www.personals.aol.com,* a chat room, or some other Web site. Describe how many of these relationships resulted in actual dating, how long they lasted, and how many of the relationships were satisfying. How many people represented themselves honestly when they were online? Do you think such relationships are different in any way from those that begin with face-to-face communication?

4. Describe a situation in which you entered into a relationship on the rebound. Analyze the positive and negative aspects of that relationship. If you were to encounter a similar situation, what, if anything, would you do differently?

5. The next time you observe a disagreement between two people, try to determine whether they are disagreeing on the content level, the relationship level, or both. Relate your observations to two other disagreements that you have experienced, and analyze those disagreements in the same way.

6. Write a paragraph describing someone you trust very much. Then write a description of someone you do not trust. Finally, elaborate on the behaviors that you want to develop and to avoid in building a trusting relationship with someone in the future.

7. Observe five communication events that illustrate five different outcomes of communication (see

Chapter 1). Analyze the events in terms of the following questions:

a.   What were the relative frequencies of confirming and disconfirming response styles for each communication event? Does there appear to be any relationship between the type of communication outcome and the predominant response style? If so, why do you think this is the case, and what implications does this have for your own communication behavior?

b.   In which communication events were trust and information sharing most apparent? Why do you think this was so?

Suggested Readings

Ahrons, Constance. *We're Still Family.* New York: HarperCollins, 2004.

A very readable book that expands the author's study of the long-term effects of divorce on children. She draws on over 150 interviews with grown children whose parents divorced and comes to some surprising conclusions.

Coontz, Stephanie. *Marriage, a History: How Love Conquered Marriage.* New York: Viking Penguin, 2006.

An important and well-written history of marriage through the ages and how it has changed in the last 200 years—the shift, in the author's words, from obedience to intimacy.

Duck, Steve. *Relating to Others,* 2nd ed. Buckingham, UK: Open University Press, 1999.

A succinct, well-written discussion of interpersonal relationships by an authority on the subject.

Gladwell, Malcolm. *Blink: The Power of Thinking Without Thinking.* New York: Back Bay Books, 2007.

An informative and entertaining book about the way people make snap judgments. Several of the leading researchers on the subject are discussed. Be sure to read about John Gottman's work on married couples.

Hendrick, Clyde, and Susan S. Hendrick, eds. *Close Relationships: A Sourcebook.* Thousand Oaks, CA: Sage, 2000.

This is a comprehensive handbook on close relationships with contributions by many eminent researchers and theorists in the field. For the advanced student.

In Her Shoes

A film about two very different siblings—their rivalries, affection, and uncommon bond.

Karbo, Karen. "Friendship: The Laws of Attraction," *Psychology Today* 39 (November/December 2006), 90–95.

A brief popular article on our choices of friends.

Knapp, Mark L., and Anita L. Vangelisti. *Interpersonal Communication and Human Relationships,* 5th ed. Newton, MA: Allyn & Bacon, 2004.

The authors analyze communication patterns in developing and declining relationships as well as the strategies and behaviors people use to maintain satisfying relationships.

My Big Fat Greek Wedding

A film about two young people of very different cultures who fall in love and decide to marry. The contrasts in family styles and expectations make for rich, good-natured comedy.

Tannen, Deborah. *I Only Say This Because I Love You.* New York: Random House, 2001.

A linguist examines how talk can build or destroy relationships within families. There are wonderful examples of actual conversations, and much can be learned, painlessly, by reading this book.

 For Supplementary Information

Log onto the Online Learning Center at *www.mhhe.com/tubbsmoss11.*

PART TWO

Contexts

9

Interpersonal Communication

Chapter Objectives

After reading this chapter, you should be able to:

1. Explain the concepts of norms, enacted roles, and role conflict and give examples of each. Discuss the effects of our expectations on close relationships.
2. Explain the dialectical approach to human interactions and identify three primary dialectics.
3. Identify four ways to assess the quality of an interpersonal relationship.
4. Explain the concept of the Johari window. Give several reasons for self-disclosure and reluctance to disclose. Discuss self-disclosure and self-presentation in Internet dating. Explain when self-disclosure is appropriate.
5. Discuss the concepts of intimacy, attachment styles in romantic relationships, unreciprocated love, and the findings on intimacy between siblings.
6. Discuss affiliation and commitment in interpersonal communication, marriage and cohabitation, the triangular theory of love, and the theory about love styles.
7. State the relationship between needs for affiliation and dominance and explain how status affects interpersonal communication.
8. Discuss dominance, status, and power in interpersonal relationships and explain the four proposed bases of gendered power.
9. Explain the differences between assertive, nonassertive, and aggressive behaviors.

In David Auburn's play *Proof,* Hal, the former graduate student of a brilliant but mentally unstable mathematician, finds a groundbreaking mathematical proof among the professor's papers after his death. The professor's younger daughter Catherine, a promising math student in her mid-twenties, has left college to care for her father, refusing to let him be institutionalized. Her stylish older sister, Claire, returns to Chicago for his funeral. By the end of Act I, Catherine claims to be the author of the proof, and Claire and Hal are sure that this cannot be true.

In a later scene the sisters confront each other after Claire suddenly announces that she has sold the family house to the university. Catherine tells Claire that at least she got to finish college:

Claire: You could've stayed in school!

Catherine: How?

Claire: I would have done anything—I told you that. I told you a million times to do anything you wanted.

Catherine: What about Dad? Someone had to take care of him.

Claire: He was ill. He should have been in a full-time professional-care situation.

Catherine: He didn't belong in the nuthouse.

Claire: He might have been better off.

Catherine: How can you say that?

Claire: This is where I'm meant to feel guilty, right?

Catherine: Sure, go for it. (Auburn, 2001, p. 44)

Very much a drama about trust, loyalties, and self-doubt, *Proof* explores relationships between siblings, parent and child, and a charged, often wary relationship between a young man and a woman. Who wrote the proof is a mystery that can only be solved by reading the play or seeing the film.

Interpersonal communication encompasses many kinds of relationships from the most casual to the most long-lasting. Two issues are central in the study of interpersonal communication. First, how many people does it involve? Second, what is the level of quality and intimacy of the communication? Certainly, interpersonal communication can occur within a small group of people—for example, within your immediate family or circle of close friends—but for the sake of simplicity much of our discussion focuses on communication that occurs between two people, as seen in our model in Chapter 1. Most scholars agree that the quality or intimacy of the communication is a crucial issue. In this chapter we focus on the many variables that play a part in the dynamics of close interpersonal relationships.

THE SOCIAL SETTING

No two people, no matter how intense their relationship, live totally untouched by the rules and expectations of society. As their relationship evolves, they also develop a kind of society in miniature, a two-person social system with some of its own rules and expectations, its own rewards and punishments.

Norms

As suggested in Chapter 4, **norms** are *rules, whether implicit or explicit, about behavior,* rules from which we develop certain expectations about how people will act. We have norms for sex, eating, visiting, grading exams, tipping, childrearing—in fact, for every aspect of human life. Even two people meeting for the first time follow norms as to appropriate communication behaviors: "There are rules for taking and terminating a turn at talking; there are norms synchronizing the process of eyeing the speaker and being eyed by him; there is an etiquette for initiating an encounter and bringing it to an end" (Goffman, 1972).

Norms exist on a number of social levels and are often transferred from one relationship to another—not always with the same measure of success. Some are shared by almost all members of a given culture, others are specific to families, ethnic groups, communities, or regions of a country. For example, in getting on a bus you're more likely to exchange greetings with the bus driver in San Diego than you are in New York.

When you and I first meet, each of us already has a great many expectations (however misguided) about how the other will behave. As we get to know one another, we may also establish some norms of our own. When dating, for example, a couple decides what are acceptable or unacceptable behaviors concerning a number of things, such as places to go, topics of conversation, sexual activity, and so on.

Sometimes the norms in an intimate relationship are made unusually explicit. For example, some couples formalize such norms in a personal marriage contract or prenuptial agreement. Such a contract can cover any number of issues: where a couple will live, whether they will have children and how they will be raised, religious commitments, household responsibilities, career arrangements, and last but not least, finances. Agreements reached by young couples just starting out sometimes concern whether one spouse will be exempt from the student debts of the other if the two split up, when will stock options earned by one spouse become marital property, supporting of a student spouse, and giving up a career to raise a family. Agreements can also be highly individual. Thus, Neil Simon, "the world's most successful playwright," agreed not to write about Dianne Lander, his third wife, because "she didn't want him observing their relationship instead of living it" (Dubin, 2001, p. 137).

Initially, it may seem that a contract will minimize power struggles and conflicts, but normative agreements may have to be changed as the people who made them change. And some contracts actually specify conditions for negotiating new terms or renewing the old ones. Criticisms of such arrangements include the view that they are businesslike, dehumanizing, and reflect a lack of trust.

Although we have no research yet on whether living with a contract influences the way a couple communicates, knowing that they have a contract probably affects their communication. For example,

> sometimes couples feel that the contract signifies ownership. Either explicitly or implicitly, messages may be based upon the fact that the other person "belongs to me"—"You're my wife and you'll do as I tell you." (Knapp and Vangelisti, 2000, p. 301)

In general, certain relationships seem to establish more norms than others. One team of researchers reports that the frequency with which norms are established is linked to the *disruptive power* each person has over the other—that is, *the power one person has to keep the other from doing what he or she wants to do*. In some relationships, one person has much more disruptive power than the other. When both have high disruptive power, they tend to establish a greater number of normative agreements—perhaps because both know that overuse of their power can destroy the relationship. When disagreements between two people are common, normative agreements often reduce the level and frequency of conflict. If Matt always prefers watching football and basketball and Stephanie always wants to go to the movies, they can decide to alternate these activities. If Stephanie has greater disruptive power than Matt, they may end up going to the movies most of the time. Either arrangement is a normative agreement.

Norms are guidelines that limit and direct behavior. We accept them because they allow us to establish standard operating procedures—ground rules, if you will—that make the behavior of others more predictable and decrease the need for communicating about that behavior. If a married couple reaches an agreement about where to spend Christmas and Easter holidays each year or about who handles the finances, there is no need to renegotiate these decisions repeatedly.

Not all normative agreements are rewarding. Some are inappropriate. Some restrict communication in an unhealthy way. Others are too rigid. For example, if a normative agreement exists between father and son that the son will never question the father's judgments or decisions, the son may forfeit his own good judgment simply because it conflicts with his father's opinion. Norms can best serve us if we know that they exist and can periodically evaluate their appropriateness.

Roles

Child-parent, student-teacher, lover-lover, friend-friend, husband-wife, player-coach, patient-doctor, employee-supervisor, grandparent-grandchild. These are just a sampling of the many sets of roles possible within a two-person relationship. The term "role" is unsettling. Actors play roles, and you might be wondering what roles have to do with human communication—especially two-person communication—in which, ideally, communication is based on mutual trust, not game-playing. Roles relate to the norms we've just been talking about. In any given culture, some norms apply to all members and others apply to only some members. A **role** is simply *a set of norms that applies to a specific subclass within the society.* Each of us assumes multiple roles. Yet, in assuming them, we do not become automatons, nor do we necessarily sacrifice our individuality.

Expected versus Enacted Roles

A person's expected and enacted roles are often quite different. A parent is expected to minister to the needs of the child, to provide financial support, and so on. But the enacted role of parent may in fact be quite different. So may the role of the child, as we see in the play *Proof.* It is Catherine, the younger daughter, who ends up caring for her father, making decisions about his welfare, and, when he has a remission, encouraging him to do work in mathematics. And in one of the play's flashbacks we see that it is the father who, despite his love and respect for academic life, foils his daughter's attempt to return to college. He needs her too much to let her go.

Even when such an obvious reversal of roles does not take place, people interpret their roles differently. For example, one man might view the role of father as a stern disciplinarian, another as a completely permissive companion, another as a firm but loving teacher.

Granted, we "enact" roles. We shall not say, however, that we are actors in a completely theatrical sense: Some roles are more central to us than others. Thus the intensity with which a person takes on various roles differs: Some will be enacted casually, with little or no involvement, and others with great commitment. When we enact a role with any measure of intensity, we communicate from within that role— that is, we take a certain stance. We also internalize certain expectations about how we should respond and how other people should respond to us. ("How dare you talk to your mother that way?" asks the outraged mother.) Most communication takes place within the boundaries of these expectations (see Box 9.1).

Of course, we are more comfortable in some roles than in others. Usually the roles we don't enjoy playing are those that create conflict. Role conflict, and the misunderstandings to which it gives rise, illustrate the interdependence of role, self-concept, and communication. Let's look at two types of role conflict, both of which tend to create problems in communication.

Interrole Conflict

A person is likely to experience **interrole conflict** when *occupying two (or more) roles that entail contradictory expectations about a given behavior.* Suppose that while you are proctoring an exam, you see a friend cheating during the test. As a proctor, you are obliged to report the cheating. As a friend, you feel that loyalty demands overlooking what you've just seen. The options in this case seem clear. The demands of each role are known. They conflict, and one must be chosen over the other.

ISSUES IN COMMUNICATION

Our Expectations in Close Relationships

Stephanie Coontz, author of *Marriage, a History* (2006a), has written incisively about the connection between marriage and closeness in other relationships, with people increasingly depending on a spouse and lessening their ties to close relationships with others including family, friends, and co-workers:

> *As Americans lose the wider face-to-face ties that build social trust, they become more dependent on romantic relationships for intimacy and deep communication, and more vulnerable to isolation if a relationship breaks down. In some cases we even cause the breakdown by loading the relationship with too many expectations. Marriage is generally based on more equality and deeper friendship than in the past, but even so, it is hard for it to compensate for the way that work has devoured time once spent cultivating friendships. (Coontz, 2006b)*

Coontz argues that we can make our marriages stronger in an unusual way:

> *. . . we should raise our expectations for, and commitment to, other relationships, especially since so many people now live so much of their lives outside marriage. Paradoxically, we can strengthen our marriages the most by not expecting them to be our sole refuge from the pressures of the modern work force. Instead we need to restructure both work and social life so we can reach out and build ties with others, including people who are single or divorced. (Coontz, 2006b)*

What are your own expectations of close relationships? Do you think that maintaining other close relationships strengthens or undermines a marriage?

Sometimes interrole conflicts occur on an ongoing basis and are very difficult to resolve. For example, Sam and Maggie have been married for six years and have two children. Both spouses are ambitious and have demanding jobs: Sam is an engineer and Maggie is a lawyer. Early on they agreed to share domestic responsibilities, but when Maggie was offered another job that required some traveling, she was torn. She would be spending even more time away from home. She knew that change would advance her career and that her salary would be considerably higher than her husband's—and they could certainly use the money. But she also knew it would take time away from being with him and the children. And she worried about how he'd feel if she were earning a much higher salary. What's interesting here is that we know from the literature on dual-career couples that Sam would be less likely to hesitate about the new job. In various forms, dual-career couples experience such conflicts over responsibilities to home and job quite often.

Intrarole Conflict

An **intrarole conflict** presents a different set of problems; it involves *contradictory expectations concerning a single role*. For example, Iyesha and Marie, two friends who are close and very supportive of each other, often discuss personal problems. Iyesha believes that Marie is making a big mistake by dropping out of school and moving in with an old boyfriend, that Marie is just compounding her problem and that she very much needs counseling. As a friend, Iyesha sees herself primarily as a listener, someone who does not interfere but allows the other person to clarify her feelings. She also thinks that friends should be truthful, but she is afraid of being intrusive or meddling. She is not at all certain how she should respond. Questions such as these about appropriate behaviors and boundaries in given roles have to do with intrarole conflict.

THE DIALECTICS OF RELATIONSHIPS

One approach to interpersonal relationships of great current interest among communication scholars is relational **dialectics**. A dialectical approach *views relationships in terms of sets of contradictory or opposing impulses that create tension between two people*—for example, the pull between the need to feel separate from the other person and the need to feel connected. But such tensions do not have negative connotations.

The dialectical approach makes several assumptions:

- "Contradictions are inherent in social life and are the basic 'drivers' of change and vitality in any social system."
- There is a dynamic tension between stability and change in all social systems.
- We are at once both actors and objects of our own actions. We make communication choices, but at the same time we are reactive.
- We can understand phenomena "only in relation to other phenomena." (Baxter and Montgomery, 2000; 1996b, pp. 326–329)

In this view, such conflicts occur in all aspects of our lives. For example, in a recent study of stepfamilies, Braithwaite and Baxter (2006) looked at the dialectic conflicts of college-age stepchildren concerning their nonresidential parents and found that the children had two contradictory perceptions about communication and were extremely ambivalent. Although they wanted more involvement and parenting by the nonresidential parent, they resisted it. And while students also wanted more openness in communicating and intimacy from the nonresidential parent, they found communication to be awkward and difficult at times.

Here we look briefly at three of the primary dialectics that create ongoing tensions between people: autonomy/connection; certainty/uncertainty; openness/closedness.

Autonomy/Connection

We want to be connected with others—to have an emotional bond with them—and yet often we want to be separate from them, autonomous. In both our marital and other personal relationships, these needs to be independent and dependent are dynamic, frequently shifting. We value them both and they are also of different intensity for different people. Rawlins, who studied friends of many ages (1992, 1994), finds that this dynamic interplay between connection and autonomy continues throughout the duration of a friendship.

In some of her research on romantic relationships, Baxter (Baxter and Montgomery, 1996a) examined what she termed the "me-we pull." She had over a hundred people who were in romantic relationships discuss the tension between their desire to be with the romantic partner and their need for a sense of separation or independence, the freedom to "do their own thing." She found that the most powerful dialectic in her study was this pull between connection and autonomy (p. 93).

Are there relationship styles we consistently use across different kinds of relationships or does a person's style change from one kind of relationship to another? Neff and Harter (2003) studied the relationship styles of autonomy, connectedness, and mutuality with romantic partners, best friends, and parents. Most people used different styles in different contexts, and a major factor in the style they used was how they perceived the power within the relationship:

> Autonomy was linked to the worst psychological outcomes with parents (in terms of relationship satisfaction, self-worth, and depression) and mutuality was linked to the best outcomes with romantic partners and best friends. (p. 8)

This study also found an association between autonomy and dominance.

Certainty/Uncertainty

One study (Rawlins, 1994) found that for lifelong friends one meaning of "certainty" was trust that, if needed, they would "be there" for one another. Most theory and research on interpersonal relationships place high value on certainty and closure, while looking upon uncertainty or unpredictability as "barriers to closeness" (Baxter and Montgomery, 1996a, p. 106). Yet in close relationships it's not always order and predictability that we seek; we look also for excitement, spontaneity—at times we want the other person to respond in a new way, to be unpredictable. For example, the prediction of the other person's behaviors, attitudes, beliefs, and personality traits is often considered desirable, as is a certain predictability about planning times for meeting, yet when a relationship becomes too predictable, people express desires for change, improvisation:

> On the one hand, I wanted there to be a set routine—you know, stuff I could count on and look forward to. At the same time, it would have been really great if once in a while we just took off and did something really wacko, for the fun of it, "Hey, let's take off and drive all night to the beach!" Just something different. But don't get me wrong—I loved the stuff we did do and enjoyed our time together. And going to the beach would be really stupid in some ways, like missing classes and work and things. But I kind of missed that spontaneous craziness kind of thing. (p. 123)

Another tension expressed in terms of certainty and uncertainty is about romantic excitement:

> I want some newness, to rekindle some romance, I guess you'd say. What I don't desire is the uncertainty that you feel at the beginning of a relationship. I don't want the same schedule every day, but I don't want to give up the security of the relationship of knowing that you're there for the other. (p. 126)

Over the course of a relationship, the interplay between certainty and uncertainty, predictability and newness, will take many forms. The constant pull between these two needs, write Baxter and Montgomery, "is a jazz ensemble that consists of many voices joined in the simultaneous play of 'the already existing' with the 'new and unrepeatable'" (p. 131).

Openness/Closedness

As we've seen in Chapter 8, theories about developing and maintaining relationships emphasize how important openness and self-disclosure are. For many communication scholars, being open, responsive, and willing to disclose information about oneself is perhaps the most highly valued aspect of interpersonal relationships. But we don't always feel like talking about our innermost feelings or problems, and perhaps we don't always feel like listening to others do it. Looked at from a dialectical point of view, self-disclosure is "relatively infrequent"; and our phatic communication or small talk—"talk for talk's sake"—is also socially significant. For it is through small talk that we signal to one another that we value our relationship just for its own sake (Baxter and Montgomery, 1996a, p. 136).

Unlike those who argue for increasingly higher levels of self-disclosure, relational dialectics theorists believe that the goal of full disclosure is unrealistic—even impossible—and that the process of self-disclosure is not linear; it does not always move to ever-higher levels of openness: rather, we keeping moving between the need to reveal and the need to conceal (Dindia, 2000, p. 161). In the following pages we will discuss this issue in greater detail.

As you read on, remember that dialectics emphasizes the dynamic and improvisational nature of communication. In this view, no relationship is completely stable. Each person is shifting, changing in response to his or her needs and the responses to those needs. Here the jazz metaphor holds up well:

> Instead of envisioning relationship development as a linear musical scale that progresses from lower to higher notes of intimacy, relationship change is more like a jazz improvisation of competing, yet coordinated musical sounds. (Baxter and Montgomery, 1996a, p. 343)

We will take a further look at the dialectics of relationships in the context of our next section.

ASSESSING THE QUALITY OF AN INTERPERSONAL RELATIONSHIP

Suppose you were to keep a journal for a week and record all your interactions with a romantic partner or same-sex friend. A recent study of close relationships (Emmers-Sommer, 2004) asked people to do just that. The researcher was interested in communication quality and quantity and how they were related to intimacy and satisfaction. She found that communication quality rather than quantity was more important for both satisfaction and intimacy in a relationship, though the number of exchanges between two people—their total time face-to-face—was also important for satisfaction. Although, as found in earlier research, the actual amount of time that two people spend together can be related to their satisfaction, intimacy in long-distance relationships does not seem to suffer as a result of less frequent contact.

Most, if not all, of our qualitatively high relationships involve only two people. In distinguishing interpersonal—that is, high-quality—from noninterpersonal—that is, low-quality—relationships, Miller and Steinberg (1975) were the first to introduce four important concepts:

In qualitatively high relationships, information about the other person is primarily psychological rather than cultural and sociological. Most cultural and sociological information is easy to come by. It includes the other person's sex, age, occupation, group memberships—in other words, information accessible to most people, even without knowing the other. But for me to have psychological information about you—to know what your likes and dislikes are, or your goals or perhaps your fears—the two of us must engage in a relationship.

Rules for that relationship are developed by the two people involved rather than being rules set by tradition. For example, our relationship may be such that although it's usually expected that a visitor calls before coming to someone's apartment, you may come to mine whenever you like—and without calling. You may open the refrigerator and help yourself. You may phone me even in the middle of the night. And you may always use my car. Remember, each interpersonal relationship establishes different rules, but they are individual rather than traditional rules.

The roles in a high-quality relationship are defined primarily by personal characteristics rather than by situation. For example, Ellen may always take care of bills, correspondence, and arranging for house repairs because Cliff, her husband, hates doing these things. In turn, he may do the weekly shopping and all the vacuuming because they agree that he is more efficient at both.

Emphasis in a qualitatively high relationship is on individual choices rather than on group choices. We shall see the importance of individual choices and psychological information—that is, knowledge of personal attitudes and beliefs, highly individualized behavior, and so on—as we discuss self-disclosure, one of several variables affecting relationship quality.

Remember that the concept of quality applies to all two-person relationships, not just intimate ones. Thus many of the variables to be examined here also have an impact on more casual relationships (power, for example, can be as much a factor in your work relationships as it is in your marriage). The first variable we shall consider is self-disclosure.

Self-Disclosure

We disclose a great deal about ourselves through our facial expression, posture, clothing, tone of voice, and countless other nonverbal cues, though much of that behavior is unintentional. But **self-disclosure** as we use the term here is *intentionally making known information about oneself*. Not only is it an integral part of two-person communication, it occurs more often in this context than in any other kind of communication.

In one study that paired young men and women who were meeting for the first time (Clark et al., 2004) the more a person disclosed in the conversation, the more favorably he or she was rated in social attractiveness and positive qualities. What's especially interesting is that this was true for both men and women—and both men and women *thought* that they would be liked more if they disclosed more.

Self-disclosure is an attempt to let authenticity enter our social relationships, and it is often linked with both mental health and self-concept development:

> Self-disclosure, depending on reactions of relationship partners, . . . plays an important role in validating self-worth and personal identity. (Greene et al., 2006, p. 409)

"I have known people," writes Jourard (1964), one of the foremost early researchers on self-disclosure, "who would rather die than become known . . . When I say that self-disclosure is a symptom of personality health, what I mean really is that a person who displays many of the other characteristics that betoken healthy personality . . . will also display the ability to make himself fully known to at least one other significant human being" (p. 24).

A variety of studies link self-disclosure with intimacy and marital satisfaction (Chelune et al., 1984). In fact, one analysis of disclosure studies (Dindia, 2002) confirms that self-disclosure causes liking, liking causes self-disclosure, and that self-disclosure is reciprocal.

The Johari Window

One of the most innovative models for conceptualizing levels of awareness and self-disclosure in human communication is the **Johari window** (Luft, 1969). ("Johari" derives from the first names of the two psychologists who developed it, Joseph Luft and Harry Ingram.) Essentially, the model offers a way of looking at the interdependence of intrapersonal and interpersonal affairs. The illustration in Figure 9.1 represents you as you relate to other human beings by four quadrants—in effect, four panes of a single window. The size of each quadrant or pane is determined by awareness, by yourself and by others, of your behavior, feelings, and motivations—and the degree to which this information is shared. Unlike most windowpanes, those of the Johari window sometimes change in size.

Each of you may be described by a Johari window. Quadrant 1, the *open quadrant,* will reflect your general openness to the world, your willingness to be known. It comprises *all aspects of yourself known to you and to others.* This quadrant is the basis for most two-person communication.

By contrast, quadrant 2, the *blind quadrant,* consists of *all the things about yourself that other people perceive but that are not accessible to you.* Perhaps you tend to monopolize conversation unwittingly, or you think of yourself as quite a wit but your friends find your humor heavy-handed. Then again you might feel quite confident and yet have several nervous mannerisms that others are aware of but you are not. The blind quadrant could contain any of the unintentional communicative stimuli mentioned in Chapter 1.

In quadrant 3, the *hidden quadrant,* you are the one who exercises discretion. This quadrant is made up of *all the things you prefer not to disclose to someone else,* whether they concern yourself or other people: your salary, your parents' divorce, your feelings about your roommate's closest friends, your overdue bills, and so on. In short, this quadrant represents your attempts to limit input or information about yourself.

The last pane, quadrant 4, is the *unknown quadrant.* The blind quadrant, quadrant 2, is unknown to you though known to others. The hidden quadrant is unknown to others but known to you. Quadrant 4 is *completely unknown. It represents everything about yourself that has never been explored, either by you or by other people*—all your untapped resources, all your potential for personal growth. You can only infer that it exists or confirm its existence in retrospect.

Configurations of the Johari window depend upon one's interaction style. Thus Dan, who is unwilling to let business colleagues or even friends learn much about him, will have a very small open area (quadrant 1) and therefore a large hidden area (quadrant 3). His brother Kirk, who is very willing to disclose information but cannot receive feedback, will have a large open area (quadrant 1) and a large blind area (quadrant 2). Numerous configurations are possible.

The four quadrants of the Johari window are interdependent: a change in one quadrant will affect others. As you disclose something from the hidden quadrant, for example, you make it part of the open quadrant; you enlarge it and reduce the size of the hidden quadrant. Should friends tell you about your nervous mannerisms, this information becomes part of the open quadrant, with a corresponding shrinkage of the blind quadrant. Such change is not always desirable. Sometimes, for example, telling a person that he or she seems nervous only makes him or her more ill at ease. Because inappropriate disclosure of a feeling or perception about another can be damaging, your friends will need to use some discretion in the feedback they give you about quadrant 2.

Basically, however, Luft proposes that it is rewarding and satisfying to enlarge the open quadrant—that is, not only to learn more about yourself and thus gain insight but to reveal information about yourself so that others will know you better too. He also believes that greater knowledge of self in relation to others will result in greater self-esteem and self-acceptance. If you can learn more about yourself and others, you can change the shape of your own Johari window. An improved window might look something like the one in Figure 9.2.

Figure 9.1   The Johari Window

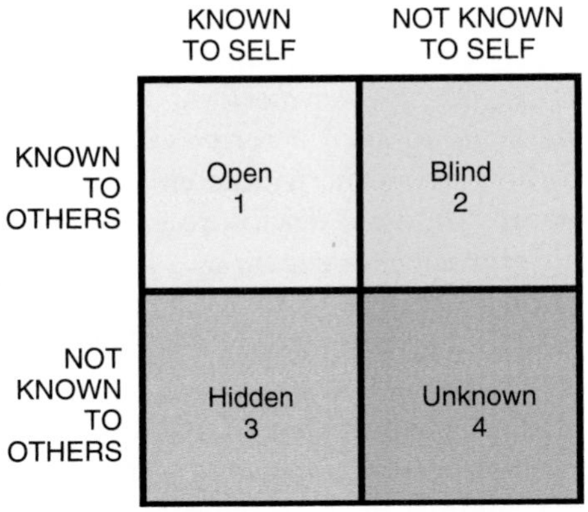

Figure 9.2   An Improved Johari Window

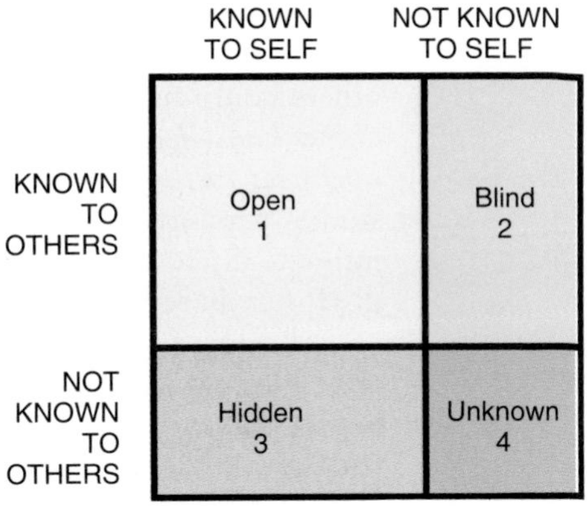

Source: From *Group Processes: An Introduction to Group Dynamics,* 3rd ed., by Joseph Luft, 1984. Reproduced with permission of The McGraw-Hill Companies.

Trust and Reciprocity

In Jhumpa Lahiri's short story "Interpreter of Maladies"(1999), Mina and Raj Das, a young couple from the United States, and their three children are touring and visiting family in India. Mrs. Das takes an interest in Mr. Kapasi, their driver and tour guide for the day, and so she learns that his other job is interpreting for the patients of a local doctor so that the doctor will understand what their ailments are. Flattered by her attention, Mr. Kapasi begins to fantasize about writing to her when she returns to the States. Later in the day Mrs. Das stays behind in the car while her husband goes on with the children to do more sightseeing. Watching as Bobby, the younger son, passes a stick back and forth to a monkey, Mr. Kapasi comments on what a brave little boy he is: Mrs. Das tells him it's not surprising because he's not her husband's son, that he's the child of one of her husband's colleagues, with whom she had a brief affair. "No one knows, of course," she tells an astonished Mr. Kapasi. "No one at all. I've kept the secret for eight whole years" (p. 62). Further disclosures about her feelings follow, but we know that Mina Das and Mr. Kapasi will never meet again.

Although at times strangers make startling self-disclosures in face-to-face encounters, these usually have few consequences. Suppose a woman sitting next to you on a transatlantic flight tells you about her concern for her teenage daughter who is living with a man twice her age. In a sense, that's an easier thing for her to tell to you, a total stranger, than to her next-door neighbors. Often when we make our supposed disclosures to strangers, we have very little to lose. And many of these so-called disclosures have to do with past events ("I was adopted," "I was in therapy for five years," and so on), rather than with present events and feelings about those events.

Authentic self-disclosure—whether between acquaintances, co-workers, friends, or lovers—is not one-sided: It tends to be reciprocal. It is an exchange process that can and often does prompt greater disclosure from the other person and often results in more positive feelings between the two. The work of Jourard (1979) and others confirms this sequence of behavior: *When one person discloses something about himself or herself to another, he or she tends to elicit a reciprocal level of openness in the second person.* Jourard calls the pattern the **dyadic effect.** Many studies support Jourard's principle: "One person's intimate disclosure encourages intimate disclosure by the listener, and superficial disclosure encourages superficial disclosure in return" (Derlega et al., 1987, p. 174).

Reciprocal self-disclosure tends to be gradual. And it seems to take place only after the two people have reached a basic level of trust (Dindia, 1996). Thus, we expect that early in a relationship disclosures will be less intimate and that as mutual trust is established, they will become more revealing. In the intensifying stage of a relationship, for example, there are often a great number of self-disclosures.

When relationships are going well, people continually match their cycles of openness. This evidence of a periodic ebb and flow "between openness and closedness, revelation and restraint" is true both for new acquaintanceships and for intact friendships and romantic relationships. VanLear's (1991) studies show that acquaintances "match the amplitude of their cycles to fit those of their partners," synchronizing the timing of cycles. In friendships and romantic relationships, partners actually perceive their own cycles of openness and those of the other person as being timed. This mutuality seems to be linked with satisfaction. If a relationship begins to deteriorate and satisfaction decreases, these cycles show increasing fluctuations.

In long-term relationships the content of disclosures tends to stabilize. For example, several studies of marital satisfaction show an interesting pattern of high self-disclosure among happily married couples—but only of positive information. In a recent novel about a couple getting a divorce, the wife's many negative comments about her present feelings toward her husband prompt him to ask that she stop telling him how she feels. "If I knew any more," he tells her, "I'd be paralyzed."

From a dialectical perspective, self-disclosure is not a single event; "it is a dynamic, continuous, and circular process." And you can never fully reveal yourself. Self-disclosure is "a life-long/relationship-long process . . . [one] that changes as individuals and relationships change" (Dindia, 2000, pp. 147, 150).

To Reveal or Conceal

You choose to be open with another person for many different reasons. It may be because something very good has happened to you (a new job) or is troubling you (a financial problem or an imminent divorce). You may wish to clarify experiences for yourself (discussing a recent family argument might be almost therapeutic), or you may be trying to get the other person to reciprocate by also talking. At times, you use selective self-disclosure to create an impression of yourself that you would like the other person to have—for example, at a party Jake may let Nicole know that he's unhappily married because he finds himself attracted to her.

A person often uses self-disclosure to maintain or develop a relationship—to keep the other person up to date on his or her life, to control and manipulate the other person, or to enhance the relationship by letting the other person know something that will increase the intimacy, depth, and breadth of their relationship (Rosenfeld and Kendrick, 1984). So we have some mixed motives for disclosure, and on occasion disclosing can be manipulative.

Indeed, self-disclosure can have many risks, and when we avoid disclosing, one of the primary reasons may be that we fear that information may be used against us. Some recent research on relationship dialectics (Dindia, 2000) has focused on the disclosure of information that is intimate, private, or risky—such as information about AIDS, sexual abuse, and homosexuality. For example, someone who is gay might reveal, then conceal, then reveal his homosexuality to others. Consider this comment:

> Coming out for me has basically moved from wanting to tell everybody, to not wanting to tell anybody, to kind of going in between those two.

Another participant said:

> I know that I've had to find a sense of equilibrium. I don't feel comfortable wearing a sign that says "I'm gay" . . . But I am becoming less tolerant as time goes on, with the "game playing" that I did in my head for a lot of years. (Dindia, 2000, p. 158)

Other reasons for not disclosing information include fear of projecting a negative image, losing control over the other person or the situation, not wanting to seem like an exhibitionist, and not wanting to commit oneself. Sometimes fear of rejection keeps us from disclosing essential aspects of ourselves, but this very withholding makes it impossible to be known.

Self-Disclosure and Self-Presentation in Internet Dating

Given that self-disclosure is an important determinant of how people develop their relationships, how does it figure in online dating? While some theorists maintain that the more limited cues and information disclosed online tend to limit sharing and intimacy, other communication scholars believe that the Internet's anonymity actually intensifies the developing intimacy between people.

How would you respond to the following statements about Internet dating?

I am always honest in my self-disclosures to those I meet online.

The things I reveal about myself to those I meet online are always accurate reflections of who I really am.

I often disclose negative things about myself to those I meet online.

On the whole, my disclosures about myself to those I meet online are more positive than negative.

When I reveal my feelings about myself to those I meet online, I consciously intend to do so. (selected from Gibbs et al., 2006, p. 173; italics in original)

A recent study of self-disclosure and Internet dating using these and other test questions finds that when people who go online are interested in having a long-term relationship that they expect will become face-to-face, they disclose more and are more honest. Their disclosures tend to be intentional, offered consciously because it's anticipated that as the relationship develops it is better to be more candid. Interestingly, such disclosures aren't always more positive—and the effect of greater honesty is not always positive either (Gibbs et al., 2006, p. 169). In this study it was experience in dating online that turned out to be the most important predictor of how successful people thought themselves to be.

"What Makes You Click?" (Hitsch, Hortacsu, and Ariely, 2005), another analysis of online dating, tracked the records of 23,000 users of an online dating service on which people posted their profiles. The authors of *Freakonomics* discuss some revealing aspects of this study—how people tend to present themselves online:

> More than 4 percent of the online daters claimed to earn more than $200,000 a year, whereas fewer than 1 percent of typical Internet users actually earn that much, suggesting that three of the four big earners were exaggerating. Male and female users typically reported that they are an inch taller than the national average. As for weight, the men were in line with the national average, but the women typically said they weighed about twenty pounds less than the national average.
>
> Most impressively, fully 72 percent of the women claimed "above average" looks, including 24 percent claiming "very good looks." The online men too were gorgeous: 68 percent called themselves "above average," including 19 percent with "very good looks." This leaves only about 30 percent of the users with "average" looks, including a paltry 1 percent with "less than average" looks— which suggests the typical online dater is either a fabulist, narcissist, or simply resistant to the meaning of "average." (Levitt and Dubner, 2006, pp. 75–76).

When Is Self-Disclosure Appropriate?

Self-disclosure is often an attempt to let authenticity enter our social relationships. At times it is an attempt to emphasize how we enact our roles rather than how others expect us to enact them. It may even be an attempt to step out of a role entirely. When does it work? When does it improve human relationships?

Luft (1969) describes five of the most important characteristics of appropriate self-disclosure:

1. It is a function of the ongoing relationship.
2. It occurs reciprocally.
3. It is timed to fit what is happening.
4. It concerns what is going on within and between persons present.
5. It moves by small increments. (1969, pp. 132–133)

By applying these standards to any of your attempts at self-disclosure that didn't come off, you may be able to determine what went wrong.

Intimacy

The quality of a two-person relationship is also measured by the degree of intimacy involved (McAdams, 1989). Intimacy has been called "the distinguishing mark of a person's most important and valued relationships," fostering both well-being and relationship satisfaction (Prager, 2000, p. 229). Many definitions of intimacy have been proposed. In his theory of love, Sternberg defines **intimacy** as *"feelings that promote closeness, bondedness, and connectedness"* (1998, p. 6). Such feelings are also present in other relationships such as those with friends and family members. It's not only what we communicate verbally. Eye contact, gestures of support, and other forms of nonverbal communication also develop and convey intimacy.

And it is not only our behaviors but our *expectations* about intimacy in a given relationship that seem to be very important. For example, a study of married couples suggests that agreement on what each spouse expects in the relationship is crucial to satisfaction and, further, that agreement about the wife's behavior is a major issue.

> It appears critical to both men and women that they agree on what level of intimacy the wife is to express in the relationship. It is possible that the wife is the relational barometer in the marriage. (Kelley and Burgoon, 1991, p. 64)

But what does "intimacy" mean to you? In a fascinating field study on the subject, Waring and his associates (1980) posed this question in interviews and found six categories of response: people associated intimacy with sharing thoughts, beliefs, fantasies, interests, goals, and backgrounds. Sexuality was not given as part of the general definition of intimacy. Intimate relationships are not necessarily sexual. Intimacy and sexuality are distinct, though in some relationships they are linked. Sexuality, as we use the term here, involves physical arousal or passion.

Of the other attempts to study and define intimacy, one of the most promising views intimacy as a relational process "in which we come to know the innermost, subjective aspects of another, and are known in a like manner" (Chelune et al., in Derlega, 1984). Beyond this, the authors argue that an intimate relationship is characterized by mutuality, interdependence, trust, commitment, and caring.

Mutuality, where partners engage "in a joint venture," must be present in any intimate relationship. Remember, the emphasis is on relationship:

> Intimate relationships have at their center a mutual process like finely choreographed dancers in which a balance of movement, of sharing, occurs. (Derlega, 1984, p. 29)

Through interdependence "partners learn in what ways they can depend upon one another for support, resources, understanding, and action, and they agree upon future dependence" (p. 31). Closely related to trust is commitment, the extent to which the two people see their relationship as continuing indefinitely and make efforts to ensure that it will continue. And caring, of course, is concern for the other's well-being and demonstrated affection for the other.

Measured by these criteria, intimacy is not characteristic of all marriages, and many intimate relationships exist that are not marriages. Intimate relationships can involve same-sex or opposite-sex partners, and there is intimacy between friends and, of course, family. As for stereotypes about same-sex couples, therapists have found that the relationships of both gay and lesbian couples are more intimate and cohesive than those of opposite-sex couples (McGoldrick, 1999, p. 235). People sometimes confuse intimacy with fusion: instead of developing an intimate relationship you try using your relationship as part of a couple to complete your self (p. 248). In addition to closeness and caregiving and the open communication, McGoldrick stresses the importance of a lack of intrusiveness:

- Respecting the need for privacy and time spent alone
- Trying not to be possessive or jealous
- Not overreacting emotionally to the other's life problems
- Not assuming you know the other person's wishes better than he or she does
- In disagreements trying not to dominate the other person or give aggressive criticism. (Adapted from 1999, p. 235)

To Be Connected or Independent

As we've seen, a dialectic approach emphasizes the tension between our need to be in-dependent (autonomous) and connected; to be on your own, deciding what you want to do and when you want to do it, and to be connected with someone close to you, sharing experience. Intimacy cannot be forced. Sometimes even talking about what's wrong only makes the other person withdraw further. In Junot Diaz's short story "The Sun, the Moon, the Stars," the narrator has taken his girlfriend Magda to the Domini-can Republic; things have not been going right between them and when he wants to talk about the day before, she puts down her pen and puts on her sunglasses, saying:

"I feel like you're pressuring me."
"How am I pressuring you?" I ask.
We get into one of those no-fun twenty-minute arguments, which the waiters keep interrupting by bringing over more orange juice and *cafe,* the two things this island has plenty of.
"I just want some space to myself every now and then. Every time I'm with you I have the sense that you want something from me."
"Time to yourself," I say. "What does that mean?"
"Like maybe once a day, you do one thing, I do another."
"Like when? Now?"
"It doesn't have to be now." She looks exasperated. "Why don't we just go down to the beach?" (Diaz, 1999, p. 22)

According to James Honeycutt and other communication scholars, we have prototypes for different kinds of relationships. A **prototype** is your "mental image of any subject that exists as [your] own personal definition of a quintessential person, place, or concept, such as a best friend, vacation spot, or marriage relationship" (Honeycutt and Cantrill, 2001, p. 39). A prototype, he explains, is "the best example illustrating a category" (p. 38).

What about your concept of love? What comes to mind? Fehr (2000) studied prototypes of love and found that people distinguish between *companionate love*, often associated with aspects of friendship, and *passionate love*. Companionate love was perceived as more central or prototypical, and people identified its essential features as trust, caring, respect, honesty, and friendship. Although passionate, romantic features were viewed as part of the concept, they were seen as peripheral rather than essential (pp. 93–94).

According to another study (Regan et al., 1998), when subjects were asked about their prototypes of romantic love, the most common characteristics mentioned were "trust, sexual attraction/desire, and acceptance/tolerance" (p. 411). Three "latent dimensions" of romantic love were also found in this study: passion, intimacy, and commitment (p. 413).

We do not all share the same prototypes, but according to this view they do guide our actions. Fehr and many other communication scholars maintain that we follow "scripts" relating to our ideal or prototypical concepts such as love:

> [T]o know the meaning of a single word such as love is to know a script, complete with antecedents, behavioral responses, beliefs, physiological reactions, and so on. We can refer to this script when deciding whether we love someone (and vice versa) or how to express our love once we have made that decision. (Fehr, 2000, p. 100)

Does the concept of a "script" seem cynical to you or is it useful in thinking about your own experience?

Magda breaks off the conversation but her half-hearted suggestion that they go for a walk on the beach does nothing to bring the two closer together.

Attachment Styles

Although a person's need for intimacy fluctuates in any close relationship, there are people who consistently fear it. Some researchers believe that our patterns and capacities for forming and maintaining intimate relationships are to some degree shaped by the quality of our first emotional bond (Feeney et al., 2000). Classic theory by John Bowlby (1973) focused on the early attachment bond between an infant and its mother or primary caretaker. Bowlby suggested that an infant learns to feel safe and secure enough to explore its environment when it makes a successful attachment to its mother. Thus, when the mother is nurturant, warm, and responsive, the infant learns to feel comfortable counting on other people, secure in the knowledge that its needs will be met. When the mother is cold, rejecting, or inconsistent, the infant learns not to rely on others for its support or comfort; instead, it tends to withdraw or to become exceptionally demanding. Studies of how an infant reacts when being separated from and then reunited with its mother (as opposed to a stranger) identified three different **attachment styles:** secure, avoidant, and anxious-ambivalent.

Studies of adults by Hazan and Shaver (1987, 1994) suggested that in later life attachment style also affects our romantic relationships. Some of their data was based on how subjects described themselves. Each of the three major attachment styles reflects our beliefs and expectancies about close relationships:

> *Secure:* Secure people are comfortable with intimacy and dependence. They describe their close relationships as characterized by love, trust, and happiness. Secure people are easy to know and have few self-doubts. They describe their relationships with their parents as warm.
>
> *Avoidant:* Closeness makes avoidant people uncomfortable. They fear the intimacy of close relationships and find it difficult to depend on others. They are not very accepting of romantic partners and don't view most of their love relationships as long-lasting, and the relationships they enter tend to decline in intensity. Avoidant people describe their mothers as cold and rejecting. Some researchers (Bartholomew, 1990) distinguish between fearful avoidance, trying to protect oneself from hurt or rejection, and dismissive avoidance, acting defensively by denying one's need for close relationships.
>
> *Anxious-Ambivalent:* Although they yearn for extremely close relationships, anxious-ambivalent people have many fears about being abandoned and unloved. They are troubled by self-doubt and may feel misunderstood. Their great need for intimacy often drives others away. Preoccupied with their love relationships, they tend to be emotionally volatile. (Feeney et al., 2000, p. 185)

In one study of marital quality among newly married couples, similarity in attachment characteristics was most accurate in predicting marital satisfaction—stronger than a couple's similarity in personality or in attitude (Luo and Klohnen, 2005).

Attachment style also plays a significant role in nonverbal communication. For example, a person who has an anxious attachment style tends to have less fluent conversation and less composure when he or she is with a romantic partner (Guerrero and Floyd, 2006, p. 153). One communication scholar explains:

> Overall, attachment security seems to act as a filter and affect both the encoding and the decoding of nonverbal behavior in close relationships. Highly anxious individuals, especially males, seem to have a general decoding deficit, to be less nonverbally expressive than other partners, and to engage in more avoidance. Thus, highly anxious individuals are likely to have difficulty in maintaining close relationships. (Noller, 2006, p. 414)

What of sexual passion and attachment style? Through an Internet survey of almost 2,000 people, researchers found that an avoidant attachment style is linked to "less overall passion and greater loss of passion over time," while sexual passion was greatest over time in those who had an anxiety-linked attachment style (Davis et al., 2004, p. 1088). Sexual passion here does not necessarily mean that the relationship was functional.

What makes for love that is not reciprocated? We all know people who tend to fall in love with people who do not feel the same way about them. You might have a friend to whom this happens over and over. One recent study identified three variables that seem to predict how intense unrequited love will be. First, and most significant, is the "perceived desirability of the partner and the relationship." The second is especially interesting: how desirable does the person perceive "the state of being in love [to be], whether reciprocated or not." There are people who feel that being in love is all that matters, that if they are not in love they are not fully alive. Third in importance is "mistakenly believing at the outset that the other [person] would reciprocate the love" (Aron et al., 2006, p. 605). This happens least to people with a secure attachment style and most often to people with an anxious-ambivalent style.

For some people the need for intimacy is never satisfied. Consider Laura, an attractive teacher in her early thirties, who has been obsessed with finding "the right one" and getting married. She has dated one man after another, often complaining to friends that it never seems to work out. When Brad, a young lawyer, came along, she expected him to spend all his free time with her. When he wanted to go to a baseball game with a friend, she became annoyed. If the two weren't together all weekend, she worried about whether he was seeing someone else. After three months, Brad broke off the relationship because, as he told his brother, Laura was "just too clingy—I feel smothered." He felt boxed in and exhausted by all the reassurance she needed. Greater awareness of your own expectations and ways of forming attachments may help you to understand and improve your own intimate relationships.

Intimacy between Siblings

As most of us know, relationships with siblings are not all roses. Think of the relationship of Catherine and Claire in *Proof*. Siblings can be intimate friends, and they can also be ardent rivals. Over the lifespan they can often be described as both. Studies of intimacy between older siblings show that relationships between siblings are unique in many ways (McGoldrick et al., 2005; Klagsbrun, 1992; Gold, 1989b, 1987). Older siblings share a history of lifetime experiences; they are usually peers and can satisfy many of the needs and desires satisfied by friends. Siblings can also offer exceptional loyalty (1989b).

Remember that each pair of siblings has a different relationship. In a family of three children, for example, the oldest and middle child may be very close, while the youngest may be more isolated—from one or both of the others. Parents often have idealized expectations that all their children will have inherently similar—and of course positive—relationships. This hoped for democracy of feeling sometimes leads to disappointment on all sides.

On the basis of her research, Gold (1989a) described five types of sibling relationships: intimate, congenial, loyal, apathetic, and hostile. In intimate relationships there is strong emotional interdependence between siblings expressed through mutual love, protection, concern, understanding, empathy, and durability (p. 42). Interestingly enough, siblings who are hostile are not indifferent. Research on how pairs of siblings interact in later life finds that in general they show greater closeness or intimacy, that this becomes an important source of satisfaction—even if the two live far apart—and that it contributes to emotional well-being. Even siblings who were not close as children frequently become closer in old age, and age differences that once seemed immense become unimportant.

One common finding in all sibling research is that the closest, most intimate relationships are between pairs of sisters. Next come brother-sister pairs:

> It is not the sister-sister combination per se that affects the quality of the interactions but rather the presence of a female as one of the dyad members. (Gold, 1987, p. 207)

Relationships between pairs of brothers are far less likely to be intimate, though the lack of intimacy is often regretted. In one study only 15 percent of brother pairs were noted as intimate, with the remaining 85 percent being rated as either hostile or apathetic. Differences in how boys and girls are socialized would seem to account for these data.

These studies offer further evidence that the need for intimacy in interpersonal relationships persists throughout our lives. Hatfield (1984) believes that each of us can develop intimacy skills. She recommends that people be encouraged "to accept themselves as they are," "to recognize their intimates for what they are," and "to also express themselves" (pp. 216, 217). Intimacy skills can also be developed by learning to deal with the responses of others—that is, learning not to apologize for your feelings or clam up and withdraw when the other person reacts negatively to what you say. Emphasis on intimacy as a process allows us to see that intimacy can be worked on—it doesn't just happen.

Affiliation and Commitment

Another important variable of relationship quality and a significant predictor of how two people will interact is the strength of their affiliative needs. The *need for affiliation* may be seen as a continuum from highly affiliative to antisocial behavior. The high affiliater, who prefers being with others to being alone, enjoys and seeks out companionship. We describe such a person as friendly, gregarious, and generally sociable. The person who is low in the need for affiliation probably prefers being alone and has much less desire for companionship. Since this behavior is not very reinforcing to other people, the low affiliater is usually described as unfriendly or unsociable.

Most of us place ourselves somewhere between the two extremes on this continuum. Since interpersonal communication is potentially the most intimate, those of us with strong needs for affiliation seem to be the most willing to make the commitment it requires. **Commitment,** as we use the term here, is *the resolve to continue in a relationship indefinitely and to make the efforts necessary to ensure that it will continue.*

You may feel committed to someone and at the same time feel the need to be independent. Or you may express your commitment verbally and yet not act on it (Duck, 1999, p. 44). This pull between commitment and autonomy exists even in very close relationships, where it may not be acknowledged. Think of the last-minute jitters some people get right before their wedding. In the story we looked at, "The Sun, the Moon, the Stars," the narrator's efforts to get Magda to go on vacation by buying her a plane ticket are resisted as "pressure," though she finally consents. She's already angry because last year he was unfaithful to her. Now the more intensely he pursues a commitment from her, the more she moves away. His own commitment has come too late.

Marriage and Cohabitation

For many the absolute commitment to another human being demanded by marriage is frightening or at best constraining. Today half the marriages in this country end in divorce, and it is still young people who are granted over half the divorces. More couples marry later though they have sex earlier; and more than half of all couples live together before they marry. Some men and women have lived with several partners. "Marriage," writes family therapist Monica McGoldrick, "is the only family relationship that we swear is forever and the only one that we swear is exclusive; yet it is the one relationship that is least likely to be exclusive or forever" (1999, p. 231).

In Chapter 2 we noted the connection between optimism and self-fulfilling prophecy. Among romantic partners, those with an optimistic outlook tended to be more satisfied in their romantic relationships. This was the case even during a conflict, with conflict partners feeling that after a week their conflicts were more successfully resolved. In a follow-up a year later the researchers found that the optimism of the male partner was a reliable predictor of the status of the relationship (Srivastava et al., 2006).

Satisfaction with relationships is also affected by self-esteem. One group of researchers recently found that people with low self-esteem, particularly women, "felt more accepted and loved by their partner on days when their professional lives were marked by success" (Murray et al., 2006, p. 866), much less so when they met with failure in their work lives. "In such ways, the successes and failures in low self-esteem people's outside lives may spill into their relationships" (p. 879).

The rapid increase in the number of unmarried couples who are living together has been well documented not only in the United States but in many other countries as well. For many couples, living together is a trial marriage of sorts, a way of getting to know each other well enough to find out whether a marriage would work. According to the 2000 Census, in the United States the number of unmarried couples living together increased tenfold between 1960 and 2000, and it increased by 72 percent from 1990 to 2000.

Yet some research shows a negative relationship between cohabitation and marital stability, with the divorce rate for couples who had lived together before marriage significantly higher than for couples who had not. Apparently this is not always the case. Researchers who compared cohabitation in 16 European countries found that stability varied significantly from one country to another. There was less stability, more risk of divorce only in countries where people who cohabited before marrying were a small minority or a large majority (Liefbroer and Dourleijn, 2006, p. 203).

But a look at the United States is instructive. For example, over a 10-year-period (1990–2000) in New York City, there was a 27 percent increase in the number of unmarried heterosexual couples who lived together. Perhaps because of the ease with which cohabiting couples can leave each other, half of such relationships tend to break up within a period of two years, and within five years only 10 percent of unmarried couples remain together (Fung, 2006, p. 27).

The lingering question is why this should be so, since living together would presumably allow people more information about each other and more time to resolve possible conflicts. Consider the relationship of a young man and woman in their twenties—let's call them Kathy and David—who have been living together for two years. During this time Kathy's job with a hotel chain has become increasingly responsible. Last year she was made director of her division and given a substantial raise. David now feels that he would like to get married, but Kathy insists that she doesn't want to spoil what she has. "David and I appreciate each other, but we don't take each other for granted. I don't feel bound to him. When I have to visit our hotels in Chicago and Los Angeles for a few days, I just take off. I don't feel guilty about leaving Dave alone. If we were married, we wouldn't be free anymore. We'd expect more things from each other." They might. On the other hand, what Kathy doesn't realize is that even by "just living together" the two have created expectations and developed certain ground rules for their behavior.

According to Knapp's theory (see Chapter 8), if a relationship reaches the integrating stage, both people must intensify at least some aspects of their personalities and minimize others. If a relationship goes on to the bonding stage, that commitment is in some sense formalized. In a romantic relationship, the commitment might be the announcement that the couple is dating exclusively, it might be an engagement or a marriage, or it might mean that a couple decide to live together.

There are, of course, people who consistently fear and avoid commitment. One reason may be that previous commitments proved disappointing or constricting. In the television series *Sex and the City*, it was not only the men who feared commitment, it was the women as well. If we think of this tendency in terms of attachment styles (see p. 290), we might describe many as "avoidant." And there are people who have never made a complete commitment to another human being. One psychologist describes the fear of commitment as characterized by "the Dance-Away Lover":

> The Dance-Away's repeated romantic disillusionments are the consequences of his discomfort with the intimacy and commitment love entails. The Dance-Away Lover is preoccupied with the fear of being trapped. He clings to his independence lest, in her eagerness to possess him, someone succeed in sucking him into a web of obligations and responsibilities. (Goldstine et al., 1977, p. 27)

Even after making a partial commitment, he or she will later maneuver to avoid intimacy by becoming unavailable—forgetting appointments, working late, withdrawing emotionally, or even withholding sexually.

Matters of the heart are elusive. Throughout history philosophers, poets, and psychologists have theorized about love—and no doubt will continue to do so in the future. Aron and his colleagues discuss seven different theories of romantic love (2006). Here we look at two current theories about love relationships that take into account intimacy, commitment, and other variables we have been discussing.

A Triangular Theory of Love

Robert Sternberg of Yale University proposes a *triangular theory of love* (1998; 1988). *Love,* he argues, *has three distinct components: intimacy, passion, and commitment.* Intimacy involves closeness, bondedness, and connection while passion is a state of physical and psychological arousal, an intense desire for the other person. Commitment, the third element, involves both the decision to love someone as well as the long-term resolve to maintain the relationship.

In Figure 9.3 you can see how different combinations of elements represent different relationships. For Sternberg, the balanced triangle at the top with three equal sides and angles represents consummate, or complete, love: all three elements—intimacy, passion, commitment—are present in equal measure. The three triangles below are unbalanced—each representing a relationship that emphasizes one component. For example, Sternberg describes commitment alone, without closeness or passion, as empty love; sometimes triangles change, so that empty love might describe the end of a relationship for two people who no longer feel connected or passionate but are staying together out of habit or convenience or a sense of

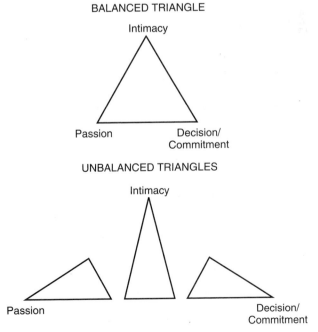

Figure 9.3

Sternberg's Love Triangles: Shape of a Triangle as a Function of Type of Love

Source: From *Cupid's Arrow: The Course of Love through Time* by Dr. Robert J. Sternberg (Cambridge University Press, 1998). Reprinted by permission of the author.

responsibility. Infatuated love involves passion alone: You are totally attracted to someone you've just seen and don't know or someone you know but with whom you have no emotional connection.

Some relationships combine two out of the three components. For example, fatuous or foolish love combines passion and commitment: "It is the kind of love we sometimes associate with Hollywood, or with a whirlwind courtship, in which a couple meet one day, get engaged two weeks later, and marry the next month" (1988, p. 59). Often such relationships don't last very long because genuine intimacy develops over time. Another type of triangle might involve emotional bonding as well as passion, in which the couple can't or are not ready to make a permanent commitment—for example, they may be young and feel that their careers would take them to very different places. Intimacy and commitment are the two components of companionate love. "Essentially," writes Sternberg, it is "a long-term, committed friendship, the kind that frequently occurs in marriages in which physical attraction (a major source of passion) has waned" (p. 21).

In one cross-cultural study that examined romantic relationships in China and the United States (Gao, 2001), the researcher found that although the expression of passion among American couples was significantly higher than among Chinese couples, levels of intimacy and commitment in the two cultures were comparable, suggesting that these are universal dimensions of love relationships.

Love Styles

When you say you love someone, how would you describe your love? Another theory about types of love is seen in the work on *love styles* by Clyde and Susan Hendrick (1986). A questionnaire appears in Table 9.1 (Hendrick et al., 1998). Before you read any further, stop and answer the questions. As you read on, you'll find out how to rate your responses.

This questionnaire—it's actually called the Love Attitudes Scale—is keyed to a set of six love types, or styles, first identified by Lee (1973):

Eros: A passionate love style. This style is marked by intense emotion, a strong erotic component, and a strong commitment to the other person. Initial physical attraction—"love at first sight"—is very common.

Ludus: A game-playing love style. This kind of lover is often manipulative. Justifying deception of one's partner as "playing the field" while having a relationship with someone else are likely to be acceptable behaviors to a ludic lover. It's a type of love that often lacks emotional intensity and commitment.

Storge: A friendship-based love style. It tends to merge love and friendship. Storgic love is down-to-earth, though not passionate. It is committed and tends to be long-lasting.

Pragma: A practical love style. This type of lover makes choices based on rationality and in selecting a partner will focus on matching desired traits.

Table 9.1 Love Attitudes Questionnaire		
At the side of each of the following statements, indicate whether you agree or disagree.	**Agree**	**Disagree**
1. My partner and I have the right physical "chemistry" between us.	___	___
2. I feel that my partner and I were meant for each other.	___	___
3. My partner and I really understand each other.	___	___
4. My partner fits my ideal standards of physical beauty/handsomeness.	___	___
5. I believe that what my partner doesn't know about me won't hurt him/her.	___	___
6. I have sometimes had to keep my partner from finding out about other lovers.	___	___
7. My partner would get upset if he/she knew of some of the things I've done with other people.	___	___
8. I enjoy playing the "game of love" with my partner and a number of other partners.	___	___
9. Our love is the best kind because it grew out of a long friendship.	___	___
10. Our friendship merged gradually into love over time.	___	___
11. Our love is really a deep friendship, not a mysterious, mystical emotion.	___	___
12. Our love relationship is the most satisfying because it developed from a good friendship.	___	___
13. A main consideration in choosing my partner was how he/she would reflect on my family.	___	___
14. An important factor in choosing my partner was whether or not he/she would be a good parent.	___	___
15. One consideration in choosing my partner was how he/she would reflect on my career.	___	___
16. Before getting very involved with my partner, I tried to figure out how compatible his/her hereditary background would be with mine in case we ever had children.	___	___
17. When my partner doesn't pay attention to me, I feel sick all over.	___	___
18. Since I've been in love with my partner, I've had trouble concentrating on anything else.	___	___
19. I cannot relax if I suspect that my partner is with someone else.	___	___
20. If my partner ignores me for a while, I sometimes do stupid things to try to get his/her attention back.	___	___
21. I would rather suffer myself than let my partner suffer.	___	___
22. I cannot be happy unless I place my partner's happiness before my own.	___	___
23. I am usually willing to sacrifice my own wishes to let my partner achieve his/hers.	___	___
24. I would endure all things for the sake of my partner.	___	___

Source: Reprinted by permission of Sage Publications, Ltd. From Clyde Hendrick, Susan S. Hendrick, and Amy Dicke, *Journal of Social and Personal Relationships,* Vol. 15 (2). Copyright 1998, Sage Publications, Ltd.

Mania: A possessive, dependent love style. This type of love often has elements of self-doubt and uncertainty about the other person. Because of their dependence, manic lovers can be very jealous and emotional.

Agape: A selfless, all-giving love. This style of love is altruistic and undemanding. It represents love without strings or qualifications.

Which love style do you think would best characterize your own? Which statements in Table 9.1 did you agree with? The questions you answered are linked to the six love styles described above. For example, agreeing with most or all of statements 1–4 would indicate someone rated high on Eros. Similarly, agreeing with statements about Ludus: 5–8; Storge: 9–12; Pragma: 13–16; Mania: 17–20; or Agape 21–24, would indicate a high rating on that attitude.

You might find that you can't be pinned down to one set of attitudes and that the way you think about love is far more complex. It's also possible that a person's love style will change over time. There's no doubt, though, that new theories about love will continue to emerge.

We spoke in the last chapter of control as a primary dimension of all relationship. It has two poles: dominance/submission. These elements are variables in all two-person relationships, as you will see in the discussion that follows.

Dominance, Status, and Power

Your mother and father have been married for 24 years. Who is the dominant partner? Who has the power? The first question is usually easy to answer. The second may be more difficult. Let's examine the issue of dominance first.

Dominance

Like the need for affiliation, the *need for dominance* can be imagined as a continuum: At one end is the person who always wants control over others; at the other end, the person with an extremely submissive style of communication. The vast majority of us fit somewhere in between.

We know some other things about people with a strong need for dominance. For example, they also tend to have a strong need for achievement. An association also seems to exist between dominance and self-concept: A person with an unfavorable self-concept tends to be submissive rather than dominant. In a dyad one person often defers to the other. This is true not only of friendships and romantic relationships but of work and classroom situations. For example, one of the authors assigned interpersonal projects to student pairs. One student, let's call him Paul, complained bitterly that Ahmed, his partner, made all the decisions and never let him participate in the planning. Yet each time the two were observed at work, Paul accepted all Ahmed's ideas and directives, making no attempt to express his own point of view. Paul's submissiveness is typical of the person with low self-esteem: unable or afraid to influence others yet resentful of always being the one who is dominated. Oddly enough, the hesitancy itself tends to intensify dominating behavior in others.

When we combine what we know about behaviors associated with the needs for affiliation and dominance (see Table 9.2), we see some of the communication patterns that are possible in an interpersonal relationship as well as in a larger group. Allowing for the uniqueness of each person, we can still make some predictions about how the two will interact if we know something about

Table 9.2	Some Behaviors Associated with Needs for Dominance and Affiliation	
	High Dominance	**Low Dominance**
High Affiliation	Advises	Acquiesces
	Coordinates	Agrees
	Directs	Assists
	Initiates	Cooperates
	Leads	Obliges
Low Affiliation	Analyzes	Concedes
	Criticizes	Evades
	Disapproves	Relinquishes
	Judges	Retreats
	Resists	Withdraws

Source: From *Reaching Out: Interpersonal Effectiveness and Self-Actualization,* 8th ed., by David W. Johnson. Published by Allyn and Bacon, Boston, MA. Copyright © 2003 by Pearson Education. Reprinted by permission of the publisher.

the strength of their individual needs for affiliation and dominance. Jennifer has a high need for dominance but a low need for affiliation, so we expect her to be analytic, to make many judgments, to be resistant, and so on; if Mark has a low need for dominance but a high need for affiliation, we expect him to acquiesce much of the time, to cooperate with Jennifer, and so on. But if, like Jennifer, Mark has a high need for dominance, there is likely to be conflict between them, or the two will have to work out some satisfactory agreements regulating their behavior—at least for a time. To put it in other terms, they themselves will have to develop rules for their relationship.

Dominance has been studied in research on relationship structure. Phillips and Wood (1983) define three relationship structures. *Complementary structures* are *based on differences between the partners;* one is dominant and the other submissive. *Symmetrical structures* are *based on similarities,* as when both partners are dominant or both are submissive. *Parallel structures,* on the other hand, *are based on some combination of complementary and symmetrical interactions;* suppose, for instance, that Javed is dominant and Shayla submissive with respect to finances, their roles reverse with respect to disciplining their two children, and both Javed and Shayla are dominant when it comes to deciding on family vacations.

Parallel structures are *the most flexible* and probably most common because they *enable us to adapt most easily to the demands of new situations.* Although the complementary relationship with the male dominant is seen as "typical," the number of such relationships seems to be declining with the rise of the dual-career marriage and the upswing in women's and minority-group rights. It's still the case, however, that the most rejected relationship is one in which the female is dominant. Some things haven't changed that much.

Status

Whether we like to acknowledge it or not, **status,** *the position of an individual in relation to another or others,* has at least some relationship to the issue of establishing control within an interpersonal relationship. "Status," write Knapp and Hall, "often connotes a socially valued quality that a person carries with her or him into different situations, whereas power and dominance are likely to be seen as a personality trait . . . in addition to a situational condition" (2002, p. 430). And as we saw in Chapter 4, status is often communicated nonverbally.

Status has marked effects on the form of all communication, no matter how unstructured, and affects content as well as communication style. There is a good chance the person with higher status will control the topics of conversation as well as the length of the discussion. Higher status may even enable that person to avoid a discussion entirely. If a bank president and a teller are conversing, for example, and the teller asks a question that seems too personal, the bank president will probably respond in a way that makes the teller uncomfortable about pursuing the subject. On the other hand, subordinates sometimes "disclose personal problems to their supervisors, but the reverse does not usually happen . . . Self-disclosures are most often employed between people of equal status" (Hargie et al., 1987, p. 192).

Perceptions of status are immediately reflected in greetings as well as in forms of address. "Hi" may be permissible for some encounters; "Hello" or "Good morning" may be more appropriate for others. The higher-status person is often addressed by title and last name ("Good morning, Dr. Jones"), and the lower-status person by first name or even a briefer version of that name ("Hi, Judy"). One sociologist observes that greetings may also affirm a subordinate's willingness to maintain lower status (Goffman, 1972). American military practice, for instance, requires that the subordinate salute first and hold the salute until it is returned by the person of higher rank. Observe people of different status greeting one another and see whether these behavior patterns are borne out by your own experience.

Power

A book on a well-known auction house tells of how its chairman, then in his late fifties, first noticed a young woman who would later become its president and CEO:

> Dede Brooks first came to the attention of Albert Taubman when he walked into a meeting where she was the only woman and asked her for a cup of coffee. "With pleasure," she replied, handing him a sheaf of documents. "And could you please photocopy these for me?" (Lacey, 1998, p. 278)

One definition of **power** is *the capacity to influence the behavior of others and to resist their influence on oneself* (Steil, 2000, p. 128). Identifying one person in a dyad as the more dominant doesn't always explain who wields the power. Power and dominance, as Wilmot (1995) reminds us, are not synonymous:

> One of the more exciting trends in the study of communication is viewing interpersonal power in relational terms. You do not have power—it is given to you by the others with whom you transact. (p. 105)

Wilmot is saying that power has to be granted by one person to the other. If I do not accept your authority, you cannot dominate me. In other words, power has much to do with how we perceive ourselves. Issues about power can occur in all kinds of interpersonal relationships from the most casual to the most intimate—those between landlord and tenant, co-workers, committee members, close friends, parent and child, siblings, and, of course, romantic partners. For a discussion about nonverbal cues of power and dominance, see page 108 in Chapter 4.

Gender and Power "There is no society," write Pratto and Walker, "in which women have greater power than men." In their survey of research (2004), they propose four bases of gendered power: force, control of resources, control of ideology, and unequal, or asymmetric, obligations. Let's consider them one by one.

Force: Men wield power not only through physical force and emotional violence but in their social roles. For example, the number of women in military, government, and political life is negligible. As heads of state, lawyers and judges, and law enforcement officials, men far outnumber women.

Resources: Social roles that have hierarchic power, as do those just described, also bring greater financial resources and such resources are predominantly held by men. To illustrate the authors point out that only 1 to 3 percent of top executives throughout the world and only 16 percent of corporate officers in this country are women. And women who do have high-status positions are paid less than men who hold the same positions. For example, "among U.S. physicians, 21 percent are women, and their median annual salary is $120,000, whereas that of male physicians is $175,000" (p. 248).

Control of ideology: It is, for the most part, men, not women, who through their roles control ideological content and how it is disseminated. This is true not only in religion and politics but in the mass media where most of the decision makers are men and influence opinion leaders, as we will see in Chapter 15. An unusual moment occurs in the television series *The West Wing* when C. J. Cregg, the White House press secretary, is chosen over her peers, all men, to become the president's new Chief of Staff. She is clearly seen by the staff as an astonishing choice.

Unequal social obligations: According to gender stereotypes, women are warm and nurturant, suggesting that they are especially suited to caregiving roles. "The obligation to provide care may well constitute the center of the feminine gender role" (p. 25). Yet often it is the obligations to provide care that undercut women's power by taking up so much of their time and limiting both their freedom and financial resources.

Contemporary marriage, many experts agree, is still "an unequal partnership": Research finds that "even wives who earn as much or more than their husbands do not achieve relationship equality"(Steil, 2000, p. 129). Steil argues that equal power between men and women cannot exist because gender roles are still separate. When women commit themselves to working outside the home, there is often no parallel commitment from their husbands to increase the work they do in the house. In family life, two of the primary gendered roles are the roles of provider and nurturer. Even when she earns more money than her husband, a woman usually views the provider role as one that interferes with her role as nurturer. Taking care of the needs of others, especially children, and sometimes parents, comes first. After a couple has children, the power balance tends to shift back to traditional marital roles (McGoldrick, 1999).

Among married couples one of the major power struggles is about money—whose it is, how it will be spent, who decides. One marital therapist writes about discovering "the golden rule: whoever has the gold makes the rules" (Carter and Peters, 1996, p. 65). Sex, and the withholding of it, is another arena of power struggles between couples. And money, because it has great symbolic value is often equated with caring.

Consider the story of Eric and Nancy, who own a summer house that they are paying off by renting it out most of the time (Tannen, 2001). When Eric informs his wife that he is buying an SUV, she is angered. He has not consulted her at all; she feels the decision to buy a car should be a joint one. She wouldn't make a decision like that without consulting him. She also feels resentful that she has deprived herself and her family of many things to keep paying off the house. Eric feels that consulting her before buying something would mean being controlled by her. "So," writes Tannen, "in addition to being a power struggle over who controls the money, it's also a connection struggle about what these maneuvers mean in terms of closeness" (p. 117).

Nancy has several alternatives. She can remain resentful without even speaking to Eric about her feelings. She might lose her temper and have a bitter argument with him. Or she might be assertive in discussing how she really feels.

In closing, we look briefly at some behaviors that can promote greater equality in our relationships and increase our sense of self-respect.

Equality and Assertiveness   Concerns about assertiveness surface in many interpersonal relationships, not just in marriage and romantic associations. Your doctor assures you that you do not need an expensive test, but you feel the test is necessary. Your landlord becomes very evasive about returning the security deposit when the lease on your apartment is up; you are getting ready to move and need the money. Your roommate constantly borrows your clothes without permission; you like your roommate but this really bothers you. Your parents are still telling you how to run your life.

When you think about behavior that is assertive, what are your first associations? For some, being called "assertive" has a negative connotation, perhaps because they equate assertiveness with aggression. Those who study assertiveness and conduct workshops on assertive training frame the concept differently. In a popular book on the subject, two psychologists write:

> Assertive behavior promotes equality in human relationships, enabling us to act in our own best interests, to stand up for ourselves without undue anxiety, to express feelings honestly and comfortably, to exercise personal rights without denying the rights of others. (Alberti and Emmons, 2001, p. 36)

Another well-known definition of assertiveness is "standing up for personal rights and expressing thoughts, feelings, and beliefs in direct, honest, and appropriate ways which do not violate another person's rights" (Lange and Jakubowski, cited in Yoshioka, 2000). Notice the word "violate." Assertive behavior is not aggressive. It acknowledges the rights of others and equality in interpersonal relationships.

Many other definitions proposed over the years seem to emphasize similar qualities: self-expression, honesty, directness, firmness. Self-expression as it is used here refers to both verbal and nonverbal communication. It's not only message content— what you say about your thoughts and feelings. It's your tone of voice and other vocal cues (do you whine or speak confidently? do you speak so that you can be heard?); your body positioning; your facial expression, and all the other nonverbal cues we discussed in Chapter 4. Think of how important these qualities would be in honest communication about sex.

Figure 9.4 highlights some of the differences between assertive, aggressive, and nonassertive behaviors—seen from the perspectives of both the sender and receiver. Nonassertive behavior (the sender on the left) is self-denying rather than self-expressive. By allowing other people to make choices for you, you often give up your own goals and desires. Behavior that is assertive (the sender on the right) allows you to be self-expressive, to make your own choices—or at least express those choices—and increase the possibility that you may achieve your own desires and goals. It also involves careful listening to how the other person responds.

Through aggressive behavior, on the other hand, you express your own thoughts and feelings and put forward your own choices—but at the other person's expense. Aggressive or forcing behaviors also include underhanded, passive actions in which you appear to be cooperative or seem to agree, but actually undercut the other person.

From the receiver's standpoint, nonassertive behavior elicits a number of responses from sympathy to contempt, impatience, or anger. Ideally, assertive behavior can lead to positive outcomes for both the sender and the receiver. As receivers of aggressive behavior we tend to feel hurt, abused, defensive, or humiliated. Anger, though sometimes suppressed, is often present—and it tends to build.

Despite the promises of assertiveness training and books on assertive behavior, assertive behavior is no guarantee that you will achieve all your goals, but it will make you feel that you are not being victimized.

Nor is assertive behavior appropriate for all situations. As one scholar suggests, the view that assertive behavior is always positive and functional in interpersonal communication may be "somewhat idealized" (Wilson, 1993, p. 56). Alberti and Emmons stress that assertive behavior is behavior "appropriate for the person and situation, not universal." In other words, it is specific to the situation and we must always "weigh the consequences" (Berko et al., 2001, p. 161). Clearly, people sometimes feel that the risks of being assertive in their closest relationships may be too great.

Suppose, for example, that Liz and Michael have been seeing one another for almost a year, and whenever they are at a party he finds ways to run her down in front of their friends. Every time it happens she feels angry and humiliated. To specify what she wants, she might explain that she wants Michael to treat her consistently, to be as thoughtful and accepting as he is when they're alone instead of using her at parties as a kind of "straight man" for his public image. She might also say that the next time it happened, she'd get up and leave the party, or that she'd end their relationship. In that case, Liz would have to be ready to follow through on what she says.

Figure 9.4 *What It Means to Be Assertive*

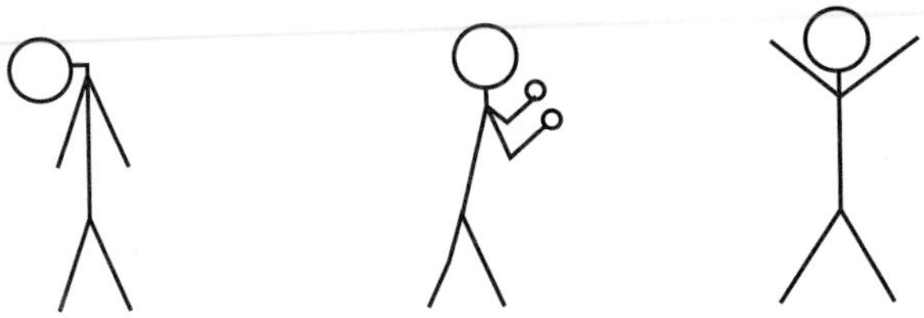

NONASSERTIVE BEHAVIOR	AGGRESSIVE BEHAVIOR	ASSERTIVE BEHAVIOR
Sender	**Sender**	**Sender**
Self-denying	Self-enhancing at expense of another	Self-enhancing
Inhibited		Expressive
Hurt, anxious	Expressive	Feels good about self
Allows others to chose	Chooses for others	Chooses for self
Does not achieve desired goal	Achieves desired goal by hurting others	May achieve desired goal
Receiver	**Receiver**	**Receiver**
Guilty or angry	Self-denying	Self-enhancing
Depreciates sender	Hurt, defensive, humiliated	Expressive
Achieves desired goal at sender's expense	Does not achieve desired goal	May achieve desired goal

Source: From *Your Perfect Right: Assertiveness and Equality in Your Life and Relationships,* 8th ed. Copyright © 2001 by Robert E. Alberti and Michael Emmons. Reproduced for Stewart Tubbs and Sylvia Moss by permission of Impact Publishers, Inc., P.O. Box 6016, Atascadero, CA 93423, USA. Further reproduction prohibited.

The effectiveness of assertive behavior will depend to a great degree on the relative strength of its rewards and how these stack up against the rewards for nonassertive behavior. Nonassertive behavior allows you to avoid conflict, anxiety, and disapproval. For example, it can be upsetting to stand up to your parents or to insist that you deserve a raise when you get a promotion. On the other hand, the increased feelings of self-respect and the satisfaction of individual needs that are often the result of a more assertive communication style are powerful rewards. As always, a reward has to be defined in terms of the individual.

In addition, a reward is also defined in terms of a given culture or co-culture. Members of various cultures and co-cultures interpret assertiveness very differently (what is assertive to you might be aggressive to me), and this is true for many interpersonal variables, as we will see in the following chapter.

Summary

Interpersonal communication is in many ways a microcosm of all larger groups and thus encompasses many kinds of relationships, from the most casual to the most intimate and long lasting. Our first major topic was the social setting within which interpersonal communication must be viewed. Members of a relationship are strongly influenced by the norms they have already adopted, and they also establish some normative agreements of their own as they interact. In addition, the roles they enact affect how they will respond to each other; we also looked at role expectations as they affect close relationships. We examined some consequences of conflicts within and between roles. We then looked at the dialectical approach, which views human relationships in terms of tensions between contradictory impulses.

Because quality is so frequently an issue in assessing relationships, we suggested several measures of high quality. We first discussed the importance of self-disclosure, its relationship

to trust, and the reasons people choose to self-disclose or to avoid disclosures. We also discussed self-disclosure and self-presentation in online dating. Intimacy was seen as a process—one that has to be developed and maintained. We also looked at a theory about attachment styles, at unreciprocated love, and at research findings on intimacy between siblings.

Affiliative need and willingness to make commitments were also seen as important variables—especially with respect to cohabitation and marriage. We considered two theories about love involving commitment and other variables that we had discussed. Dominance, status, and power were examined as other important variables. This included a discussion of the relationship between gender and power in relationships. In closing, we looked at assertiveness as a means of establishing equality and briefly at some of the differences between assertive, nonassertive, and aggressive behaviors.

Key Terms

Attachment style	Interrole conflict	Norms	Self-disclosure
Commitment	Intimacy	Power	Status
Dialectics	Intrarole conflict	Prototype	
Dyadic effect	Johari window	Role	

Review Questions

1. How are disruptive power and norms related to interpersonal communication?

2. Explain the distinction between expected and enacted roles.

3. Discuss the effects of our expectations of marriage on other close relationships.

4. Distinguish between intrarole and interrole conflict and give an example of each.

5. Explain the dialectical approach to human interactions.

6. Describe three of the primary dialectics and give an example of each.

7. What are four means by which we can assess the quality of an interpersonal relationship?

8. What are the four levels of awareness and disclosure exemplified by the Johari window?

9. State four reasons for self-disclosure and four for its avoidance.

10. What are some of the research findings on self-disclosure in Internet dating and on how people tend to present themselves in posting Internet profiles?

11. Identify five characteristics of appropriate self-disclosure.

12. Discuss at least three qualities that characterize intimacy in interpersonal communication.

13. Explain the difference between intimacy and passion.

14. Describe the concept of attachment styles as applied to romantic relationships.

15. Discuss three variables that seem to predict the intensity of unreciprocated love.

16. Discuss the research findings on intimacy in later-life relationships of siblings.

17. Explain how affiliation and commitment affect interpersonal relationships.

18. Discuss two theories about types of love relationships.

19. How are need for affiliation and need for dominance related?

20. Explain how complementary, symmetrical, and parallel relationship structures differ.

21. What are two ways in which status affects interpersonal communication?

22. What is the difference between dominance and power in an interpersonal relationship?

23. State four proposed bases for gendered power.

24. Explain the differences between nonassertive, assertive, and aggressive behavior. Give an example of each.

25. Discuss at least four qualities that characterize assertive behavior.

Exercises

1. Write a short paper in which you analyze some communication difficulties that might arise for a college student as a result of role conflicts.

2. In a small group—five people or so—have each person attempt to increase his or her awareness of self and others by telling each of the others one positive and one negative impression he or she has formed about that person. If there is time, have a discussion in which group members go into greater depth, asking for and giving further impressions.

3. Write a brief paper describing what you see as the major dialectical conflicts in your relationships with (a) one or both of your parents, (b) a close friend, and (c) someone you have dated.

4. Go to *www.web-research-design.net/cgi-bin/crq/crq.pl* and take the Close Relationships Questionnaire. After you get your test results, you can read more about attachment theory and close relationships on the same site.

5. In addition to triangles that describe the love relationships we are in, there are triangles that describe our ideal relationships. Try identifying and then drawing your real and ideal triangles.

6. After observing a conversation between two people, try to determine what specific messages (nonverbal as well as verbal) reveal the dominance

or submissiveness of each communicator. Make the same observations with respect to affiliative or antisocial behaviors. Do the characteristic roles shift from time to time?

7. Role-play the following exercises and try to use assertive (not aggressive) behaviors.

Scene 1

Bank Customer: You have been a customer of this bank for over 20 years. You request an installment loan on a new car and are refused.

Bank Employee: A long-time customer of the bank wants an installment loan to purchase a car. Current bank policy does not provide for installment loans on automobiles because the interest rates aren't profitable to the bank.

Scene 2

Bank Employee: A customer wants to cash a $10,000 check against uncollected funds (a check from another state). The bank policy requires a 10-day waiting period.

Bank Customer: You just came in from another state and you go to the bank to cash a $10,000 check drawn on an out-of-state bank. It is important that you have the cash on that day for the closing on the house you are purchasing. Because the check is drawn on an out-of-state bank, the teller refuses to give you the cash.

Suggested Readings

Alberti, Robert, and Michael Emmons. *Your Perfect Right*, 8th ed. Atascadero, CA: Impact Publishers, 2001.

This is a very popular guide to learning assertiveness skills and establishing greater equality in interpersonal relationships.

In the Mood for Love

This is a haunting, subtle, and romantic movie about a man and a woman who live in the same building and slowly discover their spouses are having an affair.

Luft, Joseph. *Of Human Interaction*. Palo Alto, CA: National Press, 1969.

The author elaborates on the rationale behind the Johari window model as well as its application. He also explains more fully the value of self-disclosure. A classic treatment of the subject.

Millman, Marcia. *The Perfect Sister: What Draws Us Together, What Drives Us Apart*. New York: Harcourt, 2004.

Based on hundreds of hours of interviews, this study of adult relationships between sisters is rich in case histories and insights. It explores the complexity of bonds between siblings as well as how long-term rifts between them can be repaired.

Proof

A play and also a film about love, family relationships, and claims of genius. Its author, David Auburn, was awarded the Pulitzer Prize.

Silver, Robert B., and Barbara Epstein, eds. *The Company They Kept*. New York: New York Review of Books, 2006.

Twenty-seven brief memoirs, each about a remarkable friend.

Sternberg, Robert J. *Cupid's Arrow: The Course of Love through Time*. New York: Cambridge University Press, 2000.

The author explains his own triangular theory of love, traces a brief history of cultural and literary conceptions of love, and goes on to examine the course of love during our lifetime.

Tannen, Deborah. *You're Wearing That? Understanding Mothers and Daughters in Conversation*. New York: Ballantine Books, 2006.

A book about mother-daughter communication by a well-known linguist with great sensitivity to dialogue.

Trillin, Calvin. *About Alice*. New York: Random House, 2006.

This is a brief and loving memoir about an extraordinary marriage—its many joys and sorrows. Superbly written with both restraint and humor.

Vanzetti, Nelly, and Steve Duck. *A Lifetime of Relationships*. Pacific Grove, CA: Brooks/Cole, 1996.

A really interesting book that covers various types of relationships from childhood to friendships, marriage, and through to retirement.

 # For Supplementary Information

Log onto the Online Learning Center at *www.mhhe.com/tubbsmoss11.*

10

Intercultural Communication

Chapter Objectives

After reading this chapter, you should be able to:

1. Define "intercultural communication," discuss three major approaches to how it is studied, and explain the concept of diaspora.
2. Discuss the differences between individualist and collectivist cultures, high- and low-context cultures, and three other dimensions that measure cultural variation.
3. State three broad communication principles with important implications for intercultural communication.
4. Explain how verbal and nonverbal messages, including those that express emotion, can interfere with communication between cultures. Give three examples of each.
5. Describe how cultural roles and norms, including norms about conflict, affect intercultural communication.
6. Discuss the effects of differences in beliefs and values on people from different cultures, identify three ethical norms that appear in a great number of them, and give an example of adapting successfully to another culture.
7. Explain the concepts of ethnocentrism, stereotyping, and polarization as they affect interethnic and interracial conflict. Discuss the research findings on intergroup relations, and explain the principles of cosmopolitanism.
8. Describe some of the personal, political, and social effects of intercultural communication and identify seven principles that would promote community building.

I came to the United States at the age of 29, excited and full of hope for the opportunities that this country has given historically to millions of immigrants. Yet I was struck by the bad image that Arabs, especially Palestinians, Muslims and women, have in this country. This was a shock to me. As a Palestinian Muslim woman I realized all of a sudden that for many people in this country I am an embodiment of what is backward and evil.

—Amari (2006, p. 36)

Anam Amari is one of the founders of the Arab American National Museum in Dearborn, Michigan. "It was this very feeling of injustice," she explains, "that pushed me and the hundreds of people involved in this project to act." The museum opened in 2005—its mission, to show that the Arab-American story was in essence the American story. Artifacts, documents, and records of oral histories all play a part.

This is increasingly a world in which differences between cultures are sometimes overemphasized and at other times ignored—a world in which fear, suspicion, or lack of knowledge about people of other cultures can set them apart, making them seem like mysterious strangers whose ways are not fully understood.

In this chapter we look at intercultural communication as it occurs in many contexts from interpersonal to mass communication. And whenever it occurs, the differences in our frames of reference make the task of communication more complex, difficult, and nuanced, for we cannot be aware of all aspects of other cultures. In fact, one reason intercultural communication has fascinated scholars is that it reveals so much about our own communication behavior that we might not have otherwise noticed as distinctive—for example, our attitudes toward time or our responses to conflict. As our involvement in intercultural communication increases—and it must—it becomes vital for each of us to understand some of its principles, problems, and implications.

A DEFINITION OF CULTURE

In Chapter 1, we defined *intercultural communication* as *communication between members of different cultures (whether defined in terms of racial, ethnic, or socioeconomic differences)*. As this definition suggests, the divisions between cultural groups are not established or absolute; we may choose one or more of a variety of characteristics to identify a group of people as having a common culture. We may, for instance, speak of natives of California, Nebraska, and New Hampshire as being from different regional cultures (West Coast, Midwest, and New England); we may identify each of them as a member of an urban or rural culture, or as a member of a Jewish or Irish culture; we may speak of them all as members of a broader Western culture. Although scholars disagree as to which of these designations may properly be said to describe a cultural group, to a certain extent all of them do.

Culture is *a way of life developed and shared by a group of people and passed down from generation to generation*. It is made up of many complex elements, including religious and political systems, customs, and language as well as tools, clothing, buildings, and works of art. The way you dress, your relationships with your parents and friends, what you expect of a marriage and of a job, the food you eat, the language you speak, are all profoundly affected by your culture. This does not mean that you think, believe, and act exactly as everyone else in your cultural group does. Not all members of a culture share all its elements. Moreover, a culture will change and evolve over time. Still, a common set of characteristics is shared by the group at large and can be traced, even through great changes, over many generations.

At the age of 19 Maude Hertelou, a native of Haiti, left her country to study in Guatemala City. Her parents gave her two suitcases "filled with farewell gifts: from a bookmark made out of dry banana leaves to family photographs" (2001, p. 89). After four years she moved to Canada, and later to Florida:

> After more than two decades away from Haiti, I still reach out for my suitcases, both physical and cultural, for all of the items in them, linked as they are to memories and traditions, that have helped me, and still continue to help me survive the immigrant life. However, my suitcase has now expanded with a few more items gathered from other cultures, with the letters and the photographs of the friends I have made in Guatemala, Canada, and Florida, with their stories and languages, and traditions that have slowly merged into my own: the particular lilt of Guatemalan Spanish that I eventually mastered, the handmade fabrics from San Andres, the *cabane à sucre* parties in Quebec City, where I indulged in maple syrup candies out on the street, along with the other residents, natives, and immigrants alike. What my own cultural isolation as an immigrant in these places has taught me is that I am part of a living culture that in no way stops being a part of me, even when I am not completely immersed in it. With everything I do and say, I am perpetuating that culture, enriching it, modifying it when necessary, but contributing to its regeneration. My suitcases, both physical and cultural, have always, and will always, make me proud of my culture. (pp. 92–93)

Culture as Learned

As we attempt to communicate with people from other cultures and reconcile our differences, it is important that we remember culture is learned. Because it is learned, not innate, an infant born in Vietnam of Vietnamese parents but brought to the United States and raised as an American will be culturally an American. Because culture is learned, it also changes as people come into contact with one another or as their experiences change their needs.

In a sense, it is the culture and its values that provide a coherent framework for organizing our activity and allowing us to predict the behavior of others. People from other cultures who enter our own may be threatening because they challenge our system of beliefs. In the same way, we ourselves may become threatening to others as we enter a foreign culture and challenge the cultural foundations of their beliefs (Neuliep and McCroskey, 1997b).

Distinctions among Cultures

Radical differences among cultures usually occur when there has been little exchange between them or, in some cases, with other cultures in general. What distinguishes one cultural group from another, however, is not always so evident. A New Yorker and a Californian will have cultural differences and similarities. Both may celebrate Thanksgiving and the Fourth of July with much the same sense of tradition associated with those holidays. On a day-to-day basis, however, they are likely to eat somewhat different foods, although probably with the same kind of utensils. They are likely to speak the same language but with different accents and a few different words or phrases. Both will speak more or less the same language as people who have always lived in England and Ontario, and they may even share many of the same values, but cultural differences are likely to become more evident as people from the United States, Canada, and England communicate with one another. Similarly, differences among cultures do not always occur abruptly at regional or national borders but gradually, over a range.

Three Approaches to Studying Culture

In the study of intercultural communication, three major approaches have emerged: social science, interpretive, and critical (Davis et al., 2000; Martin and Nakayama, 2007, pp. 52–69). Here we look briefly at each of them.

The Social Science Approach   This is the most traditional and is built on the methods and assumptions derived from psychology and sociology. It is assumed that behavior can be observed, measured, and predicted—that descriptive, often quantitative methods, can be objective—and that we can discover universals about human behavior. Here communication is seen as influenced by culture, and the primary interest is in describing and comparing cultures. For example, researchers might conduct a cross-cultural study of proxemic norms or how conflict is expressed by people from the United States, Greece, Germany, Japan, and China.

The Interpretive Approach   This approach derives its methods from anthropology and linguistics. It emphasizes the subjective experience of the individual. Its research emphasis is qualitative rather than quantitative. It makes full use of field studies and personal observation. Researchers may get to know the people they study quite well, might collect personal narratives and stories that describe the lived experience of a given culture or co-culture. Usually, the goal is understanding rather than predicting behavior, taking a perspective from *within* the culture. Communication is seen as creating and maintaining culture. For example, one well-known interpretive study examined speech codes in Teamsterville, a working-class Chicago neighborhood.

The Critical Approach   Although some of its assumptions and methods overlap with an interpretive approach, the critical approach is primarily concerned with creating change by examining power relationships within cultures. It stresses the importance of social, political, economic, and historical contexts, and its focus is on social rather than individual relations. According to this view, power relationships characterize all intercultural transactions (p. 63). Here the ultimate goal is not merely understanding behavior but producing actual change. The critical approach involves analyses of "texts" or "cultural products," including those produced by the media (e.g., newspapers, movies, television, public relations material). For example, Rey Chow, a professor of cultural studies at Brown University, writes on Chinese cinema (2007). Some other critical studies have analyzed how minorities are represented in the movies in comparison with whites or how the language of news reports contributes to a new form of racism (van Dijk, 2000).

Nick Couldry, another cultural studies scholar, writes: "We cannot oversimplify the cultural experiences of others, without caricaturing our own. Cultural studies in this sense involves an ethic of reciprocity, a mutual practice of both speaking and listening, which is inextricably tied to taking seriously the complexity of cultures" (2006, p. 54).

Although much of the research we will be looking at grows out of the first of these approaches, one view does not exclude the contributions of the others. The study of intercultural communication is enriched by all three perspectives.

Mass Migration and Diaspora

To be a colonial is to be a little ridiculous and unlikely, especially in the eyes of someone from the metropolitan country. All immigrants and their descendants are colonials of one sort or another, and between the colonial and what one might call the metropolitan there always exists a muted mutual distrust.

—Naipaul (2003, p. 38)

Migration, be it voluntary or involuntary, generally reminds me of how fragile one's name is, how fragile an allegiance to religion can prove to be, the importance of language, the importance of which *language, questions of gender.*

—Caryl Phillips (Quoted in Clingman, 2004, p. 123)

The mass movements of large groups of people whether through voluntary exile and emigration or enforced migrations and diasporas—often under extreme conditions—have marked this last century as one of displacement. The writer Salman Rushdie has described it as "this century of displaced persons" (see, for example, Clark, 2006). Although the number of refugee populations is immense, not all mass migrations are diasporas.

What do we mean when we speak of a diaspora? **Diaspora** is the Greek word for dispersal or scattering (the way grain or seeds might be scattered), and many dictionaries define diaspora as a dispersal of people from their homeland.

One scholar singles out three elements of diaspora on which most other cultural theorists agree, and to this she adds a fourth:

1. A scattering of people (whether voluntary or involuntary) to at least two destinations rather than a transfer from the homeland to a single destination.
2. Some relationship to an actual or imagined homeland.
3. Self-awareness of the group's identity.
4. A diaspora is multigenerational and must exist over at least two generations. (Adapted from Butler, 2001, pp. 192–193)

In recent years diaspora studies have become numerous and increasingly interdisciplinary. The Jewish diaspora, the Black African diaspora, and the Armenian diaspora, among others, have been studied for decades. More recently, scholars have turned their attention to such groups as the many Tibetans, including their spiritual leader, the Dalai Lama, who have left their homeland and resettled in India, the United States, and other countries. Similarly, there have been more recent studies of the two million Vietnamese, Laotians, and Cambodians who left their native countries to settle in communities in many other parts of the world.

At the PEN World Voices festival in 2006, the poet Elizabeth Alexander of Yale University spoke of her interest in teaching

> the population of young black people . . . who are as likely to have been born in Lagos or Port of Spain as in Los Angeles. The diaspora is alive and well and creative and has a new face. The black kids now—as my own children, whose father is Eritrean—describe themselves: When he was four, the eldest said to me, "Mommy, you're an African American, right?"
> And I said, "Yes."
> And he said, "And Daddy is African, right?"
> And I said, "Right."
> And he said, "So we're *African* American." (2006, pp. 109–110)

Today scholars are concerned with the way diasporic populations form bonds and maintain a sense of identity and community around the world. The well-known cultural anthropologist Arjun Appadurai (2003, 1996) believes that the two major forces with a decisive influence on the imagination and modern consciousness have been mass migration and the development of electronic media, a subject we will consider further in discussing mass communication.

SOME DIMENSIONS OF CULTURAL DIFFERENCE

The last decades have seen a dramatic increase in intercultural communication, a social change that has been brought about in part through the technological innovations of both aviation and electronic communication networks. Once an experience for the privileged few, international air travel is now routine and accessible to millions.

Satellite technology has brought the immediacy of political events into our homes, and the expansion of a vast electronic communications network now links peoples of the world many times over.

As a result, the experience of the immigrant population has also changed radically. For example, over one-third of New York City's population are immigrants—mainly from the Caribbean, Asia, and Latin America, and a variety of other nations (Foner, 2001). Many immigrants can afford to revisit their homeland regularly to see family and friends as well as conduct business. And the pervasive use of the Internet, e-mail, cell phone, and videophone, as well as other technological innovations, has brought together old and new cultures, making the understanding of cultural differences more vital than ever.

In 2002, the Census Bureau reported that the number of U.S. residents who were born outside the United States or are children of immigrants (i.e., first-generation Americans) was the highest it had ever been. About 70 percent have settled in California, Florida, Illinois, New Jersey, New York, or Texas, and over half live in large metropolitan areas (Scott, 2002).

It's not surprising, therefore, that in addition to identifying ourselves as part of a larger culture, many of us will identify ourselves as members of one or more co-cultures. It is likely, especially in a country as diverse as the United States, that groups within this culture, although they share many characteristics with members of the larger culture, will also be members of a **co-culture**—that is, *a culture within the larger culture.* That group or co-culture will often share "a specialized language system, shared values, a collective worldview, and common communication patterns" (Samovar and Porter, 2000, p. 115). Among such groups are Asian Americans, African Americans, gays, lesbians, women, people with disabilities.

On the basis of his research findings on intercultural communication, Hofstede (1980, 1991) proposed several dimensions along which cultures vary. In the pages that follow we will look briefly at each of the major variables.

Individualism-Collectivism

Many theorists regard individualism-collectivism as the central dimension within which variations between cultures may be measured. By **individualism** scholars usually mean *the tendency of people in a given culture to value "individual identity over group identity, individual rights over group rights, and individual achievements over group concerns"* (Ting-Toomey and Chung, 1996, p. 239, emphasis added). At the other end of the continuum, **collectivism** has been defined as *the tendency of people in a given culture to value "group identity over the individual identity, group obligations over individual rights, and ingroup-oriented concerns over individual wants and desires"* (p. 240).

Members of an individualist culture tend to emphasize personal goals, to think of themselves as independent, and to be direct in communicating. In an individualist culture there are many in-groups (your family, your school, your church, your occupation), but their influence is specific and often limited.

For members of collectivist cultures, the emphasis is on the importance of fitting into the group. Because they are strongly connected with the group, they tend to regard the self as interdependent and to be aware of group goals and welfare rather than focusing on individual achievements and desires. And they tend to avoid direct conflict. Unlike individualist cultures, collectivist cultures have relatively few in-groups, but these exert considerable influence.

A dramatic example of how differently actions may be interpreted in collectivist and individualist cultures was seen after the release in spring of 2004 of three young Japanese civilians who had been taken hostage in Iraq: a woman who had created a nonprofit organization that helped Iraq street children, a freelance journalist, and a photographer. They were shown on television with their kidnappers, who held knives and were threatening to slit their throats.

Two weeks after they were seen on television, the three were freed by their captors and flown home. Instead of being welcomed, they were confronted by the resentment, anger, and criticism of many of the Japanese people because, it was said, to pursue their own goals the hostages had selfishly ignored the government's advisory against travel to Iraq. "Their sin . . . was to defy what people call here 'okami,' or, literally, 'what is higher'—in this case, the Foreign Ministry" (Onishi, 2004, A1). The level of hostility was so high that the three went into seclusion, virtual prisoners in their own homes.

The response in the United States, with its mainstream individualist culture, could not have been more different. The actions of the three hostages were seen as courageous rather than reckless, compassionate and generous rather than selfish. Former Secretary of State Colin Powell praised the three as "Japanese citizens [who] were ready to put themselves at risk, for a better purpose" (A11).

Following up on earlier studies, two researchers recently studied differences in how members of Western cultures and East Asian cultures perceive the consequences of four different events, including a car accident and the firing of employees by the CEO of the firm they worked in (Maddux and Yuki, 2006). They found a greater consciousness of the "ripple effects of events" and a sense of personal responsibility among people from East Asian cultures. Their greater sense of interdependence made them more aware of social ramifications:

> Japanese participants perceived social events as affecting a larger number of
> people than did Americans; they also perceived themselves as more responsible
> for the indirect distal consequences of explicitly social events, felt worse about
> these indirect consequences, and were more likely to apologize to indirectly
> affected targets. (p. 680)

This study helps explain the response in Japan to the kidnapping of the three Japanese civilians in Iraq.

Research on cultural differences in U.S. and Japanese students also confirms that the Japanese concept of self is viewed more in terms of relatedness to others than individuality (Kanagawa et al., 2001). Another study of the individualist-collectivist dimension explored the concepts of "individual," "self," and "group" and what they mean for Japanese nationals, Japanese Americans, and European Americans (Nathan et al., 1999). The researchers suggest that we may not yet fully understand how "self" is thought of by the Japanese (and this is probably true of how "self" is thought of in other collectivist cultures as well). For example, the Japanese concept of self may have "a more spiritual or cosmic dimension . . . in accord with Buddhist concepts of the self" (p. 772). See Box 2.1 on p. 47 for a further discussion of cultural differences in self-concept.

Approximately two-thirds of the world's population are members of collectivist cultures. These include many Latino, Mediterranean, Middle Eastern, African, and Asian cultures. Despite this, researchers seem to have given more attention to individualist cultures such as the United States, Canada, Scandinavia, France, Great Britain, Germany, Switzerland, and Australia (Ting-Toomey and Chung, 1996, p. 239). (You can see a summary of differences along these dimensions in Table 10.1.)

Table 10.1 *Individualistic and Collectivistic Cultures*

Individualistic	Collectivistic
Major Characteristics	
Emphasis on individual's goals	Emphasis on in-group's goals
Self-realization	Fitting into the in-group
Little difference between in-group and out-group communication	Large difference between in-group and out-group communication
Independent self-construal	Interdependent self-construal
"I" identity	"We" identity
Saying what you are thinking	Avoiding confrontations in in-group
Low-context communication: direct, precise, and absolute	High-context communication: indirect, imprecise, and probabilistic
Example Cultures*	
Australia	Brazil
Belgium	China
Canada	Colombia
Denmark	Egypt
Finland	Greece
France	India
Germany	Japan
Great Britain	Kenya
Ireland	Korea
Israel	Mexico
Italy	Nigeria
Netherlands	Pakistan
New Zealand	Panama
Norway	Peru
South Africa	Saudi Arabia
Sweden	Thailand
Switzerland	Venezuela
United States	Vietnam

*The cultures are listed according to the *predominant* tendencies in the cultures.
Source: Adapted from *Communicating with Strangers*, 3rd ed., by William B. Gudykunst and Young Yun Kim, 1997. Reproduced by permission of The McGraw-Hill Companies.

High- and Low-Context Cultures

For students of communication, the distinction between high- and low-context cultures (Hall, 1976) is among the most fascinating. High- and low-context cultures have several important differences in the way information is coded. Members of **high-context cultures** are *more skilled in reading nonverbal behaviors; and they assume that other people will also be able to do so.* Thus, *they speak less* than members of low-context cultures *and they listen more;* in general, their communication tends to be indirect and less explicit. Members of **low-context cultures,** on the other hand, *stress direct and explicit communication. They emphasize verbal messages and the shared information they encode.* Many researchers link high-context communication style with collectivist cultures and low-context communication style with individualist cultures.

High- and low-context cultures range along a continuum, with such cultures as the Chinese and Japanese at the high end and the Scandinavian, German, and German-Swiss cultures at the low end. The United States would be within the low-context end of the spectrum, though not at the very bottom. (For a sampling of high- and low-context cultures see Figure 10.1.) In comparing people from the United States with Malays and Japanese, Althen offers a clear example of the high-context/low-context distinction:

> Americans focus on the words people use to convey their ideas, information, and feelings. They are generally quite unskilled in "reading" other people's non-verbal

Figure 10.1 High-Context versus Low-Context Rankings of Selected Countries and Groups

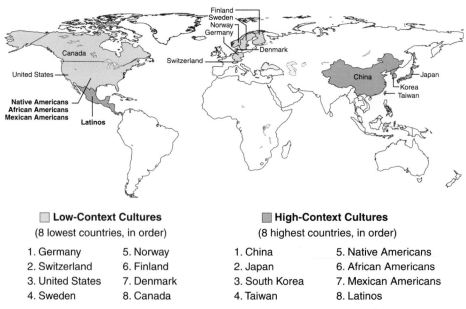

Low-Context Cultures
(8 lowest countries, in order)

1. Germany	5. Norway
2. Switzerland	6. Finland
3. United States	7. Denmark
4. Sweden	8. Canada

High-Context Cultures
(8 highest countries, in order)

1. China	5. Native Americans
2. Japan	6. African Americans
3. South Korea	7. Mexican Americans
4. Taiwan	8. Latinos

Source: From *Nonverbal Communication: Forms and Functions,* 2nd ed., by Peter A. Andersen. Copyright © 2007. Published by Waveland Press. Reprinted by of permission of Peter A. Andersen.

messages. "Oh, you Americans!" said an exasperated Japanese woman who was being pressed to express some details about an unpleasant situation, "You have to say everything!" (Althen, 1992, p. 416)

As many have pointed out, "not all members of individualist cultures are individualists, and not all members of collectivistic cultures are collectivists" (Gudykunst and Kim, 1997, p. 69). Such qualifying statements could certainly be made about other dimensions such as high- and low-context cultures. Within any dimension there will be much variation within individuals and in how each culture interprets various concepts such as self (as just discussed), community, and conflict. (For example, Yum [1997] attributes the Chinese emphasis on social relationships to the influence of Confucianism.)

Power Distance

Power distance refers to *the degree to which people accept authority and hierarchical organization as a natural part of their culture.* They expect, then, that some members of the culture have higher status and are more powerful than others. Members of high power-distance cultures (France, India, and Mexico are examples) have a more authoritarian style of communication. Among low power-distance cultures (Israel, Ireland, and Australia are examples), people emphasize and assume equality. They tend to perceive the power others have as appropriate only as it is confined to a given role, whether it be that of teacher, doctor, or government official. And when necessary, they are accustomed to questioning people in power. Power distance is thought of as present to some degree in every culture.

Masculinity–Femininity

As its name makes clear, the masculinity–femininity dimension attempts to draw a parallel with gender. According to this view, so-called *masculine cultures value work, strength, competition, and assertiveness.* Sex roles are also seen as more strictly defined. In general, the emphasis is authoritarian. *Feminine cultures place more value on such traits as "affection, compassion, nurturing, and interpersonal relationships" and tend to be more fluid.* And they give considerable importance to nonverbal communication. In case you are wondering which countries have been described in this way, here is a summary by Dodd (1999):

> The highest masculinity index scores come from Japan, Australia, Venezuela, Switzerland, Mexico, Ireland, Great Britain, and Germany. The countries with the highest feminine scores are Sweden, Norway, the Netherlands, Denmark, Finland, Chile, Portugal, and Thailand. (p. 94)

To many, the masculinity–femininity metaphor seems out of date, and it remains to be seen how useful this distinction will turn out to be. Some researchers suggest that what is being described might be better termed "achievement-nurturance" (p. 94).

Uncertainty Avoidance

How much do you have to know about people to feel comfortable in their presence? Do you have to know anything at all to feel at ease in communicating with a stranger? **Uncertainty avoidance** is *a measure of the extent to which members of a given culture attempt to avoid uncertainty or ambiguity about others.* In cultures ranked as high in uncertainty avoidance (e.g., Belgium, Greece, and Spain), people are more comfortable in situations where there is little ambiguity and a great deal of information. They prefer more rules and predictable behavior and have less tolerance for diversity. Cultures that rank low in uncertainty avoidance (Canada, Jamaica, and the United States, to name a few) are more open to change and diversity. For cultures with low uncertainty avoidance, "what is different, is curious"; for cultures with high uncertainty avoidance, "what is different, is dangerous" (Hofstede, 1991, p. 119). Yet in a country such as the United States that brings together so many cultures, we are bound to see a wide range in the tolerance for uncertainty.

INTERCULTURAL COMMUNICATION: PRINCIPLES AND PROBLEMS

Although modern means of travel and communication have brought us into contact with virtually the whole world, the technical capacity to transmit and receive messages is not, in itself, enough to allow people of vastly different cultures to communicate. Dramatic improvements in the technological means of communication have in many instances outstripped our abilities to communicate effectively with people who have different languages, different beliefs and values, and different expectations of relationships. Repeatedly, interaction between people of different cultures has created far more misunderstanding than understanding.

Of the many principles used by theorists to describe the communication process, several clearly apply to intercultural exchanges. The first is *a shared code system,* which of course will have two aspects—verbal and nonverbal. Sarbaugh (1979) argues that without such a shared system, communication will be impossible. There will be degrees of difference, but the less a code system is shared, the less communication is possible.

Second, *different beliefs and behaviors between communicators establish the basis for different assumptions from which to respond.* In fact, our own beliefs and behaviors influence our perceptions of what other people do. Thus, two people of different cultures can easily attribute different meanings to the same behavior. If this happens, the two behave differently with neither being able to predict the other's response.

A third principle discussed by Sarbaugh with important implications for intercultural communication is *the level of knowing and accepting the beliefs and behaviors of others.* Notice that there are two components: knowledge and acceptance. It isn't so much the knowledge of such differences that creates a problem. It's also the level of your acceptance. For example, writing about a tribe of African hunters called the Ik, anthropologist Colin Turnbull tried to come to terms with his own feelings of repulsion. The Ik, he knew, were uprooted hunters and the violent way they now lived—stealing each other's food, killing, and so on—could be explained by the fact that their entire society had been uprooted. Turnbull knew a great deal about the beliefs and behaviors of the Ik, but he could not accept the people of that culture. As an anthropologist, however, he still brings to his perceptions a certain objectivity—simply in declaring his responses.

The degree to which we judge a culture by our own cultural values and refuse to consider other cultural norms will determine how likely it is that effective communication takes place. At one extreme, we have participants in a transaction who both know and accept the beliefs and behaviors of others; at the other, we have those who neither know nor accept. And in this instance, the probability of a breakdown in communication is extremely high.

Adopting a shared code system, acknowledging differences in beliefs and behaviors, and learning to be tolerant of the beliefs and behaviors of others all contribute to effective communication.

Verbal Messages

Peter Hessler is the Beijing correspondent for *The New Yorker*. An American, he once taught English in China and his students still write to him. When in a letter by one of his former students we read "*I have confidence in myself that one day I will be a VIP, not like toothbrush any more,*" we know that we have come upon a Chinese word whose meaning cannot be translated literally with any ease (2006, p. 49).

Language differences can go much deeper than simple translation ambiguities. Have you ever asked someone to translate a word from another language for you, only to have him say, "Well, it doesn't translate into English exactly, but it means something like . . . "? As we saw in our discussion of the Sapir-Whorf hypothesis in Chapter 3, languages differ more than strict word-for-word translations often indicate because the people who speak the languages have different needs.

In his first year at UCLA, Wen-Shu Lee, a graduate student from Taiwan, recalls adding a Chinese summary to his English notes at the end of class. A student looking over his shoulder remarked, "That's Greek to me!"

> I promptly corrected him: "No, it's Chinese." He was shocked for about one second and then burst into laughter. We spent 20 minutes or so clarifying that "Greek" did not mean "Greek," that "Greek" meant "foreign, difficult, and mysterious stuff," and I finally agreed that my Chinese was "Greek" to him. (Samovar and Porter, 2000, p. 217)

Even when we can manage to translate from one language to another with literal accuracy, the failure to understand idioms or slang creates many misunderstandings. And the deeper meanings of individual words—with their web of rich associations—are often lost because they are rooted in the culture of the language. The English word "love" is often used to describe intense and intimate personal relationships, but Koreans use the word "jung."

Jung is a much broader concept than love. In addition to the affective aspect of love, *jung* comprises the forces of inertia of a relationship . . . *Jung* is unconscious and voluntary . . . [with] four properties: duration, togetherness, warmth, and solidarity. (Lim and Choi, 1996)

Literal translations from one language to another can also create misunderstandings because they do not account for culture-based linguistic styles. The elaborate style used in Arabic with its rhetoric of exaggeration, compliment, and multiple extended metaphors is puzzling to those unfamiliar with it:

An Arab feels compelled to overassert in almost all types of communication because others expect him to. If an Arab says exactly what he means without the expected assertion, other Arabs may still think that he means the opposite. For example, a simple "No" by a guest to a host's request to eat or drink more will not suffice. To convey the meaning that he is actually full, the guest must keep repeating "No" several times coupling it with an oath such as "By God" or "I swear to God." (Cited in Gudykunst and Kim, 1997, p. 204)

You can also get an inkling from this of how an Arab might interpret a single succinct "No" from someone speaking in English.

We can see the importance of language style as well as differences in the values placed on spoken language by looking briefly at The Hispanic Leadership project. Based in Washington D.C., it was intended to aid newly arrived Latino political leaders (Weigl and Reyes, 2001). But one of the stumbling blocks to forming political alliances and rapport between Anglos and Latinos was their contrasting views on the relationship between speech and politics:

The Anglo political style demands constant talk: to clarify a viewpoint, to plan an action, to lobby for an interest, to resolve a dispute, to establish one's authoritative public profile. . . . Within Latino worlds what you *do* is far more important then what you say . . . The constant flow of words, the frequent debate over ideology, the love of verbal analysis—basic features of local as well as national politics in Washington—seemed wasteful, foreign, and self-inflating to Latino leaders in their new U.S. home. (p. 252)

Nonverbal Messages

A recent guidebook on Vietnam, Cambodia, and Laos gives prospective tourists this advice about customs and conduct:

The head is considered pure and sacred in Buddhism; do not touch anyone, including children, on the head. The feet, which come into contact with dust on the street, are lowly; do not point your feet at anyone, or at any Buddhist image. If sitting in a temple either squat or sit with the legs tucked to the side so the soles of the feet point backward. (Buckley, 2006, p. 645)

As for facial expressions,

> An important cultural note: A smile on a Vietnamese face does not necessarily
> indicate amusement—it can also convey anger, fear, embarrassment,
> disagreement. Thus, as you pick up your mangled bicycle from a head-on
> collision with another cyclist, the other party may smile or even manage a
> nervous laugh. (Buckley, 2006, p. 645)

Nonverbal communication systems vary from culture to culture just as verbal
systems do, but often we overlook the symbolic nature of nonverbal communication. Many American travelers abroad have been embarrassed when they discovered that the two-fingered gesture they use to mean "Give me two" is assigned a
different, obscene meaning in many countries. They have also been mistaken when
they assumed that a nod always means yes. In some countries, a nod means "no";
in others a nod, or yes, simply indicates that a person understood the question. In
the United States, the gesture for "okay" is made by forming a circle with the thumb
and forefinger while the other fingers are held up. But in France this gesture means
"you're worthless," and in Greece it's a vulgar sexual invitation.

Confusion in nonverbal indicators may be much more complex. In Chapter 4
we considered some of the different ways that cultures make use of time and space.
As we discussed then, we rely on nonverbal cues to give us information about the
meaning we are to assign to a verbal message. Because we often interpret these nonverbal cues unconsciously, the message received is often very different from the one
the speaker intended. People with disabilities often remark on how often they are
affected by nonverbal behaviors:

> Even when an ablebodied person tries to "say the right thing" and communicate
> verbal acceptance to the person with the disability, the nonverbal behavior may
> communicate rejection and avoidance . . . For example, disabled people often
> report that while an ablebodied person may talk to them, they also stand at a
> greater distance than usual, avoid eye contact, avoid mentioning the disability, or
> cut the conversation short. (Braithwaite and Braithwaite, 2000, p. 139)

Vocal cues can be particularly problematic when communication is between
people from different countries. For example, in the Arab countries, men are expected to speak loudly to indicate strength and sincerity. A Saudi Arab may also
lower his voice to indicate respect to a superior. In an exchange between an American and an Arab, the confusion of signals is likely to be disastrous.

The expression of emotion is also regulated by culture. For example, the French
are often described by visitors as rude or cold, and one reason is that they usually
smile at people only after they've known them rather well:

> . . . to smile at someone you do not know and say "hello" is frequently
> considered provocative, not friendly. On the other hand, to pass a friend on the
> street or bump into family acquaintances without offering conversation would be
> considered rude. (Gannon et al., 2001, p. 71)

There are many cross-cultural studies of attitudes toward the display of emotion. For example, one study (Argyle et al., 1986) found that the Italians and the English allow more expressions of distress and anger than the Japanese. In fact, Japanese children are slower than North American children to identify anger—probably because "Japanese are socialized from an early age to avoid the expression of emotions like anger" (Gudykunst and Ting-Toomey, 1988a, p. 386). And in some cultures the display of emotions is limited to emotions that are "positive" and do not disturb group harmony (p. 396).

One aspect of a shared code system that contributes to the smooth flow of conversation and ultimately to understanding is **synchrony,** *the sharing of rhythms* (Dodd, 1999; Douglis, 1987). Goleman sees synchrony as an aspect of social intelligence:

> Synchrony lets us glide gracefully through a nonverbal dance with another person. The foundation of social facility, it is the bedrock on which other aspects [of social intelligence] build. . . . Getting in synch demands that we both read nonverbal cues instantaneously and act on them smoothly—without having to think about them. (Goleman, 2006, p. 91)

When people speak, they develop a rhythm, a dancelike beat that emphasizes and organizes meaning during conversation—a phenomenon to be observed between family members, friends, and lovers—even business associates. It is during a beat or stress that a speaker will often reveal important information or introduce a new topic into the conversation. It seems that timing in conversation can be affected even by a few microseconds, and speakers who stay in sync not only have better understanding but a better relationship.

This rhythmic pattern is also seen in the nonverbal behavior that accompanies conversation: Speaking patterns are accented by nonverbal gestures and movements that follow the beat. But when you are with someone from a different culture or linguistic background, even your expectations for speech rhythms and nonverbal behaviors may be vastly different. Consciousness about synchrony also seems to vary from culture to culture. Hall (1984) has found people from Northern Europe and North America less aware of such rhythms than people from Asia, Latin America, and Africa.

Relationships: Norms and Roles

Cultures also vary in the contexts in which verbal and nonverbal systems are used. When making friends with a foreign student or working with people abroad in business situations, it is important to remember that personal and working relationships are not the same and do not develop the same way in every culture. People in different cultures expect different behaviors from one another in a relationship. As we've seen, what you consider a friendly gesture might be considered aggressive or impertinent in another culture; your gesture of respect or deference might be interpreted as inappropriate reticence or as defiance, depending on the cultural context.

Norms

Norms, as we discussed in Chapter 9, are *established rules of what is accepted and appropriate behavior.* Although we often use these rules as if they are absolute or instinctive standards, they are actually culturally developed and transmitted. If you grew up in the United States, for instance, you may have been taught to "speak up" clearly and to look at a person who is speaking to you, and that mumbling and looking away when someone addresses you is disrespectful. But not all cultural groups interpret these behaviors as good manners. We have already seen that people in some cultures drop their voices as an indication of respect and deference. White American police officers patrolling Hispanic neighborhoods have often misinterpreted a similar gesture: Hispanic children are taught to lower their eyes, as a gesture of respect, when a person in authority addresses them. The police, who had been brought up with opposite norms, have interpreted the gesture as sullen and resentful, and reacted accordingly.

Understanding norms about conflict becomes particularly important when a disagreement seems to be brewing between two people from different cultures. One study (Ting-Toomey et al., 2000) looked at the conflict styles of acquaintances in each of four ethnic groups within the United States: African Americans, Asian Americans, Latino(a)s, and European Americans. It also studied ethnic identity (how strongly we identify with our own ethnic group) and cultural identity (in this case, how strongly members of a co-culture identified with the larger culture of the United States). Seven patterns or styles of managing conflict were seen: integrating (showing great concern for yourself and for the other person), compromising, dominating, avoiding, neglecting, emotional expression of conflict, and seeking third-party help. Here are some of the findings:

- Both Latino(a)s and Asian Americans use avoiding and seek third-party help more than African Americans do.
- Asian Americans use avoiding more than European Americans.
- African Americans tend to favor an emotionally expressive style.
- African Americans have a stronger ethnic identity and a weaker cultural identity than the other groups; European Americans have a weaker ethnic identity and a stronger cultural identity than the other groups.
- Individuals who have a strong cultural identity use more integrating, compromising, and emotionally expressive style than those who have a weak ethnic identity. (Adapted from pp. 47–48)

At least two important variables distinguish how members of a given culture view interpersonal and family conflicts: (1) expressivity, and (2) privacy and individuality (Sillars and Weisberg, 1987). Even in the United States, there is considerable cultural variation in the amount of emphasis placed on expressive communication about conflict. For example, studies have shown that Jewish families frequently value discussion and analysis so highly that by mainstream standards they may seem argumentative and that Irish families in family therapy dealt with conflicts through allusion, sarcasm, and innuendo rather than engage in verbal confrontations. In each instance, we see a set of assumptions about what constitutes conflict and how it should be negotiated or resolved—or perhaps ignored.

One reason we cannot apply the expressive norms of mainstream culture to other groups is that so many cultures place far less value on individual self-disclosures. Talking about feelings and being open about one's dissatisfactions—even with a member of your family, for example—is not always considered appropriate behavior, and many of the suggestions for resolving conflict mentioned in Chapter 6 would be difficult to apply to intercultural contexts. In fact, in many cultures keeping problems to oneself is strongly favored, and a stoic attitude often develops. For example, in working-class families, problems are frequently regarded as "lying outside the family and within the realm of natural economic, social, and biological conditions that are futile for the family to address. Thus [family members] may adopt a passive problem-solving style that emphasizes family cohesion over active problem solving" (p. 159).

The direct expression of conflict is also considered inappropriate in high-context cultures (see pp. 320–321), which deemphasize explicit verbal coding of information and pay more attention to subtle cues and indirect messages. In such cultures, discretion and indirectness are the norms for dealing with conflict, and they are upheld and understood by members. This is true of the Chinese and Japanese. So while members of low-context cultures might perceive the indirect treatment of conflict as cowardly, those from high-context cultures might perceive a more aggressive or combative response as lacking in taste (Gudykunst and Ting-Toomey, 1988b, p. 160).

Cultural norms about privacy and individuality are equally variable. In the two-person and family relationships of mainstream America, a great deal of autonomy is expected—especially among the middle class. Thus during a conflict, you may consider advice from friends and others outside your immediate family an infringement on your privacy. You might not expect others to intervene. In extended families, however, there is a more public aspect of relationships: "Because extended networks promote communal and traditional norms, there are more definite guidelines for resolving conflicts" (p. 161). There are even times when conflicts are settled not through personal communication but through the intervention of a third party. In Japan this is sometimes the case.

According to Sillars and Weisberg's survey of research (1987), emphasis on cooperation, affiliation, and dependence is stressed by such groups as Africans, Native Americans, Asians, West Indians, Japanese, Mexicans, Mormons, and Catholics. Their norms dictate that some conflicts will be minimized or even solved indirectly for the good of the group. For example, in the tribal meetings of Native Americans or Native Alaskans, it is expected that the individual will put group goals before personal ones and reach consensus (pp. 160–162). Sometimes, the mainstream American ideal of agreeing to disagree becomes "an impractical and even undesirable goal" (p. 162).

Roles

Roles, as we discussed in Chapter 9, are *sets of norms that apply to specific groups of people in a society.* Roles, too, vary markedly among cultures. Differences in the respective roles of men and women may represent some of the most apparent cultural differences in human relationships: how unmarried couples should behave and whether they should be chaperoned, how men and women should behave toward each other in business situations, what a husband's and wife's responsibilities are to one another and to their respective families.

The widowed narrator in Gish Jen's short story "Who's Irish?" (1998) is a Chinese woman who long ago immigrated to the United States. She lives with her daughter, who is the vice president of a bank, her Irish-American husband, and their small feisty daughter Sophie, whom she tries to discipline in the old Chinese way. Daughter and granddaughter object repeatedly and when asked to be "supportive," the grandmother remarks that in China the daughter is supposed to take care of the mother and that here it works the other way: "Mother help daughter, mother ask 'Anything else I can do?' Otherwise daughter complain mother is not supportive. I tell my daughter, we do not have this word in Chinese, supportive" (p. 80). By the end of the story, the grandmother is asked to move (her presence is a source of conflict in her daughter's marriage) and ends up living with her son-in-law's Irish mother.

It's not only parent-child roles that are touched on in "Who's Irish?" but also the difficulties people sometimes face when they marry someone who comes from a very different culture. Interracial marriages have been on the rise for several decades. According to the 2000 Census, in the United States "the percentage rate of mixed-race marriage has increased seven times from 1970 to 2000 and the number of [mixed-race] children has also increased four times" (Mithers, 2006, p. 102).

In interracial relationships it may be the *valued similarities* between the personal and social characteristics of two interracial partners that form the basis for their attraction to one another and that contribute to the rapport and compatibility of the partners (Gaines and Ickes, 2000). Here is part of an e-mail conversation between people on an Internet newsgroup of intercultural couples:

> My wife is Chinese—at this point, any non-Asian woman would seem more "exotic" than another Asian woman—but even a near lookalike for my wife would seem awfully strange. Then again, I'm not after "exotic and strange"—if anything, I find my wife more attractive after [more than 13] years than I did when I first met her. After all this time, racial differences are not what registers when I see her—I see *Alice,* accept no substitutes. (p. 68)
>
> I think my husband and I have much more in common mentally and personality-wise than my co-worker and her spouse. So maybe people . . . are looking for more external similarities such as race, religion, etc. While . . . people [like my husband and me] are more into inner compatibilities, so the externals are not important. (p. 69)

Nonetheless, researchers from several disciplines acknowledge that a dual-culture marriage is different from a marriage in which both partners share a common culture. The two cultures they come from may have very different definitions of marital roles. And there are also cultural differences in decision-making power and self-disclosure patterns; for example, there is generally less use of self-disclosure among northern Europeans than among people from Mediterranean cultures. "Perhaps," writes Rohrlich, "what is lacking is a set of Johari windows . . . which graphically depict the amount of open, blind, hidden and unknown areas of disclosure representative of cultures" (1988, p. 41). The author stresses that to marry someone from another culture is, in effect, marrying that culture. When one spouse fails to communicate interest or assumes that the other is not attached to his or her culture, there may be serious problems. In this view, an awareness of cultural differences must precede the development of appreciation and sensitivity: "The cultural difference is what makes the fabric of the marriage more varied, interesting, and richer" (p. 42).

Beliefs and Values

Even if you've never traveled outside the United States, you have heard stories about how U.S. politicians and presidents have inadvertently insulted Polish or Latin American audiences when trying to speak to their audiences in unfamiliar languages. Movies and television programs provide a glimpse of many ways of life, including the roles and norms of Hawaiian American, Asian, Native American, and numerous other cultures. Although the portrayals are not always accurate, they help to give us a sense of some cultural differences.

It is much more difficult to comprehend and accept the values of another culture when they differ from our own. More than any other aspect of the culture taught us from birth, our values seem to us to be universal absolutes. Values determine what we think is right, good, important, beautiful; we find it difficult to accept that what is right or good is as relative to culture as the word for "book" or "stove," or as the way our food is prepared or our clothes are made. (See Box 10.1.) It may be difficult for a Westerner to adjust to the combinations or seasonings of unfamiliar Middle Eastern or Asian cuisine. It is even more difficult to accept that some cultures eat plants or animals that we do not classify as food or to understand why, in the face of mass starvation in India, cattle wander the streets unrestrained, protected by religious taboos. People of other cultures, meanwhile, may be appalled by the willingness of people in this country to eat meat, or at the casualness with which we often have meals "on the run," without ceremony.

Ethical Values

In Chapter 7 we discussed the work of two scholars who proposed that there is a single universal principle, or **protonorm**, that underpins all systematic ethics: *the sacredness of life* (Christians and Nordenstreng, 2004). They believe it relates to at least three basic ethical principles, or "master norms": respect for human dignity, truthtelling, and nonviolence. These **master norms,** sometimes called "core values," were identified in an earlier study of ethical norms in thirteen countries across five continents. Each norm takes different forms in different countries (Christians and Traber, 1997). We consider the three briefly here.

Physical beauty seems to be valued in all cultures, and within a given culture people tend to agree on those who are physically attractive. As we saw in Chapter 2, some researchers believe that there may even be certain universal standards for beauty. (Guerrero and Floyd, 2006) In this country people who are perceived as physically attractive are also seen as socially desirable; and often the traits linked with attractive people are extraversion and dominance—both traits that our individualist culture values highly. On the other hand, research finds that in collectivist cultures—for example, Indonesia, China, and Japan—physical attractiveness is often linked with intelligence and integrity, two highly valued traits in societies that emphasize interdependence and cooperative rather than competitive behavior.

When it comes to ourselves, what qualities do we value? In one cross-cultural study, U.S. and Japanese university students were asked to identify three aspects of themselves that they would most like to change. Researchers found that more American than Japanese students opted for changes in their physical appearance, while more Japanese students were interested in changing "aspects of self pertaining to interpersonal harmony . . . American students . . . mentioned individualistic aspects of self as needing change (e.g., 'want to get more of what I deserve,' 'need to rely less on others for my happiness') more often than Japanese students" (Dion, 2002, p. 254).

Which traits do you most value and which do you link with physical attractiveness? What three aspects of yourself would you most like to change?

Respect for human dignity: This first master norm is closely linked with the acknowledgement that all life is sacred:

Native American discourse is steeped in reverence for life, an interconnectedness among all living forms . . . In communalistic African societies, *likute* is loyalty to the community's reputation, to tribal honor . . . In Islam, every person has the right to honor and a good reputation. (Christians and Nordenstreng, 2004, p. 21)

Truthtelling: Like the first, the second ethical principle is acknowledged in every culture:

The most fundamental norm of Arab-Islamic communication is truthfulness. Truth is one of the three highest values in . . . the Latin American experience of communication. In Hinduism, truth is the highest *dharma* [law] and the source of all other virtues. Among the Sushwap of Canada, truth as genuineness and authenticity is central to its indigenous culture . . . Living with others is inconceivable if we cannot tacitly assume that people are speaking truthfully. (p. 22)

Nonviolence: This third principle might be expressed as compassion, willingness to forgive, and an appeal that no harm should be done to the innocent:

Gandhi and Martin Luther King Jr. developed this principle beyond a political strategy into a philosophy of life. . . . In communalistic and indigenous cultures,

Figure 10.2 *State of the World Forum Values*

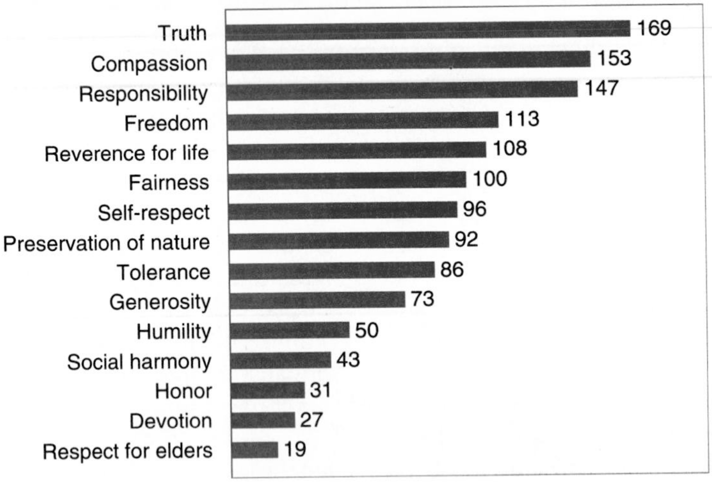

Source: From *Moral Courage*, by Rushworth M. Kidder, Figs. 2 (p. 51) and 7 (p. 73). Copyright © 2004 by Rushworth M. Kidder. Reprinted by permission of HarperCollins Publishers.

care for the weak and vulnerable (children, sick, and elderly) and sharing material resources are a matter of course. Along with *dharma, ahimsa* (nonviolence) forms the basis of the Hindu worldview. (p. 23)

In one survey of 55 possible ethical values, people from 40 countries and 50 different faith groups were asked to select the five values that were most important in their daily lives (Kidder, 2005). Their responses are summarized in Figure 10.2. Notice that truth heads the list. Which five ethical values are most important to you?

Adaptations to a New Culture

One question that has been raised is how well different groups adapt to living in another culture or country, an issue that is particularly relevant in the light of recent mass migrations and diasporas. Cross-cultural research suggests that sometimes a culture's system of beliefs and values can improve the group's ability to live in another country. A recent study of Tibetan refugees who resettled in India (de Vos, 2004) finds that they have been particularly successful in adjusting to their new environment and have made many economic and social gains. Although Tibetans in India lived within a largely Hindu culture, "they were able to educate their youth in Tibetan language, art and letters, customs, and religion. Theirs has been a very successful story of cultural conservation . . . " (p. 438).

De Vos maintains that the beliefs and values of Tibetans have given them strength, resilience, and a sense of acceptance. Values such as achievement, responsibility to and for others, and compassionate "giving and helping for the benefit of the family, community or nation" have helped to create harmony and happiness despite hardship. This confirms earlier studies. Most important, it seems, was the sense of community engendered by Tibetan religious beliefs:

> Mayahana Buddhism provides the Tibetans not only with a design for living but also with a rather positive, industrious, pragmatic, and balanced view of life . . .
>   [For the Tibetans] actions promote life affirmation based on the good deeds performed by the individual and the community. The Tibetan Buddhism worldview promotes a "can do" attitude with a healthy dose of cheerfulness. (Mahmoudi, 1992, p. 23)

Mahmoudi believes that Tibetans can provide a model for other international refugee populations.

TOWARD GREATER INTERCULTURAL UNDERSTANDING AND TOLERANCE

There is probably no more eloquent essay on what it feels like to be seen as someone *other*—someone outside society—than "Stranger in the Village" (1985) by the American writer James Baldwin, who came to stay in a village in Switzerland during the 1950s where no one had ever seen a black person before. Today, despite great technological advances and more exposure to people of other cultures, divisions between people of different cultures at times seem to have only intensified. This is true not only for people from different countries but sometimes for those who live within a single culturally diverse country such as the United States.

    In the following pages we examine some of the processes that cloud our perceptions of others, making strangers out of human beings, and then consider efforts to further greater cultural understanding and tolerance.

Ethnocentrism

Culture is like a pair of sunglasses. It shields us from external harshness and offers us some measure of safety and comfort. It also blocks us from seeing clearly through our tinted lenses because of the same protectiveness. In brief, culture nurtures our ethnocentric attitudes and behaviors.

— Ting-Toomey (1999, p. 14)

Ethnocentrism is *the tendency to judge the values, customs, behaviors, or other aspects of another culture in terms of those that our own cultural group regards as desirable or ideal.* Literally, "ethnocentrism" refers to putting one's "nation" at the center—the word is Greek in origin and derives from *ethnos* ("nation") and *kentron* ("center"). We tend to be ethnocentric about our own country, our own region, or our own ethnic group, regarding it as the best and most important—whether it is about our music, food, art, or political system. The concept of ethnocentrism is not always negative. For example, when members of a group are being attacked or threatened ethnocentrism "forms the basis for patriotism and the willingness to sacrifice for one's central group" (Neuliep and McCroskey, 1997a).

In many of our interactions, our ethnocentric attitudes interfere with our perceptions of other cultural groups. A recent study of in-group favoritism (Hammond and Axelrod, 2006) finds that ethnocentric behaviors are extremely widespread and that we are predisposed to favor in-groups. Our membership in the group fosters higher levels of cooperation, even when that cooperation has negative consequences for us: "preferential cooperation within groups occurs even when it is individually costly" (p. 926). And our ethnocentrism can also foster anxiety about members of other cultures. For example, U.S. students who rated high in ethnocentrism tended to have a higher level of anxiety about other cultural groups when they were visiting foreign countries (Stephan and Stephan, 1992).

Ethnocentrism seems to be characteristic of every culture. Yet part of the recent Pew Global Attitudes Project (*www.people-press.org*) reports that although people worldwide take pride in their own culture

> it is only in the West (North America and Western Europe) where that pride is markedly stronger among the older generations, while younger people tend to be less wedded to their cultural identities.
>
> In the U.S., 68% of those ages 65 and older agree with the statement "our people are not perfect, but our culture is superior," while only 49% of those ages 18–29 agree.

This trend seems to be true of Western Europe, but Eastern European people of all ages are "more likely to say their culture is superior." In Asia, Africa, and Latin America ethnocentric feelings seem to be uniformly stronger, with little or no generation gap (except for Japan). Perhaps you've received the "compliment" that you are not like other Americans—ethnocentric attitudes can be deeply divisive and even impede negotiations between members of different cultures.

To illustrate how pervasive ethnocentrism is, one writer refers to the maps in schoolrooms around the world. For example, on the world map that appears in many classrooms throughout this country the center of its east-west axis is the United States, which means that the Eurasian landmass is split and distorted on either side. Classroom maps from other countries are equally revealing, placing their own culture at the world's center—with all the distortions that might require. "Maps become problematic," writes Blair, "when students (and adults) forget that they are maps and start believing in the worlds they represent. The same is true of cultures: One's own culture will likely seem universal until one finds a way of stepping outside its cloaking devices at least provisionally. As an old Chinese proverb has it: the fish does not discover water" (Blair, 2000, p. 25).

But is it possible to remove the "tinted lenses" of our own culture? Blair believes that to do this we must acknowledge two principles: (1) Ethnocentrism appears to be universal; and (2) "ethnocentrisms have, in principle, an equal claim on legitimacy" (p. 32). Although we may not find these "equally attractive or admirable" (p. 32), we have to find ways of going beyond them and becoming increasingly sophisticated in our awareness of other cultures—remembering perhaps that there are alternative maps of the world, many perceptions of the same experience.

> The most promising move we can make to counter the traps that cultures set for us, lies not in seeking to get beyond culture altogether, but by changing our attitude toward whatever culture has been primary for us. Once we recognize that our own enculturation is neither universal nor authoritative for others, we can recognize it for what it is: OUR culture, one among OTHERS. [This] frees us to engage in cultural comparisons, in dialogue with OTHERS. (Blair, 2000, p. 32)

Because the Internet has become a source of increasing knowledge about the world some scholars suggest the possibility that "international news could cultivate a broad worldview, as reading international news in national and regional newspapers was found to be negatively related to ethnocentrism" (Kwak et al., 2006, pp. 192–193).

Stereotyping

As we saw in Chapter 2, we tend to impose stereotypes on groups of people, which limits our communication with those groups. It is almost impossible for us not to stereotype a group of people with whom we have no personal contact; furthermore, without personal contact, it is almost impossible for us to dispel the stereotypes we acquire about the group. We saw that stereotypes are inadequate because they are generalizations based on limited experience. Certainly, the sources of our information about people of different cultures are often inaccurate.

One recent series of studies explored how stereotypes guide **defensive projection**—that is, *seeing our own undesirable qualities in other people.* This is particularly the case when a person's self-concept is threatened in some way. In other words, our perceptions of self play a role in how much we stereotype others. Researchers also found that people who were stereotyped "are more likely to serve as targets of projection than are nonstereotyped individuals" (Govorun et al., 2006, p. 781).

Numerous cross-cultural studies identify the mass media, particularly television, as a major source of information about other cultures. Many scholars have called attention to how damaging stereotyped images can be. An example is the portrayal of Arabs, both in films and on television, as villains. This stereotyping predates 9/11, with such controversial films as *The Siege* and *Rules of Engagement*. One critic points out that since 9/11 there has been a "steady portrayal of the Arab as villain . . . CBS series, including *JAG, The District, The Agency* and *Family Law,* have represented Arabs as deceitful, brutish, lunatic terrorists and murderers . . ." (Ross, 2003, p.60). All minority cultures are greatly concerned over media representations and distortions and the stereotypes that such images create.

An implicit linguistic intergroup bias (LIB) in response to crime reporting is the subject of a recent study. Gorham (2006) looked at how people viewing a crime suspect on a television news program described him—that is, whether their choice of language was more abstract or concrete. When the suspect was African American, white adults were more likely to describe the suspect by using more abstract language;

when describing a white suspect, they used more concrete descriptive terms. The data suggest that we use language that is more abstract than concrete in describing behaviors linked with stereotypes, especially if we are describing someone who is a member of an out-group (p. 289).

Gorham (2006) emphasizes that our choice of abstract or concrete language is not a conscious one. Rather it sometimes stems from an underlying bias, "an implicit and unobtrusive way that language can reflect the dominant ideology of the race" (p. 305).

In another study of crime reporting, this one of local television news in Los Angeles and Orange County, researchers looked at how African Americans, Latinos, and whites are represented and found that

- African Americans and Latinos are significantly more likely than whites to be portrayed as lawbreakers.
- African Americans are overrepresented as lawbreakers.
- African Americans and Latinos are more likely to be portrayed as lawbreakers than as defenders; whites are significantly more likely to be portrayed as defenders than as lawbreakers. (Dixon and Linz, 2000; adapted from p. 131)

In a study of local television news coverage of members of Congress (Schaffner and Gadson, 2004), African American and nonblack members were compared. African Americans received more local coverage, but it was more race-oriented, focusing on minority issues. This was true regardless of how legislators voted. Researchers found that among African Americans in Congress, "even if their legislative record is balanced, their media coverage may not be" (p. 607):

> White voters assume that African American candidates, once elected, will pursue policies that exclusively benefit African Americans . . . Because of this prevailing view of African American incumbents, white citizens may feel that such a candidate cannot adequately represent them in Congress. (p. 606)

The mainstream bias toward African Americans is confirmed in many studies. One writer points out that today a considerable amount of racial stereotyping is nonverbal and is conveyed through "visual messages, without any explicit or overt reference to race" (Abraham, 2003, p. 90):

> A number of scholars have noted how news stories make implicit links between blacks and negative thematic concepts such as violent crime, poverty, prisons, drug-addicted babies, AIDS victims, and welfare by predominantly juxtaposing or illustrating stories with images of African Americans. (p. 91).

A new study on racial stereotyping in comedy notes the increasing number of comedies—including *I Spy, Shanghai Knights,* and *Harold and Kumar Go to White*

Castle—in which the leading men are Asian and/or African American (Park et al., 2006, p. 157). Subjects in the study watched the film *Rush Hour 2*, starring Jackie Chan and Chris Tucker as policemen in pursuit of Asian gang members involved in a counterfeiting scheme. The subjects in the study were Asian, African American, and white college students. Most were not offended by the many racial jokes—not even jokes about their own race. In the words of Justin, an 18-year-old Asian male:

> Chris Tucker and Jackie Chan complement each other. Obviously Jackie Chan is better in fighting and stuff. But Chris Tucker is better at talking and everything. So they kind of cancel each other out. They are a good combo. But I think with a White person and an Asian person, it always feels like the White person is better than the Asian person (p. 170).

The researchers note the film's sense of equality and friendship between Chan and Tucker's characters. They argue that the conventions of comedy "encourage the audience to naturalize racial difference rather than to challenge racial stereotypes"; "viewers' validation of racial stereotypes is the ideological effect of comedy that encourages them to perceive racial differences as essential and natural, not culturally constructed" (pp. 157, 174). Further research is needed to test whether the effects of racial stereotyping in comedy may be different from other kinds of programming.

There is a disturbing trend of racial stereotyping in some video games. An increasingly popular source of entertainment for young people, many of these games feature black or Hispanic male characters who are fighting—"for example, images of black youths committing and reveling in violent street crimes" (Marriott, 2004, G1). Critics worry about the effects on all children, but particularly on the self-image of minority children. (See Chapter 15 for more on video games.)

One thing we can do to overcome the effects of stereotyping is to be critical and analytic with respect to viewing mass media. See Box 10.2 for some suggestions about promoting an analytical view of film and television programs.

Theorists emphasize that in addition to creating expectations about how people will behave, stereotypes often set in motion self-fulfilling prophecies because we act on information we believe to be true. This is especially the case in intercultural communication, where our information about others tends to be so limited and the potential for interracial and interethnic conflict is immense.

Such conflicts still constitute one of our most urgent social problems. And in this country with its growing population of new immigrants, we see conflicts not only between members of mainstream and minority cultures but between one "minority" and another. For example, in the Los Angeles riots in 1992 following the Rodney King verdict, the confrontation between African and Korean Americans was fierce.

Nor are such problems about to go away. Claims by various groups for limited community resources, competition for jobs, concerns with being underrepresented in educational institutions and government, and many other factors fuel the conflicts that surface not only on the streets but in schools and colleges.

ISSUES IN COMMUNICATION

Some Guidelines for Critical Viewers of Film and Television

In her study of stereotyping, *Latin Looks: Images of Latinos and Latinas in the U.S. Media*, Clara Rodriguez suggests some guidelines for critical viewers of film and television. Here are some questions to ask yourself when watching a film or television drama. Remember, these questions are relevant for all cultural groups:

1. Who is telling this story?

2. Given the perspective of the camera, which characters does the director want us to follow? With whom do you identify? Why?

3. Can you imagine the world of the film as seen by characters who are denied a point of view in this film? Can you develop an alternative scenario around the point(s) of view of characters who function as peripheral, almost invisible, reactors to the central characters, for example, butlers, maids, waitresses, bartenders, cab drivers, and anonymous victims?

4. Where else could the camera go?

5. Who else could tell us stories?

6. What stories have not been told yet?

7. Can you provide a socioeconomic profile of the typical hero in coming-of-age films? . . . Have you observed other types of people in other situations come of age in the United States? Have you seen their stories in movies?

8. How are the answers to these questions related to who the directors, writers, producers are? to the tenor of the times? to the audience with the most money to spend? (Rodriguez, 1997, p. 240)

Source: From *Latin Looks: Images of Latinas and Latinos in the U.S. Media* by Clara Rodriguez. Copyright 1997 by Westview Press, a division of Perseus Books, L.L.C. Reprinted by permission of Westview Press, a member of Perseus Books, L.L.C.

How do members of different racial and ethnic groups react when they live with each other? In a study of intercultural contact between groups (Halualani et al., 2004), researchers chose a multicultural university in the western United States that had a commuter campus. The four groups studied were "Blacks/African Americans, Whites/European Americans, Asian Americans, and Latino/as." Despite the claims of the majority of students—70 percent of those studied said they appreciated the diversity on campus and that they participated in intercultural interactions—"student intercultural contact did not take place in community life or private homes" (p. 284). This study reflects the tendency toward insularity and ethnic enclaves in the United States.

Metamorphosis, a research project of the Annenberg School for Communication, studied fear and misperception in seven ethnic residential communities of Los Angeles (Matei et al., 2001). These researchers found that in urban areas, people's mental images of fear are influenced not so much by the likelihood that they will become victims of crimes but by communication processes and stereotyping based on ethnicity.

Hate crimes are still part of the American landscape. For example, in 1998, three white men in Jasper, Texas, brutally murdered James Byrd Jr. because he was

African American. In the same year Matthew Shepard, a 21-year-old student at the University of Wyoming, was murdered because he was gay. In fact, according to the Southern Poverty Law Center, "every day a hate crime occurs on a college campus," and "every year at least 500,000 college students are targets of bias-driven slurs or physical assaults" (2004, p. 1). In response the Center has created a guidebook for college students on counteracting hate crimes and on-campus bias: *10 Ways to Fight Hate on Campus* (see *www.tolerance.org/campus*).

Following the hijacking attacks of September 11, 2001, Arab Americans became the targets of bias crimes across the country. One source reported that between September 11 and October 2, 2001, there were over 700 reported bias crimes against Arab Americans and others including Hindus and Sikhs, who are neither Arab nor Muslim. Like the Japanese Americans in the film *Snow Falling on Cedars*, they have sometimes been seen as mysterious outsiders.

Many in the United States know little about Arab culture. Nor is there much understanding of the religion of Islam, which is not the religion of all Arabs. In some communities in the United States, fear and ignorance have turned anyone with darker skin into a focus of mistrust and anger. Sikhs have been singled out because they have beards and wear turbans (both mandated by their own religion). Several writers have pointed out that in the United States even before the events of 9/11 the turban had become a symbol for terrorism. Following 9/11, many Arab Americans lost their jobs. One Arab American who had lived in Dearborn, Michigan, all his life said:

> I don't want my kids to live the life I've had to lead, always apologizing for who I am. I can be either American or I can be an Arab, but I can't be both. You know what? I am both. (Wilgoren, 2001, p. B1)

Similarly, a young college student who had immigrated from Dar-es-Salaam, Tanzania, and described herself as a "hyphenated American" (American-Muslim), was harassed as she walked down a New York street:

> As I walked along Broadway, my headscarf was an open sign to anyone who wanted to let their frustrations out . . . by cursing, giving me dirty looks, and . . . walking into me . . . I guess one couldn't tell that my scarf was not woven with hatred for this country and it doesn't represent a defunct interpretation of Islam as a militant, bloodthirsty religion that the media often portrays it to be. And finally, I guess one couldn't tell that I, and the majority of the world's Muslims, are not responsible. (Mambani, 2001, p. 14)

In an atmosphere shadowed by fear and suspicion, and often based on lack of knowledge about members of other cultural groups, it seems important to recall two ways in which we can improve person perception: awareness that our perceptions can be inaccurate and empathy, sensitivity, or responsiveness (see pp. 65–66). And in educating ourselves about other cultures, the Internet is sometimes a valuable resource. For example, the American-Arab Anti-Discrimination Committee has a Web site that offers information about Arab American culture (see *www.adc.org*). More broad-based Web sites such as *www.tolerance.org* explore the nature of prejudice and ways to foster tolerance.

Group Polarization

A third process that can interfere with the accurate perception of others is group polarization. The Internet, with its tremendous promise for sustaining and even creating relationships between people of many cultures and co-cultures, is a source of cultural information. Yet it can also be a dangerous source of misinformation and negative stereotyping (Tolchin and Tolchin, 2006). In Chapter 7 we discussed the dangers of online bigotry and the many Web-based hate sites that now exist. Run by extremist organizations and hate groups, these sites target groups as diverse as African Americans, gays, Jews, Muslims, women, and "foreigners." Not only do they foster false information about groups of people, they often advocate violence against them.

Take a close look at Table 10.2. What you'll see is a sampling of hate sites on the Net, and the links each has to Web sites with like-minded and opposing views.

Table 10.2 *Web Links among "Hate Sites"*		
Site	**Links to Like-Minded Sites**	**Links to Opposition**
Adelaide Institute (holocaust revisionism)	16	6
Aggressive Christianity	0	0
All Men Must Die	5	0
Altar of Unholy Blasphemy	11	0
Aryan Nations	28	0
Crosstar (nationalistic)	29	0
David Duke Online	11	0
God Hates Fags	7	3
Islam Monitor	0	12
KKK.com	72	0
Martin Luther King, Jr. (revisionist view of King)	0	0
Misogyny Unlimited	92	1
National Association for the Advancement of White People	0	0
Skinheads of the Racial Holy War	100	0
Stormfront (white nationalism)	60	5
Voice of Freedom (antisemitic)	27	5
Vote for USA (antisemitic)	17	0
White Aryan Resistance	0	0
World Church of the Creator	11	0
Total (19)	14 with; 5 without	6 with; 13 without

Source: Sunstein, Cass R., *Republic.com*. Copyright 2001 by Princeton University Press. Reprinted by permission of Princeton University Press.

For example, Skinheads of the Racial Holy War is linked to 100 like-minded Web sites, but has no links to Web sites that oppose its views. What's particularly disturbing about this pattern is it can contribute to the formation of damaging stereotypes and then reinforce them even more strongly by connecting people with other representations of the same beliefs.

The pattern is part of a phenomenon called **group polarization**—that is, *"After deliberation, people are more likely to move toward a more extreme point in the direction to which the group's members were originally inclined"* (Sunstein, 2001, p. 65). For example, think of the ramifications for those who participate in the chatrooms of such sites. Each visit to a site can confirm you in your attitudes, however negative, and open up other sources of information that support your own. Many have argued, as has Cass Sunstein of the University of Chicago Law School, that the new technologies enable us to hear the views of those who agree with us and to isolate ourselves from opposing views. "For this reason alone," he writes, "they are a breeding ground for polarization, and potentially dangerous for both democracy and social peace" (p. 67). Paradoxically, the new technologies also have the potential for being more democratic in transmitting ideas and enabling group initiatives that bring people together.

Promoting Greater Tolerance and Harmony

The novel *Bel Canto* by Ann Patchett (2005) is set in an unnamed South American country. On an evening intended to celebrate the birthday of its vice president at his home, the guests, invited from all over the world, are mistakenly kidnapped by terrorists and held hostage over many days. Slowly these people, who did not know one another, come to forge a bond that goes far beyond national and linguistic boundaries. For all assembled it is an experience that changes their lives. This is a fable about what happens when people of many cultures are forced into sustained contact with one another.

Many studies have explored the effects of contact between members of different racial and ethnic groups. One important question is what, if anything, we gain from interacting with members of other cultures—does more interaction, increased communication contribute to greater rapport? *Intergroup contact theory,* proposed by Gordon Allport (1954) to explain racial and ethnic dynamics, holds that four conditions are needed for intergroup contact to be optimal—equal status between the groups, authority support, shared goals, and intergroup cooperation—so that contact between groups, if they were not competing with each other, would result in a decrease in prejudice.

The social psychologist Thomas Pettigrew later suggested that for ideal contact a fifth condition is necessary: friendship. He emphasizes the components of feeling and familiarity—that when we get to know individual people and more about their lives over a sustained period of time and when we are emotionally involved, prejudice declines and rapport increases. Pettigrew and Tropp (2006) recently examined over 500 different studies of the contact hypothesis. Their meta-analysis confirms that "intergroup contact typically reduces intergroup prejudice," and they believe that the findings can be extended to other large groups and contexts (p. 752).

Recent research on partisan social groups also finds that when we are partisan we have more misperceptions of disagreement and often overemphasize our differences of opinion with those of rival groups (out-groups) (Chambers et al., 2006; Chambers and Melnyk, 2006). And when we overemphasize disagreement with our own values, our perceptions alter how we evaluate out-group members; we tend to dislike them more, attribute negative stereotypes to them, and favor our own group more (pp. 1295, 1307). The stumbling block is our belief, sometimes unfounded, that our rivals are contesting the ideals and values we cherish most.

Several scholars are extending the study of intergroup relations. They are concerned not only with ways of reducing prejudice but with identifying variables that promote social inclusion. Nagda and others (2006) are investigating communication processes as a new dimension of intergroup contact and education. They observe that "people often long to talk about race, but may not know how to do so" (p. 557). The greater the amount of intergroup dialogue—"speaking, listening, and asking questions"—the more engaged and positive participants become. The most important variables are (1) appreciating difference, (2) engaging the self, (3) critical self-reflection, and (4) alliance building (p. 553).

In the arts an unusual example of alliance building is seen in the West-Eastern Divan Orchestra, formed by the Israeli musician and conductor Daniel Barenboim. His orchestra brings together young Arab and Jewish musicians. They have performed in many countries throughout the world including Palestine, Spain, Germany, and the United States, and their ongoing project has been described as "a symbol of hope in troubled times."

On a more practical level, there are ongoing efforts to foster understanding. For example, one reporter created a television series to explore race relations. A group of 10 strangers—5 were black, 5 were white—was sequestered and lived together for over a week, and each night they were given topics to discuss the following day. The result was a "very intense, honest, and at times politically incorrect exchange about people, stereotypes, and the reality of daily life" ("Experiment in Black and White," 2004, p. 2). Now this series is used throughout the United States to teach conflict resolution in churches, schools, and universities as well as in the workplace.

Other efforts to promote understanding and tolerance include the study circles, held in many counties and cities, in which people can speak in depth about race relations and compare experiences. In small diverse groups, participants speak from personal experience about why racial and ethnic prejudice exist and how to change such attitudes. Most important, study circles often form action groups. Group initiatives include classroom forums and advocacy for greater media coverage of minority issues as well as greater legislative representation and media ownership by minorities.

Responding to an editorial by Harvard sociologist Orlando Patterson, letters to the editor of the *New York Times* recently took up the question of living with others in a diverse society. The headline above these letters was, "Is It Who We Are, or How We Act?" Patterson (2006) proposes that it's how we act toward others, not personal concern about authenticity, that matters most:

> I couldn't care less whether my neighbors and co-workers are authentically sexist, racist or ageist. What matters is that they behave with civility and tolerance, obey the rules of social interaction and are sincere about it. The criteria of sincerity are

unambiguous: Will they keep their promises? Will they honor the meanings and understandings we tacitly negotiate? Are their gestures of cordiality offered in conscious good faith? (p. A35)

The public or looking-glass self, he argues, is "fashioned in interaction with others and by the roles we play":

This allows for change. Sincerity rests in reconciling our performance of tolerance with the people we become. And what it means for us today is that the best way of living in our diverse and contentiously free society is neither to obsess about the hidden depths of our prejudices nor to deny them, but to behave as if we had none. (p. A35)

In *Cosmopolitanism: Ethics in a World of Strangers,* Kwame Anthony Appiah, a philosopher at Princeton, argues that cultural differences are overemphasized, their significance overstated. The term *cosmopolitan,* or "citizen of the world," links back to Greek philosophers in the fourth century B.C. **Cosmopolitanism,** the approach Appiah proposes, *has two interwoven strands: The first is our obligation to others, "the recognition of our responsibility for every human being." The second is our "recognition that human beings are different and that we can learn from each other's differences."* The ideals of his philosophy are "universal concern and respect for legitimate difference"(2006, pp. 4, 7–8).

Appiah, who grew up in Ghana and has lived on three continents, believes there are ways in which we can live in harmony with others while acknowledging that differences exist and that we may not and should not expect to always persuade others of our own beliefs and values. What we do need is ongoing conversation, both in the sense of simply living, associating with one another and of genuine exchange:

Conversations across boundaries of identity—whether national, religious, or anything else—begin with the sort of imaginative engagement you get when you read a novel or watch a movie or attend to a work of art that speaks from some place other than your own. So I'm using the word "conversation" not only for literal talk but also as a metaphor for engagement with the experience and ideas of others. . . . Conversation doesn't have to lead to consensus about anything, especially not values; it's enough that it helps people get used to one another. (p. 85)

EFFECTS OF INTERCULTURAL COMMUNICATION

Effects on the Individual

Travel is easier and more affordable than it was for our parents and grandparents. Yet even within our own country we tend to stay within our own groups and subgroups. The needs and desires of many groups to affirm and preserve their cultures are reflected in demands for more bilingual education, multicultural programs and curriculums, and textbooks that better represent all cultural contributions to our literature and history. Among the swelling immigrant population in the largest cities of the United States we find ethnic groups clustering in their own neighborhoods. Take New York's "Little Bombay," for example, a densely packed area with rows of stores stocking Indian spices, saris, videos, newspapers—every imaginable evidence of this thriving culture.

For anyone who reads books and newspapers, who watches television, or gets news from the Internet and is concerned with international events, the world has grown larger. The mass media have brought us images of the war in Iraq, genocide in Darfur, bombings in London and Madrid, conflicts between Israelis and Palestinians, and the devastating tsunami in Southeast Asia as well as other natural disasters worldwide. We can no longer escape knowledge of terrorist acts or world hunger or turn away from the impact of international events.

Although it is often assumed that international understanding increases as a result of cultural and educational exchanges over an extended period of time, scholars believe that this hoped-for goal must be demonstrated empirically. Thus, there have been several studies of student exchange programs. For example, Rohrlich and Martin (1991) studied the adjustment of U.S. college students to studying abroad and found women to be more satisfied than men upon returning, perhaps because their lifestyle at home was more independent than when living with a host family. Carlson and Widaman (1988) compared students from the University of California who spent their junior year studying at a European university with students who remained on campus. At the end of the school year, the study-abroad group had higher levels of cross-cultural interest, international political concern, and cultural cosmopolitanism, as well as significantly more positive and more critical attitudes toward their own country (p. 14). So relatively long-term study abroad may contribute to more favorable attitudes and increased international understanding, but there is still much to be learned about how such attitudes develop.

Social and Political Effects

We are no longer limited to being members of our own small community; we are citizens of the world as well, affected by political, economic, and social changes.

Communications, banking, and manufacturing have become international. Companies that deal in many commodities usually have offices, factories, and distributors all over the world. They also have Web sites. As a result, the economies of the world's nations have become more and more intertwined, and the goods available in nations that trade freely are drawn from the world at large. In this country outsourcing of jobs has resulted in reverse migrations among members of some cultures—for example, some highly skilled professionals have returned to India to work and live, train others, and contribute their expertise to developing communities. Multinational manufacturing efforts and consortiums involving goods and services of every kind have been formed. Airbus Industrie, for example, is a consortium made up of the English, the French, the Germans, the Spanish, and the Dutch. That joint venture has suppliers in 27 countries including the United States and gives on-site support in 50 countries.

Not all implications of an international economy are positive, however. Concerns about oil reserves are affected by political actions. Terrorist attacks have had profound effects on business, travel, and tourism. And economic problems in many areas of the world have resulted in racial and ethnic conflict, for example, in England and Germany.

Yet our interdependence is clear. The United Nations is far more than a forum for political debate. Like many other international organizations, its agencies deal actively with "the mechanics of living," such as the needs for food, health care, and education in many countries. The humanitarian organization Doctors without Borders, awarded a Nobel Peace Prize, provides long-term and emergency medical assistance to distressed populations throughout the world. Many other organizations also work on behalf of international refugees who, according to U.N. statistics, number between 15 million and 20 million. Some international organizations help to increase productivity and raise standards of living by providing such services as literacy training, education in modern agricultural methods, and help in turning local craft production into profitable cottage industries.

Cultural Effects

Most people would not question the value of introducing sanitation methods that curb epidemics, or life-saving vaccines and medications, or agricultural methods that save thousands from starvation. But many, including a number of scholars of culture, question the value of other aspects of cultural exchange. They ask whether aboriginal communities that have been isolated for hundreds of years truly benefit from sudden contact with the outside world—whether, for example, exposure to war as well as sources of illness and pollution might outweigh what we consider the advances of civilization. The possibilities raise many ethical questions.

Some have argued that intercultural exchange leads to **cultural homogenization,** *the tendency for cultures in contact with one another to become increasingly similar to one another.* The belief the world is becoming more and more homogeneous implies that some aspects of one culture will dominate and eliminate the corresponding aspects of the other.

But to many scholars such a view of cultural influence seems simplistic. Even if we are familiar with foods from all over the world and blue jeans are as popular in Russia as in the United States, even if Shanghai has its Starbucks and McDonald's, each culture tends to modify and adapt what it receives from another. McDonald's in India serves Maharaja Macs and veggie burgers. "Local and regional ways of thinking and living do not disappear in the face of imported cultural influences," writes James Lull (2000, p. 234):

> What many contemporary observers conclude is that the global circulation of images, ideologies, and cultural styles—facilitated by the multinational culture and communications industries—actually fuels symbolic creativity, lessens homogeneity, and increases cultural diversity. (p. 232)

"The very concept of culture," Lull continues, "presumes difference" (p. 234).

Of course, awareness and understanding of difference can create greater cultural exchange. Carles Torner, a writer from Barcelona, pointed out that publishing in this country "runs the risk of helping to foster a culture in the U.S. with an increasingly narrow and insular view of other cultures. Only 3 percent of titles published in the United States are translations from other languages; in Europe it is between 20 to 40 percent" ("Mind the Gap," 2005, p. 116). Torner stressed the importance of equality in the dialogue between countries and how it can be enhanced by the availability of translations.

It is also *differences* that have become the issue in conflicts not only between racial and ethnic groups in our own country but in those of other countries. Psychiatrist Robert Jay Lifton (1992) believes that our discomfort at seeing televised images of human suffering can be a catalyst for change by evoking sympathy and compassion: "The evidence is there, on the screens, and in millions of human minds. Televised images can change the world. As survivors by proxy, can our witness be transformed into life-enhancing action . . . ?" (p. 26). Others argue that the media's commercialization of such images—for example, of Rwanda and the Sudan—create "compassion fatigue" (Moeller, 1999).

Given enough understanding of regional as well as national cultures, it is possible to preserve individual differences of many kinds and allow members of various co-cultures or groups to coexist and flourish. Indeed, Gudykunst and Kim (1997) maintain that community cannot exist without diversity. Here are the seven principles they propose for building community, principles for which each of us must be responsible:

1. *Be committed.* We must be committed to the principle of building community in our lives, as well as to the individuals with whom we are trying to develop community.

2. *Be mindful.* Think about what we do and say. Focus on the process, not the outcome.

3. *Be unconditionally accepting.* Accept others as they are; do not try to change or control them . . . Value diversity and do not judge others based only on their diversity.

4. *Be concerned for both ourselves and others.* Avoid polarized communication and engage in dialogue whenever possible. Consult others on issues that affect them and be open to their ideas.

5. *Be understanding.* Recognize how culture and ethnicity affect the way we think and behave. Search for commonalities . . . Balance emotions, anxiety, and fear with reason.

6. *Be ethical.* Engage in behavior that is not a means to an end but behavior that is morally right in and of itself.

7. *Be peaceful.* Do not be violent or deceitful, breach valid promises, or be secretive. Strive for harmony. (Adapted from pp. 381–383)

Summary

In this chapter, we discussed intercultural communication, which has become so pervasive within the last few decades. We defined "culture" as a way of life developed and shared by a people and passed down from generation to generation. Because cultures vary along a range, the differences between two cultures may be slight or very dramatic. Even when two cultural groups are very similar, however, the differences between them are likely to become more evident in intercultural communication. We looked at three major approaches to the study of intercultural communication and considered the concept of diaspora. Several dimensions of cultural variability were then examined, including collectivism-individualism, high and low context, and power distance.

Intercultural communication has increased rapidly because of mass migrations and technological advances that have made long-distance communication more feasible and more available to the general public. Despite the advances in the means of sending and receiving messages, however, there are still many obstacles. Differences in cultural variables such as language, nonverbal communication systems, relational roles and norms (particularly conflict norms), and beliefs and values that are deeply rooted in the whole cultural system often lead to intercultural misunderstanding.

Because we are not aware of the aspects of our own cultures in ourselves, the barriers to intercultural communication are complex and formidable. Ethnocentrism and stereotyping both limit our ability to deal with people beyond our own communities. And the Internet, often used as a bridge to understanding and connection, can also be used to foster division and hostility—for example, through the proliferation of hate sites. We discussed intergroup contact theory and approaches to promoting greater tolerance and harmony. We also looked at the individual and social effects of our increasingly global culture and considered some principles for building community.

Key Terms

Co-culture	Culture	High-context culture	Protonorm
Collectivism	Defensive projection	Individualism	Synchrony
Cosmopolitanism	Diaspora	Low-context culture	Uncertainty avoidance
Cultural homogenization	Ethnocentrism	Master norm	
	Group polarization	Power distance	

Review Questions

1. How do cultural groups differ from other groups that have shared characteristics?

2. Why is it important for effective intercultural communication to understand that culture is learned, rather than innate?

3. Describe the three major approaches to the study of intercultural communication and give an example of each.

4. Explain the concept of diaspora.

5. What are the main reasons that intercultural communication has increased in the last decades?

6. How do such changes affect the new immigrant population in the United States?

7. Explain two major dimensions along which cultures are thought to vary. Give an example.

8. Discuss three other dimensions that measure cultural variation. Give an example of each.

9. State three broad communication principles with significant implications for intercultural communication.

10. Explain at least three ways in which language can be an obstacle to intercultural communication.

11. Describe at least three aspects of nonverbal communication that vary from culture to culture.

12. How can cultural roles and norms affect communication between cultures?

13. Discuss two variables that influence how members of a culture view conflict. Give an example of each.

14. Explain how differences in beliefs and values can become obstacles in intercultural communication.

15. Discuss three master norms that appear to function as core values in many different cultures. Propose one underlying principle for these.

16. Describe one culture's successful adaptation to living in a new country and explain how its beliefs and values contributed to that success.

17. What is ethnocentrism? Why does it interfere with intercultural communication? Give an example.

18. Give two reasons for the stereotyping of cultural groups and discuss its effects on interethnic and interracial conflict. Explain the concept of defensive projection.

19. Explain the concept of group polarization.

20. Discuss some possible effects of the Internet on bigotry.

21. Explain the recent research findings on intergroup relations and discuss the principles of cosmopolitanism.

22. Identify several personal, political, and social effects of intercultural communication.

23. What is meant by "cultural homogenization"? How valid do you think this concept is? Support your answer with examples.

24. Explain the need for community building and state seven principles that have been proposed.

Exercises

1. Make a list of some of the cultural groups in your own region or state, including the group (or groups) that founded your community. To what extent have these groups been in contact with one another? To what extent have they remained distinct from one another? List some ways in which these cultural groups have affected your own culture, such as your traditions, religious beliefs, and language.

2. Find three current articles in print or on the Internet about a cultural group, such as a group in China, Mexico, or Israel, that has extended business, diplomatic contact, or cultural exchange with the United States. List at least five ways in which that culture, or that of the United States, has been affected by this contact.

3. Write a paragraph discussing whether you think you are prejudiced in any way. After this self-assessment, go to *www.tolerance.org* and select the heading "Dig Deeper": Take one or more of the hidden-bias tests. Compare your score with the paragraph you wrote. Discuss your agreement or disagreement with the rating.

4. List at least eight cultures, both inside and outside the United States, with which you communicate in some way (through personal contact, your work or business communication, or mass media). With which of these groups is your communication personal? With which is it institutional? In at least one case in which your contact with the other culture is primarily institutional, describe some ways in which your understanding of the people in that group is limited by your communication with them.

5. Write down what you know about Arab Americans and Arab culture. Then go to *www.adc.org* and read about Arab Americans. Afterward revise anything you wrote that was incorrect and write a one-page summary of what you have learned.

6. Think of a group of people that you feel have specific shared cultural characteristics, for

example, Californians, southerners, New Yorkers, African Americans, European Americans, Amish, Japanese, Russians, Chinese. Describe the people as a group and list the characteristics that you think distinguish that group from others. To what extent is your description a stereotype? What is the source of your information about the group? Can you think of some reasons your stereotype might be inaccurate? Can you think of some ways in which it might affect your communication with individual members of that group?

7. Find an essay or article in a book or magazine or on the Web that describes the experience of being a member of a culture other than your own. Write a brief essay comparing and contrasting it with your own experience.

Suggested Readings

Appiah, Kwame Anthony. *Cosmopolitanism: Ethics in a World of Strangers.* New York: Norton, 2006.

A philosopher from Princeton argues for both universal concern for the values of others and "respect for legitimate difference."

Braziel, Jana Evans, and Anita Mannur, eds. *Theorizing Diaspora: A Reader.* Oxford, UK : Blackwell, 2003.

An important anthology of classic and contemporary essays on diaspora studies including seminal work by Arjun Appadurai, Paul Gilroy, and Stuart Hall. For advanced students interested in an interdisciplinary approach and extensive bibliographies for further research.

Christians, Clifford, and Michael Traber, eds. *Communication Ethics and Universal Values.* Thousand Oaks, CA: Sage, 1997.

A collection of essays that looks at the value systems of individual cultures and also explores the possibility of creating a universal set of ethical norms. For the advanced reader.

Correspondents of *The New York Times. How Race Is Lived in America: Pulling Together, Pulling Apart.* New York: Henry Holt, Times Books, 2001.

The result of a journalistic project on what race relations are like today, this is a collection of individual stories from New York Times editors and writers who have covered all parts of the country. Be sure to read Ira Beskow's "The Minority Quarterback" and Don Terry's "Getting Under My Skin."

Hall, Edward T. *Beyond Culture.* Garden City, NY: Doubleday, 1976.

The author of this book, an anthropologist, is an important researcher in cultural differences and their effects on intercultural communication in business and diplomacy.

Han, Arar, and John Hsu, eds. *Asian American X: An Intersection of 21st Century Asian American Voices.* Ann Arbor, MI: University of Michigan Press, 2004.

A new generation of Asian Americans, primarily college students, examines issues of identity in this lively and surprisingly varied collection of essays.

Hessler, Peter. *Oracle Bones: A Journey Between China's Past and Present.* New York: HarperCollins, 2006.

A fascinating book of enormous range about China's people and its culture—including its many minority peoples.

House of Sand and Fog

A compelling film about the painful collision of people from two very different cultures—members of an Iranian family and a young woman born in the United States. Based on a novel by Andre Dubus III, the film stars Ben Kingsley and Jennifer Connelly.

Lester, Paul Martin, and Susan Dente Ross, eds. *Images That Injure*, 2nd ed. Westport, CT: Praeger, 2003.

Here is a collection of essays that looks at the effects of pictorial stereotypes that appear in the mass media, how they are created and how various groups of people are described and viewed by mainstream culture. There are sections on ethnic, gender, physical, sexual, and other stereotypes as well as a timely discussion of ethics and post–9/11 images.

Martin, Judith N., and Thomas K. Nakayama. *Intercultural Communication in Contexts*, 4th ed. New York: McGraw-Hill, 2007.

The authors introduce their subject from a dialectical perspective and integrate research from the social science, interpretive, and critical approaches, making use of many interesting examples.

Stewart, Frank, and Brent Fujinaka. "Beyond Words: Asian Writers on Their Work," *Mānoa* 18, no. 1 (2006).

Mānoa is an exceptional journal that brings together voices from all over Asia. In this issue writers from China, Tibet, Japan, Viet Nam, Cambodia, the Philippines, Malaysia, and Indonesia *discuss their writing, values, and beliefs.*

Stewart, Rory. *The Places in Between.* Orlando, FL: Harcourt, 2006.

This is a beautifully written account, by turns harrowing and humorous, of a young Scotsman's trip on foot across Afghanistan. Unarmed and accompanied by a mastiff he names Babur, Stewart crosses five different tribal cultures, relying on the Afghan traditions of hospitality for his food and lodging.

 # For Supplementary Information

Log onto the Online Learning Center at *www.mhhe.com/tubbsmoss11.*

Interviewing

Chapter Objectives

After reading this chapter, you should be able to:

1. Distinguish between five types of interview questions and give an example of each.
2. Identify five types of improper questions the interviewer should avoid.
3. Describe the funnel sequence as it is used in the body of an interview.
4. Describe two main advantages of the nondirective interview technique.
5. Distinguish between five types of responses to interviewers' comments in a counseling interview.
6. Identify six characteristics of successful appraisal interviews.
7. Identify five suggestions for interviewers in a selection interview.
8. Identify five suggestions for interviewees in a selection interview.

Judge a man by his questions rather than his answers.

—**Voltaire**

A young man landed his dream job a year ago. Now, he feels like he has the boss from hell. He asks you for advice on how to talk to her.

A bright young MBA grad has an employee who is technically brilliant, but rubs everyone in the work group the wrong way. He ponders how to approach this employee.

A friend comes to you asking for advice on how to be more successful in job interviews. She never uses any makeup or fixes her hair and doesn't dress well for the occasion.

What do these three situations have in common? They all involve difficult conversations. If you have ever had to have one of these difficult conversations, you know that it is like walking into a minefield. So, how do you proceed?

Kerry Patterson (2005) and his coauthors refer to these as "crucial confrontations"; Mark Gerzon (2006) uses the term "conscious conversations." We prefer the term "courageous conversations." In reality, they are actually a form of interview.

In approaching your own courageous conversations, think of the acronym SHARE to remember these five useful skills:

Suspend judgment. If you can go into a conversation with an open mind and expecting a positive outcome, it is a start. Often, based on past experience, we may have negative expectations and a chip on our shoulder that is evident to the other party, but not to us. This approach can also allow us to be open to new ideas that we may not have considered. Go into the conversation with the attitude of "no-fault" problem solving. Look for solutions rather than scapegoats. Focus on the future rather than the past. Invite the other party to help brainstorm as many ways as possible to solve the situation. Usually, this energizes both sides and creates a mutual problem-solving atmosphere rather than one of criticism resulting in defensiveness and stagnation.

Have a gentle tone. Our tone of voice should convey our sincerity and empathy for the other person. Try to stay calm. Convey calmness with your voice. Our eye contact should be direct and our body positioning should be square with the other person. All aspects of our body language should convey openness and a gentle, non-accusing style. Keep in mind how you have felt when someone has given you a break rather than nailed you when you were wrong. In negotiation it is referred to as "driving a soft bargain." A Chinese proverb says, "If you are patient in one moment of difficulty, you will escape a hundred days of sorrow."

Acknowledge, don't argue. In these situations, the other party will almost always try to convince you that they are right. They will come up with many reasons for their actions. It is usually a waste of breath to argue that they are wrong—and it isn't necessary. Instead, tell them that you understand how they feel and how they could see it from that point of view. It usually surprises them and reduces the natural need to be defensive. You may even ask them what they would do if they were in your shoes. John Steinbeck once wrote, "No one wants advice, only corroboration."

Restate and paraphrase. Once they offer their viewpoint, try as accurately as possible to restate it. Be sure to use different words—that is, to paraphrase the essence of what they have said. The intent is to see if you have accurately captured the gist of their comments. If they say, "I always try to do my best in job interviews, but I never seem to succeed," you can say, "You seem to be getting discouraged. Is that right?" After a few of these comments, they will begin to feel that you are truly listening and understanding them. Then, and only then, can you ask questions like, "If you had to guess what might make a difference in your next interview, what would you do?" That turns the conversation from focusing on the problem to focusing on the possible solutions. Then, keep asking questions like, "Would you feel comfortable trying that?" "Is that a realistic possibility for you?" Cahn and Tubbs conducted a 1983 study that found that one of the most important aspects of perceived communication effectiveness is when the other party honestly feels that you have understood them. That has to occur before they are willing to listen to any advice on how to change.

Encourage the heart. Before you conclude the conversation, be sure to offer any sincere positive comments that you have about their efforts. Compliment the efforts, if not the results. All of us have done some good things, and failing to mention them is a major mistake. Psychologists talk about the "Law of Effect," which shows that behaviors followed by a positive consequence (praise) have a much greater chance of increasing than behaviors followed by a negative consequence (criticism). Sam Horn, in her wonderful book *Tongue Fu,* writes, "The best way to get your teenager to shovel the driveway is to tell him he can use the car" (p. 63).

Finally, it is important to remember that we *can* make a difference. George Bernard Shaw once wrote, "People are always blaming their circumstances for what they are. I don't believe in circumstances. The people who get ahead in this world are the people who get up and look for the circumstances they want, and, if they can't find them, make them."

Office Team, a Menlo Park, California–based staffing service company, conducted a survey to determine some of the worst mistakes young people made when interviewing for a job. They found the following:

- A candidate ate a bag of cheese puffs while waiting for the interview. When the interviewer greeted him, he extended a hand covered with orange dust.
- A candidate who was chewing bubble gum noticed the interviewer staring at her mouth. The candidate said, "Oh, I'm sorry, did you want a piece?"
- When asked why she wanted the job, a recent graduate replied, "I'm here for a paycheck . . . Isn't everybody?" (*Detroit News,* 1998)

This chapter deals with the subject of interviewing. Even though you may not have studied interviewing before, you may have witnessed hundreds of interviews on television talk shows. Witness the success of such talk show hosts as Oprah, Jay Leno, and David Letterman.

DEFINING "INTERVIEW"

If you associate interviews only with job hunting, your definition of the term is too narrow. The interview encompasses many of the elements of all interpersonal communication. When you consult a doctor, canvass door-to-door for a political candidate, or ask a stranger for detailed instructions on how to get to a particular place, you are in some sense involved in an interview, or a "conversation with a purpose," which we think is a good definition.

Another good definition is "a process of dyadic, relational communication with a predetermined and serious purpose designed to interchange behavior and involving the asking and answering of questions" (Stewart and Cash, 1999, p. 3). However, even this definition is somewhat limited, since it limits interviews to those with a serious purpose.

Interviews serve a number of functions, as can be seen from Table 11.1. The interviewer may gather or convey information, influence people's attitudes, and at times influence their behavior. An appraisal interview, for example, often exercises a major influence on an employee's morale. The interview is also a valuable research tool. It allows the interviewer to gather more complete information than could be obtained in a questionnaire or a telephone conversation and to make full use of nonverbal as well as verbal cues. It also enables the interviewer to interpret or explain questions more easily, thus increasing the likelihood of getting answers from the respondent.

The Job Interview

The job interview is typically of great interest to most young people. If you find yourself preparing for one of these, Byham and Pickett (1999) recommend that you identify the behavioral dimensions below to get prepared. In each case, try to identify examples of each dimension that would help you convey your positive qualities to the interviewer.

PERSONAL DIMENSIONS

    Adaptability

    Building trust

    Continuous learning

    Creativity/innovation

    Energy/productivity

    Initiative/self-starting

    Integrity

    Stress tolerance

    Tenacity/sticking with a task

INTERPERSONAL DIMENSIONS

    Coaching others

    Communication

Teamwork

Valuing diversity

LEADERSHIP DIMENSIONS

    Influencing others

    Meeting participation/leadership

    Sharing responsibility for
        accomplishing tasks

DECISION-MAKING DIMENSIONS

    Problem identification

    Decisiveness

    Planning and organizing
    (pp. 49–56)

Table 11.1	Ten Interview Objectives	
Objective	**Description**	**Example**
Getting information	Interviewer gathers facts, opinions, or attitudes from respondent.	Census taker collects data.
Giving information	Interviewer presents facts, opinions, or attitudes to respondent, often as a form of instruction.	Doctor explains to patient how to maintain a balanced diet.
Persuading	Interviewer attempts to influence respondent's attitude and ultimately his or her behavior.	Student tries to convince an instructor to give a makeup exam.
Problem solving	Interviewer and respondent attempt to identify causes of a problem and together seek a possible solution.	Parent and teacher discuss child's reading difficulties.
Counseling	Respondent seeks advice from interviewer on a matter of personal concern (closely related to problem-solving interview).	Client requests legal advice from an attorney.
Job seeking or hiring	Interviewer and respondent exchange information on which to base an employment decision.	Campus recruiter meets with senior students.
Receiving complaints	Interviewer tries to minimize the respondent's dissatisfaction.	Store manager speaks with customer about defective merchandise.
Reviewing performance	Interviewer offers feedback on respondent's performance and helps establish specific goals to be met by next appraisal interview.	Editor-in-chief of newspaper gives periodic evaluation of each of the editors.
Correcting or reprimanding	Interviewer and respondent, usually in the roles of superior and subordinate, meet to discuss respondent's need to improve performance (ordinarily most effective when handled informally and with a helpful rather than critical tone).	Maintenance supervisor of airline discusses with mechanic areas in which technical competence must be improved.
Measuring stress	Interviewer determines how respondent acts under pressure.	Personnel director of large corporation selects a top executive.
Seeking information	Interviewer gathers information from a respondent who does not wish to divulge it.	Army officer questions a military prisoner.

Nonverbal Messages

As noted in Chapter 4, nonverbal communication can often speak as loud as—and sometimes louder than—words. Nonverbal cues, or body language, can make or break the interview process. Nonverbal communication also plays a large role in the interpretation of the respondents' answers. Body language can often reveal what interviewees are trying to hide, since it is much more difficult to control than the spoken word. Raudsepp (2004) gives recommendations for using unspoken communication advantageously when being interviewed: Candidates should arrive at interviews early, bring prepared notes and questions, and introduce themselves to the interviewer without hesitation. Posture is also critical in making a good impression, according to Raudsepp.

Posture is one type of important nonverbal cue during interviews; another is clothing. Choice of attire for a job interview always sends a message. Lubin (2004) focused a *Wall Street Journal* article on job interview attire for women over 50 years of age. A study revealed that of two women of this age group competing for a vice presidential position with a corporation, one dressing in an older clothing style and one dressing in a more youthful style, the one in the youthful style was perceived as "on her way up" and as a result, was offered the position. The bottom line is that companies will look at a candidate's attire to interpret if the person will fit in with their organization. A person's attire speaks loudly in the interview process. In the study it was found the companies will "pick someone who looked like them" (p. M-1).

On a similar topic, makeovers for work and leisure have recently been a prominent media theme. For example in 2004, television shows such as *Queer Eye for the Straight Guy* tout individual makeovers in our appearance-focused society. Dress for Success is a popular nonprofit organization that assists individuals in career building and employment searches, offering "makeovers for the mind, body, and soul" (Shalett, 2004, p. 1). Since 1999, Dress for Success has given business clothes to over 6,000 people needing help, so that these individuals could fit into the company cultures where they were seeking employment.

Nonverbal cues can also be an assessment tool for the respondent to silently evaluate the interviewer. Coco McCabe (2004), a reporter for the *Boston Globe,* wrote recollecting her job interview experience. McCabe realized that the interviewee can learn a lot about the interviewer from hidden meanings behind the questions asked. McCabe noted that some questions are really more about exercising authority than wanting actual answers. During an interview with a potential future supervisor, it is important to watch her behavior and how she asks questions. You can learn a lot from a boss's nonverbal behavior. Also, consider the nonverbal behavior of the interviewer and of your future boss (if they are not the same person). Their nonverbal behavior can help you as a candidate decide if this is someone that you really want to work for or with (p. G15).

Strategic Interviewing

You may be given the task of hiring someone else through job interviews. The latest view of these practices is referred to as strategic interviewing (Camp, Vielhaber, and

Simonetti, 2001). Crowley (2004, p. 13) believes that the strategic interview process is essential in hiring organizational leaders, specifically CEOs. She notes that this process provides a consistent interviewing procedure for both external and internal applicants and offers solid metrics for comparing candidates with one another. The strategic interviewing view holds that in order to hire the right person for the job, you must first conduct a careful analysis of the job requirements. Then you must interview the candidates asking questions that specifically relate to those job characteristics. Proponents of this view argue that you should not ask the following questions: Where do you want to be five years from now? If you had to pick one, what kind of a (vegetable, fruit, tree, etc.) would you be and why? These questions do not relate to the specific job that you are hiring a person to perform and therefore do not yield any useful information. A better approach is called the STAR method. This approach asks the candidate to answer in the following manner:

1. Think of a situation (S) or task (T) in which you were faced with a challenge (then fill in the type of challenge related to the job you are trying to fill), such as trying to satisfy an angry customer.

2. Describe the specific action or approach (A) that you took to handle this challenge.

3. Describe the result (R) that occurred from your actions. (Byham and Pickett, 1999)

The foundation for the strategic interviewing approach as well as for the STAR method is based on the fact that past behavior is the best predictor of future behavior. It is more reliable than first impressions or hunches or gut level reactions to people. A considerable amount of research indicates that the strategic interviewing and the STAR method create more successful interview outcomes (Camp, Vielhaber, and Simonetti, 2001).

Cognitive Interviewing

Cognitive interviewing relies on techniques that help the respondent enhance his or her recollection of an event. Ron Fisher, one of the creators of the cognitive interviewing theory, describes how the idea came about:

> The genesis of the cognitive interview was almost accidental. On several occasions, friends who had come to visit me at my apartment would misplace something. They would call me up later and ask me if it was in the apartment, and invariably, it was not. But through conversing with them and asking questions to help trigger their memories, they would then recall where they had misplaced the item. (Fisher, 2005)

A cognitive interview differs from a traditional interview in that, whereas a traditional interviewer relies on asking many questions to receive the desired information, the cognitive interviewer, instead, tries to create a social environment where the person generates information without questions being asked. "The objective is to try to elicit information, not extract information" (Fisher, 2005).

The two major types of cognitive interviewing methods are think-aloud interviewing and verbal probing (Willis, 1999). In the interview of the first type, the subject is instructed to describe the mental process the he or she uses while answering the question. Below is an example of a *think-aloud interview* found in Willis (1999).

> *INTERVIEWER (reading survey question to be tested): How many times have you talked to a doctor in the last 12 months?*
>
> *SUBJECT: I guess that depends on what you mean when you say "talked." I talk to my neighbor, who is a doctor, but you probably don't mean that. I go to my doctor about once a year, for a general check-up, so I would count that one. I've also probably been to some type of specialist a couple of more times in the past year—once to get a bad knee diagnosed, and I also saw an ENT about a chronic coughing thing, which I'm pretty sure was in the past year, although I wouldn't swear to it. . . .*

The advantages of the think-aloud technique are

1. *Freedom from interviewer-imposed bias.* The interviewer contributes little other than the reading of the survey question.
2. *Minimal interviewer training requirements.* Because the interviewer mainly reads survey questions, little training is necessary.
3. *Open-ended format.* The subject may provide information that is unanticipated by the interviewer. (Willis, 1999)

Think-aloud interviewing is, thus, "especially valuable when the subject is articulate . . . and has had significant experience with the topics covered by the survey questions" (Willis, 1999).

The disadvantages of the think-aloud technique are

1. *Need for subject training.* Thinking-aloud is unusual for most people and often requires a significant amount of training before an effective interview can take place.
2. *Subject resistance.* Even after given training, many people still tend to simply answer the questions that are asked, without elaboration.
3. *Burden [to explain] on subject.*
4. *Tendency for the subject to stray from the task.* Since the subject controls the discussion, it is very easy for a subject to deviate into irrelevant areas.
5. *Bias in subject information processing.* Because thinking-aloud forces subjects to think rather than simply provide an answer such as "yes," "no,"

or "I agree," subjects may spend a considerable effort on interpreting the questions instead of just answering them. (Willis, 1999)

Whereas the think-aloud technique places the main burden of the interview on the subject, the alternative method places more of the relative burden on the interviewer. This technique is known as *verbal probing,* as described by Willis (1999):

After the interviewer asks the survey question, and the subject answers, the interviewer then asks for other, specific information relevant to the question, or to the specific answer given. . . . The interviewer "probes" further into the basis for the response. The following list includes basic categories of cognitive probes, and an example of each:

Comprehension/ Interpretation probe:	What does the term "outpatient" mean to you?
Paraphrasing:	Can you repeat the question I just asked in your own words?
Confidence judgment:	How sure are you that your health insurance covers drug and alcohol treatment?
Recall probe:	How do you remember that you went to the doctor five times in the past 12 months?
Specific probe:	Why do you think that cancer is the most serious health problem?
General probes:	How did you arrive at that answer?
	Was that easy or hard to answer?
	I noticed that you hesitated—tell me what you were thinking.

The advantages of the verbal probing technique are

1. *Control of the interview.* The interviewer can focus on particular areas that are relevant to the discussion.
2. *Ease of training of the subject.* It is easy to induce subjects to answer probe questions, because they often do not differ from the survey question they are otherwise answering. (Willis, 1999)

The disadvantage of probing techniques is the *potential for bias,* because the use of probes may lead the respondent to particular types of responses. This problem may be overcome by unbiased phrasing of the probes (Willis, 1999).

Here is an example from a cognitive interview conducted using the verbal probing technique from Willis (1999). (The original question needed to be revised in order to elicit meaningful a response.)

Original form:

We are interested in your lifetime exercise patterns. First, when you were 14 to 19 years old:

> *How many hours a week of brisk walking did you do?*
>
> *How many hours a week of vigorous exercise such as running, cycling, swimming, or aerobics did you do?*
>
> *How many hours a week of activities that required you to be on your feet (excluding running or walking) such as dancing, hiking, . . . did you do?*

Probes:

> a. Was this hard or easy to answer? (to determine comprehension and overall ability to recall)
> b. How do you remember this? (to study recall strategy)
> c. How sure are you of your answer? (confidence probe)
> d. What, to you, is "vigorous exercise?" (comprehension/interpretation of a specific term)

Subjects found it very difficult to remember back to the time period specified, at the required level of detail. In fact, it seemed that some subjects really could not even answer this with respect to their current behavior, let alone their behavior many years ago. Recall of information . . . seemed to be the dominant problem. . . .

Suggested revision:

We are interested in your lifetime exercise patterns. When you were 14 to 19 years old, were you more active than you are now, less active than now, or about as active as now? (Willis, 1999, pp. 13–14)

Numerous studies conducted in different countries on the effectiveness of cognitive interviewing techniques have demonstrated that the cognitive interview produces between 35 and 60 percent, and in some contexts up to 100 percent, more information than the traditional interview (Fisher, 2005).

STANDARDIZED AND UNSTANDARDIZED INTERVIEWS

Whatever his or her objectives, the interviewer may use one of two approaches: standardized or unstandardized. The **standardized interview** consists of *a set of prepared questions from which the interviewer is not allowed to deviate.* The interviewer poses the questions precisely as they are worded on the form. He or she

ISSUES IN COMMUNICATION

Interviewing: Conversation with a Purpose

William C. Byham (1997) has trained people in more than 7,000 companies on the topic of how to interview and select the best job applicants. He has also developed the Situation/Task/Action/Result (STAR) method for interviewees.

Think about how you would respond to each of the following parts of the STAR method if you were in a job interview.

Situation/Task

1. Tell me about a time when you tried to satisfy a customer.
2. Tell me about a time when you had to learn something completely new.
3. Tell me about a time when you tried to persuade a person or group to do something they didn't want to do.
4. Give me an example of a time when you faced a lot of obstacles to achieving a goal.

Action

Detail the steps you took in each of the situations/tasks listed above.

1.
2.
3.
4.

Result

Detail the results that you were able to achieve in each of the situations/tasks listed above.

1.
2.
3.
4.

does not even have the option of changing their order. The standardized interview has one distinct advantage: uniform responses over a large number of interviewers and respondents. An inexperienced interviewer may still be able to conduct a fairly successful interview. As a rule, more skill is required as the interview becomes less structured.

The **unstandardized interview** *allows the interviewer as well as the respondent considerable latitude.* The interviewer may deviate from any of the prepared questions. He or she may follow up a prepared question with one of his or her own to obtain a more complete or appropriate answer. He or she may drop a question that seems unsuitable or one that might put the respondent on the defensive. If he or she suddenly discovers an interesting subject that had not been anticipated, the interviewer has the freedom to pursue this line of questioning as far as is desired. In short, the unstandardized interview gives the interviewer considerable flexibility and potential for discovery.

As we have described them, the standardized and unstandardized interviews are extremes. In fact, some standardized interviews allow some departure from the prepared questions; some unstandardized interviews do not permit the interviewer unlimited freedom. No matter how the interview is structured, however, some feedback must flow between interviewer and respondent. In the discussion that follows, let us assume that the interviewer is conducting an unstandardized interview in which he or she can make maximum use of feedback from the respondent by departing where necessary from the list of questions.

Both parties in an interview can sometimes be pretty suspicious of each other. One extreme example was the statesman Talleyrand, "who upon learning that the Russian ambassador had committed suicide, is reported to have mused, 'I wonder what he is up to?'"

TYPES OF INTERVIEW QUESTIONS

Interviewing is essentially dialogue, dialogue in which one party, the interviewer, guides the direction of the conversation by means of a series of questions. A skillful interviewer knows a great deal about the art of questioning. He or she responds to the answers received by modifying subsequent responses—particularly the kinds of questions that are being asked. We can illustrate by first looking at several categories of questions.

Open versus Closed Questions

The **open question** resembles an essay question on a test; it *places no restrictions on the length of the respondent's answer*. It also allows the respondent more latitude in interpreting the subject to be discussed. Examples of open questions would be, "Would you please summarize your work experience?" and "What are your feelings about your career?" The interviewer may want to use open questions early in the interview to get the respondent to relax and reveal more personal information.

Following are the advantages of the open question: It may reveal what the interviewee thinks is important; it may reveal an interviewee's lack of information or understanding in an area; it may bring out an interviewee's feelings on an issue, or possible prejudices and stereotypes; and it provides the interviewer with a good example of the interviewee's communication skills. The disadvantages of an open question are that it takes a great deal of time and may limit the progress of the interview, and it reduces the number of topics that can be covered (Deluca, 1997).

The **closed question** is more specific and *usually requires a shorter, more direct answer*. Contrast the following with the two open questions just given: "How many years of work experience have you had in the field?" and "What aspect of your marriage seems to trouble you most?" Closed questions may restrict the respondent still further by requiring a simple yes-or-no answer. "Would you like to work for a small corporation?" or "Do you feel you have a satisfying job?"

As you can see from these examples (and those in Table 11.2), the open questions are often more appropriate at the early part of the interview; the closed questions can be used to focus the conversation more as you go. This approach to interviewing, known as the **funnel sequence,** is illustrated in Figure 11.1. There

Table 11.2 *Open versus Closed Question*		
Interviewer	**Open Question**	**Closed Question**
Prospective employer	What do you think about money?	What starting salary were you thinking of?
Boss	What do you think about our new policy?	Do you like our new plan?
Teacher	How is your term paper coming?	Do you need help?
Doctor	How have you been feeling?	Is your back hurting again?
High school counselor	Have you thought about going to college?	Can you afford $10,000 a year tuition?

Figure 11.1 *Funnel Sequence*

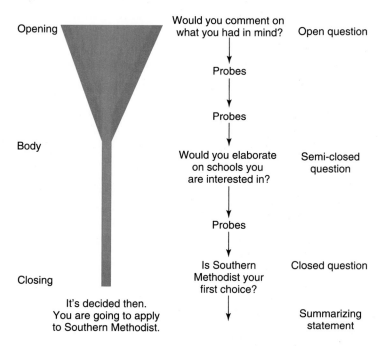

Source: Adapted from *Selection Interviewing for Managers,* by Thomas Moffatt, 1979. Reprinted by permission of the author.

are three additional interview sequences in addition to the common funnel sequence. First, the "inverted funnel" is the exact opposite of the funnel, with the interviewer first asking narrow, closed-ended questions, followed by open-ended questions. Second, the "diamond" sequence combines the two styles above, by asking specific questions, followed by open-ended questions, and ending with specific questions again that are mostly closed-ended. The final prominent style is the "tunnel." This style allows the most flexibility and comprises mostly open-ended, general questions (Coopman, 2004). Here is a funnel sequence that was used in a personal opinion survey:

1. What are your views about increasing population growth in the United States?
2. What are your feelings about controlling our population growth?
3. Do you think legalized abortion should be used to help control population in the United States?
4. Should there be restrictions on abortions?
5. What restrictions should there be?

The closed question has the following advantages: More questions can be asked in more areas and in less time than with open questions; the interviewer can guide and regulate the interview with a great deal of control; and closed questions are often easier and less threatening for the interviewee and so tend to put the interviewee at ease. Among the disadvantages of a closed question are that it provides little or no information "surrounding" the issue raised in the question, and it may close off areas that would be potentially valuable for the interviewer in his or her effort to arrive at a decision concerning the interviewee.

Primary versus Probing Questions

Primary questions *introduce a new topic in the interview.* All the examples of open and closed questions that were presented earlier are examples of primary questions. A very different type of question is called a **probe** or **secondary question.** This is *a follow-up to a primary question and is intended to elicit elaboration* from the interviewee. Such remarks as, "I see. Can you tell me more?" or "Why don't you go on?" tend to bring about further comment on a previous statement. Short pauses may elicit the same reaction, allowing the respondent to express thoughts more completely. Other examples of probes or follow-up questions are

Go on.	How do you mean?
Tell me more.	Could you elaborate?
Yes?	Would you fill me in some more on that?
Uh huh?	Do you have any other reasons?
Why?	Because of what?
Why not?	[Silence]

The probing question can significantly increase the amount of information gained from interviewees. It allows them to elaborate as much as they are willing to. The biggest disadvantage is that it can put the interviewee on the defensive. For example, "Why not?" may imply criticism. In addition, the other person may begin to resent being probed further than anticipated. This could result in an actual loss of information if the person decides to terminate or distort responses.

Leading versus Neutral Questions

Neutral questions *do not explicitly or implicitly suggest the desired answer.* **Leading questions** *are the opposite.* Obviously, the interviewer can obtain more accurate information by employing the neutral questions. The varying degrees of direction and the distinction between neutral and leading questions are illustrated below (Stewart and Cash, 1999):

LEADING QUESTIONS	NEUTRAL QUESTIONS
1. You like close detail work, don't you?	1. How do you feel about close detailed work?
2. You're going with us, aren't you?	2. Are you going with us?
3. Do you oppose the union like most workers I've talked to?	3. What are your attitudes toward the union?
4. Wouldn't you rather have a Buick?	4. How does this Buick compare to other cars in this price range?
5. When was the last time you got drunk?	5. Tell me about your drinking habits.

The Loaded Questions

A more volatile and often annoying type of leading question is the **loaded question,** which *stacks the deck by implying the desired answer.* This form of the closed question is sometimes used to back the respondent into a corner. In effect, the interviewer poses and answers his or her own questions: to a protester at a rally, "Isn't it true that violence can only make matters worse?"; to a government official at a press conference, "Hasn't your new policy been tried in the past with no success?" Such questions are emotionally charged, and they immediately put the respondent on his or her guard. Undeniably, loaded questions are sometimes used to advantage, especially in the news media. Thus, a reporter can ask a politician questions that are on the lips of many voters, forcing him or her to meet the issues head on. Nonetheless, if we are interested in getting information, the loaded question is a doubtful technique. A better way, for example, to question the official might be, "Would you explain the advantages and disadvantages of your new policy?"

The loaded question has no advantages unless the goal is to see if the interviewee can handle a threatening, hostile situation. The disadvantages are rather easy to surmise: The interviewee loses whatever trust may have existed, may become "unraveled," and may feel negatively toward the interviewer and the organization she or he represents.

SUSPECT QUESTIONS AND HOW TO HANDLE THEM

In most cases, employers ask suspect questions because they simply do not know any better and they have a genuine interest in getting to know the candidate (University of Alabama at Birmingham, 2004). However, interviewers with positive intentions can still open up an employer to increased liability if the question relates to laws protecting individuals from discrimination. These laws are in place to protect individuals from the not-so-well-intentioned employer.

Title VII of the Civil Rights Act of 1964 prohibits employment discrimination on the basis of race, color, sex, marital status, religion, or national origin. The first Civil Rights Act prohibiting discrimination was passed in 1866 (all persons were given the same rights as "white citizens"), and the latest was in 1974, the Vietnam Era Veterans Readjustment Act, which promoted the employment of Vietnam-era veterans. In addition, the 1964 Civil Rights Act was amended in 1978 to specifically cover pregnant women, and the Age Discrimination Act of 1967 was amended in 1978 to protect workers age 40 to 70 from employment discrimination. Currently, although not a federal requirement, some state, city, and local ordinances prohibit discrimination based on height, weight, and sexual orientation.

In general, questions that are lawful relate specifically to the job, attitudes about work, health if relevant to the particular work, past employment, educational background, and capabilities. Just about everything else, whether seemingly irrelevant (e.g., hobbies) or not, could be considered discriminatory.

Specifically, the Equal Employment Opportunity Commission (EEOC) has set up the following subjects as the source of discriminatory questions: change of name, maiden or former name, previous foreign address, birthplace of self or family members, religion, complexion or skin color, citizenship or national origin, foreign military service, name and address of relative to be notified ("person" is okay), arrest or conviction record, or height (unless related to the job).

Single people, for example, cannot be asked if they live with their parents, get along with them, or plan marriage. Engaged people cannot be asked if they plan to marry, what the occupation of the future spouse is, or what their plans for work after marriage are. Married people cannot be asked if they own a home or have debts, what the spouse's occupation is, whether they would relocate, (for women) what the husband thinks of their working, what the extra money will be used for, whether they have plans for a family, or the ages of their children. Questions about plans are not in themselves unlawful, but they cannot be used for unlawful screening purposes.

United States governmental agencies often have a difficult position with respect to Equal Employment Opportunity Commission guidelines. These agencies often have to obtain personal identifying information such as race and age that is unnecessary to other employers. However, the data are usually collected on a separate form to keep the information confidential and hidden from managers involved in the hiring process. In January 2004, Charles Foti broke this mold. When he was elected to the Louisiana attorney general's office, Foti put a single application form in place, which asked for an applicant's age, physical characteristics (including questions regarding tattoos, birthmarks, and other identifying factors), and race. Although the form itself was not found to be illegal, it opened up the attorney general's office to possible discrimination charges. In order to get to know them, Foti asked all of his then-current employees to complete this form on a voluntary basis to reapply for their current jobs. Although the Equal Employment Opportunity Commission does not disallow employers from asking such questions, it highly advises against it because of the risk of misuse and misinterpretation leading to discrimination charges (Scott, 2004, p. 1).

When an individual is asked an illegal discriminatory or suspect question, there are several alternatives he or she can follow:

1. Of course, if the interviewee thinks the question harmless and does not care about the fact that it could be used as an unlawful screening device, she or he may simply go ahead and answer it.

2. The interviewee can inform the interviewer that the question is a personal one and she or he would be happy to answer any questions related to qualifications necessary for the job.

3. The interviewee can ask what the thrust of the question is in relation to the job, what the interviewer wants to know.

4. The interviewee can indicate that the question is not relevant and go on to answer it (e.g., "That question has no bearing on my qualifications for the position, but I'll answer it anyway").

5. The interviewee can refuse to answer the question on the grounds that it is not related to qualifications for the job.

6. The interviewee can ignore the question and respond with an indication that she or he is willing to answer relevant questions.

7. Of course, the interviewee can stop the interviewer by expressing the belief that the question is discriminatory and (if desired) that she or he will file a complaint with the EEOC! (University of Alabama–Birmingham, 2004).

There are several problems in responding to suspect questions, most of which center around the belief that no responses or a hostile response to the question will decrease the odds of obtaining the job, and obtaining the job may be more important than the problem created by the suspect question. However, if the interviewer asks questions other than those related to qualifications for the job, and the ultimate effect is an underrepresentation of minorities and other protected groups in that employer's workforce, then the company could be vulnerable to a Title VII lawsuit. Remember that the interviewer may not realize that he or she is asking improper questions, either through a lack of familiarity with the guidelines or because he or she spontaneously asks questions without thinking about their discriminatory impact (Deluca, 1997; see also Camp, Vielhaber, and Simonetti, 2001).

TYPES OF INADEQUATE RESPONSES

Regardless of the kinds of questions chosen, the interviewer is never completely sure of obtaining the number and quality of answers he or she would like to have. Interviewing is a dynamic process, not a programmed event. It cannot move forward without the participation of the respondent. Thus another aspect of interviewing skill involves handling inadequate responses. Let us look at five that the interviewer can anticipate and try to avoid.

No Answer

First, suppose that the respondent gives no answer—that is, either refuses to answer (the familiar "No comment" or "I'd rather not say") or says nothing at all. A sufficient number of such responses will bring the interview to a dead end. The interviewer might follow up such a response with a second, related question. If necessary, the line of inquiry might be dropped altogether.

Partial Answer

Imagine instead that the respondent gives a partial answer. The interviewer might then restate the part of the question that has not been answered. If the respondent gives a good many partial answers, the interviewer should review the questions asked. Perhaps some could be subdivided and posed individually. In general, it is best to avoid asking more than one question at a time.

Irrelevant Answer

Reacting appropriately to an irrelevant answer is more complex because there are two reasons the respondent may have gone off on a tangent: He or she may not have understood the question completely or may be making a conscious effort to avoid answering it. Politicians, it seems, frequently evade questions by offering irrelevant answers.

Inaccurate Answer

Often a respondent who does not wish to disclose information will offer an inaccurate answer, especially if revealing the truth would be embarrassing. Unfortunately, an inaccurate answer is often difficult for the interviewer to detect, especially in an initial interview. Of course, the accuracy of the information the interviewer receives is determined in part by the respondent's motivation. A person who feels threatened by an interview is more inclined to provide data within what he or she perceives to be the interviewer's expectations. People sometimes respond inaccurately in an attempt to maintain their status level or achieve a higher one. It has been found, for example, that people (particularly those with high incomes) overestimate the number of plane trips they have made but play down any automobile loans they have taken out.

Whether they are intentional or not, inaccurate responses are damaging not only to the interviewer but to the respondent. If he or she will be seeing the interviewer again—as is probable after an appraisal or counseling interview—it is likely that some of these distortions will be revealed at a later date. If the interviewer finds that over a series of meetings the respondent has been giving inaccurate answers, he or she should consider possible reasons for this behavior. The interviewer has much to gain from establishing great rapport with the respondent, putting the individual at ease so that he or she feels it will not be personally damaging to tell the truth.

Oververbalized Answer

The respondent who gives an oververbalized answer tells the interviewer much more than he or she wants to know. Sometimes lengthy answers contain a great deal of irrelevant information. A high percentage of oververbalized responses will severely limit the number of topics that an interviewer can cover in the time allotted. He or she should try as tactfully as possible to guide the respondent back to the heart of the question, and to do this the interviewer may wish to increase the number of closed questions.

INTERVIEW STRUCTURE

In addition to developing skill in the art of questioning, the interviewer is sometimes responsible for giving the meeting structure. Much of what we have said thus far can be applied to relatively unstructured communication as well as to interviews. But in most cases an interview should have an apparent structure—an opening, a body, and a closing—and the interviewer will have specific responsibilities during each part.

Opening of the Interview

In beginning an interview, an interviewer has three basic responsibilities. The first is to introduce the objectives of the interview to the respondent. Although these usually seem obvious to the interviewer, a brief statement of purpose is reassuring to the other party: An employee who is called in for a routine appraisal, for example, may perceive it as a reprimand interview unless the purpose is made clear. A second task for the interviewer is to establish rapport with the respondent, to get him or her to feel that the interviewer can be trusted and that the meeting does not present a threatening situation. The interviewer's third and most important responsibility is motivating the respondent to answer questions. Sometimes the respondent's interest seems ensured. For example, a person applying for a job will probably do his or her utmost to answer questions. But what if you are conducting some research interviews? Typically, respondents consider door-to-door canvassing a nuisance, and they may be reluctant to talk. An interviewer should never assume that a potential respondent is just waiting to be interviewed. Instead, he or she should act as though the person is busy and try to show briefly why it is important that the person give a few moments of his or her time. According to Coopman (2004), the opening part of the interview can be defined as setting the tone for the rest of the interview, including "formality level," "rapport," and "orientation."

Wilson and Goodall (1991) identify three related goals of the opening part of the interview:

1. To make the interviewee feel welcomed and relaxed
2. To provide the interviewee with a sense of purpose
3. To preview some of the major topics to be covered (p. 53)

Body of the Interview

The body of the interview constitutes the major portion of time spent with the respondent, and it should be carefully planned for best results. If at all possible, it should be free from interruptions, phone calls, and other distractions so that both parties remain as relaxed as possible. We have seen that a number of different types of questions can be used in an interview. Each has advantages and disadvantages; the student of interviewing should at least be familiar with them. In addition, the sequence of questions used is important.

The first step in interview planning is to determine the topics to be covered. What, for example, is the typical content of the employment interview? One analysis of 20 employment interviews lists the topics shown in Table 11.3 as the most frequently discussed.

After selecting the topics, the interviewer then determines the actual sequence of questions. At this point the funnel sequence is often useful: *The interviewer begins with broad questions and gradually makes them more specific* (see Figure 11.1, p. 365).

Because each question in the sequence is more specific than the preceding one, the interviewer can reconstruct a more complete picture of the respondent's attitudes and at the same time evaluate specific answers in relation to the general issue. The funnel sequence may be used for any number of individual topics within the body of the interview.

Theme	Percentage*
Table 11.3 *Themes of Twenty Employment Interviews*	
Information about the company	
General organizational orientation	100
Specific job area	90
Promotion policies	60
Information about the candidate	
Job expectations	80
Academic background	75
Prepared for the interviews	75
Scholastic record	70
Military status	70
Work experience	60
Geographical preference	60
Interviewing for other jobs	50
Information about the interviewer	
Job	25
Background	25
Where he or she lives	10

*Refers to the percentage of observed interviews in which this theme occurred.
Source: Adapted from *Personnel Administration and Public Review,* September, 1971. Reprinted by permission of Professor Cal Downs.

The funnel sequence is just one of several ways of organizing the exchange. In their discussion of the research interview, Kahn and Cannell (1968) offer some advice about selecting the sequence of topics that might well apply to almost any type of interview:

> The sequence of topics themselves should be planned to make the total interview experience as meaningful as possible, to give it a beginning, a middle, and an end. More specifically, the early questions should serve to engage the respondent's interest without threatening or taxing him before he is really committed to the transaction, and to exemplify and teach him the kind of task the interview represents. The most demanding of questions might well be placed later in the interview, when respondent commitment can be presumed to have peaked—and fatigue has not yet set in. Sometimes the riskiest of questions may be put very late in the interview, so that if they trigger a refusal to continue, relatively little information is lost. This procedure seems prudent, but it risks also the possibility of an unpleasant leavetaking. (p. 578)

Conclusion

The possibility of an unpleasant or at least an unsatisfying conclusion points to the importance of skillfully terminating the interview. All too often interviews end abruptly because of a lack of time, and both parties are left feeling the need for closure, or resolution. A proper conclusion, or interview closing, should include three parts: "conclusion preparation, final summary, and post-interview discussion" (Coopman, 2004).

Almost any interview profits from a summary of the grounds covered, or final summary. It can range from a brief statement to a review of all the major points discussed. Then, if some action is to be taken as a result of the interview (e.g., hiring a person), the nature of the next contact should be agreed on. If each person thinks the other will initiate the contact, both may wait too long before following up. More than one job has been lost this way. Finally, a written summary may be sent to the respondent. In appraisal interviews this procedure is especially helpful: Both parties then have a written record of the agreed-upon objectives for the employee's future job responsibilities. The summary will also serve as a record of the employee's progress.

Whetten and Cameron (2005) offer the following checklist to use in preparing for your interview:

1. Have I determined my purpose with regard to both content and relationship with the interviewee?
2. Do my questions all relate to my purposes and agenda?
3. Are my questions worded in an unbiased manner?
4. Have I chosen an appropriate interview structure for this situation?
5. Have I chosen an appropriate physical setting?
6. Have I planned ways to deal with problems that could develop? (p. 528)

NONDIRECTIVE INTERVIEW TECHNIQUE

We have seen various ways in which the interviewer can conduct an interview or reinforce the interview structure. The nondirective interview technique, however, demands skill of a different order. In this approach, which is often used in counseling or problem solving, the interviewer tries to restate the essence of the respondent's answers without making value judgments about them or offering advice. The aim is to encourage interviewees to elaborate on previous statements in greater depth and thus gain insight into the situation so that they can help solve their own problem. It reflects the joke "How many psychiatrists does it take to change a light bulb? Only one, but the light bulb has to really want to be changed."

In the nondirective interview, you convey to the person that you are listening and empathizing with the situation. Banville (1978) illustrates the technique with an example of a problem statement that you might hear from a typical college friend and some samples of common responses:

A. "I can't figure out what's wrong, but lately I've had a tough time getting up during the week. On Saturday and Sunday when I could sleep later, I'm up at the crack of dawn!"
   1. "If I were you, I'd try getting to bed a little earlier during the week and stay up later on Friday and Saturday nights." (**Advice giving.**)
   2. "The reason you do that is because you're not happy with your job." (**Interpretation.**)
   3. "Didn't you realize when you enrolled in those classes that they would be too heavy a load for you? Why did you take eighteen units in the first place?" (**Cross-examination.**)
   4. "Oh, yeah, I know, I think that's a pretty common thing. It's nothing to be concerned about." (**Reassurance.**)
   5. "It sounds like your everyday responsibilities are getting you down." (**Paraphrasing.**) (pp. 172–173)

How would you respond to a friend who came to you with this problem? Banville offers five types of responses. The last response—paraphrasing—is the one to use in nondirective interviews.

Motivational Interviewing

The concept of motivational interviewing evolved from the experience of treating alcoholism and was first described by Miller in 1983. This basic experience was developed into a coherent theory, and a detailed description of the clinical procedure was provided by Miller and Rollnick (1991), who defined motivational interviewing as a "directive, client-centered counseling style for eliciting behavior change by helping clients to explore and resolve ambivalence" (Rubak et al., 2005). In other words, motivational interviewing is a way of helping clients recognize and do something about their problems. This technique might be useful in professions such as social work, nursing, psychology, human resources, or personal/professional training or coaching work.

In trying to accomplish this goal, the motivational interview differs greatly from traditional advice giving.

> The strategies of motivational interviewing are more persuasive than coercive, more supportive than argumentative, and the overall goal is to increase the client's intrinsic motivation so that change arises from within rather than being imposed from without. (Miller and Rollnick, 2002)

Rollnick and Miller provide the following key characteristics of motivational interviewing (Rollnick and Miller, 1995):

1. *Motivation to change is elicited from the client, and not imposed from without.*

Other motivational approaches have emphasized coercion, persuasion, constructive confrontation, and the use of external contingencies (e.g., the threatened loss of job or family). Such strategies may have their place in evoking change, but they are quite different in spirit from motivational interviewing which relies upon identifying and mobilizing the client's intrinsic values and goals to stimulate behaviour change.

2. *It is the client's task, not the counsellor's, to articulate and resolve his or her ambivalence.*

   . . . Many clients have never had the opportunity of expressing the often confusing, contradictory, and uniquely personal elements of this conflict, for example, "If I stop smoking I will feel better about myself, but I may also put on weight, which will make me feel unhappy and unattractive." The counsellor's task is to facilitate expression of both sides of the ambivalence impasse, and guide the client toward an acceptable resolution that triggers change.

3. *Direct persuasion is not an effective method for resolving ambivalence.*

   It is tempting to try to be "helpful" by persuading the client of the urgency of the problem about the benefits of change. . . . These tactics generally increase client resistance and diminish the probability of change.

4. *The counselling style is generally a quiet and eliciting one.*

   Direct persuasion, aggressive confrontation, and argumentation are the conceptual opposite of motivational interviewing and are explicitly proscribed in this approach. . . .

5. *The counsellor is directive in helping the client to examine and resolve ambivalence.*

   . . . The specific strategies of motivational interviewing are designed to elicit, clarify, and resolve ambivalence in a client-centered and respectful counselling atmosphere.

6. *Readiness to change is not a client trait, but a product of interpersonal interaction.*

   . . . Client resistance is often a signal that the counsellor is assuming greater readiness to change than is the case, and it is a cue that the therapist needs to modify motivational strategies.

7. *The therapeutic relationship is more like a partnership or companionship than expert/recipient roles.*

   The therapist respects the client's autonomy and freedom of choice (and consequences) regarding his or her own behavior.

In short, motivational interviewing differs from traditional intervention methods in that it does not

- argue that the person has a problem and needs to change;
- offer direct advice without the person's permission or without actively encouraging the person to make his or her own choices;
- use an expert stance leaving the client in a passive role;
- impose diagnostic labels;
- behave in a punitive or coercive manner. (Rollnick and Miller, 1995)

Effectiveness of motivational interviewing in promoting behavior change has made it a popular counseling tool, but it still lacks coherent theoretical foundation. Recently, an attempt has been made to interpret motivational interviewing principles in light of the self-determination theory (Markland et al., 2005). However, researchers point out that more work is needed to understand the causes underlying the success of motivational interviewing.

HELPFUL HINTS

The Interviewee

Several authors have compiled some helpful hints for achieving greater success in interviewing. Murnighan (1992) offers an excellent tip based on practical experience. He writes,

> One of my mentors gave me some terrific advice: He told me that the most important thing in an interview was to make sure they liked me. Certainly I needed to show that I knew what I was talking about. But the most important thing was personal—I should try to make sure that they liked me. I don't think he was saying that I should hide my true personality so that I could get this job—at least I hope not. Instead, he was telling me to be pleasant, smile a little here and there—in general, to be someone that they would like to have as a colleague. (p. 27)

With any economic downturn and high unemployment rate, many writers address job interviewing skills in order to prepare candidates for the highly competitive job market. Candidates are marketing themselves as commodities to compete with other available talent.

To gather first impressions, job interviewers often begin with open-ended general questions that allow the candidates to share something about themselves. Interviewees often get asked questions such as, "Tell me about yourself." Jeff Skrentny, president of a Chicago-based technical recruiting firm called the Jefferson Group, says the appropriate answer to this common interview question uses a three-step format. The first part is a quick summary of your work experience and how this experience has led to the next step in your professional career. The second step is to quickly connect part one to an accomplishment that you are proud of that relates to your career. Part three is an expression of your interest in the particular position for which you are interviewing. Skrentny believes that this approach allows candidates to truly market themselves (Kennedy, 2003, p. 22). In the world of advertising, marketing, and sales, it is the first quick impression that grabs the attention of the consumer. In the recruiting world, the interviewer is the consumer and the candidate is the product.

The job interviewee must utilize the interview process to learn more about his or her potential future supervisor. Development Dimensions International (DDI), a worldwide human resources company, urges candidates to select the right supervisor. DDI cites that 56 percent of employees leave their jobs because of their boss, whereas only 6 percent leave due to unsatisfactory compensation. In addition to asking the interviewer critical questions, the candidate should request meetings with members of the work group that report to the same supervisor to get their feedback ("Turning the Tables on the Job Interview," 2004, p. 1). The candidate or respondent should interview the interviewer!

The Interviewer

It is very important to give a realistic job explanation during interviews and to hire an individual who is the best fit for the position. Sheridan (2004) cites six important interviewer suggestions. First, Eric Chester, author and consultant on generational hiring, emphasizes that with any job it is very important to tell it like it is and not "oversell the job." Second, interviewers should familiarize themselves with the candidate's application and résumé in order to detect any variations. Third, all questions should be relevant to the open position. Fourth, interviewers should also take notes, but not so many that they would be distracting. Fifth, interviewers should also pay close attention to body language to detect attention span and personality traits. Finally, interviewers must be familiar with the law and not ask questions such as those which discuss age, national origin, or marital status (p. 26).

Interview coach Marky Stein and recruiter Tim Lawler offer some of the following tips for interviewers as noted in *The Augusta Chronicle* ("On the Job; Interview Tips," 2003, p. F01):

- Ask the candidate why she/he is interested in the job.
- Inquire what research the candidate has done on the position.
- Ask for examples from the candidate regarding relevant experience.
- Rephrase questions as necessary.
- Ask consistent questions to each candidate.
- Inquire about the candidate's work ethic.
- Continue to practice your interview skills.

Deep and Sussman (1998) offer the following suggestions:

Regardless of the specific purpose of the interview (employment, appraisal, reprimanding, or firing) there are general guidelines we can offer which should improve your performance, the performance of the interviewee, and the general climate of the interviewing session.

1. Plan the interview carefully.
2. Establish a climate of comfort and rapport with the person you are interviewing.
3. Conduct the interview in a comfortable environment.
4. Keep distractions in the situation at a minimum.
5. Be prepared to listen.
6. Try to be as objective as possible.
7. Keep the purpose of your interview in mind.
8. Frame your questions so that you get adequate responses from the person you are interviewing.
9. Decide whether open or closed questions will give you the information you want.
10. Avoid directed (leading or loaded) questions, unless they serve your specific purpose.
11. Choose language that the interviewee understands, but do not "talk down" to him or her. Be clear but not condescending.
12. Provide some kind of a summary of what was decided, discussed, and/or considered in the interview.
13. Provide the interviewee with a statement of what future action is expected from him or her based on the interview and what is expected from you based on the interview. (p. 225)

Summary

The interview is defined as "conversation with a purpose." It is more structured than dyad communication and may involve more than two people. Interview objectives, various types of questions and responses, and ways of structuring the interview were discussed. The nondirective interview technique was explained, and the chapter concluded with some practical hints for successful interviewing.

Key Terms

Advice giving	Leading question	Primary question	Unstandardized
Closed question	Loaded question	Probe	interview
Cross-examination	Neutral question	Reassurance	
Funnel sequence	Open question	Secondary question	
Interpretation	Paraphrasing	Standardized interview	

Review Questions

1. What are five different types of interview questions? Give an example of each.

2. What are five types of questions the interviewer should not ask of job applicants?

3. What is the funnel sequence?

4. Name three steps that might be used in terminating an interview.

5. Describe two main advantages of the nondirective interview technique.

6. What are five types of responses in a counseling interview? Give an example of each.

7. Identify six specific hints for success in an appraisal interview.

8. Identify five specific hints for success in a selection interview.

9. Identify five specific hints for interviewers for success in a selection interview.

Exercises

1. Videotape an interview conducted by your classmates. Play back the interview and have the class evaluate it in terms of the suggested procedures for conducting the beginning, body, and end of an interview.

2. Role-play the part of respondent to a classmate, providing inadequate responses to develop his or her ability to probe for better answers. Then switch roles and take the test yourself.

3. Role-play the following examples, attempting to use the nondirective interview technique.

Situation 1

Manager: Paul, one of the supervisors in the computer services department, has asked to see you about what he says is really "a problem." You are not really sure what the problem is, but you have heard that he is having personnel problems in his department. In thinking through the approach you might take with Paul, what things should you consider?

Employee: You are one of the supervisors in the computer services department. You have arranged to meet with your manager about a personnel problem concerning one of your employees. The problem is that this employee is competent in his job, and you really depend on him to get things done. However, he makes life miserable for everyone. He has a very negative approach toward the other employees and communicates a very "superior" attitude. Just the other day you asked him to consult with one of the other employees before

making a program revision. He did this, but the other employee was so upset with his approach that she came to you about the problem. This is really a dilemma for you because on one hand this employee does the job well, but on the other hand he causes real conflict in the department.

You really want the manager to solve the problem for you. So, you continually ask him, "What would you do?" "I need some advice." If the manager begins to use an approach that gets you to "solve your own problem," then begin to think what you can do.

Situation 2

Supervisor: It has come time for you to appraise Bill, one of your employees. Bill is the product of a misused appraisal system. Because of inflated past appraisals, he's received a couple of promotions he probably didn't deserve, judging by his present performance. He does an average job, but at his level and pay you expect a lot more from him. Bill joined your group about a year ago on a lateral transfer when another group was reducing head count. Initially you had high hopes for him based on those performance appraisals, but he hasn't lived up to your expectations. He usually gets his work done, but he sometimes misses deadlines. He never seems to be around when you need him in a hurry, and you're not sure you can count on him when the chips are down. As a result you usually end up giving the tight-deadline jobs to Ron or June.

Bill's problem is that he loves to talk, especially if there's a good rumor to be spread. He seems to know the "right" people and delights in talking about "inside information" and "political power plays." This may have been a factor in his past promotions. This not only takes him away from his job and chews up his time, but it wastes your time and other people's. You've talked to him several times about this, but somehow the message never seems to get through. In your annual appraisal of Bill you rate him as just meeting standard. Since he has been rated so high in the past, you know that he will be upset. In getting ready for your appraisal discussion, what approach would be best?

Employee: You are Bill and your supervisor has just arranged a time for you to discuss your performance appraisal. You have always received good appraisals and you really don't expect that much different this time. When your supervisor tells you that he has rated you as "just meeting standard," you get very upset. You indicate that you have always received good appraisals in the past. In fact, the last five years you have received two promotions.

You are a "talker" and you try to dominate the interview with your reactions. Hold on to your negative attitude until the supervisor does some things to make you "cool down." When he does this, begin to respond objectively.

Suggested Readings

Bolles, Charles. *What Color Is Your Parachute?* Berkeley, CA: Ten Speed Press, published annually.

An invaluable source for someone seeking a job.

Byham, William C., and Debra Pickett. *Landing the Job You Want.* Pittsburgh: Three Rivers Press, 1999.

This excellent book is based on many years of research on employment interviews. It offers practical suggestions to help you with job interviews. This book is a must read if you are going to interview for a job.

Camp, Richaurd, Mary Vielhaber, and Jack Simonetti. *Strategic Interviewing: How to Hire the Best People.* San Francisco: Jossey-Bass, 2001.

This book takes a "behavioral interviewing" approach. It is an excellent source for interviewers and interviewees alike.

Deluca, Matthew J. *Best Answers to the 201 Most Frequently Asked Interview Questions.* New York: McGraw-Hill, 1997.

This interview guide offers excellent suggestions about how to answer many of the most frequently asked interview questions. It includes tips on breaking the ice, personal questions, educational questions, stress questions, and illegal questions.

Gerzon, Mark. *Leading Through Conflict.* Boston: Harvard Business School Press, 2006.

This book focuses on ways that leaders can work through conflict with others, through using one-on-one interviews.

Kador, John. *How to Ace the Brainteaser Interview.* New York: McGraw-Hill, 2004.

This book contains 200 of the most puzzling interview questions and how to answer them.

Patterson, Kerry, Joseph Grenny, Ron McMillan, and Al Switzler. *Crucial Confrontations.* New York: McGraw-Hill, 2005.

This best seller offers extensive tips on how to conduct interviews when the parties need to resolve broken promises, violated expectations, and bad behavior.

Stewart, Charles J., and William B. Cash. *Interviewing: Principles and Practices,* 9th ed. New York: McGraw-Hill, 1999.

Excellent and comprehensive coverage of interviewing. In addition to covering the basics, the book has entire chapters on special types of interviews. It covers surveying, information gathering, employment performance appraisal and disciplining, counseling, and the persuasive interview.

 # For Supplementary Information

Log onto the Online Learning Center at *www.mhhe.com/tubbsmoss11.*

Small-Group Communication

Chapter Objectives

After reading this chapter, you should be able to:

1. Describe two theories that have been used to explain compliance with social pressure.
2. Describe the problem of "groupthink."
3. Describe the four phases of a typical group's development.
4. Describe the relationship between group size, member satisfaction, and group performance.
5. Distinguish between task and consideration functions in leadership.
6. Identify six common difficulties that small groups encounter in developing ideas and solving problems.
7. Describe four ways in which a group can arrive at a decision.

Consider the following facts:

- 11 million meetings occur in the United States each and every day.
- Professionals attend a total of 61.8 meetings per month.
- Over 50 percent of this meeting time is wasted (Meetings in America, 1998).

James Surowiecki, an author and business columnist for the *New Yorker,* states that "under the right circumstances, groups are remarkably intelligent, and are often smarter than the smartest people in them" (Hannon, 2004, p. B8). Did you know that in 2003, 17 international research labs harmonized their small-group efforts in order to unveil the SARS virus (Hannon, 2004, p. B8)?

The power of group decisions over individual decisions has been dramatically demonstrated in the popular television show *Who Wants to be a Millionaire?* As Surowiecki (2004) writes in his best-selling book *Wisdom of Crowds,* past incidents have shown that asking the crowd most of the time gave a higher chance of getting the correct answer than calling a friend through the "lifeline." This is but one of many such studies that show that groups of individuals consistently make better quality decisions than the same individuals trying to solve the same problems separately in the same amount of time (Tubbs, 2007).

Although group communication skills have been valued for many years, recently there has been a dramatic increase in the emphasis placed on this type of expertise. One professional association reported that Harvard, Syracuse, UCLA, the University of Illinois, the University of Michigan, BYU, SMU, and the University of Tennessee are just a few of the many universities that have increased their requirements for students to take group communication courses to improve their teamwork and communication skills (AACSB, 2007). One of the reasons is that more and more careers require teamwork and group committee work.

According to a national survey, the average number of meetings has jumped from 7 to 10 a week. Business and other professionals spend 25 to 60 percent of their time in meetings according to 3M Meeting Network, an online resource covering meeting issues (*www.abanet.org/buslaw/blt/7-6snap.html*). They report that as much as 50 percent of that time is unproductive and up to 25 percent of the time covers irrelevant issues. The following are a few tips on how to make meetings more useful:

- Have a reason for the meeting.
- Prepare ahead of time.
- Give participants at least one day's notice.
- Distribute an agenda ahead of time.
- Limit attendance and designate a leader.
- Encourage everyone to contribute.
- Keep a clock in the room and have a specific starting and ending time.
- Start and end on time. (Armour, 1997)

Most of us spend at least some of our time in problem-solving groups. A student council, a commission investigating the causes of prison riots, a fund-raising committee for a political party, and a tenants' association organized to fight rent increases have much in common. Despite the diverse issues that concern them, each group consists of several human beings with different ideas, skills, and levels of interest. Each group has a problem to solve and must determine the best way to go about solving it—ideally by making use of the resources of all its members.

This chapter is about the kind of communication that takes place in small groups, particularly in **problem-solving,** or *task-oriented,* **groups.** We shall focus first on the ways in which such groups typically function and second on the ways individual members can improve their effectiveness in them. In doing so, we begin to extend the communication model outlined in Chapter 1. The dyad is sometimes referred to as a "two-person group," and often two people will engage in problem solving. But in discussing the small group, particularly the problem-solving group, we shall follow the definition offered in Chapter 1—namely, that a small group is a collection of individuals who influence one another, derive some satisfaction from maintaining membership in the group, interact for some purpose, assume specialized roles, are dependent on one another, and communicate face to face (Tubbs, 2007). A small group will meet some but not necessarily all six criteria.

TYPES OF SMALL GROUPS

Small-group experience is by no means confined to problem solving. Each of us is simultaneously a member of many small groups. The first and most informal are primary groups, the basic social units to which we belong. Our first primary group is our family. Our childhood friends constitute another.

A social identity forms once a person realizes he or she belongs to a group. One of the major cognitive tools individuals use to define themselves vis-à-vis the world in which they live is social categorization, "the ordering of social environment in terms of groupings of persons in a manner which makes sense to the individual" (Gudykunst and Hammer, 1988, p. 571).

In the company of adult friends, neighbors, and others with whom we socialize—fraternity or sorority groups, classmates, teammates, even street gangs—we continue and *extend our primary-group relationships* to **casual** or **social groups.** While these relationships may be relatively short-lived, their influence on later thinking and behavior is often considerable. Newcomb (1963) found that the attitudes and values of college students were influenced significantly by the friends and acquaintances they made while at college. To a lesser degree, these changes were still present 30 years after graduation. Occasionally, members of primary or social groups solve problems together, but much of their communication is spontaneous and informal.

As members of **learning** or **education groups,** we come together in an attempt *to teach or learn something about a given subject.* Quarterback clubs meet to learn more about football. Film groups get together to share their interpretations of movies. Seminars and courses involving group interaction also constitute learning groups. Brilhart and Galanes (1998) refer to such groups as "enlightenment groups," in which members may attempt to solve problems but have no authority to implement their decisions.

Sooner or later, most of us will belong to **work groups,** which *have specific goals to achieve,* often within the context of a job. Membership may be required by virtue of employment in an organization rather than because of individual interest in the group. Group members may have little in common other than that their jobs require them to interact. That they receive payment for their individual contributions adds a unique dimension to this type of group. And whereas a member of a social or a learning group might remain relatively inactive, the consequences of not participating in a work group can be more severe (reprimands, ostracism, or even loss of employment).

The most recent innovation in work groups is the **self-directed work team** (SDWT), defined by Kimball Fisher (1999) as "a group of employees who have day-to-day responsibility for managing themselves and the work they do with a minimum of direct supervision. Members . . . typically handle job assignments, plan and schedule work, make production and/or service related decisions, and take action on problems" (p. 15).

Increasingly, modern organizations are striving to use their employees more effectively. Huszczo (2004) identifies three reasons why SDWTs seem to work so well:

1. Those closest to the work know best how to perform and improve their jobs.
2. Most employees want to feel that they "own" their own jobs and are making meaningful contributions to the effectiveness of their organizations.
3. Teams provide possibilities for empowerment that are not available to individual employees. (p. 4)

Using SDWTs allows employees to have a much greater level of empowerment, increases productivity, and lowers product costs. Pasternack and Viscio (1998) report that Mrs. Field's Cookies, Levi Strauss, AT&T, General Electric, IBM, and Xerox are just a few of the many companies using this very creative new form of leadership (p. 25). However, since the introduction of the SDWT several years ago, as Davis and colleagues write in the *Employee's Responsibility and Rights Journal* (2004), some legal questions have been raised. Teams are not legally able to make disciplinary and/or discharge decisions without exposing the organization to "wrongful discharge" allegations.

Homans (1950, p. 1) has described membership in small groups as "the first and most immediate social experience of mankind." More specifically, he defines a group as "a number of persons who communicate with one another often over a span of time and who are few enough so that each person is able to communicate with all the others, not at secondhand, through other people, but face-to-face." As you read this chapter, you might give some thought to this definition.

GROUP DYNAMICS

We are all familiar with all the problems and pleasures associated with family roles, but in the business world we discover other aspects of group membership. One of the major complaints about committees and other problem-solving small groups is that they take up too much time and seldom accomplish as much as they should. To make better use of the time spent in small groups, we have to know something about how people ordinarily behave in them.

Remember when you first came to college? You encountered a lot of situations in which you didn't know exactly how you were supposed to act. In unfamiliar situations, we all look to others for cues on what is the appropriate thing to do. In these situations we are especially vulnerable to social influence. In the movie *Big*, Tom Hanks goes to a cocktail party in a light blue tuxedo, and everybody laughs at him for not dressing appropriately. All of us have been in situations like that.

Conformity Pressure

A great deal of research has been done on conformity pressure and the effect it has on our behaviors. In one study, people had to estimate how much a point of light appeared to move in a dark room. Since the light did not move at all, the optical illusion regarding the amount of movement was highly sensitive to social influence. The researchers found that individual estimates of autokinetic movement vary a great deal. To one person it might seem that the light has moved 2 inches; to another the distance might seem to be 6 inches. Yet Sherif (1967) found that a person who first views this phenomenon when he or she is isolated from others and observes it several times under these conditions will develop a standard of his or her own so that all his or her subsequent estimates of distance fall within this range. On the other hand, when a person witnesses the autokinetic effect for the first time as a member of a group, the group establishes a norm; if that person is then exposed again to the autokinetic effect, he or she will make estimates in terms of the group norm. Moreover, a person who has made initial judgments in isolation and then overhears others estimate the distance will correct his or her own estimate so that it tends to converge with that of the others.

A more recent case of group conformity pressure was illustrated in the movie *A Few Good Men*, starring Jack Nicholson, Demi Moore, and Tom Cruise. In the film, the marines in a military unit would discipline a member of their unit who was out of line with the group's norms. This practice was referred to as a "Code Red" and usually consisted of some type of physical punishment. In this particular case it resulted in an accidental death. The entire movie illustrates several group dynamics concepts discussed in this chapter.

One of the criticisms of conformity research has been that subjects rarely get to argue their point of view against the majority opinion. Yet even in studies that allow dissenting members to present their arguments, considerable conformity behavior still occurs (Lovelace, Shapiro, and Weingart, 2001; Barr and Conlon, 1994). These studies distinguish between **private acceptance** of a judgment or opinion and **public compliance**—that is, *between whether people change their thinking as a result of hearing opinions different from their own or whether they say they agree with the group when in fact they disagree.*

Private acceptance is more likely to occur when (1) the individual greatly values membership in the group, (2) opinion is unanimously against him or her, (3) the issue in question is ambiguous to begin with, or (4) the group is under pressure to achieve an important goal (Tubbs, 2007). Public compliance usually stems from the desire to avoid the unpleasantness of conflict. After maintaining a dissenting opinion for a long time, a person may be made so uncomfortable by social pressures that as a peace-keeping gesture, he or she gives the impression of going along with the rest of the group. A number of studies have shown that the person who conforms readily tends to be (1) more submissive or dependent, (2) high in the need for social approval and low in the need to be outstanding, (3) more often female than male, and (4) lacking in self-confidence (Hare, 1962).

Social Influence

We have looked at conformity behavior in terms of the individual member. Now let us examine the behavior of the group. We know that the group tends to exert most pressure to conform on newcomers, who have not yet earned the right to deviate from group norms. Fraternities and sororities often deal out harsh criticism when rushees and pledges dress or act differently from other members of the group. Yet a great many of the same deviations are tolerated when they exist in fraternity members who are juniors or seniors. One may wonder if those involved in the abuse of the Abu Ghraib prisoners in Iraq would have participated in the abuse if acting out on their own. Or, were some conforming to the social influence of others at the prison?

Groups with a high level of cohesiveness tend to exert strong conformity pressures. It seems that the more closely knit the group, the more the members resist allowing anyone to become a member who does not share their values. Members with the greatest prestige tend to be "super representatives" of the attributes that are highly valued by the group. The typical football team captain is usually one of the best athletes on the team. Similarly, the gang leader is often one of the gang's toughest members. In each case, the person who best represents the qualities esteemed by the group has the most prestige.

How does the cohesive group behave when one of its members takes a stand quite different from that of the rest? Schachter (1951) found that initially the deviant gets most of the group's attention. Each member will probably say or do something to persuade the lone dissenter to come around to the position held by the rest of the group. These efforts may go on for some time. Eventually, the deviant either gives in—there is no way of knowing, of course, whether this is simply public compliance—or is ignored or rejected.

An explanation of what makes most of us yield to social pressure is offered by Festinger's **social comparison theory.** Festinger (1954) believes that *all human beings have a need to evaluate their own opinions and abilities and that when they cannot do so by objective nonsocial means, they compare them with those of other people.* How do you tell, for example, whether you are a good driver? Clearly, by comparing your performance with that of other drivers. Similarly, you find out whether you are liberal in your political views by comparing them with those of others. In other words, in the absence of objective criteria, you rely on the opinions of others to determine the validity of your own.

In the Schachter experiment, a discrepancy existed between the opinions of one group member and the rest of the group. Social comparison theory predicts that in such a situation group members will act to reduce the discrepancy and that the person with the discrepant opinion will tend to change his or her position so that it is closer to that of other group members. We saw this to be the case not only in the Schachter experiment but in some of the studies of the autokinetic effect, where individual judgments tend to converge with group norms. However these phenomena are explained, the tendency to conform seems clear. In the following section, we shall examine conformity as it affects group decisions.

The Quality of Group Problem Solving

The study of group dynamics raises the question "How do groups compare with individuals in problem solving?" Will the number of people in the group affect the quality of the decision? Will people meeting together generate a greater number of novel ideas than they would working in isolation? In short, how does the presence of others influence the way we think?

Acceptance of Risk

It has been established that members of groups tend to conform. As yet, however, nothing has been said about the direction of that conformity. When we call someone a "conformist," we usually think of him or her as somewhat conservative. Conformists don't rock the boat. They don't create dissension. They go along with group norms. They probably go along with group decisions. It would seem that because they conform, they take few risks, and from this we might guess that the decisions of the group would also tend to be conservative or at least cautious.

Suppose you are on your way to a meeting in which your group will advise Mr. A, an electrical engineer, about the pros and cons of a certain career choice. Should he remain in the large electronics corporation for which he works, where he is assured a high level of security and moderate financial rewards, or should he accept an offer from a small, recently founded company that will offer him a higher starting salary and a share in the firm's ownership but whose future is highly uncertain? What odds will you give—1 in 10, 3 in 10, and so on—that the new company turns out to be financially sound and, thus, that Mr. A will do better joining it than remaining where he is? Whatever the odds you choose, chances are that if a group discussion follows, it will significantly increase your estimate of Mr. A's chances for success.

The **risky shift phenomenon** is the name given this *tendency of people to increase their willingness to take risks as a result of group discussions*. It is by no means confined to decisions about careers. Here, for example, are summaries of a few of the experimental problems that have demonstrated a shift toward risk after group communication:

> A man with a severe heart ailment must seriously curtail his customary way of life if he does not undergo a delicate medical operation which might cure him completely or might prove fatal.

A captain of a college football team, in the final seconds of a game with the college's traditional rival, may choose a play that is almost certain to produce a tie score, or a more risky play that would lead to sure victory if successful, sure defeat if not.

An engaged couple must decide, in the face of recent arguments suggesting some sharp differences of opinion, whether or not to get married. Discussions with a marriage counselor indicate that a happy marriage, while possible, would not be ensured. (Wallach et al., 1962, p. 77; see also Okhuysen, 2001)

Several explanations of the risky shift phenomenon have been proposed; we shall consider three of them in brief fashion. The first is that within a group no member feels totally responsible for the decision. This might explain the actions of lynch mobs: A person who might never dare commit a murder alone suddenly helps carry out a lynching. The second possibility is that those who argue in favor of risky positions are more persuasive than those who are conservative and that they therefore influence others in favor of riskier decisions. The first two hypotheses have little experimental support. A third and more likely possibility is that Western culture tends to value risk taking over conservative behavior.

As you find yourself participating in task-oriented groups, it is important to realize that the group decision is likely to be riskier than the average of the positions taken by individual group members before their interaction.

Groupthink

In the small group, social influence is even more powerful than it is in the dyad. Moreover, as we know from the principles of balance theory, the judgments of other people affect our attitudes, beliefs, and values as well as our perceptions.

Norms need not be negative in their effect. Sometimes it's possible to establish constructive norms that will improve group functioning. Marv Patterson of Hewlett-Packard (HP) says that the norm for the company is to hire the "best of the best." This is how HP maintains a team environment that "crackles with creativity and intellectual spirit" (Kao, 1996, p. xvi). This constructive norm at HP is designed to avoid the "groupthink" problem that often occurs when subordinates in large organizations are afraid to disagree with the boss.

In general, groupthink refers to a problem-solving process in which ideas accepted by the group are not really examined, and opposing ideas are suppressed. The term "groupthink" was coined in 1972 by Irving Janis, a psychologist with Yale University. Janis defined groupthink as "a mode of thinking that people engage in when they are deeply involved in a cohesive in-group, when the members' strivings for unanimity override their motivation to realistically appraise alternative courses of action" (Schwartz & Wald, 2003, p. A15). This phenomenon has been investigated in very visible social and political arenas. For example, political critics assert that the 2003 false statements that Iraq was housing weapons of mass destruction was a result of political groupthink among the ultimate decision makers within the United States government (Lobe, 2004, p. 1). A groupthink problem has also been considered by some theorists in the February 1, 2003, failed *Columbia* space shuttle mission. Analysis of the incident raised questions about NASA regarding the decision made by Boeing engineers to allow *Columbia* to launch when there was a potential problem with a portion of the foam core detaching from the vessel. The critical group of engineers all seemed to be in agreement when the decision was made that the detached foam would not affect the mission, even though some engineers strongly disagreed at the onset of the decision-making process. The foam has now been identified as a key factor in the failure of the mission (Lobe, 2004, p. 1).

Kevin McManus, (2007) writing in the *Industrial Engineer* magazine, summarizes why the groupthink phenomenon is so powerful. First, most people are not aware of groupthink when it is occurring. Second, people are afraid to speak their minds because they don't want to appear to be an outsider or are insecure about taking a contrary position. The result is that groupthink often causes us to use limited organizational resources in suboptimal ways.

Janis (1982) lists eight main symptoms of groupthink: (1) Members share the illusion of invulnerability, providing the impetus to take extraordinary risks and fail to see early signs of danger; (2) warnings and other negative feedback are rationalized away; (3) members believe they are moral and thus can ignore the ethical implications of what they do; (4) leaders of other groups are considered evil and, therefore, not people with whom negotiations are reasonable; (5) members who stray from the group's beliefs are pressured to conform; (6) members avoid speaking out when not in favor of the group's actions, thus self-censure replaces group censure; (7) members share the illusion that agreement is unanimous; and (8) members screen the group, and especially the leader, from adverse information. With groupthink in operation, the group considers few alternatives, fails to scrutinize accepted ideas, fails to gather all the necessary information, fails to consider all the sides of an issue, and fails to consider alternative plans in the event the chosen plan is rejected by others or does not work.

Level of Creativity

Another issue concerning the kinds of solutions groups reach has to do with creativity. Consider this problem. The Lang Advertising Agency has five writers on its staff. It is bidding for the Hudson's Bay Scotch account and must submit a sales presentation and advertising program to the prospective client. Should all five writers work independently and submit their own programs to the advertising director, or should the five be brought together to tackle the problem? Which procedure will generate a greater number of original ideas?

In essence we are asking whether **brainstorming** is an effective problem-solving technique. This approach, first introduced in the advertising firm of Batten, Barton, Durstine & Osborn in 1939, was designed to offset tendencies of group members to be inhibited by pressures to conform. Brainstorming had several rules. There was to be no criticism of ideas. "Freewheeling" was encouraged: The more way out the idea, the better. Quantity was desired: The greater the number of ideas, the better. Taking off on other people's ideas—either by improving one or by showing how two different ideas could be combined—is also encouraged (Newvine, 1998). Raudsepp

(1980) cites his own research at Princeton University, which indicates that by using this technique, individuals are able to increase their creative performance by 40 to 300 percent (p. 10). (See also Lipman-Blumen and Leavitt, 1999.)

Take the example of the popular TV show *Everybody Loves Raymond*. In 2004 the show was deciding whether to run another season. Creator Phil Rosenthal and star Ray Romano were reported to "have numerous brainstorming sessions with the writing staff to determine whether there's enough life left in *Raymond*, creatively speaking, to go another season" ("Raymond Mulls Future," 2004). Their brainstorming must have worked: The show decided to tape episodes for one final season.

Tubbs (2007) offers the following list of idea killers, which often serve to reduce group creativity as well as productivity:

- That's ridiculous.
- We tried that before.
- That will never work.
- That's crazy.
- It's too radical a change.
- We're too small for it.
- It's not practical.
- Let's get back to reality.
- You can't teach an old dog new tricks.
- We'll be the laughingstock.
- You're absolutely wrong.
- You don't know what you're talking about.
- It's impossible.
- There's no way it can be done. (pp. 75–76)

On the other hand, "igniter phrases" such as those listed below often promote creativity and group productivity by establishing a psychological climate in the group that encourages creative thinking:

- I agree.
- That's good!
- I made a mistake. I'm sorry.
- That's a great idea.
- I'm glad you brought that up.
- You're on the right track.
- I know it will work.
- We're going to try something different today.
- I never thought of that.
- We can do a lot with that idea.
- Real good, anyone else?
- I like that!
- That would be worth a try.
- Why don't we assume it would work and go from there.
  (Tubbs, 2007, pp. 75–76)

For effective group creativity, a happy group yields the most positive results. Sutton (2002) recommends positive steps by the use of humor in small groups. He recommends waiting until the group has truly bonded to introduce difficult topics, teaching humor as an outlet for stress, telling stories of successful group conflict, and screening new group members to make sure that they are positive and energetic.

Additional research by Amabile (1998) found that individuals who were high producers of ideas perceived the brainstorming task as more attractive, were low in communication apprehension, and possessed higher ambiguity tolerance than those individuals low in idea productivity. The author concludes from her findings that the best brainstormers are those interested in the brainstorming topic who are not afraid to communicate their ideas. This indicates that although brainstorming may achieve its best effects by reducing the problems associated with criticism and the question of "quality," individual predispositions to communicate still play a major role in the outcome.

The Role of a Group Member

Nine psychotherapists have formed a group to help block the passage of mental health legislation that they consider repressive. Ostensibly, the group's members are equal in status. No leader has been appointed. In this context each of the therapists has the same role—that of group member. Because of your interest in small-group communication and your friendship with one of the therapists, you are allowed to attend the meetings as an observer.

After attending a few meetings, you begin to notice that Bob knows a lot about existing mental health laws. He also makes a number of suggestions for actions the group might take: contacting legislators, raising funds for a series of broadcasts on the issue, distributing handbills about the implications of the new law. Matt, another member of the group, has few ideas of his own and tends to go along with any concrete proposals for group action. "I'm for that. Why not try it?" he often says. Frank, on the other hand, has more ideas than he knows what to do with. He proposes solutions, one after another—some sound, others extreme. Initially, he is very enthusiastic, but he never seems to carry through on any of his suggestions. To the chagrin of most of the group, Kay usually punches holes in other people's arguments. "It will never work," she chides. "What do we use for money? People aren't going to contribute. They don't understand the issue."

Here are four people in the role of group member. Each interprets it somewhat differently. You think you see some individual patterns of interaction emerging, but to be accurate, you need a method of describing various behaviors.

One of the more important accomplishments of small-group research has been the development of several such systems. The most widely known is interaction process analysis (IPA), developed at Harvard University by Robert Bales (1970). The twelve categories of IPA are virtually self-explanatory (see Figure 12.1), and they offer a valuable framework from which to view the functions and patterns of communication. Each interaction is assigned to one of the categories, and when the scoring has been completed, certain behavior patterns become apparent.

Figure 12.1 *Categories for Interaction Process Analysis*

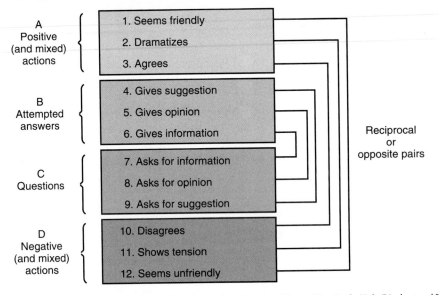

Source: From *Personality and Interpersonal Behavior* by Robert Freed Bates, (New York: Holt, Rinehart and Winston, 1970). Reprinted with permission of the author.

In the group we have been discussing, Bob's statements would tend to fall in categories 4 (gives suggestion) and 6 (gives information), Matt's in 3 (agrees), Frank's in 4 (gives suggestion), and Kay's in 10 (disagrees). The responses of other members in the group may be more diversified so that no single category or set of categories predominates, but over an extended period we could probably identify the characteristic behaviors of each member. In any case, Bales's method of classifying human interaction gives us a systematic way to analyze group communication. By means of these categories, we can classify each communicative act regardless of its content.

As you look at the list in Figure 12.1, you might ask yourself which categories describe your own actions in small groups. There is a good chance that you will find yourself performing only a limited number of these behaviors. For example, one friend of ours summed up his participation in groups by saying, "I often like to play the devil's advocate and give people a bit of a hard time." If his statement is accurate, we would expect that most of his interactions (like those of Kay in the group we described) would fall in category 10 of the IPA. There are groups that need at least one critical member, someone willing to challenge others, but the last thing in the world some groups need is another devil's advocate. In general, it seems foolish to assume that any behavior or set of behaviors is appropriate in all situations; there is much to be said for developing some degree of role flexibility.

Tubbs (2007) has adapted the following classification of roles that originated with Benne and Sheats (1948).

Group Task Roles

These behaviors are directed toward accomplishing the group's objective through problem solving:

- *Initiating-contributing:* Proposing new ideas or a changed way of regarding the group goal. This may include a new goal or a new definition of the problem. It may involve suggesting a solution or some way of handling a difficulty the group has encountered. It may also include a new procedure for the group to better organize its efforts.
- *Information seeking:* Asking for clarification, for authoritative information and facts relevant to the problem under discussion.
- *Opinion seeking:* Seeking information related not so much to factual data as to the values underlying the suggestions being considered.
- *Information giving:* Offering facts or generalizations based on experience or authoritative sources.
- *Opinion giving:* Stating beliefs or opinions relevant to a suggestion made. The emphasis is on the proposal of what ought to become the group's values rather than on facts or information.
- *Elaborating:* Expanding on suggestions with examples or restatements, offering a rationale for previously made suggestions, and trying to determine the results if a suggestion were adopted by the group.
- *Coordinating:* Indicating the relationships among various ideas and suggestions, attempting to combine ideas and suggestions, or trying to coordinate the activities of group members.
- *Orienting:* Indicating the position of the group by summarizing progress made and deviations from agreed-upon directions or goals or by raising questions about the direction the group is taking.
- *Evaluating:* Comparing the group's accomplishments to some criterion or standard of group functioning. This may include questioning the practicality, logic, or procedure of a suggestion.
- *Energizing:* Stimulating the group to action or a decision, attempting to increase the level or quality of activity.
- *Assisting on procedure:* Helping or facilitating group movement by doing things for the group—for example, performing routine tasks such as distributing materials, rearranging the seating, or running a tape recorder.
- *Recording:* Writing down suggestions, recording group decisions, or recording the outcomes of the discussion. This provides tangible results of the group's effort.

Group-Building and Maintenance Roles

The roles in this category help the interpersonal functioning of the group. They help alter the way of working; they strengthen, regulate, and perpetuate the group. This is analogous to preventive maintenance done to keep a mechanical device such as a car in better working order:

- *Encouraging:* Praising, showing interest in, agreeing with, and accepting the contributions of others; showing warmth toward other group members, listening attentively and seriously to the ideas of others, showing tolerance for ideas different from one's own, conveying the feeling that one feels the contributions of others are important.
- *Harmonizing:* Mediating the differences among the other members, attempting to reconcile disagreements, relieving tension in moments of conflict through the use of humor.
- *Compromising:* Operating from within a conflict situation, one may offer a compromise by yielding status, by admitting a mistake, by disciplining oneself for the sake of group harmony, or by coming halfway toward another position.
- *Gatekeeping and expediting:* Attempting to keep communication channels open by encouraging the participation of some or by curbing the participation of others.
- *Setting standards or ideals:* Expressing standards for the group and/or evaluating the quality of group processes (as opposed to evaluating the content of discussion).
- *Observing:* Keeping a record of various aspects of group process and feeding this information, along with interpretations, into the group's evaluation of its procedures. This contribution is best received when the person has been requested by the group to perform this function. The observer should avoid expressing judgments of approval or disapproval in reporting observations.
- *Following:* Going along with the group, passively accepting the ideas of others, serving as an audience in group discussion.

Individual Roles

These behaviors are designed more to satisfy an individual's needs than to contribute to the needs of the group. These are sometimes referred to as self-centered roles:

- *Aggressing:* Deflating the status of others, disapproving of the ideas or values of others, attacking the group or the problem it is attempting to solve, joking maliciously, resenting the contributions of others and/or trying to take credit for them.
- *Blocking:* Resisting, disagreeing, and opposing beyond reason; bringing up dead issues after they have been rejected or bypassed by the group.
- *Recognition seeking:* Calling attention to oneself through boasting, reporting on personal achievements, acting in inappropriate ways, fighting to keep from being placed in an inferior position.

- *Self-confessing:* Using the group as an opportunity to express personal, non-group-related feelings, insights, ideologies.
- *Acting the jokester:* Showing a lack of involvement in the group's task. Displaying nonchalance, cynicism, horseplay, and other kinds of "goofing-off" behaviors.
- *Dominating:* Trying to assert authority or superiority by manipulating others in the group. This may take the form of flattery, asserting a superior status or right to attention, giving directions authoritatively, and/or interrupting others.
- *Help seeking:* Attempting to get sympathy from other group members through expressions of insecurity, personal inadequacy, or self-criticism beyond reason.
- *Special-interest pleading:* Speaking on behalf of some group such as "the oppressed," "labor," "business," usually cloaking one's own prejudices or biases in the stereotype that best fits one's momentary need.

Cohesiveness

Probably one of the most important by-products of group interaction is the emotional commitment that may evolve from having worked on a problem with others. For example, many organizations use self-managed work teams to solve internal problems. These are generally small groups in which cohesiveness is a necessity. A Kansas City Harley-Davidson plant study revealed that the group members' perceptions of fair treatment within the group and control over who was on the team led to higher levels of cohesion and performance (Chansler et al., 2003, p. 101).

A classic study conducted during World War II found that women who participated in group discussions on how best to cook unpopular cuts of meat (and thus leave favored cuts for the troops overseas) were much more likely to try out new recipes than were women who simply listened to a speech intended to persuade them to do so (Cartwright and Zander, 1968). Being in a cohesive group leads to greater effectiveness from individuals in the group.

This kind of emotional commitment seems to increase as attraction to the group increases. **Cohesiveness** has been defined as *"the total field of forces acting on members to remain in the group"* (Schachter, 1951, p. 191). It may also be considered in terms of the loyalty and high morale of group members. Think of groups you have either been in or observed that were closely knit. Two groups that are not necessarily problem-solving groups but that illustrate high levels of cohesion are the Kennedy clan and Michael Jackson's family. Cohesiveness, which connotes pride of membership, often intensifies as a group becomes more successful. We are all familiar with the popular chant of crowds at sporting events, "We're number 1. We're number 1."

In general, cohesive groups have interested and committed members who enjoy each other's company. The group is not always highly productive, but its members do tend to help each other with problems, to adapt well to crisis situations, and to ask questions openly. We referred earlier to the conformity demands made by a cohesive group on its members. It is true, however, that they may sometimes feel free to disagree more openly than members of less cohesive groups.

Any discussion of emotional reactions to groups must acknowledge that things do not always turn out so positively. Working with others can also be frustrating, boring, and unsettling. The point is that the socioemotional dimension of group interaction constitutes a very real and powerful part of group behavior. Many people think that feelings have no place in a problem-solving group. On the contrary, feelings are very much involved in group behavior and should be studied as vigorously as its logical and rational aspects.

Phases of Group Development

It has been said that, like a human being, each group has a life cycle: It has a birth, childhood, and maturity, and ultimately it ceases to exist. A number of theories have been proposed about what growth typically occurs in a group, and these are based on the study of either problem-solving or therapeutic groups (especially encounter groups). Understanding the phases of group development provides a framework upon which group growth may be measured, provides a basis for making predictions about the group's progress, and allows a leader to plan interventions aimed at affecting the group's growth. Understanding allows for the best predictions, and the best predictions allow for the best responses to the group. For example, avoiding group conflict is not a good response, since conflict is a normal part of group development.

Theorists seem to agree that growth and development in the group are the result of both the needs of the individual members and the social forces created within the group itself. Typically, these forces interact in a predictable way, with the group going through several stages or phases. Some theorists identify four phases, others three, and there are other differences in interpretation as well. For example, some theorists believe that the various phases occur even if a group meets only once (Tuckman, 1965; Fisher, 1970). Others hold that the phases occur over the life history of a group that meets repeatedly (Bennis and Shepard, 1956; Thelen and Dickerman, 1949). And still a third faction contends that all the group phases occur in each meeting and continue to recur throughout the group's life history (Schutz, 1958; Bales and Strodbeck, 1951; Blanchard, 2007). This third theory seems the most likely and the most valuable in providing insight into group development. Keeping these different viewpoints in mind, let us look at the four-phase model of group development as it is represented in the literature.

Phase 1: Forming really begins prior to the first meeting, when members begin the process of separating themselves from attachments that could interfere with the group and attempt to learn about the group and/or other members. Forming lasts anywhere from one day to several weeks, as members attempt to learn about the group members and the task that needs to be accomplished. Interaction is cautious, characterized by ambiguous language and a great deal of agreement (which is easy with ambiguous statements). Minimal work is accomplished, and the phase doesn't end until the norms are relatively clear. Questions uppermost in members' minds are "What is this group about?" "Do I fit in?" "Do I want to be in or out?"

Phase 1 is also a period in which group members break the ice and begin to establish a common base for functioning. This stage is sometimes referred to as a period of "orientation," "inclusion," or "group formation." Initially, people may ask questions about one another, tell where they are from, and generally make small talk. It seems that early in the life of a group, members are interested in building a working relationship that is psychologically comfortable. Even members of the most ambitious problem-solving groups usually spend some time socializing.

Phase 2: Storming is a normal and expected response to the orientation phase: Whereas the orientation or forming phase built group solidarity, storming or conflict is the assertion of individuality (often in response to feelings of being "swallowed up" by the group). The agreement and ambiguity of the first phase give way to clear, unambiguous, and direct language, and agreement now is on specific issues, albeit agreement is low. During this phase the group loses part of its group identity, confusion over goals may increase, and minimal work is accomplished (still!). Storming usually revolves around two issues (regardless of the specific content, these two issues are usually the bottom line, the real issues): How close/how far should we be from each other emotionally, and is the leader a fool or "all wise?" Control and affection are the issues (see Chapter 6).

This period of dissent and controversy is ripe for communication failures: The more emotionally charged the discussion, the more prone group members are to jump to conclusions, lose their tempers, or interpret the comments of others as threats or criticisms. One student description clearly tracks the movement from Phase 1 to Phase 2:

> We talked about personal interests until some common ground was established, then we found we could talk about the assignment more freely. But after talking about non-subject things, it was hard to keep the line of talk on the problems at hand. Some wanted to get the assignment accomplished while two guys in the group continually swayed the conversation to things that were easier to talk about, but had nothing to do with the subject (Howard has a big thing for John Deere farm machinery). At first we were constantly trying not to hurt anyone's feelings, so we let the conversation drift. We didn't question or reject each other's ideas, and I feel we often settled for less than we should have. The longer we were in the group together, the more we got to know each other and the more times we voiced our real opinions. That's when the tempers started to flare!

Phase 3: Norming is marked by several levels of "balance" in response to the storming phase: Individuality and groupness balance, group goals and individual goals balance, closeness is balanced, and the role of the leader and the leader's authority are defined. Note that "balance" does not mean "resolved," since the balance is a delicate one easily upset.

In Phase 3, group cohesion begins to emerge, and the group starts functioning more smoothly as a unit. Here is B. Aubrey Fisher's (1991) description of Phase 3:

> Social conflict and dissent dissipate during the third phase. Members express fewer unfavorable opinions toward decision proposals. The coalition of

individuals who had opposed those proposals which eventually achieve consensus also weakens in the third phase. (p. 142)

Phase 4: Performing is the *period of consensus and maximum productivity.* Dissent is very much out of place at this time so that few negative or unfavorable comments are expressed. Group spirit is high, and a great deal of mutual back patting takes place. Group members joke and laugh and reinforce each other for having contributed to the group's success.

In an early article, Thelen and Dickerman (1949) did a good job of summarizing the group phases:

> Beginning with individual needs for finding security and activity in a social environment, we proceed first to emotional involvement of the individuals with each other, and second to the development of a group as a rather limited universe of interaction among individuals and as the source of individual security. We then find that security of position in the group loses its significance except that as the group attempts to solve problems it structures its activities in such a way that each individual can play a role which may be described as successful or not in terms of whether the group successfully solved the problem it had set itself. (p. 316)

The tail end of Phase 4 is signaled by several member behaviors: Lateness increases, absence increases, daydreaming and other signs of withdrawal increase, and the overall level of involvement in the group decreases. There is a great deal of anxiety associated with ending the group, and members respond differently to this anxiety—all the way from those who refuse to admit the group is ending and run around collecting phone numbers and addresses and planning the party, to those who talk about how terrible the group experience was and are glad it's over. Just as the preorientation stage required potential group members to begin to invest themselves in the group, the final stage requires members to divest themselves of the group.

The four phases are different, but they are not mutually exclusive: Overlap in behaviors is apparent; however, predominant behaviors are recognizable and may be used to judge the phase the group is in. "Usual" problems associated with each phase are forcing the group to jump into the problem during forming, avoiding conflict (storming) during the second phase, norming or ignoring social aspects of group life during the third phase, not allowing members to respond as they feel (e.g., taking disparaging remarks seriously) or to talk out their feelings, and not providing methods for postgroup feedback during the last phase.

Most recently, Blanchard and his colleagues (2007) cite findings from a comprehensive review of over 200 studies on group development. Their conclusion is that these four phases have been confirmed along with one other, termination, for temporary groups that disband (p. 185–186).

Of course, not every group will develop precisely along the lines described above. Nevertheless, an awareness of the recurring themes in group development should enable us to improve our perception and understanding of group dynamics.

The consequences of ignoring group dynamics was depicted on the show *The Apprentice,* hosted by Donald Trump. The teams on this show illustrate what happens when teams skip the development stages to attempt to reach the performing stage. In Episode 3 of Season 6, the team leader, Michelle, formed the team named Arrow and forced her team members to work all night. She was insistent that an all-nighter wouldn't hurt anyone. However, the team rebelled (storming). Team leaders who underestimate the team development stages as well as the importance of group cohesiveness are doomed to fail. Michelle ended up resigning, knowing that she was the most likely candidate to be fired.

GROUP STRUCTURE

The distinction between group structure and group dynamics is somewhat arbitrary, for the way a group is constituted has considerable influence on how it functions. In our discussion of structure, we shall be concerned with three communication variables: group size, networks, and leadership.

Group Size

Think back to the groups you have belonged to that ranged in size from 3 to 15 members. As the group got larger, what did you notice about the quality of the communication? How did you feel about your part in the discussions? How satisfied were you with them? It has been known for a number of years that as group size increases, the satisfaction of each member decreases. In larger groups, a few people account for almost all the talking; the rest do very little. If you remember larger groups as boring and slow-moving, you probably were among the more silent members. We have seen a number of student groups fail to develop into effective decision-making bodies because a great many people spent most of their time listening to a few long, complicated speeches made by a handful of members.

Group size affects performance as well as satisfaction. For example, larger groups tend to take more time to reach decisions, particularly if unanimity is required. We also know that as group size increases, a number of subgroups may form, and that these factions tend to polarize and to distract members from the problems at hand.

You can get some idea of the subgroups that may develop by looking at the potential communication relationships within groups of various sizes. Bostrom (1970) showed that in a dyad, for example, only two relationships are possible—A to B or B to A; but in a triad, or three-person group, there are nine possibilities:

1. A to B	4. B to C	7. A to B and C
2. A to C	5. C to B	8. B to A and C
3. B to A	6. C to A	9. C to A and B

The following table shows how rapidly complexity increases as groups gain in size. Bostrom calculated all the communication relationships possible within groups of

3 to 8 people (pp. 257–258). Small wonder that to most people, belonging to a large group is less satisfying than belonging to a small one.

Number in Group	Interactions Possible
2	2
3	9
4	28
5	75
6	186
7	441
8	1,056

For our purposes, the most practical question we can ask is: What size group seems best for problem solving? In a tongue-in-cheek discussion of government cabinets, the world's most powerful committees, Parkinson (1964) reasons that ideally a cabinet should consist of 5 members. Nevertheless, membership usually increases to 7 or 9 and then from 10 toward 20. In addition to the obvious difficulty of assembling all these people at one time, writes Parkinson,

> there is a far greater chance of members proving to be elderly, tiresome, inaudible, or deaf. Relatively few were chosen from any idea that they are or could be or have been useful. A majority perhaps were brought in merely to conciliate some outside group. The tendency is therefore to report what happens to the group they represent. All secrecy is lost and, worst of all, members begin to prepare their speeches. They address the meeting and tell their friends afterward about what they imagine they have said . . . Internal parties form and seek to gain strength by further recruitment. (p. 54)

As membership expands beyond 20, the whole quality of the committee changes so that "the 5 members who matter will have taken to meeting beforehand" (p. 55).

While not to be taken literally, Parkinson's amusing description of the life cycle of the committee has essential validity. Although it is true that a greater variety of ideas tend to be expressed in large groups, such groups have several limitations we have already mentioned. Generally, the optimum size for a problem-solving group is 5 to 7 members. This figure seems to have the greatest number of advantages.

A recent study by Roberts and colleagues (2006) showed that both group size and social presence in groups affect individual instrumental voice, value-expressive voice, and the group interaction process. The results show that by increasing social presence through the use of collaborative software (software that allows individuals to work together, implicitly communicate about work, and see other group members' work through connectivity on the computer), it is possible to lessen the negative impact of increasing group size.

Communication Networks

In *Further Up the Organization,* Robert Townsend (1985), the man who revitalized Avis Rent-a-Car and has headed numerous other business enterprises, has some provocative things to say about how management should be organized. One of his proposals is that all positions with "assistant to" in the title be abolished. In making his point, Townsend presents three charts; these are reproduced in Figure 12.2. Unlike the regular assistant, who is given authority to make decisions, the assistant-to "moves back and forth between the boss and his people with oral or written messages on real or apparent problems—overlapping and duplicating efforts and make-working." Farther on in his book, the author makes this observation about structure:

> In the best organizations people see themselves working in a circle as if around one table. One of the positions is designated chief executive officer, because somebody has to make all those tactical decisions that enable an organization to keep working. In this circular organization, leadership passes from one to another depending on the particular task being attacked—without any hang-ups. (p. 134)

Townsend is talking about communication networks, patterns of human interaction. As you read on, try to decide for yourself whether his recommendations have merit. You might reserve your judgment, however, until after you have read the section on leadership.

Figure 12.2 *Three Types of Management Organization*

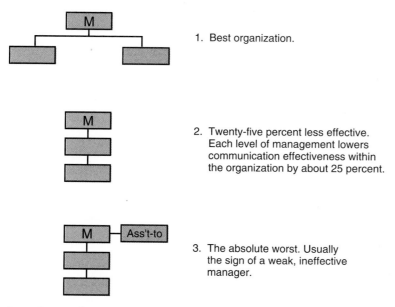

1. Best organization.

2. Twenty-five percent less effective. Each level of management lowers communication effectiveness within the organization by about 25 percent.

3. The absolute worst. Usually the sign of a weak, ineffective manager.

Source: From *Further Up the Organization* by Robert Townsend. Copyright © 1970, 1984 by Robert Townsend. (New York: Alfred A. Knopf).

In Figure 12.3 we see several frequently used communication networks: the Wheel, Chain, Y, Circle, and All-Channel networks. Note that in this illustration each is a five-person group. In the Wheel, one person—who usually becomes the leader—is the focus of comments from each member of the group. As the central person in the network, he or she is free to communicate with the other four, but they can communicate only with him or her. In the Chain network three people can communicate with those on either side of them, but the other two with only one other member of the group. The Y network resembles the Chain: Three of the five people can communicate with only one person. Unlike these systems, which are centralized and tend to have leaders, the Circle and All-Channel patterns are decentralized and sometimes leaderless. In the Circle each person may communicate with two others, those on either side of him. In the All-Channel network, sometimes called "Concom," all communication lines are open: Each member is able to communicate with all the other members.

In studying small-group communications, we want to know how the type of network used affects group performance in problem solving and how given patterns affect interpersonal relationships within the group. Much of the research on networks is based on an experiment by Leavitt (1951) in which five subjects were each given different information essential to the solution of a problem in symbol identification. By using various networks (the Y, Wheel, Chain, and Circle), Leavitt manipulated the freedom with which information could be transmitted from one subject to another, and he then compared the results. The Wheel, the most centralized of the four networks, produced the best organized and fastest performance; the Circle group, the least centralized, was the most disorganized and unstable and proved slowest in solving the problem. The biggest drawback of the Circle network, as another researcher has observed, is that it tends to generate a large number of errors as members try to communicate information around it.

Numerous studies of networks have been patterned after the Leavitt experiment, but the results are not easy to summarize. It is sometimes argued, for example,

Figure 12.3   Five Types of Communication Networks

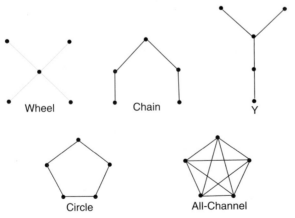

that certain networks are inherently more effective because of their structure, but Guetzkow and Simon (1955) believe that there are other factors to be considered. A particular network may handicap a group not in its ability to solve a problem but in its ability to organize itself so that it can solve the problem. This is an interesting hypothesis, especially in the light of Leavitt's original finding that Y, Wheel, and Chain groups were able to organize themselves so that each eventually established one procedure it used over and over, whereas members of Circle networks did not. Guetzkow and Simon believe that, once a group has established a procedure for working together, it can perform efficiently regardless of its type of network.

The nature of the problem to be solved also affects performance. Groups with centralized networks are better at identifying colors, symbols, and numbers and solving other simple problems. Decentralized networks have the edge over centralized ones when dealing with problems that are more complex—arithmetic, word arrangement, sentence construction, and discussion problems (Shaw, 1981).

Because most of the communication we are concerned with relates not to symbol identification and the like but to more complex issues, decentralized networks will usually be most desirable. For example, the Wheel, though efficient in its use of time, tends to lower the cohesiveness of a group, reduce its inventiveness, and make it too dependent on its leader. Another advantage of decentralized networks is that they tend to provide the most satisfaction for individual members. The All-Channel network seems desirable for a number of reasons. Although initially it tends to be more inefficient and time-consuming, it maximizes the opportunities for corrective feedback, which ultimately should result in greater accuracy. Furthermore, freedom to speak to anyone else in the group creates high morale. These findings are important to keep in mind in the event that group discussions you participate in are characterized by inaccuracy or low morale.

Virtual Groups

Technology has taken groups of all sizes to a new level of efficiency. Software has allowed groups to have virtual meetings and use video conferencing technologies that have united people across the globe instantaneously. Gerry Stahl in 2003 wrote a paper titled "Communication and Learning in Online Collaboration" to address the online communication medium and some of the benefits and shortcomings of the new technology. Groupware technologies have made instantaneous and affordable global groups possible and can create online records of all group communications for later reference. The shortcomings of the process include the inability of the group members to see the nonverbal communication of fellow group members, which makes group conflict situations much more difficult to resolve and interpret. Exchanged messages and individual technological challenges can slow interaction and conversation. Stahl recommends some of the following elements integral to successful online group communication to eliminate some of these shortcomings: The first is the necessity of constant availability of technical support. Second, there should be a way to know that other group members are logged on. Third, planned rules for decision making must be put in place proactively.

The successes of online group communication are numerous. First and foremost, online group communication technology eliminates physical boundaries and constraints. Everyone in the group can interact at different times of the day, foregoing personal timetables, to post messages for later discussion. Any visual physical bias is eliminated as group members cannot see one another (Stahl, 2003).

Videoconferencing is another form of group communication that allows real-time video discussions. This mode of communication requires set meeting times but can bring together global group members with ease. It has many benefits, including reduced cost and the ability to view the expressions and nonverbal communications of group members. The shortcomings, on the other hand, include technological problems, static movements of the group members viewed through the screen, and limitations of this technology only to group members with the availability of videoconferencing technology. However, videoconference availability and utilization is increasing. In June 2004, two United States National Guard soldiers were married via a videoconference, with the groom in Colorado and the bride in Iraq. With this type of union occurring over videoconference, the possible uses of this medium for small groups of all kinds are limitless (Associated Press, 2004, p. A2).

Leadership

The single biggest way to impact an organization is to focus on leadership development. There is almost no limit to the potential of an organization that recruits good people, raises them up as leaders, and continually develops them.
          —John C. Maxwell, *The 17 Indisputable Laws of Teamwork* (2001, p. 185)

For many years people believed that leaders are born, not made, and a search was conducted to determine the traits of the "born leader." The quest has been largely unsuccessful. We do know that usually a leader is more self-confident and more intelligent than other members of his or her group. Some studies suggest that the leader is better adjusted and more sensitive to the opinions of other group members. Nevertheless, these traits are by no means reliable predictors of leadership. No single set of traits seems important in all situations. The successful commander of an air force squadron is not necessarily effective in an administrative post at the Pentagon. The outstanding teacher is not always a worthwhile dean or department chair.

Recent studies have led us to view leadership not as a quality but as a series of functions that groups must have performed. The leader then becomes the person who successfully performs a number of these functions, and sometimes leadership will pass from one person to another or be divided among group members. Thus far, two major leadership activities have been identified: task functions and consideration functions. Neither set is in itself sufficient to satisfy all the group's needs.

Task functions are *activities that help the group achieve its goals.* In terms of the IPA categories in Figure 12.1 (on page 396), the activities might include giving and asking other members for suggestions, opinions, and information (categories 4 through 9). Other task functions might be orienting the group on how best to proceed, clarifying the remarks of others, and summarizing group process.

Consideration functions have to do with morale. They include *any activities that improve the emotional climate or increase the satisfaction of individual members:* showing agreement, support, or encouragement; gatekeeping (i.e., allowing members who might otherwise be ignored to speak); and so on.

It is often difficult for one person to perform task and consideration functions simultaneously (Tichy, 1997). Suppose that an emergency meeting of a school board is called to prevent a walkout of the teachers and that two board members monopolize the discussion in an unconstructive way. Someone will have to steer the conversation back to the problem at hand, which requires immediate action, and in doing so he or she may bruise a few egos. It takes considerable skill for the person who has done the offending to also conciliate the offended. For this reason, the group often develops two or more leaders: a task leader, whose primary concern is that the job be done and the group perform well, and a social leader, whose first interest is in maintaining the group's high morale. Nevertheless, the most valuable leaders are those able to perform both task and consideration functions successfully.

Support for the concept that leaders are made, not born, comes from the study of communication networks. Whereas in decentralized networks there was found to be little agreement among members as to the identity of the group's leader, in centralized networks such as the Wheel, Chain, and Y, people who occupied central positions and were thus able to channel communication were considered leaders. (Leadership and popularity are by no means synonymous, however.)

Although we have stressed leadership functions rather than traits, specific behaviors are often characteristic of leaders. If we compare those who get weeded out with those who emerge as leaders, we see some clear-cut differences. The first tend to be quiet, uninformed or unskilled, inflexible, and bossy or dictatorial; they also spend a great deal of time socializing. In contrast, emergent leaders tend to speak up, to have good ideas and state them clearly, to care about the group, and to make sacrifices and build cohesiveness (Bormann, 1976). In sum, leadership functions include a number of behaviors that can be learned.

Recent leadership research has focused on the notion of emotional intelligence, or EQ, analogous to IQ (Goleman, 1998; Cherniss and Goleman, 2001). Emotionally intelligent people control their emotions and act more appropriately to the situation. One extreme example of the lack of emotional control is former President Bill Clinton and his relationship with Monica Lewinsky. Emotional intelligence comprises the five components shown in Table 12.1.

In conclusion, we remember the thoughts on leadership of E. M. Estes, former president of General Motors:

> Leadership is the courage to admit mistakes, the vision to welcome change,
> the enthusiasm to motivate others, and the confidence to stay out of step when
> everyone else is marching to the wrong tune.

Table 12.1	Five Components of Emotional Intelligence	
Component	Definition	Hallmarks
1. Self-awareness	The ability to recognize and understand your moods, emotions, and drives, as well as their effect on others; self-deprecating sense of humor	Self-confidence; realistic self-assessment
2. Self-regulation	The ability to control or redirect disruptive impulses and moods; the propensity to suspend judgment—to think before acting	Trustworthiness and integrity; comfort with ambiguity; openness to change
3. Motivation	A passion to work for reasons that go beyond money or status; a propensity to pursue goals with energy and persistence	Strong drive to achieve optimism, even in the face of failure; organizational commitment
4. Empathy	The ability to understand the emotional makeup of others; skill in treating people according to their emotional reactions	Expertise in building and retaining talent; cross-cultural sensitivity; service to others
5. Social skill	Proficiency in managing relationships and building networks; an ability to find common ground and build rapport	Effectiveness in leading change; persuasiveness; expertise in building and leading teams

Sources: Adapted from Goleman (1998) and Cherniss and Goleman (2001).

CORRELATES OF EFFECTIVE GROUPS

Anyone who has participated in problem-solving group discussions knows that they can be time-consuming, boring, and sometimes infuriating. Furthermore, the decisions groups make may be of poor quality and may be ignored by those who must carry them out. Yet even totally ineffective committees are not that easily disbanded. There are countless situations in which we cannot make decisions on our own; we must work within a group.

James Surowiecki, in his book *The Wisdom of Crowds: Why the Many Are Smarter than the Few and How Collective Wisdom Shapes Business, Economics, Societies, and Nations,* believes that a group, or "the crowd," often comes up with successful solutions. He believes that a group or crowd will make good decisions if it possesses four fundamental characteristics. First, the group must contain different kinds of people, which Surowiecki defines as "diversity." Second, there should not be an ultimate team leader, known as "decentralization." Third, the group members' thoughts should be combined into a unified answer. Lastly, each group member should be self-determining about the data the group has collected; in this case, Surowiecki references the group members as "independent people" (Hannon, 2004, p. B8).

Recent research by Whetten and Cameron (2005) summarized the research findings of the correlates of high-performing teams. They

1. Get results
2. Have a specific and shared purpose
3. Have mutual internal accountability
4. Have each member responsible for numerous roles and tasks
5. Exhibit high quality in their standards of performance
6. Continuously try to improve
7. Exhibit high credibility and trust
8. Focus on the task and avoid getting distracted by extraneous events (p. 476)

A recent example of a successful group effort occurred in Ann Arbor, Michigan. On December 22, 2005, Kelly Fuks was asked to stop breast-feeding her son in the YMCA (Young Men's Christian Association) pool area. When she refused, she was ejected from the pool area. Fuks was told that her breast-feeding was creating a distraction for the male lifeguards (Gershman, 2006). A few weeks later, a group of 50 women organized a "nurse-in" at which they all breast-fed their babies at the YMCA pool to protest its policy banning breast-feeding (Gantert and Tracy, 2006). On March 7, 2006, the Ann Arbor City Council voted 8–1 to allow women to breast-feed their children anywhere in places of "public accommodation" (Gershman, 2006). This is a vivid example of the power of effective groups to exert influence.

In this section, we shall be looking at some other correlates of small-group effectiveness.

It would be nice if we could automatically improve our communication behaviors by reading about what makes small groups successful. Unfortunately, improvement is not so easily attained. It does come, however, with participation. The adage "Practice makes perfect" seems to be fairly well substantiated by small-group research. The more training and experience group members have, the better they perform as individuals and as groups.

The process by which improvement takes place is probably that of social learning. Behaviors that are productive tend to be reinforced by other members of the group, and those that are unproductive tend to be extinguished because they go unrewarded. Granted that no amount of reading can replace the experience of being part of a group, there are still some lessons we can learn from reading about communication. We can learn what behaviors make for successful groups and then try to practice them when we do participate. In some situations, we may be able to do no more than improve our own performance within the group. In other cases, we may be able to design as well as engage in more effective group activities.

Idea Development and Problem Solving

For several years communication scholars have tried to identify ways of becoming a better small-group participant. For example, Gouran and his associates (1978) found three communication behaviors that were seen by members of small groups as particularly helpful or effective in solving problems. They were (1) introducing relevant issues or ideas, (2) amplifying or expanding on ideas, and (3) documenting assertions. For example, instead of saying all members of Sigma Phi Delta fraternity are goof-offs, it would be better to state that "according to the Office of the Dean of Students, Sigma Phi Delta fraternity has the lowest grade point average of all the fraternities on campus." Two helpful procedural behaviors were singled out: (1) maintaining a goal orientation rather than getting sidetracked and (2) pursuing issues systematically rather than in a disorganized fashion (p. 62). With these findings in mind, let's look at some of the communication behaviors to avoid in small groups.

If you were to interview members of several different kinds of small groups about the difficulties they encounter in developing ideas and solving problems, you would find at least six recurring complaints: (1) Group objectives are not clearly stated or agreed upon, (2) group members do not come up with enough ideas, (3) the group does not carry through discussion of each issue until it is resolved, (4) members rarely help one another, (5) conflict between members becomes so intense that it is counterproductive, and (6) conclusions are not reached or agreed upon.

Standard Agenda

In an attempt to correct some of these shortcomings, many groups try to follow an agenda or schedule that will help them make better use of their time and resources. One of the most widely known group agendas is that adopted from a problem-solving sequence of questions developed several decades ago by John Dewey. This approach has often been called the "standard agenda" because, as you can see, the questions are broad enough to be applied to just about any problem.

1. What are the limits and specific nature of the problem?
2. What are the causes and consequences of the problem?
3. What things must an acceptable solution to the problem accomplish?
4. What solutions are available to us?
5. What is the best solution?
6. What needs to be done to implement the solution?

Brainstorming

Another popular method for generating ideas is the process called "brainstorming" (Osborn, 1957). This technique can be used to generate ideas in any part of the standard agenda. It emphasizes right-brain activity.

RULES FOR BRAINSTORMING
1. *Put judgment and evaluation aside temporarily.*
   a. Acquire a "try anything" attitude.

   b. No faultfinding is allowed. It stifles ideas, halts association.

   c. Today's criticism may kill future ideas.

   d. All ideas are at least thought starters.

2. *Turn imagination loose and start offering the results.*

   a. The wilder the ideas are, the better.

   b. Ideas are easier to tame down than to think up.

   c. Freewheeling is encouraged; ideas can be brought down to earth later.

   d. A wild idea may be the only way to bring out another really good one.

3. *Think of as many ideas as you can.*

   a. Quantity breeds quality.

   b. The more ideas there are to choose from, the more chance there is of a good one.

   c. There is always more than one good solution to any problem.

   d. Try many different approaches.

4. *Seek combination and improvement.*

   a. Your ideas don't all have to be original.

   b. Improve on the ideas of others.

   c. Combine previously mentioned ideas.

   d. Brainstorming is a group activity. Take advantage of group association.

5. *Record all ideas in full view.*

6. *Evaluate at a later session.*

   a. Approach each idea with a positive attitude.

   b. Give each idea a fair trial.

   c. Apply judgment gradually.

Leonard and Swap (1999) offer additional tips to further stimulate the creation of ideas. After ideas are generated, think of adding, subtracting, multiplying, and dividing as ways of further modifying your existing ideas. For example, the Gillette Mach 3 razor, introduced in 1998, added a third blade. Cell phones and laptop computers have been made more portable by subtracting size and weight. McDonald's has added new products by doubling its list of menu items, and many manufacturing companies have increased their cost effectiveness by dividing up their suppliers to produce larger modules such as entire seating systems. Ford Motor Co. linked up with UPS in 2001 to speed its delivery of new cars and trucks to owners. You can not only get your vehicle faster, but you can track its progress online during shipment. This idea grew out of brainstorming sessions at Ford. Transit times have been reduced by 26 percent and savings have been over $1 billion in reduced inventory costs ("Ford saving time . . . ," 2001, p. 3E).

Keep in mind that after you have generated all these ideas, you still have to go back and evaluate their usefulness (see Box 12.1).

One of the most dramatic innovations in the workplace in the past decade has been the increased use of teams, especially self-directed teams. Although the value of teamwork is certainly hard to dispute, implementing teams is not always as easy as it appears. What do you think about the two positions discussed below? How do you resolve them?

Anne Donnellon (1996) at Harvard has written the following observation: "The past 10 years of brouhaha over work teams have left managers and professionals in a quandary: We know we need teams (for at least certain organizational tasks), and we've learned a lot about them, but while the demands for high performance teams continue to increase, our ability to create and sustain them has plateaued. Where there should

be enhanced capability, greater confidence in the process, and satisfaction with outcomes, there is a growing sense of disappointment, frustration, and cynicism."

On the other hand, Noel M. Tichy (1997) at the University of Michigan writes, "Where single individuals may despair of accomplishing a monumental task, teams nurture, support and inspire each other . . . For example, Focus: HOPE [a not-for-profit organization that transforms people's lives in the inner city of Detroit]. Although each student . . . is working to improve his or her own life, the common struggle serves to unite them as a team. They know that the program requires enormous effort from each student, and they draw strength from knowing that other people have chosen to make the commitment as well."

Nominal Group Technique

The use of discussion methods is one way to increase the effectiveness of a group. One method commonly used in business and industry is the nominal group technique (NGT).

The NGT method has six phases. First there is silent, independent generation of ideas, written down on paper. The second round is a round-robin listing of ideas on a large newsprint page so everyone can see. The third step is a discussion or clarification of points but without critique. In the fourth step, everyone individually rates the ideas. The fifth step is a clarification of the vote, and the sixth is a final ranking of ideas.

This method circumvents some of the problems of groupthink, such as the focus effect and the illusion of anonymity.

When compared with unstructured groups, NGT provided better decisions (Jarobe, 1988).

No matter which problem-solving technique is used, effective groups have some elements in common. In a fascinating study comparing effective with ineffective groups, Hirokawa (1983) found

> The "successful" groups make an attempt to analyze the problem before
> attempting to search for a viable solution to the problem, while the
> "unsuccessful" groups immediately begin working on a solution to the problem
> before attempting to analyze it and understand it. (p. 304)

This research supports the problem-solving sequence advocated in all three of the approaches discussed above.

Constructive Conflict

Neil Young once said, "If you agreed with me all the time, there wouldn't be any need for one of us. Guess which one?" (Sutton, 2002).

In 2002, Sutton described two types of conflict that can apply to small-group interaction: "destructive" and "constructive" conflict. Destructive conflict is linked to emotional and personal conflict; constructive conflict is seen as "intellectual." Effective small groups take part in intellectual conflict in which discussion occurs over decision making and ideas. This type of conflict does not attack individuals, but challenges ideas. It allows the exploration of diverse solutions that would otherwise be ignored. The more ideas a small group can generate, the more effective they will be.

Additional research has revealed that groups that can laugh together are more effective in their use of constructive conflict. Humor lightens up tense moments of conflict and can help small groups address difficult topics with ease (Sutton, 2002).

Patterns of Decision Making

Decisions can be avoided, demanded, or agreed on. Assuming that decisions will actually be made, let us briefly examine four rather different ways of carrying out the process.

One writer goes quite far in stating that "achieving consensus is the essential purpose of interpersonal communication" (Phillips, 1966, p. 39). Although this position fails to account for several other important communication goals, we heartily agree that consensus is one of the most desirable outcomes of interaction in small groups. The term can mean a majority opinion, but we use **consensus** to denote *agreement among all members of a group concerning a given decision.* Juries in criminal cases must reach consensus, and those that cannot—hung juries—are ultimately dismissed.

Pace (1988) studies high- versus low-consensus groups. He has found the following differences in interaction:

HIGH CONSENSUS
1. Used more than one method of integrating or unifying diverging points of view into one decision
2. Changed integration methods from episode to episode
3. Generated a wide variety of possible solutions to the problem
4. Generated solutions to the problem in the early stages of discussion
5. Terminated episodes by voicing agreement for an idea or claim

LOW CONSENSUS
1. Rarely used more than one method of integration within a single episode
2. Repeated one type of integration method from episode to episode

3. Generated a limited number of possible solutions to the problem

4. Generated solutions to the problem in the later stages of discussion

5. Terminated episodes by changing topics or by introducing claims that went unacknowledged or undeveloped (p. 200)

Few groups are as concerned as they should be about trying to reach consensus on decisions. We tend to forget that the people who help make a decision are often those who are also expected to carry it out. And given a choice, most people who disagree will resist enacting it. Therefore, problem-solving groups should try to reach consensus to ensure maximum satisfaction and commitment to the decision by all members.

The **majority vote** represents *the wishes of at least 51 percent of a group's members.* Although it is not nearly as satisfying as consensus, it does allow some group harmony in decision making. After as much deliberation on the problem as time permits, there may still be a substantial split in opinion. The majority vote allows the group to proceed despite this. The major limitation of the majority vote is that the dissenting members may be numerous and may be bitterly opposed to the decision. If so, they may be expected to resist carrying it out. When feasible, the majority vote can be used to establish whether a group is near consensus. If a split still exists and time allows, deliberation should continue. If continued discussion does not prove fruitful, the majority vote may be used to reach the decision.

A still less desirable method of arriving at a decision is **handclasping,** or **pairing.** This term applies when various *minority members within a group form a coalition to help each other achieve mutually advantageous goals.* Their decision may not represent common sentiment in the group, but they overpower the majority by dint of their collective numbers. This pattern seems characteristic of political life. It is a common practice for legislators to vote for each other's bills in order to compel support for their own. In the short run, coalitions may be quite successful, but ultimately they can have disastrous effects on group morale. Furthermore, members of coalitions sometimes forget that these bargains exact obligations.

Most groups have at some time been the victims of **railroading,** which occurs when *one or a few group members force their will on the group.* This technique is used most frequently by a leader or a particularly influential member, and, of course, it is the one most likely to produce resentment and resistance.

Since reaching consensus is the most desirable method of decision making within the small group, it is instructive to turn to a few of the research findings on the subject. Gouran (1969) compared the conversation of groups who were able to reach consensus with that of groups who were not. He found that the discussion in the first groups had a greater proportion of "orientation statements," statements explicitly directing the group toward the achievement of its goal or helping it resolve conflict. A follow-up study reported that orientation statements contained fewer self-referent words and phrases—"I," "me," "my," "I think," and so on—and that highly opinionated statements, which were characteristic of groups that had difficulty reaching consensus, contained more self-referent words (Kline, 1970).

Findings about orientation statements bear out our commonsense expectations, but we cannot follow our hunches. We might predict, for example, that if group members expressed their ideas clearly and briefly (in one or two minutes), they would facilitate the group's progress. It has been found, however, that clarity and length of statements are not significantly related to the group's ability to reach consensus. These data need to be substantiated by further research.

Testing the Group's Effectiveness

It is to be hoped that in the near future we shall have more experimental findings pinpointing the communication behaviors that help discussion groups achieve their goals. For the time being, however, we have to agree with Mortensen (1970), who comments that "far more is known about the dynamics of groups than about the distinctive communicative properties, functions, and outcomes in groups" (p. 309).

For these reasons most of us learn about what goes on in groups from our firsthand experience as members. Sometimes, however, this knowledge can be increased through special exercises. One frequently used technique is called the "fishbowl discussion." Two groups form concentric circles. The inner group carries on a discussion; the outer comments on what it has observed. The two groups then switch positions and repeat the procedure. Each member is allowed to leave the discussion long enough to observe the behavior of the others in the group. He or she may be aided by a list of pointers about what behaviors to be looking for.

Thomas Clay (2007), a consultant with 30 years of experience in the legal profession, explains how working with dozens of law firms and many practice groups allowed him to observe six elements that drive group effectiveness. If group leaders evaluate their groups against those six elements, they can determine whether they are, individually and collectively, serving their purpose and decide what needs to be done to improve group effectiveness. The six criteria are

- Clarifying roles of the participants
- Putting the right people in leadership positions
- Requiring plans
- Getting client feedback
- Investing in the groups
- Compensating leaders the appropriately

Summary

After touching on some characteristics of cohesive groups and on the phases of group development, we considered three aspects of the structure of a group that affect its functioning: size, communication network, and leadership. Limiting the size of the group to five to seven members seems to ensure maximum performance and satisfaction. Among communication networks, the All-Channel pattern offers the greatest opportunity for corrective feedback and high morale, though the centralized systems are more efficient. Two concepts of leadership were discussed, and analysis of leadership functions rather than traits was recommended.

The last question raised was practical: How can the small group be made more effective? First, the use of an agenda makes the most of time and resources. Second, an awareness of various attitudes toward conflict allows group members to resolve conflicts in a way that respects both task and human concerns. A third correlate of small-group effectiveness is an approach to decision making that ensures commitment to the decision by all members of the group.

Key Terms

Brainstorming
Casual or social group
Cohesiveness
Consensus
Consideration function
Forming

Handclasping or pairing
Learning or education
 group
Majority vote
Norming
Performing

Private acceptance
Problem-solving group
Public compliance
Railroading
Risky shift
 phenomenon

Self-directed work team
Social comparison
 theory
Storming
Task function
Work group

Review Questions

1. Discuss two theories about compliance with social pressure. How does each explain this phenomenon?

2. How does groupthink encourage conformity?

3. Identify the four phases of group development and describe briefly the type of communication characteristic of each.

4. What is the relationship between group size, membership satisfaction, and group performance?

5. How do task and consideration functions in leadership differ?

6. What are six common difficulties that small groups encounter in developing ideas and solving problems?

7. What are four ways of arriving at a decision in a group? What are some relative advantages and disadvantages of each?

Exercises

1. Have five people solve the "sinking ship" exercise in the appendix independently. After individual solutions have been reached, ask these people to solve the same problem in a group. Compare the individual solutions with the group solution. In what ways is the risky shift phenomenon illustrated?

2. Observe an actual problem-solving group. Listen carefully for statements that indicate the four phases of group development. Record any statements that represent any of these phases. Notice also whether the group does not seem to go through these four phases. Compare your observations with others who have observed different groups. Do most of the observations correspond to the research findings?

3. Conduct an in-depth study of a group of which you are a member. Keep a journal of the group's interaction pattern and activities and write a paper in which you analyze (a) the communication network(s) of the group, (b) the leadership functions, (c) the group's cohesiveness, (d) members' satisfaction, and (e) methods of conflict resolution.

4. Analyze the most successful group discussion that you have ever participated in. What specific factors were presented that accounted for its success?

Suggested Readings

Blanchard, Ken. *Leading at a Higher Level.* Upper Saddle River, NJ: Prentice-Hall, 2007.

This excellent book has a very good chapter on groups and teams. It is well worth reading.

Donnellon, Anne. *Team Talk: The Power of Language in Team Dynamics.* Cambridge, MA: Harvard Business School Press, 1996.

This unique and excellent book looks at the role of language in the work of teams. It offers a method for analyzing team discussion to determine the group's effectiveness.

Fisher, Kimball. *Leading Self-Directed Work Teams: A Guide to Developing New Team Leadership Skills,* 2nd ed. New York: McGraw-Hill, 1999.

This book is one of the finest available on this subject. It explains in detail how to use self-directed work teams (SDWTs) in any organization. Since it is written for the practitioner, it is highly readable.

Galanes, Gloria J., Katherine Adams, and John K. Brilhart. *Communicating in Groups,* 4th ed. New York: McGraw-Hill, 2000.

This little book is one of the better texts on the subject. Especially helpful are its practical chapters: "Group Problem-Solving Procedures" and "Creative and Critical Thinking in Small Groups."

Huszczo, Gregory. *Tools for Team Leadership.* Palo Alto, CA: Davies-Black, 2004.

This book is excellent for those interested in the leadership aspect of small groups. It includes numerous self-diagnostic instruments.

Leonard, Dorothy, and Walter Swap. *When Sparks Fly.* Boston: Harvard Business School Press, 1999.

This book explores the practical applications of group creativity.

Maxwell, John C. *The 17 Indisputable Laws of Teamwork.* Nashville, TN: Thomas Nelson Publishers, 2001.

This book offers a very readable and enjoyable insight into what makes teams successful. Very practical and user-friendly.

Tubbs, Stewart L. *A Systems Approach to Small Group Interaction,* 9th ed. New York: McGraw-Hill, 2007.

A rather novel "systems approach" in the analysis of communication in the small group. Topics covered in the present chapter are dealt with in greater detail. Emphasis is on the complex interplay of 24 variables that relate to small-group processes.

Wilson, Gerald L. *Groups in Context,* 6th ed. New York: McGraw-Hill, 2003.

A well-balanced blend of theory and applications that gives students an abundant number of real-life examples to help apply principles to actual group situations.

 # For Supplementary Information

Log onto the Online Learning Center at *www.mhhe.com/tubbsmoss11.*

Public Communication

Chapter Objectives

After reading this chapter, you should be able to:

1. Define three dimensions of source credibility.
2. Describe four modes of delivery.
3. Outline five popular patterns of message organization.
4. Describe the use of at least two types of supporting materials and state the general research findings regarding the effects of using evidence in persuasive communication.
5. Distinguish between the assimilation effect and the contrast effect and describe the relevance of each to the problem of how much change a speaker should advocate.
6. Specify under what conditions one-sided and two-sided messages are most effective.
7. State the conditions under which climax- and anticlimax-order messages are most effective.
8. State the general research findings regarding the relative effectiveness of messages containing stated versus implied conclusions.

In January 2007, Delaware Senator Joe Biden stated the following about fellow Democratic presidential candidate and opponent Barack Obama: "I mean, you got the first mainstream African American who is articulate and bright and clean and a nice-looking guy . . . I mean, that's a storybook, man." Online bloggers, less constrained by editors and often highly partisan, opined that Senator Biden had received especially kind treatment from the press:

> If a Republican had said this, we'd have a national outpouring of grief
> over the residual ignorance and racial insensitivity in our country, and
> the guy would be in sensitivity training until round about the time John
> Kerry is elected president. Biden, I'm sure, will pay no consequences for his
> boneheaded comment. (Ham, 2007)

Covering the same story, MSNBC's online news included comments from Jesse Jackson, a response from Senator Obama, and further quotes from Senator Biden about other presidential candidates (Gregory, 2007). One writer (Hinds, 2007) cites experts saying that the presence of a candidate who is black (Barack Obama) and also a candidate who is female (Hilary Clinton) in the 2008 presidential campaign changes the language of campaigns from now on (p. 2C).

If you are looking for some fast tips on successful speaking, David Gergen (2000), famous speechwriter for Richard Nixon, Gerald Ford, Ronald Reagan, and Bill Clinton, wrote the following advice in what he called "Tricks of the Speech Trade":

- Prepare carefully. Speeches that appear the most effortless—and are also effective—are usually ones that require the most preparation.
- Keep it short. Twenty minutes max for a good speech.
- Keep it brisk. Don't drone on and on with a litany of statistics.
- Use the language of the living room. Don't use too many fancy words. Keep it more conversational.
- Look for catchy facts. Ronald Reagan once said, "A trillion dollars is incomprehensible . . . If you had a stack of thousand-dollar bills in your hand only four inches high, you'd be a millionaire. A trillion dollars would be a stack of thousand-dollar bills sixty-seven miles high."
- Use the occasional prop. This includes charts, graphs, PowerPoint graphics, etc.
- Be positive.
- Anticipate the critics. Use strong evidence to support your points.
- Have a good closer. This can be a quote or a touching story. (pp. 235–240)

Public speaking gives people an opportunity to market themselves. Lawyer, writer, and speaker Sean Carter advertises three tips for successful public speaking. First, Carter states that speakers must deliver their topics with enthusiasm to keep their audiences engaged in the topic. Second, humor will keep the audience attentive and engaged. Third, speakers should be methodical about planning their speaking engagements and planning what they want to say in whatever method works best for them. Carter continues with the "do's" and "don'ts" of public speaking. He includes practicing the speech, getting to the speech site ahead of time, using true stories to get points across, and having effective and memorable openings and closing as "do's." His "don'ts" include apologizing at the beginning of the speech and reading the speech (James-Enger, 2004, p. 41).

In 2007 public speaking paid quite handsomely. Bill Clinton was making $250,000 a speech; former General Electric boss Jack Welch was getting $150,000 per speech. Other top draws were Alan Greenspan, former chairman of the Federal Reserve, at $100,000; Dana Carvey at $75,000; and TV host Tucker Carlson at $25,000 per speech (Arango, 2007).

For centuries, public communication has been one of the cornerstones upon which civilizations have been built. Communication as a discipline has grown out of the traditions of the great ancient rhetoricians from Aristotle and Cicero to the modern orators such as Bill Clinton, Martin Luther King, Jr., and Elizabeth Dole. Throughout the ages, public communication has served to unite as well as inspire people to action.

An interesting recent study (Greenstein, 2006) throws light on how this country's first presidents utilized public communication.

> Washington's efforts to legitimize the new nation were grounded in his public adulation.
>
> In his first three years as chief executive, Washington paid official visits to each of the states. . . . When Washington entered a community, the ritual was for a local reception committee to welcome him, extolling his virtues and those of the nation. He then would reply in kind, praising the community and voicing patriotic sentiments. These exchanges were occasions for bonding Americans to their new government.
>
> The stiff-necked John Adams lacked a communications strategy. This is not surprising, in that he distrusted the public and scorned self-promotion. Adams spent roughly a year and a half of his four presidential years away from the seat of government and in virtual political limbo. His inaugural, state of the union, and other addresses were reported in the press, but he did not employ them to advance an overall program. (Greenstein, 2006, p. 17)

A critical element in the success of a democratic government, the U.S. government in particular, is having a public that is informed well enough to make appropriate decisions about who to select as their leaders (Fairbanks et al., 2007). Over the past several decades, scholars have noted a dramatic decline in public trust of government (Fairbanks et al., 2007). It has been suggested that this decline is a result of poor communication between government and the public, where the public feels that they are not well informed about government actions.

This chapter is designed to help you improve your public communication abilities.

A DEFINITION

In Chapter 1 we defined face-to-face communication. We have since examined two contexts in which it occurs: interpersonal and small groups. Two-person interaction comes closest to an equal exchange between communicators. Theoretically, each person is responsible for half of all the verbal and nonverbal messages transmitted; each is both speaker and listener. When we become members of problem-solving or therapeutic groups, the balance shifts and the communication process changes. We speak for shorter periods of time; we listen longer. Yet we still think of ourselves as speakers and listeners, senders and receivers of messages.

In public communication one person is designated the speaker, and the rest are cast in the complementary role of listeners, or audience members. Participants are still face-to-face and are still sending and receiving communicative stimuli. Anyone who has tried to speak before an audience whose members are reading the paper, sleeping, or doing other things that denote lack of attention knows all too well that audiences do send messages as well as receive them. But the balance of message sending is quite uneven—the speaker initiates most of the verbal messages, and, though audience members often send nonverbal messages (applause, laughter, catcalls, and so on), audiences in general are not usually expected to contribute verbal messages except in a question-and-answer period following the speech. Despite this imbalance, public communication is still face-to-face communication, and we frequently find ourselves participating in it as either speakers or listeners.

Public communication often demands that the speaker be more deliberate and organized than in private conversation, we tend to value spontaneity and informality, but the same spontaneous, unplanned approach is usually inappropriate to the public speaking situation.

Ironically, experts are leaning toward more spontaneity for speakers. Lublin (2007) cites improvisation training at comedy clubs like Second City to help speakers learn to think more quickly on their feet, like entertainers. Chicago-based Second City president Tom Yorton says that "presentation skills has become our most requested offering" (p. B1).

In addressing an audience, a speaker ordinarily has at least one of three purposes: to inform, to entertain, or to persuade listeners. When that purpose is to inform, the speaker is primarily concerned with the outcome of information gain, an aspect of understanding discussed in Chapter 1. Speaking to entertain is directed toward pleasure, a second outcome that we have discussed. Lenn Millbower, author and instructor at Disney University, has a unique view of public speaking. Millbower calls informing audiences "learnertainment." He structures his presentations on the premise that entertaining audiences results in emotion, which creates attention, involvement, meaning, and subsequently memory and retention. Too much information in a session, according to Millbower, results in "info-fog" and can inhibit the learning and attentive processes (Pawlak, 2004, p. 2).

When the speaker's intention is to persuade, the desired outcome is attitude influence. The speaker may try to establish an attitude not previously held by the listeners or to reinforce or change one that they already hold. Persuasive speeches may also attempt to elicit some action. The political candidate ultimately wants our vote, not just our agreement on various issues. The saleswoman wants us to purchase the product she is selling, not simply to be aware of its superiority to other products. Nonetheless, attitude change is the intermediate goal to achieve before prompting action.

Informing, entertaining, and persuading are by no means mutually exclusive purposes. In fact, the classification, though traditional, is thought by some to be rather arbitrary. A persuasive speech about this country's diplomatic relations with China may also be informative and entertaining. Comedians like Ellen DeGeneres and Chris Rock speak primarily to entertain, yet their material frequently includes persuasive social commentary as well. An informative lecture on animal life, delivered in an entertaining and appealing style, may yet persuade audience members of the need for establishing wildlife preserves.

Most of the public communication experiences in which you find yourself either as speaker or listener will involve some persuasion—usually in addition to information gain and perhaps entertainment. Therefore, this chapter will give more emphasis to public communication that attempts to be persuasive. We begin with a consideration of the speaker apart from his or her message.

THE SPEAKER

How will the speaker be perceived by the audience? On what basis will the audience members form their judgments? In Chapter 2, we examined some principles of person perception and talked about the basis on which we form our first impressions of others. In Chapter 8, we examined some of the bases for our most permanent attraction to other people. We also discussed trust as it affects communication, particularly informal transactions between people. We spoke of trust as facilitating human relationships. We shall speak in this chapter about another aspect of trust—usually referred to as "source credibility"—as it relates to the public communication experience.

Source Credibility

During President George W. Bush's second term in office, serious questions were raised about his ability as a communicator. Daily calendars and comic strips contained quotes of his garbled use of the English language. After President Bush and Vice President Cheney admitted that Saddam Hussein did not possess the weapons of mass destruction that had been cited as the justification for invading Iraq, some accused him of deceiving the American public about various aspects of the war in Iraq. In general, even many who supported him and voted for him began to seriously question his leadership as the Iraqi war dragged on.

During the administrations of recent presidents, the American public has become painfully aware of the term "credibility gap." In its broadest sense, credibility refers to our willingness to believe what a person says and does. It is undoubtedly the most important influence on our judgment of a speaker. One writer describes credibility as the attitude a listener holds toward a speaker (Samovar and McDaniel, 2007). Thus, credibility is in the mind of the listener.

Dimensions of Credibility

Credibility is not a new concept. In the fourth century B.C., Aristotle used the term "ethos" to refer to the personal characteristics of a speaker that influence the audience. A person with high ethos was thought to possess a high level of competence, good character, and goodwill toward his or her listeners. Aristotle believed that these qualities helped a speaker gain audience acceptance of his or her message.

Writing from the perspective of twentieth-century social psychology, Whalen (2007) identified two components of credibility as competence and honesty. The two are roughly equivalent to Aristotle's components (if you combine his concepts of good character and goodwill).

During this century, considerable research has been conducted on the subject of source credibility. Notice our use of the word "source." Although a speaker is usually perceived as the source of his or her message, this is not always the case. When a United Nations delegate addresses the General Assembly, she may not be considered the source of her message. Similarly, when an executive of a large oil company discusses Middle Eastern affairs, he may be seen not as the originator of his message but simply as a spokesperson for the firm. In most instances, however, the speaker of the message will be viewed as the source.

Credibility is not a constant. Each person's perception of a source varies. Moreover, the credibility of any source varies from topic to topic. In fact, political differences and bias can affect perceptions of source credibility. In 2004, Matt Drudge reported that Massachusetts Senator and Democratic presidential candidate John Kerry was guilty of infidelity. His story was pushed to the sidelines because of the perception that Drudge was alternative, extremist, and therefore not credible (Pappas, 2004, p. B5).

Credibility may also vary from one situation to another (e.g., a teacher may be a high-credibility source in a classroom but a low-credibility source on the witness stand in a courtroom). Nonetheless, for some time researchers have attempted to determine whether there are in fact elements of credibility that do not vary. The results of a series of such studies are summarized by Whalen (2007), who finds essentially two dimensions of ethos: authoritativeness and character. Authoritativeness, or expertise, refers to the speaker's perceived command of a given subject—how intelligent, informed, competent, and prestigious we think the speaker is. Character, a vaguer but no less important dimension, refers to the speaker's perceived intentions and trustworthiness—how objective, reliable, well motivated, and likeable the speaker seems to be. Former Secretary of State General Colin Powell is considered one of this country's finest statesmen. He illustrates both his authoritativeness and his character in a speech he gave on January 25, 2001, when he said,

> I didn't know I would be coming back into government when I left the Army seven years ago and went into private life . . . But when President [George W.] Bush asked me to consider it, I was ready for it. I was anxious to see if I could serve again. I think I have something to contribute still. And when he specifically

said, I would like you to go to the State Department, it was almost as if I had been preparing for this in one way or another for many, many years. My work in the Pentagon, my work as a Deputy National Security Advisor, National Security Advisor, Chairman of the Joint Chiefs of Staff, and seven years of private life watching the world change, suggested to me this is something I should do. (Maxwell, 2001, p. 32)

Both elements enter into our judgments of credibility. If a physician who also holds a doctorate in chemistry argues that preservatives in baby food have no adverse effects, most audiences will regard her as a high-credibility source. If it is then disclosed that she is a consultant to one of the largest producers of baby food in this country, her credibility may suffer a sharp decline. While the audience may not question her expertise, it will question her motives as well as her ability to be objective about a position from which she stands to gain. In one study, a convicted criminal produced no attitude change in his audience in arguing for greater personal freedom and less police power, but significant attitude change when he argued for greater police power. By supporting a position that seemed to be against his own interests, he increased his credibility considerably (Shaw, 1997).

Many writers on public speaking believe that a third dimension of ethos is dynamism—that is, how forceful, active, and intense the speaker seems to be. (Kouzes and Posner, 1995, call it being inspiring.) It is proposed that, other things being equal, the speaker who is self-assured and conveys a message with liveliness and vigor should be perceived as having higher credibility than a more reserved, passive, and slow-moving speaker. On the other hand, if the motivations of the more dynamic speaker are questionable (e.g., the convicted criminal arguing for greater freedom and less police power) or if the speaker's authoritativeness is in doubt, we would not expect him or her to be perceived as a high-credibility source. And if the presentation is too aggressive and vigorous, receivers may suspect that the motivation is self-interest and may doubt the speaker's capacity to be objective. Cole and McCroskey's (2004) study investigated the connection between perceived "apprehension, shyness, and verbal aggression" and perceived source credibility. They found that both apprehensive and aggressive individuals were perceived to be less credible than their counterparts (Cole and McCroskey, 2004, p. 101). We want to believe in our leaders. We want to believe that their word can be trusted, that they have the knowledge and skill to lead, and that they are personally excited and enthusiastic about the direction in which we are headed (Kouzes and Posner, 1995).

Information on sex differences and the effects on credibility are summarized by Ivy and Backlund (1994). They indicate that men and Anglo-Saxons (perceived to have high status) are considered more effective than women, Mexican Americans, and blacks (who are perceived to have low status). When sex differences exist (and there is a growing body of research that fails to find differences), male sources are perceived as more competent, and female sources are perceived as higher in trustworthiness.

Whalen (2007) offers the following suggestions: To enhance perceptions of competency, associate yourself with other high-credibility sources, use self-references to demonstrate familiarity with the topic, use the special vocabulary of the topic, and be well organized. To enhance perceptions of trustworthiness, entertain alternate points of view, make sure verbal and nonverbal behaviors are congruent, demonstrate how the listener's benefit is considered, and indicate your similarity with audience members. To enhance perceptions of dynamism, control delivery variables, use intense language, and use somewhat opinionated language so as not to appear wishy-washy.

To sum up, source credibility refers to the receiver's perception of the speaker's authoritativeness on a given topic, his or her character, and, to a lesser degree, dynamism.

Throughout our discussion of credibility let us remember the word "perception." Credibility has to do not with what the speaker is but with what the receiver perceives him or her to be. Regardless of demonstrated expertise or good character, no speaker has high credibility for every audience. The vice president of an airline may be a high-credibility source when addressing employees but not when speaking before the Federal Aviation Administration. In lecturing on the influence of mass communication on voting patterns, a sociologist from the University of Chicago may be a high-credibility source to his students; to his colleagues, however, his credibility may be considerably less.

Because it is linked to perception, a speaker's credibility varies not only from one audience to another but from one point to another during the speech. Time, then, is a variable not only in two-person and small-group communication but in public communication, where the speaker is perceived in terms of his or her extrinsic, intrinsic, and ultimately total credibility.

The scales in Table 13.1 have been developed for measuring a listener's evaluation of any speaker. Scales numbered 1, 2, and 3 measure authoritativeness; 4, 5, and 6 measure character; and 7, 8, and 9 measure dynamism. The closer the rating to the left end of the scale, the higher the perceived credibility.

Extrinsic Credibility

Extrinsic credibility refers to *the credibility a source is thought to have prior to the time he or she delivers the message.* For example, if Jesse Jackson or Gloria Steinem gives a speech on your campus, his or her reputation will undoubtedly influence your evaluation of that speech. Similarly, if the top student in your class gives a speech, your previous impression of him or her affects your attitude toward the message.

When Illinois Senator Barak Obama and former Massachusetts Governor Mitt Romney first appeared as candidates for the 2008 presidential election, both men created quite a stir with their handsome good looks and their dynamic speaking styles.

There has been ample research on the influence of extrinsic credibility. The typical study involves the delivery of the same speech (sometimes tape-recorded for greater consistency) to several audiences but with the speaker introduced differently to each. For example, a taped speech (supposedly for a radio program) favoring lenient treatment of juvenile delinquents was presented to three separate groups of high school students, but the speaker was identified to one group as a juvenile court judge, to the second as a neutral member of the studio audience, and to the

Table 13.1 Evaluating a Speaker								
1. Competent	- - -	- - -	- - -	- - -	- - -	- - -	- - -	Incompetent
2. Experienced	- - -	- - -	- - -	- - -	- - -	- - -	- - -	Inexperienced
3. Important	- - -	- - -	- - -	- - -	- - -	- - -	- - -	Unimportant
4. Honest	- - -	- - -	- - -	- - -	- - -	- - -	- - -	Dishonest
5. Open-minded	- - -	- - -	- - -	- - -	- - -	- - -	- - -	Closed-minded
6. Kind	- - -	- - -	- - -	- - -	- - -	- - -	- - -	Cruel
7. Active	- - -	- - -	- - -	- - -	- - -	- - -	- - -	Passive
8. Fast	- - -	- - -	- - -	- - -	- - -	- - -	- - -	Slow
9. Emotional	- - -	- - -	- - -	- - -	- - -	- - -	- - -	Calm

Source: From *Analyzing Human Communication*, 2nd ed., by Lawrence B. Rosenfeld, 1983. Dubuque, IA: Kendall/Hunt Publishing Company.

third as an audience member who had a criminal record and had been a juvenile delinquent himself. As might be expected, the speech that was supposedly delivered by the judge, a high-credibility source, was considered much fairer than the speech delivered by the ex-convict. The judge's speech also resulted in more attitude change than the ex-convict's.

A number of studies confirm that speakers with high credibility tend to have more influence on an audience's attitudes than do those with low credibility. One summary of the literature qualifies this statement with the observation that "the perceived-competence aspect adds to persuasive impact more than the trustworthiness aspect does. By competence we mean the perceived expertness, status, intelligence, etc., of the attributed source; by trustworthiness, we refer to his perceived disinterestedness, objectivity, and lack of persuasive intent" (McGuire, 1969, p. 187). But the credibility of the speaker does not seem to have a significant effect on the level of the audience's comprehension (Petrie, 1963). Credibility appears to be a more important consideration when we are persuading an audience than when we are informing them.

Intrinsic Credibility

Extrinsic credibility is only one aspect of credibility. Your total credibility as a speaker consists of how you are perceived by the audience before your speech plus the impressions you make while delivering it. In other words, a speaker comes into a speaking situation with some level of credibility and adds to or detracts from it by what is said. **Intrinsic credibility** is the name often given to this *image that a speaker creates as a direct result of his or her speech.*

Former President Ronald Reagan was referred to as the "Great Communicator." He gave many eloquent speeches; his actor's training allowed him to deliver effective and memorable messages such as his forceful 1987 speech at the Brandenburg Gate in a still-divided Berlin: "Mr. Gorbachev, tear down this wall!" (Reagan Foundation, 2007). Each of us may be accomplished in some way or make certain claims about our good character or even be a poised and dynamic speaker. By and large, however, we are not perceived as high-credibility sources. Our major opportunities for increasing our credibility come during the actual presentation of our speech.

One way in which you may increase your intrinsic credibility as a speaker is by *establishing a common ground* between you and your audience. This rhetorical technique has been successfully used for centuries. For example, Daniel J. Boorstin, a well-known historian, opened a speech to an audience of Associated Press managing editors with these remarks:

> Gentlemen, it's a great pleasure and privilege to be allowed to take part in your meeting. It is especially a pleasure to come and have such a flattering introduction, the most flattering part of which was to be called a person who wrote like a newspaperman.
>
> The historians, you know, sometimes try to return the compliment by saying that the best newspapermen write like historians but I'm not sure how many of the people present would consider that a compliment.
>
> This afternoon I would like to talk briefly about the problems we share, we historians and newspapermen, and that we all share as Americans. (Boorstin, 1969, p. 204)

Boorstin attempted to show his listeners that he was sympathetic to their point of view and that he and they shared certain things—notably, that they were writers, that they had some of the same problems, and that they were Americans. Balance theory predicts that similarities tend to increase liking and that in general we tend to like those who agree with us on a substantial proportion of salient issues. Thus, it is quite possible that a speaker's intrinsic credibility will increase if he or she can convince the audience that a common ground exists between them.

Another influence on the character dimension of credibility is **humor.** Many speakers use humor as a means of ingratiating themselves with the audience. In 2004, the National Speakers Association Eastern Educational Workshop offered group seminars on integrating humor into public speaking. For those humor-challenged speakers, a seminar called *"But I'm Just Not Funny! Humor for the Non-humorist"* was offered. One speaker, Kathleen Passanisi, recommended telling personal funny stories that would present something that speakers have in common with their recipients. She also recommended sharing embarrassing moments and stories with the audience to break the ice (Bess, 2004, p. C3).

Research on the use of humor in speeches indicates that though it may not increase the listeners' understanding or change their attitude toward the speaker's topic, it affects their perception of the person's character. In general, they like a speaker more when he or she uses humor (Gruner, 1970).

In a summary of research, Gruner (1985) offers suggestions for the use of humor in public communication:

1. "A modicum of . . . relevant humor in informative discourse will probably produce a more favorable audience reaction toward the speaker" (p. 142).

2. "Humor that is self-disparaging may further enhance speaker image" (p. 142).

3. "Apt, relevant humor in a speech can enhance interest in that speech; this generalization must be qualified and limited, however" (p. 143).

4. "Apt, relevant humor seems not to influence the effectiveness of persuasive speeches either negatively or positively" (p. 144).

Other variables that increase a speaker's credibility are effective delivery, apparent sincerity, the use of relevant evidence, and a clear pattern of organization. We shall have more to say about some of these variables farther along in this chapter.

Delivery

Another significant influence on how we judge the speaker is delivery. For years, two guidelines for effective delivery have been naturalness and poise. A speaker's delivery should not draw attention from the content of the message—as it might, for example, if it were overly dramatic or reflected lack of confidence. In the 2004 presidential campaign, Howard Dean, an early favorite as the Democratic nominee, destroyed his candidacy in a thank-you speech to a large crowd of fans after the Iowa primaries. One source wrote that "Dean unleashed a powerful blast of escalating oratory punctuated by the loudest cheer he could muster" (Dean, 2004). This cheer gave birth to the "I Have a Scream" label, which became directly associated with Dean. He broke the mold of typical political speeches that usually consist of a closely monitored vocal tone by yelling even louder while the crowd was cheering. The volume of Dean's voice and the expression on his face was alarming to viewers, and the subsequent commentary on his aggressiveness combined into an overall view of uncertainty about his fitness for duty as president of the United States (Dean, 2004).

This example highlights the importance of effective delivery in public speaking. Good delivery involves much more than mere fluency in speaking. It includes the effective use of many of the visual and vocal cues we discussed in Chapter 4: eye contact, hand gestures, posture, and general physical appearance as well as vocal quality, pitch, volume, and rate of speech.

For example, educators must work on their delivery every day. Educators are public speakers in classes, seminars, lectures, and panels. Their audience is a plethora of students, professionals, or academics. Germano (2003) offers several delivery tips for educators. He suggests they exude confidence, speak clearly, and engage the audience with eye contact. He addresses technology, suggests picking a primary presentation medium, and condemns the overuse of PowerPoint. He emphasizes rehearsing and planning for questions that may be asked. Lastly, Germano urges speakers to refrain from apologizing about any part of their delivery or presentation (Germano, 2003, p. B15).

According to Thomas (1998), even in the ancient days of Cicero, "delivery was a subject best learned by doing. Ancient students were drilled in voice modulation, the use of emphasis and pacing, physical stance and gestures, and the use of facial expressions and eye contact. Their curriculum sounds very much like a speech class in a university today" (p. 23).

When you see a successful presentation delivered by Bill Gates, Steve Jobs, or Bill Ford, it is tempting to believe that it is their natural public communication talent that is responsible. Do you sometimes catch yourself thinking that you are not as charismatic as those people? Here is what Carmine Gallo, the author of a highly acclaimed book, *10 Simple Secrets of the World's Greatest Business Communicators*, says about it:

> That's nonsense. When they first started, those leaders were not nearly as persuasive and electrifying as they are today. They worked—and continue to work—on their presentation skills. But above all, they believed in themselves and their message. So should you. (Gallo, 2006a)

Visual Cues

Direct eye contact with audience members is one of the most important nonverbal cues in public speaking. The speaker who spends too much time looking at note cards or staring at the floor or ceiling or the feet of various listeners fails to make use of an important advantage—the preference for direct eye contact (Tieger and Barron-Tieger, 1998).

A related aspect of delivery is facial expression. Since facial cues constitute the single most important source of nonverbal communication, audiences generally favor a speaker whose facial expression is somewhat animated and varied over a speaker whose delivery is deadpan or expressionless.

Bodily action can also add to or detract measurably from a speaker's impact on the audience. For example, a relaxed but alert posture helps to communicate poise. Lecterns may be helpful for holding note cards, but at times they seem to inhibit a speaker's gestures and movements. Moving about the room frequently adds variety and interest to a speech. The speaker may take a step forward to emphasize a point, or move from one spot to another in making a transition from one main point in the speech to another. This technique is called moving on transition. Of course, a speaker who constantly paces back and forth across the room soon calls attention to these movements and away from what is being said.

Blanchard and Thacker (1999) have offered the following practical advice for improving common mistakes in delivery: Avoid talking to the visual aid with your back to the audience. Videotape one of your presentations and view it with the sound off to concentrate on your visual delivery. Turn the overhead projector or computer projector off when you are finished showing a visual aid so that it does not distract from your message. Use multimedia when they can enhance your visual presentation (pp. 340–341).

Vocal Cues

Vocal delivery in the public speaking situation is somewhat similar to that in less formal communication settings. As we saw in Chapter 4, vocal delivery includes four types of cues: (1) volume, (2) rate and fluency, (3) pitch, and (4) quality. Because the receiver is playing a less active role, however, the message sender's vocal delivery becomes more apparent. For example, deficiencies in vocal quality—breathiness, hypernasality, poor articulation, and so on—are likely to be particularly noticeable in public speaking (Knapp and Hall, 1997).

Demands for adequate volume in public speaking are obvious. The speaker must be able to project his or her voice so that it is heard by all the members of the audience.

Both fluency and rate of speech can also have considerable influence on an audience. How many times have you heard a speaker who uses a lot of "ahs," "uhs," and "ums"? This annoying habit, along with the needless repetition of such words and phrases as "like," "well," and "you know," falls into the category of nonfluencies. We have seen in Chapter 4 that nonfluent speakers tend to be irritating and boring to listen to because their rate of speech is slower. Moreover, the image they tend to project is one of passivity and hesitancy. Each of us is nonfluent at times, and this is normal. Research on fluent and nonfluent speakers shows, however, that fluency not only enhances image in the eyes of the audience but also produces more attitude change when the speaker's speech is persuasive (McCroskey, 1993).

The rate of speech can also be too fast. Some speakers talk rapidly to ease their own anxiety. However, the audience becomes very aware of the speaker's discomfort. Attention to one's breathing will tell the speaker if he or she is talking too fast.

The solution is to become conscious of one's breathing before the speech. Begin to inhale deeply and slowly. Fill the lungs to capacity and hold for a couple of seconds, then release the air slowly and completely. Continue the breathing exercise until normal breathing is under control. These breathing exercises promote inner stability and a sense of calm.

The pitch of the voice as well as the rate of speech can affect how well a speech is received. We observed in Chapter 4 that people expect a voice to be varied in pitch and, in fact, sometimes derive information about emotions from changes in pitch.

Modes of Delivery

Modes of delivery refer to the *amount of preparation and the type of presentation a speaker employs.* There are four modes of delivery commonly used in public communication; each serves a different purpose and has some strengths and weaknesses.

The first mode, **impromptu delivery**, describes the speech presented with little preparation. In essence, the speaker stands before the audience and thinks out loud. This style has one advantage: maximum spontaneity. It suffers, however, from the lack of advance planning. Less formal kinds of communication place a high premium on spontaneity, but public address usually requires a more formal style of delivery. Impromptu speeches are usually assigned to the speaker only a moment or two before the speech is to be delivered. The speech itself may last only a minute, but almost all the elements of a speech are there for analysis (content, organization, use of language, and so on). The inherent difficulties of impromptu speaking were suggested by Mark Twain when he remarked that "it usually takes more than three weeks to prepare a good impromptu speech."

The second and the most formal mode of delivery is **reading from manuscript.** In direct contrast to the impromptu speech, this type of delivery requires complete preparation. For broadcasters, politicians, and other people whose remarks are often quoted, this technique is a valuable one. It allows the speakers to be extremely precise in phrasing a message and to minimize the possibility that it will be misconstrued. The speech is delivered exactly as it has been prepared. For the average person, however, manuscript speaking requires an unnecessarily long preparation time. It has another limitation. It makes the speaker so reliant on reading from manuscript that he or she is unable to look up at the audience, except for very brief periods of time. Thus, the ability to adapt the message to audience feedback is drastically reduced.

Memorized speech is the third mode of delivery. Here, the entire speech has been planned beforehand, written in manuscript, and then committed to memory. The speaker is therefore free to look at the audience instead of reading from notes or manuscript. Although memorized speech might sound like the most effective kind of delivery, it has two drawbacks. The first is the problem of robotlike delivery; many of the natural qualities of human communication—vocal inflection, facial expression, gesture, and so on—may be lost. Second, human memory being what it is, the speaker runs the risk of forgetting part of the message. If this happens to you and you have to sit down before you have finished, you are unlikely to forget the experience for a long time.

The fourth mode of delivery is **extemporaneous speaking,** which combines the advantages of careful speech outlining and planning with the spontaneity of impromptu speaking. The person who uses this style speaks from minimal notes (preferably on small cards).

Sedlack and colleagues (2008) recommend the following use of notes: Reduce the speech to a "key-word" outline. For easy visibility:

Use a large font size.

Capitalize trigger words or key words.

Use lots of white space between phrases to avoid confusion.

Number pages.

Generally, the speaker rehearses aloud until he or she becomes familiar enough with the speech content. The speech may be worded slightly differently each time it is rehearsed, and the precise wording is sometimes chosen only when the speech is actually delivered. Extemporaneous speaking allows the speaker to be well prepared and yet flexible enough to respond to audience feedback. For these reasons, it seems well suited to the public speaking situations that most of us will encounter. We emphasize, however, that different speaking situations unquestionably require different modes of delivery.

The Sleeper Effect

Despite its impact on an audience's receptivity, credibility does not appear to have a sustained influence on persuasion. Earlier, we mentioned a study in which a speech favoring a lenient attitude toward juvenile delinquency produced maximum attitude change when presented by a high-credibility source. This influence was greatest immediately after the speech was delivered. Differences resulting from the speaker's credibility tended to diminish over time so that the attitude change produced by the high-credibility source decreased and the message from the low-credibility source gained ground, producing more attitude change. The trend is sometimes called the **sleeper effect.**

The sleeper effect seems to result from the listener's tendency to dissociate the source and the message—presumably because he forgets who the source is. In experiments during which the listener was reminded of the source of the message, the high-credibility source regained his significantly greater influence on attitude change over the low-credibility source (Pratkanis et al., 1988). Many presidents use this tactic in press conferences when they answer questions by referring to speeches they have made in the past.

A Word about Stage Fright

Past research illustrates that public speaking phobias are very common. The general phobia, commonly called *stage fright,* includes physical symptoms such as rapid heart rate, shaking, thirst, and a fear that something terrible will happen while giving the speech. To quell the fear, column writers of the *State Register Journal* of Springfield, Illinois, share that public speakers should not be afraid of their audiences—since their audiences are generally "forgiving" because they are just happy that they are not the one having to give the speech! ("Speaking of Fears . . . ," 2004, p. 9).

Perhaps the most influential book about public communication is *How to Win Friends and Influence People* by Dale Carnegie. If you have ever gotten the jitters thinking about presenting a speech, you might be interested to know that until he published his now-famous book, Dale Carnegie had failed at almost everything he had ever tried. He never graduated from college. His attempts at careers all flopped. His first marriage ended in divorce. He lost almost all of his savings in the stock market crash of 1929. He grew up in abject poverty and was painfully shy because of his shabby clothes and downtrodden condition. He decided to write his now-famous book mostly to gain self-confidence and insight into how to turn his life around. He said in 1937, "I have blundered so often myself, that I began to study the subject for the good of my soul." To date, his book has sold over 50 million copies (Higgins, 2001, p. A5). So, if you have ever experienced stage fright, take comfort in the fact that even the best-known experts in the field have gone through the same thing.

We have tried to isolate important aspects of public communication that relate primarily to the speaker: source credibility and delivery (including how to handle stage fright). Although over time the influence of the source of the message seems to decline and the impact of the message itself gains ground, the ultimate effectiveness of any speech is determined by its appropriateness to the particular audience. So before considering how best to construct the message, let us turn our attention to the audience.

THE AUDIENCE

If delivering a speech is a new experience for you, the suggestion that you analyze your audience beforehand, or even as you are speaking, may come as something of a shock. When you stand before this group of people, you may view them only as the proverbial sea of faces. Yet some common characteristics have brought them together in the first place. Are they predominantly parents, college students, liberals, Roman Catholics, business people, educators, or anthropologists? Just about any group of listeners who gather in one place will do so for some of the same reasons. By establishing these reasons, you may find a strategy that allows you to appeal to the majority of audience members.

Audience Analysis

According to Clevenger (1966), there are at least two traditional methods by which the speaker may determine how best to adapt a message to a given audience: demographic analysis and purpose-oriented analysis.

Demographic Analysis

In demographic audience analysis, the speaker first considers some general characteristics of the audience members—age, sex, geographic background, occupation, socioeconomic level, education, religion, and so on. These known characteristics suggest inferences about the audience's beliefs, attitudes, and values. Such inferences are then used to gear the message to what seems to be the audience's level and interests. This does not mean that as a speaker you change the thrust of your argument but rather that you adapt its presentation for maximum impact.

Samovar and McDaniel (2007) recommend that you ask yourself the following questions in analyzing your audience:

What is the average age of the audience members?

What is the age range?

What is the gender breakdown of the audience?

What racial and ethnic groups are represented, in about what proportions?

What is the socioeconomic composition of the group?

What occupations are represented?

What religious groups are represented?

What is the political orientation of the group?

How homogeneous (similar) or heterogeneous (diverse) are the audience members for each of the above characteristics?

Let us consider for a moment the value to the speaker of knowing beforehand certain relevant data about the members of the audience. Imagine that you are to give a talk on the causes of inflation. It might be extremely valuable to know something about the occupations of audience members. For example, you would expect the values and viewpoints of members of a labor union to be different from those of a group of business executives.

Having knowledge of demographic variables also makes it easier for the speaker to establish some *common ground* with audience members. This is often accomplished with an anecdote, a joke, or a remark by the speaker indicating some sort of identification with the audience. It is common practice, for example, for a politician who comes from a small town to make some remark about his or her own upbringing when addressing a small-town audience. In his acceptance speech to the Democratic National Convention, former President Jimmy Carter made an appeal to delegates from many different regions of the United States when he remarked: "Now, our party was built out of a sweatshop on the old Lower East Side, the dark mills of New Hampshire, the blazing hearths of Illinois, the coal mines of Pennsylvania, the hardscrabble farmbelt, the Southern coastal plains and the unlimited frontiers of America" (Carter, 1976, p. A10).

As we shall illustrate in discussing message variables, in all public communication the construction of a message is inherently linked to the speaker's analysis of the audience. Consider, for example, selecting materials of support. Suppose a speaker knows that she is a low-credibility source for the audience. She may wish to use more evidence. Initially, at least, the use of good evidence enhances credibility. Also, the kind of evidence the speaker uses will be different for different audiences. For an audience of Hispanics being urged to take adult education courses in English, quotations from Hispanics who have moved out of the barrios and secured high-status jobs because of their bilingual skills will probably be more persuasive than quotations from English teachers who lack any knowledge of Spanish. Materials of support are covered on p. 444.

The speaker's choice of language is another variable that ideally should be influenced by a knowledge of audience characteristics. Given this audience, will the terminology be familiar? Will the connotations of the words as used by the speaker be understood by the entire group? Are the metaphors and analogies appropriate for this audience? These are some of the many considerations for any speaker who has some prior knowledge about the demographic makeup of the audience.

In adapting your speech on inflation, you would probably choose a less formal language style for the audience of union members than for the executives. You might say that large wage increases "fan the flames of inflation" rather than "perpetuate the inflationary cycle." With the executives, you might choose a statistical approach showing percentage inflationary increases; with the union audience, you might talk about the cost of an average market basket from one year to the next.

There are numerous other ways in which demographic information about audience members may be used to one's advantage. Suppose, for example, that you plan to deliver a persuasive speech on the prevention of hijacking, and you find that virtually all of your audience will be college graduates, and half will have advanced degrees. In this instance, it would be wise to take into account the finding that intelligent or better-educated audiences respond more readily to two-sided rather than one-sided appeals.

Former President Ronald Reagan used the National Republican Convention to deliver this farewell speech to the American people as well as to appeal to the television audience to vote Republican:

> Before we came to Washington, Americans had just suffered the two worst back-to-back years of inflation in 60 years. Those are the facts. And as John Adams said: "Facts are stubborn things."
>
> Interest rates had jumped to over 21 percent—the highest in 120 years—more than doubling the average monthly mortgage payments for working families—our families. When they sat around the kitchen table, it was not to plan summer vacations, it was to plan economic survival.
>
> Facts are stubborn things.
>
> Industrial production was down, and productivity was down for 2 consecutive years.
>
> The average weekly wage plunged 9 percent. The median family income fell 5½ percent.
>
> Facts are stubborn things.
>
> Our friends on the other side had actually passed the single highest tax bill in the 200-year history of the United States. Auto loans, because of their policies, went up to 17 percent—so our great factories began shutting down. Fuel costs jumped through the atmosphere—more than doubling. Then people waited in gas lines as well as unemployment lines.
>
> Facts are stubborn things. (1989, p. 11)

It is important to emphasize that gathering demographic information is only the first step in audience analysis. Very often, the speaker goes on to make *inferences about the beliefs, attitudes, and values of the audience.* Often the speaker is trying to determine in advance what position audience members are likely to have about a given issue before public communication actually takes place. This might well help him or her to decide how much attitude change to attempt in the speech. Once you determine what position audience members are likely to take on a given issue, it is probably wise to construct a persuasive appeal that is within their latitude of acceptance. Otherwise, the appeal will be too discrepant with initial attitudes and will create a boomerang effect (see "How Much Change to Attempt" on p. 456). The usefulness of the assimilation-contrast theory will depend on how well the speaker analyzes the audience. For example, given information about the average age of audience members, you might try to anticipate how discrepant your position on a particular issue would be from that of your audience. It is generally believed, for instance, that younger audiences tend to be more receptive to change and older audiences more conservative. Therefore, a speech favoring decriminalization of marijuana would probably be seen by a college-age audience as moderate but by their parents or grandparents as radical.

In certain audiences there will be more variability in important demographic characteristics. Here, the speaker might find it necessary to *appeal to a target audience* within the larger audience, especially if the speaker's aim is persuasion and it is known that there will be a distinct group of opinion leaders within the audience.

Purpose-Oriented Analysis

A second mode of adapting the message to the audience is **purpose-oriented audience analysis.** Instead of analyzing audience characteristics, *the speaker begins by asking himself or herself what information about the audience is most important for the speaker's purposes.* If you are an economist giving an informative speech about devaluation of currencies, you will want to know how much of an economics background the average listener has. Sometimes this information is easy to establish; sometimes you will have to make inferences. In any case, you begin with a general idea of audience level and constantly refer back to it as you prepare your speech. Can you assume that the listener will know what the gold standard is, or will you have to explain the concept in some detail? Will a quote from the late John Kenneth Galbraith be recognized as evidence from a high-credibility source? Will the audience be familiar with the basic concepts of statistics or probability theory? In contrast to demographic analysis, in which you gather information about the audience before preparing your speech, purpose-oriented analysis will be an ongoing part of your message preparation.

Listener Persuasibility

Persuasibility, as the term implies, refers to *a listener's susceptibility to persuasion.* A question that researchers and public speakers have often raised is whether there is a difference between men's and women's openness to persuasion.

Research indicates that women are often more readily swayed than men (Tuthill and Forsyth, 1982). This pattern was not always borne out in studies of children, however, which suggested that willingness to be persuaded might be learned as part of the female sex role. An interesting study by Montgomery and Burgoon (1977) found that *psychological sex* is a better predictor of sex differences in persuasibility than anatomical sex. Feminine females are more persuasible than masculine males, whereas androgynous males and females hardly differ.

As the female sex role in our society continues to undergo redefinition, differences in persuasibility will be less and less predictable. In fact, Rosenfeld and Christie (1974) concluded that it has become "futile to attempt to conclude that one sex is more persuasible than another" (p. 23).

A second question that has been the object of much research concerns the correlation between personality and persuasibility. Is it true, for example, that some people are resistant to changing their minds in all situations, whereas others go along with almost everything one says? Early research on the question looked for "those attitudes or personality factors leading to low or high resistance to *a wide variety of persuasive communication on many diverse topics."* Some people were more persuasible than others, regardless of the subject of the persuasive appeal. Furthermore, these people tended to be more easily persuaded in either direction on a given topic—to be more in favor of, or more opposed to, cancer research, for example (Janis and Field, 1959, emphasis added).

In another study, the same research team tried to identify the personality characteristics linked to persuasibility. It is generally agreed that persuasible people tend to have low self-esteem, a perception that presumably extends to their opinions: Such people value the opinions of others more than their own. By contrast, the person who resists persuasion is described as "likely to be little affected by external standards in other kinds of situations, to have a mature and strong self-image, to value subjective feeling and have a relatively rich inner life, to examine himself and his role in life to an extent that may include marked self-criticism, and to be independent without being rebellious" (Linton and Graham, 1959, p. 96).

Although there is little the speaker can do to control for such variables as listener persuasibility, it is still of interest to know that some personality differences affect persuasibility. This information might be especially useful in demographic audience analysis. For example, before an all-male audience, a female speaker might attempt a more thoroughgoing persuasive strategy than she would before an all-female audience that was already well-disposed toward her argument.

Persuasion theory has a lot to offer us in the way of advice on how best to go about the process of persuading others. The most famous persuasion theory is known as *Monroe's motivated sequence.* It has five steps:

1. *Attention.* First, you gain the attention of your audience. You do this in your introduction. You can show the importance of your topic, make a startling statement, tell a dramatic story, pose a rhetorical question, arouse curiosity, or use visual aids.

2. *Need.* Next, you must show that a problem currently exists. State the need clearly and dramatize it with relevant supporting materials (i.e., definitions, examples, statistics, quotes, or analogies). This arouses their need for a solution.

3. *Satisfaction.* Next, you satisfy the need by providing a solution to the problem. Make sure your plan has enough specifics to show how it satisfies the need.

4. *Visualization.* Next, help the audience visualize the plan by showing its benefits. It is important to use vividness to show how the members of the audience will benefit from adopting your plan.

5. *Action.* Finally, specify what the audience members can do. Give them an address to write to, or a phone number to call, or a place to go. Then use a strong conclusion to stimulate them to act.

THE MESSAGE

When we feel strongly enough about an issue to get up and speak in front of others, we sometimes confuse intensity with effectiveness. We may speak out passionately on a particular issue, but sometimes we fail to obtain the desired outcome—whether it be information gain, attitude change, or action.

To improve effectiveness, experts recommend the traditional use of introduction, body, and conclusion to organize a speech.

The **introduction** provides the opportunity to establish a common ground, gain the audience's attention, establish the thesis of the speech, and relate the importance of the topic or speech. A preview of what's coming is also a good idea, as this orients the audience and aids in their listening. By the end of the introduction, audience members should be attentive, should be familiar with the speaker and with what is to come, and should want to hear the speech. The introduction "sets up" the audience for the speaker and his or her speech.

The **body** of the speech presents the information and/or arguments indicated in the introduction. This is the largest part of the speech, possibly as much as 80 percent, unless the audience is hostile, in which case the introduction might be very long. In general, the body of a speech should contain few points (remember from Chapter 5 that audiences forget half of what they hear immediately after hearing it, and then lose another half within a few months). The fewer the number of points, the higher the probability the audience members will remember what is said.

The **conclusion** often gets the most attention since members know you are about to end. With this in mind, it comes as no surprise that the conclusion of the speech reviews what was said and finishes the speech with some memorable remarks. The message remembered, the "residual message," is tied significantly to the last words of the speech, so those last words must emphasize for the audience, in a memorable way, exactly what each member might best remember of the speech.

Notice the strong conclusion from General Douglas MacArthur's speech to the cadets at West Point. MacArthur was a national hero after the Korean War and was very old when he spoke. Think how you would feel if you were a cadet and were listening to this:

> The shadows are lengthening for me. The twilight is here. My days of old have vanished—tone and tints. They have gone glimmering through the dreams of things that were. Their memory is one of wondrous beauty, watered by tears and coaxed and caressed by the smiles of yesterday. I listen, then, but with thirsty ear, for the witching melody of faint bugles blowing reveille, of far drums beating the long roll.
>
> In my dreams I hear again the crash of guns, the rattle of musketry, the strange, mournful mutter of the battlefield. But in the evening of my memory, I come back to West Point. Always there echoes and re-echoes: duty, honor, country.
>
> Today marks my final roll call with you. But I want you to know that when I cross the river, my last conscious thoughts will be of the corps, and the corps, and the corps.
>
> I bid you farewell. (Safire, 1992, p. 78; see also Sprague and Stuart, 1996)

In this portion of the chapter, we shall concentrate on ways of preparing and presenting messages that will ensure optimum effectiveness. For centuries, students of public communication have discussed the subject of organizing speech material, the use of supporting materials, the speaker's choice of language, as well as several other options available to the speaker in choosing an appropriate strategy for persuasion. Only within the twentieth century, however, have experimental investigations allowed us to put some of these age-old notions to the test.

In studying **message variables,** or *alternative ways of presenting a message,* we shall review over 50 years of research. This period is one of the most fruitful in providing experimental clarification of some long-standing questions. We shall find, however, that some of the answers are more complex than we might have anticipated, that many substantive issues are still unresolved, and that there are some very important elements of speech preparation about which few research data exist.

Organization

According to many theorists, virtually all speeches consist of the three elements above: an introduction, a body, and a conclusion. At some point within the speech, there may also be a direct statement—a thesis sentence—that crystallizes the speaker's central idea. This theme, whether stated directly or not, will be elaborated in the main and subordinate points of the speaker's presentation. How the speaker chooses to organize and elaborate on speech materials is an issue of some concern, particularly for those with little experience or training in public speaking.

No research points to a single pattern of organization as the most desirable. In assembling speech materials, the speaker must find the pattern best suited to his or her particular message and to the particular audience to be addressed. (We have already discussed some aspects of the adaptation of speech materials to one's audience when we discussed audience analysis.) A speaker has many options in organizing materials. In the following pages, we shall discuss five of the more popular patterns.

Topical Organization

Among the most popular ways of ordering speech material is a **topical organization.** Here, *the speaker moves from one topic to the next in a way that clearly demonstrates how they are related.* Usually the speaker first prepares an outline in which the main points of the speech are in the form of a traditional outline and in which some concepts are subordinated to others. Making an outline is usually a part of any speech preparation, regardless of its patterns of organization. The following topical outline was prepared by a student for a speech on the human nervous system:

I.   The central nervous system consists of the brain and the spinal cord.
    A.   The brain has three distinct regions, each with a special function:
        1.   Forebrain

2. Midbrain
3. Hindbrain
B. The spinal cord has two distinct functions:
1. Sensory functions
2. Motor functions
II. The peripheral nervous system connects the central nervous system to the rest of the body.
A. Afferent nerves carry neurochemical impulses from the body to the brain
1. Somatic nerves (from the extremities)
2. Visceral nerves (from the abdomen and chest)
B. Efferent nerves carry neurochemical impulses from the brain to the body
1. Somatic nerves (to the extremities)
2. Visceral nerves (to the abdomen and chest)

Chronological Organization

Instead of arranging material topically, the speaker might choose a **chronological organization,** which uses time as an organization mechanism. Using this pattern, it is possible *to move from a review of the past into a discussion of contemporary events, and, if desirable, conclude with a projection into the future.* Or one can *start by discussing a current situation and trace its origin backward in time.*

Numerous themes—not simply historical ones—lend themselves to a chronological pattern of organization. The speaker might be discussing capital punishment, birth control, foreign affairs, or pornography.

Spatial Organization

A third method or arrangement is **spatial organization.** This pattern uses space or geographical position as an organizing principle. For example, in a speech about our solar system, one student briefly described each planet, beginning with Mercury (the one closest to the sun) and moving in order away from the sun to what was the planet Pluto. The spatial pattern is more limited as a means of organization, but it is one that is sometimes necessary. It might be well suited, for example, to the discussion of such topics as trade routes, territoriality among animals, and the distribution of bilingual communities within the United States. Moreover, there are times when a speaker makes use of spatial organization in only part of a speech. An instructor using topical organization in a lecture on Russian military history might also use spatial organization to analyze the strategy used during a single battle.

Problem Solution

Another very popular pattern of organization is **problem solution.** We find it in speeches of every kind, particularly in affirmative speeches during debates and in speeches concentrated on persuasion. *The speaker describes what he or she believes to be an existing problem and then offers a plan that will alleviate or resolve* *it.* For example, in a speech about automation one speaker first introduced a three-part problem: (1) that automation resulted in loss of jobs, (2) that many of those who lost their jobs were not easily retrained for more highly skilled jobs, and (3) that some of those who were capable of taking on such jobs were unable to relocate. Having described this problem in some detail, she proposed a three-part solution: (1) a shorter workweek, (2) the development of new domestic industries, and (3) the creation of new foreign markets for the products produced by automated processes.

Causal Organization

Like the problem-solution pattern, **causal organization** has two major divisions. *The speaker argues either from cause to effect or from effect to cause.* For example, a speaker might describe a condition such as alcoholism and the deteriorating effects it has on the human body and then go on to discuss its underlying causes. In this case, the sequence is from effect back to cause. Under other circumstances, the causes of alcoholism (unhappiness, personal failures, and so on) might be discussed first, with the speaker then going on to discuss its effects.

We have described five ways of organizing speech materials; many others are possible. To date, however, there are no acceptable data as to which pattern is most effective. This is a decision that the speaker must make on an individual basis.

Materials of Support

After deciding on the pattern of arrangement that best suits the topic, the speaker is ready to gather various **materials of support**—*forms of evidence* that develop or strengthen each of the points to be made. These materials include examples, statistics, quotations, and analogies.

As aids in gathering supporting materials, the speaker may consult some of the standard reference works, such as the Internet, *Reader's Guide to Periodical Literature, Education Index, Biography Index,* the *World Almanac,* any set of encyclopedias, *Who's Who, Psychological Abstracts,* and the *Congressional Record.* All these sources will be available in the reference section of most libraries. In most cases, such reference works will lead the speaker to the books, magazines, and journals that will be most helpful.

Examples

The use of examples is so much a part of other, less formal modes of communication that we tend to be unaware that it is frequently a method of support in speech making. By adding examples to a discussion, the speaker can make his or her presentation more concrete.

Sometimes the vivid detail available in an example gives the speaker a chance to make a presentation more dramatic. There is, for instance, a world of difference between discussing the effects of an earthquake in terms of damage costs and describing the experience of a single family whose home has been destroyed.

When examples are well chosen and representative of what they are intended to illustrate, they buttress the various points the speaker is trying to develop. How much a receiver can be led to infer from a given example depends upon his or her critical listening skills.

Statistics

Sometimes a speaker can summarize much numerical data through the use of statistics and at the same time increase his or her authoritativeness with reference to the subject being discussed. When Lee Iacocca spoke to the National Association of Manufacturers, he used statistics to dramatize the need for educational success. He said:

> We're turning out high school graduates who will have a hard time even *understanding* the problems, let alone tackling them. Somebody did a study (oh, hell, we're always doing studies). Seventy-five percent of our high school students don't know what *inflation* is . . . 66 percent don't know what *profits* are . . . and 55 percent don't have a clue as to what a government *budget deficit* is. (So the size has no meaning to them.)
>
>   Hell, 60,000 of our graduates last year could barely read their diplomas. (I couldn't read *mine* either, but it was in *Latin*. Theirs were in *English*.) (1989, p. 456)

In addition to clarifying and developing a point, statistics can sometimes present a revealing overview of the topic under consideration. Thus in one talk on job satisfaction, the speaker quoted several dissatisfied workers who had been interviewed concerning their jobs. But then he went on to show his audience a bar graph based upon Gallup polls. The bar graph illustrated that the negative reactions were not at all representative of the workforce.

In certain settings—mass and organizational communication, for example—it is common practice for a speaker to use such a visual presentation of statistics. Another popular visual presentation of statistics is the line chart. Statistics may be represented in several other graphic ways, but of course, they are most frequently introduced directly into the body of the speech. Cybele Werts (2004) suggests that statistics must be arranged into chart and graphical presentations that are easy for the audience to understand. Too much data on a chart can make the visuals difficult to read. Colors can help clarify comparisons on charts but should not be fluorescent or garish. Additionally, simple fonts should be used to make the statistical representations easy to read and understand from a distance (p. 21). In general, statistics seem most appropriate when the speaker can make a particular point more clearly and concisely with them than with elaborate description.

Quotations

The most obvious use of quotations within a speech is for the dramatic, sometimes eloquent qualities that can be conveyed to the audience. The speeches of Margaret Thatcher, Martin Luther King, Jr., John F. Kennedy, and other public figures are constantly being tapped for their power and command of language. Many phrases and sentences of their speeches have entered the language. Paraphrase would not seem to do them justice. For example, it would be difficult and self-defeating to paraphrase John Kennedy's famous exhortation from his 1961 inaugural address:

> Ask not what your country can do for you. Ask what you can do for your country.

Even speakers known for their eloquence and command of language make use of quotation for dramatic effect, particularly in the opening or conclusion of a talk. For example, in "I Have a Dream," a speech that is exemplary for its eloquence and power, Martin Luther King, Jr., concluded by quoting the words of a spiritual:

> When we allow freedom to ring, when we let it ring from every village and every hamlet, from every state and every city, we will be able to speed up that day when all of God's children, black men and white men, Jews and Gentiles, Protestants and Catholics, will be able to join hands and sing in the words of the Old Negro spiritual, "Free at last! Free at last! Thank God almighty, we are free at last!" (King, 1969, p. 294)

Of course, quotations are cited for many reasons other than eloquence. If the quoted source has knowledge or experience greater than that of the speaker, the quotation may be used to add validity to the speaker's argument and, indirectly, to enhance credibility. In our discussions of social influence and conformity, we have seen that attitudes and beliefs become more acceptable to us if we think they have been accepted by others—especially if those others are perceived as being of higher status. It is one thing for a speaker to assert that the government's fiscal policies have failed. It is quite another, however, to quote a Harvard economics professor who says exactly the same thing. To most audiences the expert's opinion is much more credible.

There are numerous other examples. In arguing about the effects of alcohol on the human body, a speaker might support his or her position with quotations from medical authorities. Lawyers in court frequently call on or cite an expert witness to establish the validity of their cases: "Ladies and gentlemen of the jury, the coroner's report showed that the cause of death was a bullet wound indicating the angle of the bullet was downward. We have established that my client is twelve inches shorter than the deceased and could not have fired the gun from such an angle. Therefore, my client could not have committed the murder."

Analogies

A speaker who draws an **analogy** makes *a comparison between two things or situations on the basis of their partial similarities.* As a method of support, an analogy can function in several different ways.

First of all, an analogy may be used for clarification. For example, one speaker was discussing the effect of a college degree on a person's earning power throughout his or her career. She compared the college graduate to a stone flung by a slingshot (education): For a short time, she explained, the college student's earning power is impeded, but the college graduate catches up and then shoots past the average wage earner who holds no degree.

An analogy may also be used to dramatize a point. Thus, a speaker might compare dumping industrial wastes into the environment to adding a spoonful of dirt to each of our meals. Or he or she might use an analogy to make a point seem less significant. The speaker might argue, for example, that the environment is so vast that pollutants have no more effect than would adding a spoonful of dirt to an ocean.

On many occasions an analogy is the most concise way to get a complex idea or point across. Often the analogy is an extended comparison, as in the following speech. After the *Challenger* astronauts were killed, President Reagan's skill made it one of his best speeches. He said,

> There's a coincidence today. On this day 390 years ago the great explorer Sir Francis Drake died aboard ship off the coast of Panama. In his lifetime the great frontiers were the oceans. And a historian later said, "He lived by the sea, died on it, and was buried in it." Today we can say of the *Challenger* crew: Their dedication was, like Drake's, complete.
>
> The crew of the space shuttle *Challenger* honored us by the manner in which they lived their lives. We shall never forget them, nor the last time we saw them—this morning, as they prepared for their journey, and waved good-bye, and "slipped the surly bonds of earth" to "touch the face of God." (Noonan, 1990, p. 257)

The use of analogy was explored more fully when we discussed critical listening in Chapter 5.

During the course of a speech a speaker sometimes makes use of many kinds of supporting materials. For example, in arguing that United States foreign aid policy was not meeting its objectives, one student gave examples of specific countries that had worsening relations with the United States even though they were receiving substantial amounts of foreign aid. He used statistics to show the increasing amount of aid to various countries over the year and the simultaneous rise of communism in some of those countries. He also gave quotations from experts on foreign relations who argued that our foreign aid policy was ineffective. Finally, he drew an analogy between the United States' giving foreign aid and a person playing the stock market: "When an investment does not pay off," he said, "it is wise to stop investing in a losing cause and reinvest in another, more profitable venture."

Visual Aids

Without question, visual aids make presentations more vivid and interesting. Visual aids include objects and models, demonstrations, illustrations (such as, artwork, photos, tables, charts, handouts), as well as audiovisuals (for example, audiotape, videotape, film, computer, and slide/tape combinations). With the increasing sophistication and availability of computers, presentations are becoming more and more dramatic with computer-generated graphics. Figures 13.1 through 13.3 give a few examples (Sedlack et al., 2008). PowerPoint is, by far, the most frequently used method for presenting via computer. Recent research has shown that using Power-Point increases an audience's enjoyment and evaluation of the speaker. However, it does not increase audience retention (Downing and Garmon, 2001).

The effective use of visual aids includes the following considerations:

1. Prepare the aids well in advance and get used to using them.
2. Keep all aids simple (based on the audience analysis; e.g., what is "simple" for IBM employees may be difficult for sixth-grade students).
3. Be sure the aids can be seen, heard, and so on.
4. When using aids that require special equipment, such as videorecorders, computers, overhead projectors, slide projectors, video projectors, and screens, make sure that the equipment is *available,* that it is *delivered* on time and to the right place, that it *works,* and that *you know how to work it.*
5. Be sure the aids suit the situation with respect to the size of the room and its capabilities (e.g., a room with an echo is problematic, as is a room without the capacity to dim the lights) and to audience expectations.
6. Be sure the aid enhances the speech or is an integral part of the speech.
7. Talk to your audience and *not* to the visual aid. (Whetten and Cameron, 2005)

Figure 13.1   *Market Planning Meeting with Computer*

***Figure* 13.2**   *Computer Graphics*

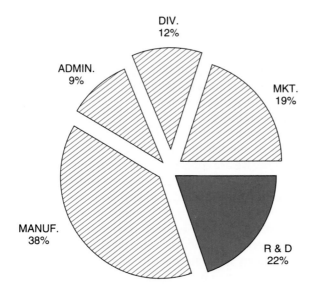

GRAPHICS IMPROVE COMMUNICATION

REVENUE DISTRIBUTION

***Figure* 13.3**   *Computer Graphics*

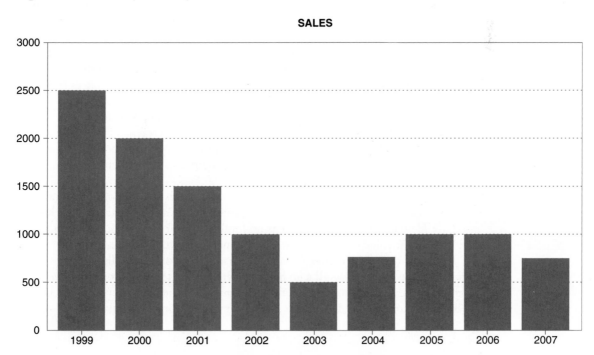

SALES

The important message here is that a visual aid is *audience* and *situation specific*. This makes it clear why an audience analysis is necessary. With the rise in popularity of PowerPoint, making really appealing visual aids has never been easier.

Language

Joan Detz, speechwriter and coach, makes suggestions involving language use in public communication. These include "simplifying your language," so that everyone in the audience can understand what you have to say, "giving it some style" including "word play," and ample rehearsal to make sure that "how" you say things makes the desired impact on the message (2004).

From the beginning of this book, we have stressed the difficulties inherent in trying to create a meaning in the mind of another human being. In two-person and small-group communication, for example, we are concerned that the connotations of the words used be similar for all the people participating in a given transaction. In broader terms, we are concerned with the use of shared, rather than private, meaning. These concerns are multiplied many times over in public communication, where a message is likely to be long and complex, feedback between sender and receiver is apt to be quite limited, and the number of receivers increases sharply. In the following pages, we shall explore some questions of style—some ways in which the clarity, appeal, and persuasiveness of a message are affected by the speaker's use of language.

Vividness

According to Collins and associates (1988), *vividness*, in the context of communication, means concrete and colorful language (p. 1). Compare, for example, the vagueness of "A period of unfavorable weather set in" with the more pointed "It rained every day of the week."

Vigorous writing and speaking are often grounded in specifics. Thus the various methods of support are important not only from a logical but from a stylistic point of view. Sometimes a speaker must discuss a subject that is relatively abstract—for example, the responsibilities of a free press or the three-part division of government—but the presentation becomes more vigorous, more capable of sustaining audience attention, if it is also somewhat concrete.

Senator George Graham Vest (Missouri) spoke eloquently about even so humble a subject as his dog. Notice how beautifully he paints a verbal picture:

> One absolutely unselfish friend that man can have in this selfish world, the one that never deserts him, the one that never proves ungrateful or treacherous is his dog . . . He will kiss the hand that has no food to offer: He will lick the wounds and sores that come in encounter with the roughness of the world . . .
>
> If fortune drives the master forth an outcast in the world, friendless and homeless, the faithful dog asks no higher privilege than that of accompanying him, to guard him against danger, to fight against his enemies. And when the last scene of all comes, and death takes his master in its embrace and his body is laid

away in the cold ground, no matter if all other friends pursue their way, there by the graveside will the noble dog be found. His head between his paws, his eyes sad, but open in alert watchfulness, faithful and true even in death. (in Safire, 1992, p. 164–165)

Metaphor

Since classical times writers have argued that the use of metaphor enhances credibility—presumably by reflecting the speaker's intelligence as well as by entertaining and pleasing the audience. In fact, Aristotle described a command of metaphor as "the mark of genius." **Metaphor** has been defined as *"language that implies a relationship, of which similarity is a significant feature, between two things and so changes our apprehension of either or both"* (Deutsch, 1957, p. 73; italics added). Metaphors differ from analogies, which we have already discussed; in an analogy the comparison is partial ("Education is *like* a slingshot" and "Dumping industrial wastes into the environment is *like* adding a spoonful of dirt to each of your meals"), whereas in a metaphor two different things are said to be equivalent ("Education *is* a slingshot").

President George H. W. Bush, in his inaugural speech, used colorful language when he said,

> Some see leadership as high drama and the sound of trumpets calling; and sometimes it is that. But I see history as a book with many pages . . .
> The breeze blows, a page turns, the story unfolds—a small and stately story of unity, diversity, and generosity, shared and written together. (Noonan, 1990, p. 337)

Theorists concerned with persuasion have long wondered whether there is any significant difference between a message that is literal and straightforward in its arguments and one that makes use of metaphor. Suppose, for example, that a speaker argues against government aid to needy students. Would she be better off saying, "In education governmental help is not compatible with our national goals," or would the listeners be more inclined to agree with the argument if the speaker used a bold metaphor such as "Governmental help is the kiss of death"?

Before we can make a definitive statement about the relationship between attitude change and the widespread use of metaphoric language, researchers will have to explore other kinds and uses of metaphor.

Intensity

Although metaphor is sometimes considered an aspect of intensity, message **intensity** is also reflected in a speaker's choice of high- and low-intensity words. In Table 13.2, we see a comparison of high- and low-intensity modifiers and verbs used in a study by McEwen and Greenberg (1970). Their research, which is a comparison of high- and low-intensity messages on the same subject, indicates that audiences regard intense messages more highly, as clearer and also more logical. In fact, audiences

	High Intensity	Low Intensity
Table 13.2 *High- and Low-Intensity Words*		
Modifiers	positively	perhaps
	greatly	possibly
	most	some
	definitely	slightly
	extremely	somewhat
Verbs	be	seems to be
	causes	may cause
	must	could

regard the sources of those messages as more trustworthy, dynamic, and competent. The researchers suggest that high-intensity messages may be more persuasive because they provide "a greater impetus to adopt the message-advocated position" (p. 341). According to an earlier study, however, language that is highly intense or emotional has a boomerang effect if the audience's initial attitude is discrepant with that of the speaker (Bowers, 1963). For example, when speaking in favor of the Equal Rights Amendment, a radical feminist would be less likely to persuade a group of women initially opposed to the amendment if her language were highly emotional than she would if she used words of lesser intensity.

In his speech to a national educator's group, Benjamin Alexander (1989) used moderately intense language, as you can see:

> When Dr. Nyangoni called and asked me to speak on the topic, "Reflections on Education and Our Society," she stated, "You will be addressing the largest professional educational association in the world."
>
> Once upon a time . . . I like that expression—so let me say it again. Once upon a time, we passed out homework in our schools . . . and not condoms, and it was not "Teacher Training and Driver Education." It was "Teacher Education and Driver Training." We trained our drivers but we educated our teachers.
>
> We did not have courses like "Physics without mathematics," "Chemistry made easy," and "Mathematics without fractions." Yes, once upon a time—we did not coddle students by passing them when they should have been held back. (p. 563)

McCroskey proposes that language that is highly intense will magnify "the perceived discrepancy of a communicator's message." He goes on to say, "Increasing perceived discrepancy tends to enhance the effectiveness of an initially high-credibility source but reduce even further the effectiveness of an initially low-credibility source" (McCroskey, 1993, p. 203). In other words, a dynamic, emotional presentation by a speaker perceived as a high-credibility source is going to be more effective than the same presentation by a speaker perceived as being low in credibility.

Transitions

It is possible to discuss transitions from the standpoint of either organization or style, for a **transition** is *the verbal bridge between two parts of a speech*. Transitions are more easily developed if the points in a speech flow somewhat logically from one to another. In speech about the planets in our solar system, the transitions were made quite easily. "Beginning with the planet nearest the sun we find Mercury," the speaker began. For the transition to the next point, he said, "Continuing our journey away from the sun we find Venus." He continued, using the analogy of a journey as a vehicle for devising smooth transitions. To avoid repeating himself, he used some variation in each transition. He said, "The third planet we encounter is Earth." Then, "As we leave the blue and green planet, we set out for the red planet, Mars." In this speech, spatial organization made the movement from one point to the next seem logical and easy to follow.

There are any number of ways of smoothly relating two concepts to each other. In discussing leadership, a speaker might move from one part of her speech to another by saying, "let us turn from the leadership of yesterday to my second concern, the leadership of tomorrow." Effective transitions add more than finishing touches to a speech. They clarify the speaker's train of thought for the listener, they help give the speech unity and coherence, and sometimes they help make the argument seem well reasoned.

Economy of Language

Those long-winded birds. They're all the same. The less they have to say, the longer it takes them to say it.
—Harry S. Truman on politicians (quoted in Miller, 1973, p. 177)

Signal-to-noise ratio, *the relationship between the essential and extraneous information contained in any message,* is a measure of interference. A concept that can be applied to all contexts of communication, it seems particularly relevant to any discussion of public speaking. Let us say at the outset that a certain amount of repetition, or redundancy, is necessary in most communication. This is certainly the case in public communication, where members of the audience have little chance to ask a speaker for clarification—at least before the question-and-answer period that may follow. A limited amount of redundancy ensures that the speaker's main points will not be misinterpreted. Nonetheless, there is little need to hammer the point home over and over again. We all know what torture it can be to sit through a public address by a long-winded repetitive speaker.

"Brevity is the sister of talent," according to the playwright Anton Chekhov (1889).

According to a recent Associated Press survey, Americans are running out of patience. We can't stand to wait more than five minutes on the phone, and we start fuming in long grocery lines. Acknowledge this reality in your talks, e-mails, phone calls, presentations, meetings, and any other type of professional communications by getting to the point. Fast. (Gallo, 2006c)

Carmine Gallo elaborates this principle with the following three tenets of effective business presentation:

TO THE POINT. In the words of the former General Electric chief executive Jack Welch, "Business is simple. No need to make it complicated."

15 MINUTES, TOPS. President John F. Kennedy's inaugural speech, one of the most inspiring speeches ever given, was 15 minutes long. President Ronald Reagan gave strict instructions to his speechwriters to avoid talks of more than 15 minutes. Segments on *60 Minutes* run no more than 15 to 17 minutes. All this is not a coincidence. Research shows that 15 minutes is the length of the average attention span, and after 15 to 20 minutes listeners' attention drops dramatically.

THREE-SLIDE LIMIT. Use no more than three slides.

Microsoft's PowerPoint program is a blessing and a curse for business professionals. Most of us use it to convey information, but many of us are bored to tears when we watch the finished product. (Gallo, 2006b)

The problem, of course, is not the software itself, but how it is used to convey information. Because the program is so easy to use and the slides are so easy to make, many presenters often succumb to the temptation of including too many slides in their presentations. This, according to Gallo, is a mistake, since it makes your audience focus on the slides instead of you, the presenter.

For example, even 30 slides in one hour are far too many for most presentations. In the case of any presentation, less really is more. Monster.com founder Jeff Taylor once told me that he can speak for 15 minutes with one slide in the background. He uses a total of 11 slides for a one hour presentation. Sybase CEO John Chen uses 15 in an hour.
That gives you an idea of just how few slides are needed to make an impact. Motivational guru Tony Robbins will show a total of only five slides in two hours! Again, he wants the focus to be on him, not the slides. And so should you. (Gallo, 2006b)

Tim Draper of Draper Fisher Jurvetson, whose firm was behind such companies as Hotmail and Skype, says that "in an initial presentation . . . he only wants to see three slides, with no more than three lines of text on each" (Gallo, 2006c).
The speaker who is concise has the gift of selection. By omitting what is unnecessary and repetitious, he or she makes every word count. Economy in the use of language is a distinct stylistic advantage. Perhaps that is what one of President Franklin Roosevelt's close associates was driving at when, early in Eleanor

Roosevelt's public speaking career, he gave her this terse bit of advice: "Have something to say, say it, and then sit down."

Humor and Satire

John F. Kennedy's use of humor was memorable. One of his best known quips was his opening remark to an audience in Paris in 1961: "I do not think it altogether inappropriate to introduce myself to this audience. I am the man who accompanied Jacqueline Kennedy to Paris and I have enjoyed it." We have already touched on the subject of humor in our discussion of credibility. We saw that although humor affects whether an audience likes a speaker, it may not influence the speaker's perceived expertness. And yet, as they prepare their speeches, there is no doubt that the majority of speakers are scrupulous about including humorous elements. Even if the subject is one of great urgency, there will often be at least some effort to win over the audience with a joke or two. In fact, opening a speech with a joke is a frequent practice and is often recommended in handbooks on public speaking. Reportedly, one of Gerald Ford's speechwriters was concerned solely with the writing of humorous material.

Does this mean that you should always open your presentation with a joke? Dennis Beaver, who teaches bankers public speaking at the Graduate School of Banking at the University of Wisconsin–Madison, doesn't believe so.

> One of the common misconceptions about public speaking is the tired advice, "Open with a funny story." This is completely wrong. If you've got a story that fits your presentation, and you are a good storyteller, then consider using it, but it's got to fit!
>
> There is a difference between humor and telling a joke. Humor is a broad concept. Audiences love to laugh, and you can get them laughing through tone of voice, your own laughter, asking ironic questions—the list is endless. Your job as a speaker is to determine well in advance, "Where and how can I lighten the mood, get 'em laughing, and enhance my credibility?" You can do this without telling a single joke.
>
> So, leave nothing to chance. Yes, humor should appear spontaneous—and sometimes will be—but a good speaker "builds in" those seemingly impromptu comments. Finally, a good speaker will laugh with the audience. (Beaver, 2006)

Appeals to Fear

You want to persuade your audience that driving without safety belts is dangerous, that smoking can cause cancer, that disarmament will be detrimental to national security. What should your strategy be? Is the audience more likely to be persuaded if you appeal to fear? And if so, what level of fear is optimal?

A number of studies have examined the relationship between fear and attitude change. Many researchers report a strong positive correlation between fear arousal and attitude change. Historically, under high-fear conditions students urged to get tetanus inoculations showed significantly greater attitude change than those given the same advice under low-fear conditions. High-fear conditions resulted in more behavior change as well: More students did get tetanus shots (Dabbs and Leventhal, 1966). In 2003, Das, de Wit, and Stroebe concluded from three studies that appeals to fear in persuasive health messages resulted in increased related preventive action steps by listeners. Those study participants who received fear appeal messages felt vulnerable, negative, and responded as hoped to quell their fears (p. 650).

Witte (1992, 1994) has hypothesized a "parallel process model" of fear appeals. She proposes that fear appeals actually arouse two parallel reactions in the receiver: first, the cognitive or rational reaction, and second, the emotional or fearful reaction. Fear appeals apparently can arouse both reactions. Her findings support earlier research findings that fear appeals are the most effective.

How Much Change to Attempt

Confrontation is a persuasive style that has come to dominate numerous public communication contexts. The use of this strategy brings up an important question: Assuming that the speaker is interested in maximum persuasion, how much change should he or she argue for?

Let us explain the question by giving an example. Suppose the issue under discussion is whether the federal government should provide welfare benefits for the unemployed. Let the continuum in Figure 13.4 represent the range of opinion on this issue, and let us assume that there are 100 possible attitudes. Suppose Greg's preferred position on welfare can be quantified at 65. Surrounding this point on the scale is a range of opinions that Greg also finds acceptable, sometimes referred to as his "latitude of acceptance." Beyond this point is a latitude of noncommitment and, finally, a latitude of rejection, a range of opinions that he finds unacceptable. Imagine that Greg's latitude of acceptance goes from 50 to 75. If the speaker advocates a position within this range—55, for example—the discrepancy between this view and Greg's favored position is relatively small. Researchers

Figure 13.4 *The Assimilation Effect: One Listener's Attitude toward Welfare*

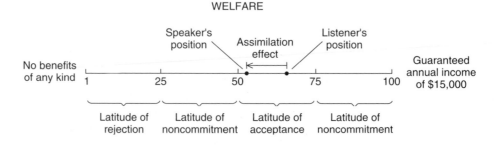

have found that, other things being equal, such a moderate discrepancy will tend to shift listener attitude toward the position advocated by the speaker (Hovland et al., 1953). That is, the listener tends to perceive the speaker's position as closer to his or her preferred position than it really is; in fact, the listener tends *to assimilate, or accept, the change in attitude urged by the speaker.* This phenomenon is often referred to as an **assimilation effect.**

In the hope of bringing about maximum attitude change, the speaker may, of course, advocate a position that falls within the listener's latitude of rejection. This is the rationale behind confrontation tactics. But the results have often been disappointing. Research has shown that when a message falls within the latitude of rejection, the listener tends to perceive the message as even more discrepant with his or her viewpoint than it actually is and therefore to reject it. Thus, instead of producing greater attitude change, the speaker elicits *a negative reaction on the part of the listener* that has variously been referred to as a **backlash, boomerang effect,** or **contrast effect.** This methodology can be used instrumentally, or can occur accidentally. Consider the following example. In 2004 a film called *Fahrenheit 9/11* was released that showed an opposing view of the Republican George W. Bush presidency through 9/11 and the war in Iraq. This brought about the question of whether a movie, geared toward a public audience, could be an effective mode of persuasive communication and influence a presidential election. Although the film showed a scathing portrayal of the Bush presidency and naturally seemed to benefit the Democrats, Republicans believed that there would be a backlash against the film that would help Bush's candidacy instead of hindering it. Republicans argued that such negative public commentary united them in their push to keep Bush in office (Ivry, 2004, p. A1). A speaker can elicit the same kind of effect as a film when attempting to persuade the public.

Bear in mind that the more deeply committed you are to your system of beliefs or to a given position, the narrower your latitude of acceptance will be. Thus, in trying to persuade listeners whose minds are fairly well made up, a speaker should advocate a relatively moderate amount of change to produce the optimum reaction.

One Side or Two Sides?

Suppose that you want to persuade a mixed (male and female) audience to be more sympathetic toward the women's movement. Should you present only your side of the issue, or should you also discuss the case against it?

We now know that if audience members are initially receptive to a message and are unlikely to hear any arguments opposing it, then a one-sided approach will probably be more persuasive than a two-sided approach. In this case, your effort would probably be directed toward reinforcing existing attitudes rather than changing values. If, on the other hand, the audience is likely to be skeptical or hostile to the speaker's point of view or will hear later arguments opposing it, a two-sided approach will probably be more effective. You can prepare a two-sided argument by listing the pros and cons of your subject and trying to anticipate the objections of the skeptical listener. If you are speaking on the women's movement, your list might look something like this:

PROS	CONS
1. Women are paid less than men for comparable jobs.	1. Women are poorer job risks than men because women often leave work soon after they marry.
2. Women are denied some legal rights of ownership.	2. Women enjoy more legal protection than men do; they also receive alimony in the event of divorce.
3. Women are always assumed to be responsible for child care and housework; these responsibilities should be shared by men.	3. Woman's natural role is in the home, and this is her highest fulfillment.

Once you have made such a list, you will find evidence that refutes or substantiates the arguments against you. As you speak, you present the first points and acknowledge the extent to which the objections are invalid and do not negate your main arguments. You then go on to cite evidence supporting your side of the issue.

Why should a two-sided approach work when the listener is likely to hear opposing arguments later on? Inoculation theory suggests an explanation in the form of a medical analogy. There are two ways in which a doctor can help a patient resist a disease: maintain the patient's state of health by prescribing a balanced diet, adequate rest, and so on, or inoculate the patient with a small amount of disease so that the patient builds up antibodies. Now, imagine that your patient, the audience member, is about to be attacked by a disease—that is, a persuasive message discrepant with your own. When you use a one-sided approach, you offer support: You give arguments in favor of your position and try to make the listener strong enough to ward off attacks. When you use a two-sided approach, you "inoculate" the listener through exposure to a weak form of the disease—the counterargument—so that he or she can refute it and thus build up defenses against future attacks. **Inoculation theory** holds that *inoculation is more effective than support in building up resistance because listeners exposed to a weak version of the counterarguments tend to develop an immunity to later arguments favoring that side.* You might try this tactic to see whether your experience corroborates the predictions of inoculation theory. Remember, though, that an inoculation must be a weak version of the disease.

A final point to be made is that the one-sided approach seems to work better if most of the members of your audience are poorly educated or of low intelligence. Perhaps in this case presenting both sides confuses listeners, leaving them uncertain which side you actually advocate.

Climax Order or Anticlimax Order?

If you had three arguments, one of which was clearly the strongest, would you use it first or save it for last? When you use the **climax order** of presentation, *you save* *your strongest argument until last;* when you use the **anticlimax order,** *you present your strongest argument first* and then proceed to the weaker arguments. Which order to use poses a serious question when you would like to change group opinion on an important issue.

Research evidence on this question does not clearly favor one approach over the other. Nevertheless, if we take into account the existing attitudes of our listeners, we are able to come up with some answers. If the audience is initially interested in your topic and favorable to your point of view, you can better afford to save your strongest argument for last. Presumably, the audience will be willing to give you the benefit of the doubt. If, on the other hand, your listeners are initially opposed to your point of view, you may be more effective if you use your most persuasive argument first (Karlins and Abelson, 1970).

Two important assumptions underlie the issue of climax versus anticlimax order. The first is that you are able to determine which of your arguments your listeners are likely to perceive as strongest or most persuasive. It is not always possible to know in advance how your audience will react to a given line of reasoning. Even seasoned public speakers have been surprised by audience response to a particular argument or, for that matter, to a casual remark. The second assumption is that you can know in advance whether most of the audience will be for or against your stand on a particular subject. In almost all cases some audience members will favor your position and others will not. Thus, you are forced to make your choices about climax or anticlimax strategy on the basis of what you know about the majority of your listeners, knowing full well that these choices will be the wrong ones for the remaining listeners. Any decision you make will win over some listeners and risk alienating others (see Conger, 1998).

Stated or Implied Conclusions?

Have you ever tried to persuade someone by hinting at something? Sometimes it works, but sometimes the other person doesn't get the hint at all. Public speakers have long wondered whether it is more persuasive to state the conclusion of a speech explicitly or to allow listeners to draw their own conclusions from the arguments presented.

One argument in favor of implicit conclusions is that if the speech is already comprehensible on its own, an explicit conclusion is unnecessary. It has also been proposed that listeners with a high level of interest or ego involvement are more likely to be persuaded by an implied than by an expressed deduction, which might offend them if they hold an opposing view.

Despite these considerations, and the fact that one early study (Thistlethwaite et al., 1955) found no difference in attitude acceptance between conclusion drawing and no-conclusion drawing, most studies confirm that you have a better chance of changing audience attitude if you state your conclusion than if you allow listeners to draw their own (Tubbs, 1968). One reason for this seems to be that in making their own summation of your argument, listeners may distort it; they may even find support for their own point of view in the new information you present.

Speak First or Have the Last Say?

In 2003 Brunel and Nelson published their research on primacy and recency effects in public advertising messages in the *Journal of Advertising Research*. They found that the order of items presented, audience gender, and perceived value of the message affected "message persuasion" (p. 330). With this in mind, now consider the situation in which two speakers, Doreen and Chris, are to debate an issue. Is it to Doreen's advantage to speak first, or would she have maximum impact if she spoke following Chris? In other terms, would learning and remembering the first argument interfere with learning and remembering the second?

According to a classic paper on the issue (Miller and Campbell, 1959), two persuasive communications are retained equally well if presented together and measured immediately. If audience attitudes are measured a week later, however, we expect a **primacy effect**—that is, *the first communication is remembered somewhat better than the second.* If there is a long delay between the two speakers and audience attitudes are measured right after the second speaker's presentation, we expect a **recency effect**—that is, *the second message is remembered somewhat better than the first.* Suppose, however, that there is a delay not only between the two speakers but in the measurement of audience attitude. In this instance, primacy and recency seem to cancel out each other, for neither message has the dominant impact.

A more recent study of the primacy-recency issue finds "the more recent information somewhat more influential shortly after the communications and the earlier information after a longer time lapse" (Luchins and Luchins, 1970, p. 68; McGuire, 1985, p. 273). Over time, however, conflicting communications tend to converge so that aspects of both communications are integrated into a more balanced view. Given these findings, the speaker's message, credibility, and delivery are likely to be more important than whether the speaker is first or last.

It is tempting to apply what is known about message variables to less formal kinds of communication. For example, if you want to persuade your parents to finance a new car for you, you might find yourself speculating about whether to hint or come right out and ask for it—and then whether to use a one-sided or a two-sided approach. The research findings we have discussed, however, are based primarily on speaker-audience situations. Although they may indicate some trends in other kinds of communication, the information about message variables is most relevant to person-to-group communication.

Summary

One of the most formal modes of human communication we experience is public, or person-to-group, communication. We have tried to view it here in terms of both the speaker's and the listener's experience, giving special attention to persuasive rather than information communication.

The single most important judgment we made about the speaker, apart from his or her message, concerns credibility. Judgments about source credibility, as we saw, are not constant; they vary not only from audience to audience but from one time to another. In general, the high-credibility source has greater influence than the low-credibility source, but the impact of credibility on persuasion is greatest immediately after the message is received. Delivery is a second important speaker variable. In this chapter, we discussed both the visual and vocal aspects of delivery and then went on to evaluate four modes of delivery: impromptu speaking, reading from manuscript, memorized speech, and extemporaneous speaking.

Our next topic was the audience itself, which we viewed from the speaker's vantage point. We described two methods—demographic and purpose-oriented analysis—that a speaker might use to adapt a message to a particular audience. Research findings on how listener persuasibility correlates with sex differences and personality traits were also examined.

Our treatment of the message itself focused on message preparation and structure rather than content. We discussed the organization of speech material, the use of supporting materials, and the speaker's choice of language, as well as several other options available to the speaker in choosing an appropriate strategy. Thus we have an opportunity to review research findings on such diverse topics as appeals to humor or fear; the degree of change to attempt in a speech; and the relative effectiveness of one-sided versus two-sided messages, climax- versus anticlimax-order messages, and stated versus implied conclusions.

Key Terms

Analogy
Anticlimax order
Assimilation effect
Backlash
Body
Boomerang effect
Causal organization
Chronological
 organization
Climax order
Conclusion

Contrast effect
Extemporaneous
 speaking
Extrinsic credibility
Humor
Impromptu delivery
Inoculation theory
Intensity
Intrinsic credibility
Introduction
Materials of support

Memorized speech
Message variables
Metaphor
Mode of delivery
Persuasibility
Primacy effect
Problem solution
Purpose-oriented
 audience analysis
Reading from
 manuscript

Recency effect
Signal-to-noise ratio
Sleeper effect
Spatial organization
Topical organization
Transition

Review Questions

1. What are three dimensions of source credibility? What are the differences between extrinsic, intrinsic, and total credibility?

2. What are the visual and vocal cues that contribute to audience judgments about delivery? Name the four modes of delivery, giving some of the advantages and disadvantages of each.

3. Discuss five possible ways of organizing speech materials.

4. Describe two methods of support and the general research finding concerning how a speaker's use of evidence affects his or her efforts to persuade.

5. What is the difference between the assimilation effect and the contrast effect? How do these concepts relate to how much change a speaker should advocate?

6. Under what conditions is a one-sided message most effective? Under what conditions is a two-sided message most effective?

7. Under what conditions is a climax-order message most effective? Under what conditions is an anticlimax-order message most effective?

8. What is the general research finding regarding the effectiveness of messages containing (1) stated conclusions, and (2) implied conclusions?

Read William Clinton's and Arnold Schwarzenegger's speeches on the Web site, and analyze each speech by answering the following questions:

1. What was the purpose of the speech?

2. What was the most probable state of the speaker's extrinsic and intrinsic credibility in terms of the three major dimensions of source credibility? What factors in the message and context of the message led you to your conclusions? What external factors have influenced your opinion?

3. What method(s) of organization does the speech illustrate?

4. What forms of support were used? How effective were they?

5. How effective was the speaker's use of language?

6. Was humor or satire used? If so, what seemed to be the speaker's purpose in using it?

7. Were fear appeals used? If so, were they used appropriately (i.e., according to research findings)?

8. Was the message one-sided or two-sided? Was it appropriate, given the conditions of the speech?

9. Was a climax or an anticlimax order used? Was it the more appropriate order for the situation in which the message was given?

10. Was the conclusion stated or implied? Was it the more appropriate technique for the situation in which the message was given?

Exercises

1. If you were asked to present a speech to the audience that heard one of the speeches used on the Web site, how would you go about analyzing the audience?

2. Making use of what is known about message variables, write a three- to four-minute extemporaneous speech to persuade and present it to your class. Remember to aim for clarity and to make your presentation relevant to your listeners' interests. You may wish to choose a topic from the list that follows these exercises.

3. Give a one-minute impromptu speech on a topic assigned to you by a classmate or by the instructor. Try to determine your purpose and organization in the short time available.

4. Take your identity and membership cards out of your wallet or purse, and conduct an audience analysis on the groups to which you belong. Write a short paper on different approaches that would be appropriate for the different groups.

5. Tape-record one of your speeches and play it back for self-analysis. What changes would you make if you were to give it again?

6. Here is a list of speech topics and thought starters for use in preparation of speeches.

Water pollution
American Indians
Latin American relations
Divorce
Wine tasing
Farm bankruptcy
Flood control
Personality—what is it?
Muslim beliefs
Causes of earthquakes
Ethnocentrism
Why the Great Lakes tilt
The continental drift theory
Hazards in the home
What makes people buy
Social stratification
Interpreting dreams
The scientific lie detector
Improving your memory
Learning to listen
Wedding customs
Plastic surgery
Trick photography
Skydiving
Taxidermy
Baseball in America
Music
Internet censorship
The importance of friendship
The honor system
The Nobel prize

Buying a car
Women leaders
Revision of the penal system
Prayer in public schools
Prostitution
Domestic violence
The overorganized society
Japanese investment in the United States
Sex education in the schools
Slaughterhouses
The space program
Speech pathology
Suicide
Tornadoes
China
The Strategic Air Command
Air traffic safety
Anarchy
Atheism
Capitalism
Culture
Body piercing
Empathy
Illiteracy
Libel
AIDS
Mental illness
Alcoholism and drug abuse
Computers
Overcrowded airports
The high cost of dying
Involuntary sterilization
The Academy Awards
Morality
Prejudice
Slander
Abortion
Birth control
Boxing
Censorship
Cigarette smoking

Conformity
Country music
Cryogenics
Pornographic films
Driver education
Drunk drivers
Cocaine
Euthanasia
The FBI
Firearms regulation
Foreign aid
Forest fires
Fraternities and sororities
Free college education
Grading systems
Hell's Angels
The John Birch Society
The Ku Klux Klan
Lecture classes
The metric system
Communism
Football for the spectator
Nuclear testing
Living together
Dieting fads
The communication gap
South Africa
Television evangelists
Urban blight
Rationalizing
Abstract art
Misleading advertising
Animal research
The armed forces
Demographic changes
Siamese twins
The laser beam
Safe sex
Medical practices
Herpes
Breast implants

Suggested Readings

Gregory, Hamilton. *Public Speaking for College and Career,* 5th ed. New York: McGraw-Hill, 1999.

Combines business and professional examples with step-by-step instruction for developing a speech. Includes techniques for doing research on the Internet.

Lucas, Stephen E. *The Art of Public Speaking,* 8th ed. New York: McGraw-Hill, 2004.

A well-written look at the topic from a skills perspective.

Safire, William. *Lend Me Your Ears: Great Speeches in History.* New York: Norton, 1992.

Contains nearly a thousand pages of some of the greatest speeches of all time. It includes speeches by Art Buchwald, George H. W. Bush, Demosthenes, Barbara Jordan, Abraham Lincoln, Malcolm X, Martin Luther King, Jr., John F. Kennedy, Jeane Kirkpatrick, Margaret Chase Smith, Elizabeth Cady Stanton, Margaret Thatcher, Sojourner Truth, and Boris Yeltsin, along with dozens of others. This is a great source of quotes as well as a rich sourcebook.

Samovar, Larry, and Edwin McDaniel. *Public Speaking in a Multicultural Society.* Los Angeles: Roxbury Publishing Company, 2007.

A classic text on this subject.

Sedlack, Robert, Barbara Shwom, and Karl Keller. *Graphics and Visual Communication for Managers.* Mason, OH: Thomson South-Western, 2008.

This little paperback has great tips for improving visuals aids in your presentations.

Sprague, Jo, and Douglas Stuart. *The Speaker's Handbook,* 4th ed. New York: Harcourt Brace, 1996.

An excellent little book with a wealth of well-organized information for all aspects of speech making.

Whalen, Joel. *The Professional Communications Toolkit.* Thousand Oaks, CA: Sage Publications, 2007.

This book offers brief yet comprehensive coverage of ways to improve public communication skills.

Whetten, David A., and Kim S. Cameron. *Developing Management Skills,* 6th ed. Upper Saddle River, NJ: Prentice-Hall, 2005.

This excellent book has a special Supplement A that offers advice on how to make oral and written presentations.

 # For Supplementary Information

Log onto the Online Learning Center at *www.mhhe.com/tubbsmoss11.*

Organizational Communication

Chapter Objectives

After reading this chapter, you should be able to:

1. Explain three functions communication performs in organizations.
2. Define and illustrate supportive supervisory communication.
3. List five ways in which people adapt to information overload.
4. Explain the law of diminishing returns as it relates to downward communication.
5. Identify the five types of power.
6. List five functions of upward communication.
7. List three ways to create change using upward communication.
8. Describe the differentiation-integration problem in organizations as it relates to horizontal communication.
9. Explain the formula that expresses the important variables in the development of rumors.
10. Describe the three types of message distortion that occur during rumor transmission.

Airbus, one of the world's leading commercial jet manufacturers, planned to launch its newest and biggest jet, the A380, in 2007. With the wings made in Britain, the horizontal tail stabilizer made in Spain, the nose section and center fuselage made in France, and the forward fuselage and vertical tail stabilizer made in Germany, this plane is the result of one of the most modern and advanced organizational communication marvels in the world. However, each plane contains over 348 miles of bundled electrical wiring. When the final assembly was attempted for the first time, they found out that the wires from front to back of the plane were too short to connect. It turns out that the engineers in Hamburg, Germany, were initially drawing on a two-dimensional computer program, while their counterparts in Toulouse, France, were working in 3-D. The delays caused Airbus enormous headaches and losses in the billions of euros—and even more in U.S. dollars (Burke, 2007).

Consider these other examples:

Ferrari, the automaker, sent a memo to its automobile dealers in the United States, instructing them to "monitor" cars that are privately imported into the United States to make sure the company was in compliance with U.S. laws, according to a report in *Auto Week*. Some dealers interpreted the memo to mean that they should intrusively inspect, and in some cases partially disassemble, certain Ferraris brought in for service to verify point-by-point compliance with a list of U.S. requirements. But by "monitor," the company meant only to inform its U.S. dealers that some privately imported Ferraris might not be in compliance and for the dealers to notify the company if they had noticed this problem.

The U.S. Army bought 461,000 helmets from the Gentex Corporation, then told the company that the helmets were unacceptable, according to a *Wall Street Journal* article. The helmets were to be manufactured with layers of Kevlar material. Apparently, the Army interpreted "layer" to be a solid sheet of material. The manufacturer interpreted "layer" to also include small scrap sheets of the material stitched together. As a result, the helmets were manufactured using layers of patchwork Kevlar material, and the Army declared the helmets to be defective (Catt et al., 2005).

By now you have probably figured out that all of these situations involve **organizational communication.** More correctly, they involve *human communication that occurs within the context of organizations*—for it is people who do the communicating, not organizations. These examples show the wide range of events that can be called "organizational communication." They also illustrate the overlap between organizational communication and the other communication contexts (interpersonal, small-group, public, and mass communication). Any and all of these four types of communication can be associated with organizations.

We spend a good part of our lives as members of organizations. Although we tend to think first of business organizations, this also includes schools, churches, military institutions, fraternities, sororities, and other social organizations. This chapter focuses on communicating in these organizations, especially communicating on the job.

The above examples are not unusual events where large companies are concerned. Carol Bobke of Mission Viejo, California, struggled for three months to resolve a problem with her health insurance company. After getting the runaround, she looked up the company's e-mail address and wrote to the president. By the next morning, the president's assistant had stepped in to fix the problem (Mulkern, 2001). If you are having a problem with a company, you can go to *www.Planetfeedback.com* to get some help. This is a firm that specializes in getting quick responses via the Internet.

ORGANIZATIONAL CULTURE

When Gordon Bethune took over as CEO of Continental Airlines, it had the worst record among the top 10 airline companies in America. The company's culture was highly bureaucratic, with a 9-inch-thick book of rules and regulations. In order to communicate his vision for a change in corporate culture, he gathered employees in a parking lot and dropped the manual in a trash can, doused it with gasoline, and burned it (Maxwell, 2001, p. 195).

In an equally dramatic example of the power of organizational culture, Julie Roehm was fired as a marketing executive at Wal-Mart after only 10 months. One of the reasons cited was that she was traveling so much that she routinely missed her immediate boss's staff meetings. In addition, her first day on the job, she brought in a painting crew and had her office painted chartreuse green with brown trim. This was within a corporate culture with plain white walls and no windows to symbolize its low-price customer image. Her flamboyant style finally caught up with her. After she was fired, one former colleague sarcastically said, "And take your paint crew with you" (Berner, 2007).

Similarly, Michael Ovitz was fired from the Disney Company after only 14 months. His colleague Michael Eisner wrote,

> He started to rub people the wrong way. We'd all take a bus (at the corporate retreat) and he had a limousine; a special driver. Everyone had a walkie talkie and you heard walkie talkies around the 30,000 acres saying, "Who was this guy and why was he demanding this?" The perception was that Michael Ovitz was a little elitist for the egalitarian Walt Disney World in Florida. It was a bad vibe. (Goffee and Jones, 2006, p. 110)

What comes to mind when you think of Southwest Airlines, Hewlett-Packard, Microsoft, or Google? How do these images compare to your images of the U.S. Postal Service, General Motors, or AT&T? The first four companies are each thought to have a culture that is highly innovative and responsive to changes in the environment. *Fortune* magazine notes that Hewlett-Packard's culture is focused on three tenets: "respect for others, a sense of community, and plain hard work." Southwest Airlines's CEO Herb Kelleher shares that the Southwest Airlines culture is based on "zealous" hiring, positive attitudes, dedicated personalities, and a sense of humor (Auxillium West, 2003). The second set of organizations is often associated with tradition and relative slowness to change. In part, each of their images is a reflection of their individual organizational cultures. The term "culture" originally comes from social anthropology. It refers to the totality of socially transmitted behavior patterns in an organization. In 2003, Auxillium West, a human resources software company, defined organizational, or corporate, culture as "the moral, social, and behavioral norms of an organization based on the beliefs, attitudes, and priorities of its members." It is important to note that most organizational cultures emerge passively over time, and cultural change is a long-term process. Many organizations consist of combinations of cultures that make it difficult to pin one down. For example, departments within companies can have varying cultures. An advertising department may be much more outgoing than an IT department, based on the combined personalities of its members (Auxillium West, 2003).

When you start your first day on a new job, you will notice that there are a lot of verbal and nonverbal cues that teach you how to fit into the organization's culture: the way people dress; how hard they work; the way space is used; the level of technological sophistication; who talks to whom and, what type of language, terminology, and acronyms they use; and so on. One young worker who joined Ford said that his co-workers used so many three-letter acronyms they had them coming out his ears. He referred to them as having TLA–OYE (three letter acronyms–out your ears). The joke seemed to fit perfectly into their culture. Schein (1997) has written extensively on the numerous communication cues that make up organizational culture.

Deal and Kennedy (1984) have identified four predominant types of culture and the leadership styles that go with each.

Tough-Guy–Macho Culture   This type of organization is typical of high-risk organizations such as police departments, and among surgeons, since they deal with life and death. Other examples are the movie industry, management consulting, sports, construction, and venture capital firms where fortunes are made and lost.

Work-Hard–Play-Hard Culture   Organizations of this type focus on sales and on meeting customers' needs. Mary Kay Cosmetics, McDonald's, Xerox, Hewlett-Packard, IBM, and Frito-Lay are examples. Sales-type organizations also celebrate a lot to keep up their energy and motivation.

Bet-Your-Company Culture   Life in this culture requires that you endure high risks but slow feedback. For example, big oil companies invest millions in exploration before seeing their success or failure. Boeing spends billions to develop a new aircraft. The same is true with NASA. Mining companies, military organizations, and architectural firms are other examples.

Process Culture   This is a low-risk, slow-feedback type of culture. Most governmental organizations, utilities, and heavily regulated industries like pharmaceutical firms fall into this category. Employees in these cultures rarely see the results of their work. They focus on the processes of how things get done. Even the most trivial event can become the subject of a memo. And numerous memos are written just to "Cover Your A—" (CYA). This culture is also known for its long, rambling meetings. However, that does not always have to be the case. Note the leadership style of the president of one private university:

> I had an accreditor once who said to me that any [curriculum] change should take two years. My response was if it takes two years we don't need it . . . We can take a program from idea to delivery in less than three months. And we do it all the time. In fact, the only time we can't do that is when accrediting agencies enter into the picture. (Hodgetts, 1998, p. 162)

Not only is the culture of many organizations changing, but the type of employees in those organizations is changing also. Lambert (1992) cites data from the Bureau of Labor Statistics that show these changes are dramatically influencing organizational communication. Historically, organizations have been overwhelmingly male and white. Even as recently as 1985, white males composed 47 percent of the workforce and white females 36 percent. As indicated in Table 14.1, the Bureau of Labor Statistics predicts that women and minorities will represent about 70 percent of net new entrants to the workforce by 2008.

Given such startling changes in demographics, it will become increasingly necessary to learn to communicate within a context of cultural diversity. And the study of human communication in organizations is more relevant today than ever before.

Cetron and Davies (1991) also predicted numerous other changes in organizations. For example, persons aged 29 to 59 will account for two-thirds of the workforce. Furthermore, almost all growth of the labor force over the decade from 1990 to 2000 would be in this age group. They also predicted that union membership will continue to decline nationally. It reached 17.5 percent in 1986. According to the United Auto Workers, it fell to 12 percent by 1995 and to less than 10 percent by the year 2000. This changing of the workforce will be another factor for new college graduates entering the workforce to contend with.

Table 14.1   Net New Entrants to the Workforce by 2008

	Population	Percent of Total	Median Age (years)	Mean Age (years)	Percent Male	Percent Female
All races	273,137	100	35.5	36.4	48.9%	51.1%
Caucasian	224,865	82.3	36.6	37.3	49.1	50.9
African American	34,948	12.8	30.1	32.1	47.5	52.5
American Indian	2,400	0.9	27.7	30.4	49.5	50.5
Eskimo, Aleut	10,924	4	31.7	32.6	47.9	52.1
Asian, Pacific Islander, and Hispanic	31,469	11.5	26.5	28.8	50.3	49.7

Source: Bureau of Labor Statistics, 2003.

IMPORTANCE OF COMMUNICATION

Chester Barnard once wrote that "the first executive function is to develop and maintain a system of communication" (1938, p. 82). Barnard's statement has proved prophetic. Some years ago, a survey of the presidents of 100 of the largest corporations in the United States found that 96 percent believed there was a "definite relationship" between communication and employee productivity. Numerous studies have shown that when managers and other responsible businesspeople are asked how much of the workday they spend communicating, their replies range from about 85 to 99 percent. Most say above 90 percent. Most recently, work by Harvard researchers Cherniss and Goleman has shown that Emotional Intelligence (primarily comprising self-awareness and social awareness, i.e., communication competence) accounts for 85 to 90 percent of a leader's success (2001, p. xv).

Surveys conducted by the University of Michigan, Pennsylvania State University, and Wake Forest University have documented the importance of communication skills to organizational success. According to one recent *Wall Street Journal* survey of employers (Safon, 2007), the following were the most highly valued attributes that recruiters were seeking in people they wanted to hire:

1. Communication and interpersonal skills (89 percent)
2. Ability to work well in teams (87 percent)
3. Analytical and problem-solving skillls (84 percent)
4. Leadership potential (73 percent)

All of these top attributes are discussed in this book.

After finishing college, young people who start new jobs often face a rude awakening. They feel that, with their up-to-date knowledge and training, they should be making a major contribution. As they enter this new world of work, however, they find that developing interpersonal skills is of overriding importance. Their frustration is expressed in the following excerpts:

> All the problems I encounter boil down to communication and human relations. (Initiate in a consumer goods company)
>
> I thought I could sell people with logic and was amazed at the hidden agendas people have, irrational objections; really bright people will come up with stupid excuses. (Initiate in an aerospace company). (Schein, 1997, p. 18)

A study by Watson Wyatt Worldwide showed that companies with the most effective communication programs returned 57 percent more to their shareholders than companies with the least effective communication programs. "The results of our study confirm that communication is a critical element in creating successful business results," says Kathryn Yates, global director of communication consulting (Watson Wyatt, 2006).

Jennings (1971) studied the common patterns of those who are promoted fastest and describes their communication style in the following way:

> Executives tend to use a feather-light touch with their subordinates and peers. The heavy hand of the lower positioned manager is frowned upon at high corporate levels. The terms "style" and "panache" are often used to mean the ability to say and do almost anything without antagonizing others. People tend to work better when they do not have to work at saving face. To be mobility-bright also means to present oneself in a manner becoming to the dignity and stature of the superiors above. It means to behave as though the executive were at a higher level than his present one. (p. 69)

One of the most wide-sweeping changes in organizational communication is the increase in teamwork. For example, Boeing announced that its new Boeing 777 jetliner was going to be built by teams. The company set up more than 200 "design-build" teams. These teams were composed of employees from engineering, quality control, finance, and manufacturing. Each one concentrates on a specific part of the aircraft. Even suppliers and potential customers are sometimes included in team meetings (Downes and Mui, 1998).

Another facet of this change is the increase in employee empowerment. Empowerment is giving workers more latitude to make decisions and to implement them. Fisher (1993) defines empowerment as:

$$\text{Empowerment} = f(A \times R \times IA)$$

$$
\begin{aligned}
\text{where} \quad & A = \text{authority} \\
& R = \text{resources} \\
& I = \text{information} \\
& A = \text{accountability}
\end{aligned}
$$

In other words, in order to be able to make decisions, workers need to be given not only the authority but sufficient training and budget, as well as critical information. Then, they must be held accountable for their decisions (Fisher, 1993, p. 14).

Conrad (1985) identified three functions communication performs in organizations:

The Command Function

Communication allows members of the organization to "issue, receive, interpret, and act on commands" (Conrad, 1985, p. 7). The two types of communication that make up this function are directions and feedback, and the goal is the successful influence of other members of the organization. The outcome of the command function is coordination among the many interdependent members of the organization.

The Relational Function   Communication allows members of the organization "to create and maintain productive business and personal relationships with other members of the organization" (Conrad, 1985, pp. 7–8). Relationships on the job affect job performance in many ways, for example, job satisfaction, the flow of communication both down and up the organizational hierarchy, and the degree to which commands are followed. The importance of good interpersonal skills is highlighted on the job when you consider that many of the necessary relationships are not chosen but forced by organizational circumstances, making the relationships less stable, more prone to conflict, less committed, and so on.

The Ambiguity-Management Function   Choices in an organizational setting are often made in highly ambiguous circumstances. For example, multiple motivations exist, given that choices affect co-workers, the organization, and oneself; the organization's objectives may not be clear; and the context within which the choice needs to be made may be unclear. Communication is the means for coping with and reducing the ambiguity inherent in the organization: Members talk with each other in an effort to structure the environment and make sense of new situations, which entails gaining and sharing information.

With the help of increased technology, the importance of communication is further demonstrated. The Internet "blog" trend has recently emerged as a way for businesses to improve communication. Blogs are "self-published chronicles of ideas, news, facts, opinions and inspirations that are frequently updated" (Aber, 2004). Businesses can use blogs in the following different ways:

- Communicate and collaborate among distributed colleagues, partners, suppliers, customers, and others.
- Use a unique, informal way to establish a company or individual's reputation or brand.
- Improve operations (as with project management or tech support knowledge-sharing).
- Demonstrate expertise.
- Establish competitive differentiation.
- Reach out to value chain members with organizational news, marketing promotions, new product announcements, and so forth.
- Share knowledge among professionals in the same industry, but not necessarily the same organization. (Aber, 2004).

In the next section, we see the critical role that the supervisor plays in the organization's success or failure.

Supervisory Communication

The Gallup Organization surveyed over one million people, including over 80,000 managers in over 400 countries, and found the single most important thing that people want to know in doing their jobs is this: Do I know what is expected of me at work? Supervisors who make this clear to workers are more likely to be successful (Rath, 2007).

If we know that communication is important to organizational success, then it becomes important to know what types of communication are most important to the organization. A recent stream of research has focused on what is known as the Leader-Member Exchange (LMX) in organizations. According to this theory, the relationship between the employee and the leaders is influenced by both parties, and the leader develops a somewhat different relationship with each of his or her employees. Avolio and Luthans (2006) found that a positive LMX is associated with employees who practice organizational citizenship behaviors, defined as employees who help others with their work even when they are not required to do so. A number of research studies have shown that the leader is the one who starts this chain of events. The question is, what communication behaviors on the part of the leader tend to create this positive climate?

Supportive Communication   Have you ever had a boss who seemed to be on your side? Or, on the other hand, one who seemed to be looking for ways to catch you in a mistake? This difference is the crux of supportive communication behaviors. Whetten and Cameron (2005) studied the effect of communication behaviors on employee creativity. They found that the following behaviors created a higher LMX score and were associated with higher employee creativity and productivity on the job. The supervisor

1. Helps employees solve problems.
2. Encourages employees to develop new skills.
3. Keeps informed about how employees think and feel about things.
4. Encourages employees to participate in important decisions.
5. Praises good work.
6. Encourages employees to speak up when they disagree with a decision.
7. Explains his or her actions.
8. Rewards employees for good performance.

These important guidelines will help improve your supportive communication behaviors as a leader.

Noncontrolling Communication   Employees also respond well when they are not micromanaged or "snoopervised." Dean (2006) found that the following communication behaviors were associated with a high LMX score and with high employee creativity and productivity. The supervisor

1. Never seems to be checking on employees' work.
2. Never forces employees to do work his or her way.

3. Gives employees a chance to make important decisions on their own.

4. Leaves it up to employees to decide how to go about doing their jobs.

These are also important guidelines to show you how to improve your noncontrolling communication behaviors as a leader.

Trust   Trust is derived from the German word *trost,* which implies "a level of comfort with the other person (Lennick and Kiel, 2005). It is based on our assessment of the other person's perceived competence at a certain task as well as his or her character.

Trust is often defined as "an individual's confidence in another person's intentions and motives, and the sincerity of that person's word" (Lennick and Kiel, 2005). Researchers have found that there are two components of trust—one cognitive or rational, the other affective or emotional. They asked people to rate a supervisor's trust using the following statements to differentiate high from low:

COGNITIVE TRUST

1. This person approaches his or her job with professionalism and dedication.

2. Given this person's track record, I see no reason to doubt his or her competence.

3. I can rely on this person not to make my job more difficult by careless work.

AFFECTIVE TRUST

1. I have a sharing relationship with this person. We can both freely share our ideas, feelings, and hopes.

2. I can talk freely to this individual about difficulties I am having at work and know that he or she will want to listen.

3. If I shared my problems with this person, I know she or he would respond constructively and caringly.

McAllister (1995) has found that both the cognitive and the affective components are important to the formation of trust between an employee and his or her supervisor.

Many experts agree that the supervisor is the one who must initiate the trusting relationship. After all, the employee who comes into the organization learns very quickly what is acceptable and unacceptable behavior in that organization. The immediate supervisor is the person who most influences the employee's perception of the organization. Again, we see the importance of the Leader-Member Exchange. Whitener and her colleagues (1998) found five important qualities that help supervisors establish that trusting relationship. These five qualities are discussed below.

Behavioral Consistency   This is also known as reliability. A friend recently described her former boss as "one person one day, and a different one on another day." She never knew which person she was going to be dealing with from day to day. Clearly, consistency is important if a person is to be able to count on his or her supervisor.

Behavioral Integrity   Employees notice agreement or lack of agreement between a supervisor's words and deeds. Behavioral integrity is often referred to as "walking the talk." Does the person tell the truth? Does the person keep promises? How often does a supervisor say, "Let's get together on this item and discuss it" (at some later time), only to forget about it? This may seem like a small thing, but it is an example of keeping a promise.

Sharing and Delegation of Control   Sharing control by inviting employee participation in decision making is the basis of a great deal of modern leadership. Delegating tasks also conveys a certain level of confidence and trust in the employee's ability to carry out the task. Both of these behaviors convey to the employee a level of respect and trust in his or her ability.

Communication   Research has shown that three factors affect perceptions of trustworthiness in communication. First, accurate information has the strongest influence upon a person's trust in a supervisor. Also of great importance are, second, explanations for decisions and, third, openness. Employees see their supervisors as trustworthy when they give out accurate information, when they are willing to explain their decisions, and when they demonstrate openness to considering suggestions from employees.

Demonstration of Concern   Employees prefer supervisors who show consideration and sensitivity for their needs and interests. They also like it when the supervisor "goes to bat" for them. People like to think that their boss will stand up for their interests if necessary. Also, employees like supervisors who avoid exploiting others for their own benefit. A classic example of this sort of exploitation is a boss taking credit for the work of an employee.

In the remaining sections of this chapter, we shall examine four other factors Dennis (1975) found under the traditional categories for analyzing organization communication: (1) downward communication, (2) upward communication, (3) horizontal communication, and (4) informal communication.

Downward Communication

Jim Donald is president of Starbucks in Seattle. He states, "I'm fanatical about communication . . . If anyone in our company e-mails me or leaves me a voicemail, they get a response, quickly. We have to operate like a store. Nobody likes to wait. I get 200 to 250 e-mails a day, and I respond to 75 percent of them." Donald maximizes his efficiency by distributing his time as follows:

44 percent talking with direct reports

28 percent traveling to stores and roasting plants

17 percent meeting with employees

11 percent strategic thinking and employee evaluations

He also says, "When I'm traveling, I visit 10 Starbucks stores a day. I walk right back to the counter, put on an apron, and start talking to our partners. You can tell how a store is doing by smelling it, so I stick my nose in the pastry display. I check out the restrooms . . . I learned this from Sam Walton, who hired me to run Wal-Mart's Supercenters six months before he died. Sam used to say, 'If you want to know what's wrong with the business, ask the front line' " (Sellers, 2006, p. 51).

After supervisory communication, the second most important factor in determining communication climate in the organization is **downward communication.** Such communication *is initiated by the organization's upper management and then filters downward through the "chain of command."* In 2004, a *Wall Street Journal* article urged executives to take full responsibility for organizational communication. They must obtain buy-in from "superiors, subordinates, and peers," while sharing critical information. Superiors, peers, and subordinates need information and should be treated equally in its dissemination. The writer also recommended that instead of making organizational decisions and drilling them down through the organization based on "what's right for the shareholders, or the executives, or the employees," executives should ask "what is right for the enterprise," or what is right for everyone, including employees at every level in the organization. To make organizations work, decisions must be made holistically and not in parts (Anonymous, 2004, p. 1).

Swift (1973) describes a problem in the downward communication that often faces managers:

> Let's suppose that everyone at X Corporation, from the janitor on up to the chairman of the board, is using the office copiers for personal matters; income tax forms, church programs, children's term papers, and God knows what else are being duplicated by the gross. This minor piracy costs the company a pretty penny, both directly and in employee time, and the general manager—let's call him Sam Edwards—decides the time has come to lower the boom. (p. 59)

If you were Sam Edwards, how would you communicate with your subordinates about this problem? First, you might consider some communication alternatives. Our model in Chapter 1 referred to these as "channels." Some typical channels of downward communication are

E-mail	Fax
Department meetings	Voice mail
Face-to-face conversation with subordinates	Telephone calls

Company newspaper   Speech to all employees

Bulletin boards   Videotape recordings

Letters sent home   Intraorganizational memos

Posters

Any of these, alone or in combination, could be employed to get the message about photocopying to your employees. However, as the chart in Figure 14.1 shows, people are so busy that they are often hard to contact.

Figure 14.1   *Daily Activities of Business Professionals*

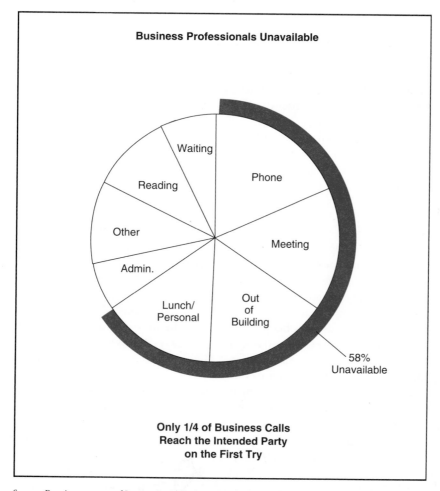

Sam Edwards of the X Corporation is an experienced manager, and he also knows that if he overloads his people with too much information, they will begin to make more errors. Given the costs and the potential benefits involved, Edwards decides to send an e-mail about the abuse of photocopying privileges. In doing so, he avoids bogging down his supervisors with more time-consuming forms of communication, such as meetings.

Scholars have identified seven ways in which people adapt to information overload. They are (1) *omission* (failing to handle all the information), (2) *error* (ignoring or failing to correct errors when made), (3) *queuing* (letting things pile up), (4) *filtering* (dealing with input in categories ranked according to a priority system), (5) *approximation* (lowering standards of precision), (6) *multiple channels* (delegation of information processing to others), and (7) *escape* (refusal to handle the input at all).

Effectiveness of Downward Communication

Research on the effectiveness of different forms of downward communication has shown that using a combination of channels tends to get the best results. Typically, channels were ranked in the following order of effectiveness (from most to least effective):

1. Combined oral and written
2. Oral only
3. Written only
4. Rumor

In other words, in terms of actually getting the information through to employees accurately, a combination of written and oral channels gets the best results. Sending the same message through more than one channel creates *redundancy,* and redundancy seems to be helpful not only in getting messages through but in ensuring that they will be remembered. For example, a busy executive may get an e-mail message reminding her of an executive committee meeting that day at one o'clock. By lunch hour, however, her busy activity schedule has caused the meeting to slip her mind. At lunch, the chairperson of the executive committee says, "Don't forget the meeting at one this afternoon." The woman replies, "Thanks for reminding me. It almost slipped my mind. It's been one of those days."

One of the paradoxes of communicating in organizations is that busy people seem to require more reminders (i.e., more message redundancy) to act on the downward communication they receive. On the other hand, as the number of memos, meetings, phone calls, and so on increases, each person becomes that much busier, since it requires time to attend to each of these messages. Therefore, an important consideration in organization communication is the so-called **law of diminishing returns,** which states that *more is better, up to a point.* For example, a more open flow of communication is good up to a point, after which the receiver may become overloaded. A supervisor of our acquaintance believed very firmly in communicating fully with subordinates.

The net result of her good intentions was that employees in the department had to check their mailboxes about every two hours to keep up with the continual barrage of memos. Naturally, this volume of communication kept employees from being as productive as they might otherwise have been. This relationship between communication frequency and desired effect is illustrated in Figure 14.2.

Another characteristic of downward communication is lack of accuracy; in other words, "people often don't get the message straight." Conboy (1976) cites a study that polled 100 industrial managers to determine what percentage of a message got through to lower organizational levels. The results are somewhat surprising:

Board of directors	100% of communication content
Vice presidents	67%
General supervisors	56%
Plant managers	40%
Foremen	30%
Workers	20% (Conboy, 1976, p. 27)

This message distortion in downward communication is humorously illustrated in the following example:

Colonel communicates to Major: At 9 o'clock tomorrow there will be an eclipse of the sun, something which does not occur every day. Get the men to fall out in the company street in their fatigues so that they will see this rare phenomenon, and I will then explain it to them. Now in the case of rain, we will not be able to see anything, of course, so then take the men to the gym.

Major passes message to Captain: By order of the Colonel tomorrow at 9 o'clock there will be an eclipse of the sun. If it rains, you will not be able to see it from the company street, so, then, in fatigues, the eclipse of the sun will take place in the gym, something which does not occur every day.

The Captain then said to the Lieutenant: By order of the Colonel in fatigues tomorrow, at 9 o'clock in the morning the inauguration of the eclipse of the

Figure 14.2

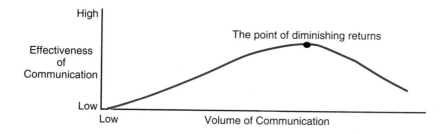

sun will take place in the gym. The Colonel will give the order if it should rain, something which does occur every day.

The Lieutenant then told the Sergeant: Tomorrow at 9, the Colonel in fatigues will eclipse the sun in the gym, as it occurs every day if it's a nice day. If it rains, then this occurs in the company street.

The Sergeant then instructed the Corporal: Tomorrow at 9, the eclipse of the colonel in fatigues will take place because of the sun. If it rains in the gym, something which does not take place every day, you will fall out in the company street.

Finally, one Private said to another Private: Tomorrow, if it rains, it looks as if the sun will eclipse the Colonel in the gym. It's a shame that this does not occur every day. (Zima, personal communication)

More will be said about message distortion in the section "Informal Communication." It seems obvious that as organizations increase in size, the frequency of these kinds of snafus* increases.

Power

Power often comes into play in organizational relationships. It is especially relevant, but not limited, to downward communication. When we think of powerful people, we think of Donald Trump or Bill Gates or Condoleezza Rice. The classic typology of power was originally written by French and Raven (1962); see also Greene and Elffers (1998). They identified five types of power: three types of power that are available to a supervisor based on his or her position in the organization and two types of personal power.

Legitimate power is *the authority a person has by virtue of her or his position.* For example, a boss can hire, give orders, authorize paychecks, and require things to be done.

Reward power is *the ability to use rewards to influence other people.* Allowing a person to take time off and giving pay increases or bonuses or awards are a few examples.

Coercive power is *the ability to influence individuals by withholding rewards* such as pay increases, promotions, business travel, or a desirable office as well as the use of punishment such as reprimands, suspensions, and ultimate termination.

Expert power, a type of personal power, is *the ability to influence another based on one's possession of knowledge, experience, or judgment that the other person needs.* Dr. Henry Kissinger has often been consulted by U.S. presidents because of his considerable expertise, even when he does not hold any position in their administrations.

Situation normal, all fouled up.

| 14.1 | **ISSUES IN COMMUNICATION** | *Managing Your E-Mail* |

According to an e-mail from the president of one of your authors' universities, in the first week of class in September 2004, there were 972,149 e-mail messages sent through the university computers! (Willis, 2004)

Have you ever felt like all of those have come to you? E-mail use is a mixed blessing. So, let's take a look at some hints to manage your e-mail messages.

- Scan first, read second. Do just a quick scan to see if it is important.
- If you can't use it, nuke it. Avoid saving messages for later if you can. They just clutter your computer.
- Thin out. If you get many messages on the same topic, delete all but the most important ones. These first three steps can reduce your in-box messages by 60 percent.
- Prioritize. Deal with the remaining e-mails in order of importance.
- Ask friends to stop sending unwanted e-mails.
- Don't be a cc rider. Ask to be removed from the cc lists you don't want to be on.
- Use your utilities. Use e-mail utilities to color code e-mails as they come into your in-box.
- Less is more. Respond only when needed.
- Avoid emotions. If you are tempted to send an angry e-mail, wait a day and read it again. Remember, "You can't unring a bell." (Cooper, 2004)

Referent power, another type of personal power, is *the ability to influence someone because of his or her desire to identify with the power source.* The so-called yes-man is someone who will do what is asked in order to please the boss. The follower who takes this behavior to the extreme is called a *sycophant.*

Pfeffer (1998) has identified several practical power strategies and tactics, which are discussed below: the selective use of objective criteria, forming coalitions, and cooptation.

All organizations make decisions according to certain criteria. Sometimes the **selective use of objective criteria** can influence decisions. For example, a member of Congress may agree to reduce the budget deficit by a certain percentage but will fight savagely to keep a military base from being closed in his or her own district in order to save jobs. In this way, the Congress member is able to use power to selectively apply the budget cuts only to other districts.

The **forming of coalitions** represents another power strategy. In union there is strength. If you want to increase your power, you can team up with someone of equal or greater power. Coalitions can be formed with other units within an organization, with an outside expert who has great credibility, or with other outside constituencies. Fraternities and sororities have practiced this for decades by forming Greek Councils. Children will attempt to influence their parents by citing what is being allowed in other families. And companies will hire expert witnesses to help win product liability suits.

The tactic of **cooptation** involves *an attempt to change the attitude of powerful individuals by bringing them into partnership*. It is a special form of coalition formation. For example, student leaders who are protesting some university policy may be invited into membership on the task force to correct the problem. Often students are invited to sit on committees in order to win their support. Similarly, complaining employees may be placed in charge of solving the problem they are concerned about. This is a special example of participative decision making, the only difference being that the individuals tend to start out antagonistic rather than neutral. Pfeffer (1998) states that the reason that cooptation is so often effective is that it increases

> identification and commitment to the organization, gives the representatives a stake and legitimate position in the organization, and motivates them to be interested in the organization's survival and success. (p. 182)

Downes and Mui (1998) have argued persuasively that the newest generation of power brokers in organizations includes those who can successfully manipulate electronic information. They write

> Every large organization has a phone system, internal mail, and other forms of regular and ad hoc communications . . . Does your organization have an "e-mail culture"? How hard would it be to add voice, video, document sharing, and other collaborative tools? (p. 209)

Tapscott (1998) has labeled this young group of workers the N Generation, with the "N" standing for (Inter)Net. He writes

> The N-Gen mind is ideally suited for wealth creation in the new economy . . . This generation is exceptionally curious, self-reliant, contrarian, smart, focused, able to adapt, high in self-esteem, and possessed of a global orientation. These attributes, combined with N-Geners' ease with digital tools, spell trouble for the traditional enterprise and the traditional manager. (p. 209)

Whether you agree with these authors or not, it certainly seems true that technology-savvy people wield a great deal of power in organizations. So if you are interested in power, there's a tip.

Upward Communication

The third and fourth most important factors in organizational communication, as studied by Dennis (1975), seem to be involved primarily with **upward communication**—*the process whereby the ideas, feelings, and perceptions of lower-level employees are communicated to those at higher levels in the organization*. The following example shows the dangers of inhibiting or not encouraging upward communication. In 2003 NASA was criticized for its lack of upward communication from frontline engineers during the time that led up to the *Columbia* shuttle crash.

Large organizations like NASA have more levels of management and authority that can act as barriers to the flow of communication and that can lead to detrimental or, in this case, disastrous results (Wessel, 2003, p. C8).

Employees must be encouraged to communicate from the bottom-up. When employees are not told why they must do things and are not shown the results of their efforts, they tend to become frustrated and disillusioned about their work.

Several barriers prevent employees from freely communicating to their superiors, including fears of bureaucracy and of retaliation. Creating incentives is one way to encourage bottom-up communication (Wessel, 2003, p. C8). One worker told us that he had worked for company X for 30 years and for all he knew he had never done anything right because he only got feedback when he did something wrong.

Research has shown that upward communication can serve at least five important functions:

1. It provides management with needed information for decision making.
2. It helps employees relieve the pressures and frustrations of the work situation.
3. It enhances employees' sense of participation in the enterprise.
4. It serves as a measure of the effectiveness of downward communication.
5. As a bonus, it suggests more rewarding uses of downward communication for the future. (Goldhaber, 1993, pp. 156–159; see also Adler and Elmhorst, 1999)

Ironically, although its importance is obvious, upward communication is not always encouraged by management. One reason for this may be that the messages superiors hear from subordinates are not always pleasant or flattering. In one rather extreme case, a foundry manager was reportedly so unreceptive to bad news that his environmental engineers were afraid to tell him the extent to which their foundry was dumping pollutants into a neighboring river. Eventually, the foundry had legal problems with another factory located downstream. The problems could probably have been averted if the manager had been more responsive to the ideas and feelings of his subordinates.

The facetious employee performance appraisal form in Table 14.2 gives examples of the type of information subordinates might want to communicate to their bosses from time to time.

Some bosses might laugh with their employees, others might not think it funny at all. The employer who can see the good-natured humor in some of the entries may be said to have a higher degree of **upward receptivity** or *willingness to receive messages from subordinates*. Upward receptivity is most often associated with the so-called open-door policy in business. If a manager has his or her door open, this signals a willingness to communicate with employees. Unfortunately, an open door does not always signify an open mind. It has been pointed out that the best open-door policy is really one in which a superior opens the door of the subordinate's

Table 14.2	*Guide to Employee Performance Appraisal*				
	Performance Degrees				
Performance Factors	Far Exceeds Job Requirements	Exceeds Job Requirements	Meets Job Requirements	Needs Some Improvements	Does Not Meet Minimum Requirement
Quality	Leaps tall buildings with a single bound	Must take running start to leap over tall buildings	Can leap over only an average building with no spires	Crashes into buildings when attempting to jump over them	Cannot recognize buildings at all, much less jump them
Timeliness	Is faster than a speeding bullet	Is as fast as a speeding bullet	Not quite as fast as a speeding bullet	Would you believe a small bullet?	Wounds self with bullet when attempting to shoot
Initiative	Is stronger than a locomotive	Is stronger than a bull elephant	Is stronger than a bull	Shoots the bull	Smells like a bull
Adaptability	Walks on water consistently	Walks on water in emergencies	Washes with water	Drinks water	Passes water in emergencies
Communication	Talks with God	Talks with the angels	Talks to himself	Argues with himself	Loses those arguments

office to initiate communication. Such action indicates even greater willingness on the superior's part to meet employees halfway in opening the communication channels.

Indeed, initiative on the part of the employer would seem to be one of the best ways to "open the door" to communication within the organization. A number of studies have shown, for example, that most subordinates feel reluctant to communicate information to superiors. That reluctance can be increased (or decreased) by a number of circumstances. In conferences between college students and their professors, students rated professors as more receptive, more trustworthy, and better qualified if they did not sit with a desk between themselves and the students (Widgery and Stackpole, 1972). And, as might be expected, nervousness on the part of the students increased their sensitivity to such variables during the conference. So even such nonverbal factors as closed doors and imposing desks can serve as additional barriers to upward communication.

A special type of upward communication is **ingratiation.** This is defined by Liden and Mitchell (1988) as *"an attempt by individuals to increase their attractiveness in the eyes of others"* (p. 572). The authors identify three main forms of ingratiation. The first is flattery. Those who are attempting to "get in good" with others above them will often flatter or compliment the other person (often falsely). The second is self-disclosures and advice requests. Ingratiators may reveal personal information or may request the advice of a superior to gain favor. Third is attitude similarity and sincerity. The ingratiator will attempt to stress any similarities between himself or herself and the target person. However, research has shown that any of the ingratiating behaviors mentioned will be effective only if the target person perceives them as sincere (pp. 580–581). Cecily Cooper (2005) hypothesized the ways that humor might also work as an attempt to gain favor with the boss. Her theory contends that it will help to improve the boss-subordinate relationship.

Upward communication is less likely to occur if there are *psychological barriers* between superior and subordinate. The literature on this point suggests that three major psychological barriers affect upward communication:

1. If a subordinate believes that disclosure of his feelings, opinions, or difficulties may lead a superior to block or hinder the attainment of a personal goal, he will conceal or distort them.
2. The more a superior rewards disclosure of feelings, opinions, and difficulties by subordinates, the more likely they will be to disclose them.
3. The more a superior discloses his own feelings, opinions, and difficulties to subordinates and his superior, the more likely subordinates will be to disclose theirs. (Manz and Sims, 2001)

These findings seem to confirm what we have learned about downward communication—that is, that the supervisor who is seen as supportive is preferred. If we feel that we can be ourselves with a superior and that he or she will not use our mistakes against us, we are much more likely to communicate openly. And as a result, the superior is likely to have a better "feel" for the workings of his or her operation. In addition, Wayne and colleagues (1997) found that employees strongly valued the freedom to speak their minds to superiors. When employees' freedom of speech is reduced, their commitment to the organization is markedly reduced.

Even when upward communication is effective, however, bosses still have a hard time picturing the organizational realities at levels below them. The reasons for this difficulty are summarized by Reich (1970):

Top executives know what they are told. In effect, they are "briefed" by others, and the briefing is both limiting and highly selective. The executive is far too busy to find out very much for himself; he must accept the information he gets, and this sets absolute limits to his horizons. Yet the briefing may be three steps removed from the facts, and thus be interpretation built upon interpretation—nearer fiction than fact by the time it reaches the man at the top. The person at the top turns out to be a broker, a decider between limited alternatives. (p. 54; see also Dutton and Ashford, 2001)

As we have observed, organizational communication style differs according to the levels of the sender hierarchy. Rice (1987) writes:

> Managers spend most of their time communicating (75–80 percent), about 60 percent of which is oral (phone, face-to-face, or in meetings). Higher-level managers spend more time communicating with subordinates than do lower-level managers; senior managers initiate more downward communication than upward communication; those at lower levels engage in more peer communication; only a small amount of managerial time is actually spent making decisions; managers communicate more in situations of greater innovation and uncertainty; and written communication is less likely to capture the attention of managers because of their fragmented, interrupted schedules. (p. 68)

Creating Change

Have you ever tried to create change in your organization when you are not the top dog? The vast majority of literature on creating change assumes that you are the top person—and even then it is a very difficult prospect. However, there is now a stream of literature that looks at change from the viewpoint of the rest of us who are not blessed (or saddled) with being the CEO.

Several scholars at the University of Michigan spearheaded by Jane Dutton and Susan Ashford (2001) have researched the processes by which change is attempted within organizations. Writing in *The Academy of Management Journal,* they state that instead of change being a singular activity conducted by the CEO, " . . . in reality, organizations are a cacophony of complementary and competing change attempts, with managers at all levels joining the fray and pushing for issues of particular importance to themselves." After collecting interview data from 82 managers in one large organization, they conclude that there are systematic and predictable competencies that people use to get top management's attention and approval for these lower level managers' priorities for change. The main categories for change strategies fall into three groups: (1) packaging, (2) involvement, and (3) process.

Packaging   The most frequent and successful change effort is to package your idea as part of the overall business strategy. This attempt involves presenting the ideas with data and carefully prepared charts that convey a logical argument to show how this effort will support the bottom line. (In a not-for-profit organization such as a university, it could be to show how to increase enrollments.) The second most frequently used packaging technique is persistence. Most ideas that get accepted have to be pitched to top leaders many times in many contexts before they are accepted.

Involvement   By now, most leaders know that people support what they help to create. But getting "buy-in" is not as simple as it may seem. First is the question of urgency. Do you have time to get others involved or should you go solo? If the building is burning, you don't stop to hold a town meeting to discuss the pros and cons of doing something. If you decide to involve others, then you have to decide who should be involved. One of the authors has an ongoing discussion with one company owner who thinks that getting employees involved is a sign that the company's leaders don't know what they are doing. However, the research shows that the more important the issue is to the company, the more people need to be involved. Then there is the question of how to involve others. Committees, task forces, and teams are the most frequently used approaches.

Process   Utilizing effective timing is perhaps the most important process skill. The most successful change attempts get other people involved at the very beginning of a change effort. Once the train has left the station, it is a lot harder to get people onboard. Knowing how to work the "informal systems" is another key process skill. We all know that if you want to get things done, you have to go to key people who may not be the designated leaders, but who have a lot of respect. They are the informal leaders. Knowing how to cut through the red tape is an essential change management skill.

These factors remind us that an organization must have effective upward communication if it is to survive.

Horizontal Communication

The survival of a modern organization often depends on the degree to which it specializes. Anyone who has visited a busy hospital, for example, will readily notice the high degree of specialization or differentiation that exists in such an organization. Medical services constitute only one part of the hospital organization. Other units that are vital to its operation include maintenance departments and administrative services such as accounting and personnel.

Coordination or integration of all these diverse units is required to keep the organization running efficiently. Many companies are trying new tactics to open up horizontal lines of communication by pushing employees out of their "comfort zones" through experiential training that will take employees with different department loyalties completely out of their element. These types of experiences (games and team challenges outside of the office and perhaps outside of departments) will open up the lines of communication and diminish obstructions to effective communication across equal levels of the organization (Mowle, 2004, p. 1). Consider the following example.

It is not unusual in a large university to find two or more departments teaching similar concepts and even using the same textbooks without knowing it because of a lack of coordination between units. This phenomenon is known as a "differentiation-integration problem" (Lawrence and Lorsch, 1969). It illustrates the intense need for effective **horizontal communication** in organizations—that is, *the exchanges between and among people on the same level of the organization.*

Horizontal communication frequently suffers in organizations because of employee loyalty to a given department. Groups within the organization compete for power and resources, and new employees are taught to be loyal to their department and not to trust or help those outside it. This situation is intensified in organizations that reward people and groups on a competitive basis. Naturally, if there are four promotions to be awarded among 10 departments, rivalries will develop.

In such situations, each department may consider itself to be at the top of the organization. In a manufacturing plant, for example, production departments consider themselves to be the "stars" of the organization and regard accountants as "paper shufflers," engineers as "geeks," and human resources specialists as "the last to know and the first to go." Obviously, members of the other departments would hardly agree.

In summarizing the literature, Goldhaber (1993) identified four functions of horizontal communication in an organization:

1. *Task coordination:* The department heads may meet monthly to discuss how each department is contributing to the system's goals. Another example of coordination is the frequent use of team-teaching or team-writing found in university communities.

2. *Problem solving:* The members of a department may assemble to discuss how they will handle a threatened budget cut; they may employ brainstorming techniques.

3. *Information sharing:* The members of one department may meet with members of another department to give them some new data. One department at a university recently rewrote its entire curriculum. In order to inform other departments about these major revisions (which affected most segments of the university), the faculty held several meetings with representatives of the other departments to explain the new curriculum.

4. *Conflict resolution:* Members of one department may meet to discuss a conflict inherent in the department or between departments. (p. 124)

Ineffective horizontal communication has been cited as one important factor in the space shuttle *Challenger* accident in January 1986. Since horizontal communication can help an organization function more effectively and may even be necessary to avoid tragic accidents, how do we bring it about?

The Linking-Pin Function

A solution offered by Likert (1967) is the **linking-pin function,** which is illustrated in Figure 14.3.

The type of structure shown in Figure 14.3 uses committees made up of people with overlapping—or linking—group memberships in the organization to help coordinate efforts upward, downward, and across the system. Unfortunately, if groups in the organization are rewarded on a competitive basis, overlapping group

Figure 14.3 *The Linking-Pin Function (indicated by arrows)*

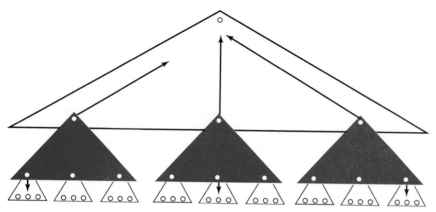

structure fails to function as intended because of the low levels of trust that exist among group members.

Reducing Barriers

Some steps can be taken to reduce the barriers to horizontal communication. Schein (1997) describes four procedures or guidelines that have proven successful in some cases:

1. Relatively greater emphasis given to *total organizational effectiveness* and the role of departments in contributing to it; departments measured and rewarded on the basis of their *contribution* to the total effort rather than their individual effectiveness.

2. *High interaction and frequent communication* stimulated between groups to work on problems of intergroup coordination and help; organizational *rewards given partly on the basis of help* that groups give to each other.

3. Frequent *rotation of members* among groups or departments to stimulate high degrees of mutual understanding and empathy for one another's problems.

4. *Avoidance of any win–lose situation;* groups never put into the position of competing for some organizational reward; emphasis always placed on pooling resources to maximize organizational effectiveness; rewards shared equally with all the groups or departments.

A number of *organizational development (OD)* strategies include one form or another of team-building activities, which are designed to implement Schein's four guidelines. Keep in mind, however, that these are only guidelines and may not apply in every situation.

Communication and Organizational Change

Precision of communication is important, more important than ever, in our era of hair trigger balances, when a false or misunderstood word may create as much disaster as a sudden thoughtless act.

—Thurber (*Leadership Now,* 2004)

In the previous section you read about creating change within organizations from a bottom-up, or upward direction. Organizations must undergo frequent adaptation and change in order to survive in today's competitive business environment. We will now address the critical role of effective communication in the organizational change process.

As noted previously, one of the most challenging types of organizational change is *cultural* change. ACA News, as reported by Auxillium West (2003), describes the aggregated results of a conglomeration of cultural change studies with a list of elements necessary for cultural change. Auxillium references the necessity of common and consistent goals within an organization, role clarity and power among leaders, accountable employees, shared rewards, and encouragement of appropriate behaviors. Communication failures during cultural change can result in inconsistencies such as "split personality work environments." Lack of appropriate communication creates a churn within the organization, and portions of the organization split off, resulting in "split personalities" within the organization. The organization's "vision," for example, should be communicated to all levels of the organization and upheld through reinforcing behavior (Auxillium West, 2002).

Ivy Sea Online, online resources for "Visionary Resources for Conscious Enterprise and Inspired Leadership" makes several comments about change and the need for effective communication within organizations. First, Ivy Sea notes that "change is constant and often uncomfortable," and they continue by noting that "skillful communication" is necessary to effectively "navigate" change. People must have information in order to tolerate and drive change ("Change & Communication," 2004).

In the current decade, chaos theory, originally a mathematical theory that evolved into a line of thought that periods of disorder result in a higher order and that sensitive nuances can lead to large scale results, has been applied to organizational structure and communication during times of change. Chaos theory states that organizations are living and breathing dynamic systems, which must continuously adapt and change in order to exist in today's challenging and ever-changing technological and economic environment. Dynamic systems like organizations are sensitive to subtle changes and must go through states of disorder before reaching states of higher order. If an organization fails to change, it will fail over time. Communication between leadership and all employees is essential in overcoming the chaos that many people feel during times of organizational change. This concept has strong implications for the field of organizational change and communication (Wheatley, 2002).

There are three major tenets of the chaotic, or evolving, organization. First, organizations are webs of relationships that make up an evolving system. Second, times of perceived chaos within an organization are actually a means to an end of a greater order within the organization. Third, tiny nuances within the organization can result in significant effects, for better or for worse. Each employee within the organization has a high impact on the ability of an organization to create positive change (London, 1996).

Margaret Wheatley, EdD, studies and writes about chaos in organizations and has developed a new science of management. Her book *The New Science of Leadership* explores the importance of chaos in organizations that strive to readapt and change to become better. She also looks at the importance of employee acceptance of change as the normal development cycle at both the organizational and employee levels. Most people do not like change, and both employees and leaders within organizations have critical roles in the change process. Employees must allow chaos to occur and work within a culture that will nourish flexibility and resilience. Accepting chaos is difficult because most people like to be in control. Leaders must help employees feel that they are in control by arming them with information through the use of effective communication (Wheatley, 2002).

These studies show that the development of information exchange systems within organizations is critical. The more that employees know, the more willing they will be to accept change and impending chaos as their organization adapts. First, there must be free flow of information at all times because lack of information leads to employee discomfort during times of change. Second, an organizational vision must be communicated across the organization. Third, buy-in must be achieved from all employees through effective communication channels. The more knowledge employees have, the less resistant they will be to change.

According to Margaret Wheatley, to adapt as an organization and survive organizational change, the whole organization must be engaged in the change effort, there should be openness and access to information, information should be reported quickly and without obstacles, and change must be accepted (Wheatley, 1999). The bottom line is that communication is essential to change. Communication arms employees with information to decrease their resistance and fear of change, allowing the organization to evolve, adapt, and reach a higher state of functioning. Wheatley notes in a 2004 article that "people deal far better with uncertainty and stress when they know what's going on" (p. 97).

Informal Communication

Last but not least, we shall examine the informal channels of communication used in organizations. Such channels are often labeled "rumor mills" and "the grapevine." The term "grapevine" is said to have originated during the Civil War. According to Smith, "In those days, intelligence telegraph lines were strung loosely from tree to tree in the manner of a grapevine, and the message was often garbled; thus, any rumor was said to be from the 'grapevine'" (Smith et al., 1972, p. 273).

Rosnow (1988) defines a rumor as "a proposition for belief . . . disseminated without official verification" (p. 14). Researchers theorize that rumors help relieve emotional tensions and generally arise under ambiguous circumstances.

It has long been known that ineffective or inadequate downward communication creates an information vacuum in an organization. This vacuum usually is filled by rumors, which are often educated guesses. For example, company X, an organization with over 10,000 employees in its home headquarters in the East, began construction of a new plant on the West Coast. Immediately, a rumor started circulating among the employees that the entire company was going to move its operation west in retaliation for severe union management problems that had recently developed. When management failed to communicate its intentions to stay in its present location in the East, great fear and unrest developed among the employees. In this case, the rumor was untrue; nevertheless, management felt that the employees' fears about their jobs might help "tame down" union activity. So they deliberately allowed the company's plans to remain ambiguous.

German and Rath (1987) stress the importance of the office "grapevine," writing that "many students tend to equate oral communication with formal public address . . . But our research indicates that much, if not most, oral communication takes place in largely informal circumstances" (p. 340). They go on to say that one manager stated that when he really needed information, he had his greatest success around the water cooler (or the copying machine).

Sostek (2006) writes that gossip actually plays a part in helping employees bond. Erik Foster, a psychologist at Temple University, states, "Gossip greases the social wheels. We need to gossip to establish trust, to feel comfortable, to find out all kinds of things that allow us to operate effectively on an everyday basis." There are two kinds of gossip: self-serving and group-serving. Self-serving is when you spread rumors that hurt others. Group-serving is when you share information about how other units in the organization are doing better. This stimulates productivity and helps the organization (Sostek, 2006, p. D1).

Variables in Rumor Development

Rosnow (1988) further proposed that rumors are a function of the ambiguity of the situation multiplied by the importance of the issue. Obviously, the loss of over 10,000 jobs in a city of about 70,000 people is a matter of critical importance. However, rumor transmission is slowed down by a person's critical sense that the rumor might not seem valid. These three variables (importance, ambiguity, and critical sense) can be expressed in the following equation:

$$R = i \times a \times 1/c$$

According to this equation, rumor R is directly encouraged by importance i and ambiguity a but inversely related to one's critical sense c. In the case of company X, for example, many employees felt that it would probably be too costly to abandon all the company's facilities and technical equipment in the East and start operations all over again in the West; these people did not believe the rumor that was circulating among the other employees and thus did nothing to help spread it.

Types of Message Change

Rumors undergo three types of message change as they pass from one person to another. These changes are (1) leveling, (2) sharpening, and (3) assimilation. **Leveling** is *the process whereby some details are omitted.* Not all the details of a message are interesting to relate, so people tend to get to the point as soon as possible, leaving out what they consider the extraneous details. **Sharpening** is *the exaggeration of certain parts of the rumor.* Suppose, for example, Professor Smith was told to leave Dean Jones's office after a heated exchange of words. When the incident was described by Jones's secretary, Professor Smith had been "thrown out" of the dean's office. And by the third transmission there had been a "fight in the dean's office." As you can see, the story gets more interesting (and less accurate) with each telling. **Assimilation,** a more complicated change, refers to *the way people distort messages to accord with their own view of things.* In a classic study by Allport and Postman (1947), a picture was shown to subjects who were to describe the picture to a second person, who would then tell a third, and so on. The picture showed the interior of a subway car with a roughly dressed white man holding a razor in his hand and talking to a well-dressed black man. In the retelling of the story, the razor was moved from the white man's hand to that of the black man. Obviously, this detail fit in more closely with racial stereotypes held by the subjects in the experiment.

Speed and Accuracy

Using a method called *Episodic Communication Channels in Organizations* (ECCO) analysis in which subjects identify persons from whom they have heard a rumor and pinpoint when they heard it, Davis (1953) and others have described several additional characteristics of grapevine communication. The grapevine, they point out, is one of the fastest methods of communicating in an organization. The grapevine is also often quite accurate. (Davis [1972] found between 80 and 90 percent accuracy in the case of noncontroversial rumors.) And the grapevine may carry a lot of information. For example, think about the information you get from friends on which courses (and professors) to take and which to stay away from. Finally, the grapevine is not considered reliable by most people in an organization—mainly because of the three types of message distortions described above.

Hendrickson and Psarouthakis (1998) surveyed chief executive officers of small entrepreneurial companies and found they used the following methods for sharing company values with employees. You might think of these as alternatives to the grapevine.

Informal conversations (one on one) with employees	32%
Bringing up values as secondary agenda of meetings	26%
Social activities	17%
Companywide meetings	6%

| Meetings with middle managers | 6% |
| Others | 13% (p. 116) |

Results of an earlier study indicate that the grapevine ranked as the second most frequently used channel of organizational communication (the most used channel was the employee's immediate supervisor). As a source of information, however, the grapevine was ranked next to last on both reliability and desirability. So the grapevine is considered by employees to be an important, but not always preferred, channel of communication within an organization.

In a new application of informal communication, some professional organizations are organizing a speed-dating format for business to improve networking with other professionals. "You don't have time to make a business deal in eight minutes, but you'll gather a great list of people that might work with you in the future," says Tom Jaffee, founder of Match Events (*www.matchevents.com*), which organizes business meet-ups from its headquarters in Delray Beach, Florida. A few companies like Match Events and eXtreme Networking (*www.extremenetworking.biz*), which is based in Chicago, use software to help make good business matches (Bick, 2007).

Summary

In this chapter, we have discussed human communication that occurs in the context of organizations. We have seen that this context involves more people and is more complex than public communication.

We discussed the growing importance of communication in a postindustrial society. Evidence indicates that quality of communication in organizations relates to overall performance goals. This has been found to be true in such widely divergent organizations as engineering firms, hospitals, manufacturing plants, and universities.

In downward communication, a basic problem is how to communicate enough information to employees without "overloading them." In this respect, a combination of written (including electronic) and oral messages seems to be more effective than either written or oral messages alone. More message distortion seems to occur at lower levels in the organization, and superior-to-subordinate communication has been shown to be the single most important component in successful organizational communication. The most desired type of supervisory communication style is the supportive style.

Upward communication, or communication from subordinate to superior, has proved valuable to upper management in maintaining an accurate picture of day-to-day organizational operations. As we have seen, however, there are numerous nonverbal as well as psychological barriers to effective upward communication. Again, a supportive or receptive supervisory style is more likely to promote upward communication.

Horizontal communication was defined as the method that helps to coordinate all the diverse functions of an organization. We saw here the paradox between the need for specialization of functions on one hand and the need for coordination of these functions on the other.

In the last section, we examined the role of informal communication in organizations. Research has shown that transmission of rumors in an organization is influenced by the importance and ambiguity of the situation as well as by the critical sense of the people involved. Leveling, sharpening, and assimilation were shown as three forms of message distortion that commonly occur in the transmission of rumors. Finally, we found that grapevine communication is a frequently used but not necessarily preferred source of information in organizations.

Key Terms

Assimilation
Coercive power
Cooptation
Downward
  communication
Expert power
Forming of coalitions

Horizontal
  communication
Ingratiation
Law of diminishing
  returns
Legitimate power

Leveling
Linking-pin function
Referent power
Reward power
Selective use of
  objective criteria

Sharpening
Upward
  communication
Upward receptivity

Review Questions

1. What are three functions communication performs in organizations?

2. What is the general research finding regarding the type of supervisory style that is preferred by employees?

3. What are five ways in which people adapt to information overload?

4. Explain the law of diminishing returns as it relates to downward communication.

5. Discuss and illustrate the five types of power.

6. What are five functions of upward communication?

7. What are two barriers to upward communication?

8. What are three ways to create change through upward communication?

9. Explain the differentiation-integration problem in organizations.

10. How does this relate to horizontal communication?

11. Explain the formula $R = i \times a \times 1/c$ as it relates to rumors.

12. Identify the three types of message distortion that occur during rumor transmission.

Exercises

1. Have the class break up into groups of five or six and discuss the following. If you were Sam Edwards and were faced with the problem of employees using the photocopier for personal business (see pp. 478–480), how would you try to solve it? Have each discussion group decide on a specific plan of attack for solving this problem. Then have the groups share their solutions with the entire class. What organizational communication issues are involved in this case problem? What other issues are indirectly related to this problem?

2. Divide the class into small groups and have each group discuss the following case problem. After each group has shared its reactions with the other groups, discuss the principles from this chapter that are illustrated by the case.

   In the men's sportswear department of Samson's Department Store, two men and four women are regularly employed as sales personnel. In addition to salary, they receive a bonus determined by how much their daily volume of sales exceeds a quota. Mr. Wilcox, the buyer, is head of the department, but during his frequent absences his assistant buyer, Ms. Jones, is in charge. In addition to six regulars, during the summer the department employs several extra salespeople. These are college students on vacation, who have been given some training by the store's personnel department. They are eager beavers and often outsell the regulars. They also work for a salary plus bonus.

During Mr. Wilcox's absence on a buying trip, the regulars complained to Ms. Jones that the extras were making it difficult for them to make their quotas, that they mixed up the stock and generally were a nuisance. Ms. Jones, a close friend of one of the regulars, ordered the extras to take care of the stock and to sell only when customers were waiting. On his return, Mr. Wilcox countermanded this order; he told the extras to get in there and sell or look for other jobs. A competitive spirit, he said, was good for the department. The regulars are now more resentful than ever; customers are beginning to notice the bad feelings, and some of them have taken their trade elsewhere.

Which one of the following comments on this situation seems to you most sound?

a.   Mr. Wilcox should return to the position taken earlier by his assistant—that is, instruct the extras to work on stock and handle customers only when no regular is free.
b.   In addition to telling the extras to sell at top capacity, Mr. Wilcox should call the regulars in, take a firm stand with them, and advise them to increase their sales or look elsewhere for work.
c.   Mr. Wilcox is right: A competitive spirit is good for the department. Beyond making this point clear, he should continue to maintain a hands-off policy and let the situation work itself out.
d.   Mr. Wilcox should pay the extras a straight hourly wage.

e.   Mr. Wilcox should investigate the activities of all employees and also check into the company's compensation plan.

3.   Have five people leave the classroom. Then bring them back into the room one at a time. Start a rumor by giving the first person a short description of an event. Be sure the story has at least a few details such as time, location, names, number of people involved, and so on. Or show a picture of an event and ask the person to describe what is going on in the picture. Then have each person in turn give his or her version of the story (or picture) to the next person who comes back into the room. Have the rest of the class try to keep track of the leveling, sharpening, and assimilation that occur as the story is told and retold.

4.   Discuss the following case and determine answers to the three questions that follow:

A clinical psychologist at a university feels that his interviews with a client should be recorded on tape and that the benefits to be derived from such recordings would be impaired if the client knew in advance that the recording was to be made. The psychologist sometimes uses these recordings in his classroom to illustrate his lectures, always without the knowledge of the client, though the client's name is not revealed to the class.

a.   What should be the university's policy in this matter?
b.   How should the policy be communicated?
c.   What considerations are there in trying to communicate this policy?

5.   Suppose you are a manager of an office and you hear that the head of your account department (who is married) is believed by many to be having an affair with a married woman in the personnel department. You (Mr. Wilson) call him (Mr. Townsend) into your office to discuss this matter. Have two people in the class role-play this conversation. How would you change the conversation if you were taking into account what we discussed about rumors in this chapter?

Suggested Readings

Argenti, Paul A. *Corporate Communication,* 2nd ed. New York: Irwin/McGraw-Hill, 1998.

This excellent book examines the subject of CorpComm. CorpComm is a term that refers to communication as one of the formal mechanisms in the organization. It covers such diverse topics as employee communication, investor relations, governmental affairs, and communication in a crisis.

Blanchard, Ken. *Leading at a Higher Level.* Upper Saddle River, NJ: Prentice-Hall, 2007.

This outstanding book synthesizes ways that leaders communicate in all aspects of the organization.

Day, George. *Peripheral Vision.* Boston: Harvard Business School Press, 2006.

This excellent book explores ways to look outside the organization to see future trends for organization success or failure.

Goffee, Rob, and Gareth Jones. *Why Should Anyone Be Led by You?* Boston: Harvard Business School Press, 2006.

This book looks at all the ways that the reader can analyze himself or herself to improve communication and leadership skills.

Goldhaber, Gerald M. *Organizational Communication,* 6th ed. Dubuque, IA: Brown, 1993.

Certainly one of the best, if not the best, book available on this subject. It is comprehensive, accurate, and very well written. Must reading for anyone wanting to know more about this subject.

Hartman, Laura P., and Joe Desjardins. *Business Ethics.* New York: McGraw-Hill, 2008.

This outstanding book offers numerous practical tips on how to apply ethics in the business organization.

Rath, Tom. *Strengths Finder 2.0.* New York: Gallup Press, 2007.

This best-selling book offers readers an assessment instrument to determine their top five interpersonal strengths. You will need to buy the book to log onto their Web site and take the test. To learn more about this, go to http://sf2.strengthsfinder.com/ learnmore.

Tapscott, Don. *Growing Up Digital.* New York: McGraw-Hill, 1998.

Looks at the impact of the Internet Generation (N-Gen) on organizations and on the entire realm of electronic communication. Includes chapters on the N-Gen culture of interaction; the mind-set of typical members of this generation; and their impact on the workplace, family, and the N-Gen leaders of the future.

Welch, Jack. *Winning.* New York: Warner Books, 2005.

This book gives great insight into how a major corporate organization (General Electric) works. Welch offers many examples of the crucial role that communication plays in an organization's success or failure.

 # For Supplementary Information

Log onto the Online Learning Center at *www.mhhe.com/tubbsmoss11.*

15

Mass Communication and the New Technologies

Chapter Objectives

After reading this chapter, you should be able to:

1. Explain how mass communication, because it is mediated, differs from personal encounters and identify four characteristics of mass communication.
2. Explain the concept of the gatekeeper, gatekeeping and war reporting, and several of the major ethical issues involving gatekeeping and the media.
3. State two theories concerning message flow from the mass media and explain the concept of the active audience.
4. Discuss the research findings on media uses and gratifications, including new research on the use of computer-mediated communication.
5. Discuss the extent to which the media disseminate information and influence attitudes. Explain the concepts of agenda setting and framing.
6. Describe the influence mass communication has on social learning, particularly in children, and discuss research on the mean world syndrome and the effects of media violence on aggression. Discuss the effects of video games.
7. Discuss the new communication technologies, including their relationship to the mass media and the rise of new alternative media.
8. Describe the effects of the new technologies on interpersonal communication, their accessibility, and their implications for global communication.

Media, information and communications technology, and popular culture permeate everyday life. Individuals everywhere exercise more autonomy than ever before as cultural decision makers. Obviously, the extent of these developments varies according to the structured circumstances in which people find themselves. But widespread global trends toward personal accessing of film, video, music, and TV "on demand" dramatically symbolize how people everywhere are expanding the range and increasing the control of their cultural experiences to accord with their particular needs, wants, and interests.

—Lull (2007, p. xii)

Mass communication as we know it—through the print media (newspapers, magazines, and books) and the electronic media (radio, film, recordings, television, and computer)—is undergoing a sustained transformation. For example, we are seeing the emergence of a new form of journalism that will include a complete spectrum of communication modalities (including 360-degree video); hyperlinks that place news in a far larger context; greater audience involvement; and news presentations that are customized for individuals (Pavlik and McIntosh, 2005). In this chapter we look at mass communication and the new technologies, the traditional media and the new media, exploring how such seemingly different experiences are related and the nature of their effects on human communication.

A FIRST DEFINITION

Mediated Encounters

As suggested in Chapter 1, every aspect of mass communication is *mediated,* and mediated encounters are different from personal encounters (Avery and McCain, 1982). First, *the sensory input potential for receivers is more limited.* Second, *receivers* of a mediated message *have little or no control over its sources*—that is, feedback is extremely limited. And finally, the *sources* of mediated messages *are known either in a limited way or not known at all, only imagined.* Put more simply, mediated experience is not direct. When you read this book, for example, your experience is mediated. The book is the means, the medium, through which we communicate. If you wanted to ask us a question about it, you would have to write, e-mail, or telephone us.

In Woody Allen's film *The Purple Rose of Cairo,* Mia Farrow plays a young woman who escapes her lackluster husband and depressing job by constantly going to the movies. One night, the young handsome hero of a movie she is watching steps off the screen and addresses her directly, asking why she has seen the movie so many times. A romance develops between Farrow and the celluloid hero, and for a time she loses her point of reference as her fantasies become real. What Woody Allen plays with here is the failure to distinguish between mediated and personal encounters—the mediated experience (of the film) becoming more real than the interpersonal.

As we amplify our definition of mass communication, keep in mind the point made by Wright (1986) that mass communication is not defined in terms of technological achievements: "Rather, it is a special kind of social communication involving distinctive characteristics of the audience, the communication experience, and the communicator" (p. 7). According to Wright, in *mass communication the audience is relatively large, heterogeneous, and anonymous to the source. The experience is public, rapid, and fleeting. The source works through a complex organization rather than in isolation, and the message may represent the efforts of many different people* (pp. 6–9).

But as the many changes in mass communication unfold, definitions will have to be qualified. One communication scholar writes:

> Thanks to the World Wide Web, one person can become a mass communicator. The full implication of this change may take some time to become clear. (Dominick, 2007, p. 11).

The Audience

Consider again the first element in this definition: the audience. Perhaps most significant for our purpose is its size. Celebrations of the New Year as it is ushered in by country after country are seen by millions of viewers around the world. And in 2001, news of terrorist attacks on the World Trade Center and the Pentagon was watched by millions on network television and CNN, who also followed the story through other media: radio, Internet, and newspapers. Although in person-to-group and organizational settings, face-to-face interaction is often possible, in mass communication the size of the audience makes it impossible for the mass communicator and audience members to interact face-to-face.

Nonetheless, there are critical times when, through the technology of mass communication, people worldwide are spurred to action in the form of donations and volunteerism. This was the case following the powerful tsunami in Southeast Asia in December 2004. And in 2005 ongoing news coverage of Hurricane Katrina's destruction of areas in the Gulf Coast, most notably New Orleans, resulted in generous donations and the mobilization of skilled groups, including firefighters and police, from across the United States to volunteer their services. The devastation was so great that media coverage of Katrina's aftereffects continues to this day.

In addition to being a diversified group, the receivers in mass communication are, for the most part, unknown to the source. This is not to say that members of a mass communication audience are isolated from other human beings. It is possible—in fact, very likely—for us to experience mass communication as members of dyads, small groups, or organizations. You may be out with a friend seeing a movie. Half the dorm may be watching reruns of *Seinfeld* on television. The day after a show opens, the entire cast of a theatrical production may be reading the newspaper reviews in the director's apartment. Or you may be online with a newsgroup, talking about politics or global warming.

The Communication Experience

As for the second element, the communication experience itself, it is intended for rapid consumption by great numbers of people. Moreover, it is characterized as public rather than private because the messages are not addressed to particular individuals. Think of a college president addressing a very large audience of parents in a public hall. Although she may not know any of them personally, she is aware of the audience as a group and is directing what is said to those people. If the same address were to be broadcast on C-Span, that message would be received by a highly diversified group of people who were, for the most part, unknown to the speaker. This is one of the important ways in which mass communication and the public, or person-to-group, communication described in Chapter 13 differ.

The Source of Communication

The third element in this definition of mass communication, the source of the communication, is usually not working in isolation but rather from within a complex organization. The message itself often represents the efforts of many individuals, which we shall understand more clearly when we discuss the concept of the gate-keeper. These people may represent a complex organization that, in countries such as the United States, is usually concerned with making a profit.

Mass communication events sometimes require not only the efforts of hundreds of people but often months of preparation and millions of dollars. Individual salaries can be spectacular. For example, David Letterman's annual salary is $31 million, and in 2006 Katie Couric reportedly negotiated a five-year contract with CBS for $60 million. Broad media coverage of sports, which brings in great advertising revenue, has enabled skyrocketing salaries for star athletes. Baseball players Alex Rodriguez, Roger Clemens, and Derek Jeter each earn $20 million or more annually. Television programming is equally costly. Oprah Winfrey once gave away 276 cars to audience members. And some movie budgets are staggering: the production costs for *Spider-Man 3* were $250 million; for *King Kong,* $207 million.

Profits in mass communication are often equally spectacular—a fact that has prompted an increasing number of corporate takeovers. Publishing, once considered a "gentleman's occupation" with little hope of great financial gain, became both profitable and competitive through the proliferation of paperback books, memoirs by celebrities and people in the public eye, the sale of book club rights, and the sale of film rights for best-selling novels. Recommendations by Oprah Winfrey have placed many novels on the best-seller list. And with the publication and film rights to the *Harry Potter* series, the British author J. K. Rowling has earned more royalties than any author in publishing history.

We have said that in the United States the mass media are usually concerned with making a profit, and a good part of that profit depends on advertising. There are countries in which the mass media are independent of such concerns, but in the United States advertising dominates mass communication. And, certainly, awareness of the extent to which advertising maintains the mass media should affect the source credibility mass communicators have for their audiences. There are many ethical considerations as well. It is estimated that by age 16 the average viewer will have seen over 600,000 commercials, yet recent studies show that children have difficulty differentiating between programs and commercials. Conflicts of interest between profit-making functions and responsibilities to the public also affect the free flow of information.

Media Consolidation

The deregulation of telecommunications through the Telecommunications Act of 1996 facilitated the creation of international conglomerates that now dominate the mass media:

> In 1983, the men and women who headed the fifty mass media corporations that dominated American audiences could have fit comfortably in a modest hotel ballroom. . . . By 2003, five men controlled all these media once run by the fifty corporations of twenty years earlier. These five, owners of additional digital corporations, could fit in a generous phone booth. Granted, it would be a tight fit, and it would be filled with some tensions. (Bagdikian, 2004, p. 27)

The five international corporations that Pulitzer Prize–winning journalist Ben Bagdikian is talking about are Time Warner, whose holdings include CNN, HBO, *Time, Fortune,* Warner Brother Pictures, AOL, and the Atlanta Braves; Disney, which owns ABC, Miramax, and Walt Disney Pictures as well as parks and resorts worldwide; News Corporation (owned by Rupert Murdoch), which includes the Fox network, Twentieth Century Fox, the publisher HarperCollins, SKY News, the *Times* of London, MySpace, and Intermix; Viacom, which includes CBS, MTV Networks, and Paramount Pictures; and Bertelsmann, a German firm whose many holdings include the largest number of English-language books in the world and 82 record labels. The total holdings of the five largest media corporations (and there are other media conglomerates) include radio and television networks, newspapers, magazines, Internet Web sites, book and music publishers, movie companies, theme parks, sports teams, and other properties (Bagdikian, 2004; Bennett, 2005; *The Nation,* 2006). For an example of one corporation's international holdings, see the media map of News Corporation in Figure 15.1.

In 2007 News Corporation also acquired the business news publisher Dow Jones & Company, the parent company of the highly influential *Wall Street Journal.* To read about the ever-changing holdings of the largest media giants, go to *www.cjr. org/resources,* where *Columbia Journalism Review* updates information on "Who Owns What." And see Box 15.1 on media consolidation and news content.

Our first concern will be with how mass communication is related to other modes of human communication. As we have seen, mass communication is not face-to-face communication. It is mediated, and this at once sets it apart from the other communication contexts we have been discussing. We have considered several defining elements of mass communication: the audience, the communication experience,

Figure 15.1   *A Media Map of a News Corporation*

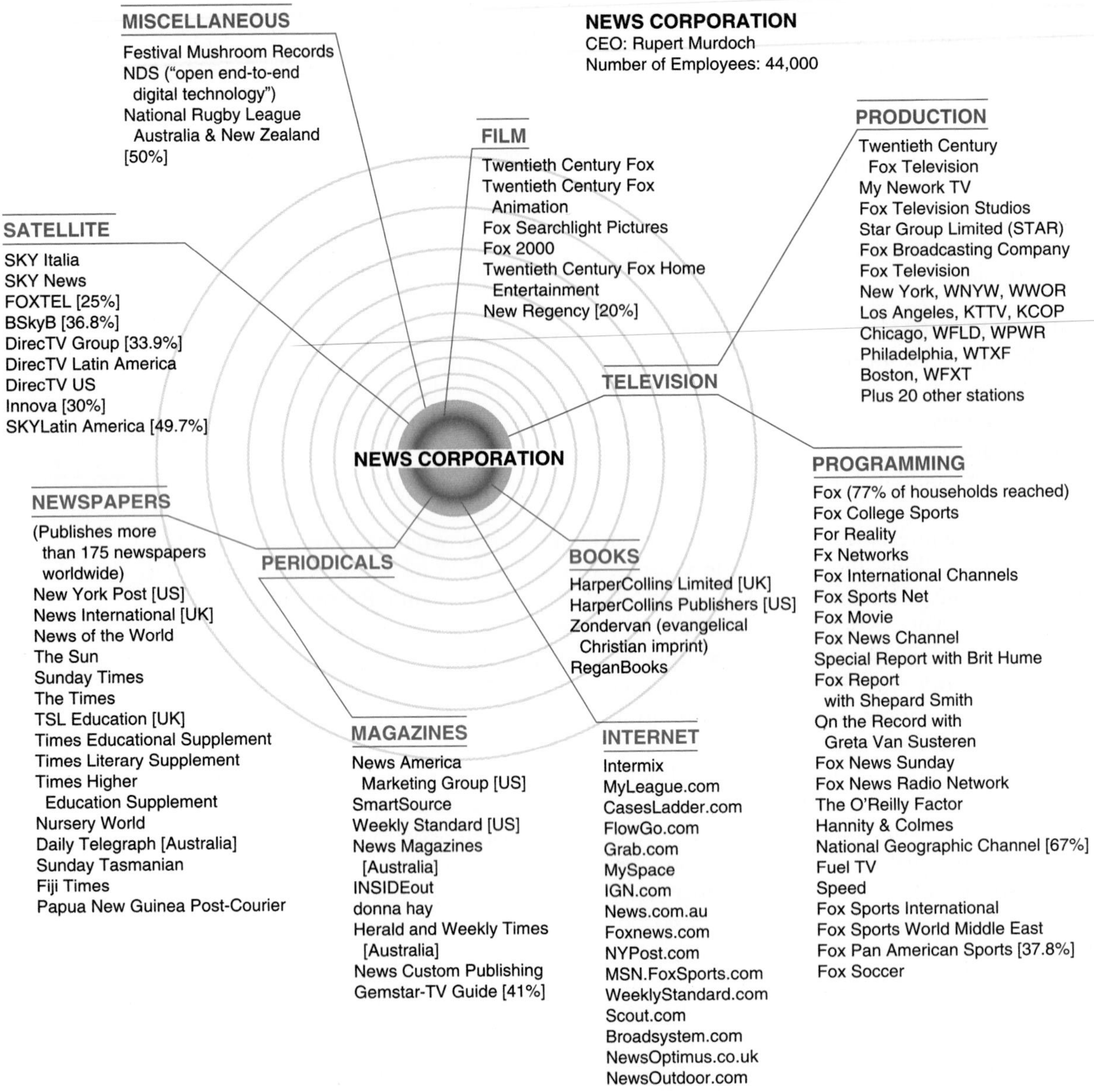

MISCELLANEOUS

Festival Mushroom Records
NDS ("open end-to-end
 digital technology")
National Rugby League
 Australia & New Zealand
 [50%]

NEWS CORPORATION
CEO: Rupert Murdoch
Number of Employees: 44,000

FILM

Twentieth Century Fox
Twentieth Century Fox
 Animation
Fox Searchlight Pictures
Fox 2000
Twentieth Century Fox Home
 Entertainment
New Regency [20%]

PRODUCTION

Twentieth Century
 Fox Television
My Nework TV
Fox Television Studios
Star Group Limited (STAR)
Fox Broadcasting Company
Fox Television
New York, WNYW, WWOR
Los Angeles, KTTV, KCOP
Chicago, WFLD, WPWR
Philadelphia, WTXF
Boston, WFXT
Plus 20 other stations

SATELLITE

SKY Italia
SKY News
FOXTEL [25%]
BSkyB [36.8%]
DirecTV Group [33.9%]
DirecTV Latin America
DirecTV US
Innova [30%]
SKYLatin America [49.7%]

TELEVISION

NEWS CORPORATION

PROGRAMMING

Fox (77% of households reached)
Fox College Sports
For Reality
Fx Networks
Fox International Channels
Fox Sports Net
Fox Movie
Fox News Channel
Special Report with Brit Hume
Fox Report
 with Shepard Smith
On the Record with
 Greta Van Susteren
Fox News Sunday
Fox News Radio Network
The O'Reilly Factor
Hannity & Colmes
National Geographic Channel [67%]
Fuel TV
Speed
Fox Sports International
Fox Sports World Middle East
Fox Pan American Sports [37.8%]
Fox Soccer

NEWSPAPERS

(Publishes more
 than 175 newspapers
 worldwide)
New York Post [US]
News International [UK]
News of the World
The Sun
Sunday Times
The Times
TSL Education [UK]
Times Educational Supplement
Times Literary Supplement
Times Higher
 Education Supplement
Nursery World
Daily Telegraph [Australia]
Sunday Tasmanian
Fiji Times
Papua New Guinea Post-Courier

PERIODICALS

BOOKS

HarperCollins Limited [UK]
HarperCollins Publishers [US]
Zondervan (evangelical
 Christian imprint)
ReganBooks

MAGAZINES

News America
 Marketing Group [US]
SmartSource
Weekly Standard [US]
News Magazines
 [Australia]
INSIDEout
donna hay
Herald and Weekly Times
 [Australia]
News Custom Publishing
Gemstar-TV Guide [41%]

INTERNET

Intermix
MyLeague.com
CasesLadder.com
FlowGo.com
Grab.com
MySpace
IGN.com
News.com.au
Foxnews.com
NYPost.com
MSN.FoxSports.com
WeeklyStandard.com
Scout.com
Broadsystem.com
NewsOptimus.co.uk
NewsOutdoor.com

Source: "The National Entertainment State" by Nation Editors, from the July 3, 2006, issue of *The Nation*. Reprinted with permission. For subscription information, call 1-800-333-8536. Portions of each week's *Nation* magazine can be accessed at http://www.thenation.com.

and the communicator. If we are to evaluate mass communication within the framework of other communication contexts, we must add still another element to this definition: the limited feedback usually possible in mass communication.

ISSUES IN COMMUNICATION

Media Consolidation and the News

Many media critics and scholars have voiced concerns about how the extreme concentration of media ownership might affect the content of the news (Chester, 2007; Kleinenberg, 2007, Bagdikian, 2004; Bennett, 2005, pp. 88–100). These concerns include:

- A focus on profits that results in less coverage of news and public affairs and more entertainment programming and "more infotainment and soft news— including news magazines, reality TV, and local TV news."
- Less competition, resulting in some independent media being forced out, and therefore less diversity and less representation of other points of view.
- News that is generic: "Innovation in packaging and branding disguises declining information diversity and content distinctiveness." (p. 89)
- Possible censorship and self-censorship motivated by self-interest.

Consider the last of these points. Media conglomerates have far-reaching interests, not only in a variety of mass media but in numerous other businesses. So what happens to news coverage in a media conglomerate when there is a breaking story about one of its many holdings? Is there self-censorship? And if not, can one division of a conglomerate report fairly and fully on another? Charles Lewis of the Center for Public Integrity says:

It means you're not going to be investigating certain subjects. It means you're not going to see NBC investigating General Electric. You're not going to have ABC doing a big investigation covering Disney. (cited in Foerstel, 2001, p. 20)

Jeff Chester, the author of *Digital Destiny*, writes: "The CEOs of many media conglomerates have a clear political allegiance either to a candidate, a political party, or an ideology" (2007, p. 5).

Do you believe conflicts of interest are inevitable? And what do you think are the obligations of those who write and report the news?

Delayed Feedback

Not all letters to the editor get published. One writer sent this e-mail to the *The New York Times:* "I have noticed that the paper rarely publishes letters that are directly critical of the paper's news coverage. Rather, letters about news articles usually convey the writer's views about the subject in question—not about the way the paper has covered it. Does this reflect a policy on the part of the *Times?*" An interesting question. The e-mail he got back informed him that an error of fact would only be mentioned on page A2 (in a small section called "Corrections"). But he had been talking about policy (Massing, 2001, p. 22).

Still, feedback is given in mass communication. It is true, for example, that television viewers often fax, e-mail, write letters, or telephone a network concerning a given program and that enough letters, calls, or responses to a rating survey will affect the future of that program. But usually those viewers will not be face-to-face with the television producer or, for that matter, with the executive in charge of programming, and the feedback will not be as immediate or complete as it would be on a face-to-face basis. And since mass communication usually involves a chain or network of individuals, the feedback intended for one person in the chain is likely to reach a different member of the chain.

Although feedback can be virtually immediate now, it is often impossible for the source in mass communication to respond to and make public all the feedback that is received. For example, large metropolitan papers such as the *Seattle Times, The Washington Post,* and *The New York Times* receive thousands of letters, faxes, and e-mails each year, of which they can print only a very small percentage. These "letters to the editor" may express praise or strong disagreement, offer observations from personal experience, comment on "shameless" editorials, or correct points of information. Today e-mails and faxes to the editor result in publication of much more rapid, indeed almost instantaneous, responses to opinion pieces. The editorial page of a metropolitan newspaper often runs several letters—pro and con—in response to an editorial that appeared only a day or two before.

So despite the striking differences that seem to set off mass communication from other kinds of human communication, there is also a degree of overlap between different modes. As we discuss the mass communication process, we shall also see some ways in which mass and face-to-face communication perform complementary functions.

THE PROCESS OF MASS COMMUNICATION

The Gatekeeper

Essential to an understanding of the workings of mass communication is the concept of the gatekeeper. A **gatekeeper** is *a person who, by selecting, changing, and/or rejecting messages, can influence the flow of information to a receiver or group of receivers.* Although the concept of the gatekeeper might be applied to other contexts of communication—think, for example, of our discussion in Chapter 14 about how rumors are created—it is particularly relevant to mass communication.

The Gatekeeper's Work

Imagine yourself for a moment as the wire editor of a metropolitan newspaper. You are looking at a computer screen. It is your job to go though all the news items provided by the various wire services to which your paper subscribes. On an average day there might be some 3,000 items, out of which only 200 will be selected. As you go over all this copy on the screen, you have to ask yourself questions: "Did we run anything in yesterday's paper that was like it?" "Will this copy be of broad enough interest for our readers?" "Are other papers covering it?" "Is there room for this story today?" "What are the chances that there will be more important stories later in the day?" "Will we make the deadline if we wait?"

These are some of the considerations that determine which items are discarded and which are selected and edited. Gatekeeping is a necessary aspect of mass communication, and gatekeepers exist in all the mass media. For example, a reader in a publishing house might select 5 out of 100 manuscripts for review by house editors. Or consider the film editor's work. For *Apocalypse Now*, a film about the Vietnam War by Francis Ford Coppola, Walter Murch had to edit 1.25 million feet of film; the final version ran 2 hours and 25 minutes. That film was released in 1979. In 2001, Coppola released *Apocalypse Now Redux*. It took Coppola and Murch six months to re-edit and remix this version of the original, adding some 53 minutes to the film and giving it the subdued, pacifist ending that Coppola had always wanted. You can get some inkling of what choices confront a film editor when you view the special features on the DVD of a current film. There you often find an interview with the director or film editor as well as scenes that were deleted from the final version.

In mass communication we find a network or *chain* of gatekeepers. The following is a simplified example of the gatekeeping process: The senior editor of a monthly travel magazine gets an article and discusses the idea with the editor-in-chief, who approves it. The senior editor then assigns it to a freelance writer and specifies the length of the article and the number of color transparencies needed for the illustrations. The writer decides which aspects of the story to include and adapts the coverage to the needs of the magazine, then selects appropriate color transparencies from several sources.

Once the article is written, it goes back to the senior editor, who reads it, suggests how much editing it needs, and then assigns the work to an assistant editor. (If it were a news article, it would—or should—be reviewed by a fact-checker.) The author of the article then reviews the changes and answers any editorial queries. The managing editor checks the color transparencies, selects half, and turns them over to the art director. The copy is set electronically, and the layout and photographs are handled by a member of the art department. Before the article appears in the magazine, it is reviewed and approved by the managing editor and the editor-in-chief.

Gatekeeping in mass communication involves a selection process that has analogies with the selection process going on in all other contexts of communication—from interpersonal to organizational.

The Gatekeeper's Choices

The gatekeeper's choices concerning what information to select and reject are influenced by many variables. Bittner (1985) identifies the following:

The first is *economics:* Most mass media in the United States are profit making, or concerned with how their money is raised and spent. Thus, advertisers, sponsors, and contributors may have a major impact on news selection and editorials. For example, some radio stations give listeners an opportunity to respond on the air to editorials with which they disagree.

Second, such *legal restrictions* as libel laws will affect media content and presentation. Federal Communications Commission regulations also have an impact, for example, on the issue of who will be allowed to own and operate a broadcasting facility. The Child Online Protection Act is a federal law designed to restrain commercial Web sites from making online pornography available to those under the age of 17.

Deadlines affect depth as well as the time available to determine the accuracy of news selected. And deadlines also affect what will be broadcast: When only a brief amount of time is available, the gatekeeper makes choices concerning relative importance. When the gatekeeper must choose between two stories of equal worth, the one that has a video story is usually selected (p. 378).

The gatekeeper's *ethics,* both personal and professional, also influence the news that will be selected. It's an ethical judgment that determines how much back-bending will take place to be "fair" to a sponsor or a cause endorsed by that sponsor. Personal ethics—and the extent of the gatekeeper's awareness of his or her own beliefs—will influence whether the gatekeeper's likes and dislikes, attitudes, and interests play a part in news selection. For example, it's possible that a financial columnist could affect a company's stock with a story and allow friends to have inside information before the story is printed.

A fifth factor is *competition among media:* In a market with several available sources, it was hoped that competition would raise the overall level of professionalism, ensuring a more objective presentation of information. Often, though, the result has been an increasing amount of "infotainment," a blurring of the lines between information and entertainment in which news stories (e.g., *Dateline*) or interviews are often sensationalized in an effort to gain a wider audience: The theory in the boardrooms is that consumers are attracted by entertainment, rather than information" (Nichols and McChesney, 2005, p. 7). In recent years competition between cable and network news has been intense, and network ratings have shown a significant decline and a definite increase in tabloid journalism.

Sixth, *news value, the intensity of an item in comparison with all others available,* and *news hole, the amount of space or time it takes to present the story,* need to be balanced. Besides balancing these two, gatekeepers must weigh the claims of local interest against those of national interest. For example, how much time should be given to a new statewide campaign to conserve water when the president has just made a major foreign policy announcement?

Another of the important variables affecting what gatekeepers select or reject is the *reaction to feedback,* although that feedback is delayed. If a political cartoon offends an ethnic group, for example, and that group has representatives who write irate letters or insist on a public apology, a magazine editor might deliberate a long time before including another cartoon of that kind. Here the gatekeeper must weigh media goals against public opinion.

Gatekeepers and War Reporting

In this profession, we are not paid to be neutral. We are paid to be fair, and they are completely different things. . . . Yes, we should be absolutely ruthless as to fact. We should not approach a story with some sort of ideological template that we impose on it. We should let the facts lead us to conclusions, but if the conclusions seem clear, then we should not avoid those on the basis of an idea we are supposed to be neutral. . . .

As far as I am concerned, when they hire me, they hire somebody who has a conscience and who has a passion about these things.
—John Burns, *The New York Times* Baghdad Bureau Chief (2003, p. 161)

During wartime one problem for the press has traditionally been access. Certainly this was true during World War II. Still, many journalists found ways to circumvent this. Denied a place among reporters who were to be on an assault craft at the start of the Allied invasion in 1944, the war correspondent Martha Gellhorn found a way to board a hospital ship and land on Omaha Beach—and was there to witness and report on D-Day (Moorehead, 2003, pp. 218–220).

Following television coverage of the Vietnam War, the relationship between the press and the military became quite strained. "When U.S. military forces stormed onto Grenada in 1983, navy gunboats kept the press away from the island" (Katovsky, 2003, p. xii). More recently, during the first Gulf War in 1992 the government had a much criticized pool system, with only a few journalists witnessing action and then reporting back to other correspondents. At the time of the Iraq war in 2003 the government's treatment of the press changed when the Pentagon reintroduced the concept of embedding, which gave reporters far more access to actual military operations than they had had for over 20 years.

Embedded and Independent Journalists: Some Differences

The pros and cons of embedding continue to be discussed at length. **Embeds** are *journalists placed in individual military units who live and travel with the troops.* In addition to the embedded journalists are many **unilaterals,** or *independent journalists.* From the standpoint of news gathering, each group has advantages and disadvantages.

During the current Iraq war, embeds had open access to all sections of the unit they were with. They had that access all the time. Sometimes they formed close personal relationships with members of the unit and therefore had more interviews and stories about the troops. They were also protected by the units they were assigned to. On the other hand, embedded journalists were also subject to censorship. They had to sign contracts and were governed by rules about what could be reported. For example, they were not allowed to reveal their locations or the destination of their unit; after Geraldo Rivera revealed his unit's military position, he was forced to leave the unit. "Embeds," comments one writer, "could only report dramatic accounts of isolated incidents" (cited in Girardi, 2004, p. 23). Often they lacked the context of the larger story, not knowing what was going on elsewhere.

Unilaterals, or independent journalists, were on their own. They had no contract with the military, hence less restrictions. Their work was not censored before being submitted to their publications. Often they could see events in a broader context, could interview all kinds of people, and attempt to travel where they wished to be or view something. On the other hand, they were not protected by the military. And often, they had very limited means of transportation and difficulty getting to sites they wanted to be at.

According to one source, there were estimates of about 600 embeds and 2,100 unilaterals in Iraq, "with a great many of the latter working for the more freewheeling European press"; a second source places the number of embeds at 775 (Katovsky, 2003, p. xiv; Girardi, 2004, p. 21). Since 2003 the death toll for journalists in Iraq, both embeds and unilaterals, has been quite high. In 2006, 55 journalists died in connection with their assignments; 32 of them were killed in Iraq (Smyth, 2006).

Issues of Objectivity

One overriding question has been whether the embedding of journalists within military units in Iraq compromises their objectivity. Ben Brown, an embed who is a special correspondent with BBC News, believes this is not the case:

> I embedded with the British. They had rather a hybrid thing. They had individual journalists embedded with frontline units, but they also had a thing called the Forward Transmission Unit, which was attached to their military headquarters of First Armored Division, which was the main British fighting force there.
>
> I don't feel that our objectivity was ever suspended, really. I was very aware that this was a very unpopular war and also that a lot of our audience—at least half, maybe a majority of our audience—were against the war in the first place. So there was no way that you could be gung-ho. The BBC policy is not to say *our* troops, it was just British troops. (2003, pp. 218–219)

Susan Glasser, a unilateral in Iraq and one of the *Washington Post's* Moscow bureau chiefs, disagrees:

> It's incredibly important to have independent reporting from a war zone. We didn't want to talk to more American soldiers, who were being wonderfully covered by a lot of our colleagues. We wanted to talk to Iraqis. The overall sense I got from the embeds was you could tell modern technology is now up to the task of covering a war on the ground and showing you things as they unfold in real time, perhaps misleadingly. The main thing it caused journalists to see is the utter uselessness of the set-piece Pentagon briefings. (Glasser and Baker, 2003, p. 298)

In studying how embedded journalists framed their television news coverage of Iraq, Pfau and others (2005) examined whether differences existed between embedded and nonembedded reports; the embedded news stories were "more favorable in overall tone toward the military, more favorable in depictions of military personnel, and featured greater use of episodic frames . . . [eliciting] somewhat more positive relational cues" (p. 468). An earlier study also found the general tone and stories about individual soldiers to be more favorable than those of independent journalists (Pfau et al., 2004).

One media critic commented on a less-than-positive story by embedded reporter William Branigin of the *Washington Post*:

Soldiers in the division killed seven women and children in a car the troops said failed to stop, despite commands and warning shots. Branigin's story quoted Capt. Ronny Johnson, who ordered the warning shots, as subsequently telling his platoon leader, "You just . . . killed a family because you didn't fire a warning shot soon enough!" (David Shaw cited in "The View from Inside the Military," 2003, p. 89)

The larger newspapers and other news media were able to supply context for the more dramatic and narrowly focused firsthand accounts of the embeds because they can also draw on the work of many independent journalists. The editor in chief of Reuters writes:

I go back to Doon Campbell on D-Day, "How to convey even a tiny detail of this mighty mosaic." No one battlefield reporter can ever make sense of a war. The challenge for a news organization is to gather and meld the fragments into a coherent and, you hope, accurate and impartial whole. ("The View from Inside," 2003, p. 88)

Gatekeeping and Ethics

[T]he job of trying to tell the truth about people whose job it is to hide the truth is almost as complicated and difficult as trying to hide it in the first place.
—**Bill Moyers (2004)**

In thinking about gatekeeping and ethics in mass communication, all the issues we looked at in Chapter 7 come into play—issues about truth telling, lying, and misrepresentation; secrecy, privacy, and disclosure; leaks and whistleblowing. We have already discussed questions concerning the growing power of media conglomerates. In this connection it is interesting to look at investigative journalism.

The Project for Excellence in Journalism finds that investigative reporting on television, though still going strong, has declined somewhat at local stations, probably because it involves risks (including lawsuits and the loss of advertising). Writing of the media conglomerates, Av Westin remarked: "Michael Eisner, Jack Welch, Mel Karmazin, and Rupert Murdoch need never worry that a story done by their news divisions is going to rip the lid off their company, because the guys down below are not going to OK it. The executive producer of *20/20* will never again approve a story investigating Disney. Why should he?" (cited in Hickey, 2001a, p. 9). For more on investigative reporting go to *www.ire.org*.

In 2001 Bill Moyers and his staff did a PBS documentary called "Trade Secrets" about the chemical industry. The PBS special was followed the next year by HBO's award-winning documentary *Blue Vinyl*, which dealt with much of the same material. The Moyers program used information from industry documents and interviews with former employees who had developed debilitating illnesses from what they considered the toxic effects of the chemicals they had worked with for years. Moyers based the two-hour special on documents that revealed what the industry withheld. The chemical industry responded by establishing its own Web site and an active campaign accusing Moyers of bias. They objected to being allowed to state their position only in the last half hour of the program and to what they saw as journalistic malpractice. Moyers's response was that "investigative journalism is not a collaboration between the journalist and the subject" (Editor's Postscript, in Moyers, 2001, p. 17).

Misrepresentations in the media can involve literally altering the way we see images. During the 2004 presidential campaign, Web viewers often saw a digitally manipulated photo of John Kerry and Jane Fonda speaking together at an antiwar rally in 1971, although they never had. On the cover of a June issue of *Time* in 1994, O. J. Simpson's face was darkened. Another example is a newspaper photo in which President George W. Bush is shown addressing what appears to be a crowd of U.S soldiers. Objections were raised when it turned out that all the soldiers had the same face and pose. Apparently, the photo had been altered digitally, making use of the image of a single soldier. The digital production of news makes it possible to manipulate digital images in three ways—adding something to an image that was not in it; removing something that had been there; or modifying the image by enhancing it, "blending two objects into one, or distorting one face into another (referred to as a morph in the movie industry)" (Pavlik, 2001, p. 87). And using digital video editors such as the Avid Media Composer, "the number one system in television newsrooms in the United States," makes it possible "to create completely realistic video sequences of events that never take place . . . 'Soon, then, the capability will be such that the recorded, digitized, sampled voice of, say, the President of the United States, could be made to sound perfectly as if he had said something he in fact had not said' "(pp. 97–98).

Issues about media intrusion and privacy are also of exceptional importance in relation to mass communication. One such issue involves media coverage of public figures and the public's hunger for information about them—for example, Princess Diana of Wales from her marriage to Prince Charles to her funeral 1997. To this day news stories about Princess Diana make good copy, and the networks have fed and sustained public interest. In 2004, for example, NBC had two hour-long programs showing videotapes of Princess Diana that were owned by the voice coach she had engaged to help her with public speaking. The tapes include many disclosures about her courtship and marriage, as well as other remarks and allegations about the royal family. The question such programming raises is whether it violates the rights and privacy of someone, now dead, who assumed that what was being taped would remain confidential.

Cass Sunstein, a professor of law at the University of Chicago, has written:

> Intrusions on the privacy of celebrities are, at least potentially, intrusions on the privacy of everyone. New technology is making it extremely difficult for both celebrities and ordinary people to insulate themselves from public view, especially at their most vulnerable moments. (1997, p. 23)

Source credibility is an essential part of all news reporting and discussion. In September 2004, a broadcast segment by Dan Rather on *60 Minutes Wednesday* critical of George W. Bush's service in the Texas National Guard became a media controversy when the authenticity of documents presented on the show was questioned.

CBS appointed an independent panel to review the segment. In 2005 the panel found no evidence of political bias and "has not been able to conclude with absolute certainty whether the Killian documents are authentic or forgeries," but made clear that CBS had failed to properly authenticate the documents and interview the controversial source who had offered them. The panel strongly criticized the "considerable and fundamental deficiencies in reporting and producing the segment," reporting that had been flawed and careless because of the rush to air the show. "This decision on timing," the panel wrote, "was driven in significant part by competitive pressures, as other news organizations were working on stories related to President Bush's TexANG service" ("What the Panel Said," 2005, C7).

As a result of the panel's report, four people at CBS News, including Mary Mapes, the program's highly respected producer, were dismissed, and Dan Rather stepped down as anchor of *CBS Evening News*.

Personal credibility was a major issue in 2005 when *USA Today* reported that Armstrong Williams had been paid to make endorsements of the Bush administration's No Child Left Behind Act (NCLB) on his television show and in his nationally syndicated newspaper columns. As part of an undisclosed contract with the Department of Education, he had agreed to promote the administration's education initiative on a regular basis, for which he was paid $240,000 (Kirkpatrick, 2005). This potential conflict of interest led to dismissal and loss of credibility for Williams and raised ethical questions about the role of government departments in promoting agendas through public relations programs.

Gatekeeper functions can also involve complex ethical questions about federal control of broadcast licensing, the general freedom of the media to present information, censorship, and the responsibilities of the mass media to the public. (See Chapter 7 for a discussion of the Valerie Plame case). Everette Dennis of Columbia University's Gannett Center for Media Studies has compared the ubiquitous nature of the mass media to "a kind of central nervous system for the nation and, perhaps, the world" (1988, p. 349), noting the "sheer, raw power" of the media and their virtual monopoly on many kinds of information. He points out that because the media make choices concerning which issues, events, or people are more important than others, they establish an agenda of sorts. If they do not tell us what to think, they "do tell us what to think about as they narrow and refine the focus of public discussion" (p. 350).

The choices made by the media have profound effects on public information, and the press tends to take seriously its watchdog function. It's not often that a newspaper admits its shortcomings:

An interesting journalistic retake on the Iraq war coverage was offered by the *New York Times*, which subsequently admitted that it had not been sufficiently independent or critical in evaluating or reporting many claims about the rationale for the Iraq War provided by administration officials and the often anonymous sources that the administration fed to reporters to construct "independent" verification of its claims. (Bennett and Serrin, 2005, p. 171)

In arguing for "responsible communication" in the media, Redding (1988) emphasized that "responsible" does not necessarily mean "safe" or "compliant." "Silence itself can be irresponsible," and irresponsible communication sometimes involves a lack of verbal messages. Martin Luther King, Jr., once said, "Our lives begin to end the day we become silent about things that matter."

Other kinds of silence are also possible. In 1992 the Gulf War presented a critical incident for journalists in many ways (Zelizer, 1992). As we have seen in the discussion of embedded journalists, during wartime one ethical dilemma for the press has usually been "how to communicate events fairly and accurately, without revealing confidential military information" (p. 68). Yet several critics maintain that editors and members of the press were too accepting about the government's press pool system: MacArthur (1992) and others have argued that government figures about Iraqi troop strength were exaggerated as were accounts of the success and importance of "smart bombs" and that, in effect, the news media were reduced to "a state of subservience" by being limited to pool coverage.

Questions about patriotism can be extremely divisive—especially in time of war. For example, is it unpatriotic to mention war casualties? In 2004 a controversy arose over Ted Koppel's program "The Fallen" on ABC's *Nightline*. To honor U.S. soldiers killed in action in Iraq, Koppel read the names and showed the faces of over 700 soldiers. This was the format of an earlier program in which he had honored the victims of September 11 by reading their names. Sinclair Broadcasting, a conservative broadcaster, accused Koppel of having a political agenda. Sinclair Broadcasting, which has several stations that are ABC affiliates, refused to air the program, after which Senator John McCain, a former Vietnam POW, accused the broadcaster of being unpatriotic ("McCain Rebukes . . . ," 2004).

Later that fall, shortly before the 2004 presidential elections, Sinclair Broadcasting planned an hour-long program that would draw heavily on an anti-Kerry film critical of the senator's antiwar activities following his service in Vietnam. The planned program provoked so much criticism before it was aired that Sinclair's stock plummeted and sponsors threatened boycotts; Sinclair softened its approach but still presented segments from the film.

It's because of incidents such as this that many media critics have questioned whether broadcaster use of publicly owned airwaves for political and other purposes calls for reinstating the Fairness Doctrine—particularly at a time when each of the media conglomerates reaches such a vast audience. Repealed during the 1980s, the Fairness Doctrine required that stations "devote a reasonable time to discussions of serious public issues and [allow] equal time for opposing views to be heard" (Bagdikian, 2004, p. 139; Rendall, 2005).

Although members of the media have traditionally regarded themselves as having a watchdog function with respect to news and government, blackouts and press controls in time of war have a long history. The ethics of censorship are still being debated. For example, when the networks ran a videotape of Osama bin Laden following the September 11 attacks, the Bush administration stated its concern that broadcasting the tapes could be used to send coded messages to other terrorists around the world as well as to incite hatred through propaganda that might result in further violence. All five major television news networks agreed to edit future tapes: to limit both their length and the rhetoric that urged violence. They also agreed not to show the excerpts repeatedly. A network executive disagreed, saying, "The videos could also appear on the Internet. They'd get the message anyway" (Carter and Barringer, 2001, p. B2).

In November 2001, representatives from both Fox News Channel and CNN made statements in support of their policy of limiting or playing down coverage of civilian casualties in Afghanistan following U.S. airstrikes. According to FAIR (Fairness & Accuracy In Reporting), "The host of Fox News Channel's 'Special Report with Brit Hume' . . . wondered why journalists should bother covering civilian deaths at all" ("Fox: Civilian Casualties . . . ," 2001). While forms of self-censorship are common in the media, critics of Internet gossip columns such as The Drudge Report point out that many stories on the Net are partisan and unsubstantiated, often based on rumor.

In an essay on fairness in journalism, Carlin Romano (1998) recalled philosopher John Rawls's principle of the veil of ignorance: "Given the powerful hold that self-interest exerts on us, fairness can only emerge from a scenario in which no one knows how the rules chosen will affect his self-interest" (p. 91). As we saw in Chapter 7, the veil of ignorance requires that we make an ethical decision in which there will be unanimity of choice—fairness: No single person or group will be favored and what is moral will be fair to all.

Romano asks us to imagine that John Rawls has just been named the new managing editor of *The New York Times*. If journalists argue that the goal now is "to get the news, to get the truth, and to get it right" while many philosophers argue that "fairness is owed to people," how would Rawls reconcile fairness to the truth with fairness to the people? A philosopher such as Rawls, Romano reminds us, would recommend that to be fair-minded, journalists should be guided by this principle:

> In deciding how to act on a day-to-day basis, they must not only take into account the interests of everybody else involved in the news process, but act according to whatever rules they think will most fairly distribute benefits and burdens among those people. (1998, p. 94)

Message Flow

Hypodermic Needle Model

Early studies of mass communication suggested that the flow of information from source to receiver was always direct and immediate. According to this view, often referred to as the **hypodermic needle model,** *each audience member receives* *messages directly from the source of a given medium.* The implication is that if the "injection" is powerful enough, it will influence the receiver in some way. A further implication of such a theory is that the mass media can have an almost magical, and sometimes a potentially dangerous, effect on audiences (especially if the media are used to mount massive propaganda campaigns).

Opinion Leaders and the Two-Step Flow Model

In 1948 a study changed the direction of thinking about message flow in mass communication. The researchers analyzed the general impact of mass media on voting behavior and especially on the people who changed their voting intention during the course of the 1940 presidential campaign. One important finding was that broad coverage of the campaign by the mass media simply reinforced the initial preferences of the voters. Even more significant, for people who did change their minds about how they would vote, the major source of influence was *personal influence—the influence of other people.* In other words, even in mass communication contexts, the receiver had to be viewed within a larger social setting (Lazarsfeld et al., 1968). The findings of Lazarsfeld and others take this a step further, suggesting that within the groups to which we belong, certain people have a particularly strong influence. Such a person has been called an **opinion leader**—*"someone who, through day-to-day personal contacts and communication, influences someone else's opinions and decisions . . . fairly regularly"* (Wright, 1986, p. 89). And the decisions concern all kinds of matters, not just voting—for example, what type of car to buy, the most fashionable way to dress, the best school to attend, and so on.

Opinion leaders can come from any social, economic, or occupational level. Within different levels of society, there are different opinion leaders. They all tend to be better informed. They read more newspapers and magazines; they watch the coverage of political and social issues by the broadcast media. And in addition to receiving greater exposure to mass media, they tend to be influenced by them. This influence, in turn, is passed on to others in face-to-face communication.

It was this discovery that generated a **two-step flow model** of mass communication. According to this theory, on many occasions *information is passed from the various mass media to certain opinion leaders and from these leaders to other people within the population.* Some studies suggest that it is often more accurate to think in terms of a *multiple,* or *n-step, flow model,* since opinion leaders may also be consulting with others whom they consider opinion leaders. "An opinion leader can best be thought of as a group member playing a key communications role" (Katz and Lazarsfeld, 1964). See Simonson (2006) for a reevaluation of this theory.

The Active Audience

Implicit in the hypodermic needle model is the concept of a passive audience, a group of rather compliant people who, given a potent enough message, receive and absorb whatever was intended by the mass media. Such an audience could be manipulated into buying whatever product was given the most advertising nationwide or voting

When you watch or read an interview, is the person being interviewed answering the question? According to Bob Schieffer of *Face the Nation*, these days almost all the people interviewed by the press are "professional talkers." Very often we are watching politicians, public officials, and corporate executives who have been coached on how to speak with the press by "media trainers, who receive between $4,000 and $10,000 a day." The aim, writes the journalist Trudy Lieberman, is to control information in the interview (2004, p. 41). Among the techniques she identifies are these:

> **Taking control** *with comments such as "Let's move on to other matters. I think we've covered this" or "What I'd like to talk about . . . ," or "I want to turn to . . . ,"—all without fully answering the question posed by the host/journalist/ interviewer. "One of the first rules of media training is to seize control of the interview, and skillful guests can do it from the very beginning" (pp. 40–41).*

> **Dodging the question** *is another often used technique. "When guests don't want to answer, they use phrases such as: That's such a complex subject . . . Your question is not relevant . . . You bring up an interesting point, but before I discuss it, I want to talk about . . ." (p. 41)— after which the guest may go on to repeat the message he or she really wants to get across.*

> **Telling stories** *through anecdotes, personal observations, or recollections of personal experience all take up time and tend to head off a follow-up question by the interviewer, often because of interview time constraints. People are*

> *coached not to return to the original question, to offer context in place of an answer—in short, not to allow the interviewer a second chance to ask the question differently.*

> *By* **answering what's easy** *a guest can often navigate a two-part question, responding to the easier question at such length that the interviewer never gets around to follow-up on the second unanswered one. Thus the guest gets away with saying the question was answered.*

Journalists sometimes lose control of interviews when they can't pin down the guest or follow up sufficiently. We know from reading about interviewing (see pp. 364–366) that open questions facilitate talking—in public and mass communication they also empower people to say what they want to say. And of course open-ended questions can also be subverted by simple answers such as "Absolutely" or "Absolutely not."

Lieberman tells us that journalists also fear straining the guest's—and the audience's—tolerance of follow-up questions. There is a certain level of courtesy that interviewers wish to maintain so that important guests will be willing to return (Lieberman, 2004, pp. 40–43).

Set yourself the task of listening critically to radio, television, or cable interviews—and perhaps reading sections of them in the newspapers or online. Ask yourself how directly and completely the person being interviewed has answered the questions. How much information have you received? How skilled was the interviewer in posing the questions and following up on them?

for the candidate who had the most exposure on radio and television. It is an audience made up of people who do not interact with other human beings or accept group norms, people who are not, in fact, seen as living within a social context.

But today the receivers of mass communication are often conceptualized as an **active,** or obstinate audience, (Webster, 1998). You have already seen some reference to this concept in Chapter 5, in our discussion of critical listening. Schramm and Roberts (1971) characterize this view of the mass communication audience well:

> . . . an intensely active audience, seeking what it wants, rejecting far more content than it accepts, interacting both with the members of the groups it belongs to and with the media content it receives, and often testing the mass media message by talking it over with other persons or comparing it with other media content. (p. 191)

Perhaps the most obvious way an audience is active is in its selection of the mass communication to which it will be exposed. You buy the newspaper of your choice. You choose the programs you watch on television, and if you find something you don't like, you turn it off. In many ways, we can control this aspect of communication more readily than we can control face-to-face communication. It is much easier, for example, to turn off the television set if we dislike a program or even to walk out of a theater in the middle of a bad film than it is to conclude face-to-face communication so abruptly. Widespread use of the DVD player and VCR have had an impact not only on family interaction but on the mass media with a decline in movie-going and an increase in viewing movies at home. Today it offers a significant challenge to research in mass communication.

Selective Exposure

To put it another way, the person who watches a particular television program to the end or finishes reading a particular newspaper editorial tends to agree with the attitudes and opinions being presented. These are examples of **selective exposure,** *the tendency to choose communication that will confirm your own opinions, attitudes, or values.* This is a broad concept. In Chapter 8 we saw how it works on a one-to-one basis. We tend to like and seek out those whose beliefs, attitudes, and values are similar to our own, and to dislike and avoid people we perceive as different from us in these respects. Selective exposure is equally present in mass communication, where, for example, the vast majority of people who read the *National Review* are conservatives, and most of the people who read *The Nation* are liberals. See Chapter 10, pp. 340–341, for a discussion on how Internet use can reinforce the beliefs of like-minded people.

Selective Attention

In addition to the selective nature of our exposure to the mass media, our perception itself is selective. In Chapter 2 we spoke about **selective attention,** in which *the receiver processes certain of the available stimuli while filtering out others.* This screening process takes place in mass communication just as it does in other contexts of human communication. It takes place whether we are watching a situation comedy, a political debate, or a sports event.

Selective attention is well illustrated by examples from the political arena. In the televised Bush–Kerry debates, Bush supporters tended to see Bush as the "winner," and Kerry supporters tended to see Kerry as the "winner." As we assess the various outcomes of mass communication, we shall see other ways in which beliefs, attitudes, and values of the receiver influence his or her perceptions.

In discussing selective attention, we use the word "receiver" rather than "audience member" to emphasize the continuity between the receiving function in face-to-face communication and in mass communication. Message reception is an active process: It is behavior. Watching television is behavior, reading a best seller or a newspaper is behavior, and so is surfing the Net. When engaged in any of these activities, individual receivers are selecting and processing information.

At the other end of the communication cycle is a parallel selection process at work in the gatekeeping function. The flow of information from the mass communicator to the individual receiver sometimes involves opinion leaders and therefore face-to-face communication, so that at times there is a multiple-step flow rather than a direct flow of information. Similarly, the flow of feedback from the individual receiver to the mass communicator can also involve several steps. For example, parents concerned about violence in children's television programs may take group action through an organization such as Action for Children's Television, which in turn gives feedback not only to various television stations but to governmental agencies that regulate the broadcast media.

Another way of looking at the selectivity of receivers of mass communication is to examine how and when they use particular mass media as well as the basis for their choices.

Media Uses and Gratifications

The relationship between personal and mediated communication—including the new media technologies—continues to be an important area of research (Fallows, 2004; Flanagin and Metzger, 2001; Morrison and Krugman, 2001; Wanta, 1997). For example, recent research finds that among college students the five most often used sources of news were "hometown newspapers, comedy news, cable news, Internet news, and broadcast news" and that habit turns out to be the best predictor of news consumption (Diddi and LaRose, 2006, p. 193). Those who study the interface between mass and interpersonal communication stress that the media to which we attend are an integral part of our interpersonal world. One earlier comparison of how various media and interpersonal communication sources are used finds that "media and interpersonal sources serve similar functions . . . They are both used by people 'to connect (or sometimes disconnect) themselves . . . with different kinds of others (self, family, friends, nation, etc.)'" (Rubin et al., 1988, p. 607). Moreover, Rubin and Rubin (1985) argue that mass media use is goal directed—that is, people make choices about what media they will use for particular reasons.

Although computer-mediated communication has sometimes been said to decrease our social interactions, many researchers disagree. For example, one study comparing the social role of television and computers in the home found that in homes with more advanced media technology, television is used for entertainment whereas the computer and related technologies are used for entertainment and information as well as their communication capacities. In fact, people who were high-technology users regarded their computer as a "lifeline" (Morrison and Krugman, 2001, p. 153).

Other studies by UCLA's Center for the Digital Future (now part of USC's Annenberg School; *www.digitalcenter.org*) and Stanford University (*www.stanford.edu/group/siqss*) focus specifically on how people use the Internet. Regardless of the media chosen, the researchers find the same communication needs served including information, learning, leisure, solving problems, social bonding, maintaining relationships, and so on. There has been increasing use of e-mail and other forms of computer-mediated communication for social purposes. And the Internet, rather than television, is increasingly used as a source of information. Others suggest that in addition to extending our capabilities in several ways, ultimately the new technologies are "folded in with more traditional media" and are used in the same ways (Flanagin and Metzger, 2001, p. 175).

At this point in our chapter, we turn to examine some of the effects and outcomes of mass communication. We hope first to illustrate more concretely the concepts we have been talking about and, second, to evaluate some of the various effects and outcomes of mass communication, particularly as they relate to less formal communication contexts.

SOME EFFECTS AND OUTCOMES

Most closely related to the concept of message flow is the study of how the mass media disseminate information.

The Diffusion of Information

Through the mass media we learn about innovations, discoveries, accidents, assassinations, revolutions, and natural disasters. How soon after these events we hear about them and what the sources of our information were are questions that preoccupy those interested in the **diffusion of information**—that is, *how quickly news or information travels and the communication channels through which it spreads to a community of receivers.*

Everett Rogers defines diffusion as "the process by which an innovation is communicated through certain channels over time among the members of a social system" (1995, p. 5). Although news events are ideas, their diffusion is similar to that of technological innovations (p. 75). "Diffusion" as we use it here refers to the spread of all kinds of information—not just news that generates shock or excitement. Thus, news of a flu immunization program or a citywide transportation strike is usually diffused to the public through several media.

After the attacks of September 11, 2001, the diffusion of information was virtually instantaneous. The collapse of the Twin Towers was seen by many who had already been watching the burning towers on television. A study by the Pew Research Center finds that while 79 percent of all Americans got more of their news information from television, others turned to the radio (7 percent) and newspapers (7 percent), with less to the telephone (2 percent) and Internet (2 percent). In the days right after September 11, Internet use declined somewhat, but those who were online used it mainly to supplement other news sources and to e-mail family. Table 15.1 outlines the findings. For more on this report, go to *www.pewinternet .org/ppf/r/45/report-display.asp.*

The most thoroughgoing examination of news diffusion focused on another unanticipated news event of major proportions: the assassination of President John F. Kennedy on November 22, 1963. The diffusion of news was rapid, and it was complete. One researcher writes, "The murder of President Kennedy concentrated all channels of communication—both mass media and person to person—on a single incident at the same time" (Greenberg, 1965, p. 89).

This single focus of all communication channels is certainly not the case for the diffusion of all public information. In most instances, 90 percent of those who are aware of a given news event first learn about it through the mass media. In the

---

Table 15.1 *Mass Media and Internet Use Right After the Attacks of September 11, 2001*

Even the most wired Americans were wedded to the television and the telephone after the attacks.

	All Americans	The Heaviest Internet Users*
Main source of information		
Television	79%	80%
Radio	7	6
Newspaper	7	7
Internet	2	6
Talking with others	2	1
Communication activities: The phone was also used more by Internet users than by the general population.		
Phone family member about attack	63%	75%
E-mail family member		38
Phone friend about attack	55	70
E-mail friend		47

*The heaviest Internet users are those who have more than three years experience online and who log on from home every day. They make up about 20 percent of all Internet users and about 11 percent of the whole U.S. population.
Source: "How Americans Used the Internet After the Terror Attack," by Lee Rainie, September 15, 2001, Pew Internet & American Life Project, *www.pewinternet.org.*

past radio and television have predominated as the first sources of such information, with newspapers usually being the first source for less significant events.

There is some evidence that the way in which information will be disseminated depends on the importance of that information. Person-to-person communication will have a major role in disseminating information about lesser-known events. For news events of intermediate levels of importance, however, the mass media will be the most pervasive first source of information.

It is important to think of the roles of face-to-face and mass communication as complementary rather than mutually exclusive. At times, meeting a friend who tells you about a recent news event prompts you to turn to one of the mass media for further information. Or something you learned from the mass media prompts a discussion with someone who then adds to your knowledge of the event by mentioning details that were not part of the magazine article you read or the televised news summary you heard. And then there are times when we experience mass communication in the company of others (e.g., family members, friends, co-workers), so that there is a constant interplay between what is being conveyed through the mass media and the awareness of personal responses to those communicative stimuli.

We have been speaking essentially about message flow and the spread of information through a community of receivers. But as you know from our discussion of persuasion in Chapter 13, some message senders have as their primary intention not information gain but attitude influence, and even messages intended primarily to inform often make persuasive appeals. Thus, once a message has been received, its persuasive impact must be evaluated.

Attitude Influence

Because politicians believe that attitudes can be influenced through the media the sums spent on political advertising grow higher with each election: "The 2004 U.S. presidential election was a close, hard-fought, negative election campaign that cost candidates and special interest groups more than one billion dollars, much of it spent in efforts by candidates to get their message through the media to the voters" (Drew and Weaver, 2006, p. 25).

Did the media matter in the 2004 presidential election? Drew and Weaver have analyzed data from the last four elections and report a significant correlation between voting intentions and attention to television news, televised debates, and the Internet. (Attention given to radio news was also of some importance.)

According to recent surveys by the Pew Research Center and other groups, the audience for online politics continues to grow. The Internet has emerged as one of the major sources of news about political campaigns: "Overall, 41% of voters say they got at least some of their news about the 2004 election online. Further, 21% relied on the Internet for most of their election news, nearly double the number in 2000 (11%)" (*www.people-press.org*).

There was also increased interest in news of the presidential election among young voters. In 2004 a higher percentage registered to vote and young voters also felt prior to the election that the debates would be important to them in choosing a candidate (*www.people-press.org/commentary*). (For other sources of news about the presidential election, see Table 15.2.)

It was Howard Dean, an early Democratic candidate for president in 2004, who first used the Internet so successfully to mount a grassroots movement and gain significant contributions for his campaign (only to be undone by a highly emotional speech). Regaining credibility, he was elected Chairman of the National Democratic Committee in 2005.

Early in 2007 hopefuls for the 2008 presidential election began using the Internet to announce their candidacy and to raise funds. The first was Senator Barack Obama, who posted a video on his Web site, quickly followed by Senator Hillary Rodham Clinton and others. According to a recent study—*Election 2006 Online*—by the Pew Internet & American Life Project, "The number of Americans using the Internet as their main source of political news doubled since the last midterm election" (Rainie and Horrigan, p. 2):

THE AMERICAN NEWS MEDIASCAPE IS IN FLUX.

The news market has been fracturing for more than a decade and news audiences have become increasingly politicized as trust in the mainstream media has declined and public perceptions of the credibility of mainstream news sources has fallen. Over this period the Internet is playing an ever-more-important role in the news diet of Americans. A decade ago, just one-in-fifty Americans got the news with some regularity from what was then a brand new source—the Internet. Today, nearly one-in-three regularly gets news online. (pp. 3–4)

Table 15.2 summarizes the results of the Pew study.

Table 15.2 *The Internet and Campaign 2006: Summary of Findings at a Glance*
• The number of Americans using the Internet as their main source of political news doubled since the last mid-term election.
• 31% of Americans used the Internet during the 2006 campaign to get political news and information and discuss the race through e-mail. We call them campaign Internet users.
• Relatively young broadband users say the Internet is a more important political news source than newspapers.
• A new online political elite is emerging as 23 percent of campaign Internet users became online political activists.
• While mainstream news sources still dominate the online news and information gathering by campaign Internet users, a majority of them now get political material from blogs, comedy sites, government Web sites, candidate sites, or alternative sites.
• While most campaign Internet users say convenience is a major reason they use the Internet, more than half cite the Internet's breadth of information and perspectives as a major reason for their online activity.
• Republicans and Democrats were equally likely to rely on the Internet—but there were partisan trends in usage of other political news sources.

Source: Adapted from Election 2006 Online, by Lee Rainie and John Horrigan. Washington, DC: Pew Internet & American Life Project and Pew Research Center for The People & The Press (January 17, 2007), p. vi. *www.pewinternet.org/pdfs/PIP_Politics_2006.pdf.*

Despite the growing influence of the Internet, however, the Pew study affirms the importance of television:

TELEVISION STILL WINS THE POLITICAL NEWS HORSERACE—BY A WIDE MARGIN.

As it has been said for generations, television remains ahead of other media in 2006 as a news source. . . . When it comes [to] the political news, television's lead is even more pronounced. Fully 69% of all Americans said they went to the television for most of their news about the campaign—twice the proportion of those who cited newspapers (34%), four times the proportion who singled out radio (17%) and the Internet (15%). (Rainie and Horrigan, 2006, p. 7)

One of the ways in which attitude influence has been studied is through the history of televised presidential debates. How presidential debates are presented on television has drawn much attention. One recent study focused on the effects of split-screen coverage on our evaluation of a presidential debate (Scheufele et al., 2007). Before the 2004 Bush–Kerry debates, a "Memorandum of Understanding," agreed on by both candidates, stipulated that both broadcast and cable television networks could show the candidates only while they were speaking and could not use reaction shots or split-screen shots. But many stations ignored that agreement, arguing that the technique would not make a difference. The study concluded that despite "postdebate coverage, discussing the potential damaging impact of George W. Bush's supposed expressions of anger, frustration, and arrogance" (p. 4), "the predominant mode of coverage for this debate was much kinder to Bush than it was to Kerry" (p. 20).

Roughly 70 million out of the 107 million adults in the United States either watched or listened to the first of four debates between John Kennedy and Richard Nixon in 1960. Moreover, many who did not see or hear the debates through the broadcast media soon read about them in the newspapers. But the consensus of opinion is that exposure to the Kennedy–Nixon debates through the mass media had little effect on changing initial voting intentions. As many studies have noted, when viewers were asked about who had "won," Kennedy supporters tended to see Kennedy as the winner of the debates, while Nixon supporters, for the most part, saw Nixon as the winner. We have seen more recent examples of this effect in the 1996 debates between Bill Clinton and Robert Dole, the 2000 debates between George W. Bush and Al Gore, and the 2004 debates between Bush and John Kerry.

Other studies of presidential debates and elections (Wayne, 1992, 1996), attitude influence, and voting behavior suggest that, in addition to reinforcing previous attitudes, debates can sometimes influence attitudes when the voters are independent, less partisan, or undecided—and in some cases change perceptions. As a result of watching the debates, some people learn more about the issues, but they also form impressions of the candidates through the debaters' nonverbal cues. In the first presidential debate of the 2000 campaign, Al Gore's sighs and eye-rolling made him look arrogant and impatient. The second debate was in the format preferred by George W. Bush: The two men were seated at a table and Bush seemed more confident and at ease. In 1992 during the second presidential debate between Bill Clinton, George Bush, and Ross Perot, newspapers were quick to pick up on a moment when Bush looked at his watch while one of the other candidates was speaking. This was variously interpreted in the press; some read the gesture as discomfort, others

When Ira Glass of National Public Radio was interviewed about his new television show *This American Life,* he was asked if he wrote or read fiction. "No. No. No. No," he joked. "I don't know how to read. I get all my news from Jon Stewart every day" (Solomon, 2007, p. 15). John Stewart's *Daily Show* has over 1.2 million viewers.

Communication and political science scholar Robert Entman (2006) cites a Pew survey: For 28 percent of those studied, late-night TV programs such as those of Jay Leno and David Letterman were a source of news about the 2004 presidential campaign. For those under age 30, late-night TV programs were twice as important as they were for older Americans. "Although this appears troubling," writes Entman, "it is worth noting that politically oriented comedians and satirists have been with us for centuries":

> Mark Twain, Will Rogers, even Benjamin Franklin are some of the rather distinguished progenitors of today's Bill Maher and Jon Stewart. . . . in some cases, in part because such commentators are not bound by news conventions (timeliness, balance) that can turn journalists into tools of spin doctors and public relations operatives, they have the ability to speak truths that elude the front page or the network news. (Entman, 2006, pp. 57–58)

Which media sources do you turn to for information about politics and news? Which do you feel are the most reliable?

as boredom. From facial expression, tone of voice, posture, hand movements, and other cues, viewers also tend to form stronger personality impressions of the candidates. But as is true in other communication contexts, increased understanding does not ensure persuasion or attitude influence.

It seems, then, that exposure to other points of view through the mass media often serves simply to strengthen or reinforce the receiver's initial attitudes and opinions. Many studies of voting behavior confirm this tendency. And although there are far more sophisticated formats and technologies possible for coverage of current presidential debates, since the election of 1964 the number of voters has decreased. Studies have shown that in the past people tended to seek political information from newspapers, but the declining number of newspaper readers may be the reason for declining voter turnout (see Box 15.3).

When do presidential debates matter; when do they influence attitudes? According to the Pew Research Center, from an historical standpoint, the debates have been most influential when the presidential race is close or when there are unresolved issues concerning the personal character of either or both of the candidates.

Often we listen and watch the debates through a filter—that of the press, which has the ability to frame what we see. Communication scholars Kathleen Hall Jamieson and Paul Waldman (2003) point out that:

- Opinion about debates is often shaped more by the post-debate interpretation than by the exchanges between the candidates.
- The power of the press's interpretation of debates takes on greater importance as audiences of debates decline.

- Debate coverage presents in miniature the press's approach to the campaign and candidates. (pp. 30–31)

During the presidential election of 2000, television analysts started calling the election prematurely in Gore's favor, which resulted in a night of confusion and a loss of credibility for the networks. According to a poll by CNN, 79 percent of Americans felt the networks had not acted in a responsible way—though that night there were the most viewers since the Nielsen ratings began in the 1960 Kennedy–Nixon race (Hickey, 2001b, p. 35).

One study (Cappella and Jamieson, 1997) suggests that the way the mass media cover political news and various issues has contributed, even activated, a "spiral of cynicism" among voters. The deciding factors are the emphasis on politics as a game and the coverage given to discussion of various political strategies. Cynicism, the authors suggest, is contagious, and they discuss ways to break this spiral. Another well-known study by Kathleen Hall Jamieson (1996) traces the media campaigns of many American presidents throughout history: her work reveals that political advertising—despite its sometimes questionable practices—plays an important role in "packaging" presidential candidates.

Issues of Importance and How We Think About Them

Agenda Setting

Look at the front page of your newspaper over several days or the lead stories on the television news night after night and you stand to learn a great deal about mass media agendas. There might be a string of stories about policy making and the Iraq war, or the firing of district attorneys by the Department of Justice, or a series of investigative articles about global warming or corporate corruption. An *agenda* in the mass media, explains communication scholar Maxwell McCombs, is "strictly a descriptive term for a prioritized list of items, the major topics found in newspapers, televisions news programs, and other mass media messages" (2005, p. 156).

Almost 40 years ago McCombs and his colleague Donald Shaw (1972) developed a highly influential theory on the agenda-setting function of the press. According to **agenda-setting theory**, which has generated much research, *the press tells us what to think about by establishing the relative importance of certain issues*. And through framing, the press can also tell us *how* we should think about them.

Agenda setting works largely through "repetition of the major issues in the news day after day." If, for example, the press chooses to emphasize an ethical issue, the public is given more information on it and given that coverage more frequently. When the press ignores or avoids an issue, we, the public, receive little or no information about it. So the potential for influencing our attitudes is there just by raising the level of our consciousness.

How can you figure out what a newspaper's agenda is? In addition to identifying which issues the paper singles out, you can learn a lot from other cues. For example, ask yourself these questions:

- How long are the articles?
- How large are the headlines?
- What page numbers are the stories covered on? Is the story on the front page, in the middle of the paper, or at the end?
- Is the article at the top of the page or possibly at the very bottom? (Adapted from McCombs, 2005, p. 156)

McCombs points out that there are comparable cues and patterns in other mass media including television news. He also discusses the relative influence of newspapers versus television:

> For agenda-setting effects, a rough rule of thumb is that about half the time, there is no difference in the influence of newspapers and television. For the other half of the time, newspapers have greater influence about twice as often as television. There are ready explanations for this contradiction of the conventional wisdom about the power of television. First, television news is analogous to the opening pages of the newspapers, which means that newspaper readers frequently have a longer time to learn the emerging issue agenda. Second, citizens in many countries are aware that television is under a significant degree of influence from the government or a dominant political party. (McCombs, 2006, p. 160)

But who, it's often asked, sets the agenda for the agenda setters? We know that there is a public agenda, that the government has a policy agenda, and that other groups have agendas as well. For example, communication scholar Em Griffin observes:

> Current thinking on news selection focuses on the crucial role of public relations professionals working for government agencies, corporations, and interest groups. Even prestigious newspapers with large investigative staffs such as the *Washington Post* and the *New York Times* get over half of what they print straight from press releases and press conferences. (Griffin, 2006, pp. 399–400)

Awareness of agenda-setting efforts can make you a more critical viewer of the mass media. And as we'll see, the concept of framing is closely linked with agenda setting.

Framing in the Media

What we perceive is colored, of course, by our own experience and biases—our own selective attention. But in mass communication our perceptions and attitudes are also influenced by how the information we receive—news stories are a good example—is ordered, framed by the media. Framing is also an aspect of politics. One definition of **framing** is *"choosing a broad organizing theme for selecting, emphasizing, and linking the elements of a story"* (Bennett, 2005, p. 37). In a classic analysis, communication scholar Robert Entman explains that frames function in four ways. They

- *Define problems*—determine what a causal agent is doing with what costs and benefits, usually measured in terms of common cultural values.

- *Diagnose causes*—identify the forces creating the problem.
- *Make moral judgments*—evaluate causal agents and their effects.
- *Suggest remedies*—offer and justify treatments for the problems and predict their likely effects. (1993, p. 52)

Above all, a frame is a narrative, a way of telling a story from a particular point of view. Like the frame of a picture, then, a frame of a story not only encloses but also leaves some things out:

> Frames select and call attention to particular aspects of the reality described, which logically means that frames simultaneously direct attention from other aspects. Most frames are defined by what they omit as well as include. (p. 55)

In a recent study on framing and the limits of press independence, scholars analyzed the coverage of the Abu Ghraib prison scandal by *The Washington Post*, the CBS Evening News, and a range of national newspapers (Bennett et al., 2006). The story was framed as an isolated instance of prisoner abuse but a counterframe might have presented Abu Ghraib as reflecting a policy of torture:

> Despite available evidence and sources to support a counterframing of the Abu Graib prison story in terms of a policy of torture, the leading national news organizations did not produce a frame that strongly challenged the administration's claim that Abu Ghraib was an isolated case of appalling abuse perpetrated by low-level soldiers. (p. 467)

Further, Bennett and his colleagues argue, "'torture policy' was a counterframe worthy of public discussion, . . . a frame supported by evidence and sources available to mainstream journalists" (p. 471).

When reading a news story, or comparing two accounts, it's important to read critically, asking yourself what information might be missing, what might have been left out.

Choice of language also contributes significantly to framing. Political leaders and reporters frame their arguments and statements in many ways. In January 2007, for example, a dispute arose when Secretary of State Condoleezza Rice appeared before the Senate Foreign Relations Committee. Questioning her about President Bush's plan to increase the number of new troops sent to Iraq by approximately 22,000, members of the committee referred to the increase as an "escalation." Rice countered that it was not, but rather an "augmentation"—a disagreement that was not resolved ("Senate Opposition to Bush Plan . . . ," 2007).

Language often frames debates in political campaigns. For example:

- Tax cuts or tax relief?
- Religious or faith-based?
- Death penalty or execution?

- Estate tax or death tax?
- Civilian deaths or collateral damage? (Jamieson and Waldman, 2003, p. xiv)

Or notice how adding "gate" to the end of a word in a news story—especially in a headline—carries with it, whether legitimate or not, the suggestion of scandal. And the press might mention an accusation, but not comment on its later being discounted. "It is important," advises one scholar, "to detect and discard loaded descriptions and buzz words. Terms like *leftist, right-winger, big government, freedom,* and even *well-placed* or *informed sources* can set up information for very selective interpretations" (Bennett, 2005, p. 244). Attention to language is another essential part of critically viewing the media.

Social Learning through Role Models

In learning new behaviors, it is not always necessary for you to perform behaviors and be reinforced; you also learn new responses simply by observing them in others. This process is known as *modeling,* or *imitation.* Modeling goes on throughout one's lifetime but is especially important during childhood (see also p. 260 for information on family and gender). Today, movies, books, and radio and television programs set before children a truly bewildering number of models for behavior. It is in part through such sources that children acquire information about the world and develop conceptions about their future roles.

Through the mass media, children build up some ideas about various occupations and the status and material gain accorded people on the basis of their jobs. For example, 7 out of every 10 television dramas seen on prime time are about science and technology, so that each week the average viewer sees one or two scientists and 11 doctors. The mass media make available a number of other role models. One study notes how the media tend to describe women in politics in domestic terms— for example, during Hillary Rodham Clinton's senatorial campaign, framing her in terms of being more cooperative and caring as well as more willing to collaborate with others on legislation. These are traits stereotypically associated with women (Vavrus, 2002).

In the 1960s, the occupational roles portrayed on television programs gave the viewer an unrealistic representation of the lives of both males and females. For the most part, it was men who held the lucrative and more interesting jobs, and beyond that the proportion of working men to working women was in no way an accurate reflection of the status quo. From the 1950s through the 1970s male characters outnumbered female characters by three to one; in action-adventure shows there was a five to one ratio (U.S. Department of Health and Human Services, 1982, p. 54). Between 64 and 70 percent of the women characters portrayed on television did not hold jobs, and over 90 percent of the prestigious jobs represented were held by male characters. What's more, women were overrepresented as victims, with heroic roles usually being assigned to men (U.S. Department of Health and Human Services, 1982, p. 54).

How far have the media come from that image? A recent content analysis of newspapers shows that a reporter's gender influences source selection in news stories: "male sources and subjects received more mentions and were placed more prominently in the stories" except when female reporters had a byline (Armstrong, 2004, p. 139). One important study (Signorelli and Kahlenberg, 2001) examines how television portrayed occupations and the world of work during the 1990s. Researchers found that despite a more equal representation of men and women in the professions, there was job stereotyping of married women. Women who had authority and expertise in their work were often portrayed as single, always struggling for personal happiness and fulfillment. Despite the high number of married women who are employed, on television married women are more likely to be portrayed as not working or having lower status and lower paying jobs. In short, "married women are still portrayed with reduced options, for they can rarely successfully combine marriage and employment" (p. 20). The unspoken message for young viewers is that you can't have it all.

Another interesting research question is how women are portrayed using computer technology. White and Kinnick (2000) found that in television commercials, female computer users are more likely to be seen in clerical jobs and are rarely shown playing computer games or surfing the Net. "Males are the only ones shown embracing the technology as 'fun'" (p. 407), mastering it, so to speak. There are no role models here for women as computer experts.

In a recent study Hylmö found that films targeted to teenage girls downplayed the importance of careers for young women. "Instead, they are asked to continue to look toward their fathers and boyfriends for protection, guidance, and financial support" (2006, p. 167). At the University of Delaware a study by Signorelli examined gender roles portrayed in media used by teenage girls (Smith, 1997). On the positive side, in films and on television, women and girls were portrayed as intelligent and often were seen as good problem solvers. Yet, on television, only 28 percent of women were portrayed as working. And in films as well as television, women and girls were far more preoccupied than males with romance and with their appearance.

Although there have been some steps forward—for example, the Web site and TV network for women that was started by Oxygen Media in 2000—Kim Walsh-Childers observes that the images of women in the mainstream media are still as sex partners: "Two types of stereotypes seem to exist, one primarily focused on how sexy women look and the other on what might be called sexual response" (2003, p. 151).

Gender-role stereotyping for girls exists in many forms and comes from many sources, not only the mass media. Yet current studies and theories express the hope that exposure to role models provided by the media, particularly television, can help to change this—for example, by using women scientists as role models. And the recommendation is that this be done early on.

On television, higher achieving women are noticeable—to a great degree because there are not that many of them. For example, on programs such as *CSI: Miami* and *Law and Order* women are sometimes portrayed as forensic specialists, assistant district attorneys, or lawyers. And on *The West Wing,* as we've noted, in a time of crisis the press secretary, C. J. Gregg, was promoted to chief of staff; there was also one woman military commander in the Situation Room, and the president's wife was a doctor, but didn't seem to practice.

As for films, women have long held a place in American movies, and there have been some serious, even profound characterizations of women. Yet in many of today's films, women have stereotypically been portrayed as sex objects, vamps, nurturant mothers, and "airheads." In 1991 Susan Sarandon and Geena Davis starred in *Thelma and Louise*, once described as a perverse buddy movie. This film made sparks fly. One critic believes that the stereotyping of women exists because films are "tailored to the appetites of young men . . . Sixty years ago no one needed hope; the screens teemed with movies about women. Strong women, saintly or desperate ones, but always smart. . . . They had sexual equality, emotional superiority" (Corliss, 1996, p. 56).

Looking at how women were viewed during the 1990s, Corliss notes only "a handful of strong female roles"; he cites such films as *The First Wives' Club, Waiting to Exhale, Clueless, Dangerous Minds, Sense and Sensibility,* and *Pocahontas.* More recent additions would include Hilary Swank in *Million Dollar Baby*, Maggie Cheung in *Hero*, Helen Mirren in *Elizabeth*, Keira Knightley in *Pride and Prejudice*, and Jennifer Hudson in *Dreamgirls*. Still, women also want to be perceived not only as strong and attractive but as effective, successful, and realistically represented in the workforce.

Social Learning and Media Violence

According to a recent media study, although network ratings are down, children are watching more television than ever, particularly on cable networks. The average television set is on more than seven hours each day, and there are now TV sets in 98 percent of all American homes. Today children are exposed to television virtually from birth. Even the average six-month-old can be found positioned before the set for almost an hour and a half each day. From ages 2 to 11, children watch television an average of three to four hours a day.

From the middle school years onward, we see an increase in the use of print media, and during adolescence a definite increase in the use of radio. But the impact of television is primary (Pecora et al., 2006). For example, one study (Van der Molen et al., 2000) finds that for children the main source of information about news is television and that they recall television news better than they do print news. For the first 10 years of their lives, television is the dominant mass medium to which American children are exposed. It is not surprising, therefore, that much of the attention given to possible effects of media violence on children should center on television.

Cultivation Theory and the Mean World Syndrome

For over 30 years the late George Gerbner, who was Dean Emeritus of the Annenberg School for Communication at the University of Pennsylvania, studied the effects of

In their efforts to persuade us and to influence our attitudes and our actions, both advertising and public relations make use of mass communication. Yet the functions of these industries are different, although many of the largest public relations firms maintain a connection with advertising agencies.

Advertising has been defined as "any form of nonpersonal presentation and promotion of ideas, goods, and services usually paid for by an identified sponsor" (Dominick, 2007, p. 321).

Although there are thousands of advertising agencies throughout the country, the concentration of agencies is in large cities such as New York. These agencies plan ad campaigns; they do copywriting and create videos, along with graphics; and they also place their work with various media.

When we see advertising, we, the audience, know the source and can usually assume that what we're seeing has been paid for. And sometimes that knowledge helps us evaluate the credibility of the message—whether the advertising is about a new kind of Coca-Cola, a sports utility vehicle, a breakfast cereal, a mutual fund, or a political candidate. If we don't like what we see or hear, presumably we can also provide feedback to that source. For example, women's organizations such as NOW have objected to television spots and magazine ads that they found offensive to women; objections that Camel's cigarette advertising encouraged smoking among young people led to several advertising changes. On the other hand, it's far more difficult to police the presentation or claims of advertising appearing on the Web.

In some ways describing the functions of public relations is more complex—in part because instead of marketing or selling directly, public relations serves a management function. It is dealing, literally, with relations with the public—although sometimes that public may

be a selected group of people who are opinion makers, leaders in a field, for a given industry or organization. (And at times a public relations firm is engaged by an individual—e.g., a political candidate or a film star.)

Public relations firms plan strategies for disseminating information about a company (or an individual or organization) to a particular audience, they articulate an organization's goals, they increase an organization's visibility and highlight company expertise and accomplishments. One of their major concerns is public image.

Suppose a technology company came to a public relations firm. The firm may initiate surveys; create lists of influential media for their clients; write press releases and backgrounders (informational writing about a client's organization); plan meetings and other events that will bring information to targeted segments of the public.

But unlike the ads we see, the source of work by public relations firms may be unknown to us. For example, we may read an article in a newspaper or magazine or see someone interviewed on television and not be aware that public relations may have led to the representation or discussion of what we see. In addition, the demand for 24-hour coverage has increased the reliance of the media on public relations press release as "news."

Another pivotal aspect of public relations is crisis management—suppose, for example, that your pharmaceutical company puts out a drug that has to be withdrawn from the market because of toxic side effects. Or suppose that the head of a public organization makes a speech that is offensive to members of an ethnic group. Whether it's setting the record straight or "damage control," the shaping and dissemination of this kind of information is often handled by a public relations firm.

Continued

The U.S. Department of Labor projects that jobs for advertising, marketing, and public relations managers will increase faster than the average for all occupations through 2014 (2006, p. 29). The department expects keen competition for jobs as advertising, marketing, promotions, and public relations managers. Earnings can be high and the positions may involve considerable travel. "College graduates with related experience, a high level of creativity, and strong communication skills should have the best job opportunities. In particular, employers will seek those who have the computer skills to conduct advertising, marketing, promotions, public relations, and sales activities on the Internet" (p. 29).

You can learn more about careers in advertising at *www.aaaa.org* and *www.aaf.org*. For more information about careers in public relations, log onto *www.prsa.org*.

television on our society. **Cultivation theory,** which evolved out of his work, views television as our major storyteller:

> . . . telling most of the stories to most of the people, both in the United States and internationally . . . *television cultivates, like parents, peers, the clergy, and teachers, through its stories, common world views, common values, and common perspectives on how men and women should think, behave, and act.* (Signorelli and Kahlenberg, 2001, p. 4, italics added; Gerbner et al., 1994)

According to cultivation theory, the greater the amount of television you watch, the more your worldview comes to accord with the beliefs, values, and attitudes you see on the screen. Thus people with heavy viewing habits come to share the mainstream views that television presents.

Through the Cultural Indicators Project, Gerbner and other researchers have monitored prime time television dramas and children's Saturday-morning cartoons. They found an average of 5 violent scenes an hour on prime time and over 20 per hour on Saturday cartoons. Researchers also found that people with heavy viewing habits have a disproportionate fear of becoming crime victims. They perceive their chances of risk as much higher than they actually are. They are also more mistrustful of other people and think it best to protect themselves by acting defensively. Gerbner called *this set of attitudes that the world is a relatively mean and dangerous place* the **mean world syndrome.** Gerbner's project is not about how watching television results in violent behavior; it is about the altered perceptions of the world—a mistrustful view that he believed affects your attitudes toward others, quality of life, and even your political views (Gerbner et al., 1994). Gerbner believed that television violence is driven by global marketing, not popularity.

Do you think you are less influenced by media messages than other people are? If so, you are not alone. Research over more than 20 years confirms the existence of a **third-person effect**—that is, *we perceive others as more influenced by media content than we are ourselves.* This is true whether it's rap music, pornography, television drama, or political advertising. This perception is also true of attitudes toward televised violence and, to some degree, the mean world syndrome. People were much less willing to admit that viewing violence affected their own aggressive tendencies, and "the more people liked violent television, the less effect they saw on themselves relative to others for mean world perception" (Hoffner et al., 2001, p. 294).

Aggression and Televised Violence

For many years researchers argued over whether viewing violence on television teaches children to be more aggressive, and some identified media violence as a cause of juvenile delinquency. Others countered that watching televised violence has no effects or that it has cathartic value for viewers, working as a kind of escape valve for violent emotion. Today there is no evidence that viewing violence has any cathartic effects.

On the contrary, we now have an extensive body of research on media violence. In 1982, the National Institute of Mental Health completed a two-volume report, *Television and Behavior,* which explored a broad spectrum of issues and summarized the massive research of earlier studies. Concerning violence and aggression, the report concluded: "Violence on television does lead to aggressive behavior by children and teenagers who watch the programs. Not all children become aggressive, of course, but the correlations between violence and aggression are positive" (U.S. Department of Health and Human Services, 1982, p. 6).

According to the report, children who watch television may learn to accept violent behavior as normal. And in their face-to-face encounters, children imitate the aggressive models they see on television. This relationship between televised violence and aggressive behavior exists in both boys and girls and extends from preschoolers to older adolescents.

The American Psychological Association's Commission on Youth and Violence (Cited in Bok, 1998) identifies four effects of media violence: *greater aggression, fear, desensitization,* and *appetite for violence.* One member of the commission has referred to these effects as "the aggressor effect, the victim effect, the bystander effect, and the appetite effect":

> [H]igher levels of viewing violence on television are correlated with increased acceptance of aggressive attitudes and increased aggressive behavior . . .

- Viewing violence increases fear of becoming a victim of violence, with a resultant increase in self-protective behaviors and increased mistrust of others;
- Viewing violence increases desensitization to violence, resulting in calloused attitudes toward violence directed at others and a decreased likelihood to take action on behalf of the victim when violence occurs (behavioral apathy); and

- Viewing violence increases viewers' appetites for becoming involved with violence or exposing themselves to violence. (Cited in Bok, 1998, pp. 57–58)

The *National Television Violence Study* is a research project that was conducted at the universities of California, North Carolina, Texas, and Wisconsin (1997, 1998). Content analysis shows, for example, that out of every four violent acts represented on television, only one is punished—and one is actually rewarded. And of films shown on television about 90 percent contain violence. In general, cable programming, including films, tends to have more violence than broadcast network programming. But even 38 percent of programming such as news contains violent events or actions.

Recent research also offers evidence that young people with aggressive tendencies choose media content (including on the Internet) that is violent. Slater and others (2003) propose the theory that exposure to media violence then leads to a downward spiral of further aggression.

Of course, reports of violent events such as the Columbine shootings are not confined to television. In 1998, within the space of a few months, national newspapers gave special prominence to several incidents of school shootings by teenagers. Nigel Wade, editor-in-chief of the *Chicago Sun-Times,* made a conscious decision that the story of the Springfield, Oregon, school shootings should not be placed on the front page—so he ran the complete story, along with photos, on pages 2 and 3. Wade's long experience as a newspaperman had convinced him that the news teenagers see and read can be a powerful influence. With this way of presenting the news, Wade attempted to balance the newspaper's responsibility to society as a whole against its responsibility to present the news fully and accurately (p. A15).

In 2007, following the Virginia Tech shootings several national news programs aired a 10-minute video from the shooter along with his digital photographs and text. This decision raised great debate over the ethics of such graphic coverage.

Ours is by any standards a violent age, and we cannot single out the mass media as the source of all our social ills. We must remember, too, that mass communication is in essence a human creation and that some of its most important effects are indirect and cumulative.

IMPLICATIONS OF THE NEW COMMUNICATION TECHNOLOGIES

We take for granted cell phones, personal computers, fax machines, e-mail, and satellites. Electronic document interchange has revolutionized business communications by transferring information from one computer to another over telephone lines. And some experts believe that the "mediated home" will soon herald a new information age with the widespread use of interactive television. Through interactive television and other technologies, specialists hundreds of miles away can examine and diagnose patients in small hospitals or clinics in rural areas. At colleges and universities many courses are offered online, and the potential of cable and closed-circuit television is certainly being tapped.

One of the many changes made possible by the new technologies is the media trend toward narrowcasting as opposed to broadcasting. **Narrowcasting** refers to *programming designed to target a specific segment of the media audience.* Through sophisticated research techniques that take into account information about audience characteristics, lifestyles, needs, and preferences, the media often tailor their programs (and often their advertising) to various subgroups or selected audiences, for example, Spanish-speaking people, or teenagers, or people between the ages of 20 and 30. This means a media shift toward increasingly smaller audiences (Straubhaar and LaRose, 2000, p. 17; Pavlik and McIntosh, 2005). The consequences of narrowcasting are not yet fully understood, though some critics feel that this trend toward greater and greater audience selectivity could result in a more fragmented society as audiences filter out what they do not wish to see (Sunstein, 2001).

The new technologies have increased the *speed* of communication at an exponential rate. International meetings are set up and documents exchanged at a previously unimagined pace. You can fax your résumé to a prospective employer on the same day you see a job listing. And you may have found the listing on the Internet. Essential equipment for every office and many homes, fax machines allow people to send and receive messages almost instantaneously. We have also seen major changes in the *volume of information* transmitted, stored, and retrieved. For example, type is set electronically, and desktop publishing and online publishing have dramatically increased the number of books, magazines, and newsletters available to us.

By means of the computer, scanner, camera phone, and fax, we can also transmit great numbers of images—visual materials such as graphs, maps, and photographs. The visual capabilities of the new technologies have had a powerful impact on how the media present news and other information. As a result of these and other changes, we have become an *increasingly visual society.*

Williams (1992) suggests that the new technologies can be thought of as "media extensions"—that while the media function "as extensions of our basic senses and communication modes . . . the new media are not usually systems in themselves. Instead, they extend existing systems."

Many of the new technologies are linked with traditional levels of communication. We have been examining these links throughout our text not only in organizational communication but in interpersonal and intercultural contexts as well as in our study of person perception. In the pages that follow we will look at some of these connections more closely.

The Convergence of Computing, Telecommunications, and Media

Among the most striking results of technological advances is the trend toward **convergence,** *the merging or "coming together of computing, telecommunications, and media in a digital environment"*—for example, the future convergence of television and the PC (Pavlik and McIntosh, 2005, p. 547).

How will convergence affect our lives at home? Over a decade ago one vision of the future household included wireless fax and personal computer links; dial-up educational and television services; improved online banking and home shopping; integrated emergency alarm systems for fire, police, and medical assistance; customized electronic newspapers; as well as other services needed to work from one's home. Now much of this vision has become a reality—but only for the limited segment of the population who can afford it.

In the past, our views of mass communication assumed distinctions between the various media—print, film, broadcasting, and so on. What we are seeing now, in many aspects of our lives, is a blurring of distinctions between the media and an increasing overlap in functions. Writing of how the new media are transforming journalism, Pavlik (2001) argues that convergence is "neither inevitable nor necessarily good: Convergence merely holds the promise of a better, more efficient, more democratic medium for journalism and the public in the twenty-first century" (p. xiii).

Computer-Mediated Communication

Currently, it's estimated that there are 1.1 billion people online throughout the world. Asia has 418 million—the largest number of Internet users; Europe, 322 million; North America, 233 million; Latin America, 110 million; Africa, 34 million; the Middle East, 20 million; and Australia/Oceana, 19 million ("Internet Usage Statistics," 2007). Remember, of course, that the number of people online increases every day.

The Internet

In large part because of the Internet, *a global "network of computer networks,"* the computer is used not only for its word processing and graphic functions but for an everexpanding range of interactive activities (Dominick, 2007, p. 263, italics added). In the online world of computer networks—the term "cyberspace" was coined by William Gibson in his 1984 novel *Neuromancer*—you can participate in conferences, electronic brainstorming, newsgroups, support groups, and any number of online communities.

Through the Internet you can also keep in touch with friends halfway across the world, conduct research, or look for an apartment in another state. Currently, the 10 most popular Internet activities are sending e-mail, finding information through a search engine, searching for driving directions or maps, answering a specific question through an Internet search, researching services or product information, getting weather reports, searching for information about interests or hobbies, getting travel information, getting the news, and shopping ("Most Popular Internet Activities," 2007).

Many believe that the *World Wide Web* has changed the way we read and write. Online publishing now includes e-zines, out-of-print books, author home pages, searchable classics libraries. And during recent years several scholars have published full documentation of their new books online because the footnotes, filling hundreds of pages, were just too extensive to be printed within the book. The Google Cyber-library Project in its initial stages will make vast numbers of books available online by scanning from the collections of the New York Public Library, and the libraries of Oxford, Stanford, and the University of Michigan. Harvard University, a more limited contributor, will make 40,000 books available for the project.

USC's Center for the Digital Future has issued a new report (2007) on American use of the Internet. Here are some highlights:

Americans on the Internet—more than three-quarters of Americans are Internet users; 77.6 percent of Americans age 12 or older go online.

The Internet at home—more than two-thirds of Americans (68.1 percent) use the Internet at home, a substantial increase from the 46.9 percent . . . in 2000.

Hours online—the number of hours online continues to increase, rising to an average of 8.9 hours per week. . . .

The Internet and television: how important as sources of information and entertainment?— . . . the Internet has a solid position as an important source of information and entertainment for the vast majority of users, consistently outranking television.

Information on the Internet: is it reliable and accurate?— . . . Well over half of users (55.2 percent) say that most or all of the information online is reliable and accurate. . . .

The Internet and political knowledge—Belief that the Internet can be a tool for learning about the political process continues to remain high, with 59.3 percent of users agreeing that by using the Internet, people can better understand politics. . . .

Using the Internet at work: hours online— . . . Internet users who go online at work say that they actively use the Internet for work an average of 7.8 hours each week—an increase from 5.6 hours in 2005 . . . ("Online World . . . ," pp. 1–2, 4)

One of the most important long-term questions still to be answered is how Internet use will affect children.

E-Mail

Along with other research, a study from the Stanford Institute for the Quantitative Study of Society in 2005 finds that the most popular online activity is reading, sending, or answering *e-mail,* or electronic mail (46.6 percent of time is devoted to this), followed by Internet browsing (33.7 percent), and instant messaging (6.8 percent). In all, the Stanford study reports, 57 percent of time spent on the Internet is devoted to communicating with others—a combination of e-mail, instant messaging, and chat rooms (*www.stanford.edu/group/siqss*).

For many, messages sent via e-mail and fax have replaced letters, not only in businesses but in personal life. Through e-mail you keep in touch with friends and family in a rapid and informal way. According to a 2004 survey by the Pew Internet & American Life Project, almost three-quarters of young people between ages 12 and 17 who are online use instant messaging to speak with friends—and over a third of them use it every day.

As we've seen in earlier chapters, e-mail is an essential part of organizational communication. But unlike letters, electronic mail is not necessarily private. The casual nature of e-mail messages within an organization became an issue in a 1998 lawsuit against Microsoft in which e-mail messages were used as evidence, prompting several large corporations to require that their employees periodically destroy "sensitive" e-mail messages. On a personal level, too, lack of privacy can become an issue. As we mentioned in Chapter 7, there is growing surveillance of e-mail by employers. At one firm the intimate e-mail messages of an employee were posted on the company bulletin board (Wood and Smith, 2001). As with the use of other technologies, an etiquette for using e-mail seems to be needed.

Teleconferencing

With the growing popularity of **teleconferencing**—*holding a meeting with people who are in different, often distant locations*—have come many changes. If you have ever participated in a conference call, you know that the telephone technology is relatively simple. This is a form of *audioconferencing* used, for example, by many businesses and other organizations over the years as a substitute for face-to-face communication—one that drastically cuts down on business expenses and may result in greater and more rapid exchange of ideas and problem solving. For example, a cargo airline with international routes conducts daily morning briefings through audioconferencing.

Accomplished through the use of both video and audio links, videoconferencing is a form of conferencing we now take for granted as television viewers. For example, on news programs such as *Face the Nation* or *Meet the Press,* a moderator may interview a Washington correspondent and a senator in Idaho to discuss the implications of an upcoming election. The people being interviewed respond to questions, discuss their own views, listen to opposing views, and speak directly to each other. And you can see each person "live" and watch how he or she answers questions. All the nonverbal cues discussed in Chapter 4 also come into play as you watch.

Videoconferencing has many applications in the workplace, and its use is increasing not only by banks, law firms, architectural offices, but also medical providers and universities. Even many small companies can now afford videoconferencing systems. They are being used for everything from sales presentations, creative meetings, brainstorming, to job interviews. The chances are that at some time you will be participating in them.

Cell Phones

The growing popularity of the cell phone, sometimes called "the communications Swiss Army knife," is confirmed in a joint study by Pew Research Center's Internet

& American Life Project, the Associated Press, and AOL (Rainie and Keeler, 2006). People use cell phones not only to make and receive calls but to send and receive text messages, take still pictures, access the Internet, trade instant messages, play music, watch video and TV programs as well as engage in other activities.

As of 2006 there were 208 million cell phone users in the United States, a number that is sure to increase. Young adults are the largest population of users. Interestingly, 22 percent of people who own cell phones admit "they are not always truthful about exactly where they are when they are on the phone. Younger users are much more likely to say that they are not always honest about where they are: 39% of cell users ages 18–29 say that" (p. 3). The Pew study identifies several implications of their findings, among them:

> Cell phones enable real-time action and engagement.
> Cell phone use is encouraging people to reallocate portions of their time and their communications patterns.
> Cell phone use is changing expectations about when and how others are available to us. (p. 11)

Telecommuting

In **telecommuting,** sometimes called *telework, people work at various locations outside the main office, often at home, and are usually connected to a main office by computer and a high-speed modem.* Newer technology and increasing use of broadband also offer people who telecommute an array of options that merge home and office including the fax, voice mail, cell phone, e-mail, and videoconferencing. For example, e-mail makes it possible to transmit and receive files almost instantaneously. All this can create far more flexible work arrangements.

Once considered experimental, telecommuting is becoming part of "mainstream practices" at some firms and will certainly have an impact on social, family, and professional relationships. For many, telecommuting is offered as an employee benefit, and over 50 percent of North American firms allow their employees to telecommute. Some people telecommute two or three days out of the workweek, and it is estimated that in addition to cutting costs, telecommuting can increase productivity by from 5 to 20 percent.

Despite the convenience and benefits, however, not everyone wishes to work from home. A computer specialist we know was startled and somewhat disappointed when the firm she worked for decided that all employees would switch from working at home one or two days a week to working at home every day. The firm's potential savings in overhead were clear, but she regretted the lack of face-to-face contact with her colleagues.

Video Games

The range of video games is enormous, extending from *Madden NFL,* currently a best-selling game about football, to the so-called God games such as *The Sims.*

Despite their wide popularity, however, video games are controversial (Vorderer and Bryant, 2006). Some critics believe that playing video games can become addictive; that they may divert time from studies; that they are violent (*Grand Theft Auto*, for example); and that they ultimately reinforce aggressive behavior, particularly among adolescents.

A number of psychologists argue that the category of addiction usually cannot be applied to this type of game playing. As for how video games affect learning, some educators believe that the educational benefits are limited. For example, Howard Gardner of Harvard argues that video games have too much emphasis on competition, that they appeal more to boys than to girls, and that simulation is "a powerful technique . . . but it's not the same as real life" (Cited in Glazer, 2006, p. 953).

Others believe that selected video games and other digital media can actually enhance learning, problem-solving abilities, and creativity. Consider *SimCity:* "A sizable number of players . . . first became interested in urban design as a result of the game [and] have gone on to become architects and designers, making SimCity arguably the single most influential work of urban-design theory ever created" (Seabrook, 2006, p. 95). Will Wright is the creator of *The Sims* and *SimCity*. His newest game is *Spore*, which includes "creative toolkits for making everything from creatures and vehicles to plants and buildings" (cited in Glazer, 2006, p. 945).

As we discussed in Chapter 10, violent video games and the stereotypes that they often promote are of great concern. Some studies have found that violent video games can promote aggressive behavior (Anderson et al., 2006). Here again it is not digital media per se, but the uses to which they are put that is most important.

The New Alternative Media

There have always been some alternatives to mainstream media from ham radio operators to independent publishers of political newsletters. But the growing dissatisfaction with traditional media along with advances in digital technologies that include greater interactive capability are enabling numerous efforts of individuals and groups to explore new media alternatives. *Columbia Journalism Review* refers to "a new age of alternative media." Some even believe that the new alternatives have the ability to "change some of the terms in the unwritten contract between the press and the people" ("The New Age," 2003, p. 20). Here we look briefly at two of these alternative media.

News-Related Blogs

In recent years there has been a proliferation of blogs of all kinds on the Internet. A **blog,** or *Weblog,* is *"a Web site where information is updated frequently and presented in reverse chronological order . . . [newest material coming first]. Typically, each post contains one and often several hyperlinks to other Web sites and stories, and usually . . . a standing list of links to the author's favorite bookmarks"* (Welch, 2003, p. 21).

As of 2006, a study by the Pew Internet & American Life Project reported that there were about 12 million bloggers in the United States (as of this writing that number must be even higher), and "thirty-four percent of them consider blogging to be a form of journalism" (cited in Lemann, 2006, p. 44). The technology for creating blogs is now so inexpensive that people can create their own for as little as $200 or far less. In the last few years, bloggers have influenced public opinion and events in many ways—for example, by criticizing political issues as well as politicians and media figures from Senators Trent Lott and Senator John McCain to Bill O'Reilly and Don Imus. And there are blogs that post eyewitness accounts of important events worldwide. In fact, writers of blogs are sometimes referred to as "amateur journalists" or "citizen journalists."

Much of the information on blogs as it relates to news is inaccurate and undocumented. And much of it is partisan—often it is a criticism of mainstream media. Yet one journalist writes that while 90 percent of news-related blogs may be mediocre, "the top 10 percent is among the most exciting new trends the profession has seen in a while" (Welch, 2003, p. 26). Nicholas Lemann, professor and dean of Columbia University's Graduate School of Journalism, disagrees. Of the work of so-called "citizen journalists" that appears on the Internet, including their press criticism, Lemann writes, "none of that yet rises to the level of a journalistic culture rich enough to compete in a serious way with the old media" (2006, p. 47).

The mainstream media also have an increasing number of Weblogs. *The Wall Street Journal* (*www.opinionjournal.com/best*), ABC News (*http://abcnews.go.com/Politics/TheNote*), and MSNBC (*www.msnbc.com/id/3032105*) are just a few.

Media Reform Organizations

"Don't hate the media, be the media" is the much-quoted slogan of one of the many media reform organizations using the Web to inform the public, heighten awareness of media bias, and promote greater interactivity between the press and the public. Some groups mobilize their audiences toward grassroots activism.

Media reform organizations cover the political spectrum. For example, compare Accuracy in Media (*www.aim.org*) and Fairness & Accuracy In Reporting (FAIR) (*www.fair.org*), which among other things, advise activist groups in such activities as documenting hate speech on the radio. While some reform groups are well-established organizations run by journalists and political scientists that now include a Web site, others have emerged that are thoroughly Web-based.

Recently formed, The Free Press (*www.freepress.org*) is interested in working toward "a more competitive and public interest–oriented media system" and advising start-up activist groups. And the Indymedia (independent media) movement is a group of individual collectives in places as farflung as Seattle, Prague, and Mexico City. The collectives are run by volunteers and may use a number of different media—video, radio, print, and so on—to reach their audiences, but it is the Internet (*www.indymedia.org*) that unites them (Beckerman, 2003). Their focus is on noncorporate news coverage and activism or protest politics through the Internet on a national or worldwide level (Bagdikian, 2004, p. 132). Currently, there are over 150 independent media centers around the world, each with its own Web page.

Other new media alternatives that are emerging include the small low-power FM radio stations. These neighborhood stations, often run by volunteers, are noncommercial and offer programming of special interest to their listeners. For example, for its Hispanic community, WSBL-LP in South Bend, Indiana, broadcasts in Spanish and also plays current Hispanic music; during breaks listeners can hear English-language lessons in vocabulary (Kelliher, 2003, p. 31).

Effects on Interpersonal Communication

How are the new technologies affecting interpersonal communication? For at least a segment of our population, a number of face-to-face transactions are now mediated by computers and other interactive technologies. This does not necessarily mean that there will be less interpersonal communication. For example, Skype is a "peer-to-peer" telephone network on the Internet that enables people to do voice and videoconferencing at no cost (*www.skype.com*). Through Skype a friend of this author who lives in Connecticut is able to speak with and see her two children online every day: They work in Mauretania and India.

Applications of technological advances (e.g., customized television feeds) also intensify the *selectivity* of the mass communication audience. Conversely, technology has enabled the mass media to become far more selective. For example, in publishing, books can now be printed as needed, with specific sections added or dropped, according to the demands of a given readership.

As we've seen, certain technological innovations are well suited to enhancing rather than limiting communication. In organizational communication, for example, many companies use videoconferencing on a routine basis. The global nature of telecommunications has changed the structure of business today. As members of increasingly multinational businesses and institutions, we have opportunities to extend our relationships across local and national boundaries.

There have been many theories about the effects of interactive computing (Porter, 1997; Kiesler, 1996; Turkle, 1995). For example, in *Life on the Screen: Identity in the Age of the Internet,* Sherry Turkle argues that communicating in cyberspace is affecting our sense of a unified self and increasing our feeling that each of us has multiple and contradictory selves. She also suggests that we have a feeling that we "know" computers even though we don't understand how they work. Byron Reeves and Clifford Nass take this a step further: In *The Media Equation* (1996) they argue that we treat computers, mass media, and new media as though they were "real people and places."

Several researchers view the Internet as a rapidly diffusing technology that extends social contact. But does using technology really affect our sense of well-being and connectedness? In particular, is the Internet isolating or does it extend social contact and enhance communication? These questions have been the subject of much ongoing research and debate. For example, in Chapter 2 we looked at new studies that find shy people reduce their levels of shyness online and then sometimes reduce their levels of shyness offline (Roberts et al., 2000). (We also discussed first impressions that are formed through computer-mediated communication.) And in Chapter 8 we saw that some people who meet online do go on to develop interpersonal relationships.

A study by Robert Kraut and colleagues at Carnegie Mellon University (1998) found that people who used the Internet at home (including the most social forms such as e-mail and chat rooms) showed higher levels of loneliness and depression than people who did not. Time people spent online seemed to correlate with less family interaction and a declining number of friends. In a later study (2002), Kraut and his colleagues changed their minds. "Internet Paradox Revisited," their follow-up study, finds that Internet use may not cause loneliness and depression, though it increases stress. Better outcomes for social well-being and connectedness are seen for extroverts than for introverts or others with less social support *(www.cmu.edu/cmnews)*.

Other studies that support a positive view include the Pew Internet & American Life Project (Howard et al., 2001). This research finds that Internet use fosters social connection, particularly through e-mail to communicate with family and keep in touch with friends. Boundaries between home and office Internet use are blurring so that, on the job, people sometimes do other Internet activities unrelated to work, and at home they may do Internet activities that are work-related. All studies show greater amounts of communication, particularly through e-mail.

New research on the use of social networks in the United States finds that 55 percent of online teenagers use social networking on such Web sites as Facebook and MySpace, and 55 percent have posted an online personal profile (Lenhart and Madden, 2007, p. 2). The most popular site is MySpace, which "dominates the social networking world" (p. 4). Almost half of online teenagers access social networking sites daily, and two-thirds have limited the access to their profiles. Girls from ages 15 to 17 are even more likely to use them.

This survey examines five ways in which these sites are used: "The vast majority . . . say they use the sites to maintain their *current* friendships, while half report using the sites to make *new* friends":

To stay in touch with friends you see a lot: 91 percent

To stay in touch with friends you rarely see in person: 82 percent

Make plan with friends: 72 percent

Make new friends: 49 percent

Flirt with someone: 17 percent (adapted from Lenhart and Madden, 2007, pp. 2, 5)

Norman Nie, coauthor of Stanford University's "Internet and Society" survey (Nie and Erbring, 2002), is one exception; he disagrees with the more positive views of the Internet's social effects. He found that with the growing use of the Internet, people are spending more time at their jobs and less time with their families and friends (Nie, 2001). Their social isolation also increased steadily with the amount of time they spend online. Nie is also concerned that Internet use in telecommuting will undercut the social aspects of work. A later Stanford University study directed by Nie (Nie et al., 2005) seemed to add weight to his concerns. It reports that people spend one-third of online time at work; the other time they spend online takes away twice as much from time spent with family as from time spent watching television (*www.stanford.edu/group/siqss*). For Nie, no technology can replace the immediacy and warmth of face-to-face communication as it affects both individual well-being and our sense of connection with others.

Yet a recent and very extensive review of research on personal relationships both online and offline reports "little evidence of the Internet harming social relationships or detracting from time spent socializing in person" (Boase and Wellman, 2006, p. 713). The authors find that

(1) Internet use is not associated with decreases in time spent on social activities. Internet use is associated with relatively high levels of offline contact with friends, but not family.

(2) Only a small percentage of Internet users meet new people online. Relationships formed online rarely stay there. [They then become face-to-face relationships.]

(3) Internet use has the potential to enhance neighborhood relationships. (p. 717)

Boase and Wellman believe that changes in social networks reflect changing social patterns that have been developing for over a century: "All in all, . . . the Internet is neither destroying nor radically enhancing society. Rather, the Internet is adding to the overall volume of communication, helping to maintain the kinds of relationships that have existed for decades" (p. 721).

Gender differences also have to be considered (Tannen, 2006). A study of the use of personal e-mail (Boneva et al., 2001) suggests gender differences in the way men and women maintain interpersonal relationships: Apparently, women are more likely to maintain relationships with family and to keep up long-distance relationships with friends through e-mail, and in general they take more pleasure in this type of exchange. They are used to the role of facilitating communication. The authors of the study speculate that "e-mail fits better with women's expressive style of relationship maintenance, with its emotional intimacy and sharing of personal information. In contrast, men's more instrumental style . . . with its emphasis on joint activities, is hard to accomplish with distant partners through computer-mediated communication" (p. 546). Haythornthwaite (2001) proposes that the Internet is best viewed not as a separate activity, but one potentially complementing the other activities in which people are involved.

Technological Literacy and the Digital Divide

There is growing concern that *technology is creating a gap between those who can use, afford, and understand it and those who cannot.* This is sometimes referred to as the **digital divide** or the technology gap.

According to government reports from 2000 and 2002, in the United States the divide is narrowing and rural areas are now approaching major cities in their access to the Internet. Despite this optimistic picture, recent research points out flaws in several studies and some disturbing findings about social problems (Mossberger et al., 2003). *The CQ Researcher* (2004) confirms that access to the Internet is more limited for those who are less educated or have lower household incomes. Race or ethnicity also affects Internet access. So the divides we have in the United States no longer seem to be geographic, but they remain racial, ethnic, and economic. In developing countries the divide continues to widen (van Dijk, 2005). Only a select group of people at the higher socioeconomic levels will have and understand how to use state-of-the-art technology not only at work but in their homes.

Prospects for a Global Human Community

For diasporic South Asian, West Indian, and African (as well as many other) viewers, particularly those located in non-metropolitan centers in North America, it became possible to watch cricket games live and uninterrupted from a library in Amherst, Massachusetts, at home in Madison, Wisconsin, or in cyber-cafes around the world . . . simply by logging on to one's computer. Access to the World Wide Web allowed certain diasporic communities to connect with the [homeland] . . . in ways that have not been possible in the past.

—Mannur (2003, p. 286)

[I]n global terms, how can we talk about the empowering potential of computers, the Internet, and information technology for India, China, and most countries in Africa and Southeast Asia when the vast majority of families there don't yet have a telephone?

—Lull (2000, p. 8)

The hope that technological advances would contribute to a global human community— a world of "free-flowing information, borderless communities [and] increased democratization" (p. 356)—has been voiced by communication theorists for many years. One group of scholars (Kwak et al., 2006) writes of the potential to connect people from many nations and create what they characterize as "a psychological sense of belonging to the international community":

> [T]he Internet matters for international engagement. . . . the Internet connects individuals to the international community by helping them increase their knowledge of the world, facilitating their sense of belonging in the greater world, and motivating them to participate in international events and foreign volunteer opportunities. (p. 207)

As we saw in Chapter 10, the new communication technologies have vastly increased the amount of intercultural communication. People of different cultures have more information about each other and are more accessible than ever before. They are also more interdependent. Yet we've also seen how the use of new technologies can also result in more group polarization—as in the case of hate sites on the Web (see pp. 340–341). Thus the new media may have the potential for fostering extremism because they enable people to isolate themselves from opposing views and reinforce their own attitudes (Tolchin and Tolchin, 2006).

The new technologies have also been used to implement political or social change. People around the world have used electronic mail and the Internet to mount high-tech campaigns; for example, at times they have documented atrocities that they claim were not reported by the media, and they have organized protest rallies in many cities around the world. In general, online activism has become much more widespread. For example, there are Web sites on environmental concerns such as global warming. Web sites on human rights include *www.amnesty.org* (Amnesty International) and *www.aiusa.org* (the U.S. branch), which are concerned with human rights violations; and *www.oneworld.net,* a site with concerns about global issues, has established a portal promoting universal high-quality education. Numerous Web sites also deal with censorship issues and freedom of the press—for example, *www.dfn.org* (Digital Freedom Network).

We also know that through global communications many diaspora or refugee communities are able to maintain their identifications with their country of origin. When it is accessible, they use the new media, including the Internet, to promote both human and cultural rights along with "new forms of cosmopolitan democracy" (Gillespie, 2000, p. 178; Braziel and Mannur, 2003).

Today we communicate across both real and electronic spaces. The long-term implications of the new technologies are still unfolding. Some communication scholars are especially concerned that within technologically rich societies an emphasis on the use and ongoing development of technology will overshadow human issues. Yet for the vast majority of the world's population, access to technology remains limited and a mediated home environment seems very far away.

The potential for creating a global community in the twenty-first century is in our hands, within our reach, but it will be determined not by the nature of the technology itself but the human uses to which technology is put. Ultimately, it may depend on our willingness to redefine our own self-interest so that it includes rather than excludes other groups of people. Communications scholar Nick Couldry writes:

> Since media are the principal means through which the world's realities are presented, media ethics is a necessity. . . . But media ethics, like all ethics, starts from where we find ourselves, not from where we would like to be. Ethics is a framework for building consensus, even where none seems available; without it . . . we shall not survive. (2006, p. 140)

Summary

In this chapter, we saw that mass communication, by its very nature, is mediated. We defined the audience in mass communication as relatively large, heterogeneous, and anonymous to the source. The experience itself was characterized as public, rapid, and fleeting, and the source was seen as often working through a complex organization. It was also pointed out that the feedback in mass communication was often limited and not as complete as it is in interpersonal communication.

We also discussed the mass communication process in terms of the gatekeeper concept and influences on gatekeeper choice. We gave special attention to gatekeeping and media conglomerates, war reporting, and ethical issues. We also looked at various theories about how messages flow from source to receiver, and at the concept of the active audience. We saw that the flow of information from the mass communicator to individual receivers sometimes involves opinion leaders, with mass and face-to-face communication playing complementary roles.

The next section of this chapter assessed some of the effects and outcomes of mass communication. Although the mass media are often extremely effective in disseminating information, information gain by no means ensures attitude influence. Often, exposure to several points of view through the mass media simply reinforces the receiver's initial attitudes, particularly with respect to voting intentions. We gave special attention to agenda setting and framing in news reporting. We then looked at the functions of advertising and public relations. We also examined some of the female role models presented by the media and the many effects of media violence on social attitudes and on aggressive behavior.

In a final section of our chapter, we looked at several of the new communication technologies and explored some of their implications. Despite increases in the selectivity, speed, volume, and visual nature of communication, the new media were seen primarily as extensions of existing media. The convergence of computing, telecommunications, and media, as well as some effects on interpersonal communication were discussed. We also looked at the new alternative media and the problem of technological literacy. In closing, we tried to make clear that so-called revolutions in technology have historical precedents and that the possibility of a global human community will depend on the human application of technology rather than on technology itself.

Key Terms

Active audience	Diffusion of	Hypodermic needle	Selective exposure
Agenda-setting theory	information	model	Telecommuting
Blogs	Digital divide	Mean world syndrome	Teleconferencing
Convergence	Embeds	Narrowcasting	Third-person effect
Cultivation	Framing	Opinion leaders	Two-step flow model
theory	Gatekeeper	Selective attention	Unilaterals

Review Questions

1. Identify three aspects of mass communication that are mediated.

2. What are four distinguishing characteristics of mass communication?

3. Discuss the concept of the gatekeeper. Give one example of how gatekeeping in mass communication differs from gatekeeping in face-to-face communication.

4. What are six variables that may influence the information a gatekeeper chooses to select or reject?

5. Identify three concerns about the concentration of media ownership and its possible effect on news content.

6. Discuss the problems of gatekeepers during wartime and the pros and cons of embedded versus independent journalists.

7. Explain some of the major ethical problems with respect to gatekeeping and mass communication.

8. Identify some of the ways in which guests attempt to control media interviews and some of the problems interviewers have in getting them to answer questions.

9. Discuss two different theories about how messages flow from the mass media to individual receivers.

10. What is meant by the concept of the active audience?

11. What are some of the research findings on media uses and gratifications and the way the new technologies are used?

12. What is the general research finding concerning the relationship between a news event's importance and the channels through which it is disseminated?

13. How effective are the mass media in influencing the receiver's attitudes? Support your answer with an example.

14. Explain the concepts of agenda setting and framing in the media. How does the use of language contribute to framing? Give two examples.

15. What are the functions of advertising and public relations, how do they differ, and what is the relationship of both to mass communication?

16. How does mass communication affect the social learning process in children? Support your answer with an example.

17. Discuss the mean world syndrome in light of the research on cultivation theory.

18. Explain the third-person effect.

19. What is the consensus of opinion about whether viewing media violence influences our behavior in face-to-face encounters?

20. Explain the relationship between the new technologies and the mass media as traditionally conceived. Discuss the possible effects of video games.

21. What are two of the effects of the growing convergence of computing and telecommunications?

22. What are some of the ways in which the new technologies might affect interpersonal communication and media and what are the recent findings of a long-term study of Internet trends in this country?

23. Discuss the rise of the new alternative media and give two examples.

24. Discuss the digital divide and its possible effects on communication.

25. Discuss the new communication technologies and speculate upon their possible effects in bringing about a global human community.

Exercises

1. Follow a major news event as covered by a weekly magazine, a metropolitan newspaper, a local newspaper, and two Web-based news sites, both domestic and international—for example, *www.washingtonpost.com* and *www.bbc.co.uk*. Relate your findings to what you have read about the gatekeeping function of the media.

2. Identify a current issue related to fairness and accuracy in reporting by going to *www.fair.org* (this site has good Web links) or *www.ire.org* and compare the treatment of the subject with the coverage of a newspaper and television station. If there are differences, what are they? Did you use any of the Web links and, if so, what did they add to your understanding?

3. Watch a controversial television program (preferably a panel discussion or a talk show) in the company of at least five other people and observe the quality of their interaction and their comments about the program. Do the responses of the receivers reinforce each other? Is there an opinion leader in the group?

4. Compare the coverage of an event of moderate importance as presented by a newspaper, a television newscast, a radio program, and a news site on the Web. Which was the most comprehensive? Which seemed most objective and which most partisan? Give examples.

5. Select four children's programs at random from the daily television programming offered during after-school hours. Watch each of the programs and then discuss the presentation of sex-linked and occupational roles as well as the degree of violence, if any, that you observed. Compare your own observations with the discussion of role models, the mean world syndrome, and media violence in this chapter.

6. Do a content analysis of the news as presented by two different networks and two cable stations for the same evening. Discuss what each chose to emphasize and further discuss the worldview implied by each of the four choices. Compare these with an Internet newsgroup discussion and a news Web site from another country.

Suggested Readings

Alterman, Eric. *What Liberal Media? The Truth About Bias and the News.* New York: Basic Books, 2003.

The author takes an intensive look at political bias and argues that the media are actually more conservative than liberal. His examples are detailed and numerous.

Bagdikian, Ben H. *The New Media Monopoly.* Boston: Beacon Press, 2004.

A classic on the subject by a Pulitzer Prize–winning media critic and journalist. This edition has been completely revised and updated.

Bennett, W. Lance. *News: The Illusion of Politics,* 7th ed. New York: Pearson, 2007.

A well-written and lively examination of the relation between the news media and politics with interesting examples. The author looks at information biases in the news, freedom of the press issues, and the complex relationship between media and government.

Chester, Jeff. *Digital Destiny: New Media and the Future of Democracy.* New York: The New Press, 2007.

A book about current media policy, the special interests trying to shape it, and the future of digital technology in a democracy. Bill Moyers has called its author "the Paul Revere of the media revolution."

Christians, Clifford G., Mark Fackler, Kim B. Rotzoll, and Kathy Brittain McKee. *Media Ethics: Cases and Moral Reasoning,* 7th ed. Reading, MA: Allyn & Bacon, 2004.

An excellent and comprehensive treatment of media ethics with detailed case studies on each of the issues discussed.

Good Night, and Good Luck

An award-winning film about Edward R. Murrow, the legendary broadcaster at CBS, and his challenge, through television programming, to the intimidation and fear tactics of Senator Joseph McCarthy, who was head of the House Un-American Activities Committee during the 1950s.

Jamieson, Kathleen Hall, and Paul Waldman. *The Press Effect: Politicians, Journalists, and the Stories That Shape the Political World.* New York: Oxford University Press, 2003.

A superb book on the many ways in which news stories can be presented or framed. The authors focus on how the press presented the presidential campaigns of Bush and Gore and the controversy over the 2000 election.

Katovsky, William, and Timothy Carlson. *Embedded: The Media at War in Iraq.* Guilford, CT: Globe Pequod Press, 2003.

An important collection of interviews with embedded and independent journalists on their experiences in Iraq during 2003. Be sure to read the introductory essay.

Lull, James. *Media, Communication, Culture: A Global Approach,* 2nd ed. New York: Columbia University Press, 2000.

An interdisciplinary approach to the interaction of mass media and information technology, human communication, and the social construction of cultures from around the world. *Excellent examples throughout.*

Overholser, Geneva, and Kathleen Hall Jamieson, eds. *The Press, Institutions of American Democracy Series.* New York: Oxford University Press, 2005.

A comprehensive collection of essays by distinguished communication scholars on numerous aspects of the press including essays on the nature of the press, the First Amendment, the watchdog function of the press, minority concerns and Net neutrality, and the role of the press in a democracy.

Pavlik, John V., and McIntosh, Shawn. *Converging Media.* Boston: Pearson, 2005.

This is a comprehensive text on communication and new media. John Pavlik is also the author of a book on journalism at the beginning of the twenty-first century.

Sunstein, Cass. *republic.com.* Princeton, NJ: Princeton University Press, 2001.

A provocative book. The author discusses such issues as the consequences of the new technologies, particularly the Internet, for free speech, patterns of belief, and democracy.

 For Supplementary Information

Log onto the Online Learning Center at *www.mhhe.com/tubbsmoss11*.

GLOSSARY

Active audience: The concept that receivers of mass communication seek out and select the media content that they want.

Advice giving: A judgmental method of counseling implying the other person can't find the solution.

Agenda setting: The theory that the press tells us what to think about by establishing the relative importance of certain issues.

Analogy: A form of supporting material comparing two things or ideas.

Anticlimax order: A method of presentation in which the speaker presents the strongest argument first.

Appeasement: Giving in to the other party in a conflict situation.

Arousal level: The level of mental alertness relating to one's readiness to listen.

Assimilation: A way people distort messages to agree with their own view of things.

Assimilation effect: An effect that occurs when a listener tends to accept a change in attitude urged by a speaker and perceives the speaker's position as closer to his or her preferred position than it really is.

Attachment style: A person's capacities and patterns of forming and maintaining intimate relationships, shaped in part by the quality of the first emotional bond with the mother or other primary caregiver.

Avoidance: Not dealing with a conflict between two or more parties.

Avoiding topics: Not bringing up topics that are sensitive in a conflict situation.

Backlash: When a person reacts in the opposite way intended by the speaker (same as boomerang effect).

Bandwagon appeal: A propaganda device using statistics to indicate that many people are doing something.

Behavior attribution: Seeing your own behavior as a response to the demands of a situation but the same behavior in others as generated by their dispositions.

Blog: A Weblog or "Web site where information is updated frequently and presented in reverse chronological order. Typically, each post contains one and often several hyperlinks to other Web sites and stories."

Body: The main part of a speech.

Boomerang effect: When the listener reacts opposite to that intended by the speaker (same as backlash).

Brainstorming: A group technique designed to create as many ideas as possible.

Breadth: The variety of topics communicated.

Casual or social group: A group intended for purely pleasurable purposes.

Categorical imperative: A command or obligation to act that is absolute and without exceptions or conditions.

Causal organization: A pattern of organization that tries to identify causes of problems.

Charisma: "Personal magnetism that enables an individual to attract and influence people."

Chronemics: The study of how human beings communicate through their use of time.

Chronological organization: An organizational pattern that follows an idea through time.

Climax order: A way of ordering main points in a speech that builds from weaker arguments to the strongest.

Closed question: A form of question requiring a short answer such as a yes or no.

CMC: Computer-mediated communication.

Co-culture: A group or culture within the larger culture that will often share a specialized language system, values, a collective worldview, and common communication patterns.

Coercive power: A type of power in which threat or coercion is used.

Cohesiveness: The total field of forces acting on members to remain in a group.

Collectivism: The tendency of people in a given culture to value group identity over individual identity, group objectives over individual rights, and group-oriented concerns over individual wants and desires.

Commitment: The resolve to continue in a relationship indefinitely and to make the efforts necessary to ensure that it will continue.

Communication: The process of creating a meaning between two or more people.

Communication climate: The social-psychological context of a relationship.

Communication context: The situation in which communication occurs (interpersonal, intercultural, interviewing, small group, public, organizational, and mass).

Competition: Where one party tries to use aggression or power to beat the other party in a conflict situation.

Concentration: A person's ability to focus his or her mental faculties.

Conclusion: The closing part of a speech.

Confirmation: Any behavior that causes another person to value herself or himself more.

Conflict: An expressed struggle between at least two interdependent parties each of whom perceives incompatible goals, scarce rewards, and interference from the other, in attempts to achieve goals.

Connotation: The secondary associations a word has for one or more members of a linguistic community.

Consensus: Agreement among all members of a group concerning a given decision.

Consideration function: A role intended to build the rapport with other group members.

Context: The setting and social-psychological climate within which communication takes place.

Contrast effect: Trying to make a point by contrasting it with something very different.

Convergence: The merging or "coming together of computing, telecommunications, and media in a digital environment."

Cookies: Small files that Web sites place within the computers of visitors to track their preferences.

Cooptation: A way to get people to accept an idea by getting them involved.

Cosmopolitanism: The philosophy that our two governing principles should be universal concern for others and respect for legitimate differences.

Critical listening: Being able to detect flaws in a speaker's arguments.

Cross-examination: Using too many questions in a row resulting in the person feeling uncomfortable.

Cultivation theory: The view that through the stories it tells, television "cultivates" or promotes common worldviews, values, and perspectives on how we should think and behave.

Cultural frame of reference: A person's point of view based on his or her cultural background.

Cultural homogenization: The view that there is a tendency for cultures in contact with one another to become increasingly similar.

Culture: A way of life developed and shared by a group of people and passed down from generation to generation.

Defensive climate: Evaluative or judgmental atmosphere established through communication that arouses behaviors used to protect ourselves from what we perceive to be a threat.

Defensive projection: Seeing our own undesirable qualities in other people.

Defensiveness: Behavior that results from perceiving or anticipating a threat by a person or group.

Denial: A negotiation tactic in which one party does not admit to an earlier agreement.

Denotation: The primary associations a word has for most members of a given linguistic community.

Depth: The intimacy of what is communicated.

Dialectics: An approach that views relationships in terms of sets of contradicting or opposing impulses that create tensions between two people.

Diaspora: The dispersal or scattering of people from their homeland (whether voluntary or involuntary) to more than one destination.

Diffusion of information: The dissemination of news or information through communication channels to a community of receivers.

Digital divide: The gap between those who can use, afford, and understand technology and those who cannot.

Disconfirmation: Any behavior that causes another person to value herself or himself less, behavior rejecting both who the person is and what the person has to say.

Discriminative listening: Understanding and remembering a speaker's points.

Downward communication: Communication initiated by an organization's upper management, which then filters downward through the chain of command.

Dyadic effect: Eliciting a reciprocal level of openness from another person by disclosing something of oneself.

Embeds: Journalists placed within individual military units who live and travel with troops and whose work is censored by the military.

Empathic listening: Being able to demonstrate empathy for the speaker.

Empathy: Experiencing the other person's perception—that is, seeing and feeling things as the other person does.

Ethical protonorms: Underlying presuppositions that function as core values.

Ethics: The study of the general nature of morals and of the specific moral choices to be made by a person.

Ethnocentrism: The tendency to judge the values, customs, behaviors, or other aspects of another culture in terms of those that our own cultural group regards as desirable or ideal.

Example: A method of supporting material using a case or instance to illustrate a point.

Expert power: A type of power in which knowledge is used to influence someone.

Expressiveness: A dimension of nonverbal communication linked with animation, dynamism, expansiveness, and intensity.

Extemporaneous speaking: A mode of speech delivery in which minimal notes are used and that combines the advantages of careful speech outlining and planning with the spontaneity of impromptu speaking.

Extrinsic credibility: The credibility that a source is thought to have prior to the time when he or she delivers a message.

Family: Networks of people who share their lives over long periods of time; who are bound by ties of marriage, blood, or commitment, legal or otherwise; who consider themselves as family; and who share future expectations of connected relationship.

Feedback: The return of behavior you have generated.

Forming: The first stage of a group's development.

Forming of coalitions: Joining forces with others.

Framing: The use of a broad organizing theme to select, emphasize, and link the elements of a news story.

Funnel sequence: A method of interviewing in which an interviewer begins with broad questions and gradually proceeds to more specific questions.

Gatekeeper: A person who, by selecting, changing, and/or rejecting messages, can influence the flow of information to a receiver or group of receivers.

Gender: An aspect of self-concept shaped in part by culture and including one's "biological sex (male or female), psychological characteristics (femininity, masculinity, androgyny), attitudes about the sexes, and sexual orientation."

Golden mean: The Greek philosopher Aristotle's principle that morality is to be found in moderation and moral virtues are viewed as choices or modes of choice. Each virtue is seen as the middle path between the extremes of excess and deficiency.

Group polarization: After deliberation, people are more likely to move toward a more extreme point in the direction in which the group's members were originally inclined.

Handclasping (pairing): A coalition between minority members of a group, formed for the purpose of helping one another to achieve mutually advantageous goals.

Haptics: The study of how we use touch to communicate.

Hasty generalization: Jumping to a conclusion on the basis of very limited information.

Hate site: A Web site that disseminates inaccurate information and supports violence or unreasonable hostility toward an individual, organization, or group of people singled out because of race, religion, ethnic group, sexual orientation, or disability.

Hearing problems: Problems in the physiological process of receiving aural stimuli.

High-contact culture: A culture in which people touch each other more often, sit or stand closer to each other, make more eye contact, and speak louder than they do in low-contact cultures.

High-context culture: A culture whose members tend to be more skilled in reading nonverbal behaviors and to be more indirect and less explicit than members of low-context cultures.

Horizontal communication: Communication across the same level of an organization.

Humor: Using surprise with a funny ending to make a speech more interesting.

Hypodermic needle model: A view of communication in which each audience member receives messages directly from the source of a given medium.

Impromptu delivery: A mode of delivery requiring no advance planning.

Individualism: The tendency of people in a given culture to value individual identity over group identity, individual rights over group objectives, and personal needs and desires over those of the group.

Ineffective listening: When a receiver fails to understand or comprehend a speaker's message.

Ingratiation: A method of influencing others by complimenting them.

Inoculation theory: A theory that offers the listener a small exposure to an idea so that they will accept a stronger exposure later.

Input: All the stimuli, both past and present, that give us our information about the world.

Intensity: A measure of the power of words.

Interference: A general term used to describe anything that interferes with the communication process.

Intergroup conflict: Conflict between groups.

Intergroup contact theory: The theory that given certain conditions including equal status, shared goals, and group cooperation, sustained contact between noncompeting groups will result in decreased prejudice.

Interpersonal conflict: Conflict between individuals.

Interpersonal distance: Four distance zones within which different human interactions occur: intimate, personal, social, and public distance.

Interpersonal sensitivity: "Success in decoding nonverbal communication."

Interpretation: Trying to guess the other person's reasons for how he or she feels.

Interrole conflict: Conflict that is likely to be experienced when a person occupies two (or more) roles that entail contradictory expectations about a given behavior.

Intimacy: Feelings that develop a sense of closeness, bondedness, and connection.

Intragroup conflict: Conflict within a group.

Intrapersonal conflict: Conflict within an individual.

Intrarole conflict: Conflict experienced because of contradictory expectations concerning a single role.

Intrinsic credibility: A speaker's credibility or reputation as a direct result of his or her speech.

Introduction: The first part of a speech.

Johari window: A model for conceptualizing levels of awareness and self-disclosure in human communication: a way of looking at the interdependence of intrapersonal and interpersonal affairs.

Kinesic slips: Contradictory verbal and nonverbal messages.

Kinesics: The study of body movements (including the head and face) in communication.

Law of diminishing returns: The effectiveness of messages increases with the frequency up to a point and then diminishes.

Leading question: Suggesting the desired answer to the question.

Leak: A method of communicating information in which previously unknown information is made known to others, but its source remains anonymous to the general public.

Leakage: Signals of deception.

Learning or education group: A group primarily intended to be used as a vehicle to educate its members.

Legitimate power: A type of power based on a person's job position (i.e., the boss).

Leveling: A part of rumors in which details are left out.

Lie: An intentionally deceptive message that is stated.

Linking-pin function: Connecting parts of an organization by having members of different groups represent the groups in other overlapping groups.

Loaded question: Stacking the deck by implying the correct answer to the question.

Looking glass self: A sense of self that develops out of our relations and interactions with others; evaluating ourselves on the basis of how we think others perceive and evaluate us.

Low-contact culture: A culture in which people touch each other less often, maintain more interpersonal distance, make less eye contact, and speak in a lower, softer tone of voice.

Low-context culture: A culture whose members tend to emphasize verbal messages and stress direct and explicit communication.

Majority vote: A method of decision making in which the decision is determined by a simple majority of votes.

Master norm: One of a group of core ethical values; each norm takes different forms in different countries.

Materials of support: Methods of developing a point that make the point more interesting, understandable, and/or persuasive.

Mean world syndrome: The theory that heavy viewers of television come to believe that the world is a mean and dangerous place.

Memorized speech: A mode of delivery in which the speaker commits the entire speech to memory.

Memory structure approach: The view that our expectations are influenced by past experiences, what we have seen in the media, observations of others, and what we imagine and fantasize.

Message variables: Factors that a speaker can change to make a speech more effective.

Messages: Any type of verbal or nonverbal, conscious or unconscious communication.

Metacommunication: Communication about communication.

Metaphor: A comparison between two or more things or ideas.

Minimal daters: "A unique population of individuals who have few dates in a specific period of time . . . feel inhibited around members of the opposite sex . . . and are dissatisfied with their current dating frequency."

Mode of delivery: One of four methods for delivering a speech (impromptu, reading from manuscript, memorized, and extemporaneous).

Monochronic culture: A culture in which time is compartmentalized, viewed as segmented and linear. Emphasis is on tasks and agendas—doing one thing at a time.

Moral courage: The courage to be moral, involving three interrelated elements: commitment to one's moral principles, awareness of danger in supporting them, and willingness to endure the danger.

Narrowcasting: Programming designed to target a specific segment of the media audience.

Neutral question: Asking a question that does not suggest the desired answer.

Noise: A general term used to describe anything that interferes with the communication process.

Nonverbal communication: All the messages we convey, whether intentionally or unintentionally, without words or over and above the words we use.

Norming: The third phase in a group's development.

Norms: Rules, whether explicit or implicit, about behavior.

Objectics: The study of how we select and make use of physical objects in our nonverbal communication.

Oculesics: The study of the role of eye behaviors, including eye contact, eye movements, and pupil dilation in communicating.

Open question: Resembles an essay question on a test. It places no restrictions on the length of the answer.

Opinion leaders: People who have a particularly strong influence on others in forming opinions and making decisions.

Orientation: The angle of your body as you interact with another person.

Overload: Having to attend to too many stimuli.

Paralinguistics: The study of vocal phenomena beyond or in addition to language itself: voice qualities (such as pitch and resonance) and vocalizations (noises without linguistic structure such as sighs and groans).

Paraphrasing: Using your own words to express or restate someone else's words or ideas. Also an interview technique that restates the content as well as the emotions of the other person's answer.

Perceived reciprocity of liking: Feeling that people you like you.

Perceptual filters: Physiological limitations that are built into human beings and cannot be reversed.

Performing: The fourth phase in a group's development.

Personal space: A person's portable territory, which each individual carries along wherever he or she may go.

Persuasibility: A person's level of receptivity toward being persuaded.

Plagiarism: Using or presenting as your own the ideas, images, or words of another source—for example, from books or online information—without acknowledgment or permission.

Plain folks: A propaganda technique of using testimony to falsely appear like the listener.

Pleasurable listening: Listening for social enjoyment.

Polychronic culture: A culture in which time is seen as flexible and many things are done simultaneously. There is more emphasis on commitment to human relationships than on keeping to schedules.

Postponement: Putting off an agreement in a negotiation.

Power: "The capacity to influence the behavior of others and to resist their influence on oneself."

Power distance: The degree to which people accept authority and hierarchical organizations as a natural part of their culture.

Prescription: A competitive tactic in communication, referred to in Sillars's schema, in which a confrontational person makes requests, demands, threats, or arguments for a given behavior change in another person, with the goal of helping to resolve conflict.

Presumptive attribution: Making statements that attribute to another person's feelings, thoughts, or motives that he or she does not acknowledge.

Primacy effect: In impression formation, the belief that the first information we receive about a person is the most decisive in forming our impression.

Primary question: Questions that introduce a new topic in an interview.

Principled negotiation: An approach to negotiation in which an issue is decided on the basis of its merits rather than by taking positions and trying to get the other parties to change their positions; developed by Roger Fisher and his colleagues at Harvard University.

Private acceptance: A true measure of a person's level of commitment to an idea.

Private theory of personality: How we select and organize information about others on the basis of what behaviors we think go together.

Probe: A type of secondary question intended to follow up on earlier questions.

Problem-solving group: A group that is primarily intended to solve problems and make decisions.

Problem solution: An organizational pattern of a speech, going from the problem to the proposed solution.

Protonorm: A single universal principle that underpins all systematic ethics.

Prototype: A mental image of a subject that is your personal definition of a quintessential person, place, or concept.

Proxemics: The study of how human beings use space to communicate nonverbally.

Proximity: Geographic closeness.

Psychological sets: Expectancies or predispositions to respond that have a profound effect on one's perception of objects.

Public compliance: Forcing a person to go along with the group. This may be quite different from his or her private acceptance.

Purpose-oriented audience analysis: A method for analyzing an audience that examines the information the audience most needs to know.

Qualification: A collaborative tactic to help resolve conflict, which involves disclosing one's own thoughts and feelings and soliciting disclosures from the other person.

Railroading: A style of group decision making in which one person may force the rest of the group to go along.

Rapid thought: Our brains can process words many times faster than the normal rate of speaking.

Reading from manuscript: A mode of delivery in which the speaker first prepares a word-for-word copy of the speech.

Reassurance: Attempting to make the other party feel comfortable.

Recency effect: An effect in which the most recent arguments are the strongest in influencing the listener's attitude.

Referent power: A type of personal power that has the ability to influence someone because of his or her desire to identify with the power source.

Relationship disengagement: The dissolution of a relationship.

Relationship maintenance: Behaviors by which people sustain close and satisfying relationships—whether routinely or strategically.

Remembering: Retaining points a speaker has made.

Reward power: A type of power in which rewards or incentives are used to gain cooperation.

Risky shift phenomenon: The tendency of people to increase their willingness to take risks as a result of group discussions.

Roles: A set of norms that applies to a specific subclass within the society.

Sapir-Whorf hypothesis: A hypothesis that the world is perceived differently by members of different linguistic communities and that this perception is transmitted and sustained by language.

Secondary question: A follow-up to a primary question, intended to elicit elaboration from the interviewee.

Selective attention: The receiver processes certain of the available stimuli while filtering out others.

Selective exposure: The tendency to choose communication that will confirm your own opinions, attitudes, or values.

Selective use of objective criteria: When objective criteria are only used some of the time.

Self-concept: Your relatively stable impressions about yourself.

Self-directed work team: A form of work group that does not have a boss.

Self-disclosure: Intentionally making known information about oneself.

Self-esteem: Your feelings of self-worth.

Self-expansion model: "Including others in the self through close relationships so that the other's resources, perspectives, and identities are treated to some extent as one's own."

Self-fulfilling prophecy: Expectation about another's behavior influences and unwittingly leads to the predicted behavior.

Semantic focus: An attempt to avoid a conflict in which a person focuses on what is being said and then makes statements about what the words mean or how to characterize the ongoing conflict.

Semantic interference: Interference that occurs when a receiver does not attribute the same meaning to a signal that the sender does.

Setting: Physical environment.

Sexist language: Language reflecting a negative bias toward one gender.

Shadow page: A page established anonymously on a Web site to destroy the reputation of a person, group, or organization, or another Web site.

Shared meanings: Some correspondence between the message as perceived by the sender and the receiver.

Sharpening: A part of rumors in which details are exaggerated or distorted.

Shifting: Changing your requirements within the course of a negotiation.

Signal-to-noise ratio: A measure of interference that looks at the relationship between essential and extraneous information contained in a message.

Sleeper effect: An effect in which the source of a message is forgotten over time.

Social comparison theory: A theory based on the idea that each person decides what is true in relation to other people.

Spatial organization: An organizational pattern that is based on locations.

Standardized interview: A set of prepared questions from which an interviewer is not allowed to deviate.

Statistics: Numerical methods of describing events or ideas.

Status: The position of an individual in relation to another or others.

Stereotype: A generalization, based on limited experience, about a class of people, objects, or events that is widely held by members of a given culture.

Storming: The second phase of group development.

Supportive climate: Nonjudgmental atmosphere established through communication that conveys empathy and equality.

Synchrony: The sharing of rhythms between speakers, which helps to emphasize and organize meaning during conversation.

Task function: A role designed to help a group accomplish work.

Technical interference: Factors that cause a receiver to perceive distortion in the intended information or stimuli.

Telecommuting: Working at various locations outside the main office, often at home; telecommuters are usually connected to a main office by computer and high-speed modem.

Teleconferencing: Using audio and/or video links to hold a meeting with people who are in different, often distant, locations.

Testimony or quotations: A method of supporting materials in which the speaker quotes other sources.

Third-person effect: Your perception that others are more influenced by media content than you are yourself.

Topical organization: A method of arranging a presentation in which a speaker moves from one topic to the next in a way that clearly demonstrates how the topics are related.

Touch avoidance: "A negative attitude toward touch that also affects proxemic behavior and other types of nonverbal communication."

Transition: A verbal bridge connecting two parts of a speech.

Two-step flow model: A theory that information is passed from the various mass media to certain opinion leaders and from these leaders to other people within the population.

Uncertainty avoidance: A measure of the extent to which members of a culture attempt to avoid uncertainty or ambiguity about others.

Underresponsiveness: When the other party is not responding to your communication efforts.

Unilaterals: Journalists who are independent, do not travel within an individual military unit, and are not protected or censored by the military.

Unstandardized interview: An interview that allows the interviewer as well as the respondent considerable latitude.

Upward communication: Communicating to those higher in the organization.

Upward receptivity: The willingness to receive messages from subordinates.

Utilitarianism: A doctrine that places primary value on the outcomes or consequences of our actions rather than our moral intentions.

Veil of ignorance: A principle of justice or fairness that insures protection of those whose position is weakest; according to this view, proposed by contemporary American philosopher John Rawls, what is moral is what is fair for all.

Verbal message: Any type of spoken communication that uses one or more words.

Whistleblowing: A member of a group makes a charge about the violation of ethical standards or norms within that group itself.

Work group: A type of group designed to accomplish a specific task.

REFERENCES

Chapter 1   The Process of Human Communication

Albom, Mitch. *Tuesdays with Morrie* (New York: Doubleday, 1997).

Avery, Robert K., and Thomas A. McCain. "Interpersonal and Mediated Encounters: A Reorientation to the Mass Communication Process," in Gary Gumpert and Robert Cathcart, eds., *Inter/Media: Interpersonal Communication in a Media World*, 2nd ed. (New York: Oxford University Press, 1982), 29–40.

Barbaro, Michael. "Wal-Mart Enlists Bloggers in P.R. Campaign," *New York Times* (March 7, 2006).

Batista, E. "She's Gotta Have It: Cell Phone." *Wired News, 11.05* (May 16, 2003). Retrieved from *www.wired.com/news/culture/0,1284,58861,00.html*.

Begley, Sharon, and Fiona Gleizes. "My Granddad, Neanderthal?" *Newsweek* (October 16, 1989), 70–71.

Bishop, Todd. "Microsoft Files Patent for 'Immortal Computing,'" *Ann Arbor News* (January 23, 2007), D3.

Braud, Gerard. "What Does That Mean?" *Communication World* 24, no. 1 (January/February 2007).

Byrne, Zinta S., and Elaine LeMay. "Different Media for Organizational Communication: Perceptions of Quality and Satisfaction," *Journal of Business and Psychology* 21, no. 2 (Winter 2006).

Camp, Richaurd, Mary Vielhaber, and Jack L. Simonetti. *Strategic Interviewing: How to Hire Good People* (San Francisco: Jossey Bass, 2001).

Carr, Nicholas. "Lessons in Corporate Blogging," *BusinessWeek Online* (July 18, 2006).

Chin, Chen-Oi, John Gu, and Stewart L. Tubbs. "Developing Global Leadership Competencies," *The Journal of Leadership Studies* (Winter/Spring, 2001), 20–31.

Clark, Don. "Managing the Mountain," *Wall Street Journal* (June 21, 1999), R4.

Correia, A. C., and E. L. Menezes De Faria. "An Intranet Success Story," *Computers & Auditing* 61, no. 3 (2004), 32–34.

Dempsey, J. "Information Overload Increasing Stress, Illness," *San Diego Union–Tribune* (December 4, 2003), E3.

Dvorak, Phred. "MBA Programs Hone 'Soft Skills,'" *Wall Street Journal* (February 12, 2007), B3.

"Editorial," *Greensboro News Record* (February 20, 2004), A14.

Finney, John, "A World of Difference: A New Study by Watson Wyatt Worldwide Finds that Successful Companies Recognize the Value of Global Internal Communication and Develop Policies to Make It Happen," *Communication World* 23, no. 4 (July 1, 2006).

Freud, Sigmund. *The Psychopathology of Everyday Life*, in A. A. Brill, ed. and trans., *The Basic Writings of Sigmund Freud* (New York: Modern Library, 1938).

Garrett, Wilbur E., ed. *National Geographic* 176 (October 1989), 560.

Giussani, Bruno. "How About an E-mail on That?" *BusinessWeek Online* (August 21–28, 2006).

Glassman, Audrey. *Can I Fax a Thank-You Note?* (New York: Berkley Books, 1998).

Goldberg, Bernard. *Bias: A CBS Insider Exposes How the Media Distort the News.* (Washington, DC: Regnery Publishing, 2002).

Goldhaber, Gerald M. *Organizational Communication*, 5th ed. (Dubuque, IA: Brown, 1990).

Gudykunst, William B., and Young Yun Kim. *Communicating with Strangers*, 2nd ed. (New York: McGraw-Hill, 1992).

Hailey, D., and Christine Hailey. "Hypermedia, Multimedia and Reader Cognition: An Empirical Study," *Technical Communication* 45, no. 3 (1998), 330–342.

Haney, William V. *Communication and Interpersonal Relations*, 6th ed. (Homewood, IL: Irwin, 1992).

Harmon, Amy. "Internet Use Increases Depression, Loneliness," *Ann Arbor News* (August 30, 1998), A4.

Howard, M. "How Babies Learn to Talk," *Baby Talk, New York* 69, no. 3 (April 2004), 69.

Imamoglu, Salih Zeki. "An Empirical Analysis Concerning the User Acceptance of E-Learning," *Journal of American Academy of Business* (Cambridge) 11, no. 1 (March 2007).

Kageyama, Yuri. "Farmer Beeps Until the Cows Come Home," *Ann Arbor News* (July 11, 1992), A3.

Kanaley, Reid. "Cell Phones Raise Privacy Concerns," *Detroit Free Press* (May 14, 2001), 8F.

Kaweevisultrakul, Tanin, and Peng Chan. "Impact of Cultural Barriers on Knowledge Management Implementation: Evidence from Thailand," *Journal of American Academy of Business* (Cambridge) 11, no. 1 (March 2007).

Kelley, Robert E. *How to Be a Star at Work* (New York: Times Books, 1998).

Kenny, Shirley Strum. *Reinventing Undergraduate Education* (Washington, DC: Carnegie Foundation for the Advancement of Teaching, 1998).

Knapp, Mark L., and Judith A. Hall. *Nonverbal Communication in Human Interaction,* 4th ed. (New York: Harcourt Brace, 1997).

Larkin, T. J. "Change the Communication Channel: Web, Paper or Face-to-Face: Knowing the Strengths and Weaknesses of Each Channel Can Help You Choose the One that Best Suits Your Message," *Communication World* (November–December 2005).

LeDuc, Doug. "Teens Become Big Cell Phone Market," *Detroit Free Press* (May 14, 2001), 3F.

"Lessons from a Blackout," *New York Times* (April 12, 2004), A18.

Liker, Jeffrey. *The Toyota Way.* (New York: McGraw-Hill, 2004).

Lucas, Stephen. *The Art of Public Speaking,* 7th ed. (New York: McGraw-Hill, 2001).

Maxwell, John C. *The 17 Indisputable Laws of Teamwork: Embrace Them and Empower Your Team* (Nashville: Thomas Nelson Publishers, 2001).

Oglesby, C. "What's Behind the Curb-Your-Carbs Craze?" *CNN.com* (June 18, 2004). Retrieved from *www.cnn.com/2004/HEALTH/diet.fitness/06/carbohydrate.overview/ind_ex.html.*

Rosenberg, Morris. *Conceiving the Self* (New York: Basic Books, 1979).

Schein, Edgar H. *Career Dynamics: Matching Individual and Organizational Needs* (Reading, MA: Addison-Wesley, 1978).

Schellenberger, Sue. "Dealing with the Dead Zone: Spouses Too Tired to Talk," *Wall Street Journal* (February 22, 2007), D1.

Spyridakis, J. "Guidelines for Authoring Comprehensible Web Pages and Evaluating Their Success," *Technical Communication* (1998).

"Staffer of New Orleans Mayor Responds to Error in Press Release Regarding Carnival 2004," *New Orleans City Business,* (Metairie, LA) (March 1, 2004), 1.

Stewart, John, ed. *Bridges, Not Walls,* 4th ed. (Reading, MA: Addison-Wesley, 1986).

Stone-Palmquist, Peri. "Popular Revealing Attire Is Now Taboo," *Ann Arbor News* (August 24, 2001), A1.

Sultan, F., et al. "A Meta-Analysis of Applications of Diffusion Models," *Journal of Marketing Research* 27 (February 1990), 70–77.

Tubbs, Stewart L. *A Systems Approach to Small Group Interaction,* 9th ed. (New York: McGraw-Hill, 2007).

Valentis, J. "How 'Heart' Smart," *Lancaster (PA) Intelligencer Journal* (April 20, 2004), 1.

Vandermeer, Jim. "Seven Habits of Highly Successful Enterprise E-mail Managers," *EDPACS* (Reston) 34, no. 2 (August 2006).

"Wall Street Journal Examines New Hospital Communications Standards Examined to Prevent Medical Errors," *Medical News Today* (June 30, 2006). Retrieved from http://wwwmedicalnewstoday.com/medicalnews.php?newsid=46175.

Whetten, David A., and Kim S. Cameron. *Developing Management Skills,* 6th ed. (Upper Saddle River, NJ: Prentice-Hall, 2005).

Williams, M. "Dean's Campaign Finally Flickers Out; Once-Hot Candidacy Cooled Fast," *Austin American Statesman* (February 19, 2004), A1.

Chapter 2   Person Perception

Adelmann, Pamela. "Possibly Yours," *Psychology Today* 22 (April 1988), 8, 10.

"Anorexia's Web," *Current Events* 101 (September 7, 2001), 3–6.

Aron, Arthur, and Elaine Aron. *Love and the Expansion of Self* (New York: Hemisphere, 1986).

Aron, Arthur, Helen E. Fisher, and Greg Strong. "Romantic Love," in Anita Vangelisti and Daniel Perlman, eds., *Cambridge Handbook of Personal Relationships* (New York: Cambridge University Press, 2006), 595–614.

Asch, S. E. "Forming Impressions of Personality," *Journal of Abnormal and Social Psychology* 41 (1946), 258–290.

Asch, Solomon E., and M. Zukier. "Thinking about Persons," *Journal of Personality and Social Psychology* 46 (1984), 1230–1240.

Asendorpf, Jens B. "Shyness and Adaptation to the Social World of the University," in W. Ray Crozier, ed., *Shyness: Development, Consolidation and Change* (London: Routledge, 2000), 103–120.

Baron-Cohen, Simon. *The Essential Difference* (New York: Basic Books, 2003).

Baumeister, Roy F. "The Self," in Daniel Gilbert, Susan Fiske, and Gardner Lindzey, eds., *Handbook of Social Psychology,* 4th ed., vol. 2 (New York: McGraw-Hill, 1998), 680–740.

Baumeister, Roy F., Laura Smart, and Joseph M. Boden. "Relation of Threatened Egotism to Violence and Aggression: The Dark Side of High Self-Esteem," in Roy F. Baumeister, ed., *The Self in Social Psychology* (Philadelphia: Psychology Press, 1999), 240–279.

Beall, Anne E., Alice H. Eagly, and Robert J. Sternberg. "Introduction," in Alice H. Eagly, Anne E. Beall, and Robert J. Sternberg, eds., *The Psychology of Gender,* 2nd ed. (New York: Guilford Press, 2004), 1–8.

Berscheid, Ellen, and Harry T. Reis. "Attraction and Close Relationships," in Daniel Gilbert, Susan Fiske, and Gardner Lindzey, eds., *Handbook of Social Psychology,* 4th ed., vol. 2 (New York: McGraw-Hill, 1998), 193–281.

Best, Deborah L., and Jennifer J. Thomas. "Cultural Diversity and Cross-Cultural Perspectives," in Alice H. Eagly, Anne E. Beall, and Robert J. Sternberg, eds., *The Psychology of Gender,* 2nd ed. (New York: Guilford Press, 2004), 296–327.

Bodenhausen, Galen V., and C. Neil Macrae. "Putting a Face on Person Perception," *Social Cognition* 24, no. 5 (2006), 511–515.

Boone, R. Thomas, and Ross Buck. "Emotional Expressivity and Trustworthiness: The Role of Nonverbal Behavior in the Evolution of Cooperation," *Journal of Nonverbal Behavior* 27 (Fall 2003), 163–182.

Brown, Roger. *Social Psychology,* 2nd ed. (New York: Free Press, 1986).

Bruner, Jerome. *Actual Minds, Possible Worlds* (Cambridge, MA: Harvard University Press, 1986).

Bussey, Kay, and Albert Bandura. "Social Cognitive Theory of Gender Development and Functioning," in Alice H. Eagly, Anne E. Beall, and Robert J. Sternberg, eds., *The Psychology of Gender,* 2nd ed. (New York: Guilford Press, 2004), 92–199.

Cheek, Jonathan, and Bronwen Cheek. *Conquering Shyness* (New York: Dell, 1990).

Cherlin, Andrew J. "By the Numbers," *New York Times Magazine* (April 5, 1998), 391.

Christiansen, Neil D., Shaina Wolcott-Burnam, Jay E. Janovics, Gary N. Burns, and Stuart W. Quirk. "The Good Judge Revisited," *Human Performance* 18, no. 2 (2006), 123–149.

Cunningham, Michael R., Anita P. Barbee, and Correna L. Philhower. "Dimensions of Facial Physical Attractiveness," in Gillian Rhodes and Leslie A. Zebrowitz, eds., *Facial Attractiveness: Evolutionary, Cognitive, and Social Perspectives* (Westport, CT: Ablex, 2002), 193–238.

Davis, Mark H., and Linda A. Kraus. "Personality and Empathic Accuracy," in William Ickes, ed., *Empathic Accuracy* (New York: Guilford, 1997), 144–168.

Deaux, Kay, and Marianne LaFrance. "Gender," in Daniel Gilbert, Susan Fiske, and Gardner Lindzey, eds., *Handbook of Social Psychology,* 4th ed., vol. 1 (New York: McGraw-Hill, 1998), 788–827.

DePaulo, Bella M., and Howard Friedman. "Nonverbal Communication," in Daniel Gilbert, Susan Fiske, and Gardner Lindzey, eds., *Handbook of Social Psychology,* 4th ed., vol. 2 (New York: McGraw-Hill, 1998), 3–40.

Dion, Karen. "Cultural Perspectives on Facial Attractiveness," in Gillian Rhodes and Leslie A. Zebrowitz, eds., *Facial Attractiveness: Evolutionary, Cognitive, and Social Perspectives* (Westport, CT: Ablex, 2002), 239–260.

Fletcher, Garth J. O., Jacqueline M. Tither, Claire O'Loughlin, Myron Friesen, and Nickola Overall. "Warm and Homely or Cold and Beautiful? Sex Differences in Trading Off Traits in Mate Selection," *Personality and Social Psychology Bulletin* 30 (June 2004), 659–672.

Gardner, Wendi L., and Shira Gabriel. "Gender Differences in Relational and Collective Interdependence," in Alice H. Eagly, Anne E. Beall, and Robert J. Sternberg, eds., *The Psychology of Gender,* 2nd ed. (New York: Guilford Press, 2004), 169–191.

Graham, Lawrence. *Member of the Club* (New York: HarperCollins, 1995).

Graham, Tiffany, and William Ickes. "When Women's Intuition Isn't Greater Than Men's," in William Ickes, ed., *Empathic Accuracy* (New York: Guilford, 1997), 117–143.

Gudykunst, William, and Stella Ting-Toomey. *Culture and Interpersonal Communication* (Newbury Park, CA: Sage, 1988).

Guerrero, Laura, and Kory Floyd. *Nonverbal Communication in Close Relationships* (Mahwah, NJ: Erlbaum, 2006).

Gustafson, Robert, Mark Popovich, and Steven Thomsen, "Subtle Ad Images Threaten Girls More," *Marketing News,* 35 (June 4, 2001), 12–13.

Hall, Judith A. "Women's and Men's Nonverbal Communication," in Anita Vangelisti and Daniel Perlman, eds., *Cambridge Handbook of Personal Relationships* (New York: Cambridge University Press, 2006), 201–218.

Hall, Judith A., Nora Murphy, and Marianne Mast. "Recall of Nonverbal Cues: Exploring a Definition of Interpersonal Sensitivity," *Journal of Nonverbal Behavior* 30 (Winter 2006), 141–155.

Han, Arar, and John Hsu, eds. *Asian American X: An Intersection of 21st Century Asian American Voices* (Ann Arbor: University of Michigan Press, 2004).

Hancock Jeffrey T., and Philip J. Dunham. "Impression Formation in Computer-Mediated Communication Revisited: An Analysis of the Breadth and Intensity of Impressions," *Communication Research* 28 (2001), 325–347.

Harper, Marcél, and Wilhelm J. Schoeman. "Influences of Gender as a Basic-Level Category in Person Perception on the Gender Belief System," *Sex Roles* 49, no. 9/10 (2003), 517–526.

Haslam, Nick, and Paul Bain. "Humanizing the Self: Moderators of the Attribution of Lesser Humanness to Others," *Personality and Social Psychology Bulletin* 33 (January 2007), 57–68.

Haslam, Nick, P. Bain, L. Douge, M. Lee, and B. Bastian. "More Human than You: Attributing Humanness to Self and Others," *Journal of Personality and Social Psychology* 89 (2005), 937–950.

Hiller, D., and W. Philliber. "Predicting Marital and Career Success among Dual-Working Couples," *Journal of Marriage and Family* 44 (1982), 53–62.

Hinde, Robert A., Catrin Finkenauer, and Ann Elisabeth Auhagen. "Relationships and the Self-Concept," *Personal Relationships* 8 (2001), 187–204.

Honeycutt, James M., and James G. Cantrill. *Cognition, Communication, and Romantic Relationships* (Mahwah, NJ: Lawrence Erlbaum, 2001).

Ivy, Diana K., and Phil Backlund. *Genderspeak: Personal Effectiveness in Gender Communication,* 3rd ed. (New York: McGraw-Hill, 2004).

Jacobson, David. "Impression Formation in Cyberspace," *JCMC* 5 (September 1999).

James, William. *Principles of Psychology,* vol. I (New York: Dover, 1950).

Johnson, Kirk. "Self-Image Is Suffering from Lack of Esteem," *New York Times* (May 5, 1998), F7.

Jones, Melinda. "Stereotyping Hispanics and Whites: Perceived Differences in Social Roles as a Determinant of Ethnic Stereotypes," *Journal of Social Psychology* 131 (1991), 469–475.

Kagan, Jerome. *Unstable Ideas: Temperament, Cognition, and Self* (Cambridge: Harvard University Press, 1989).

Kanagawa, Chie, Susan E. Cross, and Hazel Rose Markus. "Who Am I? The Cultural Psychology of the Conceptual Self," *Personality and Social Psychology Bulletin* 27 (2001), 90–103.

Keating, Caroline F. "Charismatic Faces: Social Status Cues Put Face Appeal in Context," in Gillian Rhodes and Leslie A. Zebrowitz, eds., *Facial Attractiveness: Evolutionary, Cognitive, and Social Perspectives* (Westport, CT: Ablex, 2002), 153–192.

Kernis, Michael H., ed. *Self-Esteem Issues and Answers: A Sourcebook of Current Perspectives* (Philadelphia, PA: Psychology Press, 2006).

Kleinke, Chris L. *Meeting and Understanding People* (New York: Freeman, 1986).

Kutner, Lawrence. "Parent and Child," *New York Times* (January 2, 1992), C12.

LaFrance, M., and C. Mayo. "A Review of Nonverbal Behaviors of Women and Men," *Western Journal of Speech Communication* 43 (1979), 76–95.

Lewandowski, Gary W., Jr., Arthur Aron, Sharon Bassis, and Johanna Kunak. "Losing a Self-Expanding Relationship: Implications for the Self-Concept," *Personal Relationships* 13 (2006), 317–331.

Luchins, A. S. "Primacy-Recency in Impression Formation," in Carl I. Hovland et al., eds., *The Order of Presentation in Persuasion,* vol. I (New Haven, CT: Yale University Press, 1957), 33–61.

Madon, Stephanie, Jennifer Willard, Max Guyll, Linda Trudeau, and Richard Spoth. "Self-Fulfilling Prophecy Effects of Mothers' Beliefs on Children's Alcohol Use," *Journal of Personality and Social Psychology* 90 (June 2006), 911–926.

Malpass, Roy, and Jerome Kravitz. "Recognition for Faces of Own and Other Race," *Journal of Personality and Social Psychology* 13 (1969), 330–334.

Maner, Jon K., Douglas T. Kenrick, D. Vaughn Becker, Andrew W. Delton, et al. "Sexually Selective Cognition: Beauty Captures the Mind of the Beholder," *Journal of Personality and Social Psychology* 85 (December 2003), 1107–1120.

Mansfield-Richardson, Virginia. *Asian Americans and the Mass Media* (New York: Garland, 2000).

Mast, Marianne Schmid, and Judith A. Hall. "Women's Advantage at Remembering Others' Appearance,"

Personality and Social Psychology Bulletin 32 (March 2006), 353–364.

McCroskey, J. C., and V. P. Richmond. "Power in the Classroom I: Teacher and Student Perceptions," *Communication Education* 32 (1983), 175–184.

Mead, George Herbert. *Mind, Self, and Society* (Chicago: University of Chicago, 1934).

Monin, Benoit. "The Warm Glow Heuristic: When Liking Leads to Familiarity," *Journal of Personality and Social Psychology* 85 (December 2003), 1035–1048.

Noller, Patricia. "Nonverbal Communication in Close Relationships," in Anita Vangelisti and Daniel Perlman, eds., *Cambridge Handbook of Personal Relationships* (New York: Cambridge University Press, 2006), 403–420.

Nurmi, Jari-Erik. "The Effect of Other's Influence, Effort, and Ability Attributions on Emotions in Achievement and Affiliative Situations," *Journal of Social Psychology* 131 (1991), 703–715.

Pearson, Judy Cornelia, Lynn H. Turner, and William Todd-Mancillas. *Gender and Communication,* 3rd ed. (Dubuque, IA: Benchmark/Brown, 1995).

Penton-Voak, Ian S., Nicholas Pound, Anthony C. Little, and David I. Perrett. "Personality Judgments from Natural and Composite Facial Images: More Evidence for a 'Kernel of Truth' in Social Perception," *Social Cognition* 24 (October 2006), 607–640.

Perrett, D. I., K. J. Lee, I. Penton-Voak, et al. "Effects of Sexual Dimorphism on Facial Attractiveness," *Nature* 394, no. 6696 (August 27, 1998), 884–886.

Random House Webster's College Dictionary (New York: Random House, 2000), p. 223.

Rhodes, Gillian, Sakiko Yoshikawa, Alison Clark, Kiernan Lee, Ran McKay, and Shigeru Akamatsu. "Attractiveness of Facial Averageness and Symmetry in Non-Western Cultures," *Perception* 30 (2001), 611–625.

Rhodes, Gillian, and Leslie A. Zebrowitz, eds. *Facial Attractiveness: Evolutionary, Cognitive, and Social Perspectives* (Westport, CT: Ablex, 2002).

Rimm, Sylvia. *See Jane Win: The Rimm Report on How 1,000 Girls Became Successful Women* (New York: Crown, 1999).

Riniolo, Todd C., Katherine C. Johnson, Tracy R. Sherman, and Julie A. Misso. "Hot or Not: Do Professors Perceived as Physically Attractive Receive Higher Student Evaluations?" *Journal of General Psychology* 133 (January 2006), 19–35.

Roberts, Lynne D., Leigh M. Smith, and Clare M. Pollock. "'U r a lot bolder on the net': Shyness and Internet Use," in W. Ray Crozier, ed., *Shyness: Development, Consolidation and Change* (London: Routledge, 2000), 121–138.

Rosenthal, R., and B. M. DePaulo. "Expectancies, Discrepancies, and Courtesies in Nonverbal Communication," *Western Journal of Speech Communication* 43 (1979), 76–95.

Rosenthal, Robert, and Leonore Jacobson. *Pygmalion in the Classroom,* newly expanded ed. (New York: Irvington, 1992).

Sargent, Michael J., and Amy L. Bradfield. "Race and Information Processing in Criminal Trials," *Personality and Social Psychology Bulletin* 30 (August 2004), 995–1008.

Schütz, Astrid. "Self-Esteem and Interpersonal Strategies," in Joseph P. Forgas, Kipling D. Williams, and Ladd Wheeler, eds., *The Social Mind: Cognitive and Motivational Aspects of Interpersonal Behavior* (New York: Cambridge University Press, 2001), 157–176.

Segall, M. H., D. T. Campbell, and M. J. Herskovits. "Cultural Differences in the Perception of Geometric Illusions," in D. R. Price-Williams, ed., *Cross-Cultural Studies* (Baltimore: Penguin, 1969), 95–101.

Shorter Oxford English Dictionary on Historical Principles, 5th ed., vol. 1 (Oxford, UK: Oxford University Press, 2002), 382.

Srivastava, Sanjay, Kelly M. McGonagal, Jane M. Richards, Emily A. Butler, and James J. Gross. "Optimism in Close Relationships," *Journal of Personality and Social Psychology* 91 (July 2006), 143–153.

Sternberg, Robert J., and John Kolligian, Jr., eds. *Competence Considered* (New Haven, CT: Yale University Press, 1990).

Storms, Michael D. "Videotape and the Attribution Process: Reversing Actor's and Observer's Point of View," *Journal of Personality and Social Psychology* 27 (1973), 165–175.

Sunnafrank, Michael, and Artemio Ramirez Jr. "At First Sight: Persistent Relational Effects of Get-Acquainted Conversations," *Journal of Social and Personal Relationships* 21, no. 3 (2004), 361–379.

Surawski, Melissa K., and Elizabeth P. Ossoff. "The Effects of Physical and Vocal Attractiveness on Impression Formation of Politicians," *Current Psychology* 25 (Spring 2006), 15–27.

Taylor, Charles R., and Barbara B. Stern. "Asian-Americans: Television Advertising and the 'Model Minority' Stereotype," *Journal of Advertising* 26, no. 2 (1997), 47–61.

Ting-Toomey, Stella. *Communicating Across Cultures* (New York: Guilford, 1999).

Todorov, Alexander, Anesu N. Mandisodza, Amir Goren, and Crystal C. Hall. "Inferences of Competence from Faces Predict Election Outcomes," *Science* 308 (2005), 1623–1626.

Trenholm, S., and T. Rose. "The Complaint Communicator: Teacher Perceptions of Appropriate Classroom Behavior," *Western Journal of Speech Communication* 45 (1981), 13–26.

Veenendall, Tom, and Rita Braito. "Androgeny in Spouse Interaction," in Lea P. Stewart and Stella Ting-Toomey, eds., *Communication, Gender, and Sex-Roles in Diverse Interaction Contexts* (Norwood, NJ: Ablex, 1987), 31–48.

Watzlawick, Paul, Janet Helmick Beavin, and Don D. Jackson. *Pragmatics of Human Communication* (New York: Norton, 1967).

Willis, Janine, and Alexander Todorov. "First Impressions: Making Up Your Mind After a 100-Ms Exposure to a Face," *Psychological Science* 17 (July 2006), 592–598.

Zebrowitz, Leslie A. *Reading Faces: Window to the Soul?* (Boulder, CO: Westview Press, 1997).

Zebrowitz, Leslie A., and Gillian Rhodes. "Nature Let a Hundred Flowers Bloom," in Gillian Rhodes and Leslie A. Zebrowitz, eds., *Facial Attractiveness* (Westport, CT: Ablex, 2002), 261–293.

Zhang, Liqing, and Roy F. Baumeister. "Your Money or Your Self-Esteem," *Personality and Social Psychology Bulletin* 32 (July 2006), 881–893.

Zimbardo, P. "Psychological Power and Pathology of Imprisonment," unpublished manuscript, Stanford University, Palo Alto, CA, 1971.

———. *Shyness* (Reading MA: Addison-Wesley, 1990).

Chapter 3   The Verbal Message

Adams, Scott. *Dilbert.* Retrieved January 16, 2007, from *www.unitedmedia.com/comics/dilbert/*.

Applebome, Peter. "The Birth of a Novel: Up North, Down South," *New York Times* (May 19, 1998), E1.

Becker, Carl. "Reasons for the Lack of Argumentation and Debate in the Far East," in Larry A. Samovar and Richard Porter, eds., *Intercultural Communication: A Reader*, 6th ed. (Belmont, CA: Wadsworth, 1991), 234–243.

Bell, Robert A., Nancy L. Buerkel-Rothfuss, and Kevin E. Gore. "Did You Bring the Yarmulke for the Cabbage Patch Kid?" *Human Communication Research* 14 (1987), 47–67.

Berryman, C. L., and L. R. Wilcox. "Attitudes toward Male and Female Speech: Experiments on the Effects of Sex-Typed Language," *Western Journal of Speech Communication* 44 (1980), 50–59.

Blumenthal, Michael. "The Eloquence Gap," *New Republic* (November 14, 1989), 18–19.

Bostrom, Robert, John R. Basehart, and Charles Rossiter. "The Effects of Three Types of Profane Language in Persuasive Messages," *Journal of Communication* 23 (1973), 461–475.

Bott, Jennifer. "Amway Changes Name, Mission," *Detroit Free Press* (October 25, 2000), F1.

Bradac, J. J., M. R. Hemphill, and C. H. Tardy. "Language Style on Trial: The Effects of 'Powerful' and 'Powerless' Speech upon Judgments of Victims and Villains," *Western Journal of Speech Communication* 45 (1981), 327–341.

Bradac, J. J., and A. Mulac. "A Molecular View of Powerful and Powerless Speech Styles," *Communication Monographs* 51 (1984), 307–319.

Brown, Roger, and Eric Lenneberg. "A Study in Language and Cognition," *Journal of Abnormal and Social Psychology* 49 (1954), 454–462.

Burgoon, M., J. P. Dillard, and N. E. Doran. "Friendly or Unfriendly Persuasion: The Effects of Violations of Expectations by Males and Females," *Human Communication Research* 10 (1983), 283–294.

Cameron, Deborah, ed. *The Feminist Critique of Language* (London: Routledge, 1990).

Candlish, S. "Private Language," *The Stanford Encyclopedia of Philosophy*, 2004.

Carmody, Deirdre. "College Recruiters and Counselors Share Some Tips from the Trenches," *New York Times* (October 11, 1989), B6.

Carroll, Raymonde. *Cultural Misunderstandings*, trans. by Carol Volk (Chicago: University of Chicago Press, 1988).

Chandler, T. "The Laureate's Choice—Re-seeing and Re-thinking the Familiar," *Providence Journal* (February 24, 2002), p. I9.

Condor, Bob. "Prunes Get an Image Makeover," *Detroit Free Press* (February 6, 2001).

Crane, Loren, Richard Dieker, and Charles Brown. "The Physiological Response to the Communication Modes: Reading, Listening, Writing, Speaking, and Evaluating," *Journal of Communication* 20 (1970), 231–240.

Davis, Hayley. "What Makes Bad Language Bad?" *Language and Communication* 9, no. 23 (1989), 1–9.

Durkel, J. C. "Non-Verbal Communication: Cues, Signals, and Symbols." Retrieved August 21, 2007, from *www .tsbvi.edu/Education/vmi/nonverbal.htm.*

Friedlander, John. "Abstract, Concrete, General and Specific Terms." Retrieved January 20, 2007, from *http://faculty.southwest.tn.edu/jfriedlander/abstract_ and_concrete.htm.*

Galvin, Kathleen M., and Bernard J. Brommel. *Family Communication: Cohesion and Change* (New York: HarperCollins, 1991).

Gordon, Peter. "Numerical Cognition Without Words: Evidence from Amazonia," *Science* 306, no. 5695 (October 15, 2004), 496–499.

Griffin, Em. *A First Look at Communication Theory* (New York: McGraw-Hill, 1991).

Hamilton, William L. "Low Down, Repulsed, Yet Watching All the Same," *New York Times* [Electronic version] (December 6, 2006), section 4, p. 5.

Haney, William V. *Communication and Organizational Behavior* (Homewood, IL: Irwin, 1992).

Haslett, B. J. *Communication: Strategic Action in Context* (Hillsdale, NJ: Erlbaum, 1987).

Hayakawa, S. I. *Language in Thought and Action,* 4th ed. (Orlando, FL: Harcourt Brace Jovanovich, 1978).

Heilbrun, A. B. "Measurement of Masculine and Feminine Sex-Role Identities as Independent Dimensions," *Journal of Consulting and Clinical Pathology* 44 (1976), 183–190.

Hood, James. "AT&T Plans to Kill Cingular Name," *Consumer Affairs.com* (May 4, 2006).

"House Restaurants Change Name of 'French Fries' and 'French Toast,'" *CNN.com* (March 11, 2003). Retrieved July 1, 2004, from: *www.cnn.com/2003/ ALLPOLITICS/03/11/freedom.fries/index.html.*

Kirkwood, William G. "Truthfulness as a Standard for Speech in Ancient India," *Southern Communication Journal* 54 (1989), 213–234.

Laing, R. D. *Self and Others,* 2nd ed. (New York: Penguin, 1972).

Lavoie, Denise. "Case Seeks Redefinition of 'Mother.'" *Ann Arbor News* (August 31, 2001), A7.

Legum, Colin. "The End of Cloud-Cuckoo-Land," *New York Times Magazine* (March 28, 1976), 18–19.

Lei, Xiaolan. "Sexism in Language," *Journal of Language and Linguistics* 5, no. 1 (2006).

Liska, J., E. W. Mechling, and S. Stathas. "Differences in Subjects' Perceptions and Believability between Users of Deferential and Nondeferential Language," *Communication Quarterly* 29 (1981), 40–48.

Losoncy, Lewis. *Best Team Skills* (Boca Raton, FL: St. Lucie Press, 1997).

Mabry, Edward. "A Multivariate Investigation of Profane Language," *Central States Speech Journal* 26 (1975), 39–44.

Ministry of Education. "Exploring Language Online," *Learning Media Limited* (1996). Ministry of Education, Wellington, New Zealand.

Motley, Michael. "Mindfulness in Solving Communicator's Dilemmas," *Communication Monographs* 59 (1992), 306–314.

Motluk, Alison. "You Are What You Speak," *New Scientist* 176, no. 2371 (2002), 34.

NetLingo. *http://www.netlingo.com,* accessed July 2007.

Osgood, Charles E. "Probing Subjective Culture Part 1. Crosslinguistic Tool-Making," *Journal of Communication* 24 (1974a), 21–35.

———. "Probing Subjective Culture Part 2. Crosscultural Tool-Using," *Journal of Communication* 24 (1974b), 82–100.

Osgood, Charles, George Suci, and Percy Tannenbaum. *The Measurement of Meaning* (Urbana: University of Illinois Press, 1957), chaps. 1–4.

Pearson, Judy Cornelia, Lynn H. Turner, and William Todd-Mancillas. *Gender and Communication,* 2nd ed. (Dubuque, IA: William C. Brown, 1991).

Quina, Kathryn, Joseph A. Wingard, and Henry G. Bates. "Language Style and Gender Stereotypes in Person Perception," *Psychology of Women Quarterly* 11 (1987), 111–122.

Reuters News Agency. "SPAM (the lunch), Spam (the junk mail), Make Their Peace," *Wall Street Journal* (May 31, 2001), B13.

———. "Gossip," *Detroit Free Press* (September 4, 2001), 5A.

Rossiter, Charles, and Robert Bostrom. "Profanity, 'Justification,' and Source Credibility," paper delivered at the annual conference of the National Society for the Study of Communication, Cleveland, OH, 1968.

Salant, Jonathon D. "FCC: Don't Use the F-word," *Ann Arbor News* (March 19, 2004), C1.

Samovar, Larry A., and Richard Porter, eds. *Intercultural Communication: A Reader,* 6th ed. (Belmont, CA: Wadsworth, 1991).

"Sapir-Whorf-Hypothesis Redux." *ETC: A Review of General Semantics* (Concord) 59 (Winter 2002/2003), 456–457.

Scotton, Carol M. "Self-Enhancing Codeswitching as Interactional Power," *Language and Communication* 8, no. 34 (1988), 199–212.

"Shoemaker's Foot in Mouth," *Detroit Free Press* (February 20, 1997), E1.

Sillars, Alan L., and Judith Weisberg. "Conflict as a Social Skill," in Michael E. Roloff and Gerald R. Miller, eds., *Interpersonal Processes: New Directions in Communication Research* (Newbury Park, CA: Sage, 1987), 140–171.

Stoltz, Paul G. *Adversity Quotient* (New York: John Wiley and Sons, 1997).

Tan, Amy. "Mother Tongue," in Joyce Carol Oates, ed., *The Best American Essays 1991* (New York: Ticknor and Fields, 1991).

Tannen, Deborah. *You Just Don't Understand: Women and Men in Conversation* (New York: Ballantine Books, 1990).

Tubbs, Stewart L. *A Systems Approach to Small Group Interaction,* 9th ed. (New York: McGraw-Hill, 2007).

Turkington, D., and D. G. Kingdon. "Cognitive Behaviour Therapy of Schizophrenia," in T. Wykes, N. Tarrier, and S. Lewis, eds., *Outcome and Innovation in Psychological Treatment of Schizophrenia* (Chichester, UK: Wiley, 1998), 59–79.

Urban Dictionary. *http://www.urbandictionary.com,* accessed July 2007.

Wain, M. "African Wildlife Photography: Communication Components." Retrieved on May 19, 2004, from M. Wain Web site: *www.mcdcwain.freeserve.co.uk/behaviour7.htm.*

Whiteman, Thomas, Sam Verghese, and Randy Peterson. *The Complete Stress Management Workbook* (Grand Rapids, MI: Zondervan Publishing House, 1996).

Whorf, Benjamin Lee. *Language, Thought, and Reality,* ed. John B. Carroll (Cambridge, MA: MIT Press, 1956).

"Words Can Heal." Retrieved May 21, 2004, from *Words Can Heal* Web site: *www.wordscanheal.com/aboutus/whoinvolved.htm#Advisors.*

Chapter 4   The Nonverbal Message

Alvarez, Julia. *In the Time of the Butterflies* (Chapel Hill, NC: Algonquin Books, 1994).

Andersen, Peter. *Nonverbal Communication: Forms and Functions* (Mountain View, CA: Mayfield, 1999).

Andersen, Peter, and Laura Guerrero, eds. *Handbook of Communication and Emotion* (San Diego, CA: Academic Press, 1998).

Anderson, P. A., and K. K. Sull. "Out of Touch, Out of Reach: Tactile Predispositions as Predictors of Interpersonal Distance," *Western Journal of Speech Communication* 49 (1985), 57–72.

Anolli, Luigi, and Rita Ciceri. "The Voice of Deception: Vocal Strategies of Naive and Able Liars," *Journal of Nonverbal Behavior* 21 (Spring 1997), 248–259.

Argyle, Michael. *The Psychology of Interpersonal Behavior,* rev. ed. (Baltimore: Penguin, 1985).

Barnlund, Dean C. *Interpersonal Communication: Survey and Studies* (Boston: Houghton Mifflin, 1968).

Baron-Cohen, Simon. *The Essential Difference: The Truth About the Male and Female Brain* (New York: Basic Books, 2003).

Bates, Brian, with John Cleese. *The Human Face* (London: BBC, 2001).

Biehl, Michael, David Matsumoto, Paul Ekman, et al. "Matsumoto and Ekman's Caucasian Facial Expressions of Emotion (JACFEE): Reliability Data and Cross-National Differences," *Journal of Nonverbal Behavior* 21 (Spring 1997), 3–21.

Birdwhistell, Ray L. *Introduction to Kinesics* (Louisville, KY: University of Louisville Press, 1952).

———. *Kinesics in Context* (Philadelphia: University of Pennsylvania Press, 1970).

Bodenhausen, Galen V., and C. Neil Macrae. "Putting a Face on Person Perception," *Social Cognition* 24, no. 5 (2006), 511–515.

Buller, David B., Krystyna D. Strzyzewski, and Frank G. Hunsaker. "Interpersonal Deception: II. The Inferiority of Conversational Participants as Deception Detectors," *Communication Monographs* 58 (1991), 25–38.

Burgoon, Judee K., David B. Buller, and W. Gill Woodall. *Nonverbal Communication: The Unspoken Dialogue* (New York: McGraw-Hill, 1996).

Burns, Nick. "One Hairy Lip, A Mix of Messages," *New York Times* (November 2, 2006), G3.

Caso, Letizia, Fridanna Marricciolo, Marino Bonaiuto, Aldert Vrij, and Samantha Mann. "The Impact of Deception and Suspicion on Different Hand Movements," *Journal of Nonverbal Behavior* 30 (March 2006), 1–19.

Chang, Eileen. "Red Rose, White Rose," in Eileen Chang, *Love in a Fallen City,* Karen S. Kingsbury, trans. (New York: New York Review Books, 2007).

Corbin, Martin. "Response to Eye Contact," *Quarterly Journal of Speech* 48 (1962), 415–418.

Darwin, Charles. *Evolution and Natural Selection,* ed. by Bert James Loewenberg (Boston: Beacon, 1959).

Dibiase, Rosemarie, and Jaime Gunnoe. "Gender and Culture Differences in Touching Behavior," *Journal of Social Psychology* 144, no. 1 (2004), 49–62.

Doherty, R. William. "The Emotional Contagion Scale: A Measure of Individual Differences," *Journal of Nonverbal Behavior* 21 (Summer 1997), 131–154.

Einstein, Elizabeth, and Lindsy Van Gelder. "Crowning Glories," *Allure* (August 2004), 105–108, 110.

Ekman, Paul. "Differential Communication of Affect by Head and Body Cues," *Journal of Personality and Social Psychology* 2 (1965), 726–735.

Ekman, Paul, and Wallace V. Friesen. "Constants across Cultures in the Face and Emotion," *Journal of Personality and Social Psychology* 17 (1971), 124–129.

———. *Unmasking the Face: A Guide to Recognizing Emotions from Facial Cues*, 2nd ed. (Palo Alto, CA: Consulting Psychologists Press, 1984).

Ekman Paul, and Maureen Sullivan. "Who Can Catch a Liar?" *American Psychologist* 46 (1991), 913–920.

Elfenbein, Hillary Anger. "Learning in Emotion Judgments Training and the Cross-Cultural Understanding of Facial Expressions," *Journal of Nonverbal Behavior* 30 (Spring 2006), 21–36.

Forgas, Joseph P. "The Role of Physical Attractiveness in the Interpretation of Facial Cues," *Personality and Social Psychology Bulletin* 13 (1987), 478–489.

Frank, Mark G., and Paul Ekman. "Appearing Truthful Generalizes Across Different Deception Situations," *Journal of Personality and Social Psychology* 86, no. 3 (2004), 486–495.

Goldin-Meadow, Susan. *Hearing Gesture* (Cambridge, MA: Belknap Press, 2003).

Greene, J. O., H. D. O'Hair, M. J. Cody, and C. Yen. "Planning and Control of Behavior during Deception," *Human Communication Research* 11 (1985), 335–364.

Guerrero, Laura, and Kory Floyd. *Nonverbal Communication in Close Relationships* (Mahwah, NJ: Lawrence Erlbaum, 2006).

Hall, Edward T. *The Silent Language* (New York: Fawcett, 1959).

———. *The Dance of Life* (Garden City, NY: Doubleday/Anchor, 1984).

———. "Monochronic and Polychronic Time," in Laura K. Guerrero et al., eds., *The Nonverbal Reader: Classic and Contemporary Readings*, 2nd ed. (Prospect Heights, IL: Waveland Press, 1999), 237–240.

Hall, Edward T., and William Foote Whyte. "Intercultural Communication: A Guide to Men of Action," in Alfred G. Smith, ed., *Communication and Culture: Readings in the Codes of Human Interaction* (New York: Holt, Rinehart and Winston, 1966), 567–576.

Hall, Judith A. "Women's and Men's Nonverbal Communication," in Anita Vangelisti and Daniel Perlman, eds., *Cambridge Handbook of Personal Relationships* (New York: Cambridge University Press, 2006), 201–218.

Hall, Judith A., Nora Murphy, and Marianne Mast. "Recall of Nonverbal Cues: Exploring a Definition of Interpersonal Sensitivity," *Journal of Nonverbal Behavior* 30 (Winter 2006), 141–155.

Hancock, Jeffrey T., and Philip J. Dunham. "Impression Formation in Computer-Mediated Communication Revisited," *Communication Research* 23 (June 2000), 325–347.

Hargie, Owen, Christine Saunders, and David Dickson. *Social Skills in Interpersonal Communication* (Cambridge, MA: Brookline Books, 1987).

Heingartner, Douglas. "It's the Way You Say It, Truth Be Told," *New York Times* (August 1, 2004), G1, 7.

Heslin, R., and T. Alper. "Touch: The Bonding Gesture," in M. Wiemann and R. P. Harrison, eds., *Nonverbal Interaction* (Beverly Hills, CA: Sage, 1983).

Hess, E. H. "Attitude and Pupil Size," *Scientific American* 212 (April 1965), 46–54.

———. *The Tell-Tale Eye* (New York: Van Nostrand Reinhold, 1975).

Jacobson, David. "Impression Formation in Cyberspace," *JCMC* 5 (September 1999).

James, Caryn. "After All That Goodness, A Sudden Fall from Grace," *New York Times* (January 22, 2007), E7.

Jones, Stanley E. "Communicating with Touch," in Laura Guerrero et al., eds., *The Nonverbal Communication Reader: Classic and Contemporary Readings*, 2nd ed. (Prospect Heights, IL: Waveland Press, 1999), 192–201.

Jones, S. E., and E. Yarbrough. "A Naturalistic Study of the Meanings of Touch," *Communication Monographs* 52 (1985), 19–56.

Kawamura, Satoru, and Keiko Kageyama. "Smiling Faces Rated More Feminine than Serious Faces in Japan," *Perception & Motor Skills* 103 (August 2006), 210–214.

Kinzel, August. "Towards an Understanding of Violence," *Attitude* 1 (1969).

Kleinke, C. R. *Meeting and Understanding People* (New York: Freeman, 1986).

Knapp, Mark L., and Judy A. Hall. *Nonverbal Communication in Human Interaction*, 5th ed. (Belmont, CA: Wadsworth, 2002).

Lahiri, Jhumpa. "A Temporary Matter," in Jhumpa Lahiri, *Interpreter of Maladies* (Boston: Houghton Mifflin, 1999), 1–22.

Lakin, Jessica L., Valerie E. Jefferis, Clara Michelle Cheng, and Tanya L. Chartrand. "The Chameleon Effect as Social Glue," *Journal of Nonverbal Behavior* 27 (Fall 2003), 145–162.

Levine, Robert. *A Geography of Time* (New York: Basic Books, 1997).

Libby, William L., and Donna Yaklevich. "Personality Determinants of Eye Contact and Direction of Gaze Aversion," *Journal of Personality and Social Psychology* 27 (1973), 197–206.

Lohr, Steve. "Slow Down, Brave Multitasker; And Don't Read This in Public," *New York Times* (March 25, 2007), 1, 27.

Mast, Marianne Schmid, and Judith A. Hall. "Women's Advantage at Remembering Others' Appearance," *Personality and Social Psychology Bulletin* 32 (March 2006), 353–364.

Matsumoto, David. "Culture and Nonverbal Behavior," in Valerie Manusov and Miles Patterson, eds., *The SAGE Handbook of Nonverbal Communication* (Beverly Hills, CA: Sage, 2006), 219–235.

McDaniel, Ed, and Peter A. Andersen. "International Patterns of Interpersonal Tactile Communication," *Journal of Nonverbal Behavior* 22, no. 1 (Spring 1998), 58–72.

Mehrabian, Albert. "Orientation Behaviors and Nonverbal Attitude Communication," *Journal of Communication* 17 (1967), 324–332.

———. "Communication without Words," *Psychology Today* 2 (1968), 53–56.

Morris, Desmond, Peter Collett, Peter Marsh, and Marie O'Shaughnessy. *Gestures* (New York: Stein and Day, 1979).

Mottet, Timothy P., Steven A. Beebe, Paul C. Raffeld, and Michelle L. Paulsel. "The Effects of Student Verbal and Nonverbal Teachers' Liking of Students and Willingness to Comply with Student Requests," *Communication Quarterly* 52, no. 1 (Winter 2004), 27–38.

Moynihan, Colin. "City of a Thousand Handshakes," *New York Times* (May 22, 2004), B1, 4.

Nelson, Audrey, with Susan Golant. *You Don't Say: Navigating Nonverbal Communication between the Sexes* (New York: Prentice Hall, 2004).

Noller, Patricia. "Nonverbal Communication in Close Relationships," in Anita Vangelisti and Daniel Perlman, eds., *Cambridge Handbook of Personal Relationships* (New York: Cambridge University Press, 2006), 403–420.

Parnes, Amie. "Dress-Down Is Down if Not Quite Out," *New York Times* (June 13, 2001), G1.

Pearson, Judy Cornelia, Lynn H. Turner, and Wm. Todd-Mancillas. *Gender and Communication,* 3rd ed. (Dubuque, IA: Brown and Benchmark, 1994).

Pease, Alan, and Barbara Pease. *The Definitive Book of Body Language* (New York: Bantam Books, 2006).

Penton-Voak, Ian S., Nicholas Pound, Anthony C. Little, and David I. Perrett. "Personality Judgments from Natural and Composite Facial Images: More Evidence for a 'Kernel of Truth' in Social Perception," *Social Cognition* 24 (October 2006), 607–640.

"Phones Are the New Cars." In "Technology Quarterly," in *The Economist* (December 2, 2006), 16–18.

Prager, Karen. "Intimacy in Personal Relationships," in Clyde Hendrick and Susan S. Hendrick, eds., *Close Relationships: A Sourcebook* (Thousand Oaks, CA: Sage, 2000), 229–242.

Robinson, Jeffrey D. "Nonverbal Communication and Physician-Patient Interaction Review and New Directions," in Valerie Manusov and Miles Patterson, eds., *The SAGE Handbook of Nonverbal Communication* (Beverly Hills, CA: Sage, 2006), 437–459.

Rodgers, Joan Ellison. "Flirting Fascination," *Psychology Today* (January/February 1999), 37–70.

Rosenfeld, Howard M. "Effect of Approval-Seeking Induction in Interpersonal Proximity," *Psychological Reports* 17 (1965), 120–122.

Scheflen, Albert E. "Quasi-Courtship Behavior in Psychotherapy," *Psychiatry* 28 (1965), 245–257.

Semic, Beth. "Vocal Attractiveness," in Laura Guerrero et al., eds., *The Nonverbal Communication Reader: Classic and Contemporary Readings,* 2nd ed. (Prospect Heights, IL: Waveland Press, 1999), 149–155.

Simpson, Jeffry A., Steven W. Gangestad, and Michael Biek. "Personality and Nonverbal Social Behavior: An Ethological Perspective of Relationship Initiation," *Journal of Experimental Social Psychology* 29 (1993), 434–461.

Smith, Jack. "To Say Luxury in Chinese, Start by Sitting in the Back," *New York Times* (October 27, 2004), G14.

Sommer, Robert. *Personal Space: The Behavioral Basis of Design* (Englewood Cliffs, NJ: Prentice-Hall, 1969).

Soskin, William F., and Paul E. Kauffman. "Judgment of Emotion in Word-Free Voice Samples," *Journal of Communication* 11 (1961), 73–81.

Stewart, J., and G. D'Angelo. *Together: Communicating Interpersonally,* 2nd ed. (New York: Random House, 1980).

Storace, Patricia. *Dinner with Persephone* (New York: Vintage, 1997).

Ting-Toomey, Stella. *Communicating Across Cultures* (New York: Guilford, 1999).

Trager, George L. "Paralanguage: A First Approximation," *Studies in Linguistics* 13 (1958), 1–12.

Tusing, Kyle James, and James Price Dillard. "The Sounds of Dominance: Vocal Precursors of Perceived Dominance During Interpersonal Influence," *Human Communication Research* 26, no. 1 (2000), 148–157.

Vrij, Aldert. "Nonverbal Communication and Deception," in Valerie Manusov and Miles Patterson, eds., *The SAGE Handbook of Nonverbal Communication* (Beverly Hills, CA: Sage, 2006), 341–359.

Vrij, Aldert, Lucy Akehurst, Stavroula Soukara, and Ray Bull. "Detecting Deceit via Analyses of Verbal and Nonverbal Behavior in Children and Adults," *Human Communication Research* 30, no. 1 (2004), 8–41.

Walther, Joseph B. "Nonverbal Dynamics in Computer-Mediated Communication," in Valerie Manusov and Miles Patterson, eds. *The SAGE Handbook of Nonverbal Communication* (Beverly Hills, CA: Sage, 2006), 461–479.

Watts, Geoff. "You Need Hands," *The Lancet* 367 (April 29–May 5, 2006), 1383–1384.

Willis, F. N., and H. K. Hamm. "The Use of Interpersonal Touch in Securing Compliances," *Journal of Nonverbal Behavior* 5 (1980), 49–55.

Winstead, Barbara A., Valerian J. Derlega, et al. "Friendship, Social Interaction, and Coping with Stress," *Communication Research* 19 (1992), 193–211.

Zebrowitz, Leslie A. "Finally, Faces Find Favor," *Social Cognition* 24, no. 5 (2006), 657–701.

Chapter 5   Listening

Acuff, Frank L. *How to Negotiate Anything with Anyone Anywhere Around the World,* 2nd ed. (New York: AMACOM, 1997).

Andre, Rae. *Positive Solitude* (New York: Harper-Collins, 1991).

Armstrong, A. "Critical Listening," *About, Inc.* Retrieved June 1, 2004, from About, Inc. Web site: *http://stereos.about.com/cs/trainingyourear/a/listening.htm.*

Athos, Anthony G., and John J. Gabarro. *Interpersonal Behavior: Communication and Understanding in Relationships* (Englewood Cliffs, NJ: Prentice-Hall, 1978).

Barker, Larry. *Listening Behavior* (Englewood Cliffs, NJ: Prentice-Hall, 1971).

Barker, L., R. Edwards, C. Gaines, K. Gladney, and F. Holley. "An Investigation of Proportional Time Spent in Various Communication Activities by College Students," *Journal of Applied Communication Research* 8 (1981), 101–109.

Beagrie, Scott. "How to Listen Meaningfully," *Personnel Today* (April 26, 2005), 23.

Blanchard, G. "Is Listening Through a Stethoscope a Dying Art?" *Boston Globe* (May 25, 2004), C1.

Bostrom, Robert. "Patterns of Communicative Interaction in Small Groups," *Speech Monographs* 3 (1970), 257–263.

Bostrom, Robert N., and Enid S. Waldhart. "Memory Models and the Measurement of Listening," *Communication Education* 37 (1988), 1–13.

Brilhart, Barbara. "The Relationship between Some Aspects of Communicative Speaking and Communicative Listening," *Journal of Communication* 15 (1965), 35–46.

Broadbent, Donald. *Perception and Communication* (Elmsford, NY: Pergamon, 1958).

Brooks, Bill. "The Power of Active Listening," *The American Salesman* 51, no. 6 (June 2006), 12.

Brooks, William D. *Speech Communication,* 4th ed. (Dubuque, IA: Brown, 1981).

Cohen, L. "Few of Us Are Really Good at Listening," *Boston Globe* (February 27, 2003), H5.

Covey, Stephen. *The 7 Habits of Highly Effective People* (New York: Simon and Schuster, 1990).

Crane, Loren, Richard Dicker, and Charles Brown. "The Physiological Response to the Communication Modes: Reading, Listening, Writing, Speaking, and Evaluating," *Journal of Communication* 20 (1970), 231–240.

Dulye, Linda. "Get Out of Your Office," *HR Magazine* 51, no. 7 (July 2006), 99–101.

Fox News Channel. "Statement from Cubs Fan Steve Bartman" (October 15, 2003), from *www.foxnews.com/story/0,2933,100218,00.html.*

Fuimano, J. "Sharp Listening Skills Point Staff in Right Direction," *Nursing Management* 35 (May 2004), 12.

Goss, Blain. *Processing Information* (Belmont, CA: Wadsworth, 1982).

Guttman, Howard M. "Power Listening," *Leadership Excellence* (Provo) 22, no. 2 (February 2005), 18.

Hargie, Owen, Christine Saunders, and David Dickson. *Social Skills in Interpersonal Communication* (Cambridge, MA: Brookline Books, 1987).

Keefe, William. *Listen, Management* (New York: McGraw-Hill, 1971).

Keller, P. "Major Findings in Listening in the Past Ten Years," *Journal of Communication* 10 (1960), 29–30.

Kern, E. "The Brain: Part II: The Neuron," *Life* (October 22, 1971).

Losoncy, Lewis. *Today* (Boca Raton, FL: St. Lucie Press, 1998).

Malone, Patrick. "A Prelude to Profit: The Finest Listening Skills in the World," in Melanie Bullock, Charla Friday, Kathy Belcher, Bonnie Bisset, Simon Hurley, Casey Foote, and Diem Thai, *1998 International Conference on Work Teams Proceeding* (Dallas, TX), 199.

McCormack, Mark. *What They Don't Teach You at Harvard Business School: Notes from a Street Smart Executive* (New York: Bantam, 1984).

Moore, Kenny. "Become a Better Communicator by Keeping Your Mouth Shut," *The Journal for Quality and Participation* 28, no. 2 (2005), 8–10.

Moray, Neville. *Listening and Attention* (Baltimore: Penguin, 1969).

Munoz, Gisela M. "The Five R's of Listening," *Practical Lawyer* 52, no. 2 (April 2006), 11–18.

Murphy, Kevin J. *Effective Listening* (Salem, NH: 1992).

Nadig, L. *Tips on Effective Listening.* (April 7, 2004). Retrieved May 24, 2004, from Larry Alan Nadig, PhD, Clinical Psychology, Marriage and Family Therapist Web site: *www.drnadig.com/listening.htm.*

Nadler, Scott, and Roy L. Simerly. "The Effect of Listening on the Formation of Students' Trust and Commitment in Academic Advising: A Study at a United States University," *International Journal of Management* 23, no. 2 (2006), 215–221.

Nichols, Ralph. "Listening Is a 10-Part Skill," *Nation's Business* 45 (1957), 56–60.

Pearce, C. Glenn. "Learning How to Listen Empathically," *Supervisory Management* 36, no. 11 (1991).

Pearce, L., and S. Newton. *The Conditions of Human Growth* (New York: Citadel Press, 1963).

Pollitt, David. "Training to the Beat of a Different Drum," *Training & Management Development Methods* (Bradford, England) 20, Iss. 1–5 (2006), 305–312.

Rankin, Paul. "The Measurement of the Ability to Understand Spoken Language," unpublished PhD dissertation, University of Michigan, 1926, 43.

Reik, Theodore. *Listening with the Third Ear* (New York: Grove Press, 1948).

Rogers, Carl. *On Becoming a Person* (Boston: Houghton Mifflin, 1961).

Rowh, Mark. "Listen Up!" *Career World* 34, no. 6 (April/May 2006), 22–24.

Schmid, John. "Driven to Distraction: Put that BlackBerry Down and Listen Up, Author Advises," *Milwaukee Journal Sentinel* (January 8, 2007).

Tannen, Deborah. *You Just Don't Understand: Women and Men in Conversation* (New York: Ballantine Books, 1990).

Walston, Sandra Ford. "Hello Saturn! Hello Neptune!" *Strategic Finance* 87, no. 12 (June 2006), 61. Retrieved June 24, 2007, from *www.walstoncourage.com/pages/articles/saturnneptune.shtml.*

Walters, Jamie. "Fostering a Culture of Deep Inquiry and Listening," *The Journal for Quality and Participation* (Cincinnati) 28, no. 2 (Summer 2005), 4–7.

Chapter 6   Conflict and Negotiation

Akin, J. "Escalation Limiting Language," *Beyond Intractability.org.* (2003). Retrieved July 7, 2004, from Beyond Intractability Web site: *www.beyondintractability.org/m/escalation-limiting_language.jsp.*

Bester, Helmut, and Karl Warneryd. "Conflict and the Social Contract," *Scand. J of Economics* 108, no. 2 (2006), 231–249.

Brahm, E. "Conflict Sages," *Beyond Intractability.org* (2003). Retrieved July 7, 2004, from Beyond Intractability Web site: *www.beyondintractability.org/m/conflict_stages.jsp.*

"Canton Township Paints Over Big Boy Statue Controversy," *America's Newspapers* (July 13, 2004), 10A. Retrieved from *infoweb.newsbank.com/iwsearch/we/InfoWeb?p_action=doc&p_docid=103D53F0168BBDCF&p_docnum=11&NBID=G5EB50WIMTA5MDQzMDY2IC41Mjg3MTM6MTo2OjE2NC43Ng.*

Cheung, Sai On, Tak Wing Yiu Yiu, and Sau Fung Yeung. "A Study of Styles and Outcomes in Construction Dispute Negotiation," *Journal of Construction Engineering and Management* (August 2006).

Cloke, Kenneth, and Joan Goldsmith. *Resolving Conflicts at Work,* 2nd ed. (San Francisco: Jossey-Bass, 2005).

Coase, Ronald H. "The Problem of Social Cost." *Journal of Law and Economics* 3 (October 1960), 1–44.

Cohen, Herb. *You Can Negotiate Anything* (Secaucus, NJ: Lyle Stuart, 1996).

Covey, Stephen. *The 7 Habits of Highly Effective People* (New York: A Fireside Book, 1990).

Deep, Sam, and Lyle Sussman. *Yes You Can!* (Reading, MA: Addison-Wesley, 1998).

Dzwonkowski Ron, "Let's Have a Heart-to-Heart Every Day," *Detroit Free Press* (July 5, 1998), 2H.

Fisher, Roger, William Ury, and Bruce Patton. *Getting to Yes,* 2nd ed. (New York: Penguin Books, 1991).

Goleman, D., *Emotional Intelligence: Why It Can Matter More than IQ* (London: Bloomsbury, 1995).

———. "Emotional Intelligence: Issues in Paradigm Building," in G. Cherniss and D. Goleman, eds., *The Emotionally Intelligent Workplace* (San Francisco: Jossey-Bass, 2001), 13–26.

Goleman, D., R. Boyatzis, and A. McKee. *The New Leaders: Transforming the Art of Leadership into the Science of Results* (London: Little Brown, 2002), 182.

———. *Primal Leadership: Learning to Lead with Emotional Intelligence* (Boston: Harvard Business School Press, 2004).

Goudakov, Vladimir. "Gumilev and Huntington: Approaches and Terminologies," *Diogenes* 210 (2006), 82–90.

Hede, Andrew. "The Shadow Group: Towards an Explanation of Interpersonal Conflict in Work Groups," *Journal of Managerial Psychology* 22, no. 1 (2007), 25–39.

Hoffmann, Michael H. G. "Logical Argument Mapping: A Method for Overcoming Cognitive Problems," *International Journal of Conflict Management* 16, no. 4 (2005), 305–335.

Horn, S. *Tongue Fu: How to Deflect, Disarm, and Defuse any Verbal Conflict.* (New York: St. Martin's Press, 1996).

———. "Ten Tongue Fu!® Tips," *Samhorn.com.* (2004). From *www.samhorn.com/article_10_Tongue_Fu_Tips .html.*

J. D. Power and Associates. "The Saturn Way" (September 1992). Los Angeles: J. D. Power and Associates. Retrieved from *http://home.business.utah.edu/mgths/ pdf/CMR11.PDF.*

Jannetta, Candy. "Handling Gatecrashers: Conflict Management and Resolution," *Legal Information Management* 6 (2006), 28–30.

Kilmann, R., and K. W. Thomas. "Interpersonal Conflict– Handling Behavior as Reflections of Jungian Personality," *Psychological Reports* 37 (1975), 971–980.

Kyriacou, Andreas P. "Functional, Overlapping, Competing, Jurisdictions and Ethnic Conflict Management," *Kyklos* 59, no. 1 (2006), 63–83.

Lage, L. "Dumars: Pistons in 'Same Neighborhood' with Rasheed Wallace," (July 16, 2004). Retrieved from *www.mlive.com/sportsflash/michigan/index.ssf?/base/ sports-8/1089969540293320.xml.*

Lewicki, Roy, Bruce Barry, and David Saunders. *Negotiation: Readings, Exercises and Cases,* 5th ed. (New York: McGraw-Hill, 2007).

Lewicki, Roy J., Joseph A. Litterer, John W. Minton, and David M. Saunders. *Negotiation,* 3rd ed. (New York: Irwin/McGraw-Hill, 1998).

Lim, John, and Yin Ping Yang. "Enhancing Negotiators' Performance with Computer Support for Pre-Negotiation Preparation and Negotiation: An Experimental Investigation in an East Asian Context," *Journal of Global Information Management* 15, no. 1 (January-March 2007), 1–2.

Losoncy, Lewis. *Best Team Skills* (Boca Raton, FL: St. Lucie Press, 1997).

———. *Today! Grab It* (New York: St. Lucie Press, 1998).

Molm, Linda D., Jessica L. Collett, and David R. Schaefer. "Conflict and Fairness in Social Exchange," *Social Forces* 84, no. 4 (June 2006), 2331–2352.

Nibler, R., and K. Harris. "The Effects of Culture and Cohesiveness on Intragroup Conflict and Effectiveness," *The Journal of Social Psychology* 143, no. 5 (October 2003), 613.

Sillars, A. L. "Procedures for Coding Interpersonal Conflict," Department of Communication Studies, University of Montana, 1986.

Sillars, Alan L., and Judith Weisberg. "Conflict as a Social Skill," in Michael E. Roloff and Gerald R. Miller, eds., *Interpersonal Processes: New Directions in Communication Research* (Newbury Park, CA: Sage, 1987), 140–171.

Ury, William. *Getting Past No* (New York: Bantam Books, 1993).

Walker, Michael A., and George L. Harris. *Negotiations: Six Steps to Success* (Upper Saddle River, NJ: Prentice-Hall, 1995).

Wilmot, William, and Joyce Hocker. *Interpersonal Conflict,* 5th ed. (New York: McGraw-Hill, 1998).

Chapter 7   Ethics and Communication

Abelson, Raziel. "History of Ethics," in Paul Edwards, ed., *The Encyclopedia of Philosophy,* vol. 3 (New York: Macmillan and Free Press, 1967), 81–117.

American Heritage Dictionary of the English Language. (Boston: Houghton Mifflin, 2004).

Aristotle. *Introduction to Aristotle,* Richard McKeon, ed. (New York: Random House, Modern Library, 1947).

Augustine. *Enchiridion,* Henry Paolucci, ed. (Chicago: Regnery, 1961).

Barringer, Felicity. "Newsday Refuses to Reveal Source of Thomas Report," *New York Times* (February 14, 1992), A20.

Barry, Dan, David Barstow, Jonathan D. Glater, Adam Liptak, and Jacques Steinberg. "Times Reporter Who Resigned Leaves Long Trail of Deception," *New York Times* (May 11, 2003), A1.

Bavelas, Janet Beavin, Alex Black, Nicole Chovil, and Jennifer Mullett. *Equivocal Communication* (Newbury Park, CA: Sage, 1990).

Bok, Sissela. *Secrets: On the Ethics of Concealment and Revelation* (New York: Vintage, 1989).

———. *Lying: Moral Choice in Public and Private Life,* 2nd ed. (New York: Vintage, 1999).

Carr, David. "Skipping Merrily Along as Others Take the Heat," *New York Times* (February 5, 2007), C1–C7.

Christians, Clifford, and Kaarle Nordenstreng. "Social Responsibility Worldwide," *Journal of Mass Media Ethics* 19, no. 1 (2004), 3–28.

Christians, Clifford G., Mark Fackler, Kim B. Rotzoll, and Kathy Brittain. *Media Ethics: Cases and Moral Reasoning,* 5th ed. (Reading, MA: Addison-Wesley, 1998).

Christians, Clifford, and Michael Traber, eds. *Communication Ethics and Universal Values* (Thousand Oaks, CA: Sage, 1997).

Colvin, Geoffrey. "Wonder Women of Whistleblowing," *Fortune* 146, no. 3 (2002), 56.

Couldry, Nick. *Listening Beyond the Echoes: Media, Ethics, and Agency in an Uncertain World* (Boulder, CO: Paradigm Publishers, 2006).

Donadio, Rachel. "Nadine Gordimer and the Hazards of Biography," *New York Times Sunday Book Review* (December 31, 2006).

Ekman, Paul. *Telling Lies* (New York: Norton, 1985).

Farhi, Paul. "U.S. Media Settle with Wen Ho Lee," *Washington Post* (June 3, 2006), A1.

Fox, Richard Wightman. "A Heartbreaking Problem of Staggering Proportions," *Journal of American History* 90 (March 2004), 1341–1346.

Franklin, Nancy. "Show and Tell: When Did Privacy Go Public?" *New Yorker* (August 24–31, 1998), 11–12.

Freedman, Samuel G. "The Predictable Scandal," *Columbia Journalism Review* 44 (March/April 2006), 50–53.

Glazer, Sarah, "Combating Scientific Misconduct: The Issues," *CQ* (January 10, 1997), 3–23.

Gorney, Carole. "Litigation Journalism Is a Scourge," *New York Times* (February 15, 1993), A15.

Griffin, Em. *A First Look at Communication Theory,* 6th ed. (New York: McGraw-Hill, 2006).

Hafner, Katie. "Lessons in the School of Cut and Paste," *New York Times* (June 28, 2001), G1, 6.

Hassan, Adeel. "Blair's Victims: That Helpless Feeling," *Columbia Journalism Review* 42 (July/August 2003), 19–22.

Hauser, Marc D. *Moral Minds: How Nature Designed Our Universal Sense of Right and Wrong* (New York: HarperCollins, 2006).

Interlandi, Janeen. "An Unwelcome Discovery," *New York Times Magazine* (October 22, 2006), 98–103.

Jensen, J. Vernon. *Ethical Issues in the Communication Process* (Matawah, NJ: Erlbaum, 1997).

Kant, Immanuel. *Foundations of the Metaphysics of Morals,* Lewis White Beck, trans. (Indianapolis: Bobbs-Merrill, Library of Liberal Arts, 1959).

Kidder, Rushworth M. *Moral Courage* (New York: HarperCollins, 2005).

Kiernan, Matthew, ed. *Media Ethics* (London and New York: Routledge, 1998).

Kleinfield, N. R. "Mideast Tensions Are Getting Personal on Campus at Columbia," *New York Times* (January 18, 2005), B1.

Knapp, Mark L. "Lying and Deception in Close Relationships," in Anita Vangelisti and Daniel Perlman, eds., *Cambridge Handbook of Personal Relationships* (New York: Cambridge University Press, 2006), 517–532.

Knapp, Mark L., and Anita L. Vangelisti. *Interpersonal Communication and Human Interaction,* 4th ed. (Boston: Allyn and Bacon, 2000).

Lacayo, Richard, and Amanda Ripley. "Persons of the Year 2002: Cynthia Cooper, Coleen Rowley and Sherron Watkins." *www.time.com/time/personoftheyear/2002/poyintro.html.*

Lea, Martin, and Russell Spears. "Love at First Byte? Building Personal Relationships over Computer Networks," in Julia T. Wood and Steve Duck, eds., *Under-Studied Relationships: Off the Beaten Track* (Thousand Oaks, CA: Sage, 1995), 197–233.

Levitt, Steven D., and Stephen J. Dubner. *Freakonomics: A Rogue Economist Explores the Hidden Side of Everything,* revised and expanded ed. (New York: HarperCollins, 2006).

Lippard, Paula. "Ask Me No Questions, I'll Tell You No Lies," *Western Journal of Speech Communication* 52 (Winter 1988), 91–103.

Liptak, Adam. "Reporters Face Scrutiny in C.I.A. Leak Inquiry," *New York Times* (September 28, 2004), A18.

"Media Advisory: FAIR Calls for Revealing Sources in Plame, Lee Cases" (September 5, 2004). From *www .fair.org/press-releases/plame-lee.html.*

Mieth, Dietmar. "The Basic Norm of Truthfulness," in Clifford Christians and Michael Traber, eds., *Communication Ethics and Universal Values* (Thousand Oaks, CA: Sage, 1997), 87–103.

Mill, John Stuart. *Selected Writings of John Stuart Mill,* Maurice Cowling, ed. (New York: New American Library, 1968).

Noller, Patricia. "Nonverbal Communication in Close Relationships," in Anita Vangelisti and Daniel Perlman, eds., *Cambridge Handbook of Personal Relationships* (New York: Cambridge University Press, 2006), 403–420.

"NSA Whistleblower Tells House Subcommittee Domestic Spying Could Effect [*sic*] 'Millions of Americans,'" Federal News Service (Washington, DC: February 14, 2006).

Posner, Richard A. *The Little Book of Plagiarism* (New York: Pantheon, 2007).

Rainie, Lee, Susannah Fox, and Mary Madden. "One Year Later: September 11 and the Internet." (September 11, 2004). From *www.pewinternet.org/PPF/r/69/ report)display.asp.*

Rawls, John. *A Theory of Justice* (Cambridge, MA: Harvard University Press, 1971).

Rost, Peter. *The Whistleblower: Confessions of a Healthcare Hitman* (New York: Soft Scull Press, 2006).

Rowley, Coleen. "Coleen Rowley's Memo to FBI Director Robert Mueller," *Time* (May 21, 2002). From *www .time.com/time/covers/110120603/memo.html.*

Schuller, Robert H. *Life's Not Fair but God Is Good* (Nashville, TN: Thomas Nelson, 1991).

Schwartz, John. "As Big Brother Watches, Users Encounter Frustration," *New York Times* (September 5, 2001), A1.

"See Evil, Hear Evil, Speak Evil," *New York Times* (March 19, 2001), 7.

Simpson, Kevin. "To ID or Not to ID: Debate Renewed on Rape Victims," *Denver Post* (October 17, 2004), C1.

Smith, Richard Norton. "'The President Is Fine' and Other Historical Lies," *Columbia Journalism Review* (September/October 2001), 30–32.

Stanley, Alessandra. "Poet Told All: Therapist Provides the Record," *New York Times* (July 15,1991), A1.

Weiner, Jon. *Historians in Trouble* (New York: New Press, 2007).

"Whistleblowing Workers: Becoming an Endangered Species?" *HR Focus* 83, no. 6 (2006), 9.

Williams, Patricia J. "Shrieking Violets," *Nation,* (February 14, 2005), p. 9.

Wood, Andrew F., and Matthew J. Smith. *Online Communication: Linking Technology, Identity, and Culture* (Mahwah, NJ: Erlbaum, 2001).

Chapter 8   Relationships in Process

Ablow, Keith. "Finding New Passion After the Pain of Infidelity," *New York Times* (June 20, 2006), F5.

Acitele, L. K. "When Spouses Talk to Each Other about Their Relationship," *Journal of Social and Personal Relationships* 5 (1987), 185–199.

Altman, I., and D. Taylor. *Social Penetration: The Development of Interpersonal Relationships* (New York: Irvington, 1983).

Aron, Arthur, Helen E. Fisher, and Greg Strong. "Romantic Love," in Anita Vangelisti and Daniel Perlman, eds., *Cambridge Handbook of Personal Relationships* (New York: Cambridge University Press, 2006), 595–614.

Baxter, Leslie. "Strategies for Ending Relationships: Two Studies," *Western Journal of Speech Communication* 46 (1982), 223–241.

———. "Trajectories of Relationship Disengagement," *Journal of Social and Personal Relationships* 1 (1984), 223–241.

———. "Forms and Functions of Intimate Play in Interpersonal Relationships," *Human Communication Research* 18 (1992), 336–363.

Baxter, Leslie A., and Dawn O. Braithwaite. "Introduction: Meta-Theory and Theory in Family Communication Research," in Dawn O. Braithwaite and Leslie A. Baxter, eds., *Engaging Theories in Family Communication: Multiple Perspectives* (Thousand Oaks, CA: Sage, 2006).

Berscheid, Ellen, and Harry T. Reis. "Attraction and Close Relationships," in Daniel Gilbert, Susan Fiske, and Gardner Lindzey, eds., *Handbook of Social Psychology,* 4th ed., vol. 2 (New York: McGraw-Hill, 1998), 193–281.

Bochner, Arthur P., and Eric M. Eisenberg. "Family Process: System Perspectives," in Charles R. Berger and Steve H. Chaffee, eds., *Handbook of Communication Science* (Newbury Park, CA: Sage, 1987), 540–563.

Boone, R. Thomas, and Ross Buck. "Emotional Expressivity and Trustworthiness," *Journal of Nonverbal Behavior* 27, no. 3 (2003), 163–182.

Buber, Martin. "Distance and Relation," *Psychiatry* 20 (1957).

Bury, Martine. "You and Me Against the World," in Edwidge Danticat, ed., *The Butterfly's Way* (New York: Soho Press, 2001), 101–108.

Buss, David. M., Todd K. Shackelford, Lee A. Kirkpatrick, and Randy J. Larsen. "Human Mate Selection," *American Scientist* 73 (January–February, 1985), 47–51.

———. "A Half Century of Mate Preferences: The Cultural Evolution of Values," *Journal of Marriage & the Family* 63 (May 2001), 491–503.

Bussey, Kay, and Albert Bandura. "Social Cognitive Theory of Gender Development and Functioning," in Alice H. Eagly, Anne E. Beall, and Robert J. Sternberg, eds., *The Psychology of Gender,* 2nd ed. (New York: Guilford Press, 2004), 92–119.

Byrne, Donn. "An Overview (and Underview) of Research and Theory within the Attraction Paradigm," *Journal of Social and Personal Relationships* 14 (1997), 417–431.

Canary, Daniel J., and Marianne Dainton, eds. *Maintaining Relationships through Communication: Relational, Contextual, and Cultural Variations* (Mahwah, NJ: Erlbaum, 2003).

Canary, Daniel J., and Laura Stafford. "Relational Maintenance Strategies and Equity in Marriage," *Communication Monographs* 59 (1992), 243–267.

———, eds. *Communication and Relational Maintenance* (San Diego, CA: Academic Press, 1994).

Chan, Darius K.-S., and Grand H.-L. Cheng. "A Comparison of Offline and Online Friendship Qualities at Different Stages of Relationship Development," *Journal of Social and Personal Relationships* 21, no. 3 (2004), 305–320.

Cheever, John. "Goodbye, My Brother," in *The Stories of John Cheever* (New York: Knopf, 1978), 3–21.

Chelune, G. J., J. T. Robison, and M. J. Kommor. "A Cognitive Interaction Model of Intimate Relationships," in V. J. Derlega, ed., *Communication, Intimacy, and Close Relationships* (Orlando, FL: Academic Press, 1984).

Coleman, Marilyn, Mark A. Fine, Lawrence H. Ganong, Kimberly J. M. Downs, and Nicole Pauk. "When You're Not the Brady Bunch: Identifying Perceived Conflicts and Resolution Strategies in Step Families," *Personal Relationships* 8 (2001), 55–73.

Coontz, Stephanie. *Marriage, a History* (New York: Viking Penguin, 2006a).

——— "Marriage as Social Contract/The Decline in Married Couple Households," *Philadelphia Inquirer* (October 20, 2006b). Retrieved July 19, 2007, from *www.stephaniecoontz.com/articles/article31.*

Dindia, Kathryn. "Relational Maintenance," in Clyde Hendrick and Susan S. Hendrick, eds., *Close Relationships: A Sourcebook* (Thousand Oaks: Sage, 2000), 287–298.

Duck, Steve. "A Topography of Relationship Disengagement and Dissolution," in Steve Duck, ed., *Personal Relationships 4: Dissolving Personal Relationships* (London: Academic Press, 1982).

———. *Human Relationships,* 2nd ed. (London: Sage, 1992).

———. "Steady as (S)he Goes," in Daniel J. Canary and Laura Stafford, eds., *Communication and Relational Maintenance* (San Diego, CA: Academic Press, 1994), 45–60.

———. *Relating to Others* (Buckingham, UK: Open University Press, 1999).

Duck, Steve, and Garth Pittmann. "Social and Personal Relationships," in Mark L. Knapp and Gerald R. Miller, eds., *Handbook of Interpersonal Communication,* 2nd ed. (Thousand Oaks, CA: Sage, 1994), 676–695.

Enright, Elizabeth. "A House Divided," *AARP* (July/August, 2004), 60–64.

Fehr, Beverly. "The Life Cycle of Friendship," in Clyde Hendrick and Susan S. Hendrick, eds., *Close Relationships: A Sourcebook* (Thousand Oaks, CA: Sage, 2000), 71–84.

Festinger, Leon, Stanley Schachter, and Kurt Back. *Social Pressures in Informal Groups* (New York: Harper and Row, 1950).

Galvin, Kathleen M., Carma L. Bylund, and Bernard J. Brommel. *Family Communication: Cohesion and Change,* 6th ed. (Boston: Allyn & Bacon, 2003).

Gergen, Kenneth J. *The Saturated Self: Dilemmas of Identity in Contemporary Life* (New York: Basic Books, 2000).

Gibb, Jack R. "Defensive Communication," *Journal of Communication* 11 (1961), 141–148.

Gilligan, Carol. *In a Different Voice: Psychological Theory and Women's Development* (Cambridge, MA: Harvard University Press, 1993).

Gilligan, Carol, Janie Victoria Ward, and Jill McLean Taylor, eds., *Mapping the Moral Domain* (Cambridge, MA: Harvard University Press, 1989).

Gladwell, Malcolm. *Blink: The Power of Thinking Without Thinking* (New York: Little, Brown, 2005).

Guerrero, Laura, and Kory Floyd. *Nonverbal Communication in Close Relationships* (Mahwah, NJ: Erlbaum, 2006).

Hawken, Leila, Robert L. Duran, and Lynne Kelly. "The Relationship of Interpersonal Communication Variables to Academic Success and Persistence in College," *Communication Quarterly* 39 (1991), 297–308.

Heider, Fritz. *The Psychology of Interpersonal Relations* (Hillsdale, NJ: Lawrence Erlbaum, 1983).

Hendrick, Clyde, and Susan S. Hendrick, eds. *Close Relationships: A Sourcebook* (Thousand Oaks, CA: Sage, 2000).

Honeycutt, James M. "Memory Structures for the Rise and Fall of Personal Relationships," in Steve Duck, ed., *Individuals in Relationships* (Thousand Oaks, CA: Sage, 1993), 60–86.

Honeycutt, James M., and James G. Cantrill. *Cognition, Communication, and Romantic Relationships* (Mahwah, NJ: Lawrence Erlbaum, 2001).

Houston, Pam. "The Best Girlfriend You Never Had," in Amy Tan, ed., *Best American Short Stories of 1999* (Boston: Houghton Mifflin, 1999), 143–163.

Ivy, Diana K., and Phil Backlund. *Genderspeak: Personal Effectiveness in Gender Communication,* 3rd ed. (New York: McGraw-Hill, 2004).

Kaplan, Daniel L., and Christopher B. Keys. "Sex and Relationship Variables as Predictors of Sexual Attraction in Cross-Sex Platonic Friendships between Young Heterosexual Adults," *Journal of Social and Personal Relationships* 14 (1997), 191–206.

Knapp, Mark. *Interpersonal Communication and Human Relationships* (Boston: Allyn and Bacon, 1984).

———. "Lying and Deception in Close Relationships," in Anita Vangelisti and Daniel Perlman, eds., *Cambridge Handbook of Personal Relationships* (New York: Cambridge University Press, 2006), 517–532.

Knapp, Mark L., and Gerald R. Miller, eds. *Handbook of Interpersonal Communication,* 2nd ed. (Thousand Oaks, CA: Sage, 1994).

Knapp, Mark L., and Anita L. Vangelisti. *Interpersonal Communication and Human Relationships,* 4th ed. (Newton, MA: Allyn and Bacon, 2000).

Leary, Timothy. *Interpersonal Diagnosis of Personality* (New York: Ronald Press, 1957).

Leck, Kira. "Correlates of Minimal Dating," *Journal of Social Psychology* 146, no. 5 (2006), 549–567.

Lehr, Andrew T., and Glen Geher. "Differential Effects of Reciprocity and Attitude Similarity Across Long-Versus Short-Term Mating Contexts," *Journal of Social Psychology* 146, no. 4 (2006), 423–439.

Lippard, Paula V. "'Ask Me No Questions, I'll Tell You No Lies': Situational Exigencies for Interpersonal Communication," *Western Journal of Speech Communication* 52 (Winter 1988), 91–103.

Lund, M. "The Development of Investment and Commitment Scales for Predicting Continuity of Personal Relationships," *Journal of Social and Personal Relationships* 2 (1985) 3–23.

Madden, Mary, and Amanda Lenhart. "Online Dating," *Pew Internet & American Life Project* (March 5, 2006). Retrieved July 16, 2007, from *www.pewinternet.org*.PIP_Online_Dating.pdf.

Maeda, Eriko, and L. David Ritchie. "The Concept of *Shinyuu* in Japan," *Journal of Social and Personal Relationships* 20, no. 6 (2003), 579–598.

McGoldrick, Monica, and Betty Carter. "Remarried Families," in Betty Carter and Monica McGoldrick, eds., *The Expanded Family Life Cycle,* 3rd ed. (Needham Heights, MA: Allyn & Bacon, 1999), 417–435.

"Melting At Last?" *Wilson Quarterly* 24 (Winter 2000), 11.

Millar, Frank, and L. Edna Rogers. "Relational Dimensions of Interpersonal Dynamics," in Michael E. Roloff and Gerald R. Miller, eds., *Interpersonal Processes: New Directions in Communication Research* (Beverly Hills, CA: Sage, 1987), 117–139.

Newcomb, Theodore M. *The Acquaintance Process* (New York: Holt, Rinehart and Winston, 1961).

Pearce, L., and S. Newton. *The Conditions of Human Growth* (New York: Citadel, 1963).

Pearson, Judy C. *Communication in the Family,* 2nd ed. (New York: Harper and Row, 1993).

Petronio, S., J. Martin, and R. Littlefield. "Prerequisite Conditions for Self-Disclosing: A Gender Issue," *Communication Monographs* 51 (1984), 268–273.

Previti, Denise, and Paul R. Amato. "Is Infidelity a Cause or a Consequence of Poor Marital Quality?" *Journal of Social and Personal Relationships* 21, no. 2 (2004), 217–230.

Roker, Al. *Don't Make Me Stop This Car!* (New York: Scribner, 2000).

Ruesch, Jurgen, and Gregory Bateson. *Communication: The Social Matrix of Psychiatry* (New York: Norton, 1968).

Satir, Virginia. *The New Peoplemaking* (Mountain View, CA: Science and Behavior Books, 1988).

Schachter, Stanley. *The Psychology of Affiliation* (Palo Alto, CA: Stanford University Press, 1959).

Schimel, Jeff, Tom Pyszcynski, Jamie Arndt, and Jeff Greenberg. "Being Accepted for Who We Are,"

Journal of Personality and Social Psychology 80 (2001), 35–52.

Shaw, Robert Bruce. *Trust in the Balance* (San Francisco: Jossey-Bass, 1997).

Shellenbarger, Sue. "No Comfort in Numbers: Divorce Rate Varies Widely from Group to Group," *Wall Street Journal* (April 22, 2004), D1.

Sieberg, Evelyn, and Carl Larson. "Dimensions of Interpersonal Response," paper delivered at the annual conference of the International Communication Association, Phoenix, April 1971.

Sprecher, Aron, Elaine Hatfield, et al. "Love: American Style, Russian Style, and Japanese Style," *Personal Relationships* 1 (1994), 349–369.

Stafford, Laura, Susan L. Kline, and Caroline T. Ranking. "Married Individuals, Cohabiters, and Cohabiters Who Marry: A Longitudinal Study of Relational Well-Being," *Journal of Social and Personal Relationships* 21, no. 2 (2004), 231–248.

Tannen, Deborah. *You Just Don't Understand: Women and Men in Conversation* (New York: Ballantine Books, 1990).

———. *I Only Say This Because I Love You* (New York: Random House, 2001).

Watzlawick, Paul, Janet Helmick Beavin, and Don D. Jackson. *Pragmatics of Human Communication* (New York: Norton, 1967).

Zajonc, Robert B. "Attitudinal Effects of Mere Exposure," *Journal of Personality and Social Psychology* 9 (1968), 1–29.

Chapter 9   Interpersonal Communication

Alberti, Robert, and Michael Emmons. *Your Perfect Right* (Atascadero, CA: Impact Publishers, 2001).

Aron, Arthur, Helen E. Fisher, and Greg Strong. "Romantic Love," in Anita Vangelisti and Daniel Perlman, eds., *Cambridge Handbook of Personal Relationships* (New York: Cambridge University Press, 2006), 595–614.

Auburn, David. *Proof* (London: Faber & Faber, 2001).

Bartholomew, K. "Avoidance of Intimacy: An Attachment Perspective," *Journal of Social and Personal Relationships* 7 (1990), 147–148.

Baxter, Leslie A., and Barbara Montgomery. *Relating: Dialogues and Dialectics* (New York: Guilford, 1996a).

———. "Rethinking Communication in Personal Relationships from a Dialectical Perspective," in Steve Duck, ed., *Handbook of Personal Relationships*, 2nd ed. (New York: Wiley, 1996b), 325–349.

———. "Rethinking Communication in Personal Relationships from a Dialectical Perspective," in Kathryn Dindia and Steve Duck, eds., *Communication and Personal Relationships* (Chicester, UK: Wiley, 2000), 31–54.

Berko, R. M., A. D. Wolvin, and D. R. Wolvin. *Communicating: A Social and Career Focus*, 8th ed. (Boston: Houghton Mifflin, 2001).

Bowlby, John. *Attachment and Loss: vol. 2, Separation: Anxiety and Anger* (New York: Basic Books, 1973).

Braithwaite, Dawn O., and Leslie A. Baxter. "You're My Parent but You're Not," *Journal of Applied Communication Research* 34 (February 2006), 30–48.

Carter, Betty, and Joan K. Peters. *Love, Honor and Negotiate* (New York: Pocket Books, 1996).

Chelune, G. J., J. T. Robison, and M. J. Kommor. In V. J. Derlega, ed., *Communication, Intimacy, and Close Relationships* (Orlando, FL: Academic Press, 1984).

Clark, Ruth Anne, Michael Dockum, Heidi Hazeu, Meikuan Huang et al. "Initial Encounters of Young Men and Women: Impressions and Disclosure Estimates," *Sex Roles* 50 (2004), 699–709.

Coontz, Stephanie. *Marriage, a History: How Love Conquered Marriage* (New York: Viking Penguin, 2006a).

———. "Too Close for Comfort," *International Herald Tribune* (November 7, 2006b), *www.iht.com/bin/print/.php?id=3430735*.

Davis, Deborah, Philip R. Shaver, and Michael L. Vernon. "Attachment Style and Subjective Motivations for Sex," *Personality and Social Psychology Bulletin* 30 (August 2004), 1076–1090.

Delia, J. G. "Some Tentative Thoughts Concerning the Study of Interpersonal Relationships and Their Development," *Western Journal of Speech Communication* 44 (1980), 97–103.

Derlega, V. J., ed. *Communication, Intimacy, and Close Relationships* (Orlando, FL: Academic Press, 1984).

Derlega, V. J., and J. Grzelal. "Appropriateness of Self-Disclosure," in G. J. Chelune, ed., *Self-Disclosure* (San Francisco: Jossey-Bass, 1979).

Derlega, Valerian J., Barbara A. Winstead, Paul T. P. Wong, and Michael Greenspan. "Self-Disclosure and Relationship Development: An Attributional Analysis," in Michael E. Roloff and Gerald R. Miller, eds., *Interpersonal Processes: New Directions in Communications Research* (Beverly Hills, CA: Sage, 1987), 172–187.

Diaz, Junot. "The Sun, the Moon, the Stars," in Amy Tan, ed., *Best American Short Stories of 1999* (Boston: Houghton Mifflin, 1999), 15–28.

Dindia, Kathryn. "Self-Disclosure, Self-Identity, and Relationship Development: A Transactional/Dialectical Perspective," in Steve Duck, ed., *Handbook of Personal Relationships,* 2nd ed. (New York: Wiley, 1996), 411–426.

———. "Self-Disclosure, Identity, and Relationship Development: A Dialectical Perspective," in Kathryn Dindia and Steve Duck, eds., *Communication and Personal Relationships* (New York: Wiley, 2000), 147–161.

———. "Self-Disclosure Research: Knowledge through Meta-Analysis," in Mike Allen, Raymond W. Preiss, Barbara Mae Gayle, and Nancy A. Burrell, eds., *Interpersonal Communication: Advances through Meta-Analysis* (Mahwah, NJ: Erlbaum, 2002), 169–186.

Dubin, Arlene G. *Prenups for Lovers* (New York: Villard, 2001).

Duck, Steve. *Relating to Others* (Buckingham, UK: Open University Press, 1999).

Emmers-Sommer, Tara M. "The Effect of Communication Quality and Quantity Indicators on Intimacy and Relational Satisfaction," *Journal of Social and Personal Relationships* 21 (2004), 399–411.

Feeney, Judith A., Patricia Noller, and Nigel Roberts. "Attachment and Close Relationships," in Clyde Hendrick and Susan S. Hendrick, eds., *Close Relationships: A Sourcebook* (Thousand Oaks, CA: Sage, 2000), 185–201.

Fehr, Beverly. "How Do I Love Thee? Let Me Consult My Prototype," in Steve Duck, ed., *Individuals in Relationships* (Newbury Park, CA: Sage, 2000), 87–120.

Fung, Amanda. "Love and No Marriage," *Crain's New York Business* (February 13, 2006), 27–28.

Gao, Ge. "Intimacy, Passion, and Commitment in Chinese and US American Romantic Relationships,"*International Journal of Intercultural Relations* 25 (2001), 329–342.

Gibbs, Jennifer, Nicole B. Ellison, and Rebecca D. Heino. "Self-Presentation in Online Personals," *Communication Research* 33 (April 2006), 152–177.

Goffman, Erving. *Relations in Public: Microstudies of the Public Order* (New York: Harper and Row, 1972).

Gold, Deborah T. "Siblings in Old Age: Something Special," *Canadian Journal on Aging* 6 (1987), 199–215.

———. "Men and Their Siblings," paper presented at the 42nd Annual Scientific Meeting of the Gerontological Society of America, Minneapolis, November 1989a.

———. "Sibling Relationships in Old Age: A Typology," *International Journal of Aging and Human Development* 28 (1989b), 37–51.

Goldstine, Daniel, et al. *The Dance-Away Lover and Other Roles We Play in Love, Sex, and Marriage* (New York: Morrow, 1977).

Greene, Kathryn, Valerian J. Derlega, and Alicia Mathews. "Self-Disclosure in Personal Relationships," in Anita Vangelisti and Daniel Perlman, eds., *Cambridge Handbook of Personal Relationships* (New York: Cambridge University Press, 2006), 409–427.

Guerrero, Laura, and Kory Floyd. *Nonverbal Communication in Close Relationships* (Mahwah, NJ: Erlbaum, 2006).

Hargie, Owen, Christine Saunders, and David Dickson. *Social Skills in Interpersonal Communication* (Cambridge, MA: Brookline Books, 1987), 187–208.

Hatfield, Elaine. "The Dangers of Intimacy," in V. J. Derlega, ed., *Communication, Intimacy, and Close Relationships* (Orlando, FL: Academic Press, 1984).

Hazan, Cindy, and Phillip Shaver. "Romantic Love Conceptualized as an Attachment Process," *Journal of Personality and Social Psychology* 52 (1987), 511–524.

———. "Attachment as an Organizational Framework for Research on Close Relationships," *Psychological Inquiry* 5 (1994), 1–22.

Hendrick, Clyde, and Susan Hendrick. "A Theory and Method of Love," *Journal of Personality and Social Psychology* 50 (1986), 392–402.

Hendrick, Clyde, Susan Hendrick, and Amy Dicke. "The Love Attitudes Scale: Short Form," *Journal of Social and Personal Relationships* 15, no. 2 (1998), 147–159.

Hitsch, Gunter J., Ali Hortaçsu, and Dan Ariely. "What Makes You Click? An Empirical Analysis of Online Dating," *www.aeaweb.org/annual_mtg_papers/2006/0106_0800_0502.pdf.*

Honeycutt, James M., and James G. Cantrill. *Cognition, Communication, and Romantic Relationships* (Mahwah, NJ: Lawrence Erlbaum, 2001).

Jourard, Sidney M. *The Transparent Self, Self-Disclosure and Well Being* (Princeton, NJ: Van Nostrand, 1964).

———. *Self-Disclosure: An Experimental Analysis of the Transparent Self* (Melbourne, FL: Kreiger, 1979).

Kelley, Douglas L., and Judee K. Burgoon. "Understanding Marital Satisfaction and Couple Type as Functions of Relational Expectations," *Human Communication Research* 18 (1991), 40–69.

Klagsbrun, Francine. *Mixed Feelings: Love, Hate, Rivalry, and Reconciliation among Brothers and Sisters* (New York: Bantam, 1992).

Knapp, Mark L., and Judy Hall. *Nonverbal Communication in Human Interaction,* 5th ed. (New York: Harcourt Brace Jovanovich, 2002).

Knapp, Mark L., and Anita L. Vangelisti. *Interpersonal Communication and Human Relationships,* 4th ed. (Newton, MA: Allyn and Bacon, 2000).

Lacey, Robert. *Sotheby's—Bidding for Class* (Boston: Little, Brown, 1998).

Lahiri, Jhumpa. *Interpreter of Maladies* (Boston: Houghton Mifflin, 1999), 43–69.

Lee, J. A. *The Colors of Love* (Don Mills, Ontario: New Press, 1973).

Lehr, Andrew T., and Glen Geher. "Differential Effects of Reciprocity and Attitude Similarity across Long-Versus Short-Term Mating Contexts," *Journal of Social Psychology* 146, no. 4 (2006), 423–439.

Levitt, Steven D., and Stephen J. Dubner. *Freakonomics,* rev. ed. (New York: HarperCollins, 2006).

Liefbroer, Aart C., and Edith Dourleijn. "Unmarried Cohabitation and Union Stability," *Demography* 43 (May 2006), 203–221.

Luft, Joseph. *Of Human Interaction* (Palo Alto, CA: National Press, 1969).

Luo, Shanhong, and Eva C. Klohnen. "Assortative Mating and Marital Quality in Newlyweds," *Journal of Personality and Social Psychology* 88 (2005), 304–326.

McAdams, Dan P. *Intimacy: The Need to Be Close* (New York: Doubleday, 1989).

McGoldrick, Monica. "Becoming a Couple," in Betty Carter and Monica McGoldrick, eds., *The Expanded Family Cycle,* 3rd ed. (Boston: Allyn & Bacon, 1999), 231–248.

McGoldrick, Monica, Marlene Watson, and Waymon Benton. "Siblings through the Life Cycle," in Betty Carter and Monica McGoldrick, eds., *The Expanded Family Life Cycle,* 3rd ed. (Boston: Allyn and Bacon, 2005).

Miller, G. R., and M. Steinberg. *Between People* (Chicago: Science Research Association, 1975).

Murray, Sandra L., Dale W. Griffin, Paul Rose, and Gina Bellavia. "For Better or Worse? Self-Esteem and the Contingencies of Acceptance in Marriage," *Personality and Social Psychology Bulletin* 32 (July 2006), 866–880.

Neff, Kristin D., and Susan Harter. "Relationships Styles of Self-focused Autonomy, Other-focused Connectedness, and Mutuality across Multiple Relationships," *Journal of Social and Personal Relationships* 20, no. 1 (2003), 81–89.

Noller, Patricia. "Nonverbal Communication in Close Relationships," in Anita Vangelisti, and Daniel Perlman, eds., *Cambridge Handbook of Personal Relationships* (New York: Cambridge University Press, 2006), 403–420.

Phillips, G. M., and J. T. Wood. *Communication and Human Relationships* (New York: Macmillan, 1983).

Prager, Karen. "Intimacy in Personal Relationships," in Clyde Hendrick and Susan S. Hendrick, eds., *Close Relationships: A Sourcebook* (Thousand Oaks, CA: Sage, 2000), 229–242.

Pratto, Felicia, and Angela Walker. "The Bases of Gendered Power," in Alice H. Eagly, Anne E. Beall, and Robert J. Sternberg, eds., *The Psychology of Gender,* 2nd ed. (New York: Guilford Press, 2004), 242–268.

Rawlins, William K. *Friendship Matters* (Hawthorne, NY: Aldine de Gruyter, 1992).

———. "Being There and Growing Apart: Sustaining Friendship during Adolescence," in Daniel J. Canary and Laura Stafford, eds., *Communication and Relational Maintenance* (New York: Academic Press, 1994), 275–296.

Regan, Pamela C., Elizabeth R. Kocan, and Teresa Whitlock. "Ain't Love Grand! A Prototype Analysis of the Concept of Romantic Love," *Journal of Social and Personal Relationships* 15, no. 3 (1998), 411–420.

Rosenfeld, L. B., and W. L. Kendrick. "Choosing to Be Open: Subjective Reasons for Self-Disclosing," *Western Journal of Speech Communication* 48 (1984), 326–343.

Srivastava, Sanjay, Kelly M. McGonagal, Jane M. Richards, Emily A. Butler, and James J. Gross. "Optimism in Close Relationships," *Journal of Personality and Social Psychology* 91 (July 2006), 143–153.

Steil, Janice M. "Contemporary Marriage: Still an Unequal Partnership," in Clyde Hendrick and Susan S. Hendrick, eds., *Close Relationships: A Sourcebook* (Thousand Oaks, CA: Sage, 2000), 125–136.

Sternberg, Robert J. *The Triangle of Love: Intimacy, Passion, Commitment* (New York: Basic Books, 1988).

———. *Cupid's Arrow: The Course of Love Through Time* (New York: Cambridge University Press, 1998).

Tannen, Deborah. *I Only Say This Because I Love You* (New York: Random House, 2001).

VanLear, C. Arthur, Jr. "The Formation of Social Relationships: A Longitudinal Study of Social Penetration," *Human Communication Research* 13 (1987), 299–322.

———. "Testing a Cyclical Model of Communicative Openness in Relationship Development: Two Longitudinal Studies," *Communication Monographs* 58 (1991), 337–361.

Waring, E. M., et al. "Concepts of Intimacy in the General Public," *Journal of Nervous and Mental Disease* 168 (1980), 471–474.

Wilmot, William. *Relational Communication,* 4th ed. (New York: McGraw-Hill, 1995).

Wilson, Keithia. *Assertiveness and Its Social Context* (New York: Pergamon Press, 1993).

Yoshioka, Mariane. "Substantive Differences in the Assertiveness of Low-Income African American, Hispanic and Caucasian Women,"*Journal of Psychology* 134, no. 3 (2000).

Chapter 10   Intercultural Communication

Abraham, Linus. "Media Stereotypes of African Americans," in Paul Martin Lester and Susan Dente Ross, eds., *Images that Injure: Pictorial Stereotypes in the Media* (Westport, CT: Praeger, 2003), 87–92.

Alexander, Elizabeth. In "Africa and the World," *Pen America: A Journal for Writers and Readers,* no. 7 (2006), 104–118.

Allport, Gordon W. *The Nature of Prejudice* (Cambridge, MA: Addison-Wesley, 1954).

Althen, Gary. "The Americans Have to Say Everything," *Communication Quarterly* 40 (1992), 413–421.

Amari, Anan. "An American Story: The Arab American National Museum," *Museum News* 85 (November/ December 2006), 34–41.

Appadurai, Arjun. *Modernity at Large: Cultural Dimensions of Globalization* (Minneapolis: University of Minnesota Press, 1996).

———. "Disjuncture and Difference in the Global Cultural Economy," in Jana Evans Braziel and Anita Mannur, eds., *Theorizing Diaspora* (Oxford, UK: Blackwell Publishing, 2003), pp. 25–48.

Appiah, Kwame Anthony. *Cosmopolitanism: Ethics in a World of Strangers* (New York: Norton, 2006).

Argyle, M., et al. "Cross-Cultural Variations in Relationship Rules," *International Journal of Psychology* 21 (1986), 287–315.

Baldwin, James. "Stranger in the Village," in James Baldwin, *The Price of the Ticket: Collected Nonfiction 1948–1985* (New York: St. Martin's, 1985), 79–90.

Blair, John G. "Thinking Through Binaries: Conceptual Strategies for Interdependence," *American Studies International* 38, no. 2 (2000), 23–38.

Braithwaite, Dawn G., and Charles A. Braithwaite. "Understanding Communication of Persons with Disabilities as Cultural Communication," in Larry A. Samovar and Richard E. Porter, eds., *Intercultural Communication: A Reader,* 9th ed. (Belmont, CA: Wadsworth, 2000).

Buckley, Michael. *Moon Handbook: Vietnam, Cambodia & Laos,* 4th ed. (Emeryville, CA: Avalon Travel Publishing, 2006).

Butler, Kim. "Defining Diaspora, Refining a Discourse," *Diaspora* 10, no. 2 (Fall 2001), 189–220.

Carlson, Jerry S., and Keith F. Widaman. "The Effects of Study Abroad during College on Attitudes toward Other Cultures," *International Journal of Intercultural Relations* 12 (1988), 1–17.

Chambers, John R., Robert S. Baron, and Mary L. Imman. "Misperceptions in Intergroup Conflict," *Psychological Science* 17, no. 1 (2006), 38–45.

Chambers, John R., and Darya Melnyk. "Why Do I Hate Thee? Conflict Misperceptions and Intergroup Mistrust," *Personality and Social Psychology Bulletin* 32 (October 2006), 1295–1311.

Chow, Rey. *Sentimental Fabulations, Contemporary Chinese Films* (New York: Columbia University Press, 2007).

Christians, Clifford, and Kaarle Nordenstreng. "Social Responsibility Worldwide," *Journal of Mass Media Ethics* 19, no. 1 (2004), 3–28.

Christians, Clifford, and Michael Traber, eds. *Communication Ethics and Universal Values* (Thousand Oaks, CA: Sage, 1997).

Clark, Bruce. *Twice A Stranger* (London: Granta Books, 2006).

Clingman, Stephen. "Other Voices: An Interview with Caryl Phillips," *Salmagundi,* no. 143 (Summer 2004), 113–140.

Couldry, Nick. *Listening Beyond the Echoes: Media, Ethics, and Agency in an Uncertain World* (Boulder, CO: Paradigm Publishers, 2006).

Davis, Olga I., Thomas K. Nakayama, and Judith N. Martin. "Current and Future Directions in Ethnicity and Methodology," *International Journal of Intercultural Relations* 24 (2000), 525–539.

De Vos, George A., and Eric De Vos. *Cross-Cultural Dimensions in Conscious Thought* (Lanham, MD: Rowman & Littlefield, 2004).

Dion, Karen. "Cultural Perspectives on Facial Attractiveness," in Gillian Rhodes and Leslie A. Zebrowitz, eds., *Facial Attractiveness: Evolutionary, Cognitive, and Social Perspectives* (Westport, CT: Ablex, 2002), 239–260.

Dixon, Travis L., and Daniel Linz. "Overrepresentation and Underrepresentation of African Americans and Latinos as Lawbreakers on Television News," *Journal of Communication* 50 (Spring 2000), 131–154.

Dodd, Carley H. *Dynamics of Intercultural Communication,* 5th ed. (New York: McGraw-Hill, 1999).

Douglis, Carole. "The Beat Goes On," *Psychology Today* 21 (November 1987), 36–42.

"Experiment in Black and White," *Letters & Science Today* (University of Wisconsin–Madison) 9, no. 2 (Spring 2004), 1–2.

Foner, Nancy. *New Immigrants in New York* (New York: Columbia University Press, 2001).

Gaines, Stanley O., Jr., and William Ickes. "Perspectives on Interracial Relationships," in William Ickes and Steve Duck, eds., *The Social Psychology of Personal Relationships* (Chicester, UK: Wiley, 2000), 55–78.

Gannon, Martin J., Peter Brown, and Sharon Ribas. "French Wine: An Illustration of a Cultural Metaphor," in Martin J. Gannon, ed., *Cultural Metaphors* (Thousand Oaks, CA: Sage, 2001), 59–78.

Goleman, Daniel. *Social Intelligence* (New York: Bantam Books, 2006).

Gorham, Bradley W. "News Media's Relationship with Stereotyping: The Linguistic Intergroup Bias in Response to Crime News," *Journal of Communication* 56, no. 2 (2006), 289–308.

Govorun, Olesya, Kathleen Fuegen, and B. Keith Payne. "Stereotypes Focus Defensive Projection," *Personality and Social Psychology Bulletin* 32 (June 2006), 781–793.

Gudykunst, William B., and Young Yuri Kim. *Communicating with Strangers: An Approach to Intercultural Communication,* 3rd ed. (New York: McGraw-Hill, 1997).

Gudykunst, William B., and Stella Ting-Toomey. "Culture and Affective Communication," *American Behavioral Scientist* 31 (1988a), 384–400.

————. *Culture and Interpersonal Communication* (Newbury Park, CA: Sage, 1988b).

Guerrero, Laura, and Kory Floyd. *Nonverbal Communication in Close Relationships* (Mahwah, NJ: Erlbaum, 2006).

Hall, Edward T. *The Silent Language* (New York: Doubleday, 1959).

————. *Beyond Culture* (Garden City, NY: Doubleday, 1976).

————*The Dance of Life: The Other Dimension of Time* (New York: Anchor Books, 1984).

Halualani, Rona Tamiko, Anu S. Chitgopekar, Jennifer Huynh Thi Ahn Morrison, and Patrick Shaou Whea Dodge. "Diverse in Name Only? Intercultural Interaction at a Multicultural University," *Journal of Communication* 54, no. 2 (2004), 270–286.

Hammond, Ross A., and Robert Axelrod. "The Evolution of Ethnocentrism," *Journal of Conflict Resolution* 50, no. 6 (2006), 926–936.

Hertelou, Maude. "My Suitcases," in Edwidge Danticat, ed., *The Butterfly's Way* (New York: Soho Press, 2001).

Hessler, Peter. *Oracle Bones: A Journey Between China's Past and Present.* (New York: HarperCollins, 2006).

Hofstede, Geert. *Culture's Consequences* (Newbury Park, CA: Sage, 1980).

————. *Culture and Organizations* (New York: McGraw-Hill, 1991).

Jen, Gish. *Who's Irish?* (New York: Knopf, 1999).

Kanagawa, Chie, Susan E. Cross, and Hazel Rose Markus. "'Who Am I?' The Cultural Psychology of the Conceptual Self," *Personality and Social Psychology Bulletin* 27 (2001), 90–103.

Kidder, Rushworth M. *Moral Courage* (New York: HarperCollins, 2005).

Kwak, Nojin, Nathaniel Poor, and Marko M. Skoric. "Honey, I Shrunk the World! The Relation Between Internet Use and International Engagement," *Mass Communication & Society* 9, no. 2 (2006), 189–213.

Lifton, Robert Jay. "Can Images of Bosnia's Victims Change the World?" *New York Times* (August 23, 1992), 26.

Lim, Tae-seop, and Soo Hyang Choi. "Interpersonal Relationships in Korea," in William B. Gudykunst, Stella Ting-Toomey, and Tsukasa Nishida, eds., *Communication in Personal Relationships across Cultures* (Thousand Oaks, CA: Sage, 1996).

Lull, James. *Media Communication, Culture: A Global Approach* (New York: Columbia University Press, 2000).

Maddux, William W., and Masaki Yuki. "The 'Ripple Effect': Cultural Differences in Perceptions of the Consequences of Events," *Personality and Social Psychology Bulletin* 32 (May 2006), 669–683.

Mahmoudi, Kooros M. "Refugee Cross-Cultural Adjustment: Tibetans in India," *International Journal of Intercultural Relations* 16 (1992), 17–32.

Mambani, Zehra. "When a Hyphen Barely Holds Up," *Barnard: Special Section: The Aftermath of September 11* (Fall 2001), 14.

Marriott, Michel. "The Color of Mayhem," *New York Times* (August 12, 2004), G1, 7.

Martin, Judith N., and Thomas K. Nakayama. *Intercultural Communication in Contexts*, 4th ed. (New York: McGraw-Hill, 2007).

Matei, Sorin, Sandra J. Ball-Rokeach, and Jack Linchuan Qiu. "Fear and Misperception of Los Angeles Urban Space," *Communication Research* 28 (2001).

"Mind the Gap," *PEN America: A Journal for Writers and Readers* 3, no. 6 (2005), 114–120.

Mithers, Carol. "Interracial Families," *Ladies' Home Journal* 123 (July 2006), 102–103.

Moeller, Susan D. *Compassion Fatigue* (New York: Routledge, 1999).

Nagda, Biren (Ratnesh) A. "Breaking Barriers, Crossing Borders, Building Bridges: Communication Processes in Intergroup Dialogues," *Journal of Social Issues* 62 (September 2006), 553–576.

Naipaul, V. S. "East Indian," in V. S. Naipaul, *Literary Occasions: Essays* (New York: Knopf, 2003), 35–44.

Nathan, Jeffrey H., Anthony J. Marsella, Ann Marie Horvath, and Frederick L. Coolidge. "The Concepts of Individual, Self, and Group in Japanese National, Japanese-American, and European American Samples: A Semantic Differential Analysis," *International Journal of Intercultural Relations* 23 (1999), 711–725.

Neuliep, James, and James C. McCroskey. "The Development of a U.S. and Generalized Ethnocentrism Scale," *Communication Research Reports* 14 (1997a), 385–398.

———. "The Development of Intercultural and Interethnic Communication Apprehension Scales," *Communication Research Reports* 14 (1997b), 145–156.

Onishi, Norimitsu. "Freed from Captivity in Iraq; Japanese Return to More Pain," *New York Times* (April 23, 2004), A1, A11.

Park, Ji Hoon, Nadine G. Gabbadon, and Ariel R. Chernin. "Naturalizing Racial Differences through Comedy," *Journal of Communication* 56 (2006), 157–177.

Patchett, Ann. *Bel Canto* (New York: HarperCollins, 2005).

Patterson, Orlando. "Our Overrated Inner Self," *New York Times* (December 26, 2006), A35.

Pettigrew, Thomas F., and Linda R. Tropp. "A Meta-Analytic Test of Intergroup Contact Theory," *Journal of Personality and Social Psychology* 90 (May 2006), 751–783.

Pew Global Attitudes Project. Retrieved November 9, 2004 from *www.people-press.org/commentary/display.php3?AnalysisID=86*.

Rodriguez, Clara E. "Promoting Analytical and Critical Viewing," in Clara E. Rodriguez, ed., *Latin Looks: Images of Latinas and Latinos in the U.S. Media* (New York: Westview Books, HarperCollins, 1997).

Rohrlich, B. F. "Dual-Culture Marriage," *International Journal of Intercultural Relations* 12 (1988), 35–44.

Rohrlich, Beulah, and Judith N. Martin. "Host Country and Reentry Adjustment of Student Sojourners," *International Journal of Intercultural Relations* 15 (1991), 163–182.

Ross, Susan Dente. "Unequal Combatants on an Uneven Media Battlefield: Palestine and Israel," in Paul Martin Lester and Susan Dente Ross, eds., *Images that Injure: Pictorial Stereotypes in the Media* (Westport, CT: Praeger, 2003), 58–63.

Samovar, Larry A., and Richard Porter, eds. *Intercultural Communication: A Reader,* 9th ed. (Belmont, CA: Wadsworth, 2000).

Sarbaugh, L. E. *Intercultural Communication* (Rochelle Park, NJ: Hayden, 1979).

Schaffner, Brian F., and Mark Gadson. "Reinforcing Stereotypes? Race and Local Television News Coverage of Congress," *Social Science Quarterly* 85 (September 2004), 604–621.

Scott, Janny. "Foreign Born in U.S. at Record High," *New York Times* (February 7, 2002), A26.

Sillars, Alan L., and Judith Weisberg. "Conflict as a Social Skill," in Michael E. Roloff and Gerald R. Miller, eds., *Interpersonal Processes: New Direction in Communication Research* (Newbury Park, CA: Sage, 1987), 140–171.

Southern Poverty Law Center. "Conference Addresses Hate Studies Program," *SPLC Report* 34, no. 1 (2004), p. 5.

Stephan, Cookie White, and Walter G. Stephan. "Reducing Intercultural Anxiety through Intercultural Contact," *International Journal of Intercultural Relations* 16 (1992), 89–106.

Sunstein, Cass. *republic.com* (Princeton, NJ: Princeton University Press, 2001).

Ting-Toomey, Stella. *Communicating Across Cultures* (New York: Guilford, 1999).

Ting-Toomey, Stella, and Leeva Chung. "Cross-Cultural Interpersonal Communication: Theoretical Trends and Research Directions," in William B. Gudykunst, Stella Ting-Toomey, and Tsukasa Nishida, eds.,

Communication in Personal Relationships across Cultures (Thousand Oaks, CA: Sage, 1996), 237–261.

Ting-Toomey, Stella, Kimberlie K. Yee-Jung, Robin B. Shapiro et al. "Ethnic/cultural Identity Salience and Conflict Styles in Four US Groups," *International Journal of Intercultural Relations* 24 (2000), 47–81.

Tolchin, Martin, and Susan J. Tolchin. *A World Ignited* (Lanham, MD: Rowan & Littlefield, 2006).

Tropp, Linda. "Valuing Diversity and Interest in Intergroup Contact," *Journal of Social Issues* 62 (September 2006), 533–551.

Van Dijk, Teun A. "New(s) Racism: A Discourse Analytical Approach," in Simon Cottle, ed., *Ethnic Minorities and the Media* (Buckingham, UK: Open University Press, 2000), 33–49.

Weigl, Robert C., and Jesus M. Reyes. "Latino and Anglo Political Portraits: Lessons from Intercultural Field Research," *International Journal of Intercultural Relations* 25 (2001), 235–259.

Wilgoren, Jodi. "A Nation Challenged: Arab American: Struggling to Be Both Arab and American," *New York Times* (November 4, 2001), B1.

Yum, June Ock. "The Impact of Confucianism on Interpersonal Relationships and Communication Patterns in East Asia," in Larry Samovar and Richard E. Porter, eds., *Intercultural Communication: A Reader,* 8th ed. (Belmont, CA: 1997), 78–88.

Chapter 11   Interviewing

Banville, Thomas G. *How to Listen—How to Be Heard* (Chicago: Nelson-Hall, 1978).

Byham, William C. *Landing the Job You Want: How to Have the Best Job Interview of Your Life.* (New York: Three Rivers Press, 1997).

Byham, William C. and Debra Pickett. *Landing the Job You Want,* 2nd ed. (Pittsburgh, PA: Three Rivers Press, 1999).

Cahn, Dudley D., and Stewart L. Tubbs. "Management as Communication: Performance Evaluation and Employee Self-Worth," *Communication* 12 (1983), 46–54.

Camp, Richaurd, Mary Vielhaber, and Jack Simonetti. *Strategic Interviewing: How to Hire the Best People* (San Francisco: Jossey-Bass, 2001).

Coopman, Stephanie. "Conducting the Information Interview," (2004). From Web site: *www.roguecom .com/interview/module5.html.*

Crowley, E. "Making CEO Selection Work," *Directorship* 30, no. 2 (February 2004), 13–16.

Deep, Sam, and Lyle Sussman. *Yes, You Can* (Reading, MA: Addison-Wesley, 1998).

Deluca, Matthew J. *Best Answers to the 201 Most Frequently Asked Interview Questions* (New York: McGraw-Hill, 1997).

Fisher, Ron. "Q&A with Ron Fisher, Ph.D. Cognitive Interview," NTSB Training Center (2005). *http:www .ntsb.gov/tc/courseinfo/QandA_Fisher.pdf.*

Gerzon, Mark. *Leading Through Conflict* (Boston: Harvard Business School Press, 2006).

Kabateck, J. "Interview with 'Hire' Goal in Mind: Building the Best Employee Team," *Nation's Restaurant News,* New York, 37, no. 1 (May 2003), 27.

Kahn, Robert L., and Charles F. Cannell. *The Dynamics of Interviewing: Theory, Technique and Cases,* 2nd ed. (New York: Wiley, 1968).

Kennedy, J. "Killer Interview Tactic Can Help Candidate Score," *Milwaukee Journal Sentinel* (April 2003), 22.

Lubin, J. "Dated Clothes, Dirty Nails Can Tip Balance If You're Job Hunting," *Wall Street Journal, Deseret News,* (June 2004), M1.

Markland, David, Richard M. Ryan, Vannessa Jayne Tobin, and Stephen Rollnick. "Motivational Interviewing and Self-Determination Theory," *Journal of Social and Clinical Psychology* (September 2005).

McCabe, C. "Interview Is about Boss, Too, Not Just Job Hunter," *Boston Globe* (June 2004), G15.

Miller, W. R. "Motivational Interviewing with Problem Drinkers," *Behavioural Psychotherapy* 11 (1983), 147–172.

Miller, W. R., and S. Rollnick. *Motivational Interviewing: Preparing People to Change Addictive Behavior* (New York: Guilford Press, 1991).

———. *Motivational Interviewing: Preparing People to Change Addictive Behavior* (New York: The Guilford Press, 2002).

Murnighan, J. Keith. *Bargaining Games* (New York: William Morrow, 1992).

"On the Job; Interview Tips," *Augusta (GA) Chronicle* (January 2003), F1.

Patterson, Kerry, Joseph Grenny, Ron McMillan, and Al Switzler. *Crucial Confrontations* (New York: McGraw-Hill, 2005).

Ramundo, Bernard A. *Effective Negotiation* (New York: Quorum, 1992).

Raudsepp, E. "Body-Language Tactics That Sway Interviewers," *Career Journal* (2004). Retrieved July 13, 2004, from *Career Journal*

Web site: *www.careerjournal.com/jobhunting/ interviewing/20021205-raudsepp.html.*

Rollnick, S., and W. R. Miller. "What Is Motivational Interviewing?" *Behavioural and Cognitive Psychotherapy* 23 (1995), 325–334. Retrieved July 29, 2007, from *www.motivationalinterview.org/clinical/ whatismi.html.*

Rubak, Sune, Annelli Sandbæk, Torsten Lauritzen, and Bo Christensen. "Motivational Interviewing: A Systematic Review and Meta-analysis," *British Journal of General Practice* (April 2005).

Scott, T. "Foti's New Applications Ask for Age, Race; Forms Not Illegal but May Expose Agency to Lawsuits," *New Orleans Times-Picayune* (April 2004), 1.

Shalett, K. "Steps to Success; Appearance Opens Doors," *New Orleans Times-Picayune,* (May 2004), 1.

Sheridan, M. "The Ten-Minute Manager's Guide to Interviewing New Hires," *Restaurants & Institutions* 114, no. 1 (January 2004), 26.

Stewart, Charles J., and William B. Cash. *Interviewing: Principles and Practices,* 9th ed. (New York: McGraw-Hill, 1999).

"Turning the Tables on the Job Interview," *PR Newswire* (New York) (May 2004), 1.

University of Alabama at Birmingham. Illegal Interview Questions, *UAB Career Services* (2004) from UAB Career Services Web site: *www.careercenter.uab.edu/ gethired/interview/illegalquest.htm.*

Whetten, David, and Kim Cameron. *Developing Management Skills,* 6th ed. (Upper Saddle River, NJ: Prentice-Hall, 2005).

Willis, Gordon B. "Cognitive Interviewing: A 'How To' Guide," *Reducing Survey Error through Research on the Cognitive and Decision Processes in Surveys.* Short course presented at the 1999 meeting of the American Statistical Association. Retrieved July 29, 2007, from *http://appliedresearch.cancer.gov/areas/cognitive/ interview.pdf.*

Wilson, Gerald L., and H. Lloyd Goodall, Jr. *Interviewing in Context* (New York: McGraw-Hill, 1991).

Chapter 12   Small-Group Communication

AACSB. "Responses to Customers Drives Curriculum Changes," *American Assembly of Collegiate Schools of Business Newsline* 22 (Summer 1992), 1–3.

Amabile, Teresa. "How to Kill Creativity," *Harvard Business Review* (September–October, 1998), 77–87.

Armour, Stephanie. "Team Efforts, Technology Add New Reasons to Meet," *USA Today* (December 9, 1997), 1A.

Associated Press, "Soldiers Marry by Videoconference," *Dubuque (IA) Telegraph-Herald* (June 10, 2004), A2.

Bales, Robert. *Personality and Interpersonal Behavior* (New York: Holt, Rinehart and Winston, 1970).

Bales, Robert, and Fred Strodbeck. "Phases in Group Problem Solving," *Journal of Abnormal and Social Psychology* 46 (1951), 485–495.

Barr, Steve H., and Edward J. Conlon. "Effects of Distribution of Feedback in Work Groups," *Academy of Management Journal* (June 1994), 641–655.

Benne, Kenneth D., and Paul Sheats. "Functional Roles of Group Members," *Journal of Social Issues* (1948), 41–49.

Bennis, Warren G., and Herbert A. Shepard. "A Theory of Group Development," *Human Relations* 9 (1956), 415–457.

Blanchard, Ken. *Leading at a Higher Level* (Upper Saddle River, NJ: Prentice Hall, 2007).

Bormann, Ernest. *Discussion and Group Methods,* 2nd ed. (New York: McGraw-Hill, 1976).

Bostrom, Robert. "Patterns of Communicative Interaction in Small Groups," *Speech Monographs* 37 (1970), 257–263.

Brilhart, John, and Gloria Galanes. *Effective Group Discussion,* 9th ed. (Dubuque, IA: Brown, 1998).

Cartwright, Dorwin, and Alvin Zander. *Group Dynamics,* 3rd ed. (New York: Harper and Row, 1968), 139–151.

Chansler, P., P. Swamidass, and C. Cammann. "Self-managing Work Teams: An Empirical Study of Group Cohesiveness in 'Natural Work Groups' at a Harley-Davidson Motor Company Plant," *Small Group Research* 343, no. 1 (February 2003), 101–120.

Cherniss, Cary, and Daniel Goleman, eds. *The Emotionally Intelligent Workplace* (San Francisco: Jossey-Bass, 2001).

Clay, Thomas. *A Litmus Test for Practice Group Effectiveness* (Newtown Square, PA: Altman Weil Publications, 2007).

Davis, W., C. Carson, and R. Robinson. "Employment Decisions in Self-Directed Work Teams: A Regulatory Compliance Perspective." *Employee Responsibilities and Rights Journal,* 16 (2004), 179–194.

Donnelon, Anne. *Team Talk: The Power of Language in Team Dynamics* (Cambridge, MA: Harvard Business School Press, 1996).

Druskat, Vanessa Urch, and Steven B. Wolff, "Building The Emotional Intelligence of Groups," *Harvard Business Review* (March 2001), 81–90.

Festinger, Leon. "A Theory of Social Comparison Processes," *Human Relations* 7 (1954) 117–140.

Fisher, B. Aubrey. "Decision Emergence: Phases in Group Decision Making," *Speech Monographs* 37 (1970), 53–66.

Fisher, Kimball. *Leading Self-Directed Work Teams: A Guide to Developing New Team Leadership Skills,* 2nd ed. (New York: McGraw-Hill, 1999).

"Ford Saving Time, Cash on Deliveries," *Detroit Free Press* (February 22, 2001), 3E.

Goleman, Daniel. "What Makes a Leader?" *Harvard Business Review* (November–December 1998), 93–102.

Gouran, Dennis. "Variables Related to Consensus in Group Discussions of Questions of Policy," *Speech Monographs* 36 (1969), 387–391.

Gouran, Dennis S., Candace Brown, and David R. Henry. "Behavioral Correlates of Quality in Decision-Making Discussions," *Communication Monographs* 45 (1978), 51–63.

Gudykunst, William, and Mitchell R. Hammer. "The Influence of Social Identity and Intimacy of Interethnic Relationships on Uncertainty Reduction Processes," *Human Communication Research* 14 (1988), 569–607.

Guetzkow, Harold, and Herbert A. Simon. "The Impact of Certain Communication Nets upon Organization and Performance in Task-Oriented Groups," *Management Science* 1 (1955), 233–250.

Hannon, K. "Group Wisdom Is More Widespread Than We Know," *USA Today* (June 2004), B8.

Hare, A. Paul. *Handbook of Small Group Research* (New York: Free Press, 1962).

Hirokawa, Randy Y. "Group Communication and Problem-Solving Effectiveness: An Investigation of Group Phases," *Human Communication Research* 9 (1983), 291–305.

Homans, George C. *The Human Group* (San Diego, CA: Harcourt Brace Jovanovich, 1950).

Huszczo, Gregory. *Tools for Team Leadership* (Palo Alto, CA: Davies-Black, 2004).

Janis, Irving L. *Group Think,* 2nd ed. (Boston: Houghton Mifflin, 1982).

Jarobe, Susan P. "A Comparison of Input-Output, Process-Output, and Input-Process-Output Models of Small Group Problem-Solving Effectiveness," *Communication Monographs* 55 (1988), 121–142.

Kao, John. *Jamming* (New York: Harper Business, 1996).

Kline, John. "Indices of Orienting and Opinionated Statements in Problem-Solving Discussion," *Speech Monographs* 37 (1970), 282–286.

Leavitt, Harold J. "Some Effects of Certain Communication Patterns on Group Performance," *Journal of Abnormal and Social Psychology* 46 (1951), 38–50.

Leonard, Dorothy, and Walter Swap. *When Sparks Fly* (Boston: Harvard Business School Press, 1999).

Lipman-Blumen, Jean, and Harold J. Leavitt. *Hot Groups* (New York: Oxford University Press, 1999).

Lobe, J. "Iraq: A Certified Case of 'Chickenhawk Groupthink,'" *Global Information Network* (May 12, 2004), 1.

Lovelace, Kay, Dera L. Shapiro, and Laurie R. Weingart, "Maximizing Cross-Functional New Product Teams' Innovativeness and Constraint Adherence: A Conflict Communications Perspective," *Academy of Management Journal,* 44 (2001), 779–793.

Lowry, Paul Benjamin, Tom Roberts, Nicholas C. Romano, Paul Cheney, and Ross Hightower. "The Impact of Group Size and Social Presence on Small-Group Communication: Does Computer-Mediated Communication Make a Difference?" *Small Group Research (SGR),* 37, no.6 (2006), 631–661.

Maxwell, John C. *The 17 Indisputable Laws of Teamwork* (Nashville, TN: Thomas Nelson Publishers, 2001).

McManus, Kevin. "Have You Been to Abilene?" *Industrial Engineer* (March 2007), 20.

Meetings in America: A Study of Trends, Costs and Attitudes toward Business Travel, Teleconferencing, and Their Impact on Productivity. MCI Networking white paper (Greenwich, CT: INFOCOMM, 1998), 3.

Mortensen, C. David. "The Status of Small Group Research," *Quarterly Journal of Speech* 56 (1970), 304–309.

Newcomb, Theodore M. "Persistence and Regression of Changed Attitudes: Long Range Studies," *Journal of Social Issues* 19 (1963), 3–14.

Newvine, Colleen. "Meeting Mania," *Ann Arbor News* (June 7, 1998), E1.

Okhuysen, Gerardo Andres. "Structuring Change: Familiarity and Formal Interventions in Problem-Solving Groups," *Academy of Management Journal,* 44 (2001), 794–808.

Osborn, Alex F. *Applied Imagination* (New York: Scribner, 1957).

Pace, Roger C. "Communication Patterns in High and Low Consensus Discussion: A Descriptive Analysis," *Southern Speech Communication Journal* 53 (1988), 184–202.

Parkinson, Cyril Northcote. *Parkinson's Law* (New York: Ballantine, 1964).

Pasternack, Bruce A., and Albert J. Viscio. *The Centerless Corporation* (New York: Simon and Schuster, 1998).

Phillips, Gerald. *Communication and the Small Group* (Indianapolis, IN: Bobbs-Merrill, 1966).

Raudsepp, Eugene. *More Creative Growth Games* (New York: Perigee, 1980).

"Raymond Mulls Future," *CNN.com* (February 11, 2004). From *www.cnn.com/2004/SHOWBIZ/02/11/showbuzz/index.html*.

Schachter, Stanley. "Deviation, Rejection and Communication," *Journal of Abnormal and Social Psychology* 46 (1951), 190–208.

Schutz, William. *FIRO: A Three-Dimensional Theory of Interpersonal Behavior* (New York: Holt, Rinehart and Winston, 1958).

Schwartz, J., and M. Wald. "Is 'Groupthink' Part of Problem with NASA Again?" *Grand Rapids Press* (March 23, 2003), A15.

Shaw, Marvin E. *Group Dynamics: The Psychology of Small Group Behavior,* 3rd ed. (New York: McGraw-Hill, 1981).

Sherif, Muzafer. *Social Interaction: Process and Products* (Chicago: Aldine, 1967).

Stahl, G. "Communication and Learning in Online Collaboration." College of Information Science and Technology, Drexel University (2003). From Web site: *www.cis.drexel.edu/faculty/gerry/publications/conferences/2003/group/group03.doc*.

Surowiecki, James. *The Wisdom of Crowds: Why the Many Are Smarter Than the Few and How Collective Wisdom Shapes Business, Economies, Societies and Nations* (London: Little Brown, 2004).

Sutton, R. "Why Innovation Happens When Happy People Fight," *Ivey Business Journal* 67, no. 1 (November/December 2002).

Thelen, Herbert, and Watson Dickerman. "Stereotypes and the Growth of Groups," *Educational Leadership* 6 (1949), 309–316.

Tichy, Noel M., with Eli Cohen. *The Leadership Engine* (New York: Harper Business, 1997).

Townsend, Robert. *Further Up the Organization* (New York: Knopf, 1985).

Tubbs, Stewart L. *A Systems Approach to Small Group Interaction,* 9th ed. (New York: McGraw-Hill, 2007).

Tuckman, Bruce. "Developmental Sequence in Small Groups," *Psychological Bulletin* 63 (1965), 384–399.

Wallach, Michael A., Nathan Kogan, and Daryl J. Bem. "Group Influence on Individual Risk-Taking," *Journal of Abnormal and Social Psychology* 65 (1962), 75–86.

Whetten, David, and Kim Cameron. *Developing Management Skills,* 6th ed. (Upper Saddle River, NJ: Prentice-Hall, 2005).

Chapter 13   Public Communication

Alexander, Benjamin. "Reflections on Education and Our Society," *Vital Speeches of the Day* 55 (1989), 563–565.

Arango, Tim. "Speech Impediments," *Fortune* (March 19, 2007), 35.

Beaver, Dennis. "Warning: Humor Can Be Hazardous," *ABA Banking Journal* 98, no. 10 (October 2006), 72.

Bess, A. "Convention Helps Public Speakers Find Their Voice—and Funny Bone," *St. Louis Post-Dispatch* (February 29, 2004), C3.

Blanchard, P. Nick, and James W. Thacker. *Effective Training* (Englewood Cliffs, NJ: Prentice-Hall, 1999).

Boorstin, Daniel J. "Dissent, Dissension, and the News," in Wil A. Linkugel, R. R. Allen, and Richard L. Johannesen, eds., *Contemporary American Speeches,* 2nd ed. (Belmont, CA: Wadsworth, 1969), 203–211.

Bowers, John Waite. "Language Intensity, Social Introversion, and Attitude Change," *Speech Monographs* 30 (1963), 345–352.

Brunel, F., and M. Nelson. "Message Order Effects and Gender Differences in Advertising Persuasion," *Journal of Advertising Research* 43, no. 3 (September 2003), 330.

Carter, Jimmy. "Address Accepting Democratic Nomination for Presidency," *New York Times* (July 16, 1976), A10.

Chekhov, Anton. *Letter to A. P. Chekhov* (April 11, 1889).

Clevenger, Theodore, Jr. *Audience Analysis* (Indianapolis, IN: Bobbs-Merrill, 1966).

Cole, J., and J. McCroskey. "The Association of Perceived Communication Apprehension, Shyness, and Verbal Aggression with Perceptions of Source Credibility and Affect in Organizational and Interpersonal Contexts," *Communication Quarterly* 51, no. 1 (Winter 2004), 101.

Collins, Rebecca, et al. "The Vividness Effect: Elusive or Illusory?" *Journal of Experimental Social Psychology* 24 (1988), 1–18.

Conger, Jay A. *Winning 'Em Over* (New York: Simon and Schuster, 1998).

"The Credibility Question," *PC World* (San Francisco) 22, no. 4 (April 2004), 86.

Dabbs, J. M., Jr., and H. Leventhal. "Effects of Varying the Recommendations of a Fear-Arousing

Communication," *Journal of Personality and Social Psychology* 4 (1966), 525–531.

Das, E., J. de Wit, and W. Stroebe. "Fear Appeals Motivate Acceptance of Action Recommendations: Evidence for a Positive Bias in the Processing of Persuasive Messages," *Personality and Social Psychology Bulletin* 29, no. 5 (May 2003), 650.

Dean, Howard. "I Have a Scream Speech: The Making of A Media Event." From Rachet Up Digiteyes Web site: *ratchetup.typepad.com/eyes/2004/03/howard_deans_i_.html*.

Detz, J. "10 Tips for Better Speeches," (2004). From Joan Detz Web site: *www.joandetz.com/tips.html*.

Deutsch, Babette. *Poetry Handbook: A Dictionary of Terms* (New York: Funk and Wagnalls, 1957).

Downing, Joe, and Cecile Garmon. "Teaching Students in the Basic Course How to Use Presentation Software," *Communication Education* 50 (2001), 218–229.

Fairbanks, Jenille, Kenneth D. Plowman, and Brad L. Rawlins. "Transparency in Government Communication," *Journal of Public Affairs* (February 2007).

Gallo, Carmine. "Terminate Your Public Speaking Fears," *Business Week Online* (May 22, 2006a).

———. "How to PowerPoint Like a Pro," *Business Week Online* (June 2, 2006b).

———. "How to Be an Ace Speaker," *Business Week Online* (June 15, 2006c).

Gergen, David. *Eyewitness to Power* (New York: Simon & Schuster, 2000).

Germano, W. "The Scholarly Lecture: How to Stand and Deliver," *Chronicle of Higher Education,* 50, no. 14 (November 28, 2003), B15.

Greenstein, Fred. "Presidential Difference in the Early Republic: The Highly Disparate Leadership Styles of Washington, Adams, and Jefferson," *Presidential Studies Quarterly* 36, no. 3 (September 2006).

Gregory, David. "Sen. Biden Apologizes for Remarks on Obama," *NBC Nightly News.* Retrieved July 12, 2007, from *www.msnbc.msn.com/id/16911044*.

Gruner, C. R. "The Effect of Humor in Dull and Interesting Informative Speeches," *Central States Speech Journal* 21 (1970), 160–166.

———. "Advice to the Beginning Speaker on Using Humor—What Research Tells Us," *Communication Education* 34 (1985), 142–147.

Ham, Mary Katherine. *Townhall* (January 31, 2007). Retrieved July 8, 2007, from *www.townhall.com/blog/MaryKatherineHam/page30*.

Higgins, Sean. "Dale Carnegie Influenced Many People," *Investors' Business Daily* (October 24, 2001), A5.

Hovland, Carl, Irving Janis, and Harold Kelley. *Communication Persuasion* (New Haven, CT: Yale University Press, 1953).

Iacocca, Lee. "The Will to Take Leadership," *Vital Speeches of the Day* 55 (1989), 454–458.

Ivry, B. "Can a Movie Halt Making of 'Bush II'?; Political Camps Debate Impact of 'Fahrenheit 9/11,'" *Bergen County (NJ) Record* (July 2, 2004), A1.

Ivy, Diana K., and Phil Backlund. *Exploring Gender Speak* (New York: McGraw-Hill, 1994).

James-Enger, K. "Talk It Up," *The Writer* (Boston) 117, no. 5 (May 2004), 41–42.

Janis, Irving, and Peter Field. "Sex Differences and Personality Factors Related to Persuasibility," in Carl Hovland and Irving Janis, eds., *Personality and Persuasibility* (New Haven, CT: Yale University Press, 1959), 55–68.

Karlins, M., and H. Abelson. *Persuasion: How Opinions and Attitudes Are Changed,* 2nd ed. (New York: Springer, 1970).

King, Martin Luther, Jr. "I Have a Dream," in Wil Linkugel, R. R. Allen, and Richard L. Johannesen, eds., *Contemporary American Speeches,* 2nd ed. (Belmont, CA: Wadsworth, 1969), 290–294.

Knapp, Mark L., and Judith A. Hall. *Nonverbal Communication in Human Interaction,* 4th ed. (New York: Harcourt Brace, 1997).

Kouzes, James M., and Barry Z. Posner. *Credibility* (San Francisco: Jossey-Bass, 1995).

Linton, Harriet, and Elaine Graham. "Personality Correlates of Persuasibility," in Carl Hovland and Irving Janis, eds., *Personality and Persuasibility* (New Haven, CT: Yale University Press, 1959), 96.

Luchins, Abraham S., and Edith H. Luchins. "The Effects of Order of Presentation of Information and Explanatory Models," *Journal of Social Psychology* 80 (1970), 63–70.

Maxwell, John C. *The 17 Indisputable Laws of Teamwork* (Nashville, TN: Thomas Nelson Publishers, 2001).

McCroskey, James C. *An Introduction to Rhetorical Communication,* 6th ed. (Upper Saddle River, NJ: Prentice Hall, 1993).

McEwen, William J., and B. S. Greenberg. "The Effects of Message Intensity on Receiver Evaluations of Source, Message, and Topic," *Journal of Communication* 20 (1970), 340–350.

McGuire, William J. "Personality and Susceptibility to Social Influence," in E. F. Borgatta and W. W. Lambert, eds.,

Handbook of Personality Theory and Research (Chicago: Rand McNally, 1968), 1130–1187.

———. "The Nature of Attitude Change," in Gardner Lindzey and Elliot Aronson, eds., *The Handbook of Social Psychology*, 2nd ed., vol. III, *The Individual in a Social Context* (Reading, MA: Addison-Wesley, 1969), 136–314.

———. "Attitudes and Attitude Changes," in Gardner Lindzey and Elliot Aronson, eds., *The Handbook of Social Psychology*, 3rd ed., vol. II (New York: Random House, 1985), 233–346.

Miller, Merle. *Plain Speaking: An Oral Biography of Harry S. Truman* (New York: Berkley Publishing, 1973).

Miller, N., and C. T. Campbell. "Recency and Primacy in Persuasion as a Function of the Timing of Speeches and Measurements," *Journal of Abnormal and Social Psychology* 59 (1959), 1–9.

Montgomery, C. L., and Michael Burgoon. "An Experimental Study of the Interactive Effects of Sex and Androgyny on Attitude Change," *Communication Monograph* 44 (1977), 130–135.

Noonan, Peggy. *What I Saw at the Revolution: A Political Life in the Reagan Era* (New York: Random House, 1990).

Pappas, J. "The Greatest Story Never Told," *Washington Times* (February 22, 2004), B5.

Pawlak, J. "Add Some Show Biz to Seminars," *Arlington Heights (IL) Daily Herald* (January 9, 2004), 2.

Petrie, C. "Informative Speaking: A Summary and Bibliography of Related Research," *Speech Monograph* 20 (1963), 79–91.

Pratkanis, Anthony R., et al. "In Search of Reliable Persuasion Effects: The Sleeper Effect Is Dead, Long Live the Sleeper Effect," *Journal of Personality and Social Psychology* 54 (1988), 203–218.

Reagan Foundation. "Tear Down This Wall," *www.reaganfoundation.org/reagan/speeches/wall.asp*, retrieved July 8, 2007.

Reagan, Maureen. *First Father, First Daughter: A Memoir* (Boston: Little, Brown, 1989).

Reagan, Ronald. "We the People," *Vital Speeches of the Day* 55 (1989), 10–13.

Rosenfeld, Lawrence, and Vickie Christie. "Sex and Persuasibility Revisited," *Western Speech* 38 (1974), 244–253.

Safire, William. *Lend Me Your Ears: Great Speeches in History* (New York: W. W. Norton, 1992).

Samovar, Larry, and Edwin McDaniel. *Public Speaking in a Multicultural Society* (Los Angeles: Roxbury Publishing, 2007).

Sedlack, Robert, Barbara Shworn, and Karl Keller. *Graphics and Visual Communication for Managers* (Mason, OH: Thomson South-Western, 2008).

Shaw, Robert Bruce. *Trust in the Balance* (San Francisco, CA: Jossey-Bass, 1997).

"Speaking of Fears . . . " *Springfield (IL) State Journal Register* (April 27, 2004), 9.

Sprague, Jo, and Douglas Stuart. *The Speaker's Handbook*, 4th ed. (New York: Harcourt Brace, 1996).

Sterman, John, and Linda Booth Sweeney. "Understanding Public Complacency about Climate Change: Adults' Mental Models of Climate Change Violate Conservation of Matter," *Climatic Change* 80 (2007), 213–238.

Thistlethwaite, D. L., H. De Haan, and J. Kamenetzky. "The Effect of 'Directive' and 'Non-Directive' Communication Procedures on Attitudes," *Journal of Abnormal and Social Psychology* 51 (1955), 107–118.

Thomas, Martha W. "Business Communication in the Modern Age," *Business and Economic Review*, (July–September 1998), 20–23.

Tieger, Paul D., and Barbara Barron-Tieger. *The Art of Speed Reading People* (Boston: Little, Brown, 1998).

Tubbs, Stewart. "Explicit versus Implicit Conclusions and Audience Commitment," *Speech Monographs* 35 (1968), 14–19.

Tuthill, D. M., and D. R. Forsyth. "Sex Differences in Opinion Conformity and Dissent," *Journal of Social Psychology* 116 (1982), 205–210.

Werts, C. E. "Before-and-After Magic," *Information Outlook* 8, no. 3 (March 2004), 21–24.

Whalen, Joel. *The Professional Communications Toolkit* (Thousand Oaks, CA: Sage Publications, 2007).

Whetten, David A., and Kim S. Cameron. *Developing Management Skills*, 6th ed. (Upper Saddle River, NJ: Prentice-Hall, 2005).

Witte, Kim. "Putting the Fear Back into Fear Appeals: The Extended Parallel Process Model," *Communication Monographs* 59 (December 1992), 329–349.

———. "Fear Control and Danger Control: A Test of the Extended Parallel Process Model (EPPM)," *Communication Monographs* 6 (June 1994), 113–134.

Chapter 14   Organizational Communication

Aber, R. "The Bottom Line in Business Blogs," *Entrepreneur.com*. August 1, 2004.

Adler, Ronald B., and Jeanne Marquardt Elmhorst. *Communicating at Work*, 6th ed. (New York: McGraw-Hill, 1999).

Allport, Gordon, and Leo Postman. *The Psychology of Rumor* (New York: Holt, 1947).

Anonymous. "Sentencing Corporate America: Ethical or Not?" *PR Newswire* (New York) (March 17, 2004), 1.

Auxillium West. "Corporate Culture." (2003). From Auxillium West: Human Resources Software Web site: *www.aulillium.com/culture.shtml.*

Avolio, Bruce, and Fred Luthans. *The High Impact Leader* (New York: McGraw-Hill, 2006).

Barnard, Chester I. *The Functions of the Executive* (Cambridge, MA: Harvard University Press, 1938).

Berner, Robert. "My Year at Wal-Mart," *Business Week* (February 12, 2007), 70–74.

Bick, Julie. "Speed-dating Format Adapted for Business," *Ann Arbor News* (January 3, 2007), C3.

Burke, Doris. "Anatomy of an A380: Missed Connections," *Fortune* (March 5, 2007), 101–108.

Catt, Stephen E., Donald S. Miller, and Nitham M. Hindi. "Don't Misconstrue Communication Cues: Understanding Miscues Can Help Reduce Widespread and Expensive Miscommunication," *Strategic Finance* (June 2005), 51.

Cetron, Marvin J., and Owen Davies. *Crystal Globe: The Haves and Have-Nots of the New World Order* (New York: St. Martin's Press, 1991).

"Change & Communication." (2004). From Ivy Sea Online Web site: *www.ivysea.com/pages/change_mgt_issueportal.html.*

Cherniss, Cary, and Daniel Goleman, eds. *The Emotionally Intelligent Workplace* (San Francisco: Jossey-Bass, 2001).

Conboy, William A. *Working Together . . . Communication in a Healthy Organization* (Columbus, OH: Merrill, 1976).

Conrad, C. *Strategic Organizational Communication: Cultures, Situations, and Adaption* (New York: Holt, Rinehart and Winston, 1985).

Cooper, Cecily. "Just Joking Around? Employer Humor Expression as an Ingratiatory Behavior," *Academy of Management Review* 30, no. 4 (2005), 765–776.

Cooper, Cord. "Ease Your E-mail Angst," *Investor's Business Daily* (January 15, 2004), A3.

Davis, Keith. "A Method of Studying Communication Patterns in Organizations," *Personnel Psychology* 6 (1953), 301–312.

———. *Human Behavior at Work* (New York: McGraw-Hill, 1972).

Deal, Terrence E., and Allan A. Kennedy. *Corporate Cultures* (Reading, MA: Addison-Wesley, 1984).

Dean, Peter. *Leadership Is for Everyone* (New York: McGraw-Hill, 2006).

Dennis, Harry S. "The Construction of a 'Managerial Communication Climate' Inventory for Use in Complex Organizations," paper presented at the annual convention of the International Communication Association, New Orleans, April 1975.

Downes, Larry, and Chunka Mui. *Unleashing the Killer App* (Cambridge, MA: Harvard Business School Press, 1998).

Dutton, Jane E., Susan J. Ashford, Regina M. O'Neill, and Katherine A. Lawrence. "Moves That Matter: Issue Selling and Organizational Change," *Academy of Management Journal* 44 (August 2001), 716–726.

Fisher, Kimball. *Leading Self-Directed Work Teams: A Guide to Developing New Team Leadership Skills* (New York: McGraw-Hill, 1993).

French, John R. P., and Bertram Raven. "The Bases of Social Power," in Dorwin Cartwright and Alvin Zander, eds., *Group Dynamics: Research and Theory* (Evanston, IL: Row, Peterson, 1962), 607–623.

German, Carol J., and William R. Rath. "Making Technical Communication a Real-World Experience," *Journal of Technical Writing and Communication* 14 (1987), 335–346.

Goffee, Rob, and Gareth Jones. *Why Should Anyone Be Led by You?* (Boston: Harvard Business School Press, 2006).

Goldhaber, Gerald M. *Organizational Communication,* 6th ed. (Dubuque, IA: Brown, 1993).

Greene, Robert, and Joost Elffers. *The 48 Laws of Power* (New York: Viking, 1998).

Hendrickson, Lorraine, and John Psarouthakis. *Dynamic Management of Growing Firms,* 2nd ed. (Ann Arbor: University of Michigan Press, 1998).

Hodgetts, Richard M. "An Interview with Ed Kurtz," *Journal of Leadership Studies* 5 (Winter 1998), 156–162.

Jennings, Eugene E. *Routes to the Executive Suite* (New York: McGraw-Hill, 1971).

Lambert, Jack. *The Work Force Challenges of the 21st Century* (Washington, DC: National Association of Manufacturers, 1992).

Lawrence, Paul R., and Jay W. Lorsch. *Developing Organizations: Diagnosis and Action* (Reading, MA: Addison-Wesley, 1969).

Lennick, Doug, and Fred Kiel. *Moral Intelligence* (Upper Saddle River, NJ: Wharton School Publishing, 2005).

Liden, Robert C., and Terence R. Mitchell. "In Behaviors in Organization Settings," *Journal of Management Review* 13 (1988), 572–578.

Likert, Rensis. *The Human Organization* (New York: McGraw-Hill, 1967).

London, S. "The New Science of Leadership: An Interview with Margaret Wheatley," (1996). From Insight & Outlook Web site: *www.scottlondon.com/insight/scripts/wheatley.html.*

Manz, Charles C., and Henry P. Sims, Jr. *The New Superleadership* (San Francisco: Berrett-Koehler Publishers, 2001).

Maxwell, John C. *The 17 Indisputable Laws of Teamwork* (Nashville, TN: Thomas Nelson Publishers, 2001).

McAllister, Daniel. "Affect and Cognition-Based Trust as Foundations for Interpersonal Cooperation in Organizations," *Academy of Management Journal* 36 (1995), 24–59.

Mowle, J. "Local Corporate Learning Center Pushes Executives Out of Their Comfort Zones," *Colorado Springs Business Journal* (January 30, 2004).

Mulkern, Anne. "More Consumers Are Calling The Shots," *Detroit Free Press* (July 2, 2001), 6F.

Pennsylvania State University survey, personal correspondence, April 6, 1992.

Pfeffer, Jeffrey. *The Human Equation* (Cambridge, MA: Harvard Business School Press, 1998).

Rath, Tom. *Strengths Finder 2.0* (New York: Gallup Press, 2007).

Reich, Theodore. *The Greening of America* (New York: Random House, 1970).

Rice, Ronald E. "Computer Mediated Communication and Organizational Innovations,"*Journal of Communication* 37 (1987), 64–94.

Rosnow, Ralph. "Rumor as Communication: A Contextualist Approach," *Journal of Communication* 38 (1988), 12–28.

Safon, Vicente. "Factors That Influence Recruiters' Choice of B-Schools and Their MBA Graduates: Evidence and Implications for B-Schools." *The Academy of Management Learning and Education* 6 (June 2007), 217–233.

Schein, Edgar. *Organizational Culture and Leadership,* 2nd ed. (San Francisco: Jossey-Bass, 1997).

Sellers, Patricia. "A Double Shot of Productivity," *Fortune* (October 16, 2006), 51.

Smith, Ronald L., Gary A Richetto, and Joseph P. Zima. "Organizational Behavior: An Approach to Human Communication," in Richard W. Budd and Brent D. Ruben, eds., *Approaches to Human Communication* (New York: Spartan Books, 1972).

Sostek, Anya. "Studies Shows a Bit of Office Talk Can Boost Productivity," *Pittsburgh Post-Gazette* (May 2006).

Swift, Marvin H. "Clear Writing Means Clear Thinking Means . . . ," *Harvard Business Review* (January–February 1973), 59–62.

Tapscott, Don. *Growing Up Digital* (New York: McGraw-Hill, 1998).

Watson Wyatt Worldwide, Inc. *Press Release* (July 16, 2006). *www.watsonwyatt.com.*

Wayne, Sandy J., Lynn M. Shore, and Robert C. Liden. "Perceived Organizational Support and Leader-Member Exchange: A Social Exchange Perspective," *Academy of Management Journal* 40 (1997), 82–111.

Wessel, H. "Talking It Up: Business Works Best when Lower-level Workers Have a Say," *San Diego Union-Tribune* (March 17, 2003), C8.

Wheatley, M. "When Complex Systems Fail: New Roles for Leaders," Leader to Leader Institute Web site. (1999). From *pdf.org/leaderbooks.L2L/winter99/wheatley. html.*

———. "When Change Is Out of Our Control," Margaret Wheatley Web site (2002). From *www.margaretwheatley.com/articles/whenchangeisoutofcontrol.html.*

———. "Is the Pace of Life Hindering Our Ability to Manage?" *Management Today* (March 2004). From Margaret Wheatley Web site: *www.margaretwheatley.com/articles/thepaceoflife.html.*

Whetten, David A., and Kim S. Cameron. *Developing Management Skills,* 6th ed. (Upper Saddle River, NJ: Prentice-Hall, 2005).

Whitener, Ellen M., Susan E. Brodt, M. Audrey Korsgaard, and Jon M. Werner, "Managers as Initiators of Trust: An Exchange Relationship Framework for Understanding Managerial Trustworthy Behavior," *The Academy of Management Review* 23, no. 3 (July 1998), 513–530.

Widgery, Robin, and CecilStackpole, "Desk Position, Interviewee Anxiety, and Interviewer Credibility: An Example of Cognitive Balance in a Dyad," *Journal of Counseling Psychology* 19, no. 3 (May 1972), 173–177.

Willis, Craig. "Remarks to the Board of Regents," Eastern Michigan University (September 21, 2004).

Chapter 15 Mass Communication and the New Technologies

Anderson, Craig A., Douglas A. Gentile, and Katherine E. Buckley. *Violent Video Game Effects on Children and Adolescents* (New York: Oxford University Press, 2006).

Avery, Robert K., and Thomas A. McCain. "Interpersonal and Mediated Encounters," in Gary Gumpert and

Rob Cathcart, eds., *Inter/Media: Interpersonal Communication in a Media World*, 2nd ed. (New York: Oxford University Press, 1982).

Bagdikian, Ben H. *The New Media Monopoly* (Boston: Beacon Press, 2004).

Beckerman, Gal. "Edging Away from Anarchy," *Columbia Journalism Review* (September/October 2003), 27–30.

Bennett, W. Lance. *News: The Politics of Illusion*, 6th ed. (New York: Pearson, 2005).

Bennett, W. Lance, Regina G. Lawrence, and Steen Livingston. "None Dare Call It Torture: Indexing and the Limits of Press Independence in the Abu Ghraib Scandal," *Journal of Communication* 56 (September 2006), 467–485.

Bennett, W. Lance, and William Serrin. "The Watchdog Role," in Geneva Overholser and Kathleen Hall Jamieson, eds., *The Press,* Institutions of American Democracy Series (New York: Oxford University Press, 2005), pp. 169–188.

Bittner, John R., *Fundamentals of Communication* (Englewood Cliffs, NJ: Prentice-Hall, 1985).

Boase, Jeffrey, and Barry Wellman. "Personal Relationships: On and Off the Internet," in Anita Vangelisti and Daniel Perlman, eds., *Cambridge Handbook of Personal Relationships* (New York: Cambridge University Press, 2006), 709–723.

Bok, Sissela. *Mayhem: Violence as Public Entertainment* (Reading, MA: Addison-Wesley, 1998).

Boneva, Bonka, Robert Kraut, and David Frohlich. "Using E-Mail for Personal Relationships," *American Behavioral Scientist* 45 (2001), 530–549.

Brown, Ben. "War Junkie," in William Katovsky and Timothy Carlson, *Embedded: The Media at War in Iraq* (Guilford, CT: Globe Pequod Press, 2003), 217–221.

Burns, John. "The Moral Compass of Iraq," in William Katovsky and Timothy Carlson, eds., *Embedded: The Media at War in Iraq* (Guilford, CT: Globe Pequod Press, 2003), 155–163.

Cappella, Joseph N., and Kathleen Hall Jamieson. *Spiral of Cynicism: The Press and the Public Good* (New York: Oxford University Press, 1997).

Carter, Bill, and Felicity Barringer. "U.S. Shifts Focus of Attack in Afghanistan by Bombing Ground Forces of Taliban," *New York Times* (October 11, 2001), A1, B2.

Chester, Jeff. *Digital Destiny: New Media and the Future of Democracy* (New York: The New Press, 2007).

Corliss, Richard. "The Ladies Who Lunge," *Time Australia*, no. 41 (October 7, 1996), 56–57.

Couldry, Nick. *Listening beyond the Echoes: Media, Ethics, and Agency in an Uncertain World* (Boulder, CO: Paradigm Publishers, 2006).

CQ Researcher. "Does a 'Digital Divide' Cut Low-Income Citizens Out of 21st Century Politics," vol. 14, no. 32 (September 17, 2004), 757–780.

Dennis, Everette. "American Media and American Values," in *Vital Speeches of the Day* 54, no. 11 (March 15, 1988), 349–352.

Diddi, Arvind, and Robert LaRose. "Getting Hooked on News," *Journal of Broadcasting & Electronic Media* 50 (June 2006), 193–210.

Dominick, Joseph R. *The Dynamics of Mass Communication: Media in the Digital Age,* 9th ed. (New York: McGraw-Hill, 2007).

Drew, Dan, and David Weaver. "Voter Learning in the 2004 Presidential Election: Did the Media Matter?" *Journalism and Mass Communication Quarterly* 83 (Spring 2006), 25–42.

Entman, Robert M. "Framing: Toward Clarification of a Fractured Paradigm," *Journal of Communication* 43, no. 4 (1993), 51–58.

———. "The Nature and Sources of News," in Geneva Overholser and Kathleen Hall Jamieson, eds., *The Press,* Institutions of American Democracy Series (New York: Oxford University Press, 2006), 48–65.

Fallows, Deborah. "The Internet and Daily Life," *Pew Internet & American Life Project* (August 11, 2004). Retrieved September 11, 2004, from *www.pewinternet.org/PPF/r/131/report-display-asp.*

Flanagin, Andrew J., and Miriam J. Metzger. "Internet Use in the Contemporary Media Environment," *Human Communication Research* 27 (2001), 153–181.

Foerstel, Herbert N. *From Watergate to Monicagate: Ten Controversies in Modern Journalism and Media* (Westport, CT: Greenwood Press, 2001).

"Fox: Civilian Casualties Not News." *www.fair.org* (posted Number 8, 2001). Retrieved July 2007 from *www.fair.org/index.php?=1668.*

Gerbner, George, et al. "Growing Up with Television: The Cultivation Perspective," in Jennings Bryant and Dolf Zillmann, eds., *Media Effects: Advances in Theory and Research* (Hillsdale, NJ: Erlbaum, 1994), 17–42.

Gillespie, Marie. "Transnational Communications and Diaspora Communities," in Simon Cottle, ed., *Ethnic Minorities and the Media* (Buckingham, UK: Open University Press, 2000), 164–178.

Girardi, Michelle. "Lens Crafters," *The New Media and the Law* (Spring 2004), 21–23.

Glasser, Susan, and Peter Baker. "Marriage Under Fire," in William Katovsky and Timothy Carlson, eds., *Embedded: The Media at War in Iraq* (Guilford, CT: Globe Pequod Press, 2003), 287–298.

Glazer, Sarah. "Video Games: The Issues," *CQ Researcher* (November 10, 2006), 939–954.

Greenberg, Bradley S. "Diffusion of News about the Kennedy Assassination," in Bradley S. Greenberg and Edwin B. Parker, eds., *The Kennedy Assassination and the American Public* (Stanford, CA: Stanford University Press, 1965), 89–98.

Griffin, Em. *A First Look at Communication Theory*, 6th ed. (New York: McGraw-Hill, 2006).

Haythornthwaite, Caroline. "Introduction: The Internet in Everyday Life," *American Behavioral Scientist* 45 (2001), 363–382.

Hickey, Neil. "Where TV Has Teeth," *Columbia Journalism Review* (May/June 2001a), 6–10.

———. "Election Night: The Big Mistake," *Columbia Journalism Review* (January/February 2001b), 32–35.

Hoffner, Cynthia, Richard S. Plotkin, Martha Buchanan et al. "The Third-Person Effect in Perception of the Influence of Television Violence," *Journal of Communication* 51 (2001), 283–299.

Howard, Philip E. N., Lee Rainie, and Steve Jones. "Days and Nights on the Internet," *American Behavioral Scientist* 45 (2001), 383–404.

Hylmö, Annia. "Girls on Film," *Western Journal of Communication* 70 (July 2006), 167–185.

"Internet Usage Statistics: The Big Picture." *Internet World Stats*. Retrieved July 22, 2007, from *internetworldstats.com/stats.htm*.

Jamieson, Kathleen Hall. *Packaging the Presidency: A History and Criticism of Presidential Campaign Advertising* (New York: Oxford University Press, 1996).

Jamieson, Kathleen Hall, and Paul Waldman. *The Press Effect: Politicians, Journalists, and the Stories That Shape the Political World* (New York: Oxford University Press, 2003).

Katovsky, William. "Introduction," in William Katovsky and Timothy Carlson, eds., *Embedded: The Media at War in Iraq* (Guilford, CT: Globe Pequod Press, 2003), xi–xix.

Katz, Elihu, and Paul Lazarsfeld. *Personal Influence: The Part Played by People in the Flow of Mass Communications* (Glencoe, IL: Free Press, 1964).

Kelliher, Laurie. "Low Power, High Intensity," *Columbia Journalism Review* (September/October 2003), 31–33.

———. "Fox Watch," *Columbia Journalism Review* (March/April 2004), 8.

Kiesler, Sara, ed. *Culture of the Internet* (Mahwah, NJ: Erlbaum, 1996).

Kirkpatrick, David. "TV Host Says U.S. Paid Him to Back Policy," *New York Times* (January 8, 2005), A1, 12.

Kleinenberg, Eric. *Fighting for Air: The Battle to Control America's Media* (New York: Metropolitan Books, 2007).

Kovach, Bill, and Tom Rosenstiel. *The Elements of Journalism* (New York: Crown, 2001).

Kraut, Robert, Sara Kiesler, Bonka Boneva, et al. "Internet Paradox Revisited," *Journal of Social Issues* 58, no. 1 (2002).

Kraut, R., M. Patterson, V. Lundmark, S. Kiesler, T. Mukhopadhyay, and W. Scherlis. "Internet Paradox: A Social Technology that Reduces Social Involvement and Psychological Well-Being?" *American Psychologist* 53, no. 9 (1998), 1017–1031.

Kwak, Nojin, Nathaniel Poor, and Marko M. Skoric. "Honey, I Shrunk the World! The Relation Between Internet Use and International Engagement," *Mass Communication & Society* 9, no. 2 (2006), 189–213.

Lazarsfeld, Paul, Bernard Berelson, and H. Gaudet. *The People's Choice* (New York: Columbia University Press, 1968).

Lemann, Nicholas. "Amateur Hour," *The New Yorker* (August 7 & 14, 2006), 44–47.

Lenhart, Amanda, and Mary Madden. "Pew Internet Project Data Memo: Social Networking Websites and Teens: An Overview," *Pew Internet & American Life Project* (January 7, 2007) *www.pewinternet.org*.

Lester, Paul Martin, and Susan Dente Ross, eds., *Images that Injure* (Westport, CT: Praeger, 2003), 51–55.

Lieberman, Trudy. "Answer the &%$#* Question!" *Columbia Journalism Review* (January/February 2004), 40–43.

Lull, James. *Media, Communication, Culture: A Global Approach* (New York: Columbia University Press, 2000).

———. *Culture-On-Demand* (Malden, MA: Blackwell Publishing Ltd, 2007).

MacArthur, John. *Second Front: Censorship and Propaganda in the Gulf War* (New York: Hill and Wang, 1992).

Mannur, Anita. "Postscript: Cyberscapes and the Interfacing of Diasporas," in Jana Evans Braziel and Anita Mannur, eds., *Theorizing Diaspora* (Oxford, UK: Blackwell Publishing, 2003), 283–290.

Massing, Michael. "Times Letters Unfit to Print," *The Nation* (April 16, 2001), 20–21.

"McCain Rebukes Sinclair's 'Nightline' Decision." *www.cnn.com* (posted April 30, 2004). Retrieved July 13,

2007, from *www.cnn.com/2004/showbiz/tv/04/30/abc* *.nightline/index.html.*

McCombs, Maxwell. "The Agenda-Setting Function of the Press," in Geneva Overholser and Kathleen Hall Jamieson, eds., *The Press*, Institutions of American Democracy Series (New York: Oxford University Press, 2005), 156–168.

McCombs, Maxwell, and Donald Shaw. "The Agenda-Setting Function of Mass Media," *Public Opinion Quarterly* 36, no. 2 (1972), 176–185.

Moorehead, Caroline. *Gellhorn: A Twentieth-Century Life* (New York: Holt, 2003).

Morrison, Margaret, and Dean M. Krugman. "A Look at Mass and Computer Mediated Technologies: Understanding the Roles of Television and Computers in the Home," *Journal of Broadcasting & Electronic Media* 45 (2001), 135–161.

Mossberger, Karen, Caroline J. Tolbert, and Mary Stansbury. *Virtual Inequality: Beyond the Digital Divide* (Washington, DC: Georgetown University Press, 2003).

"Most Popular Internet Activities." *Infoplease.com*. Retrieved July 22, 2007, from *www.infoplease.com/ipa/A0921862.html.*

Moyers, Bill. "Journalism & Democracy: On the Importance of Being a Public Nuisance," *The Nation* (May 7, 2001), 11–17.

———. "Journalism Under Fire" (posted September 18, 2004). Retrieved July 22, 2007, from *www.alternet .org/mediaculture/19918.*

The Nation. "10th Anniversary, The National Entertainment State" (July 3, 2006), insert.

National Television Violence Study, vol. 1 (Thousand Oaks, CA: Sage, 1997).

———. vol. 2, edited by the Center for Communication and Social Policy, University of California, Santa Barbara (Thousand Oaks, CA: Sage, 1998).

"The New Age of Alternative Media." *Columbia Journalism Review* (September/October 2003), 20.

Nichols, John, and Robert McChesney. *Tragedy and Farce: How the American Media Sell Wars, Spin Elections, and Destroy Democracy* (New York: The New Press, 2005).

Nie, Norman H. "Sociability, Interpersonal Relations, and the Internet: Reconciling Conflicting Findings," *American Behavioral Scientist* 45 (2001), 420–435.

Nie, Norman H., and Lutz Erbring. "Internet and Society: A Preliminary Report," *IT & Society 1*, no. 1 (2002), 275–283.

Nie, Norman H., Irena Stepanikova, Heili Pals, Lu Zheng, and Xiaobin He. "Ten Years after the Birth of the Internet: How Do Americans Use the Internet in Their Daily Lives?" *Stanford Institute for the Quantitative Study of Society 2005 Report*. Retrieved July 23, 2007, from *www/stanford.edu/group/siqss/researchtimes_ study_files/ProjectReport2005.pdf.*

"Online World as Important to Internet Users as Real World?" *2007 Digital Future Report*. Retrieved July 22, 2007, from *www.digitalcenter.org/pdf/2007-Digital-Future-Report-Press-Release-112906.pdf.*

Pavlik, John V. *Journalism and New Media* (New York: Columbia University Press, 2001).

Pavlik, John V., and Shawn McIntosh. *Converging Media* (Boston: Pearson, 2005).

Pecora, Norma, John P. Murray, and Ellen Ann Wartella, eds. *Children and Television: Fifty Years of Research* (Mahwah, NJ: Erlbaum, 2006).

Pfau, Michael, Michel M. Haigh, et al. "Embedded Reporting during the Invasion and Occupation of Iraq," *Journal of Broadcasting & Electronic Media* 49 (December 2005), 468–487.

Pfau, Michael, Michel Haigh, Mitchell Gettle et al. "Embedding Journalists in Military Combat Zones," *Journalism and Mass Communication Quarterly* 81 (Spring 2004), 74–88.

Porter, David, ed. *Internet Culture* (New York: Routledge, 1997).

Rainie, Lee, and John Horrigan. "Election 2006 Online," *Pew Internet & American Life Project, www .pewinternet.org.*

Rainie, Lee, and Scott Keeler. "Pew Internet Project Data Memo" (April 2006). Retrieved July 22, 2007, from *www.pewinternet.org/pdfs/PIP_Cell_phone_study.pdf.*

Redding, W. Charles. "The Enemies of Responsible Communication," *Vital Speeches of the Day* 54, no. 22 (September 1, 1988), 702–704.

Reeves, Byron, and Clifford Nass. *The Media Equation* (New York: Cambridge University Press, 1996).

Rendall, Steve. "The Fairness Doctrine," *www.fair.org/ index/php?page=2053.*

Roberts, Lynne D., Leigh M. Smith, and Clare M. Pollock. "'U r a lot bolder on the net': Shyness and Internet Use," in W. Ray Crozier, ed., *Shyness: Development, Consolidation and Change* (London: Routledge, 2000), 121–138.

Rogers, Everett M. *Diffusion of Innovations*, 4th ed. (New York: Free Press, 1995).

Romano, Carlin. "All Is Not Fair in Journalism," *Media Studies Journal* (Spring–Summer 1998), 90–95.

Rubin, Alan M., and Rebecca B. Rubin. "Interface of Personal and Mediated Communication: A Research Agenda," *Critical Studies in Mass Communication 2* (1985), 36–53.

Rubin, Rebecca B., Elizabeth M. Perse, and Carole A. Barbato. "Conceptualization and Measurement of Interpersonal Communication Motives," *Human Communication Research* 14 (1988), 602–628.

Scheufele, Dietram A., Kim Eunkyung, and Dominique Brossard. "My Friend's Enemy: How Split-Screen Debate Coverage Influences Evaluation of Presidential Debates," *Communication Research* 34 (February 2007), 3–24.

Schramm, Wilbur, and Donald F. Roberts, eds. *The Process and Effect of Mass Communications,* rev. ed. (Urbana: University of Illinois Press, 1971).

Seabrook, John. "Game Master," *New Yorker* (November 6, 2006), 89–99.

"Senate Opposition to Bush Plan Grows." *MSNBC* (January 11, 2007). Retrieved July 24, 2007, from *www.msnbc.msn.com/id/16579285.*

Signorelli, Nancy, and Susan Kahlenberg. "Television's World of Work in the Nineties," *Journal of Broadcasting & Electronic Media* 45 (Fall 2001), 4–22.

Simonson, Peter, ed. *Politics, Social Networks and the History of Mass Communications Research: Rereading* Personal Influence (Thousand Oaks, CA: Sage, 2006).

Slater, Michael D., Henry L. Kimberly, Randall C. Swaim, and Lori L. Anderson. "Violent Media Content and Aggressiveness in Adolescents," *Communication Research* 30 (2003), 713–736.

Smith, Dinitia. "Media More Likely to Show Women Talking about Romance than a Job," *New York Times* (May 1, 1997), 15.

Smyth, Frank. "2006: A Deadly Year for Journalists," *Democracy Now!* (December 29, 2006). Retrieved February 24, 2007, from *www.democracynow.org/article.p/?sid+06/12/29/1446225.*

Solomon, Deborah. "This American TV Show," *New York Times Magazine* (March 4, 2007), p. 15.

Straubhaar, Joseph, and Robert LaRose. *Media Now,* 2nd ed. (Belmont, CA: Wadsworth, 2000).

Sunstein, Cass R. "Reinforce the Walls of Privacy," *New York Times* (September 6, 1997), sec. 1, 23.

———. *republic.com* (Princeton, NJ: Princeton University Press, 2001).

Tannen, Deborah. *You're Wearing That? Understanding Mothers and Daughters in Conversation* (New York: Ballantine Books, 2006).

Tolchin, Martin, and Susan Tolchin. *A World Ignited* (Lanham, MD: Rowan & Littlefield, 2006).

Turkle, Sherry. *Life on the Screen: Identity in the Age of the Internet* (New York: Simon and Schuster, 1995).

U.S. Department of Health and Human Services. *Television and Behavior: Ten Years of Scientific Progress and Implications for the Eighties,* vol. I, Summary Report (Washington, DC: Government Printing Office, 1982).

U.S. Department of Labor and Bureau of Labor Statistics. *Occupational Outlook Handbook 2006–2007 Edition* (Indianapolis, IN: JIST Works, 2006).

Van der Molen, Juliette H. Walma, and Tom H. A. Van der Voort. "The Impact of Television, Print, and Audio on Children's Recall of the News," *Human Communication Research* 26 (2000), 3–26.

van Dijk, Jan A. G. M. *The Deepening Divide: Inequality in the Information Society* (Thousand Oaks, CA: Sage, 2005).

Varvrus, Mary Douglas. *Postfeminist News: Political Women in Media Culture* (Albany: State University of New York Press, 2002).

"The View from Inside the Military," *Nieman Reports* (Summer 2003), 88–89.

Vorderer, Peter, and Jennings Bryant, eds. *Playing Video Games: Motives, Responses, and Consequences* (Mahwah, NJ: Erlbaum, 2006).

Wade, Nigel. "The Story We Didn't Print on Page 1," *New York Times* Op-Ed (May 23, 1998), A15.

Walsh-Childers, Kim. "Women as Sex Partners," in Paul Martin Lester and Susan Dente Ross, eds., *Images that Injure* (Westport, CT: Praeger, 2003), 151–156.

Wanta, Wayne. *The Public Agenda and the National Agenda: How People Learn about Important Issues* (Mahwah, NJ: Erlbaum, 1997).

Wayne, Stephen J. *The Road to the White House 1992: The Politics of Presidential Elections* (New York: St. Martin's, 1992).

———. *The Road to the White House 1996: The Politics of Presidential Elections* (New York: St. Martin's, 1996).

Webster, James G. "The Audience," *Journal of Broadcasting and Electronic Media* 42 (Spring 1998), 190–207.

Welch, Matt. "Blogworld and Its Gravity," *Columbia Journalism Review* (September/October 2003), 21–26.

"What the Panel Said about the '60 Minutes' Report on Bush's Guard Service," *New York Times* (January 11, 2005), C7.

White, Candace, and Katherine N. Kinnick. "One Click Forward and Two Clicks Back," *Women's Studies in Communication* 23 (2000), 392–412.

Williams, Frederick. *The New Communications,* 3rd ed. (Belmont, CA: Wadsworth, 1992).

Wood, Andrew F., and Matthew J. Smith. *Online Communication* (Mahwah, NJ: Lawrence Erlbaum, 2001).

Wright, Charles R. *Mass Communication—A Sociological Perspective,* 3rd ed. (New York: Random House, 1986).

Zelizer, Barbie. "CNN, the Gulf War, and Journalistic Practice," *Journal of Communication* 42 (1992), 66–82.

CREDITS

Page 58: Definition of *charisma* from *Oxford English Dictionary*, 1989. Reprinted by permission of Oxford University Press.

Figure 3.2, page 84: From *Language in Thought and Action*, 4th ed., by S. I. Hayakawa. Copyright © 1978. Reprinted with permission of Heinle, a division of Thomson Learning: *www.thomsonrights.com*. Fax 800-730-2215.

Figure 3.3, page 87: Reprinted from the *Journal of Applied Behavioral Science* 6, "The Fifth Achievement" by Blake and Mouton, p. 418. Copyright © 1970. Reprinted by permission of Sage Publications via Copyright Clearance Center.

Table 3.1, page 93: From *Gender and Communication* by Judy Cornelia Pearson. Copyright © 1985. Reprinted by permission of the author.

Figure 3.4, page 95: © Scott Adams, Inc./Dist. by UFS, Inc.

Figure 4.1, page 104: From *The Essential Difference* by Simon Baron-Cohen. Copyright © 2003. Reprinted by permission of Basic Books, a member of Perseus Books Group and Penguin Group (UK).

Figure 4.2, page 111: From *The Silent Language* by Edward T. Hall, copyright © 1959, 1981 by Edward T. Hall. Used by permission of Doubleday, a division of Random House, Inc.

Figure 4.3, page 113: "A Range of Selected High- and Low-Contact Cultures" from *Nonverbal Communication: Forms and Functions*, 2nd ed., by Peter A. Andersen. Copyright © 2007. Published by Waveland Press. Reprinted by permission of Peter A. Andersen.

Figure 4.4, page 114: Adapted from *Social Skills in Interpersonal Communication* by Hargie et al., 1987. Reprinted by permission of Taylor & Francis.

Table 4.1, page 116: From *Understanding Cultural Differences* by Edward T. Hall and Mildred R. Hall. Copyright © 1990 Edward T. Hall Associates. Published by Intercultural Press, Inc.

Figure 4.5, page 122: From *Nonverbal Communication in Human Interaction*, 5th ed., by Mark L. Knapp and Judith A. Hall. Copyright © 2002. Reprinted with permission of Wadsworth, a division of Thomson Learning: *www.thomsonrights.com*. Fax 800-730-2215.

Figure 4.6, page 125: From *Gestures* by Desmond Morris, P. Collett, P. Marsh, and M. O'Shaughnessy, 1979. Reprinted by permission of Desmond Morris.

Table 4.2, page 136: From *Nonverbal Communication in Close Relationships* by Laura Guerrero and Kory Floyd (Lawrence Erlbaum, 2006), p. 181.

Figure 5.1, page 145: From "An Investigation of Proportional Time Spent in Various Communication Activities by College Students," *Journal Of Applied Communication Research* 8, 1981, pp. 101–109. Used by permission of the National Communication Association.

Figure 6.1, page 176: This two-dimensional model of conflict handling is adapted from "The Kilmann-Thomas Conflict Model" by Kenneth Thomas. Reprinted by permission of Grid International, Inc.

Figure 7.1, page 219: From *Moral Courage* by Rushworth M. Kidder, Figs. 2 (p. 51) and 7 (p. 73). Copyright © 2004 by Rushworth M. Kidder. Reprinted by permission of HarperCollins Publishers.

Table 8.1, page 238: *Pew Internet & American Life Project Online Dating Survey*, September–December 2005 (retrieved July 16, 2007 from *www.pewinternet.org/pdfs/PIP_Online_Dating.pdf*).

Table 8.2, page 242: From "Defensive Communications" by Jack R. Gibb, *Journal of Communication*, 11(3), 1961, pp. 141–148. Reprinted by permission of the International Communication Association.

Figure 8.2, page 249: From *Interpersonal Communication and Human Relationships*, 4th ed., by Mark L. Knapp & Anita L. Vangelisti. Published by Allyn and Bacon, Boston, MA. Copyright © 2000 by Pearson Education. Reprinted by permission of the publisher.

Figure 8.3, page 253: From *Personal Relationships 5: Repairing Personal Relationships* by Steve Duck, 1984. Reprinted by permission of Elsevier.

Table 8.3, page 259: National Center for Health Statistics, Adapted from Sue Shellenbarger, "No Comfort in Numbers: Divorce Rate Varies Widely from Group to Group," *The Wall Street Journal*, April 22, 2004, D1 (with change in title of table). Copyright © 2004 Dow Jones and Co. Reprinted by permission of Dow Jones and Co. via Copyright Clearance Center.

Figure 9.1, page 283: From *Group Processes: An Introduction to Group Dynamics*, 3rd ed., by Joseph Luft, 1984. Reproduced with permission of The McGraw-Hill Companies.

Figure 9.3, page 295: From *Cupid's Arrow: The Course of Love through Time* by Dr. Robert J. Sternberg (Cambridge University Press, 1998). Reprinted by permission of the author.

Table 9.1, page 297: Reprinted by permission of Sage Publications, Ltd. From Clyde Hendrick, Susan S. Hendrick, and Amy Dicke, *Journal of Social and Personal*

Relationships, Vol. 15 (2). Copyright 1998, Sage Publications, Ltd.

Table 9.2, page 299: From *Reaching Out: Interpersonal Effectiveness and Self-Actualization*, 8th ed., by David W. Johnson. Published by Allyn and Bacon, Boston, MA. Copyright © 2003 by Pearson Education. Reprinted by permission of the publisher.

Figure 9.4, page 304: From *Your Perfect Right: Assertiveness and Equality in Your Life and Relationships*, 8th ed. Copyright © 2001 by Robert E. Alberti and Michael Emmons. Reproduced for Stewart Tubbs and Sylvia Moss by permission of Impact Publishers, Inc., P.O. Box 6016, Atascadero CA 93423, USA. Further reproduction prohibited.

Table 10.1, page 319: Adapted from *Communicating with Strangers*, 3rd ed., by William B. Gudykunst and Young Yun Kim, 1997. Reproduced by permission of The McGraw-Hill Companies.

Figure 10.1, page 320: Map, "High-Context versus Low-Context Rankings of Selected Countries and Groups" from *Nonverbal Communication: Forms and Functions*, 2nd ed., by Peter A. Andersen. Copyright © 2007. Published by Waveland Press. Reprinted by permission of Peter A. Andersen.

Figure 10.2, page 332: From *Moral Courage* by Rushworth M. Kidder, Figs. 2 (p. 51) and 7 (p. 73). Copyright © 2004 by Rushworth M. Kidder. Reprinted by permission of HarperCollins Publishers.

Box 10.2, page 338: From *Latin Looks: Images of Latinas and Latinos in the U.S. Media* by Clara Rodriguez. Copyright 1997 by Westview Press, a division of Perseus Book, L.L.C. Reprinted by permission of Westview Press, a member of Perseus Books, L.L.C.

Table 10.2, page 340: Sunstein, Cass R., *Republic.com*. © 2001 Princeton University Press. Reprinted by permission of Princeton University Press.

Figure 11.1, page 365: Adapted from *Selection Interviewing for Managers* by Thomas Moffatt, 1979. Reprinted by permission of the author.

Table 11.3, page 373: Adapted from *Personnel Administration and Public Review,* September 1971. Reprinted by permission of Professor Cal Downs.

Figure 12.1, page 396: From *Personality and Interpersonal Behavior* by Robert Freed Bales (New York: Holt, Rinehart and Winston, 1970). Reprinted with permission of the author.

Figure 12.2, page 405: From *Further Up the Organization* by Robert Townsend. Copyright © 1970, 1984 by Robert Townsend (New York: Alfred A. Knopf).

Table 13.1, page 429: From *Analyzing Human Communication*, 2nd ed., by Lawrence B. Rosenfeld, 1983 (Dubuque, IA: Kendall/Hunt Publishing Company).

Figure 14.1, page 479: Reprint courtesy of International Business Machines Corporation. Copyright © 1992 International Business Machines Corporation.

Figure 15.1, page 506: "The National Entertainment State" by Nation Editors, from the July 3, 2006, issue of *The Nation*. Reprinted with permission. For subscription information, call 1-800-333-8536. Portions of each week's *Nation* magazine can be accessed at *http://www.thenation.com*.

Table 15.1, page 523: "How Americans Used the Internet After the Terror Attack," by Lee Rainie, September 15, 2001, Pew Internet & American Life Project, *www.pewinternet.org*.

Table 15.2, page 525: Adapted from Election 2006 Online, by Lee Rainie and John Horrigan. Washington, DC: Pew Internet & American Life Project and Pew Research Center for The People & The Press (January 17, 2007), p. vi. *www.pewinternet.org/pdfs/PIP_Politics_2006.pdf*.

Photo Credits

Page 2: © Doug Menuez/Getty Images. **Page 34:** © Monica Lau/Getty Images. **Page 38:** © Image Source. **Page 70:** © Bananastock/PictureQuest. **Page 102:** © Will & Deni McIntyre/Corbis. **Page 142:** © RubberBall Productions/Getty Images. **Page 168:** © Stockbyte/Punchstock Images. **Page 198:** © Royalty-Free/Corbis. **Page 230:** © Ryan McVay/Getty Images. **Page 270:** © Colin Young-Wolff/PhotoEdit. **Page 310:** © Digital Vision. **Page 352:** © Digital Vision Ltd./SuperStock. **Page 384:** © PhotoAlto. **Page 420:** © Bob Daemmrich/The Image Works. **Page 448:** © John Madere/Corbis. **Page 466:** © Ryan McVay/Getty Images. **Page 500:** AP Photo/Lefteris Pitarakis.

NAME INDEX

Redding, W. Charles, 516
Reeves, Byron, 545
Regan, Pamela, 289
Reich, Theodore, 487
Reik, Theodore, 158
Reis, Harry T., 54, 233
Rendell, Steve, 516
Reyes, Jesus M., 324
Rhodes, Gillian, 55–56, 60
Rice, Condoleezza, 482, 530
Rice, Ronald E., 488
Richards, Michael, 72
Richmond, V. P., 62
Rimm, Sylvia, 44
Riniolo, Todd C., 57
Ripley, Amanda, 221
Ritchie, David, 257
Rivera, Geraldo, 511
Roberts, Donald F., 520
Roberts, Lynne D., 46, 546
Roberts, Ronald Suresh, 216
Robinson, Jeffrey D., 114, 121
Rock, Chris, 425
Rodgers, Joan Ellison, 123
Rodriguez, Alex, 504
Rodriguez, Clara E., 338
Roehm, Julie, 469
Rogers, Carl, 151
Rogers, Edna L., 245
Rogers, Everett M., 522
Rohrlich, Beulah, 344
Roker, Al, 239
Rollnick, S., 375, 377
Romano, Carlin, 517
Romney, Mitt, 428
Roosevelt, Eleanor, 454–55
Roosevelt, Franklin D., 454
Rosenberg, Morris, 6
Rosenfeld, Howard M., 109
Rosenfeld, Lawrence, 439
Rosenfeld, L. B., 285
Rosenthal, R., 62
Rosenthal, Robert, 48
Rose, T., 62
Rosnow, Ralph, 493–94
Rossiter, Charles, 92
Ross, Susan Dente, 335
Rost, Peter, 221
Rowley, Coleen, 220
Rowling, J. K., 504
Rubak, Sune, 375
Rubin, Alan M., 521
Ruesch, Jurgen, 239

Rushdie, Salman, 315
Russert, Tim, 224

Safire, William, 441, 451
Salant, Jonathan, 72
Salinger, J. D., 216
Samovar, Larry A., 80, 317, 323, 425, 436
Sanders, Tim, 5
Sarandon, Susan, 533
Sarbaugh, L. E., 322
Sargent, Michael J., 51
Satir, Virginia, 261, 263
Schachter, Stanley, 236, 390, 399
Schaffner, Brian F., 336
Scheflen, Albert E., 113, 122
Schein, Edgar H., 26, 470, 472, 491
Schellenberger, Sue, 4
Scheufele, Dietram A., 526
Schieffer, Bob, 519
Schimel, Jeff, 242
Schlesinger, Laura, 172
Schmid, John, 150
Schoeman, Wilhelm J., 42
Schramm, Wilber, 520
Schuller, Robert H., 202
Schütz, Astrid, 44
Schutz, William, 400
Schwartz, J., 392
Schwartz, John, 218
Schwartz, Morris, 19
Scott, Janny, 317
Scotton, Carol M., 81
Scott, T., 369
Seabrook, John, 543
Sedlack, Robert, 434, 448
Segall, M. H., 39
Sellers, Patricia, 478
Semic, Beth, 134
Serrin, William, 516
Sexton, Anne, 216–17
Shalett, K., 358
Shapiro, Dera L., 389
Sharpton, Al, 172
Shaver, Phillip, 290
Shaw, David, 513
Shaw, George Bernard, 108, 355
Shaw, Marvin E., 407
Shaw, Robert Bruce, 245, 427
Sheats, Paul, 396
Sheen, Martin, 217
Shellenbarger, Sue, 259
Shepard, Hebert A., 400
Sheridan, M., 378

Sherif, Muzafer, 389
Sieberg, Evelyn, 239–40
Signorelli, Nancy, 532
Sillars, A. L., 98, 177, 179, 181, 327–28
Simerly, Roy L., 147
Simonetti, Jack L., 20, 358–59, 370
Simon, Herbert A., 407
Simon, Neil, 273
Simonson, Peter, 518
Simpson, Jeffry A., 123
Simpson, Kevin, 217
Simpson, O. J., 514
Sims, Henry P., 487
Slater, Michael D., 537
Smith, Dinitia, 532
Smith, Jack, 129
Smith, Matthew J., 213, 222, 541
Smith, Richard Norton, 217
Smith, Ronald L., 493
Solomon, Deborah, 527
Sommer, Robert, 109
Soskin, William F., 130
Sostek, Anya, 494
Spears, Russell, 213
Sprague, Jo, 441
Sprecher, Aron, 234
Spyridakis, J., 13
Srivastava, Sanjay, 48, 293
Stafford, Laura, 244
Stahl, Gerry, 407, 408
Stanley, Alessandra, 217
Steil, Janice M., 301
Steinberg, Jacques, 206
Steinberg, M., 280
Stein, Marky, 378
Stephan, Cookie White, 334
Stephan, Walter G., 334
Stern, Barbara B., 60
Sternberg, Robert J., 43–44, 287, 295–96
Stern, Howard, 72, 172
Stewart, Charles J., 356, 367
Stewart, J., 104
Stewart, John, 6, 527
Stewart, Martha, 127–28
Stoltz, Paul G., 82
Stone-Palmquist, Peri, 16
Storace, Patricia, 116
Storms, Michael D., 49
Straubhaar, Joseph, 538
Strodbeck, Fred, 400
Stroebe, W., 456
Strong, Greg, 291, 295
Stuart, Douglas, 441

SUBJECT INDEX

Page references followed by *fig* indicate an illustrated figure; those followed by *t* indicate a table.